Learn at Home
Grade 6

From the Editors of American Education Publishing

Table of Contents

Learn at Home, Grade 6

Table of Contents

Welcome!

Congratulations on your decision to educate at home! Perhaps you are a bit nervous or overwhelmed by the task ahead of you. *Learn at Home* will give you the guidance you need to provide your child with the best sixth-grade education possible. This book is only a guide, however, and you are encouraged to supplement your child's sixth-grade curriculum with other books, activities and resources that suit your situation and your child's unique interests.

Create an inviting learning environment for your child. It should be comfortable and attractive, yet a place in which your child can work without distractions. Your child's work area should include a desk or table for the child, a chalkboard or dry-erase board, an easel, appropriate writing and art materials, a cozy area for reading (perhaps with pillows or a bean bag chair), a bulletin board for displaying work and shelves for books and storage. Hang a clock and a calendar in the room as well. You may wish to purchase a calculator, tangrams, a protractor, Cuisenaire rods, fraction models and base-ten blocks for your child to use when studying math concepts. Collect inexpensive materials from around your home for your child to use in art projects, as math manipulatives or for language activities. Bottle caps, cardboard tubes, dried pasta and beans, old magazines, egg cartons, small tiles and wooden cubes are certain to come in handy throughout the year.

The Learn at Home Series

The Learn at Home series is an easy-to-use line of resource guides for parents who have chosen to teach at home. The series covers grades K through 6, one volume per grade level. Each book in the series is organized the same. An introductory section called **Background Information and Supporting Activities** provides general information and activity ideas for each area of the curriculum. This section is then followed by 36 weeks of instruction in six curricular areas. At the sixth-grade level, these areas include Reading, Language Skills, Spelling, Math, Science and Social Studies.

Each of the 36 weeks is then further divided into three sections: **Lesson Plans**, **Teaching Suggestions and Activities** and **Activity Sheets**. Each week's **Lesson Plan** includes lessons and activity suggestions for all six curricular areas. Though divided into separate areas of the curriculum, many of these activities are actually cross-curricular in nature. The lesson plans are brief, but further explanations are often provided in the next section, **Teaching Suggestions and Activities**. This section generally contains detailed directions for activities mentioned in the lesson plans, as well as a variety of suggestions for related activities and extensions. **Activity Sheets** round out each week's materials. These sheets are grouped by subject and arranged in the order in which they appear in the lesson plans. Activity sheets are referred to by name and page number and are highlighted by **bold** print throughout this book.

Answer Key Pages are included in the final pages of this book for your convenience.

Background Information and Supporting Activities

LANGUAGE SKILLS

▶ BACKGROUND

Language skills should be taught in real context and in all subject areas, rather than in isolation. The skills covered in this book include vocabulary development, parts of speech, sentence structure, paragraph structure, punctuation, using resources, poetry, public speaking, research reports, story elements and the writing process. Try to integrate your teaching of these skills with other areas of the curriculum.

▶ THE WRITING PROCESS

Engage your child in meaningful writing activities each week. Use a writing lesson as an opportunity to stress a newly learned grammatical skill. While the focus of some writing activities will be correctness, others will encourage fluency. Devote at least 30 minutes each day to writing, whether it be creative writing or writing in other areas of the curriculum. The writing process is ongoing but generally includes these steps:

Prewriting The writer brainstorms ideas, gathers and organizes information.

Drafting The writer composes or writes a rough draft using prewriting ideas. Your child should not worry about mistakes at this stage. The emphasis here is on fluency, not accuracy. Have your child date the drafts and keep them in a writing folder.

Revising The writer rereads the draft, checking to see that it is fluent, interesting and stays on topic. Then, he/she reads the rough draft to another person to gather feedback on word choice, fluency, clarity and interest. The writer makes changes as needed.

Editing Together, the parent and child proofread the revised piece of writing for proper spelling, capitalization and grammar.

Publishing The writer copies the corrected proof and prepares to present it.

▶ PUBLISHING YOUR CHILD'S WORK

When writing, it is important to keep in mind one's audience. Most of the writing we do as adults has a real audience. Establish an audience and a purpose for your child's writing by publishing his/her work. Writing with the reader in mind may motivate your child to express him/herself clearly and accurately.

There are many ways to publish your child's work. Have your child turn a revised and edited story into a book, adding illustrations and a cover. Maintain a "library" of your child's writings. Arrange for your child to read some of his/her written work to an audience, such as young children or the elderly. Help your child submit a revised and edited piece to a children's magazine like *Cricket, Stone Soup* or *Highlights for Children*. Or, help your child create a literary magazine for publishing his/her best and favorite poems, stories, articles and essays. Help your child edit and arrange the pieces to form a magazine. Supplement with pictures, ads, puzzles, riddles and editorials. Make copies of the magazine to send to relatives and friends.

▶ WRITING TOPICS

Assign a writing topic every Monday or allow your child to choose a topic. Brainstorm a list of topics at the beginning of the year—try to include topics from all areas of the curriculum. Some topics may require research, while others may only require imagination. Have your child keep this list of topics in a writing folder. He/she may refer to the list whenever he/she needs an idea for a writing project. Your child should follow the writing process for any writing assignment.

Make opportunities for your child to write every day. For example, have your child answer a question, voice an opinion or describe a character in writing. Ask your child to write an advertisement or illustrate and caption a comic strip. Write an intriguing sentence on the chalkboard and have your child turn it into a story. Encourage your child to write letters to friends and family.

▶ PERSONAL DIARY

Have your child keep a personal diary. The objective is to help your child build fluency by writing regularly. Though you may occasionally need to suggest writing topics, allow your child to write about anything in his/her diary. Your child's diary can be a place for personal reflection, current events, lists, jokes and riddles, descriptions of wonderful or terrible things, ideas for stories and much more.

▶ LANGUAGE CENTER

Establish a language center in your classroom. Fill a file box with a collection of activities that reinforce or enrich language skills. Allow your child to work at his/her leisure on word games, puzzles and other language activities. There are many commercial games and books available.

Learn at Home, Grade 6

SPELLING

▶ BACKGROUND

Spelling is applicable to all areas of study, so work to integrate it into all areas of the curriculum. As your child encounters new terms in social studies, science and math, add that vocabulary to the weekly spelling lists. Add words from your child's own writing as well. Repeating spelling words during the week will help your child memorize words for a test, but it will not help him/her retain the words for the long term. The most effective technique for retaining accurate spelling is to use the words in context. Each week, engage your child in a writing activity using the spelling words. Steady exposure to words through reading will also improve your child's ability to spell.

▶ TEACHING SPELLING SKILLS

Each weekly lesson plan contains a list of 18 vocabulary words for your child to learn. Review weeks are the only exceptions—the spelling lists for Weeks 9, 18, 27 and 36 are generated by you and your child, based on words from previous weeks' lists that need to be reviewed. Follow the schedule below for each week's spelling lessons.

Monday

1. Give your child a pretest of the new word list. Read each word, use it in a sentence, then read the word again. Enunciate each word clearly to avoid confusion.

2. Have your child correct his/her own pretest as you read the word aloud and spell it. Ask your child to make a check mark next to each word that is spelled correctly and circle each word that is misspelled. Have your child write each misspelled word correctly next to the incorrect spelling. These words will comprise the study list for the week.

3. Add words to the list from your child's written work or from other curriculum areas. Keep the list at around 18 words. Have your child copy the study list twice: once for him/herself and a second time for your records.

4. Discuss any spelling rules that apply to the words in the list.

Tuesday

1. Have your child complete the provided activity sheet. Have your child write any additional words that fit in the category on the back of the sheet.

2. Have your child practice spelling each word aloud through games and physical activity. Play games such as "Hangman," "Boggle" or "Scrabble."

Wednesday

1. Have your child use each spelling word in a meaningful sentence.

2. Have your child read the completed sentences aloud.

Thursday

1. Have your child complete an activity that involves writing, forming, tracing or reading the spelling words repeatedly. Several activity suggestions are included on page 8.

2. Have your child practice using the spelling words orally.

Friday

1. Give your child a final test on the words studied this week. Add words from previous weeks to assess whether your child has retained the correct spellings.

2. Correct the test. Add any misspelled words to future study lists.

▶ WORD BANK

Provide your child with a stack of index cards and a file box for maintaining a word bank throughout the year. Have your child record spelling words (one word per card) and file them alphabetically. Add words from the spelling lists each Friday. Add misspelled words that are found in writing and challenging words from other curricular areas. You can also add dictionary skills lessons to the word bank. For each word, have him/her write a definition, part of speech, pronunciation and a sample sentence.

▶ SPELLING ACTIVITIES

The following activities can be used with or adapted to just about any word list. Employ a variety of activities in your teaching to keep your child challenged and motivated.

1. Have your child alphabetize the list of words.

2. Have your child write a story using the spelling words, then underline each spelling word used.

3. Have your child create word searches, crossword puzzles and other word games.

4. Copy the spelling words onto index cards, omitting the vowels. Have your child identify the spelling words and write out each word three times (with vowels). Repeat, omitting the consonants.

5. Write sentences on the chalkboard using the spelling words. Erase the spelling words in each sentence. Have your child read each sentence and fill in the missing word, based on context.

6. Play charades.

7. Assign each letter of the alphabet a numerical value. Have your child choose a spelling word and write it on the chalkboard. Have your child write the assigned value of each letter, add the values and write the sum of the word. Repeat for each spelling word.

8. Choose random pairs of spelling words. Have your child write an alphabetical sentence incorporating both words. Your child does not need to start at the beginning of the alphabet each time.
   Example: A big <u>caterpillar</u> doesn't eat <u>furiously</u>.

9. Choose a spelling word. Have your child say the word, then spell it out, clapping each consonant and snapping each vowel.

10. Have your child look up a spelling word in the dictionary. Have him/her copy the guide words from the top of the page, write the word with diacritical marks or divide the word into syllables.

11. Have your child make up a mnemonic device to help him/her remember a difficult spelling.
    Example: geography—<u>G</u>eorge <u>E</u>lliott's <u>o</u>ld <u>g</u>randmother <u>r</u>ode <u>a</u> <u>p</u>ig <u>h</u>ome <u>y</u>esterday.

12. Using grid paper and a pencil, have your child write spelling stairs. Have your child write the first letter of the spelling word in a box on the first line. On the second line, directly below the first letter, have him/her write the first and second letters of the word in two boxes. Continue until the entire word has been written. Have your child count how many steps make up the staircase and write the number at the top of the steps. Repeat with other spelling words.

Learn at Home, Grade 6

READING

▶ BACKGROUND

Reading ability and interests vary greatly at this age, so choose books that are appropriate for your child. You may follow the book suggestions in the lesson plans or choose your own. Use a variety of books or a basal reader for your reading curriculum. Go at an appropriate pace for your child. Read each book before you introduce it so that you will be prepared to lead a discussion, ask questions and suggest activities. Encourage your child to read material for a natural purpose as well. Make available magazines, newspapers, comics, maps and other reading materials. Set aside 30–45 minutes each day for your child to do silent reading. You might also choose to read books aloud to your child. This is a great opportunity to model your own love for reading and to talk about the content of a book. For more information on this subject, see *The New Read-Aloud Handbook* by Jim Trelease.

▶ CHOOSING A BOOK

There is no such thing as a sixth-grade level book. Determine if a book is appropriate for your child by having him/her read a short passage. Evaluate your child's fluency, understanding and interest. If your child reads without hesitation, the book is probably at his/her independent reading level. If your child cannot decode several words on a single page and loses track of the meaning, the book is at your child's frustration level. Struggling through the book could turn your child against reading. Choose a book at your child's instructional level when you will be reading together. Your child should recognize about 85–90% of the words on his/her own and be able to answer 75% of the comprehension questions.

Survey your child's interests periodically. Choose some books based on your child's interests; choose others because they are examples of fine literature. Have your child read a variety of books: biography, fiction, nonfiction, historical fiction, mystery, adventure, mythology, science fiction and poetry. Here is a list of books to get you started:

The Adventures of Robin Hood by Roger L. Green
Anne of Green Gables by L. M. Montgomery
The Bellmaker by Brian Jacques
Beyond the Divide by Kathryn Lasky
Big Red by Jim Kjelgaard
The Black Stallion by Walter Farley
The Blue Door by Ann Rinaldi
Caddie Woodlawn by Carol Ryrie Brink
Children of the Dust Bowl: A True Story of the School at Weedpatch Camp by Jerry Stanley
The Diary of Anne Frank with an introduction by Eleanor Roosevelt
The Egyptian Cinderella by Shirley Climo
The Endless Steppe by Esther Hautzig
The Great Depression (a Cornerstones of Freedom Book) by Richard Conrad Stein
Greek Myths by Ingri and Edgar Parin D'Aulaire
Gulliver's Travels by Jonathan Swift
Hans Brinker by Mary Mapes Dodge
Harriet the Spy by Louise Fitzhugh
The High King by Lloyd Alexander

Immigrant Kids by Russell Freedman
Just So Stories by Rudyard Kipling
Letters from Rifka by Karen Hesse
The Manhattan Project (a Cornerstone of Freedom Book) by Richard Conrad Stein
My Friend Flicka by Mary O'Hara
The Odyssey retold by Robin Lister
The Red Badge of Courage by Stephen Crane
Robinson Crusoe by Daniel Defoe
The Secret Garden by Frances Hodgson Burnett
Song of the Gargoyle by Zilpha Keatley Snyder
The Swiss Family Robinson by Johann Wyss
Tales From Shakespeare by Charles and Mary Lamb
Treasure Island by Robert Lewis Stevenson
The Trojan War by Olivia Coolidge
20,000 Leagues Under the Sea by Jules Verne
The Vietnam War by John Devaney
Walk Two Moons by Sharon Creech
When Hitler Stole Pink Rabbit by Judith Kerr
White Fang by Jack London
The Wind in the Willows by Kenneth Grahame

▶ READING CONFERENCE

Hold a reading conference with your child twice a week to discuss the current book. Discuss the characters and plot of the story. Have your child complete a copy of Story Organizer (p. 19) as he/she reads each book. The lesson plans suggest topics for discussion and activities that focus on a variety of reading and language skills. Use the reading book to demonstrate a language skills concept, such as subject/verb agreement. Choose other activities that will sharpen your child's analysis, comprehension and interpretive skills. Ask your child to recall details, sequence events, analyze a character, compare and contrast, predict outcomes, draw conclusions and interpret facts. When you notice yourself using a particular skill in your own reading, call attention to it. Discuss how you used the skill. Mastery of these skills will help your child become an independent reader.

When your child finishes a book, have him/her complete a project that involves thinking about the content and meaning of the material. Ask your child to write a sequel, rewrite the ending, create a diorama, make a mobile, pen a letter to the author or critique the book.

▶ READING JOURNAL

Have your child keep a Reading Journal. Assign questions for your child to answer in the journal or allow your child to write on other topics related to the book. The best questions will ask your child to express an opinion, make a recommendation, criticize a decision or debate an issue presented in the book.

▶ INCENTIVES

Reading can be its own reward, but your child may need a little encouragement at times. Choose an incentive that fits your child's interests and your own philosophy.

1. Make a record sheet like the one shown here. After your child finishes a book, have him/her complete one line on the chart. When each line of the chart is filled—you decide how many lines it should have—let your child choose an activity as a reward. You could play a game together, bake cookies or go ice-skating.

Title	Author	Main Idea	Rating

2. Set a reading goal. Choose a theme that will motivate your child. Design a bulletin board display around the theme. For each book your child reads, add something to the display. When the display is full, your child earns a reward related to the theme. **Example:** Draw a large pizza. Have your child add a mushroom or piece of pepperoni to the pizza for each book he/she reads. Have your child write the title of the completed book on each mushroom or piece of pepperoni. When the pizza is full of toppings, your child earns a pizza lunch with someone special.

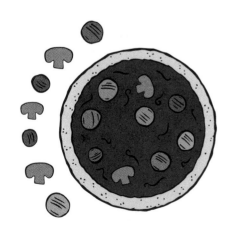

Learn at Home, Grade 6

MATH

▶ BACKGROUND

This sixth-grade math curriculum is filled with activities and exercises designed to help your child comprehend the logic behind math operations. Your child will learn about multiplication, division, geometry, fractions, decimal fractions, percents, ratios and integers. He/she will also learn about statistics and graphing. Whatever the topic, look for opportunities to relate the math concepts to your child's own world. Show your child the practical applications of mathematics.

▶ PROGRESS CHART

Have your child practice graphing skills while keeping a record of personal progress each quarter. Using a sheet of graph paper, have your child design a graph to record the name of each skill or assignment, the date and a range of scores (from 0 to 100 in increments of 5). For each assignment completed, your child will color in his/her score. Set a standard of excellence, such as 90%, that your child should strive to attain. Provide opportunities for your child to improve low scores, whether it be repeating an assignment after further instruction or completing a related assignment.

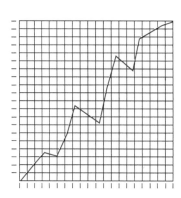

▶ BOOK OF PROBLEMS

Provide a notebook for creating and solving situational problems, or word problems. Have your child design two or three situational problems using current math concepts each week. Encourage your child to relate the math concept to his/her own experience—daily activities or themes from other curricular areas. This activity will stress the importance of the math concepts and teach that they have practical applications. Have your child leave the problems unsolved until the review week. Use the term situational problem rather than word (or story) problem to encourage your child to see math in real-life situations. You may also wish to act out, draw or model problems in order to increase your child's understanding.

▶ VOCABULARY

As new vocabulary is introduced in the math lessons, have your child record and define them in the "Book of Situational Problems." During review weeks, have your child define the terms and provide examples, when appropriate. You may also choose to add some of these terms to your child's weekly spelling lists.

11

SCIENCE

▶ BACKGROUND

In sixth-grade science, your child will explore the systems of the human body. He/she will study how these systems function together and how exercise and good nutrition are vital to its well-being. Your child will also learn about the immune system and diseases, such as asthma and AIDS, that can affect it.

This year's curriculum will also cover the study of chemistry. Your child will learn about mixtures, solutions, molecules, acids and bases through experimentation and observation. This book will also cover the fascinating study of light and sound.

Finally, your child will learn about ecology. He/she will discover different biomes and the unusual organisms that inhabit them, discuss endangered species and learn how to help save our environment and conserve precious resources.

▶ SPECIAL SCIENTIST

Feature a different "Special Scientist" in each 9–week quarter. Provide information about the scientist and his/her work. On the bulletin board, frame a large sheet of paper with a decorative border. Near the top of the frame, write the name of the scientist and display his/her picture. (Copy a picture from an encyclopedia or other resource.) Write some facts about the scientist and his/her work within the frame. Supply resource books about the scientist and his/her field. Invite your child to read and write about the scientist. Some suggestions for "Special Scientist" include Edmond Halley, Wernher von Braun, Dorothy Crowfoot Hodgkin, Alessandro Volta, John F. Enders and Helen Brooke Taussig.

▶ THE SCIENTIFIC METHOD

Encourage your child to follow the scientific method whenever he/she has a question related to science or when exploring a new idea.

1. A science lesson may begin with a question that sparks the curiosity of your child. **Example:** I wonder what will happen if I leave this half-eaten apple on the counter. Encourage your child to state a possible *hypothesis*.

2. Follow the question with an *exploration* that involves observation, play, debate, experimentation and other methods of inquiry. Encourage your child to use descriptive language, measure when appropriate and keep a journal of observations.

3. The next step involves proposing *explanations* and *solutions* for the initial question. An explanation may prove or disprove the earlier hypothesis. This is a time of writing, talking and evaluating. After this step, your child may need to return to the second step of the cycle, exploring the topic further.

4. *Applying* the knowledge to your child's world makes the event more meaningful. *Where have you seen this happen before? What will you do differently because of the experiment?* This fourth step may also spark a new question that will begin the cycle again.

▶ SCIENCE LOG

Once your child has mastered the Scientific Method, he/she will be able to apply it to all areas of science covered this year. Have your child keep a Science Log to help him/her work through experiments and other problems methodically.

12

SOCIAL STUDIES

The sixth-grade social studies curriculum consists of an in-depth study of American history from the period following the Civil War to the present. Gather relevant posters, videotapes, films, magazines, books, audiotapes, CD-ROMs and resource books for your child's reference. Use primary sources as often as possible. Have your child read excerpts from A History of the United States, a series by Joy Hakim (published by Oxford University Press). This year, your child will also study geography, including the hemispheres, longitude and latitude, landforms and boundaries of North America and South America.

▶ COMMUNITY INVOLVEMENT

Get your child involved in the community this year. Each Friday, have your child perform some sort of community service. Here are some suggested activities:

1. Tutor a young child in the primary grades.

2. Read aloud to a young child or an older adult.

3. Volunteer at the local library to straighten shelves, dust or make photocopies.

4. Help out Habitat for Humanity in some way to build a home for a low-income family.

5. Organize a fund-raising project such as a book fair, garage sale or bake sale to raise money for a community organization.

6. Help out at a local humane society.

7. Volunteer at a community organization and learn more about their work.

8. Plan and prepare a warm meal for someone who is ill, elderly or busy with a new baby.

9. Run errands for someone who is ill, elderly or busy with a new baby.

10. Collect clean, used clothing and nonperishable food items for someone in need. Donate to a shelter, church or mission.

11. Work in a food pantry or other type of distribution center.

12. Pick up litter in a park or other public area.

▶ SOCIAL STUDIES CENTER

Set up an area in the classroom called the Social Studies Center. If possible, put the center near a bulletin board where you can mount a large map of the United States and a time line to be completed as the year progresses. Suggested supplies and materials for the center include the following: maps, a globe, an atlas, books about U.S. history, weekly news magazines, almanacs, encyclopedias, video and auditory tapes, pictures of times past, copies of historical documents, games and biographies of famous people.

▶ SOCIAL STUDIES JOURNAL

A journal is an important tool for encouraging your child to reflect on new learning. Help your child make it a habit to write in the Social Studies Journal at least once a week. You will see a reminder each Friday in the lesson plans. You might ask your child to reflect on a specific aspect of the week's lessons. A journal is an excellent place for your child to voice opinions and ask questions.

Language Skills	Spelling	Reading
Fun With Words Review the concept of alliteration. Discuss why people use alliteration (to sound nice or to be silly). *See* Language Skills, Week 1, number 1. Have your child choose a topic, make a plan for writing, then begin working on a rough draft. Encourage your child to make up a title for the writing project that incorporates alliteration.	Pretest your child on these spelling words: accept different really accurate install recess arrange necessary support ballot occasion surround commit opposite terrible common quarrel tomorrow Correct the pretest, add personalized words and make two copies of this week's study list.	**Purpose for Reading** With your child, brainstorm a list of the type of things a person can read. Then, discuss the different reasons for reading each. *See* Reading, Week 1, number 1. Take your child to the library to look at possible books to read this semester. Have your child make a list of books that interest him/her. Check out enough books to last a few weeks.
Give your child three or four examples of anagrams: tire (rite or tier), flea (leaf), stain (saint), hewn (when). Then, ask him/her to define the term *anagram*. *See* Language Skills, Week 1, number 2.	Study this week's spelling words. Have your child complete **Seeing Double** (p. 18).	Hold a reading conference in which you introduce the book your child will read first. *See* **Reading Conference** (p. 10). Focus on prior knowledge (relating your child's past experiences to the topic). Give your child a copy of **Story Organizer** (p. 19) to complete as he/she reads the story.
Review *similes* and *metaphors*. Have your child compare how they are similar yet different. Discuss the purpose for using these figures of speech. Have your child write sentences containing metaphors and similes. *See* Language Skills, Week 1, numbers 3 and 4. Ask your child to incorporate at least one metaphor and one simile into this week's writing project.	Have your child use each of this week's spelling words correctly in a sentence.	Teach a vocabulary lesson using difficult words from the current reading book. Write the words on the chalkboard, followed by the page numbers on which they are found. Have your child write the words and the sentences they appear in on index cards. *See* Reading, Week 1, number 2. Have your child rewrite each sentence in his/her own words to show the meaning of the vocabulary word(s).
Review *hyperbole*. Discuss the purpose for using hyperbole (to emphasize a point). *See* Language Skills, Week 1, number 5. Have your child write several sentences containing hyperbole.	Have your child study this week's spelling words. *See* **Spelling Activities** for activity ideas (p. 8).	Have your child write in his/her Reading Journal about the book he/she is reading. Ask him/her to explain something, persuade someone of a certain point of view, argue a point raised in the book, criticize a character's actions or imagine a variation of an episode in the book.
Select a passage to read aloud that expresses a mood. Have your child describe the mood and identify the words from the passage that help to establish it. *See* Language Skills, Week 1, number 6. Have your child create a word web around a mood word of his/her choice. Then, have your child incorporate those words into a paragraph.	Give your child the final spelling test. Have your child record pretest and final test words in his/her word bank.	Discuss the current reading book in a conference. Focus on character analysis. *See* **Reading Conference** (p. 10).

Rows labeled (left margin): Monday, Tuesday, Wednesday, Thursday, Friday

Learn at Home, Grade 6

Math	Science	Social Studies
Place Value Review place value with your child. *See* Math, Week 1. Have your child read *How Much Is a Million?* by David Schwartz. Make large-number flash cards. Write large numbers in numeral form on one side and in words on the reverse side. Use the cards to practice reading and writing numbers. This is a great self-checking activity. *See also* Math, Week 1, number 1.	**The Human Body** Ask your child to name the major systems of the human body (skeletal, muscular, digestive, respiratory, circulatory, urinary, reproductive, nervous and endocrine). *See* Science, Week 1. Over the next 9 weeks, your child will learn about some of these systems. Follow the lesson plans or encourage your child to study and report on two or three systems in depth.	**Reconstruction** Show your child pictures taken during the Civil War period. Review and discuss the causes of the Civil War, where it was fought, the damage it caused on both sides and the possible feelings of the victors and losers. Have your child imagine that he/she had a brother who served in the Civil War (on either side). Have your child write an imaginary diary entry as the brother dated sometime in 1865.
Continue to give your child practice reading and writing large numbers in numeral and word form. Review the spelling rules concerned with writing numbers. *See* Math, Week 1, number 2. Add appropriate math vocabulary to this week's spelling list. Have your child complete **Down the Ladder** (p. 20).	Have your child complete **Anticipation Guide** (p. 21) before reading about the human body. Then, have your child do research on the human body to confirm or refute each statement. If the statement is false, have your child write a related true statement.	Introduce the concept of Reconstruction. *See* Social Studies, Week 1, number 1. Ask your child to imagine what the most difficult thing to reconstruct after the Civil War was. Have him/her write a paragraph about it.
Review how to read decimals with your child. *See* Math, Week 1, number 3. Have your child color models of decimal fractions. Have the child draw a large box to represent a whole, then use a ruler to divide the box into tenths, hundredths, thousandths or ten thousandths. Name decimal fractions, such as 0.93 or 0.641, for your child to illustrate.	**Skeletal System:** The skeleton is a support system that gives a body shape. The human body has 206 bones that protect the organs and act as a system of levers, helping the body to move. Discuss *endoskeletons* and *exoskeletons*. Discuss examples of animals that have each type of skeleton. Have your child draw a picture of an animal with an exoskeleton in his/her Science Log.	Provide your child with a list of questions related to Reconstruction and a selection of appropriate resources. *See* Social Studies, Week 1, number 2. Have your child take notes while reading about Reconstruction and answer the questions provided.
Have your child create a cross-number puzzle using number words as clues. Sample clue: three hundred sixty-five and twelve hundredths. Answer: 365.12 Keep the finished puzzle for future use. Give your child the puzzle to solve tomorrow or next week.	Have your child study and memorize the parts of the skeleton on **The Skeletal System** (p. 22). Help the child locate these bones on his/her own body. Then, have your child read more about the human skeleton in a resource book. Have your child locate and label other bones: *radius, ulna, carpals, metacarpals, phalanges, tarsals, metatarsals, ilium, ischium, maxilla, mandible, sternum.*	Hold a discussion about Reconstruction. Use the questions and research from yesterday as a guide and starting point.
Review the rules for rounding numbers with your child. *See* Math, Week 1, number 4. Write a large number (such as 2,375.382613) on the chalkboard. Then, ask your child to round the number to different places. Have your child write his/her answers on the chalkboard.	Have your child read more about bones, then complete **The Supportive System** (p. 23).	Arrange for your child to perform a community service. Have your child write in his/her Social Studies Journal.

TEACHING SUGGESTIONS AND ACTIVITIES

LANGUAGE SKILLS (Fun With Words)

▶ 1. *Alliteration* is the repetition of the beginning sounds in a sentence or phrase. Alliteration can be effective in a title or in poetry. Alliteration may also be used to grab the attention of the reader or to add a sense of fun.

Examples: She says Sally seems silly. Introducing Magnificent Max, the Mad Magician!

Have your child write several sentences containing alliteration.

▶ 2. An *anagram* is a word that can be scrambled to form a new word. Write the following words on the chalkboard and challenge your child to find as many anagrams as possible: *trace, pots, nips, least, emits, scrape, cast, miles, tones, pets, ropes, read, eats, lame, meat, reteach, reaps, wets, cares, tries, hoes, wane, stake, naps, hams, dens, tear, tens, sprite, own, star, dealer, tar, reread, peal, inch.*

▶ 3. Write several sentences on the chalkboard. Have your child rewrite the sentences by adding words and images to form similes. It is okay to change the order of the words to maintain the sense of the sentences.

Example: The race cars were loud as they sped around the track.
The race cars were *as loud as thunder* as they sped around the track.

▶ 4. Copy the following sentences for your child. Have him/her rewrite the sentences and replace the underlined words with specific images to form metaphors.

Example: The leaves *covered* the forest floor. The leaves *made a beautiful carpet* for the forest floor.

▶ 5. *Hyperbole* is an exaggeration that emphasizes a real characteristic.

Example: *The basketball player was so tall, he could touch the top of the Empire State Building.*

Have your child write sentences using hyperbole to exaggerate the following topics: a lot of snow, long fingernails, taking a long time to finish a task, a very angry boy, a very pretty flower.

▶ 6. After reading the paragraph, create a word web. To do this, ask your child to identify the mood of the paragraph. Write the mood in the center of the paper and draw a circle or oval around the word or phrase. Draw radiating lines from the center and write the words that helped establish the feeling at the end of each line.

READING (Purpose for Reading)

▶ 1. Have your child name different things that he/she reads—novels, history books, letters, magazines, recipes, directions, labels, etc. List these ideas on a sheet of paper. Next, have your child group the items on the list into categories of purpose: enjoyment, learning facts, locating important details, answering questions, following directions. Understanding the purpose for reading may help your child to focus when it comes time to read.

▶ 2. Vocabulary should be taught in context as much as possible. When you choose vocabulary words, note the page numbers so your child may reread the sentences. Have your child read the sentences and try to explain the meanings to you. Then, ask your child to confirm his/her understanding by looking in the dictionary. Use the dictionary to confirm pronunciation as well.

MATH (Place Value)

BACKGROUND

Our numbering system is a base-ten system. Once you understand the pattern through 100, you can count indefinitely, simply by following the same repeating pattern. *Place value* is the name of this repeating pattern. The *value* of a digit is determined by the *place* in which it rests. For example, a 2 in the ones place has a value of *two*—a 2 in the hundreds place has a value of *two hundred*. Study the place-value chart that follows with your child. As you study the chart, explain to your child the following four points:

- Numbers are composed of ones, tens and hundreds.
- Each group of ones, tens and hundreds is called a *period*.

Learn at Home, Grade 6

- Periods are separated by commas.
- Read large numbers from left to right. Name the value of the period, then state the period. **Example:** The number 3,246,030,005,700 should be read as follows: *three trillion, two hundred forty-six billion, thirty million, five thousand, seven hundred.* **Note:** the word *and* is not used between periods.

▶ 1. Make a second set of index cards (using a different color) with a place value named on each card. Have your child choose a numeral card and a place-value card, then name the digit in the given place.

▶ 2. Review some spelling rules for writing numbers.

   a. Number words between 21 and 99 are written with a hyphen (with the exceptions of 30, 40, 50, 60, 70, 80 and 90). **Example:** 34 is written as *thirty-four.*

   b. Place a comma between the *periods*—just as when writing a number with digits. **Example:** 1,200 is written as *one thousand, two hundred.*

▶ 3. Numerals to the left of the decimal point are read as whole numbers. Numerals to the right of the decimal point are read as a place value. Read the decimal point as *and.* **Example:** 341.25 is read as *three hundred forty one and twenty-five hundredths.* The first decimal place is tenths, the second is hundredths, the third is thousandths and the fourth is ten thousandths.

▶ 4. When rounding a number to a certain place, first look at the number in the place immediately to the right. If that number is less than 5, stay the same. If that number is 5 or greater, round up. All numbers to the left of the place being rounded to remain the same; all numbers after the place being rounded to are dropped. **Example:** 254.136 rounded to the nearest hundredth equals 254.14, rounded to the nearest tenth equals 254.1, rounded to the nearest ten equals 250.

SCIENCE (The Human Body/Skeletal System)

BACKGROUND
The human body is composed of several systems that work together to make the body function. Good nutrition, regular exercise and proper hygiene enable these systems to run smoothly. Poor nutrition, pollution, lack of exercise and disease, however, can cause the body to function poorly. Provide plenty of resource books and materials about the human body for your child's reference.

SOCIAL STUDIES (Reconstruction)

▶ 1. Have your child look up reconstruction/Reconstruction in the dictionary. When capitalized, the term refers to a 12–year period after the Civil War. Have your child mark this period on a time line. Reconstruction refers to not only a physical rebuilding after the war (mostly in the South) but also the re-establishment of relationships between North and South. This included punishment of Confederate leaders, ensuring the rights and protection of freed slaves and bringing the seceded states back into the Union.

▶ 2. Provide your child with the following directions and questions to guide his/her research:

   Describe President Lincoln's plan for Reconstruction.

   Describe President Johnson's plan for Reconstruction.

   How did the Ku Klux Klan develop? What was their purpose?

   Why was Tennessee the first of the eleven Southern states to be readmitted to the Union?

   What were the Reconstruction Acts?

   What were the black codes?

   Who were the carpetbaggers?

   What was the attitude of many Southern whites?

   What good came out of Reconstruction? What was not accomplished?

   When and why did Reconstruction end?

Seeing Double

accept
accurate
arrange
ballot
commit
common
different
install
necessary
occasion
opposite
quarrel
really
recess
support
surround
terrible
tomorrow

Add letters to the double consonants to spell the words on the list and complete each short phrase.

1. _ _ ll _ _ box

2. _ _ mm _ _ a crime

3. _ _ rr _ _ _ _ day

4. _ cc _ _ _ it

5. _ _ _ _ _ _ ll a program

6. _ _ _ ll _ nice

7. _ _ _ _ ss time

8. _ rr _ _ _ _ neatly

9. special _ cc _ _ _ _ _ _

10. _ _ mm _ _ name

11. _ _ pp _ _ _ group

12. lover's _ _ _ rr_ _

13. _ _ ff _ _ _ _ _ choice

14. _ _ rr _ _ _ _ sound

15. _ pp _ _ _ _ _ _ end

16. _ cc _ _ _ _ _ _ count

17. _ _ _ _ _ ss _ _ _ work

18. a new _ _ _ _ rr _ _

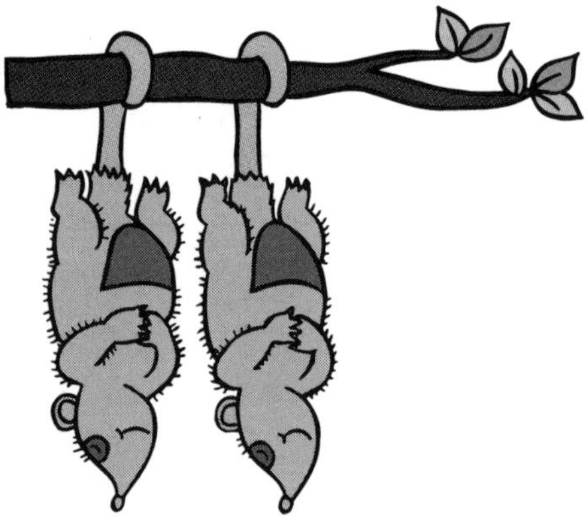

Choose eight words from the list. Separate the words into syllables and **rewrite** them below.

_____   _____

_____   _____

_____   _____

_____   _____

Learn at Home, Grade 6

Story Organizer

Week 1

Author ______________________________ Date ____________

Title ____

Vocabulary **Definitions**

______________ ______________________________

______________ ______________________________

______________ ______________________________

______________ ______________________________

______________ ______________________________

Setting: ____

Characters: ____

____

Problem: ____

____

Events: ____

____

____

____

Solution: ____

____

____

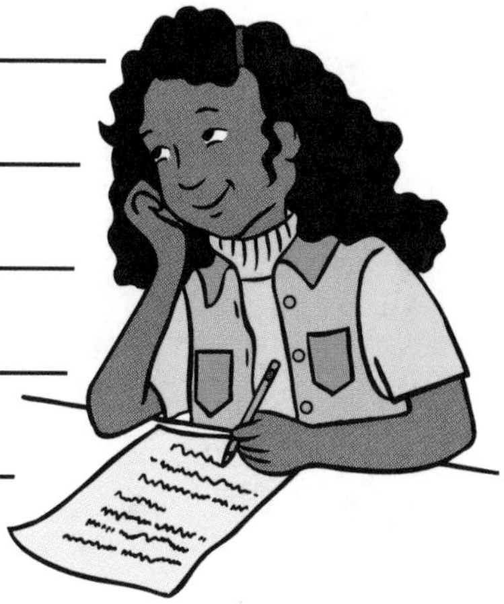

Did you enjoy this story? 1 2 3 4 5 6

Not at all — Very much!

Down the Ladder

Follow the directions to get to the bottom of the ladder.
Start with this number.

4,351,614,926

Add 4,000,000 to the number.

Subtract 40,000 from the number.

Decrease the number by 4,000.

Increase the number by 3,000,000.

Increase it by 5,000,000.

Subtract 10 from the number.

Subtract 40,000 from the number.

Add 30,000 to the number.

Increase the number by 2,000.

YOU MADE IT TO THE BOTTOM!

A quick review:

99 plus 1,001 equals _____

999 plus 100,001 equals _____

9,999 plus 100,001 equals _____

20

Learn at Home, Grade 6

Anticipation Guide

Read each statement and **circle** true or false in the left column. **Read** from a variety of resources to check the accuracy of your answers. Then, **circle** true or false in the right column as you prove or disprove statements. On another sheet of paper, **rewrite** each false statement as a true statement.

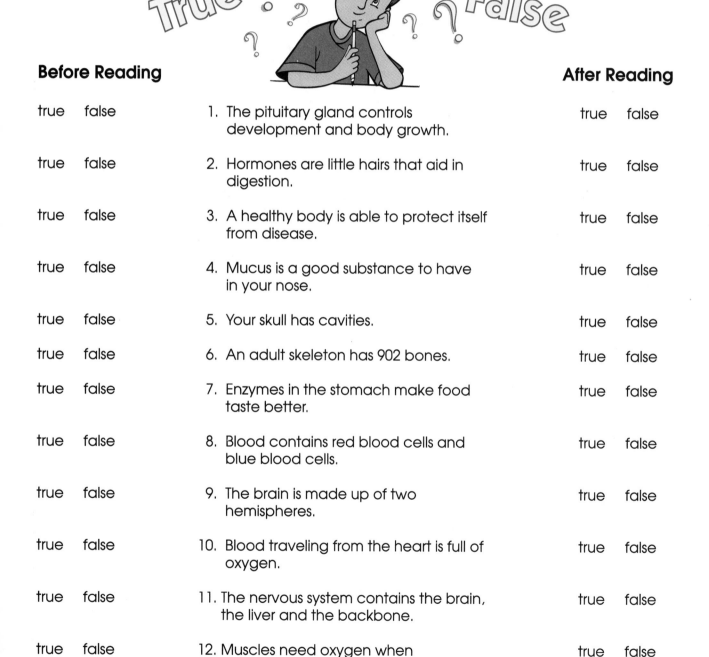

Before Reading			After Reading	
true	false	1. The pituitary gland controls development and body growth.	true	false
true	false	2. Hormones are little hairs that aid in digestion.	true	false
true	false	3. A healthy body is able to protect itself from disease.	true	false
true	false	4. Mucus is a good substance to have in your nose.	true	false
true	false	5. Your skull has cavities.	true	false
true	false	6. An adult skeleton has 902 bones.	true	false
true	false	7. Enzymes in the stomach make food taste better.	true	false
true	false	8. Blood contains red blood cells and blue blood cells.	true	false
true	false	9. The brain is made up of two hemispheres.	true	false
true	false	10. Blood traveling from the heart is full of oxygen.	true	false
true	false	11. The nervous system contains the brain, the liver and the backbone.	true	false
true	false	12. Muscles need oxygen when they are active.	true	false

21

The Skeletal System

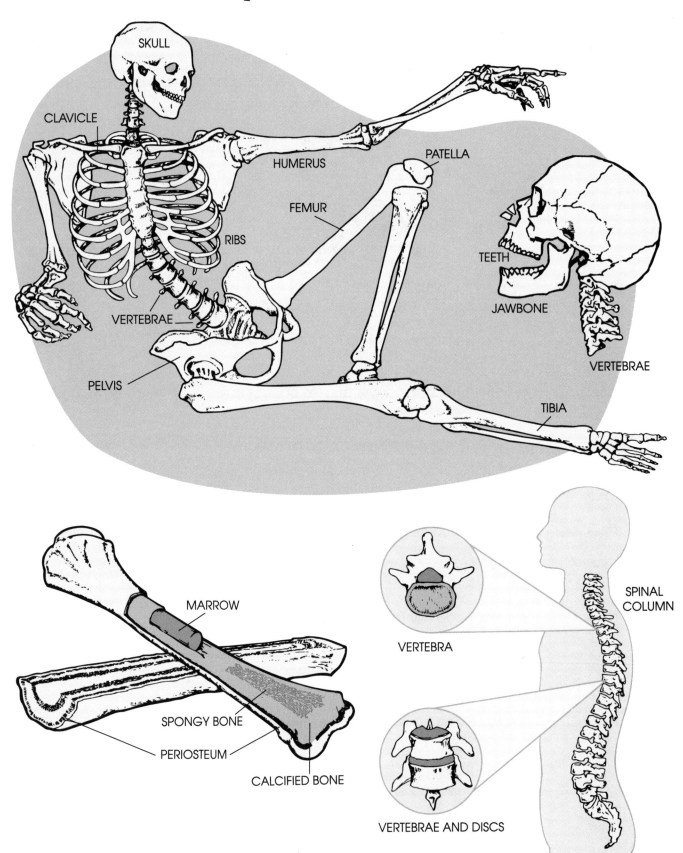

SKULL

CLAVICLE

HUMERUS

PATELLA

FEMUR

RIBS

TEETH

JAWBONE

VERTEBRAE

PELVIS

VERTEBRAE

TIBIA

MARROW

SPONGY BONE

PERIOSTEUM

CALCIFIED BONE

VERTEBRA

SPINAL COLUMN

VERTEBRAE AND DISCS

22

Learn at Home, Grade 6

The Supportive System

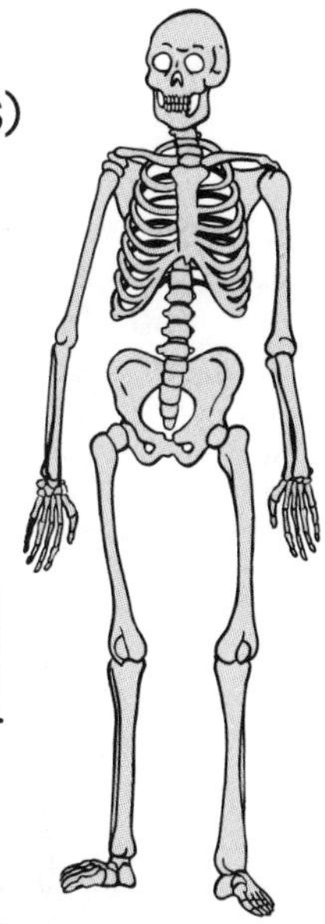

The bones are the body's supportive system. They are usually divided into two major groups—bones of the middle (skull, backbone and ribs) and bones of the arms and legs (including the shoulder and hip bones). When you were born, your skeleton was made of soft bones called **cartilage**. As you grew, most of that cartilage turned into bone. However, all people still have some cartilage in their bodies. Our noses and our ears are cartilage, and there are pads of cartilage between sections of the backbone that acts as cushions.

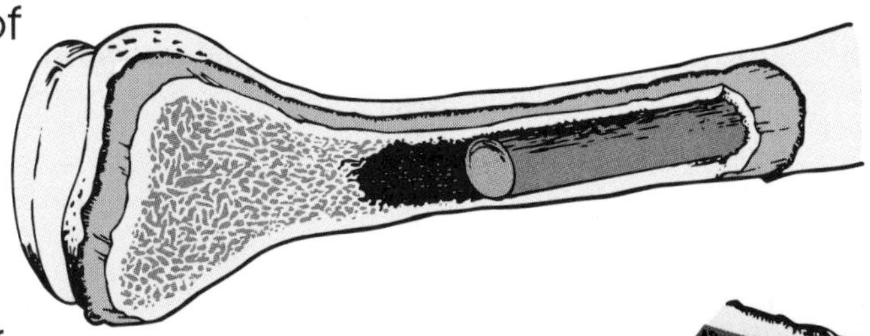

Bones do more than just support the body. The center of the bone, called **bone marrow**, makes new blood cells for our body. Bones are also a storage house for important minerals like calcium and phosphorous.

Answer the questions below. Use a science book or an encyclopedia if necessary.

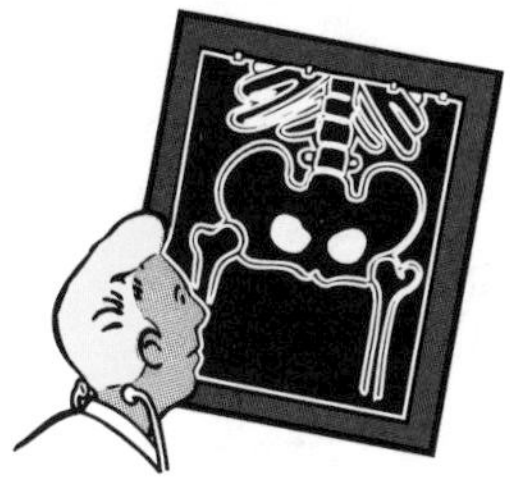

1. What are the main functions of the skeletal system?

   _____

   _____

   _____

   _____

2. What is the largest bone in your body?_____

3. What is the smallest bone in your body?_____

4. What do bones first develop as?_____

5. What does bone marrow do?_____

6. Do all bones have real bone marrow?_____

7. What is the outer layer of a bone called?_____

8. Where two bones meet is called a_____

Fascinating Fact! Did you know that a giraffe has the same number of vertebrae in its neck as you?

	Language Skills	Spelling	Reading
Monday	**Personification** Review the concept of *personification*. Discuss the purpose for using personification (to have fun with words and to create a strong image for the reader). *See* Language Skills, Week 2, number 1. Have your child write several sentences containing personification. Provide interesting pictures to spark your child's imagination.	Pretest your child on these spelling words: anywhere headache meanwhile copyright however nighttime earthquake landslide otherwise earthshaking lifeguard skewbald farewell lifetime skinflint gentleman mantelpiece throughout Correct the pretest, add personalized words and make two copies of this week's study list.	**Vocabulary** Help your child choose a nonfiction book to read this week. Discuss what he/she would like to learn from the book. Teach your child to browse through the book and look at chapter titles, bold subtitles and other organizers before reading. This will help him/her gain a sense of how the book is organized and what will be covered. *See* Reading, Week 2, number 1.
Tuesday	**Affixes:** Review *prefixes* and *suffixes*. Help your child make a list of common prefixes and suffixes. Have him/her write the meaning of each affix. Then, have your child use the list of affixes to build new words. Point to an affix and have your child name four words that contain it. Repeat with other affixes.	Study this week's spelling words. Have your child complete **Earthshaking Adventure** (p. 28).	Discuss the current reading book in a conference. Check your child's understanding of the concepts in the book. Review how to take notes.
Wednesday	Provide your child with a list of words containing affixes. Have your child underline the root word in each word on the list, then write a definition of the word combined with the affix. *See* Language Skills, Week 2, number 2 for a list of words containing affixes.	Have your child use each of this week's spelling words correctly in a sentence.	When your child encounters a difficult word in his/her reading, he/she may be able to determine its meaning by looking at the context. *See* Reading, Week 2, numbers 2 and 3. Have your child use the dictionary to confirm meaning and check pronunciation.
Thursday	Generate a list of root words. Have your child add prefixes and suffixes to the root words to create new words. Encourage your child to have fun creating lots of new words. *See* Language Skills, Week 2, number 3 for a list of root words.	Have your child study this week's spelling words. *See* **Spelling Activities** for activity ideas (p. 8).	Choose unfamiliar nouns from the dictionary. Read each definition aloud. Have your child make a sketch to illustrate the meaning of each new word. *See* Reading, Week 2, number 4.
Friday	Have your child scan the book you are reading for words containing affixes. Have your child make a chart of the words he/she finds. The chart should contain three columns: *prefix*, *root word* and *affix*. Have your child break up each word and write its components in the correct columns.	Give your child the final spelling test. Have your child record pretest and final test words in his/her word bank.	Hold a reading conference with your child to discuss the nonfiction book he/she is reading this week. Focus on summarizing and reporting information.

Learn at Home, Grade 6

Math	Science	Social Studies
Measurement Introduce the concept of measurement. *See* Math, Week 2. Ask your child to imagine a day without measuring time. *How would things be different?* Research together how people first started measuring time. Then, look at a map of world time zones. Discuss how people across the world adhere to a standard measurement of time. *See* Math, Week 2, number 1.	**Skeletal System** Continue to discuss and explore the human skeletal system. Have your child complete **Count Them** (p. 32).	**Post-Civil War U.S.** Reconstruction did not bring racial harmony to the South. Discuss some of the problems that Southern blacks encountered in their first years of freedom. Have your child read the fourteenth and fifteenth Amendments to the Constitution. *What was the impact of these two amendments?*
Adding and subtracting time can be difficult since time is not measured in base ten. Have your child add 4 hours to the current time. Observe how he/she calculates the new time. Offer your child any strategies that might help him/her determine the time more quickly. Have your child complete **What Time?** (p. 29).	Have your child read about *joints* in a reference book. *See* Science, Week 2, number 1. Have your child complete **Meeting Places** (p. 33).	During Reconstruction in the South, the United States purchased Alaska from Russia. Have your child read about the history of Alaska. *How much did Secretary of State Seward pay for the Alaskan Territory? What industry in Alaska made it a worthy purchase?*
Look around your house for devices used to measure temperature (an oral thermometer, a candy or meat thermometer, an outdoor thermometer, a thermostat, etc.). Discuss which common appliances must contain some kind of thermometer in order to maintain a given temperature. Have your child locate the temperature controls on these appliances. *See* Math, Week 2, number 2.	Have your child read about ligaments in a reference book. *Ligaments* join bones at a joint. They can be as strong as a rope. A sprain is actually a stretch or tear in a ligament. Ligaments can take a long time to heal. *See* Science, Week 2, number 2.	Have your child read about westward expansion after the Civil War. Have him/her draw a map of the United States in the 1860 and 1870s, showing with symbols and writing what was happening at that time in the Plains States.
With your child, discuss the difference between the Celsius and Fahrenheit scales. Teach your child the formula for converting degrees Celsius to degrees Fahrenheit and vice versa: $$°F = (°C \times {}^9/_5) + 32$$ $$°C = (°F - 32) \times {}^5/_9$$ Have your child complete **Thermometers** (p. 30).	**Muscular System:** The human body contains three types of muscles: skeletal, cardiac and smooth. *See* Science, Week 2, number 3 for information on these three types of muscles. Have your child read about how skeletal muscles work in tandem to move a limb. Have your child draw a diagram that demonstrates this in his/her Science Log.	Have your child read about the battle between the Sioux Indians and Lieutenant Colonel George A. Custer. Ask your child to write from the perspective of Sitting Bull or Crazy Horse. *Why was this battle worth fighting?*
In the U.S. Customary System, weight is measured in pounds and ounces; length is measured in feet and inches. Have your child complete **Mean Monster Locks Up Wrestling** (p. 31).	Have your child conduct an experiment to find out how temperature affects the movement of muscles. *See* Science, Week 2, number 4.	Arrange for your child to perform a community service. Have your child write in his/her Social Studies Journal.

TEACHING SUGGESTIONS AND ACTIVITIES

LANGUAGE SKILLS (Personification/Affixes)

▶ 1. *Personification* is the literary technique of lending human qualities and capabilities to inanimate objects.

   Example: The vegetables were swimming in butter.

   In the example, the human ability to swim is assigned to the vegetables to stress the fact that there was a lot of butter.

▶ 2. Here is a list of words containing affixes to get you started:

preschooler	semisweet	forehand	unkind	impolite
cooperate	biweekly	antifreeze	dissatisfied	careful
teacher	comfortable	mistreat	secretly	loudly
noticeable	movement	permitting	placement	changing
westward	friendliest	speaker	cooperate	teacher
triangles	hopeful	childishly	thankless	movement

▶ 3. Here is a list of root words to get you started:

school	sweet	view	kind	proper
talk	change	aware	care	hope
beauty	neat	free	happy	stand
cycle	use	year	lie	walk

READING (Vocabulary)

▶ 1. When a reading assignment involves gathering information, encourage your child to browse through the whole book first. Have him/her look at the table of contents and index to find specific topics. This prereading will enable your child to read more efficiently and with better understanding. Then, have your child read the parts that are interesting or relevant to his/her purpose.

▶ 2. Write sentences on the chalkboard containing nonsense words. Ask your child to read each sentence and describe the meaning of the nonsense word. This exercise will help reinforce the idea that your child can determine the meaning of a new word by looking at its context. Ask your child to name the part of speech of each nonsense word. Discuss how he/she was able to tell so much about the words.

   Examples: The rabbit stood *priled* when it became aware of the hunter's presence.
   We *caufled* loudly when our team scored.
   The *zebulot* box was so big that we could not get it through the door.

▶ 3. Use a *cloze* text to stress that context clues help when reading new vocabulary. Copy a passage from a book your child has not read. Use correction fluid to cover some key words in the text. Ask your child to read the passage and fill in the missing words.

   Example: Madeline stood quietly _____ her teacher whose back was to the _____. Madeline leaned over, glancing left and right in synchronized _____ with Mrs. Gramme, searching for the ____ polka-dot Minnie Mouse _____. Wait! What was that _____ the desk?

   Answers: behind, class, movement, red, earring, under

▶ 4. Have your child sketch the following vocabulary words.

   a. A *caduceus* is a winged staff (wand) with two serpents wrapped around it. It is used as a symbol of the medical profession.

   b. A *galleon* was a large sailing ship with three masts and square rigging. It was used from the fifteenth to the seventeenth century.

Learn at Home, Grade 6

c. The projection on a sundial that casts a shadow is called a *gnomon*.

d. A *torii* is the gateway of a Shinto temple, consisting of two uprights holding a curved piece of wood across the top and a straight piece of wood under the top curved one.

e. A *stalactite* is an icicle-shaped mineral deposit that hangs from the roof of a cave.

MATH (Measurement)

BACKGROUND

Measurement is a part of our daily lives. We measure time with a clock, an egg timer, a sundial and other creative devices. We measure length in *inches, centimeters, miles, kilometers* and other units. We measure weight with a bathroom scale, a kitchen scale and a balance scale, among other methods. We may measure temperatures to determine health, weather or the proper cooking environment. Measurements vary in accuracy depending on the tools used and the purpose for taking the measurements. The best way to teach measurement is to have your child design and complete a project that requires him/her to use a variety of measurement tools, units and methods. A construction project that includes a variety of materials may be ideal. Visit a science lab where tiny units of measure are used. Visit a machine shop where large units of measure are used. Explore and discover the importance of accurate measurement.

▶ 1. Have your child research and draw some of the devices used over the years to measure time.

▶ 2. Have your child choose one of the thermometers found around your house to take a temperature reading every hour throughout the day. Your child may choose to use the outdoor thermometer to record the temperature outside every hour. Have your child plot the temperatures on a line graph and analyze the changes throughout the day. Ask your child if he/she has ever wondered if his/her normal body temperature is actually 98.6°F? Have your child take his/her body temperature every hour throughout the day, then plot the temperatures on a graph. Have your child write a paragraph about his/her observations.

SCIENCE (Skeletal System/Muscular System)

▶ 1. Have your child perform the following tasks, carefully observing the movements of the joints and bones:

write	throw a ball	walk	bend over
sit	jump	swing your arms	tilt your head
make a fist	turn your head	swing your leg	walk on tiptoe

▶ 2. *Ligaments* are strong tissues that hold the bones together at the joints. Have your child try to feel the ligaments on the inside of his/her elbow or knee. It may help to demonstrate the ligament on an uncooked chicken wing or leg.

▶ 3. *Skeletal muscle*, which is striated muscle, covers the skeleton and makes up a large part of body weight. These muscles can usually be moved voluntarily. Skeletal muscles work together in pairs to provide movement. *Cardiac muscle* (also striated) is found only in the heart. *Smooth muscle* makes up the stomach, intestines, blood vessels and diaphragm. Smooth muscles are also called involuntary muscles.

▶ 4. Have your child write his/her name twenty times on a sheet of paper. Then, have your child hold some ice cubes in his/her writing hand for 1 minute. Have your child dry his/her hands quickly, then write his/her name another twenty times. Next, have your child place his/her hand in a bowl of warm water for 1 minute. Have your child dry his/her hands quickly, then write his/her name another twenty times. Ask your child to examine his/her handwriting. Discuss how each type of water affected the writing. *Do muscles work better when they are warm or when they are cold?*

Earthshaking Adventure

Locate each spelling word in the word search. Words can be found up, down, forward and backward.

anywhere   copyright   earthquake

earthshaking   farewell   gentleman

headache   however   landslide

lifeguard   lifetime   mantelpiece

meanwhile   nighttime   otherwise

skewbald   skinflint   throughout

```
T U O H G U O R H T L M N D J E H R F A R E W E L L V O E
H P L O L N J H M L P O E B L E E D Y N O T H E R W I S E
E J I W D R A U G E F I L P I Z A N E M N B E L J E S E M
M V C E B N R O U S E L Q U E L S T C O P Y N E U V K K I
E M I V T H G I N C O P Y R I G H T S R T E E S N Y I S T
F A H E A D A C H E A E A R T H Q U A K E W V E R E N K E
O P D R A W S E T F A M E A N P L I L E P L E B R E F N F
R W S T I N L E M I T T H G I N B A C K E P R D L P L E I
E A N Y W H E R E N E I F H B O R D S K E W B A L D I R L
E L I H W N A E M N A M E L T N E G J O W E V V V R N Y U
M I E D I L S D N A L E R E M T I A C E B L R R Q U T N F
K I L O O M N B M A N T E L P I E C E D W H R R E A N Y K
G N I K A H S H T R A E T H R O U G L M N O H H E A D E D
```

Learn at Home, Grade 6

What Time?

1. Mary was out of bed at 6:30 a.m. She had lunch 6 hours later. What time did Mary have lunch?

   6 hours **Ahead** = _____ p.m.

2. Mary returned from school at 4:00 p.m. Mary had left for school $8\frac{1}{2}$ hours earlier. What time did Mary leave for school?

   $8\frac{1}{2}$ hours **Back** = _____ a.m.

3. Mary ate breakfast at 7:00 a.m. and ate dinner 11 hours later. What time did she eat dinner?

   11 hours _____ = _____

4. Mary started her homework at 7:30 p.m. and studied for $3\frac{1}{2}$ hours. What time did she stop studying?

   $3\frac{1}{2}$ hours _____ = _____

5. On Saturday, Mary baby-sat a neighbor's child. The parents returned at 3:00 p.m. They had been gone 5 hours. At what time did Mary start baby-sitting?

   5 hours _____ = _____

6. Mary's party started at 8:00 p.m. and was over $2\frac{1}{2}$ hours later. Mary spent $1\frac{1}{2}$ hours cleaning up after the last guest left. What time was Mary through cleaning?

   _____ hours _____ = _____

7. Mary's math class starts at 2:30 p.m. Her music class starts $4\frac{1}{2}$ hours earlier. What time does Mary's music class start?

   _____ hours _____ = _____

8. School is out at 3:00 p.m. Baseball practice lasts 2 hours, and then the team takes $\frac{1}{2}$ hour to shower and get dressed. What time does the team leave school?

   _____ hours _____ = _____

29

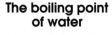
Thermometers

Write each temperature in degrees Celsius (°C).

The boiling point of water	The freezing point of water	Our normal body temperature	Freezer section of a grocery store
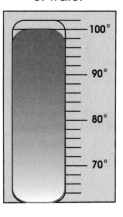	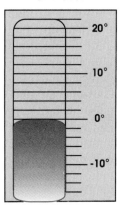	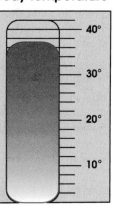	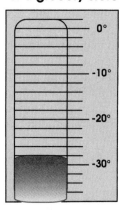
_____°C	_____°C	_____°C	_____°C

1. How many degrees Celsius does our body remain above the freezing point of water? _____

2. On the Celsius thermometer, how many degrees difference is there between the freezing and boiling points of water? _____

Write each temperature in degrees Fahrenheit (°F).

The boiling point of water	Everything outside freezes	Our normal body temperature	A hot day in Phoenix
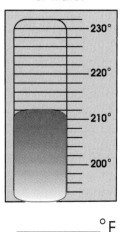	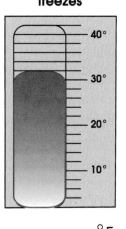	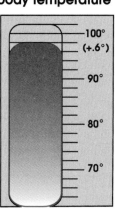	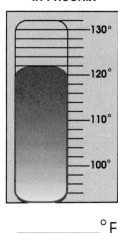
_____°F	_____°F	_____°F	_____°F

1. How many degrees difference is there on the Fahrenheit thermometer between the freezing and boiling points of water? _____

2. How many degrees difference is there between a hot day in Phoenix, Arizona, and the boiling point of water? _____

30

Learn at Home, Grade 6

Mean Monster Locks Up Wrestling

Mean Monster, a great defensive back in football, decided to take on all the top wrestlers in order to keep in shape during the off-season. He weighed 569 lb. 7 oz. and stood 7 ft. 3 in. tall. (Remember: 1 lb. = 16 oz. and 1 ft. = 12 in.)

Solve the problems on another sheet of paper. **Write** your answer in the space provided.

1. Mean Monster's first bout was with Harry the Hammer who weighed 397 lb. 4 oz. How much more did Mean Monster weigh than Harry the Hammer?

2. Mean Monster did so well in his first round that he faced Marvelous Marvin Morton in the next event. Marvelous Marvin stood 6 ft. 9 in. tall. How much taller was Mean Monster?

3. Awesome Albert Alston was 167 lb. 11 oz. lighter than Mean Monster. What did Awesome Albert weigh?

4. Irwin the Icebox weighed 478 lb. 14 oz. He and Mean Monster stood together on the scale. What did it read?

5. Dreadful Dan the Mighty Man weighed 777 lb. 7 oz. What was his weight in ounces?

6. Ivan the Incredible ate an 18 lb. 8 oz. meal before his bout. Mean Monster had only 188 oz. of food before the match. How much more did Ivan eat?

7. Melvin the Magnificent was a dainty 478 lb. 15 oz. He stood with Mean Monster and Dreadful Dan on the same scale. What was their total weight?

8. Mean Monster's brother, Itty Bitty Monster, weighed 134 lb. 15 oz. less than his big brother. What did Itty Bitty weigh?

31

Count Them

Count some of the bones in your body. Use a science book or an encyclopedia to help you answer the questions below.

1. How many cavities are there in your skull?_____What are they for?

   _____

2. How many bones do you feel in your upper arm?_____ How many are there?_____
   In your lower arm?_____ How many are there?_____How many bones are in
   your arms (counting your hands)? _____

3. How many bones do you feel that form one palm of your hand? _____
   These are called _____ How many are there?_____

4. How many bones do you feel in the fingers and thumb of one of your
   hands?_____ How many are there? _____These are called _____
   Which finger has fewer bones than the others? _____

5. How many pairs of ribs do you count? _____ How many are there? _____
   How many pairs are attached to the sternum?_____

6. How many bones do you feel in one of your legs?_____ How many are there? _____

7. The skeleton makes up about 18% of the body's weight. How much do you
   weigh?_____ How much do your bones weigh?_____

8. What is the longest single bone in your body? _____ This bone accounts for
   $\frac{1}{4}$ of your height. About how long is this bone? _____

9. An adult human skeleton has 206 bones. There are 26 vertebrae.
   What percentage of the body's bones comprise the backbone?_____

10. How many bones do you have altogether in your hands? _____What other
    part of your body has the same number of bones? _____

Fascinating Fact! Did you know babies are born with about 350 separate bones?

Learn at Home, Grade 6

Meeting Places

The place two bones meet is called a **joint**. Joints allow us to bend, twist and turn our bodies. The human body has several different types of joints. Each allows a different kind of movement. Read the descriptions below. Then, **write** examples of the joints below each description.

Hinge Joints — These joints can only move in one direction, like a door hinge. One bone works against another. Movement is back and forth on one plane. **Examples:**

_____

Ball-and-Socket Joints — These joints provide us with swinging and rotating movements. Make a fist with one hand. Cup the fingers of the other. Put your fist inside the cupped hand. You can turn your fist (the ball) in any direction within your cupped hand (the socket). **Examples:**

_____

Saddle Joints — These joints move in two directions, back and forth, up and down or in rotation. **Examples:**

_____

Sliding Joints — In a sliding joint, several bones next to one another bend together in limited gliding motion. **Examples:**

_____

Pivot Joints — These joints give us a rotating motion. **Examples:**

_____

Fixed Joints — With these types of joints, bones are fused together and permit no movement. **Examples:**

_____

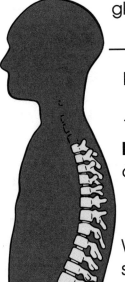

What part of your body can move forward, backward, side to side and around on top of a vertical axis and is not one of the above?

_____

33

	Language Skills	**Spelling**	**Reading**
Monday	Help your child choose a writing assignment for this week. Encourage your child to incorporate figurative language into his/her piece. *See* Language Skills, Weeks 1 and 2. Have your child choose a topic, make a plan for writing, then begin working on a rough draft.	Pretest your child on these spelling words: cymbal pare principal symbol pear principle hangar pause tacks hanger paws tax muscle plain waist mussel plane waste Correct the pretest, add personalized words and make two copies of this week's study list.	Introduce this week's reading selection. Suggestion: *The Lion, the Witch, and the Wardrobe* by C. S. Lewis.
Tuesday	Review the writing process with your child. *See* **The Writing Process** (p.5). Have your child read through his/her rough draft from yesterday and underline all the verbs.	Study this week's spelling words. Have your child complete **Mussel With Muscle** (p. 39).	Hold a reading conference in which you discuss characterization. Have your child think about the characters he/she has encountered so far in this week's book. Which characters does your child trust? Which characters does he/she predict are headed for trouble?
Wednesday	**Verbs:** There are three principal parts of every verb: *present, past* and *past participle*. Have your child write sentences using these forms. *See* Language Skills, Week 3, numbers 1 and 2. Write ten sentences on the board. Have your child underline the main verb in each and tell whether the verb form is past, present or past participle. *See* Language Skills, Week 3, number 3.	Have your child use each of this week's spelling words correctly in a sentence.	Review the purpose of library resources such as almanacs, atlases, encyclopedias, thesauri and dictionaries. Give your child sentences containing the following words underlined: *file, party, passage, row, spectacles* and *wind*. Have your child read each sentence and look up the underlined word in a dictionary. Can he/she find the appropriate definition in the dictionary? Have your child complete **The Right Stuff** (p. 40).
Thursday	Review the past, present and future tenses of verbs. Have your child state a sentence as an example of each tense. Have your child complete **Verb Tense** (p. 38).	Have your child study this week's spelling words.	**Main Idea:** Even good readers may not concentrate enough during reading to reflect on the main idea. Have your child read short passages of the text, then summarize the main ideas. Give your child more practice determining main idea. Have your child complete **What's the Idea?** (p. 41).
Friday	Teach your child how to conjugate verbs. To conjugate means to place the tenses in order with the first-, second- and third-person forms. *See* Language Skills, Week 3, number 4. Have your child conjugate the verb *to give*. The principal parts of the verb are *give, gave* and *has/have/had given*.	Give your child the final spelling test. Have your child record pretest and final test words in his/her word bank.	Hold a reading conference to discuss the messages or lessons of this week's book. Reflect on and discuss symbolism. Have your child complete a book project. *See* **Reading Conference** (p.10).

Learn at Home, Grade 6

Math	Science	Social Studies
Measurement In the metric system, length is measured in *millimeters, centimeters, meters* and *kilometers*. Discuss when it is appropriate to use each unit. For example, if you needed to know how far it was to your grandma's house, what unit would you use? Have your child complete **Metric Units of Length** (p. 42).	**Nervous System** Have your child read about the function of the brain, spinal cord and nerves. *See* Science, Week 3, number 1. Have your child complete **The Body's Communication System** (p. 44).	Have your child read "The Old Days," a poem by Baxter Black found in *Coyote Cowboy Poetry*. Discuss the imagery of the poem. Then, have your child read about the life of a cowboy in the late 1800s. Why did the need for cowboys decrease in the 1890s?
Have your child use a centimeter ruler and a meterstick to draw a room to scale. Have your child include details such as windows, doors, closets and furniture.	The three major parts of the brain include the *cerebrum, cerebellum* and *medulla*. Have your child read about the job of each part in an encyclopedia. *See* Science, Week 3, number 2. Have your child draw and label a diagram of the human brain in his/her Science Log. Provide magazines and articles for your child to read about current neurological research.	Have your child describe the elements of a cowboy's traditional attire and explain the function of each piece. Have him/her draw a diagram of a cowboy in "full costume."
Review the U.S. Customary units for measuring volume or capacity. There are many different units that measure capacity: *cups, pints, quarts, gallons.* Your child can also learn a lot about capacity by working in the kitchen with recipes. Guide your child in making a favorite recipe. Have your child complete **Units of Capacity** (p. 43).	Some actions do not involve the brain. These actions are called *reflexes*. The message of pain is sent to the spinal cord and the message is quickly sent back to remove the body from the source of pain. *See* Science, Week 3, number 3. Have your child complete **Think Fast** (p. 45).	**Industrial Revolution:** Introduce the terms *urban* and *rural*. Discuss the differences between urban and rural areas—the types of homes, the landscape, the types of jobs people have, etc. Ask your child what type of work he/she would find the most rewarding. Have your child explain the reasons for his/her choice.
Review metric units of *volume* or capacity. *See* Math, Week 3, number 1. Have your child use a metric measuring cup to determine the capacity of the following: a can of soda, a mug, a cereal bowl and a drinking glass. Have your child choose the correct unit of measure to use in a given situation. *See* Math, Week 3, number 2.	Review the five senses: *touch, sight, smell, sound* and *taste*. Discuss their importance in communicating with the brain. Have your child draw a diagram of the brain receiving messages from the senses.	Discuss the meaning of the word *revolution*. The Industrial Revolution was so named because industry changed drastically in a short period of time. *See* Social Studies, Week 3, number 1. Have your child read about the Industrial Revolution. Provide him/her with a list of questions to guide his/her research. *See* Social Studies, Week 3, number 2.
Review concepts of *place value, rounding* and *measurement*. Give your child several measurements. Have him/her round each measurement to the nearest place or to the nearest cup, foot, degree, etc.	Have your child write a poem about the five senses, using descriptive language. *See* Science, Week 3, number 4.	Arrange for your child to perform a community service. Have your child write in his/her Social Studies Journal.

~~TEACHING SUGGESTIONS AND ACTIVITIES~~

LANGUAGE SKILLS (Verbs)

▶ 1. The principal parts of two verbs are listed below.

Present	**Past**	**Past Participle**
sell	sold	have/has/had sold
learn	learned	have/has/had learned

▶ 2. The following sentence is written three times, each with a different principal part of the same verb. Have your child follow this example to practice writing sentences with the three principal parts.

The flowers bloom in my garden.

The flowers bloomed in my garden.

The flowers have bloomed in my garden.

▶ 3. You may choose to write your own sentences or use the ten sentences below for this activity:

A queen honeybee lays about 2,000 eggs in 1 day.

She has produced many fertilized eggs that will become female worker bees.

The unfertilized eggs she has placed in the brood nest will become male drones.

Worker bees work very hard during their lifetime of only 6 weeks.

Worker bees dance to tell other bees in the hive where to find flowers for food.

Some workers danced in a circle to explain that the food was nearby.

The youngest worker bees in the hive cleaned the empty cells.

They feed "royal jelly" to the larvae in the hive.

Young worker bees build the honeycomb.

Honeybees have helped us by making honey and wax and by fertilizing flowers.

▶ 4. **Present tense:**

	Singular	Plural
First person:	I ride	we ride
Second person:	you ride	you ride
Third person:	he, she, it rides	they ride

Past tense:

	Singular	Plural
First person:	I rode	we rode
Second person:	you rode	you rode
Third person:	he, she, it rode	they rode

Future tense:

	Singular	Plural
First person:	I will ride	we will ride
Second person:	you will ride	you will ride
Third person:	he, she, it will ride	they will ride

MATH (Measurement)

▶ 1. The metric units of capacity are milliliters (mL) and liters (L). There are 1000 mL in 1 L. One mL is equal to 0.001 L. A liter is just a little bit more than a quart. There are about 5 mL in a teaspoon.

▶ 2. Copy the following sentences. Have your child choose the appropriate unit of measure in each.

a. Michele's dad used 40 (**mL L**) of paint to cover the outside of their house.

b. Jeff filled his aquarium with 30 (**mL L**) of salt water.

36

c. After just a few days, 6 (**mL L**) of salt solution in a jar had evaporated.

d. Heather used 2 (**mL L**) of milk to make homemade ice cream.

e. Jolie drank 320 (**mL L**) of grape juice with her lunch.

f. Juan used 10 (**mL L**) of cooking oil in the bread he was making.

Science (Nervous System)

▶ 1. The brain and nervous system work together to control all actions and reactions of the body. Present the following questions and discuss the involvement of the brain in each situation.

What happens when you touch something extremely hot?

What is your brain doing when you read a book?

What type of music do you like?

How is your brain similar to a computer program?

How are you aware that you are eating a banana or that a candle is burning?

▶ 2. The largest part of the brain is called the *cerebrum*. It appears wrinkled and deeply grooved. The cerebrum controls sight, hearing, thinking and voluntary muscle movement. The cerebrum is made up of a right and left hemisphere. Each hemisphere is made up of lobes.

The *cerebellum* is located at the back of the brain and under the cerebrum. The cerebellum controls balance and coordination of movement.

The *medulla*, also known as the brain stem, connects the spinal cord and the cerebrum. The medulla controls involuntary movements, such as the heart, eyes, lungs, stomach and intestines.

▶ 3. Discuss the action of your reflexes in response to the following stimuli: touching a sharp pin, tickling your nose with a feather, a loud explosion, slipping on a wet floor.

▶ 4. Have your child write a sensory poem in which each line includes a description based on a different sense. Encourage your child to use metaphor, hyperbole, similes and other figurative language in his/her poem.

Chimpanzees have long, soft hair (touch)
The deep brown of dark chocolate. (taste)
They yell like excited ghosts (sound)
Flying across the sky on a dark night. (sight)
They smell like banana cream pie. (smell)

Social Studies (Industrial Revolution)

▶ 1. Prior to the late 1800s, most industry was small. Small business owners learned a trade and sold their products and services locally. With the invention of efficient electric machines, the nature of labor changed. Machines could do the work of people faster and cheaper. Goods were grown or manufactured by large industries and shipped across the country at lower costs. Many people were needed to work the large machines. Jobs were created in the shipping industry and in the production of power. Many people left small skilled jobs to work at boring assembly-type jobs. Discuss the changes in personal job satisfaction and attitudes toward work.

▶ 2. Check out several library materials on the Industrial Revolution for your child to read. Have your child use the following as a study guide.

What was life like before the Industrial Revolution?

Explain how the division of labor increases productivity.

How did life in cities change with the rise of the Industrial Revolution?

What were some of the major inventions during the American Industrial Revolution?

What did the revolution in transportation involve?

What were some of the negative effects of the Industrial Revolution? How were workers treated?

Verb Tense

The **present tense** tells what is happening now.
    Example: Jamie runs today in the big race.
The **past tense** tells about an action which happened in the past.
    Example: Jamie ran in the preliminary race yesterday.
The **future tense** tells about an action which will occur in the future. It is formed by using the helping verb will with the present tense of the verb.
    Example: Jamie will run in the Olympics someday.

Underline the verb in each sentence. Tell whether the verb is in the present tense, past tense or future tense.

1. Thousands of years ago, the Chinese used more than one name. _____

2. Today, the Chinese still give their children three names. _____

3. Family names, or last names, came about in various ways. _____

4. These names will remain for centuries into the future. _____

5. Some writers use "pseudonyms," or fictitious names. _____

6. Eric Blair wrote under the assumed name George Orwell. _____

7. Immigrants will introduce new names to the United States. _____

8. Some people use nicknames instead of their legal names. _____

Fill in the chart below.

Verb	Present Tense	Past Tense	Future Tense
see	see, sees	saw	will see
hide			
swim			
catch			
leave			
run			
throw			

Learn at Home, Grade 6

Mussel With Muscle

Write the correct homophone from the spelling words under each picture.
Write the matching homophone below it.

cymbal	symbol	hangar	hanger	muscle
mussel	pare	pear	pause	paws
plain	plane	principal	principle	tacks
tax	waist	waste		

_____

_____

_____

_____

_____

_____

_____

_____

_____

_____

_____

_____

_____

_____

_____

_____

_____

_____

The Right Stuff

Circle the resource book you would use to find . . .

1. A recipe for baking homemade bread.

    encyclopedia   cookbook   *The Life of a Beaver*

2. A description of how beavers make dams.

    almanac   *The Life of a Beaver*   *The Guinness Book of World Records*

3. A map of the United Kingdom.

    thesaurus   world atlas   *The Guinness Book of World Records*

4. The ingredients for Turkish delight.

    The Life of a Beaver   world atlas   cookbook

5. Information about the author, C. S. Lewis.

    almanac   encyclopedia   *Guidebook for Art Instructors*

6. The name of the world's most massive dam.

    The Guinness Book of World Records   dictionary   thesaurus

7. The oldest words in the English language.

    almanac   atlas   *The Guinness Book of World Records*

8. Another word for "trouble."

    thesaurus   atlas   cookbook

9. Why a beaver slaps its tail.

    dictionary   *The Life of a Beaver*   atlas

10. The pronunciation of "courtier."

    The Hobbit   dictionary   almanac

11. What camphor is used for.

    dictionary   *The Life of a Beaver*   thesaurus

What's the Idea?

Circle the sentence that best expresses the main idea of each paragraph.

1. Edmund began to question whether or not the lion in the Queen's courtyard was alive. The large creature looked as if it were about to pounce on a dwarf. But it did not move. Then Edmund noticed the snow on the lion's head and back. Only a statue would be covered like that!
   - The statue is snow-covered.
   - Edmund wonders if the lion is alive.
   - The lion is ready to jump.

2. The resting party of children and beavers heard the sound of jingling bells. Mr. Beaver dashed out of his hiding place and soon called the others to join him. He could hardly contain himself with excitement. Father Christmas is here!
   - Mr. Beaver is a brave animal.
   - Father Christmas has come to Narnia.
   - The group hears a jingling sound.

3. Poor Edmund! Because he came to the Queen, he expected her to reward him gratefully with Turkish delight. After all, he had traveled so far and had suffered miserably in the cold. When the Queen finally commanded that he receive food and drink, the cruel dwarf brought Edmund a bowl of water and a hunk of dry bread.
   - Edmund is not rewarded as he expects.
   - The young boy suffered from the cold.
   - Edmund receives bread and water.

4. Peter knew he must rescue Susan from the wolf. When the wolf charged, Susan climbed up a nearby tree. The wolf's snapping and snarling mouth was inches away. When Peter looked more closely, he realized that his sister was about to faint. Rushing in with his sword, Peter slashed at the beast.
   - Peter kills the wolf.
   - Peter realizes he must save his sister.
   - The wolf snarls at Susan.

Choose one of the following sentences as your main idea and **write** a paragraph.

1. The Queen demands that Edmund be returned to her.
2. Aslan's army loses the Queen and her dwarf.
3. Father Christmas gives gifts to the beavers and the three children.

_____

_____

_____

_____

Metric Units of Length

1 cm = 10 mm

mm

cm

0.5   1.5   2.5   3.5   4.5   5.5
1   2   3   4   5   6

Hint: If it's 0.5 or greater, round up to the next cm. If it's less than 0.5, round down.

Complete each conversion.

30 mm = _____ cm	8.5 cm = _____ mm	50 mm = _____ cm
80 mm = _____ cm	38 mm = _____ cm	5.9 cm = _____ mm
14.2 cm = _____ mm	4.7 cm = _____ mm	900 mm = _____ cm

Measure each section of the rocket to the nearest millimeter.

A = _____ mm

B = _____ mm

C = _____ mm

D = _____ mm

E = _____ mm

F = _____ mm

G = _____ mm

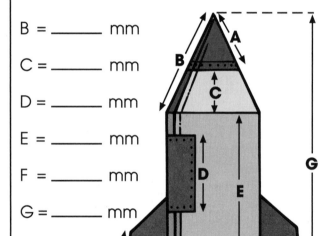

Measure each section of the hot air balloon to the nearest half centimeter.

A = _____ cm

B = _____ cm

C = _____ cm

D = _____ cm

E = _____ cm

F = _____ cm

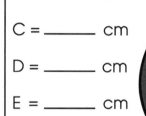

Measure in millimeters and to the nearest centimeter.

1. Width of your thumbnail _____ mm _____ cm

2. Distance between your eyes _____ mm _____ cm

3. Length of the pencil you're using right now _____ mm _____ cm

4. Thickness of your front door _____ mm _____ cm

5. Length of a book _____ mm _____ cm

6. Length of your shoe _____ mm _____ cm

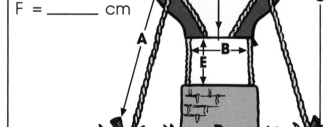

    Learn at Home, Grade 6

Units of Capacity

Complete each equation so that it equals 1 gallon.

1. 3 qt. + ____ qt. = 1 gal.

| 1 pt. = 2 c. | 1 qt. = 2 pt. | 1 gal. = 4 qt. |

2. 4 c. + 2 pt. + ____ qt. = 1 gal.

3. 2 c. + 1 pt. + ____ qt. = 1 gal.   5. 2 pt. + ____ qt. + 1 qt. = 1 gal.

4. 3 qt. + 2 c. + ____ c. = 1 gal.   6. 6 c. + ____ c. + 2 qt. = 1 gal.

Match each equivalent capacity.

 = 1 c.   = 1 pt.   = 1 qt.   = ¹/₂ gal.   = 1 gal.

1.  _____   a.

2. _____   b.

3.  _____   c.

4. _____   d.

Which unit would best measure each example below?

1. Amount of water used to take a shower _____

2. Amount of flour to make bread _____

3. Amount of water to fill your pool _____

4. A single serving of yogurt _____

5. A container of motor oil _____

| gallons |
| cups |
| pints |
| quarts |

Learn at Home, Grade 6

The Body's Communication System

Your body's **central nervous system** is made up of two parts: the **brain** and the **spinal cord**. The rest of the system consists of nerves coming from the brain and the spinal cord. These nerves are called **sensory nerve cells** and **motor nerve cells**. A stimulus causes your sensory nerve cells to carry messages from your skin and sense organs to your brain.

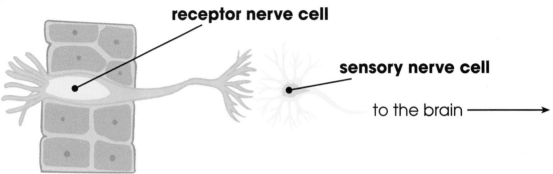

receptor nerve cell

sensory nerve cell

to the brain ⟶

Imagine you see a bee coming to sting you. Your sensory nerve cells carry this message to your brain. Your brain is the control center that interprets the message. Motor nerve cells carry the message (Run!) back from the central nervous system to the muscles. Your response (running) then occurs.

Listed below are different kinds of stimuli. **Write** how you would respond to each stimulus in the Response column.

Example: Stimulus — Feel pain in chest **Response** — Dial 9-1-1.

Stimuli	Response
Smell of burning food	
Bad odor from outside	
Sit on sharp object	
Traffic light turns green	
Bathtub overflowing	
Dog darts in front of car	
Pitcher throws ball at you	
Gale force wind blowing	

Fascinating Fact! Did you know your nervous system contains more than 10 billion nerve cells?

Learn at Home, Grade 6

Think Fast

While riding your bike down the street, a car suddenly pulls out in front of you. Your eyes send a message to your brain. Your brain sends a message to your muscles to apply the brakes. How long did it take you to stop? This time is called your **reaction time**.

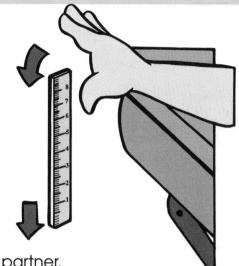

Conduct a simple experiment to test your reaction time. You will need a 30 cm ruler and a partner.

1. Place your left arm on your desk with your hand over the edge.

2. Hold your thumb and index finger apart a little more than the thickness of the ruler.

3. Your partner will hold the high (high number) end of the ruler. The lower (low number) end will be level with the top of your index finger.

4. Your partner will say "ready," pause a few seconds and drop the ruler.

5. You will catch the ruler and check the distance by reading the level at the bottom of the index finger.

6. Record your results.

7. Now, try the experiment again using your right hand.

Trial	Left Hand	Right Hand
1		
2		
3		
4		
5		

Average: _____ _____

Which hand had the fastest reaction time? _____

	Language Skills	Spelling	Reading
Monday	Choose several intriguing pictures or photographs for your child to study. Ask him/her to imagine what has just happened or what is about to happen in one of the pictures. Have him/her make a plan to turn it into a story. Have your child begin working on a rough draft.	Pretest your child on these spelling words: compact impact rebel conduct insult record conflict object refund content permit refuse contest present subject convict protest suspect Correct the pretest, add personalized words and make two copies of this week's study list.	**Using Reference Materials** Introduce this week's reading selection or continue with the book from last week.
Tuesday	**Verbs:** Helping verbs, or auxiliary verbs, work with the main verb. They can be used to form several different verb forms. *See* Language Skills, Week 4, number 1. Have your child scan his/her current reading book for helping verbs. Have him/her copy the sentences onto a sheet of paper, underlining the verb phrases and circling the helping verbs.	Study this week's spelling words. Review homographs with your child. *Homographs* are words that are spelled alike but have different meanings. Have your child complete **Present a Present** (p. 51).	Discuss the current reading book in a conference. Focus on comparison. Have your child compare the current reading book to a similar book using a Venn diagram.
Wednesday	The verb *to be* can be used as either a helping verb or a linking verb. Linking verbs do not show action; they show states of being. **Examples:** My coat *is* dirty. I *am* in sixth grade. The food *was* ready. The spiders *were* in the barn. Have your child complete **Linking or Helping Verbs** (p. 50).	Have your child use each of this week's spelling words correctly in a sentence.	With your child review how to use a table of contents and an index. *What kind of information can a person find in these pages of a book? See* Reading, Week 4, number 1.
Thursday	Action verbs express what someone or something is doing. *See* Language Skills, Week 4, number 2. Generate a list of action verbs with your child. Challenge your child by asking him/her to list synonyms for common action verbs such as *run, say* and *do*. Then, ask your child to write ten sentences using verbs from the list. Encourage your child to relate the sentences so they form a short story.	Have your child study this week's spelling words.	Nonfiction materials often contain visuals such as graphs, maps, charts, tables and time lines. These visuals help present information to the reader in a clearer format than text. Have your child look through newspapers, magazines and books to find examples of graphs, charts, etc. Have your child make a chart or graph to illustrate given information. *See* Reading, Week 4, number 2.
Friday	Cut out ten pictures from magazines. Attach each picture to a sheet of colored construction paper and glue an index card below each picture. Have your child write three sentences about each picture: The first sentence should contain an action verb; the second sentence should contain a linking verb; and the third sentence should contain a helping verb.	Give your child the final spelling test. Have your child record pretest and final test words in his/her word bank.	Discuss the current reading book in a conference. Focus on plot.

Learn at Home, Grade 6

Math	Science	Social Studies
Geometry Review and identify *points, lines, rays, line segments, angles* and *planes*. Discuss the information presented on **Geometric Figures** (p. 52), then have your child complete questions 1–6 on the activity sheet. Have your child complete **What Am I?** (p. 53).	**Respiratory System** Have your child read about the respiratory system. Review the function of the structures within the respiratory system: *nose, mouth, pharynx, larynx, trachea, bronchial tubes, lungs* and *diaphragm*. *See* Science, Week 4, number 1.	**Industrial Revolution** Explain the concept of supply and demand that forms the basis of the economy in the U.S. *See* Social Studies, Week 4, number 1. Have your child draw a diagram of a business that acts as both a producer and a consumer.
Review *intersecting lines, parallel lines* and *perpendicular lines*. Use a neighborhood or city map to discuss intersecting, perpendicular and parallel lines. *See* Math, Week 4, numbers 1 and 2.	Have your child draw a diagram of the respiratory system in his/her Science Log. Have him/her draw and label arrows to show what happens when we breathe.	The oil and steel industries were major influences during the American Industrial Revolution. Have your child read about the influence of steel and oil production on other industries in the U.S. Have your child read about the Standard Oil Company.
Review vocabulary associated with angles: *acute, obtuse, right, vertex, degrees* and *straight angle*. Then, teach your child about the different types of triangles. Have your child complete **Classifying Triangles** (p. 54).	Help your child conduct a simple experiment to learn about the respiratory system. Have your child count the number of breaths he/she takes in a minute before, during and after physical activity. *See* Science, Week 4, number 2.	Help your child make a list of inventions that arose during the Industrial Revolution. *See* Social Studies, Week 4, number 2. Have your child draw a detailed picture of one or more inventions from the nineteenth century.
Review the different types of quadrilaterals, or four-sided polygons: *trapezoid, parallelogram, rhombus, rectangle* and *square*. Have your child complete **Classifying Quadrilaterals** (p. 55). Have your child find quadrilaterals around the house. Ask him/her to identify each shape.	Discuss respiratory problems and diseases, such as tuberculosis, asthma, emphysema, pneumonia, lung cancer, bronchitis and the common cold. Have your child choose one respiratory ailment to research. Have him/her write a paragraph about how the ailment or disease is contracted and how it can be treated. *Is there a known cure?*	Have your child read about three business moguls of the late nineteenth century: Andrew Carnegie, J. Pierpont Morgan and John D. Rockefeller. All three were wealthy businessmen during the Industrial Revolution. Help your child find resources containing information about these influential men. Have your child write about the positive and negative (harmful) situations that emerged as a result of each man's story.
Congruent figures have equal sides and angles. Use a ruler and compass to draw triangles and quadrilaterals. Then, have your child draw congruent figures. Have your child measure the angles in a variety of triangles and quadrilaterals. Have him/her add the measurements within each figure. What does he/she discover? (All triangles add up to 180°, all quadrilaterals add up to 360°.)	Help your child conduct an experiment to analyze the chemical make-up of the air we exhale. *See* Science, Week 4, number 3.	Arrange for your child to perform a community service. Have your child write in his/her Social Studies Journal.

TEACHING SUGGESTIONS AND ACTIVITIES

LANGUAGE SKILLS (Verbs)

▶ 1. Helping verbs include *has, have, had, is, are, was, were, do, does, did, could, can, would, should, will, shall, may* and *might.*

Example: I *was happy* to see my dog.

The verb phrase *was happy* contains the helping verb *was.*

▶ 2. Verbs that show action are called action verbs.

Examples: My mom *baked* a cake.

The lion *roared.*

The friends *giggled.*

READING (Using Reference Materials)

▶ 1. Give your child a fiction book that has a table of contents. Discuss how reading the table of contents can prepare you for reading a particular book. Then, give your child a nonfiction book that contains an index, appendix, glossary and/or bibliography. Discuss how an index differs from a table of contents. Discuss the purposes of the appendix, glossary and bibliography. Ask your child to find specific information using these resources.

▶ 2. Copy the following paragraph for your child to read. Have him/her organize the information into a chart or graph. Then, discuss which format is easier to read and analyze.

The ticket office at the science museum kept track of attendance at a special exhibit, *Space 2100.* On Monday, the museum was closed. When the museum opened on Tuesday, there was a long line of people waiting to see the special exhibit. That day, 416 people saw the exhibit. It snowed on Wednesday, so attendance was down—only 93 people visited the exhibit. On Thursday, 247 people viewed the space exhibit. On Friday, 189 people attended. Three hundred eighty-seven people visited the museum on Saturday. On the last day of the exhibit, 756 people purchased tickets.

Analysis of the information: What is the average attendance per day? Which day brought the most people? How many more people attended the exhibit on Sunday than on Wednesday?

MATH (Geometry)

▶ 1. As you look together at a map, ask your child to identify streets that fit the following descriptions: (Fill in street names from your local map.)

Name two streets that run parallel to _____

Name two streets that are not parallel to _____

Name a street that intersects _____

Are _____ Rd. and _____ St. perpendicular or parallel to each other?

Does _____ St. intersect _____ Ave. or is it parallel?

Name the first street directly south of _____ St. and parallel to it.

Which street runs perpendicular to _____ St. and is the street farthest south shown on the map?

Which two streets intersect directly west of the school?

Name three roads that do not run directly north and south or east and west.

▶ 2. Have your child create a map of an imaginary town based on your descriptions. Dictate the layout of the streets, rivers, railroad tracks, etc. for your child to map out on paper. Describe the location of the streets using directions (*north, south, east, west*) and the terms *perpendicular, parallel* and *intersect.* Once your child has completed the map, have him/her give the town a name and describe its layout to you.

Learn at Home, Grade 6

SCIENCE (Respiratory System)

▶ 1. Provide your child with resource materials on the respiratory system. The main function of the respiratory system is to provide the body with the oxygen it needs to function. We need oxygen just to breathe, but our blood and all other cells need oxygen as well. Respiration involves two separate actions: inspiration (or inhalation) and expiration.

▶ 2. Time your child while he/she counts the number of breaths taken in a minute. Then, have your child do the same while lying down, sitting, standing, walking after jumping rope and after jogging in place. Have your child organize the results of this experiment in a simple chart, then analyze the results. Discuss why the number of breaths per minute changes.

▶ 3. This experiment uses a chemical indicator to measure the acidity of exhaled air dissolved in water.

You will need: a plastic freezer bag, a rubber band, bromothymol blue indicator, a drinking straw, a metric measuring cup, ammonia, a plastic cup, water and an eyedropper.

Background: When carbon dioxide dissolves in water, it forms a carbonic acid.

Directions: Pour 100 mL of water in a freezer bag and add three drops of bromothymol blue indicator. Swirl the bag gently to mix. Make a mental note of the color. Place the drinking straw in the top of the bag and fasten the bag tightly with the rubber band. Take a deep breath and blow into the bag through the straw. Remove the straw and hold the the bag shut and swirl the solution gently for about 10 seconds.

Remove the rubber band and pour the contents of the bag into the plastic cup. Note the change in color. Using an eyedropper, add ammonia (a base) to the solution. Count the number of drops it takes to return the solution to its original color. Discuss the results. What gas did you exhale? How can you tell? What did the ammonia do to the color? Why?

SOCIAL STUDIES (Industrial Revolution)

▶ 1. Define the terms consumer and producer. Then, ask the following questions to help your child understand the concept of supply and demand.

When are you a consumer? Are you a producer?

Are members of your family consumers or producers?

Can consumers be producers and producers be consumers?

What must you have to be a consumer? How does one obtain this?

When the demand for a product goes up, how do producers respond?

What may happen to the cost of a product when it is in great demand?

What causes a demand for a product?

What may happen if demand goes down and there is an oversupply of a product?

▶ 2. List some names and dates of nineteenth-century inventions for your child to organize on a time line. Late nineteenth-century inventions include the typewriter (1867), barbed wire (1873), the electric motor (1873), the telephone (1876), the phonograph (1877), the incandescent light (1879) and the gasoline-powered automobile (1885). Discuss the impact of these inventions on everyday lives and practices.

Linking or Helping Verbs

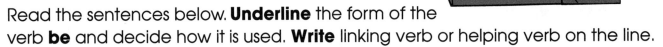

The verb **be** (and its various forms) can be used as either a linking verb or a helping verb.

Examples: Sarah **is** a fine skater. (linking verb)
Gregory **is** helping Dad clean. (helping verb)

Read the sentences below. **Underline** the form of the verb **be** and decide how it is used. **Write** linking verb or helping verb on the line.

1. In ancient times, no one was using money. _____

2. Later on, they were trading goods and services. _____

3. The trading of goods and services is called bartering. _____

4. Finally, people were accepting certain objects as payment. _____

5. These objects were valuable to everyone. _____

6. The objects were anything from animal skins to shells. _____

7. Some of the objects were metal. _____

8. Gold and silver were demanded by many people. _____

9. Governments were given the power to mint coins. _____

10. One of the first coin-makers was an ancient Roman. _____

11. The first paper money was Chinese. _____

Write sentences using each verb as indicated.

is (linking verb)

_____

is (helping verb)

_____

are (helping verb)

_____

are (linking verb)

_____

was (linking verb)

_____

was (helping verb)

_____

Learn at Home, Grade 6

Present a Present

compact
conduct
conflict
content
contest
convict
impact
insult
object
permit
present
protest
rebel
record
refund
refuse
subject
suspect

Fill in the blank with the correct homograph. Place an accent mark on the appropriate syllable of each homograph.

1. They had to _____ the _____ for committing another terrible crime.

2. A young_____ will often _____ against parents or teachers.

3. I am _____ with the _____ of my research paper.

4. The nasty_____ used to _____ him made him feel bad.

5. I will_____ myself to this _____ .

6. Someday, my parents will _____ me to get my driver's_____ .

7. The singer hopes to _____ a hit _____.

8. My mom will _____ if I throw this_____.

9. We are expected to _____ ourselves with self-control and overall good _____ .

10. I will _____ her with a lovely_____.

11. I _____ to touch that stinky_____.

12. I _____ he is the guilty _____ .

Write the six homographs that were not used in the correct category. For each homograph, place an accent mark on the appropriate syllable.

Verbs: _____   Nouns:_____

_____   _____

_____   _____

_____   _____

_____   _____

Geometric Figures

Example	Description	Symbol	Read
Point  •A	A point is an end of a line segment (an exact location in space).	A	point A
Line 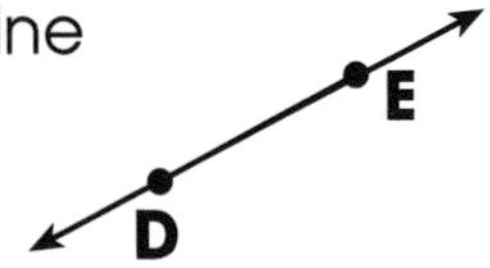 E D	A line is a collection of points in a straight path that extends in two directions without end.	$\overleftrightarrow{DE}$	line DE
Line Segment  R ——— S	A line segment is part of a line with two endpoints.	$\overline{RS}$	segment RS
Ray  B C	A ray is part of a line having only one endpoint.	$\overrightarrow{BC}$	ray BC
Angle 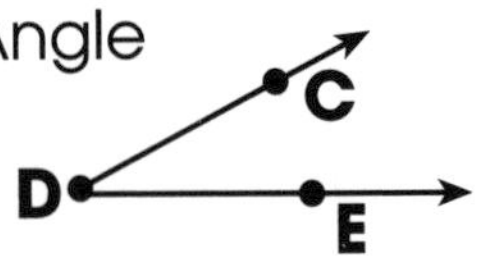 C D E	An angle is two rays having a common endpoint.	$\angle CDE$	angle CDE
Plane 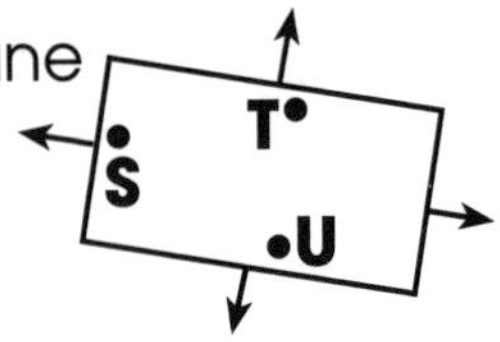 T• S •U	A plane is an endless flat surface.	plane STU	plane STU

Use the figure to **write** the symbol for each.

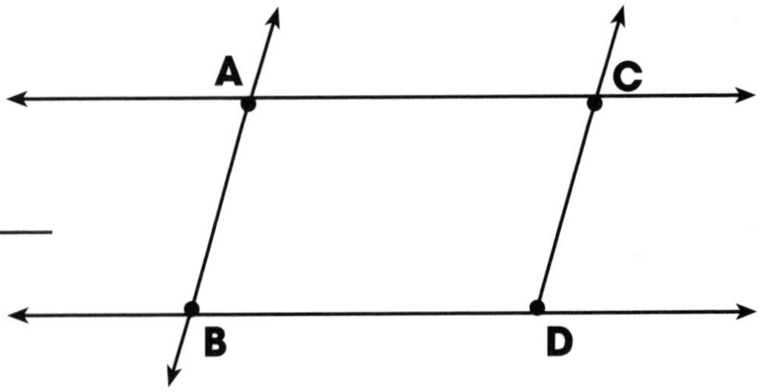

1. 1 ray _____

2. a plane _____

3. 3 points _____, _____, _____

4. 2 lines _____, _____

5. 3 angles _____, _____, _____

6. 3 line segments _____, _____, _____

Learn at Home, Grade 6

What Am I?

To find the answers to the two riddles below, find the answer that matches each figure and **write** the figure's corresponding letter above it.

What is the most prevalent form of life on Earth?

___ ___ ___ ___ ___ ___ ___
$\overleftrightarrow{AB}$ $\overline{AB}$ $\overrightarrow{MN}$ $\overrightarrow{NM}$ Point Point Plane
G C A

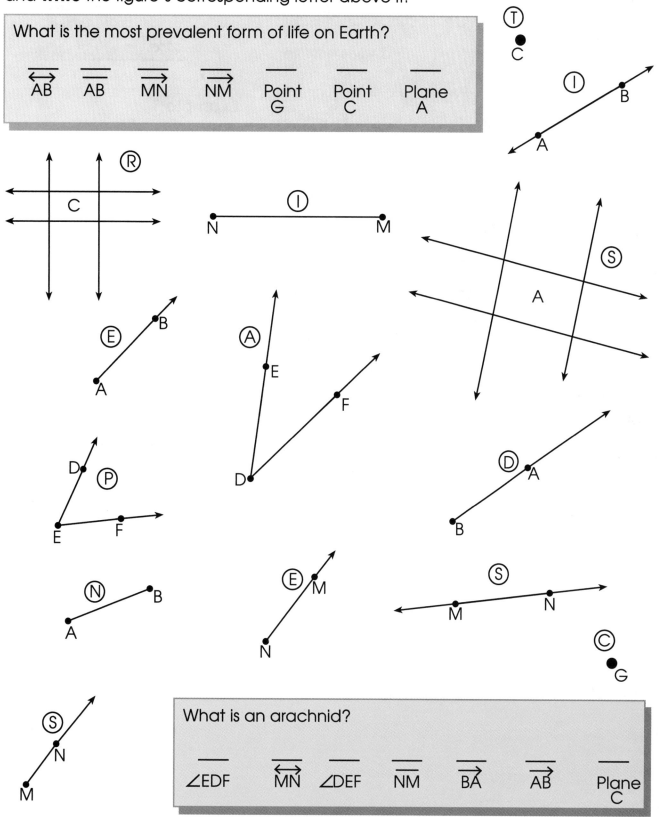

What is an arachnid?

___ ___ ___ ___ ___ ___ ___
∠EDF $\overleftrightarrow{MN}$ ∠DEF $\overline{NM}$ $\overrightarrow{BA}$ $\overrightarrow{AB}$ Plane
C

Classifying Triangles

The sum of the angles in any triangle is 180°.

Example	Name	Description
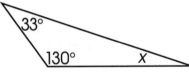	acute	3 angles less than 90°
	obtuse	1 angle greater than 90°
	right	a 90° angle
	scalene	no equal sides
	isosceles	2 equal sides
	equilateral	3 equal sides

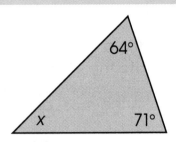

Find x.

Example 1

64° + 71° = 135°
180° − 135° = 45°
x = 45°

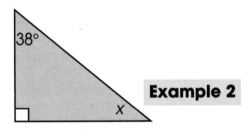

Example 2

90° + 38° = 128°
180° − 128° = 52°
x = 52°

Write two names for each triangle and find x.

1._____
2._____

x = _____

1._____
2._____

x = _____

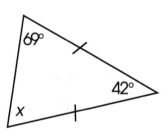

1._____
2._____

x = _____

1._____
2._____

x = _____

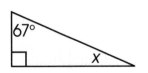

1._____
2._____

x = _____

1._____
2._____

x = _____

Learn at Home, Grade 6

Classifying Quadrilaterals

The sum of the angles in any quadrilateral is 360°.

Name	Description	Example
trapezoid	1 pair of opposite sides parallel	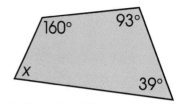
parallelogram	opposite sides parallel, opposite sides and opposite angles conguent	
rhombus	parallelogram with all sides congruent	
rectangle	parallelogram with four right angles	
square	rectangle with four congruent sides	

Find x.

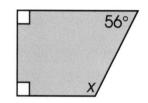

Example 1

93° + 39° + 160° = 292°
360° − 292° = 68°
x = 68°

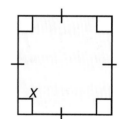

Example 2

90° + 90° + 56° = 236°
360° − 236° = 124°
x = 124°

Give all names for each quadrilateral. Then, find each missing angle measure.

1.

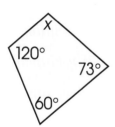

2.

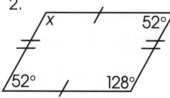

3.

4.

5.

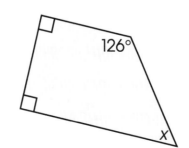

6.

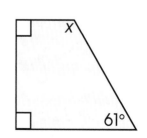

55

Language Skills	**Spelling**	**Reading**
Monday For this week's writing assignment, have your child choose a topic from the spelling list. Your child may choose to write about a natural disaster, such as a cyclone or typhoon, or about a giant python or an evil tyrant. Once your child has chosen a topic, have him/her make a plan for writing and begin working on a rough draft for the story.	Pretest your child on these spelling words: bylaw gyrate hypothesis cycle hydrant lyre cyclone hydraulic python dynamic hydrogen typhoon dynamite hygiene typist dynasty hyphen tyrant Correct the pretest, add personalized words and make two copies of this week's study list.	Introduce this week's reading selection or continue with the book from last week.
Tuesday **Verbs:** Discuss *irregular verbs* and *regular* verbs. A verb is irregular if it changes form in the past and past participle. (Regular verbs retain their spelling but add *d* or *ed* to form the past.) A dictionary shows the principal parts of most verbs following the entry word. Have your child make a chart classifying verbs as regular or irregular. *See* Language Skills, Week 5, number 1.	Study this week's spelling words. Have your child complete **Y Says "I"** (p. 60).	Discuss the current reading book in a conference. Focus on the author's purpose in writing the book.
Wednesday The past and past participle forms of irregular verbs, such as *eat* and *choose*, are formed with a change in spelling. Give your child practice in distinguishing past and past participle forms of irregular verbs. *See* Language Skills, Week 5, numbers 2 and 3.	Have your child use each of this week's spelling words correctly in a sentence.	**Dictionary Skills:** With your child, discuss the purpose of guide words in a dictionary. Give your child a list of vocabulary words to look up in the dictionary. Have your child locate the words and list the guide words found at the top of each page. Then, have your child read the definition for each vocabulary word. *See* Reading, Week 5, number 1. Have your child complete **Summer Daze** (p. 61).
Thursday There are several verbs that are often misused in everyday speech and writing. Refer to a grammar book to help teach your child the correct usage of the following verbs: *lie, lay; sit, set; may, can; teach, learn; lend, borrow; rise, raise; let, leave.* Have your child define and list the principal parts of each of these verbs.	Have your child study this week's spelling words.	Have your child study the pronunciation guide found at the bottom of each or every other dictionary page. Have your child practice making the sounds described in each example. Then, have your child look up words in the dictionary that have more than one pronunciation. *See* Reading, Week 5, number 2.
Friday Have your child use each of the verbs discussed yesterday in a sentence to demonstrate its correct usage. Have your child write pairs of related sentences to emphasize the distinction. **Examples:** My brother lent me $5 last week. I borrowed $5 from my brother last week.	Give your child the final spelling test. Have your child record pretest and final test words in his/her word bank.	Hold a reading conference to discuss the outcome of the current reading book. Have your child complete a book project. *See* **Reading Conference** (p. 10).

Learn at Home, Grade 6

Math	Science	Social Studies
Geometry Review the concept of *congruence*. Congruent shapes have the same size angles and corresponding sides. Copy and enlarge the pattern found in Math, Week 5, number 1 (or make your own pattern using two or three different sized triangles or squares repeatedly). Have your child find and color congruent shapes within the figure.	**Circulatory System** The circulatory system includes the heart, the blood and the blood vessels. Have your child read about the circulatory system. *See* Science, Week 5, number 1.	**Industrial Revolution** Teach your child about the concept of a monopoly. *See* Social Studies, Week 5, numbers 1 and 2.
The study of geometry involves spatial relations. Have your child manipulate geometric shapes in order to create a hexagon. Have your child complete a copy of **Hexagon Puzzles** (p. 62).	Have your child read about the composition of blood. *See* Science, Week 5, number 2. Have your child complete **The Circulatory System I** (p. 64).	Have your child read about the government's decision to break up the Standard Oil Company. *See* Social Studies, Week 5, number 3.
Polygons are found everywhere: in art, design, architecture, nature and in mathematics. Help your child create a mosaic with polygon shapes. *See* Math, Week 3, number 2 for a list of materials and directions.	Introduce the two circulatory systems in the body: systemic circulatory system and pulmonary circulatory system. Have your child complete **The Circulatory System II**.	Have your child read about other key figures in business during the Industrial Revolution. Have your child make a chart listing the following men and their accomplishments: Cornelius Vanderbilt, Gustavus Swift, Philip Armour, Charles Pillsbury, Andrew Mellon and James Duke.
Review the geometric solids: *sphere, cube, rectangular solid, pyramid, cone* and *cylinder*. Obtain a model of each shape for your child. Have your child make a chart that describes and compares the attributes of each type of solid. The chart headings should include *name, number of sides, number of faces* and *number of corners*. Have your child construct each geometric solid by folding, cutting and gluing paper.	Discuss pulse, the rhythm at which the heart pumps blood through the arteries. The throbbing sensation felt on the inside of the wrist or on the neck next to the windpipe is an artery expanding and contracting. Activity can greatly affect a person's pulse rate. Have your child measure his/her own pulse rate after different activities, then record them on a chart. *See* Science, Week 5, number 3.	Have your child read about some of the large corporations that were established during the Industrial Revolution. What did they do that appealed to the consumers of the time? Are any of them still in existence? *See* Social Studies, Week 5, numbers 4 and 5.
Teach your child to identify polyhedrons. A *polyhedron* is a three-dimensional figure that has many flat faces, each shaped like a polygon. Have your child complete **Polyhedrons** (p. 63).	With your child, discuss the importance of exercise and a proper diet in preventing heart disease.	Arrange for your child to perform a community service. Have your child write in his/her Social Studies Journal.

TEACHING SUGGESTIONS AND ACTIVITIES

LANGUAGE SKILLS (Verbs)

▶ 1. Give your child the following list of verbs: *choose, like, talk, do, buzz, move, take, choose, say, rush, grow, fly, throw, wish, speak, teach, swim, cross, write, ride, join, sing, watch* and *begin.* Tell your child to write the principal parts of each verb and identify the verb as regular or irregular. Then, have your child organize this information to create a chart with three columns: *present, past* and *past participle.*

▶ 2. Write a series of eight to ten sentences modeled on the following:

Justin (sang, sung) _____ a funny song accompanied by piano.

Maria has (wrote, written) _____ a song to play on her saxophone.

Write your own sentences using other irregular verbs such as *eat, fall, steal, choose, rise* and *give.* Have your child complete each sentence using the correct form of the irregular verb shown in parentheses.

▶ 3. Have your child complete the following chart.

Present	Past	Past Participle
1. Bill *chooses*	*chose*	(has, have) *chosen*
2. Alexa *says*		(has, have)
3. Eva *speaks*		(has, have)
4. David *throws*		(has, have)
5. Monica *teaches*		(has, have)
6. Gwen *swims*		(has, have)
7. Cheryl *rides*		(has, have)
8. Thomas *writes*		(has, have)

READING (Dictionary Skills)

▶ 1. Have your child look up the word *beat.* Note that the word is listed as an entry word more than once. Ask your child to differentiate the meanings listed for the word within one entry and in the separate entries. Ask your child: *Why do some meanings merit a separate entry? Is it related to part of speech?* Next, have your child look up the words *clash, fit, grade, hose, none* and *round.*

▶ 2. Some words may be pronounced in more than one way. For example, the word *gnu* many be pronounced "noo" or "nyoo." Have your child use a dictionary to find all the accepted pronunciations of the following words: *tomato, practically, vase, bouquet, catsup, protocol, rodeo, horror, pajamas.* Have the child list each pronunciation next to the word.

Math (Geometry)

▶ 1. Copy and enlarge the sunburst pattern at right. Have your child choose a shape in the design, then color all the congruent shapes the same color. Have your child choose a second shape and color all the congruent shapes a different color from the first group. Repeat until all the shapes are colored.

▶ 2. *You will need:*

cardboard box (any size, $^1/_8$" thickness)   mixing bowl
utility knife   rolling pin
plaster of Paris   scissors
2 cups flour   plastic butter knife
1 cup table salt   wax paper
$^3/_4$ cup water   old spoon or stick
food coloring   paper towels

Directions:

a. Use the utility knife to cut off the sides of the box. Leave the bottom and an edge of $^3/_4$".

b. Cut a second piece of cardboard the same dimensions as the bottom of the box. Place the rectangle inside the box bottom so it has a double bottom. This will prevent leakage.

c. Stir together the flour, water and salt. Divide the dough and make several different colors of dough by adding food coloring to each division.

Learn at Home, Grade 6

d. On wax paper, roll out the dough to a $1/2$" thickness with a rolling pin. Cut out polygon shapes with the plastic knife. Cut out several shapes and colors. Lay the shapes out on a fresh sheet of wax paper to dry and harden.

e. After the shapes have hardened, lay them in an attractive design on the bottom of the box.

f. Mix the plaster of Paris with water in the mixing bowl until watery in texture. **Note:** Mix together only as much as you can use right away. Plaster of Paris hardens quite quickly.

g. Pour the plaster of Paris between the polygon shapes. With a wet paper towel, wipe away the plaster that covers the shapes.

h. When the plaster of Paris dries completely, tear away the cardboard to reveal your mosaic.

SCIENCE (Circulatory System)

▶ 1. The circulatory system carries blood to all parts of the body. The blood supplies food and oxygen to the cells of the body and carries away carbon dioxide and other wastes from all parts of the body. The circulatory system also helps carry substances throughout the body that protect the body from disease. The heart is the pump that sends the blood coursing through the body's vast network of blood vessels.

▶ 2. Blood is made up of plasma, red blood cells, white blood cells and platelets. Have your child read in an encyclopedia or other resource about the function of each of these types of cells. Review the distinction between warm-blooded and cold-blooded animals. Humans and other mammals are warm-blooded—their blood maintains a constant temperature. Birds and reptiles are cold-blooded—their body temperature takes on the temperature of the environment. How is blood circulation related to body heat?

▶ 3. Show your child how to measure his/her pulse at the wrist or neck. Have him/her child count the number of beats for 15 seconds, then multiply that number by 4 to get his/her pulse rate for 1 minute. Next, have your child make a chart with six rows and four columns. Across the first row, have him/her write the headings: *Activity, Pulse Rate for 15 Seconds, x 4 =, Pulse Rate per Minute.* Then, have your child measure his/her pulse after sitting still for 10 minutes, after running in place for 3 minutes, after finishing lunch or dinner, while still in bed in the morning and after getting ready for school. Ask your child to study the completed chart and discuss how each activity affected his/her heart rate.

SOCIAL STUDIES (Industrial Revolution)

▶ 1. A monopoly exists when a single company is the only supplier of a product. When a company has no competition, it has the power to control the entire industry, set prices and offer consumers little or no choice. The opposite of a monopoly is competition. Competition between companies with the same or similar products may encourage those companies to try harder to please the customer and keep prices competitive (thereby winning the customer's business).

▶ 2. Play the game "Monopoly" with your child. Talk to your child about how the game demonstrates the meaning of the word *monopoly*. Discuss the exponential earnings that one player acquires when he/she holds the wealth. Relate the strategy of the game to the strategy of Mr. Rockefeller with Standard Oil.

▶ 3. Mr. Rockefeller's monopoly gave him total control in the oil industry. He lowered prices and put smaller oil companies out of business. Control of pricing can benefit the consumer but only if quality is maintained. Read about the intent of the Sherman Antitrust Act. Antitrust laws were established to restrict the purchasing of companies when the purpose is to reduce competition and control pricing in the industry. Have your child add the name of this law to the time line under 1890.

▶ 4. Some of the businesses from this period still have recognizable names today. Have your child write to one of these companies and request information on its history.

▶ 5. Make arrangements to take your child on a tour of a nearby manufacturing plant. Have your child prepare for the trip by making a list of things to look for and questions he/she would like to ask. Arrange for a company spokesperson to explain how the products are designed, produced and distributed. Inquire about how the raw materials are procured. Ask for a demonstration of how the costs and profits are determined. After the visit, have your child draw a diagram of the manufacturing process. Have your child write a thank you note to the person who directed the tour.

Y Says "I"

Match each spelling word from the list to its proper pronunciation. Refer to a dictionary, if necessary.

bylaw
cycle
cyclone
dynamic
dynamite
dynasty
gyrate
hydrant
hydraulic
hydrogen
hygiene
hyphen
hypothesis
lyre
python
typhoon
typist
tyrant

_____ **hī** fən

_____ **dī năm** ĭk

_____ **hī** jēn

_____ **tī** pĭst

_____ **jī** rāt

_____ **sī** kəl

_____ **bī** lô

_____ **dī** nə mīt

_____ tī **foon**

_____ **pī** thŏn

_____ **hī** drənt

_____ **dī** nə stē

_____ hī **drô** lĭk

_____ hī **pŏth** ĭ sĭs

_____ **sī** klōn

_____ **tī** rənt

_____ **hī** drə jən

_____ līr

Write a metaphor using spelling words. A metaphor is a direct comparison that does not use **like** or **as** to compare one thing to another. **Example:** The typhoon was an enraged monster destroying the small oceanside town.

_____

_____

Learn at Home, Grade 6

Summer Daze

Write the number of the definition that applies to each **bold** word.

_____ 1. When Mr. Wong works, he never **putters** around.

_____ 2. Mabel would **cop** the prize as the best stickball player in the

sixth grade.

_____ 3. The two small girls will **stalk** the tiger swallowtail very carefully.

_____ 4. The **cop** smiled as Shirley humbly scurried by.

_____ 5. I would wear gloves if I wished to climb that **spruce** in the forest.

_____ 6. Shirley imagined spiders **stalking** her in the furnace room.

_____ 7. She never considered that she might **cop** fruit from the market.

_____ 8. Will the students **spruce** up the playground before they leave

for the summer?

_____ 9. The **putter** missed the ninth hole by a mile.

_____ 10. Shirley discovered that she liked celery **stalks** very much.

Glossary

stalk   1) a plant stem 2) to stealthily pursue one's prey
3) to walk with a slow, stiff stride

putter   1) a golf club used on the green 2) a golfer who putts 3) to work slowly

cop   1) to steal 2) to capture 3) a police officer

spruce   1) an evergreen tree 2) the wood from this tree 3) to make neat

Hexagon Puzzles

Each of the puzzles H, E, X and A will fit on the hexagon outline. **Cut out** one set of pieces at a time and use them to make the hexagon.

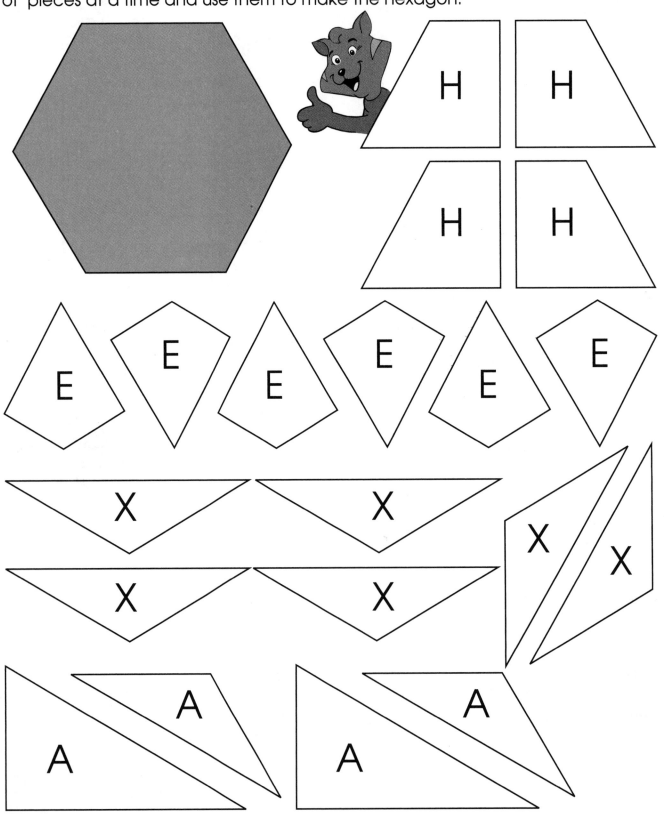

Learn at Home, Grade 6

Polyhedrons

A **polyhedron** is a space figure with many flat faces shaped like polygons.

Parts of a Polyhedron

Faces: flat surfaces (sides) **F = 4**

Vertices: corners or points (where 3 edges meet) **V = 4**

Edges: parts of a line (where 2 faces meet) **E = 6**

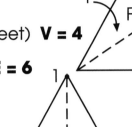

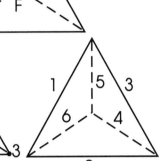

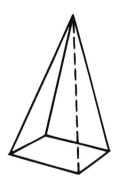

Use this formula to tell if a space figure is a polyhedron.

$$E = F + V - 2$$

Example: $6 = 4 + 4 - 2$
$8 - 2$
$6 = 6$

Find the parts of the figures and tell if they are polyhedrons.

1. F = ___
    V = ___
    E = ___
    E = F + V − 2
    Yes ___ No ___

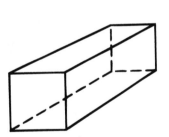

2. F = ___
    V = ___
    E = ___
    E = F + V − 2
    Yes ___ No ___

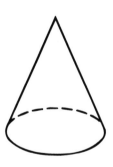

3. F = ___
    V = ___
    E = ___
    E = F + V − 2
    Yes ___ No ___

4. F = ___
    V = ___
    E = ___
    E = F + V − 2
    Yes ___ No ___

The Circulatory System I

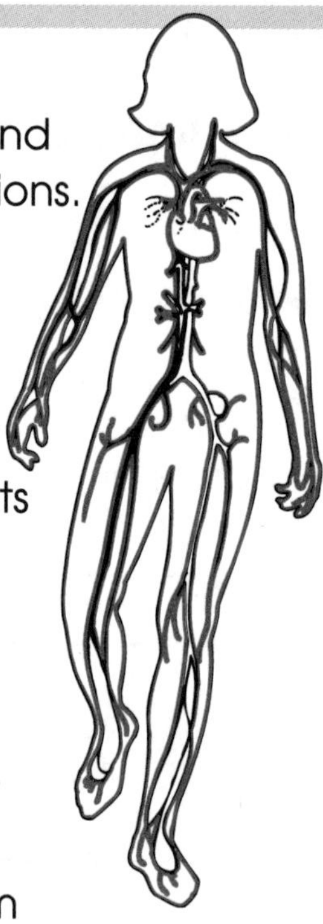

Read the information below. **Underline** the two main functions and the main organ of the circulatory system. Then, answer the questions.

The circulatory system is responsible for transporting materials throughout the body and for regulating body temperature.

The heart is vital to the circulatory system. It pumps blood to all parts of the body. The blood then carries nutrients and other important materials to the cells. Blood also carries waste products away from cells to disposal sites like the liver, lungs and kidneys.

The circulatory system also acts as a temperature control for the body. Warmer blood from the center of the body is brought to the surface to be cooled. On a cold day, the blood vessels contract very little allowing little blood to flow through. This is why skin might appear pale, or even blue. However, in hot weather, blood vessels widen and more blood is able to flow through them to increase the loss of heat. Thus, your skin looks pinker and feels warmer.

1. What are the two main functions of the circulatory system? _____
   _____

2. The blood carries important nutrients to the _____ .

3. Blood carries _____ away from cells and to the _____
   , _____ and _____ .

4. Warmer blood is brought from the _____ of the body to the _____
   _____ of the body to be cooled.

5. In cold weather, why does your skin appear pale, or even blue? _____
   _____

A "Hearty" Experiment 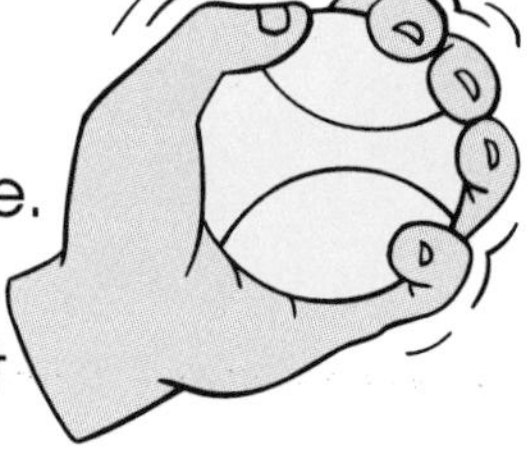
You will need: a tennis ball and a watch with a second hand
Hold the tennis ball in your stronger hand and give it a hard squeeze. This is about the strength it takes your heart muscle to contract to pump one beat. Squeeze the ball as hard as you can and release it 70 times in 1 minute.

Record how your hand feels. _____

Conclusion: _____

The Circulatory System II

There are two circulatory systems in the human body. Each begins and ends in the heart. The larger system is called the **systemic circulatory system**. It branches out to all parts of the body with oxygenated blood and returns to the heart with "bad blood." The smaller system is called the **pulmonary circulatory system**. It is much shorter because it travels only to the lungs and back to the heart with oxygenated blood.

Blood vessels that carry blood to the heart are called **veins**. Those that carry it away are called **arteries**. Blood from the systemic circulatory system flows from the **superior and interior vena cavas** into the **right atrium**, then into the **right ventricle** and out through the **pulmonary arteries** to the lungs. At the same time, blood from the lungs enters the atrium from pulmonary veins, drops into the **left ventricle**, is pumped into the body's largest artery, called the **aorta**, then flows into blood vessels that carry it to various parts of the body.

Follow the directions below.

1. **Color** the systemic circulatory system red.

2. **Color** the pulmonary circulatory system grey.

3. **Draw** blue arrows to show the flow of the systemic circulatory system.

4. **Draw** black arrows to show the flow of the pulmonary circulatory system.

5. **Label** the parts of the circulatory system listed in the box. If a number in parentheses follows a part, label it that many times.

aorta
superior and inferior vena cava
right and left atriums
right and left ventricles
pulmonary veins (2)
arteries leading from aorta
pulmonary arteries (2)

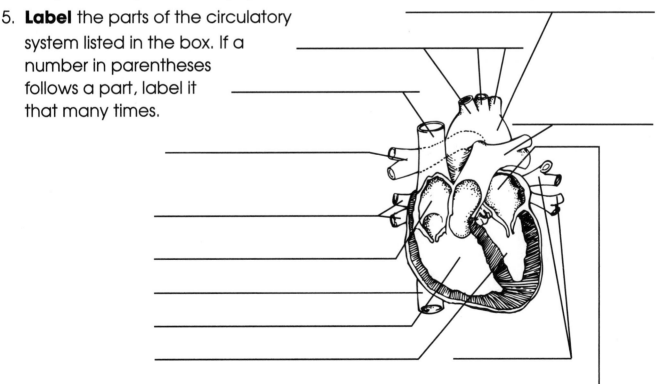

	Language Skills	Spelling	Reading
Monday	Have your child choose a topic, make a plan for writing and begin working on a rough draft.	Pretest your child on these spelling words: banjo portfolio studio buffalo ratio tobacco echo rodeo tomato halo silo tornado mosquito soprano tuxedo patio stereo zero Correct the pretest, add personalized words and make two copies of this week's study list.	**Apostrophe** Review the rules for using apostrophes. Also discuss the difference between a singular and plural possessive. *See* Reading, Week 6.
Tuesday	**Verbs:** Explain subject/verb agreement. Provide several examples for your child. Have your child complete **Agreement of Subject and Verb** (p. 70).	Study this week's spelling words. Have your child complete **Tony's Tuxedo** (p. 71).	**Historical Fiction:** Choose for your child to read this. Suggestion: *Sadako and the Thousand Paper Cranes* by Eleanor Coerr.
Wednesday	Give your child additional practice with subject/verb agreement and compound subjects. *See* Language Skills, Week 6, number 1. Have your child write five sentences that contain compound subjects. Have him/her check each sentence carefully to make sure the subjects and verbs are in agreement.	Have your child use each of this week's spelling words correctly in a sentence.	Hold a reading conference to discuss the setting for the story. Have your child find the setting on a map, then discuss the historical perspective of the story.
Thursday	A *collective noun* describes several things or people as one unit. Examples include *family, crowd, team* and *group*. A collective noun usually takes a singular verb. Except when the members of the group are seen as individuals. **Example:** The faculty *are* required to turn in the final grades. Give your child practice recognizing singular, plural and collective nouns. *See* Language Skills, Week 6, numbers 2 and 3.	Have your child study this week's spelling words.	Review the format of a friendly letter. Just as Sadako's classmates wrote to her, have your child write to someone he/she knows who is ill. Have him/her write a friendly, upbeat letter that shows interest in and care for the recipient.
Friday	Teach your child to maintain the same tense throughout a sentence. *See* Language Skills, Week 6, number 4.	Give your child the final spelling test. Have your child record pretest and final test words in his/her word bank.	Hold a reading conference to discuss the message of peace in the book. What can your child do to demonstrate that peace is an important issue?

Learn at Home, Grade 6

Math	Science	Social Studies
Geometry Review *perimeter* and *area*. With your child, discuss real-life applications for finding the perimeter or area of a figure. For example, a person would need to find the perimeter of a floor to purchase baseboard molding. A person would need to know the area of a floor to lay tile or carpeting. Have your child complete **Perimeter** (p. 72).	**Digestive System** Give your child a copy of **The Digestive/Urinary System** (p. 76) to study. Discuss the importance of the digestive and urinary systems. Have your child read more about the path food takes through the body. Provide an encyclopedia and other resources for your child's reference.	**Industrial Revolution** Help your child define the term *capitalism*. Have your child write about how capitalism allowed for the rapid growth of the Industrial Revolution.
Review the formula for finding the area of a rectangle or square (base x height). Then, review the formula for finding the area of a triangle (base x height ÷ 2). Explain to your child that he/she can find the area of an oddly shaped figure by counting the number of square units within the figure. Have your child complete **Area** (p. 73).	Have your child draw and label a diagram of the digestive system in his/her Science Log.	With your child, discuss how a business is created. Discuss the elements of a successful business. *See* Social Studies, Week 6, number 1.
Your child has already learned that volume is a measure of how much a container will hold. *Volume* can also be described as the measure of space occupied by a three-dimensional figure. Have your child complete **Volume** (p. 74).	Have your child chew a saltine cracker. Ask your child to describe what is happening. Discuss the role of chewing in the digestion process. Have your child complete **Traveling the Alimentary Canal** (p. 77).	Many businesses must borrow money to get started. With your child, discuss the concepts of loans, interest and dividends. Have your child start a simple business. Use this opportunity to discuss the difficulties that any business owner must face. *See* Social Studies, Week 6, number 2.
To find the volume of a rectangular prism, multiply the length x width x height (*l* x *w* x *h*). To find the volume of a nonrectangular prism, you must first find the area of the base. Then, multiply the base area x the height (*B* x *h*) of the figure. The volume of a figure is always expressed in cubic units. (m^3 or in.^{3}) Have your child complete **Volume of Prisms** (p. 75).	Review the four tastes: *salty, sweet, bitter* and *sour*. Perform a taste bud test with your child. *See* Science, Week 6, number 1. Have your child create a crossword puzzle using vocabulary related to the digestive system. Clues may be in the form of definitions or a diagram (with organs labeled as 2 across, 1 down, etc.).	Introduce the stock market as a means for businesses to secure investors. *See* Social Studies, Week 6, numbers 3 and 4.
Give your child some geometry-related brainteasers to solve. *See* Math, Week 6, number 1.	Have your child write a story about a character's imaginary trip in a food capsule traveling through the human alimentary canal. Encourage your child to include descriptions of unusual events along the journey, such as burps, hiccups and stomach growls to make the trip more exciting.	Arrange for your child to perform a community service. Have your child write in his/her Social Studies Journal. Save the stock market listings from the Sunday newspaper for next Monday's lesson (Week 7).

LANGUAGE SKILLS (Verbs)

▶ 1. Write the following sentences (as written) on the chalkboard. Have your child correct the mistakes.

My brothers and sister eats corn on the cob noisily.

Ty and Lyle is good at shooting free throws.

Neither Sylvester nor Twyla were present at the opening.

Either the clouds or the dark sky hint at the coming rain.

The television and the radio is on at the same time.

Blue and purple was my favorite colors.

▶ 2. Copy the following sentences for your child. Have him/her underline the subject in each and circle the correct verb. Then, ask him/her to identify whether the subject is singular, plural or collective.

The boys (is, are) members of the hockey team.

They (practice, practices) daily during hockey season.

The quarterback (pass, passes) the ball to the wide receiver.

The girls' team (play, plays) hard every Saturday morning.

You (was, were) lucky to be able to see that terrific game.

Tired runners (race, races) across the finish line.

The crowd (stand, stands) up for the national anthem.

The skiers (finish, finishes) the slalom run in record time.

▶ 3. Give your child a noun and a choice of verbs to incorporate into an original sentence.

I _____ (am, are)   Players _____ (try, tries)   The team _____ (plays, play)

▶ 4. A sentence that begins in one tense must stay in that tense.

Incorrect: The cow **jumps** over the moon and **ran** away with the spoon.

Correct: The cow **jumped** over the moon and **ran** away with the spoon.

Give your child the following sentences. Have him/her rewrite each sentence with the correct verbs.

My brother runs track and walked every day.

We are happy to see Mom as she walked in the door.

I turned on the light and pick up a book to read.

The sailors raised the sails and we sail to the island.

READING (Apostrophe)

An apostrophe is used in contractions to represent missing letters and in possessive nouns to show ownership. Dictate the following sentences to your child. Have him/her write each sentence, adding apostrophes where needed.

The doctor's decision was helpful to Sadako.

Sadako's classmates sent her a Kokeshi doll.

Sadako wasn't very hungry when her mother brought the food.

The golden cranes' wings blew in the wind.

Eiji's paper donation smelled of candy.

Sadako's good luck cranes became a symbol for peace and hope.

"I'll get better," said Sadako over and over.

There wasn't enough room on the table for all the paper cranes so Masahiro
hung Sadako's cranes from the ceiling.

68

MATH (Geometry)

▶ 1. Copy the following brainteasers for your child to solve.

a. Remove three pieces to leave three squares.

c. How many triangles are there in the figure?

_____

b. Remove six pieces to leave three squares.

d. How many triangles are there in the figure?

_____

SCIENCE (Digestive System)

▶ 1. Have your child mix four mystery solutions: 1 teaspoon sugar dissolved in 1 cup water
1 teaspoon salt dissolved in 1 cup water
1 teaspoon lemon juice mixed in 1 cup water
1 teaspoon vinegar mixed in 1 cup water

Have your child dip a clean cotton swab into one solution and touch the back, middle, sides and tip of his/her tongue with it. Have your child record his/her findings. Have him/her drink some regular water to cleanse the palate between solutions. What does your child discover? Have him/her draw a diagram of the tongue, pointing out the location of the four types of taste buds.

SOCIAL STUDIES (Industrial Revolution)

▶ 1. Every business begins by seeking to fill a need. Ask your child to think of something that people want. Encourage him/her to be creative. Ask your child if the "want" requires a product or a service. Guide your child in planning a business to fill that want. List what will be needed to start the business (money, building, land space, labor, equipment, etc.). Have your child draw a diagram of how the product will be produced (if applicable) and describe how the product or service will be managed, advertised and sold. If the business is a success, explain what the next step will be.

▶ 2. Plan a business that your child can actually carry out, such as a lemonade stand, a leaf-raking service or newspaper delivery. Help your child keep track of the costs, supplies and profits. Ask your child to analyze the following questions.

What equipment or supplies do you need?

How much money do you need to borrow to get started?

When will you pay back the money?

How will you convince someone to lend you money?

What can you do with profits to make the business even better?

▶ 3. When a person or a group of people wants to start a business or company, that person or group needs capital, or start-up money. Sometimes people will use money from a personal savings account. Oftentimes, they are able to get a loan from a bank. Another method of acquiring start-up money is to sell shares of stock in the new company. This is a commitment on the part of the investor to invest now with the understanding that the company will pay back the investment, with interest, when the company becomes profitable. Investors take a risk because the company may never become profitable; investors invest in the company because they believe it _will_ become profitable.

▶ 4. Investors who wish to buy a portion of a company buy shares. Such a business transaction is executed at a brokerage house where stockbrokers connect companies with investors by selling shares. The New York Stock Exchange, the largest and best known of the exchanges in the U.S., was started in 1792 by a group of brokers who met under a tree on Wall Street.

Agreement of Subject and Verb

A **singular subject** takes a singular verb.
Example: Bill washes the dishes.

A **plural subject** takes a plural verb.
Example: They watch television.

A **compound subject** connected by **and** takes a plural verb.
Example: Mary and Bill read books.

For a **compound subject** connected by **either/or** or **neither/nor**, the verb agrees with the subject closer to it.
Examples: Either my aunt or my uncle takes us to games. Neither my grandfather nor my grandmothers are over 85 years old.

A **singular indefinite pronoun** as the subject takes a singular verb (anybody, anyone, everybody, everyone, no one, somebody, someone, something).
Example: Everyone enjoys games.

Write the correct present-tense form of each verb on the line.

1. Everyone _____ wearing interesting hats. (enjoy)

2. Many people _____ hats for various activities. (wear)

3. One factory _____ only felt hats. (make)

4. Either bamboo grass or the leaves of a pine tree _____ wonderful straw hats. (make)

5. Factories _____ straw hats, too. (produce)

6. Somebody _____ the straw material. (braid)

7. Either machines or a worker _____ the braided material. (bleach)

8. Chemicals and gelatins _____ straw hats. (stiffen)

9. Ironing _____ the hat-making process. (finish)

Learn at Home, Grade 6

Tony's Tuxedo

banjo
buffalo
echo
halo
mosquito
patio
portfolio
ratio
rodeo
silo
soprano
stereo
studio
tobacco
tomato
tornado
tuxedo
zero

Write the spelling words in the correct category. The first one is done for you.

Two-Syllable Words

b a n • j o

___ ___ ___ • ___ ___

___ ___ ___ • ___ ___

___ ___ ___ • ___ ___

___ ___ ___ • ___ ___

Three-Syllable Words

___ • ___ ___ ___ • ___

___ • ___ ___ • ___

___ • ___ ___ • ___ ___

___ ___ • ___ ___ • ___

___ • ___ ___ • ___

___ ___ • ___ • ___

___ ___ • ___ • ___

___ • ___ ___ • ___

___ • ___ ___ • ___

___ • ___ ___ • ___

___ • ___ ___ • ___

Four-Syllable Word

___ ___ ___ • ___ ___ • ___ ___ • ___

Alliteration is a poetic device that groups words together with the same initial sound. **Write** a sentence using alliteration that includes at least two of your spelling words.
Example: Tony the tourist tried to tuck in his untidy tuxedo during a terrible tornado in town.

_____

_____

Perimeter

Perimeter is the distance around an area. Find the perimeter of each figure.

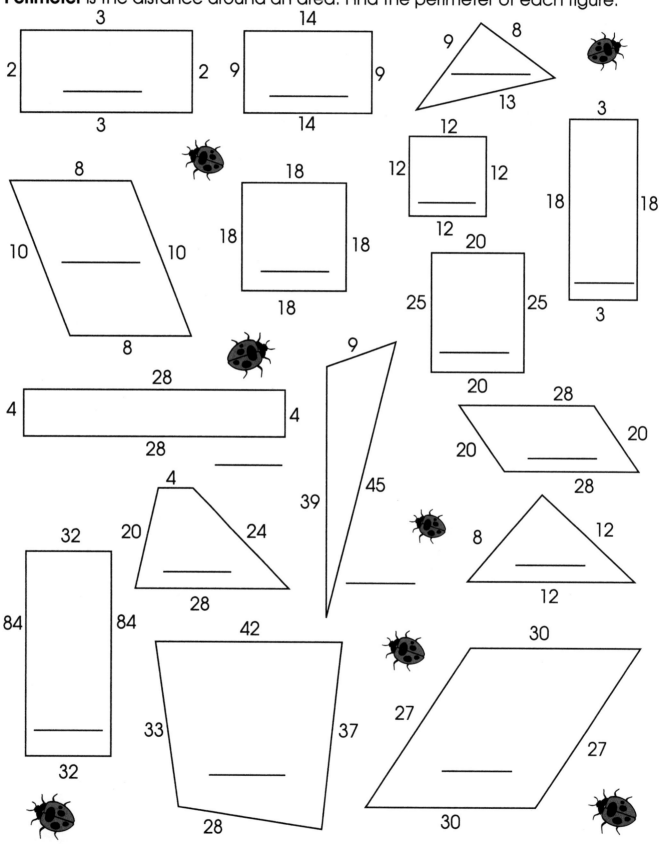

Learn at Home, Grade 6

Area

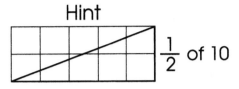

Area is the number of square units contained in a surface. Find the area of each outlined shape by counting units.

Hint 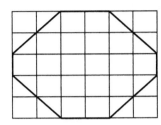 $\frac{1}{2}$ of 4

Hint 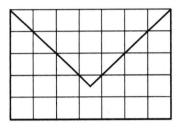 $\frac{1}{2}$ of 10

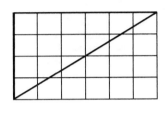

_____

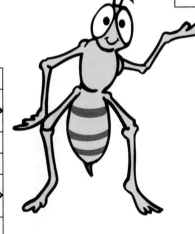

_____

_____

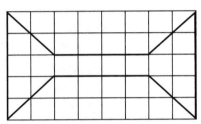

_____

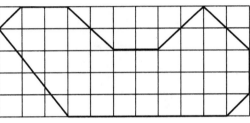

_____

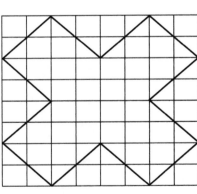

_____

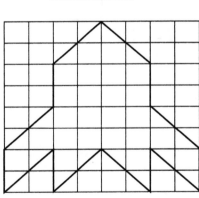

_____

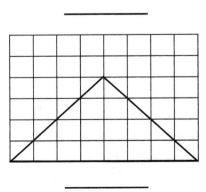

_____

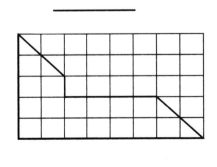

_____

73

Volume

Volume is the measure of the inside of a figure. Find the volume. Count the boxes.

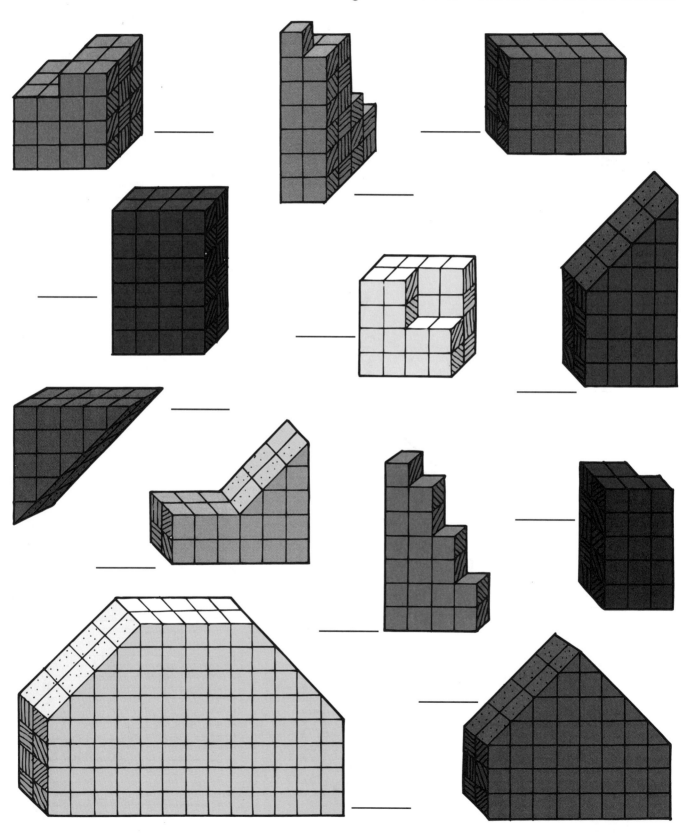

Learn at Home, Grade 6

Volume of Prisms

Volume is measured in cubic units.

Volume of a **nonrectangular prism** = base area • height

$V = b \cdot h$

$V = (\frac{1}{2} \cdot 4 \cdot 6) \cdot 12$

$V = 144 \text{ in}^3$

4 in.

6 in.

12 in

Volume of a **rectangular prism** = l • w • h

$V = 8 \cdot 5 \cdot 3$

$V = 120 \text{ m}^3$

8 m

3 m

5 m

Find the volume of each prism

1.

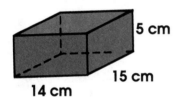

5 cm

15 cm

14 cm

4.

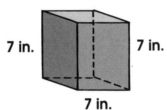

7 in.

7 in.

7 in.

7.

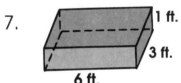

1 ft.

3 ft.

6 ft.

2.

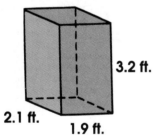

3.2 ft.

2.1 ft.

1.9 ft.

5.

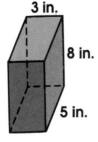

4 cm

$\frac{1}{5}$ cm

$1\frac{1}{2}$ cm

8.

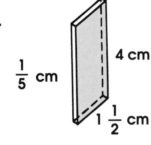

5 m

4 m

5 m

6 m

3.

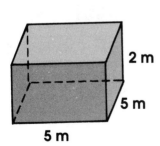

2 m

5 m

5 m

6.

3 in.

8 in.

5 in.

The Digestive/Urinary System

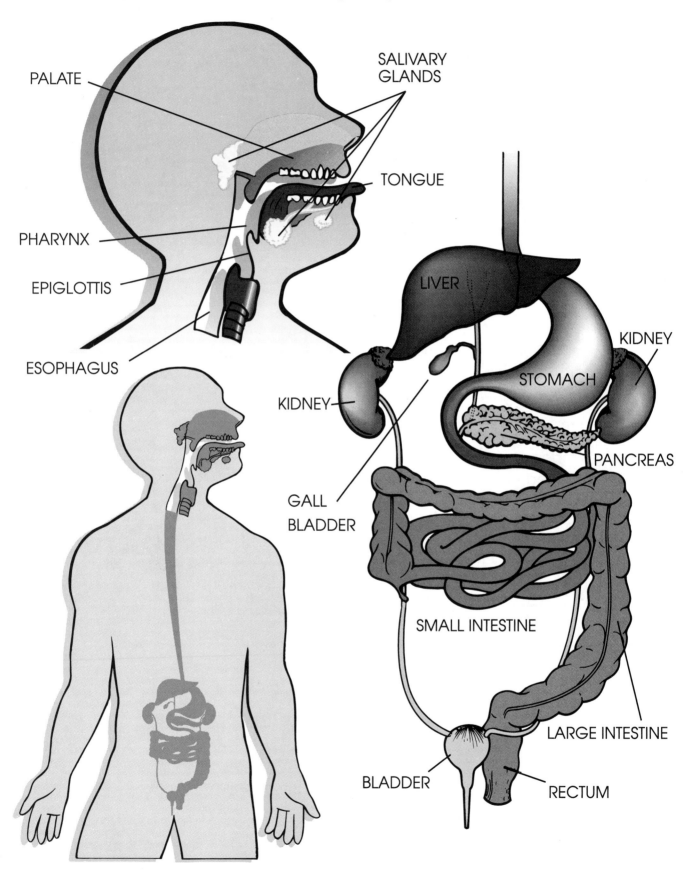

PALATE

SALIVARY GLANDS

TONGUE

PHARYNX

EPIGLOTTIS

ESOPHAGUS

LIVER

KIDNEY

STOMACH

KIDNEY

KIDNEY

PANCREAS

GALL BLADDER

SMALL INTESTINE

LARGE INTESTINE

BLADDER

RECTUM

Learn at Home, Grade 6

Traveling the Alimentary Canal

After you take a bite of food, it travels along a path through the human body called the **alimentary canal**, or the digestive tract. The canal, as it is shown here, is not how it actually is inside the body. Inside your body, it is folded back and forth so that it fits.

Fill in the missing words in the paragraph below. Use the words in the Word Box. You might also need a science book or an encyclopedia to help you.

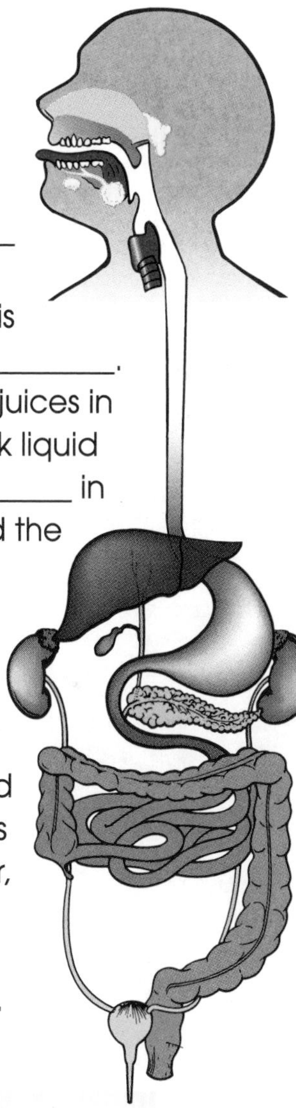

Food and water enter the alimentary canal by way of the
_____. Digestion of food begins here where it is_____
and broken into smaller pieces. Digestive enzymes, produced
by_____ _____, help to break down food further before it is
swallowed and passed through the _____ into the _____.
In the stomach, the food is mixed with _____ and digestive juices in
a churning motion. As the food is digested, it changes into a thick liquid
called _____. The chyme passes into the _____ _____ in
small amounts. The _____ produces pancreatic juices, and the
_____ produces _____ which is stored in the
_____ _____. These are released into the
small intestine as needed to work with intestinal juices and
contractions made by the intestine's walls to move the chyme
along. The digested food is absorbed by tiny_____ and
lymph vessels in the _____ of the small intestine and carried
through the _____ system to feed the body. Small amounts
of water and minerals are removed from undigested food matter,
and this and waste food products are stored in the _____
_____. This waste becomes a solid, brown material called
_____, which is finally eliminated through the_____.

salivary glands	enzymes	large intestine	chyme
pancreas	mouth	small intestine	esophagus
rectum	stomach	gall bladder	feces
circulatory	chewed	blood	walls
liver	bile		

Fascinating Fact! Did you know that during your lifetime, your digestive system may process between 60,000 and 100,000 pounds of food?

	Language Skills	**Spelling**	**Reading**
Monday	Have your child choose a topic, make a plan for writing, then begin working on a rough draft.	Pretest your child on these spelling words: clergy · error · referee clerk · fern · reserve concern · fertilizer · serpent derby · intern · sherbet desert · merchant · temperature dessert · mercury · thermostat Correct the pretest, add personalized words and make two copies of this week's study list.	Introduce this week's reading selection or continue with the book from last week.
Tuesday	**Adjectives:** Review adjectives. *Adjectives* modify nouns. They limit (how many), qualify (what kind), specify (which one) or distinguish the nouns that they precede. Brainstorm a list of adjectives with your child. *See* Language Skills, Week 7, number 1. Have your child write three sentences using as many adjectives as possible without losing the sense of the sentences.	Study this week's spelling words. Have your child complete **Desert Merchant** (p. 83).	Discuss the current reading book in a conference. Focus today on the main character's strengths and weaknesses.
Wednesday	Special forms of adjectives are used to show comparison. The *comparative* form is used to compare two nouns: The red car was *faster* than the blue car. The *superlative* is used to compare three or more nouns: The green car was *fastest* of all the cars. Have your child complete **Comparing With Adjectives** (p. 82).	Have your child use each of this week's spelling words correctly in a sentence.	**Reading Comprehension:** Give your child a short article to read carefully. Explain that you will be asking comprehension questions once the child is finished. Ask pointed questions. Suggest a few tips to increase comprehension: Skim the piece to determine general content. Predict what you might learn from the reading. Read the piece once. Reflect on what you read. Reread parts that were unclear.
Thursday	Have your child create a chart showing the comparative and superlative forms of several adjectives. *See* Language Skills, Week 7, number 2.	Have your child study this week's spelling words.	Have your child read an article and answer questions based on the reading. Have your child read **Rembrandt** (p. 84), then answer the questions about the article found on **Understanding Rembrandt** (p. 85).
Friday	Have your child represent comparative and superlative adjectives visually. Fold a sheet of paper in half the long way, then into thirds. When the paper is unfolded, there should be six boxes. Have your child choose two adjectives, then draw pictures illustrating each adjective and its comparative and superlative forms. For the word tall, for example, your child could draw a basketball player, a tree and a flagpole.	Give your child the final spelling test. Have your child record pretest and final test words in his/her word bank.	Hold a reading conference to discuss how the conflict in the story develops and how it is ultimately solved.

Learn at Home, Grade 6

Math	Science	Social Studies
Multiplication Review the properties of multiplication: *associative property, commutative property, identity (one) property* and *zero property.* These properties are useful in finding products. *See* Math, Week 7, number 1. Have your child use multiplication flash cards to practice solving one-digit multiplication facts with speed and accuracy.	**Skin** The skin is by far the largest organ of the body. It has three layers: *epidermis, dermis* and *subcutaneous tissue.* Have your child read about the make-up of the different layers of the skin in an encyclopedia. Have your child draw and label a cross section of the skin in his/her Science Log.	**Industrial Revolution** Newspapers record the daily activity of all the stocks traded on the stock exchanges. Have your child look through the listings for familiar companies. Help your child read the stock page to determine the cost of a share of a familiar stock. *See* Social Studies, Week 7, numbers 1 and 2. Over the next 4 weeks, have your child complete **The Stock Market** (p. 87).
Review the concept of multiples. Review how to find *common multiples* and *least common multiples.* Have your child list or state the multiples (up to 100) of the numbers 1–9. **Example:** The multiples of 3 are 0, 3, 6, 9, 12, 15, 18, 21, 24, 27, 30, 33, 36, 39, 42, 45, 48, 51, etc.	One of the jobs of the skin is to regulate body temperature. Have your child participate in a strenuous physical activity and observe the perspiration that forms on his/her skin. The role of perspiration is to cool the body when it becomes overheated. When a person becomes too cold, the skin reacts by narrowing blood vessels near the surface, thus allowing less heat to escape. *See* Science, Week 7, number 1.	Discuss the role of the stock market in the Industrial Revolution. Be sure your child understands that the stock market provided the funds that helped industries grow. Discuss the different stock exchanges. What are some of the world's best-known stock exchanges? Have your child look up the following terms: NYSE, NASDAQ, Dow Jones and AMEX. Under which exchange is your child's stock listed?
A *prime number* is a number that is divisible only by itself and by one. These numbers are not multiples of any number. Have your child complete an activity that will lead him/her to discover the prime numbers through 50. *See* Math, Week 7, number 2.	The skin also helps to prevent harmful chemicals and diseases from entering the body. Discuss the importance of keeping the skin (especially cuts on the skin) clean.	North America was the first continent to have a transcontinental railroad. The transcontinental railroad was completed in 1869. This helped expand development to the western U.S. very rapidly. Discuss how the railroad affected the growth of the Industrial Revolution. Have your child read about the construction of the first transcontinental railroad. What impact did this and other such railways have on settlement, trade and industry?
Squaring is multiplying a number by itself. 5^2 (read "five squared") means 5 x 5. *See* Math, Week 7, number 3. Have your child write equations to show what numbers are squared to make these products: 9, 16, 25, 784, 100, 1,600, 625, 1,849, 3,600, 400, 2,401, 2,025, 900, 484, 961, 1,369 **Example:** 15^2 or 15 x 15 = 225	Have your child read about the production of pimples or acne. Ask the child to draw a diagram of a pimple and write a paragraph explaining how to reduce the likelihood of developing acne.	Have your child read the ballad and stories about John Henry, a man who worked on the railroad. The true story involves a steam engine that was brought in to replace workers. John Henry raced against the machine. He was able to beat the machine but then died when a rock from a tunnel fell on him. Have your child add the presidents who served from 1877 to 1897 to the time line.
Review multiplying by one digit. Have your child complete **Multiplication** (p. 86).	Have your child read about skin color. How is skin color determined? *See* Science, Week 7, number 2.	Arrange for your child to perform a community service. Have your child write in his/her Social Studies Journal. Have your child continue to update his/her activity sheet on the stock market.

TEACHING SUGGESTIONS AND ACTIVITIES

LANGUAGE SKILLS (Adjectives)

▶ 1. *Adjectives* modify nouns or pronouns. Adjectives can tell which one, what kind and how many. Have your child brainstorm examples of each type of adjective.

Which one? *that, these, this, those*

What kind? *cute, excited, graceful, yellow*

How many? *one, ten, several, few*

▶ 2. Provide your child with a list of adjectives (examples below). Have your child make a three-column chart showing the comparative and superlative forms of each adjective.

pretty	tremendous	fresh	tedious
efficient	wonderful	quick	tangy
playful	energetic	common	delicious
beautiful	frivolous	slender	strange

MATH (Multiplication)

▶ 1. *Associative Property of Multiplication:* The way the factors are grouped does not change the product.
Example: $(8 \times 3) \times 2 = 8 \times (3 \times 2)$

Commutative Property of Multiplication: The order of the factors does not change the product.
Example: $6 \times 4 = 4 \times 6$

Identity (one) Property of Multiplication: The product of any number and one is that number.
Example: $348 \times 1 = 348$

Zero Property of Multiplication: The product of any number and zero is 0.
Example: $6{,}290 \times 0 = 0$

▶ 2. Copy the following chart for your child.

1	2	3	4	5	6	7	8	9	10
11	12	13	14	15	16	17	18	19	20
21	22	23	24	25	26	27	28	29	30
31	32	33	34	35	36	37	38	39	40
41	42	43	44	45	46	47	48	49	50

Read aloud the directions below to your child. He/she must follow the directions carefully to find the prime numbers between 1 and 50.

   a. Cross out number 1.

   b. Circle the next number. 2 is a prime number.

   c. Cross out all the numbers divisible by 2.

   d. Circle the next number. 3 is a prime number.

   e. Cross out the numbers divisible by 3.

   f. Circle the next number that is not crossed out or circled. 5 is a prime number.

Learn at Home, Grade 6

g. Cross out all the numbers divisible by 5.

h. Circle the next number that is not crossed out or circled. 7 is a prime number

i. Cross out all the numbers that are divisible by 7.

j. Continue in this manner until all the numbers have been crossed out or circled.

What are the prime numbers between 1 and 50? *2, 3, 5, 7, 11, 13, 17, 19, 23, 29, 31, 37, 41, 43, 47*

How many of the prime numbers are even? *one*

How many of the prime numbers are odd? *fourteen*

Extension: Have your child follow the pattern to find the prime numbers between 51 and 100.

▶ 3. The small number 2 in 5^2 is called the *exponent*. The *exponent* tells how many times the base number will be multiplied by itself. For example, the number 6^2 means 6 x 6. The number 7^3 means 7 x 7 x 7.

SCIENCE (Skin)

▶ 1. Your child may be interested in learning more about perspiration. Here are some questions that may spark his/her curiosity:

Sweat glands are not evenly distributed over the body. Where are they concentrated?

How does a deodorant work?

Why do people sweat when they are nervous?

Do people only sweat when it is hot?

▶ 2. There is a wide variation in human skin color. Skin color is determined by heredity and by exposure to sunlight. Everyone has the same number of cells that produce skin color. What varies from person to person is the amount of brown pigment, or *melanin*, that those cells produce. The melanocyte cells of dark-skinned people produce more melanin than those of light-skinned people.

SOCIAL STUDIES (Industrial Revolution)

▶ 1. Have your child look around the house for products made by well-known manufacturers. Then, have your child look at the stock listings in the Sunday edition of the newspaper to see how many of those corporations are listed on the various stock exchanges.

▶ 2. Choose a familiar entry and note the abbreviated name. After the company's name, the high and low prices of the week are given, as well as the stock's *closing price per share* and the *net change*. The closing price on one day is the opening price the next day. Have your child look up values of Disney, McDonald's (McDnlds), Toys R Us (ToyRU), Kellogg or any other stock that interests him/her.

Comparing With Adjectives

The **comparative** form of an adjective is used to compare two nouns. It is formed in two ways: by adding the suffix **er** to the adjective or by using the words **more** or **less** with the adjective.

Examples:

David is a fast**er** runner than Thomas.
David is **more** diligent at track practice than Thomas.

The **superlative** form of an adjective is used to compare three or more nouns. It is also formed in two ways: by adding the suffix **est** to the adjective or by using the words **most** or **least** with the adjective.

Examples:

David is the fast**est** runner on the track team.
David is the **most** diligent worker on the track team.

Circle the adjective of comparison in each of the following sentences. On the line, **write** if the adjective is written using the comparative form or the superlative form.

1. Central High has the shortest basketball team in the league. _____

2. One of their most skillful plays is to pass the ball through their opponents' legs. _____

3. Central wins a lot of games because the team's players are more clever dribblers than the opposing players. _____

4. The opposing team is dizzier because Central dribbles circles around them. _____

5. The toughest game of the year was against South High._____

6. Central's captain won the game with the fanciest shot of the game.

   _____

Desert Merchant

clergy
clerk
concern
derby
desert
dessert
error
fern
fertilizer
intern
merchant
mercury
referee
reserve
serpent
sherbet
temperature
thermostat

Write a spelling word to complete each phrase.
Be sure to **write** the possessive form when it's required.

Possessive Nouns

1. _____ merchandise
2. _____ chemical symbol
3. _____ decision
4. _____ temperature
5. _____ scales
6. _____ patients
7. _____ church
8. _____ store
9. _____ sand

TODAY'S SPECIALS
FREE HOT COFFEE
ICE $20.00

CACTUS JOE'S MARKET

Nouns

10. man's felt   _____
11. patio's potted   _____
12. Susie's orange   _____
13. gas tank's   _____
14. diner's delicious   _____
15. mathematician's   _____
16. farmer's   _____
17. Carol's constant   _____
18. sick child's   _____

Use the nouns from the list to form possessives in a few sentences.

_____

_____

_____

Learn at Home, Grade 6

Rembrandt

Rembrandt was one of the greatest artists of all time. He was born on July 15, 1606, in Leiden, Holland. Rembrandt began painting at an early age. At the age of fifteen, he traveled to Amsterdam to study art but soon returned home to paint on his own.

Rembrandt's first paintings were of subjects from the Bible and from history. He used bright colors and glossy paints. These paintings were very popular, and soon, Rembrandt became well-known in his community.

In 1628, Rembrandt began to teach art. He was a respected teacher with many students.

In 1632, Rembrandt moved back to Amsterdam, where he began to paint portraits of many well-known people. He soon became famous in Holland for his beautiful portraits.

In 1634, he married a wealthy and educated girl named Saskia. They moved into a large home where Rembrandt hung many of the paintings he had collected.

Rembrandt continued to succeed as an artist, but tragedy struck. Three of Rembrandt's four children died very young. And, in 1642, his wife Saskia died.

Rembrandt became very sad. He began to paint with darker colors. But somehow, his painting grew even more beautiful. He used dark colors around the figures in his paintings. The figures themselves were painted as if a soft light were shining on them.

Rembrandt began to paint more for himself and less for other people. Although his work was brilliant, he was not able to make enough money to keep his house. In 1657, his house and his possessions were auctioned off. Rembrandt was bankrupt.

Rembrandt continued to paint until he died on October 4, 1669. His most famous painting was titled *The Night Watch.*

Rembrandt created over 600 paintings, 300 etchings and 1,400 drawings. Some of his most fascinating paintings were the one hundred portraits he painted of himself. These self-portraits are a remarkable record of his life.

Learn at Home, Grade 6

Understanding Rembrandt

Answer the questions below from your reading of Rembrandt.

True or False

Rembrandt . . .

_____ was one of the greatest artists of all time.

_____ was born on July 15, 1606, in Florence, Italy.

_____ began painting at an early age.

_____ traveled to Amsterdam at the age of fifteen to study architecture.

Check and write:

Rembrandt used ☐ soft ☐ bright colors and _____ paints.

Underline:

In 1634, Rembrandt married . . .

    a wealthy and educated girl named Saskia.

    a poor girl from Amsterdam named Saskia.

Check and write:

Although Rembrandt was successful as an artist,

☐ tragedy ☐ good fortune began to strike his family.

Three of his _____ children died at a very early age.

In 1642, ☐ Rembrandt's father died. ☐ Rembrandt's wife died.

Rembrandt's sadness caused him to use ☐ darker ☐ lighter colors.

Check, circle and write:

Rembrandt died on October 4, ☐ 1669. ☐ 1700.

Rembrandt's most famous painting was called _____.

Rembrandt's works included:

☐ paintings ☐ drawings ☐ etchings ☐ self-portraits

Multiplication

Multiply.

1. 649
    x 8

2. 858
    x 7

3. 7,642
    x   5

4. 8,219
    x   3

5. 5,238
    x   6

6. 8,249
    x   4

7. 6,518
    x   7

8. 8,943
    x   9

9. 3,268
    x   5

10. 4,637
    x   8

11. 5,387
    x   4

12. 8,264
    x   9

13. 4,875
    x   7

14. 5,689
    x   8

15. 9,243
    x   4

16. 8,540
    x   6

17. 3,726
    x   5

18. 83,243
    x   6

19. 74,254
    x   7

20. 62,435
    x   9

21. 73,643
    x   8

22. 51,476
    x   4

23. 73,629
    x   5

24. 87,642
    x   7

25. 25,624
    x   4

26. 98,215
    x   6

27. 41,826
    x   9

28. 53,214
    x   8

29. 83,265
    x   4

30. 65,429
    x   5

31. 46,254
    x   7

32. 91,242
    x   8

33. 73,263
    x   6

34. 35,584
    x   2

35. 79,267
    x   2

Learn at Home, Grade 6

The Stock Market

Choose a stock to follow for the next 4 weeks. **Fill in** the information about your stock in the box below. Then, track the information you find in the newspaper on the chart.

Name of stock _____

Original price per share_____

Number of shares you wish to buy _____

Date of purchase _____

Total cost _____

Date	High	Low	Close	Net Change

Date	High	Low	Close	Net Change

After 4 weeks, complete the following analysis of your stock's performance.

1. What was the highest price per share during the past 4 weeks? _____
2. At that price, what would have been the total value of your stock? _____
3. If you had sold your shares that day, what would have been your profit or loss? _____
4. What was the lowest price per share during the past 4 weeks? _____
5. At that price, what would have been the total value of your stock? _____
6. If you had sold your shares that day, what would have been your profit or loss? _____

	Language Skills	**Spelling**	**Reading**
Monday	Have your child choose a topic, make a plan for writing, then begin working on a rough draft.	Pretest your child on these spelling words: breakfast heavy thread breath instead threat cleanse leather tread dread meant wealth feather spread weapon health sweat weather Correct the pretest, add personalized words and make two copies of this week's study list.	**Historical Fiction** Introduce this week's reading book. Suggestion: *The Return of the Indian* by Lynne Reid Banks.
Tuesday	**Adjectives:** Your child has learned how to form comparative and superlative adjectives by adding *er* or *est*. These two forms of certain adjectives are formed differently when the adjective is irregular. *See* Language Skills, Week 8, number 1. Have your child rewrite several sentences using the correct forms of comparative and superlative adjectives. *See* Language Skills, Week 8, number 2.	Study this week's spelling words. Have your child complete **Scrambled Eggs** (p. 94).	Hold a reading conference to discuss the history and lifestyle of the Iroquois Indians. Focus on the distinction between fact and fantasy.
Wednesday	Teach your child to use comparative language carefully so that the meaning of a sentence is not confused. *See* Language Skills, Week 8, number 3. Have your child write ten sentences using comparative and superlative adjectives. Have him/her compare two things in some sentences and three or more things in other sentences.	Have your child use each of this week's spelling words correctly in a sentence.	Have your child research one of the following topics related to the Iroquois: religious beliefs, superstition, family structure, the longhouse, fortification of the village, food or history. Have your child write a summary of the information gathered, including appropriate illustrations.
Thursday	Discuss adjectives that indicate which one. Have your child complete **This, That, These, Those** (p. 92).	Have your child study this week's spelling words.	Discuss the fact that many different Native American Indian tribes shared common languages. Have your child demonstrate these connections among tribes visually by completing **A Land of Many Peoples** (p. 95).
Friday	*Proper adjectives* come from proper nouns that are used as adjectives. For example, the F in French fries is capitalized because France is a proper noun. *See* Language Skills, Week 8, number 4. Have your child complete **Proper Nouns and Adjectives** (p. 93).	Give your child the final spelling test. Have your child record pretest and final test words in his/her word bank.	Hold a reading conference to discuss the climax of the book. Have your child complete a book project. *See* **Reading Conference** (p. 10).

Learn at Home, Grade 6

Math	Science	Social Studies
Multiplication Teach your child the importance of estimating an answer before multiplying. *See* Math, Week 8, number 1. Teach your child to round each factor, then multiply the rounded factors to obtain an estimated product. Have your child estimate the products of given multiplication problems by rounding the factors. *See* Math, Week 8, number 2.	**Immune System** With your child, discuss the role of the immune system. *See* Science, Week 8, number 1. Have your child add an immune system glossary page to his/her Science Log. *See* Science, Week 8, number 2.	**Industrial Revolution** Have your child read about common working conditions during the Industrial Revolution. *See* Social Studies, Week 8, number 1. Ask your child to think about the type of work he/she would like to do. Have your child list the working conditions (enjoyable work, clean environment, good pay, benefits, etc.) that he/she feels are necessary for him/her to take a job.
Provide your child with situational problems that involve multiplication. Have your child complete **Many Times Over** (p. 96).	Discuss the difference between a*ctive immunity* and *passive immunity*. *See* Science, Week 8, number 3.	The American Federation of Labor (AFL) was founded in 1886. Have your child add this date to the time line. The labor movement was an organized attempt to give workers some power against big corporations. Have your child read about the AFL's methods for gaining a voice. Have your child write a paragraph describing how labor unions improved working conditions for the laborers.
Multiplication is also known as *times*. The phrase *4 times as much,* for example, indicates that you should *multiply* by 4. Read a number riddle aloud to your child. *See* Math, Week 8, number 3. Have your child complete **Millions Mysteries** (p. 97).	Allergies are a result of the immune system reacting to a usually harmless substance. Allergens, such as dust, pollen and animal dander, can stimulate mucous production, itching and headaches in some people. Have your child do some research to find out the most common allergens and the percentage of people who have allergies. Have your child make a graph to show this information.	Have your child make a chart that compares and contrasts the life of a ten-year-old today with the life of a ten-year-old during the Industrial Revolution.
Review multiplication with regrouping (carrying). Have your child solve the problems on **Multiplication** (p. 98).	Good personal hygiene can help prevent the transmission of diseases. Review good hygiene practices with your child. Have your child write a summary of how to handle food properly in order to prevent the spread of disease.	Have your child read about and discuss the following question: *What was the effect of the Industrial Revolution on farmers? See* Social Studies, Week 8, numbers 2 and 3. Have your child compare the life of a farmer today with the life of a farmer in the late 1800s.
With your child, review how to use multiplication to find area. Have your child complete **Problem Solving** (p. 99).	Have your child read in a variety of resources about HIV and AIDS and the resulting breakdown of the immune system that occurs. Be sure your child knows the facts about HIV—who is at risk, how the virus is transmitted, etc. Have your child read about current AIDS research, then have him/her write an article about a current issue related to the AIDS virus.	Have your child make a chart about the changes in American lifestyles brought about by the Industrial Revolution. Encourage your child to use textbooks and other resources to help complete the chart. *See* Social Studies, Week 8, number 4. Have your child continue to update his/her activity sheet on the stock market.

TEACHING SUGGESTIONS AND ACTIVITIES

LANGUAGE SKILLS (Adjectives)

▶ 1. Most adjectives take an *er* or *est* ending to form the comparative or superlative forms. Some adjectives are irregular in the formation of these forms. Here are some of those exceptions:

bad / worse / worst good / better / best   little / less / least

many, much / more / most   ill / worse / worst

▶ 2. Write several sentences on the chalkboard that contain incorrect adjective forms. Have your child rewrite each sentence using the correct form of the comparative or superlative adjective.

Jane had the worstest headache she could remember.

Mother makes the goodest cookies of anyone I know.

There are many boys than girls on the team.

There is littler cake on the platter than on the plate.

It is least likely that the blue team will win than the red team.

▶ 3. Sometimes comparisons can be confusing. In the following sentence, for example, it is not clear whether Richard likes school better than he likes Harry or if he likes school better than Harry likes school: *Richard likes school better than Harry.* Encourage your child to avoid ambiguity (unless intentional) in his/her writing.

▶ 4. Other proper adjectives come from names of geographical places, people, nationalities and names of languages. Have your child brainstorm some common adjective/noun pairs that include a proper adjective (French fries, Italian leather, Cartesian coordinates, Indian food, Paris fashion, Swiss cheese). Product names are also sometimes used as proper adjectives.

MATH (Multiplication)

▶ 1. Estimation is an important skill in many everyday situations. Tell your child about instances when you regularly estimate sums or products (when purchasing something, when deciding how many eggs to cook for breakfast, etc.). When you estimate an answer, you are thinking about what a logical answer would be. If your calculation is very different, you know you have to recalculate. It is easy to make a mathematical mistake—estimating first helps you catch your mistakes.

▶ 2. Provide your child with 10 to 15 multiplication problems. Have your child round the factors and estimate the products. Some problems are provided here for your convenience.

48	29	42	63	51	37	35
x 23	x 21	x 28	x 31	x 44	x 14	x 19

32	105	48	1,998	64	19	77
x 9	x 32	x 12	x 215	x 27	x 38	x 51

▶ 3. Read the following challenge to your child, one clue at a time. Allow your child time to think before reading the next clue. Repeat the clues if necessary. Have your child solve for the mystery number.

The mystery number has five digits. No numeral is repeated. The first digit is an odd number, and it is five times as much as the last digit. The second digit is two times the third digit. The fourth digit multiplied by 8 is 0. The sum of the digits is 15. Can you name the mystery number? (56301)

SCIENCE (Immune System)

▶ 1. The immune system is the body's system of self-defense against diseases. This complex system of organs and cells in the body recognizes foreign substances and helps destroy them. Viruses, bacteria, fungi and other parasites which affect the good health of a person are called *pathogens*. The white blood cells are the body's main protector against pathogens.

Learn at Home, Grade 6

▶ 2. Add the following words to your child's weekly spelling list. Have him/her look up each word in a dictionary or science resource. Discuss the meaning of each. Have your child make a glossary of these terms in his/her Science Log. Have your child arrange the entries in alphabetical order and write a definition for each.

pathogens	immunity	viruses	bacteria
parasites	fungi	antibody	antigen
antibiotic	vaccinations	lymph	pathology
immunization	white blood cells	allergy	autoimmunity

▶ 3. There are two types of immunity: *active* and *passive*.

Active immunity involves the body's own reaction to disease. The human body naturally produces its own antibodies that fight disease and continue to protect the person after the illness has passed. A vaccination produces active immunity to a disease. Measles, mumps, smallpox, chicken pox, polio, tetanus and whooping cough are some of the diseases that can be prevented through vaccinations.

Passive immunity is produced outside the infected person by an animal or another person. An example of passive immunity occurs when a mother passes antibodies to a baby through the placenta or mother's milk.

SOCIAL STUDIES (Industrial Revolution)

▶ 1. Prior to and during the Industrial Revolution, working conditions in some factories were very poor. Workers labored long hours for low wages. Young children and women were paid even lower wages despite working long hours. Discuss how such poor conditions could be harmful. How could the workers have demonstrated their displeasure about the poor working conditions?

▶ 2. Farmers today represent a small percentage of the population. Although there are fewer farms today, they are much larger than they were a hundred years ago. These large farms ship meat and produce all around the country and to all parts of the world. Competition keeps prices very low, so many farmers have a difficult time making a living today.

▶ 3. Discuss today's organic farms. With the growing awareness of chemical fertilizers and preservatives, many people are seeking organically grown produce from smaller local growers. The costs for the small farmer are very high. These costs are passed on to the consumer.

▶ 4. Have your child make a chart showing the changes in lifestyle based on class. Using the format shown here (or something similar), have your child show who was affected by specific changes in industrialization, why they were affected and how they reacted to the change.

	Change Brought About by Industrialization	Reason	Response to Change
Upper Classes			
Middle Classes			
Lower Classes			

This, That, These, Those

The adjectives **this** and **that** are singular. The adjectives **these** and **those** are plural. **This** and **these** refer to things that are nearby. **That** and **those** refer to things that are farther away.

Examples: **This** elevator we are riding is called a "lift" in England.
Those apartments across the street are called "flats."

Use **this** and **that** correctly in the sentences below.

1. _____ cookie I have in my hand is called a "biscuit" in England.

2. _____ car trunk over there is called a "boot."

3. _____ parking lot is called a "car park."

4. _____ vacation we took last year would be called a "holiday."

5. _____ box of French fries Monica has is called "chips."

6. _____ can of fruit on the shelf is called a "bottle" of fruit.

Use **these** and **those** correctly in the sentences below.

1. _____ dollars she is handing you are the English form of currency called "pounds."

2. Isn't it interesting how _____ baby carriages across the street are called "prams"?

3. _____ bathrooms we just passed are called "loos."

4. _____ 7 gallons of gas you purchased at the last gas station would be called "petrol" in England.

5. All _____ soccer games you had fun playing in would be called "football games."

6. _____ differences show that even though people in both countries speak English, we are separate and unique in our own language.

Learn at Home, Grade 6

Proper Nouns and Adjectives

Proper nouns and **adjectives** always begin with a capital letter.

Examples: Mount Rainier
the Sahara Desert (**the** is usually not capitalized)
the English language
Italians

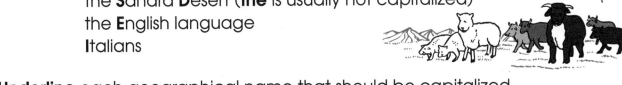

Underline each geographical name that should be capitalized.

australia is the smallest continent on Earth. The western half of this continent is dominated by the great sandy desert, the gibson desert and the great victoria desert. Two mountain ranges, the macdonnell range and the musgrave range, are located in this area. The great dividing range is a long mountain chain that runs along australia's eastern coastline. Surrounding this small continent are the indian ocean, the timor sea, the arafura sea, the coral sea and the pacific ocean. You may have read about the great barrier reef, which lies between its northeast shoreline and the coral sea.

australia is divided into six main areas: western australia, south australia, the northern territory, queensland, new south wales and victoria. The capital of australia is canberra, which is located in new south wales. Its highest point is mt. kosciusko, which is southwest of canberra. Two large lakes, lake eyre and lake torrens, lie in south australia. The darling, warrego and murray rivers flow through the southeast corner. Much of australia's land is used for grazing sheep and cattle.

Underline each word that should be capitalized.

1. americans and the english speak the english language.

2. english is a germanic language, as are german and dutch.

3. swedish, norwegian and danish are also germanic languages.

4. italian and spanish are two romance languages.

5. The romance languages come from latin, the language of all romans.

6. The languages of the russians, poles, czechs and slavs have a common origin.

7. Many africans speak hebrew and arabic.

8. The language of indians and pakistanis is hindustani.

9. Many american students study french and german.

10. spanish and latin are also often studied.

Scrambled Eggs

breakfast
breath
cleanse
dread
feather
health
heavy
instead
leather
meant
spread
sweat
thread
threat
tread
wealth
weapon
weather

Unscramble each group of letters to spell a word from the list.

trlehae _____   hhetal _____

lwehat _____   tnmea _____

tsewa _____   dhtrae _____

rddae _____   tterah _____

ayveh _____   eteharw _____

dtare _____   oanwpe _____

tekarbasf _____   sdatnei _____

dsarpe _____   cesenal _____

herfate _____   ebhatr _____

Which sound does **ea** make in each word? _____

Write two other words that have the **ea** combination and make the short **e** sound.

1. _____   2. _____

A **couplet** is a two-line poem that rhymes. **Write** a pair of couplets (two sets of two) using at least four words from the list.

Example:

When my button fell off, I meant to buy thread,
But I was tempted to buy pink bubble gum instead.

This unfortunate mistake now fills me with dread.
Before Mother sees me, to my room I will tread.

_____

_____

_____

_____

Learn at Home, Grade 6

A Land of Many Peoples

The Iroquois were a group of tribes joined together by a common language. Their enemies, the Algonquin, were several tribes of another language group.

Listed below are the names of some Native American tribes and the states that claim them. Remember that Native Americans often moved from state to state.

Write each tribe's name in or by its state name on the map. Then, **color** each state the correct color. The colors symbolize common language groups.

Ojibway (green)
Wisconsin

Arapaho (green)
Colorado

Leni Lenape (green)
Delaware

Illinois (green)
Illinois

Penobscot (green)
Maine

Algonquin (green)
Massachusetts

Powhatan (green)
Virginia

Nez Perces (lt. blue)
Idaho

Yakimas (lt. blue)
Washington

Sioux (yellow)
South Dakota

Osage (yellow)
Kansas

Crow (yellow)
Montana

Ute (tan)
Utah

Shoshoni (tan)
Wyoming

Iroquois (red)
New York

Cherokee (red)
Tennessee

Chickasaw (blue)
Mississippi

Seminole (blue)
Florida

Navajo (orange)
New Mexico

Apache (orange)
Texas

Shasta (violet)
California

Many Times Over

Mrs. Ten-twenty's class was studying multiples. Each student wrote a problem for the others to solve. **Write** the number sentence and answer for each problem.

1. If it takes the average student 10 minutes to finish 20 problems, how long would it take to finish 40?

   _____

2. If it takes 20 minutes to write 15 number facts, how long would it take to write 45?

   _____

3. The design received 30 points. If the points were tripled, how many points would the design have received?

   _____

4. Each flower on the bush had 7 pink petals. If there were 20 flowers on the bush, how many petals would there be altogether?

   _____

5. Baby Rita's shoe weighs 2 oz. Debbie's shoe weighs 10 times as much. How much does Debbie's shoe weigh?

   _____

6. Tyrone kept a bug collection in 10 boxes that each held 20 different kinds of bugs. Nikki had 30 boxes of 20 bugs each. How many bugs did they have altogether?

   _____

7. Barbara was making glitter stars for her wizard costume. If it took her 36 minutes to make 16 stars, how long would it take her to make 40 more stars?

   _____

8. The boy scouts were making model cars. Each model car had 62 parts. If they made 8 model cars, how many total parts would there be?

   _____

Learn at Home, Grade 6

Millions Mysteries

Follow the clues to **fill in** the mystery numbers.

1. Use the numbers 3 to 9. Each is used only once.
2. The ones, tens and hundreds are odd numbers.
3. The hundred thousands, ten thousands and thousands are in backwards counting order.
4. There are 3 times as many hundreds as ones.
5. There are 2 times as many hundred thousands as millions.

1. Use the numbers 2 to 8. Each is used only once.
2. The hundreds, tens and ones are in counting order.
3. The sum of the ones, tens and hundreds is 9.
4. There are 2 times as many ten thousands as tens.
5. There are 2 times as many thousands as ones.
6. The sum of the millions, hundred thousands and ten thousands is 18.

Multiplication

1. 467
x 35

2. 538
x 47

3. 393
x 82

4. 304
x 529

5. 246
x 824

6. 146
x 532

7. 308
x 236

8. 326
x 92

9. 735
x 45

10. 268
x 39

11. 486
x 513

12. 314
x 249

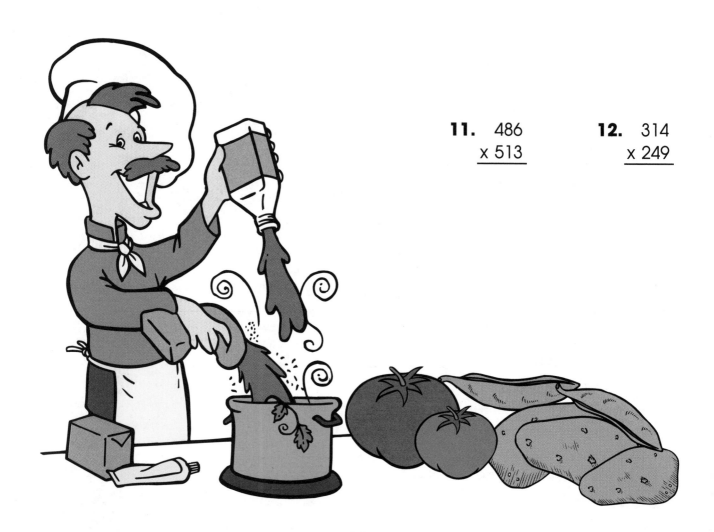

Learn at Home, Grade 6

Problem Solving

Mr. Solve-It's class measured the school and the school grounds when solving problems dealing with area, perimeter and volume.

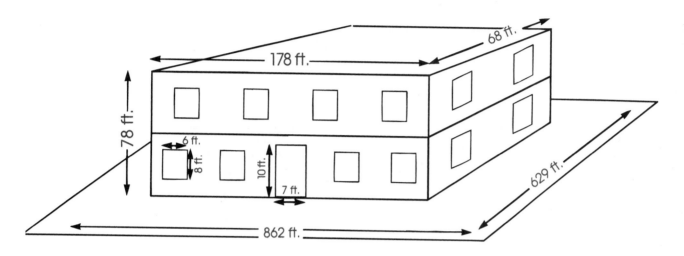

1. What is the perimeter of the building? _____

2. What is the area of the front door? _____

3. What is the area of a window? _____

4. There are the same number of windows on the other two sides of the school.

   If glass for the windows costs $8.25 a square foot, how much would it cost to

   replace the glass in all the windows? _____

5. What is the perimeter of the property? _____

6. What is the area of the property? _____

7. What portion of the property is not used for the school building? _____

   _____

8. What is the volume of the school building? _____

Find the dimensions of your home and yard. Work problems 1 to 8 using those figures on another sheet of paper.

	Language Skills	**Spelling**	**Reading**
Monday	Have your child write a descriptive paragraph about a familiar place, activity or person, such as his/her bedroom, a hike in the woods or a close friend.	Select words from the past 8 weeks for this week's pretest. Correct the pretest and make a list of any misspelled words. Have your child study the list this week.	**Nonfiction** Choose a nonfiction book for this week's reading lesson. Let your child choose the topic—it should be something of special interest to him/her. Then, help him/her find an appropriate book to read on that topic.
Tuesday	**Adverbs:** Review *adverbs*. Ask your child to compare the function of adverbs to the function of adjectives. How are they alike? How are they different? Have your child complete **Adjectives and Adverbs** (p. 104).	Have your child sort spelling words from the past 8 weeks according to number of syllables. Have him/her keep the two-syllable words separate for tomorrow's activity.	Discuss the current reading book in a conference. Focus on what your child wants to learn from the book. Have your child explain how he/she will find the answers to his/her questions.
Wednesday	Adverbs may modify verbs, adjectives or other adverbs. They add an element of intensity to an existing adjective or adverb. For example, add the adverb *really* to the following sentence to add intensity to the adverb *hard*: Chopping wood is *really hard* work. *See* Language Skills, Week 9, numbers 1 and 2. Have your child complete **More About Adverbs** (p. 105).	Have your child write all the two-syllable words from the past 8 weeks on index cards—the first syllable on one card, the second on another, and so on. Mix up the cards, then have your child match the syllables to form the spelling words.	Review the purpose and format of a glossary. Have your child read one chapter from this week's reading book. Have your child create a glossary of at least ten terms from the chapter. Encourage your child to look up definitions in a dictionary, but explain that the glossary should contain definitions written in his/her own words. Have your child list the words in alphabetical order.
Thursday	Explain the correct usage of the words *good, well, bad, badly, sure, surely, real* and *really*. Which are adjectives? (good, bad, sure, real) Which are adverbs? (well, badly, surely, really) Which adverb can be used as an adjective in some cases? (well) Have your child complete **Confusing Adjectives and Adverbs** (p. 106).	Have your child write a story using as many words as possible from the spelling lists of the past 8 weeks. Once the story is complete, have him/her read through it and underline each spelling word.	Review the purpose and format of an index. Assign the same chapter as yesterday in the nonfiction book. Have your child create an index for the chapter. *See* Reading, Week 9. Have your child complete **Keep Behavin'** (p. 107).
Friday	Teach your child about the comparative and superlative forms of adverbs. *See* Language Skills, Week 9, number 3.	Give your child the final spelling test.	Hold a reading conference in which you encourage your child to ask questions about the topic of this week's reading. Discuss ways in which your child could find answers to his/her questions.

Learn at Home, Grade 6

Math	**Science**	**Social Studies**
Multiplication Teach your child the distributive property. *See* Math, Week 9, number 1. Have your child complete **Even Distribution** (p. 108).	**Health and Nutrition** With your child, discuss the role of good nutrition in the health of the human body and the effects of poor nutrition. Ask your child to define the term *malnutrition*. *See* Science, Week 9, number 1. Have your child research a topic related to nutrition. Have your child write a report or present his/her findings in a creative format. *See* Science, Week 9, number 2.	**Immigration** Help your child map out his/her family tree. Have him/her list the country where each family member was born. *See* Social Studies, Week 9, number 1.
Explain the use of *exponents* to your child Teach him/her the different forms that are equivalent. *See* Math, Week 9, number 2. Have your child write numbers in several forms. *See* Math, Week 9, number 3.	Have your child create a poster that teaches others about the essential foods in a balanced diet. Refer to the food pyramid. *See* Science, Week 9, number 3. Encourage your child to use magazine pictures, drawings or a combination of both to make the poster. The poster should include the types of foods that are part of a healthy diet, as well as the recommended number of servings of those foods.	Help your child locate data concerning the immigrant population of the U.S. in the early 1890s and today. Have your child make a double bar graph or two graphs to display this information.
Scientists sometimes work with very, very large numbers. When they need to write a number with a lot of zeros, they use scientific notation. *Scientific notation* describes a number as a whole number between 1 and 10 times a power of ten: $1,000 = 1 \times 10^3$; $6,000 = 6 \times 10^3$; $40,000,000 = 4 \times 10^7$. Give your child extremely large numbers to write using scientific notation.	Have your child complete a nutritional analysis of one day's meals. Have your child analyze the amount of calories, fat, protein, minerals and vitamins and carbohydrates. Have your child write a summary of the healthfulness of his/her daily diet. How does it compare to the recommended daily diet of the food pyramid? Which foods should he/she eat less often? Which foods should he/she eat more often?	Give your child an outline map of the world. Have your child label and color all the countries from which his/her ancestors came. Then, have him/her label and color all the countries from which other friends and their families have come.
Scientific notation is also used with very, very small numbers. When the exponent is a negative number, it indicates the number of places to the right of the decimal that the initial number is placed. For example, 0.00006 written in scientific notation is 6×10^{-5}. Give your child extremely small numbers to write using scientific notation.	Review the systems of the human body studied over the past 8 weeks. Try to answer any questions your child may have.	Discuss the ways in which immigrants have enriched the culture of the United States. *See* Social Studies, Week 9, number 2.
Give your child the first 9-week test to assess his/her understanding of work completed so far. Reteach concepts if necessary. Have your child complete **Nine-Week Test** (p. 109).	Have your child research professions associated with the human body.	Arrange for your child to perform a community service. Have your child write in his/her Social Studies Journal. Have your child update his/her activity sheet on the stock market.

TEACHING SUGGESTIONS AND ACTIVITIES

LANGUAGE SKILLS (Adverbs)

▶ 1. Copy the following phrases on the board for your child. Have him/her write an appropriate adverb on each line, then use each phrase in a sentence.

_____ beautiful hawk _____ helpless chick _____ cleverly

_____ rough nest _____ heavily _____ carefully

▶ 2. Adverbs can have four functions: they can tell where, when or how, or they can serve to intensify an adjective or other adverb. Discuss the following examples with your child.

The children play outside.	Have your child underline the adverb in the sentence. (outside) Ask what it tells. (where) Adverbs of place tell where.
The plane arrived early.	Have your child underline the adverb. (early) Ask what it tells. (when) Adverbs of time tell when.
He walked slowly.	Have your child underline the adverb. (slowly) Ask what it tells. (how) Adverbs of manner tell how.
He walked extremely slowly.	Have your child underline *extremely*. Adverbs of degree are also called intensifiers.

▶ 3. Most adverbs have a descriptive (or positive), comparative and superlative form. The *positive* describes but does not show comparison, the *comparative* compares two things and the *superlative* compares three things. Write an example on the chalkboard and discuss.

Positive: Katja performed *skillfully* on the piano.

Comparative: Steven plays *more skillfully* on the viola than he does on the violin.

Superlative: Cheryl played the *most skillfully* of all the cellists.

READING (Nonfiction)

Gather several nonfiction books. Have your child observe the indexes of these books. After your child reads the assigned chapter in this week's reading book, ask him/her to reflect on the words and topics that should be indexed. Have him/her make an alphabetical list of those topics. Then, have your child list the pages wherever that word or concept appears.

MATH (Multiplication)

▶ 1. It is important that your child understands the distributive property of multiplication—some aspects of algebra rely on this property. The property states that *if several numbers are multiplied by the same factor and then added, the addends may be grouped and then multiplied by the common factor.*

Examples: $(3 \times 5) + (4 \times 5) + (2 \times 5) + (10 \times 5) = (3 + 4 + 2 + 10) \times 5$
$4 \times (9 + 3) = (4 \times 9) + (4 \times 3)$

▶ 2. The exponent form 7^3 is read *seven to the third power*. Its factor form is written as $7 \times 7 \times 7$. Standard form of the same number is 343.

▶ 3. Test your child's understanding of exponent, factor and standard forms with the following problems:

a. Write each in exponent form.

$5 \times 5 \times 5$ $8 \times 8 \times 8 \times 8$ $3 \times 3 \times 3 \times 3 \times 3 \times 3$ $9 \times 9 \times 9 \times 9 \times 9 \times 9 \times 9 \times 9$

b. Write each in factor form.

four to the fifth power   six to the third power   twelve to the fifth power

c. Write each in standard form.

five to the third power 4^4 $2 \times 2 \times 2 \times 2$ 7^3 5^6

Learn at Home, Grade 6

SCIENCE (Health and Nutrition)

▶ 1. Good nutrition is an essential element of a healthy life. Nutrition affects alertness, health, attitude, mood, intelligence and many other aspects of a person's life. It is important to make good nutritional choices. It is wise to choose foods that are from a variety of food groups, foods low in sugar and fat, and whole grains and unprocessed foods. A person who is malnourished suffers from poor health and is more susceptible to disease and illness.

▶ 2. Have your child research a topic related to health and nutrition. Below are some questions that may spark an idea for a topic:

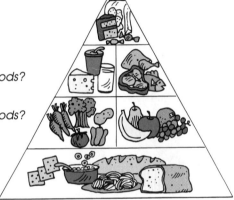

What efforts are made to help feed hungry people?

What conditions lead to hunger and starvation?

What types of foods are necessary for a balanced diet?

What can you learn about foods from nutrition labels?

What can you learn from the list of ingredients on packaged foods?

What are calories?

How do you calculate the percentage of calories from fat in foods?

▶ 3. Study the food pyramid at the right. The foods at the bottom, or in the largest section of the pyramid, are the foods you should eat in large quantities. The foods at the top, or in the smallest section of the pyramid, are the foods you should eat in only small quantities.

SOCIAL STUDIES (Immigration)

▶ 1. The population of the United States has been blessed with a wealth of immigrants from hundreds of different countries. The U.S. was at one time called a "melting pot". This image illustrated the idea that people from all different countries and cultures came together and became one in the United States. A more modern image is one of a "tossed salad". In this image, the people from different cultures come together in a tasteful blend while they strive to keep their individual identities. Encourage your child to discover the diversity in his/her own ancestry. Through marriage, some families have blends of many different cultures and backgrounds. Others have maintained a single regional ancestry. Discuss traditions your child follows that stem from old family traditions—particularly those that have been passed down from other countries.

▶ 2. If there is any evidence of foreign influence in your community, provide opportunities for your child to experience, firsthand, a broad perspective of the cultures present in this country.

Visit a museum that displays some of the art and customs of people who have immigrated to the U.S.

Have your child listen to the music of immigrants who have made America their home.

Have your child talk to a recent immigrant about his/her experience.

Visit a restaurant that serves ethnic food.

Cook some international recipes.

Make a list of foods, such as tacos, crepes, latkas and spaghetti, that are part of our culture now but were adopted from another country.

Adjectives and Adverbs

Adjectives describe or modify nouns.
They tell what kind, how many or which one.
Examples: a **tall** building (what kind)
                   three buildings (how many)
                   that building (which one)

Adverbs usually describe or modify verbs.
They tell how, when and where the action of a verb is performed.

Examples: He ran **quickly**. (how) He ran **today**. (when) He ran **away**. (where)

Circle the adjectives and **underline** the adverbs.
In the blank, **write** what each one tells about the noun or verb it modifies.

1. a fast sailboat _____

2. rapidly blinked _____

3. ran outside _____

4. the speckled egg _____

5. seven tailors _____

6. discussed later _____

7. that rose _____

8. quickly covered _____

9. played again _____

10. four kittens _____

11. fell forward _____

12. woke early _____

13. the tired worker _____

14. several pages _____

15. softly whistled _____

16. hidden nearby _____

Rewrite each sentence adding an adjective and an adverb. **Circle** all the adjectives and **underline** all the adverbs in the new sentences.

1. The pond melted in the sunshine. _____

_____

2. Frogs croaked while sitting on the lily pads. _____

_____

3. Birds warbled in the trees. _____

_____

4. Turtles sunned themselves on the rocks. _____

_____

Learn at Home, Grade 6

More About Adverbs

Adverbs that modify verbs function as adverbs of time, place or manner. Adverbs that modify adjectives or other adverbs function as adverbs of degree, also called intensifiers.

Examples: We went to the big game **today**. (time)
People were selling programs **everywhere**. (place)
He was **really** tired after his workout. (degree)

Circle each adverb. Tell if it is an adverb of time, place, manner or degree.

1. The roads were impassable because it snowed today. _____

2. We unwillingly resigned ourselves to staying at home. _____

3. Could we travel there in this storm? _____

4. We would be greatly cheered by a weather change. _____

Circle each intensifier, or adverb of degree. **Draw** an arrow to the word it modifies. On the line, identify the modified word as an adverb or adjective.

1. She was quite easily upset by any change in plans. _____

2. We made rather extensive plans for our summer vacation. _____

3. We are planning an extremely exciting trip. _____

4. She very firmly refused to go at all. _____

Many adverbs have a **positive**, a **comparative** and a **superlative** form.

| soon, softly | sooner, more softly | soonest, most softly |

Rewrite each sentence twice. Use the comparative form of the underlined adverb first, then use the superlative form.

1. He ran <u>fast</u> in the race. _____

_____

2. She walked home from school <u>quickly</u>. _____

_____

Learn at Home, Grade 6

Confusing Adjectives and Adverbs

Good, bad, sure and real are adjectives. They modify nouns.
Examples: That was a **good** dinner. He made a **bad** choice.

Badly, surely and really are adverbs.
They modify verbs, adjectives and other adverbs.
Examples: He ran **badly**. He **really** wanted to go.

Better, worse, best and worst are adjectives if they modify nouns. They are adverbs if they modify verbs, adverbs or adjectives.
Examples: That's my **best** work. (adjective)
He sang **best** last night. (adverb)

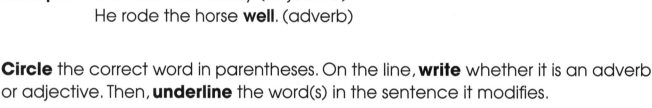

Well is an adjective if it refers to health.
Well is an adverb if it tells how something is done.
Examples: She feels **well** today. (adjective)
He rode the horse **well**. (adverb)

Circle the correct word in parentheses. On the line, **write** whether it is an adverb or adjective. Then, **underline** the word(s) in the sentence it modifies.

1. Tim was (sure, surely) he could go to the museum. _____

2. He wanted to go with his friends (bad, badly). _____

3. He (sure, surely) could finish his work before noon. _____

4. Susan had done a (good, well) job of convincing him to try. _____

5. Tim thought he could manage (good, better) with a schedule. _____

6. He could make (better, well) time if he was organized. _____

7. His list of chores was (worse, bad) than he thought. _____

8. Tim first cleaned up his room (real, really) well. _____

9. He just had to see the (real, really) dinosaur fossil. _____

10. Tim felt (well, good) and whistled as he worked. _____

11. He always worked (best, good) under pressure. _____

12. It turned out to be a (real, really) pleasure to help. _____

Learn at Home, Grade 6

Keep Behavin'

It was time for another of Mr. Fridley's science classes on behaviors. This time, the class was going to discuss learned behaviors. Mr. Fridley explained that learned behaviors are behaviors that change as a result of experience.

First, Mr. Fridley explained learning by association. This type of learning connects a stimulus with a particular response. He asked if anyone could give him an example. Lee suggested that when the bell rings at the end of class, the students put away their pens and pick up their books. Mr. Fridley congratulated Lee on his answer and said that the students learned to associate the stimulus of the bell with the response of leaving class.

There are several kinds of learning by association. One results in a conditioned response—a desired response to an unusual stimulus. Mr. Fridley reminded them of Ivan Pavlov's experiments with dogs. In the experiments, Pavlov found that dogs salivated when they smelled meat. Pavlov began ringing a bell every time he was about to give meat to a dog. In time, the dog salivated when the bell rang, whether or not there was any meat. Pavlov had trained the dogs to respond to the bell instead of the food.

Another kind of learning by association involves teaching animals to act in a certain way by rewarding them for their behavior. This is called positive reinforcement and may be as simple as a rat pressing a lever to get food. This type of learning, however, may also involve a complex series of tasks.

Match:

conditioned response   study hard—get a good grade

positive reinforcement   hear siren—panic

Underline:

Both types of learning by association involve . . .
  a stimulus.   a learned association.

  a response.   experiments.

Circle:

If a squirrel learns to climb into a bird feeder to obtain food, it has learned by . . .

  conditioned response.   unconditioned response.

  positive reinforcement.   negative reinforcement.

Write examples of something you have learned by conditioned response and something you have learned by positive reinforcement. _____

_____

Even Distribution

Some students in Ms. Statistic's class used their own experiences to study the distributive property.

1. Marcus bought three sets of baseball cards each time he went to the store. The first week, he went to the store twice. The second week, he went once. The third week, he went four times. How many sets of cards did he buy during the three weeks? _____

2. Jessie found six seashells and three sand dollars on her first visit to the beach. With the same luck, how many shells and sand dollars would she find in three visits? _____

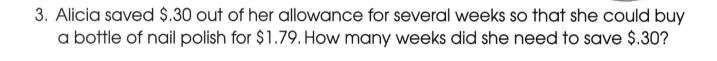

3. Alicia saved $.30 out of her allowance for several weeks so that she could buy a bottle of nail polish for $1.79. How many weeks did she need to save $.30?

   _____

4. Kim hit one single, one double and two home runs in her first softball game this season. If she could continue at this rate, how many home runs, singles and doubles would she have after six games?

   _____

   _____

5. Each person in the class was given two sheets of green construction paper, one sheet of brown and three sheets of orange. There are 27 students in the class. How many sheets of colored paper did Ms. Statistic need?

   _____

6. Tony, a novice runner, ran $\frac{1}{2}$ mile on his first try, $1\frac{1}{4}$ miles on his second try and 2 miles on his third try. How far would he run in 2 weeks if he ran the same distances the next week?

   _____

Extension: Design an art project. Figure how much of each type of material you will need.

Learn at Home, Grade 6

1. **Write** the number 3,512,978 in words.

   _____

   _____

2. Subtract the following from the number 2,846,238:

   4,000 _____

   20,000 _____

   600,000 _____

3. Round 38.462 ... to the nearest tenth. _____

   to the nearest ten. _____

   to the nearest hundredth. _____

4. **Draw** a triangle on another sheet of paper with the following specifications:

   $\overline{AB}$ is perpendicular to $\overline{AC}$.

   $\overline{AB}$ is 10 cm.

   $\angle ACB$ is 45°

5. Name the type of triangle. _____

6. Calculate the area. If $\overline{BC}$ is 14cm, what is the perimeter?

   area   _____

   perimeter _____

7. Multiply.

78	48	362	40,286
x 3	x 12	x 38	x 245

8. **Write** 6^4 in factor form and standard form.

   _____

	Language Skills	**Spelling**	**Reading**
Monday	Have your child write a story about a mythical beast. Encourage your child to imagine how the beast looks and acts, its name and where it lives. Have your child imagine the problem and events of the story, make a plan for writing, then begin work on a rough draft.	Pretest your child on these spelling words: beast freak plead beneath greasy release breathe increase repeat defeat lease scream disease leave weave eavesdrop meager wreath Correct the pretest, add personalized words and make two copies of this week's study list.	Introduce this week's reading selection or continue with the book from last week.
Tuesday	**Pronouns:** Review *pronouns*. Teach your child about four types of pronouns: *subject, object, possessive* and *indefinite*. *See* Language Skills, Week 10, number 1. Have your child create a four-column chart to list the pronouns in each category. Then, discuss the correct usage of each type of pronoun.	Study this week's spelling words. Have your child complete **Easygoing** (p. 117).	Discuss the current reading book in a conference. Focus on reading with expression.
Wednesday	Help your child identify possible pronoun errors in his/her own writing. The most common error is to confuse subject and object pronouns. Have your child complete **Pronoun Blunders** (p. 114).	Have your child use each of this week's spelling words correctly in a sentence.	**Scanning Text:** Teach your child the skill of scanning text. Demonstrate how to use an index card or your fingertips to guide your eyes as you read quickly through text. The goal is not to read every word but to look for a signal. When you find that signal, you can slow down and read carefully. *See* Reading, Week 10, numbers 1 and 2.
Thursday	Introduce reflexive pronouns: *myself, yourself, herself, himself, itself, ourselves, yourselves* and *themselves*. A reflexive pronoun reflects the action of a verb back to the subject. Write some examples on the chalkboard. Have your child draw a line under the reflexive pronoun and draw an arrow back to the subject. Have your child complete **Reflexive Pronouns** (p. 115).	Have your child study this week's spelling words.	Have your child scan the newspaper for an article on literacy. Then, have him/her read the article and write a summary.
Friday	Introduce personal, interrogative and relative pronouns. *See* Language Skills, Week 10, number 2. Have your child complete **Pursuing Pronouns** (p. 116).	Give your child the final spelling test. Have your child record pretest and final test words in his/her word bank.	Hold a reading conference in which you compare this week's reading book with another book. Ask your child to compare the settings, the characters, the styles of the authors and the conflicts faced by the main characters.

     Learn at Home, Grade 6

Math	Science	Social Studies
Division With your child, review simple rules for determining if a number can be divided evenly by 2, 3, 5, 9 and 10. *See* Math, Week 10, number 1. Have your child write down the ages of several family members, then list all the numbers by which each age is divisible. Have him/her try the same with other numbers found in the newspaper or around the house.	**Chemistry** Introduce your child to the science of chemistry. *See* Science, Week 10, numbers 1 and 2. Have your child draw a picture of a chemist in his/her Science Log. Then, have your child write a paragraph describing what he/she thinks a chemist does or studies.	**Immigration** At the turn of the century, many European immigrants came to America through New York City. They came to the U.S. because it was known as the land of opportunity. Families sailed across the ocean in ships to Ellis Island. Have your child read *Ellis Island: New Hope in a New Land* by William Jay Jacobs. Gather other books as well for your child to read more about Ellis Island.
Review the idea that division is the opposite operation of multiplication. Ask your child to demonstrate this concept. Have your child complete **Mr. Quotient's Class Divides** (p. 118).	What is matter? Explain that matter is anything that occupies space and can be observed by at least one of the senses. There are three states of matter: solid, liquid and gas. Perform a simple demonstration to show your child the three states of matter. *See* Science, Week 10, number 3. Have your child identify the states of matter of several substances, such as those listed in Science, Week 10, number 1.	Many immigrants' first sight of America was the Statue of Liberty. Have your child read about the Statue of Liberty. Where did it come from? What did it symbolize? Have your child add the year the statue was installed (1886) to the time line. Have your child read the poem inscribed on the pedestal of the statue. (It was added in 1903.) Ask your child to memorize the poem—or at least the final six lines of the poem—for tomorrow.
Many children find division especially difficult. Review the steps involved to solve a sample division problem. *See* Math, Week 10, number 2. Have your child complete twelve division problems. *See* Math, Week 10, number 3.	Help your child set up an experiment to discover whether hot or cold water freezes faster. Have your child read the information on **Freezing Hot Water** (p. 119) and plan the experiment. Your child will actually perform the experiment tomorrow. It is very important that he/she is deliberate in the planning.	Discuss why some immigrants were resented. *See* Social Studies, Week 10. Discuss some of the laws that were adopted to restrict the number of Asians and Europeans allowed to enter the United States. Have your child consider the issue of immigration carefully. What are his/her opinions on the issue? Should there be restrictions regarding who is allowed to enter the U.S.? *See* Social Studies, Week 10, numbers 1–6.
Review how to check division. Multiply the divisor by the quotient and add the remainder. Have your child check his/her work from yesterday using multiplication and addition.	Have your child perform his/her experiment and record the results on a chart or table. Ask him/her to include comments about where the ice freezes first in each ice cube tray. Then, have your child draw a conclusion from the experiment. Was his/her hypothesis correct?	At the turn of the century, New York City contained several ethnic neighborhoods. When immigrants arrived, they sought out others who had come from the same country and settled near each other in tenement houses. Have your child read about life in one of these ethnic neighborhoods. Have him/her write a journal entry as a young immigrant (near your child's own age) living in New York in the early 1900s.
Ask your child to generate twelve division problems, all with a quotient of 25. **Examples:** 125 ÷ 5 16,025 ÷ 641 475 ÷ 19	Help your child conduct a black box experiment. To make a black box, cover a small box and its cover with black construction paper. Make sure the cover is removable. Place one object (marble, nail, paper clip, cotton ball, juice box) at a time in the box. Put a large rubber band around the box to keep it closed. Ask your child to shake the box and describe the attributes (and state of matter) of the mystery object inside.	Have your child complete the activity sheet on the stock market begun in Week 7. Discuss the information. Arrange for your child to perform a community service. Have your child write in his/her Social Studies Journal.

Learn at Home, Grade 6

TEACHING SUGGESTIONS AND ACTIVITIES

LANGUAGE SKILLS (Pronouns)

▶ 1. Teach your child to recognize four types of pronouns: *subject, object, possessive* and *indefinite*.

   Subject: I, you, he, she, it, we, they

   Object: me, you, him, her, it, us, them

   Possessive: my, your, his, her, its, our, their (indicates ownership of noun that follows)
   mine, yours, his, hers, its, ours, theirs (used alone without noun following)

   Indefinite: anybody, somebody, everybody, something, anyone, someone, everyone, no one

▶ 2. *Personal pronouns* take the place of one or more nouns. **Examples:** *I, him, they, she, we, it*
   Interrogative pronouns introduce questions. **Examples:** *Which, what, where, when*
   A *relative pronoun* introduces a phrase that acts like an adjective. **Example:** The first astronauts *who* were chosen for the space program needed to have a degree in engineering.

READING (Scanning Text)

▶ 1. Scanning is a skill that can be used to locate specific information. A person may scan a newspaper looking for interesting topics or scan a book about frogs for information on what they eat. Scanning is not the same as reading. Discuss instances when your child would want to scan text rather than read carefully.

▶ 2. Give your child the following resources and directions to practice scanning.

   Nonfiction books: Look for an answer to a specific question.

   Newspapers: Look for an article on a given topic.

   Word lists: Look for a given word.

   Word search: Look for words on a list.

   Internet: Locate an article on a given topic.

MATH (Division)

▶ 1. The following hints will help your child determine the divisibility of a number:

   A number is divisible by 2 if it is even (ends in 0, 2, 4, 6, 8).

   A number is divisible by 5 if it ends in a 0 or 5.

   A number is divisible by 10 if it ends in 0.

   A number is divisible by 3 if the sum of the number's digits is divisible by 3.

   A number is divisible by 9 if the sum of the number's digits is divisible by 9.

▶ 2. Review the process of division. The steps are explained here for the auditory learner.

   a. Determine where to place the quotient.

   b. Estimate how many times the divisor divides into the first one or two digits in the dividend and place this number in the quotient.

   c. Multiply the number you placed in the quotient by the divisor and place the product below the portion of the dividend with which you are working. If the product is larger than the portion of the dividend with which you are working, estimate a smaller quotient.

   d. Subtract the product from the portion of the dividend with which you are working. If the difference is larger than the divisor, estimate a larger quotient.

   e. Bring down the next digit in the dividend.

   f. Repeat the above steps until all the numbers have been brought down from the dividend.

   g. Write the final difference as a remainder.

   These steps are usually summarized as DIVIDE, MULTIPLY, SUBTRACT and BRING DOWN.

Learn at Home, Grade 6

▶ 3. Have your child write the following twelve division problems on lined paper and solve.

3,216 ÷ 8 (402)	11,336 ÷ 52 (218)	933 ÷ 22 (42 R9)	15,552 ÷ 64 (243)
462 ÷ 33 (14)	2,467 ÷ 30 (82 R7)	1,248 ÷ 18 (69 R6)	24,314 ÷ 27 (900 R14)
7,155 ÷ 9 (795)	11,346 ÷ 36 (315 R6)	8,046 ÷ 9 (894)	618 ÷ 4 (154 R2)

SCIENCE (Chemistry)

▶ 1. Gather and display the following items for your child: a glass of water, copper wire, a piece of aluminum foil, a penny, a light bulb, household ammonia, baking soda, a match, a carbonated beverage, an inflated balloon and table salt. Explain that each of these items represents a form of matter and that matter is made up of elements. The science of chemistry is the study of the elements that make up all matter in the universe and the reactions that occur among them. Everything in the universe is composed of specific substances called elements. Each element has its own unique properties and characteristics. As an introduction, tell your child the following facts that may sound familiar:

Water (H_2O) contains the elements hydrogen and oxygen.

Copper wire and aluminum foil are metallic elements.

A penny is a mixture of copper and zinc.

Baking soda contains sodium, carbon, hydrogen and oxygen.

A carbonated beverage contains water and carbon dioxide gas.

An inflated balloon contains a mixture of oxygen, nitrogen and other gases.

▶ 2. Add the following chemistry terms to the weekly spelling lists as they are discussed. Over the next 8 weeks, your child should come to understand each of these terms. As each word is introduced, have your child define it in his/her spelling word bank.

acid	base	ion	molecule	periodic table
atom	compound	matter	neutron	proton
atomic mass	electron	metal	nonmetal	salt
atomic number	element	mixture	nucleus	solution

▶ 3. Hold a tray of ice cubes over a steaming pot of water. Have your child observe what happens (condensation). Ask your child where the water is coming from. (The steam is cooling and returning to a liquid state.)

SOCIAL STUDIES (Immigration)

Some people feel that the influence of immigrants is negative. Citizens worry about job competition. They believe that immigrants lower wages because they are willing to work for less money. Others blame immigrants for overcrowding, poverty and crime. Some people even resent immigrants because they are different: they speak different languages, eat different foods and practice different customs and religions.

▶ 1. List standards you believe immigrants must comply with in order to gain entry into the U.S.

▶ 2. List reasons you think are valid to deny an immigrant entry into the U.S.

▶ 3. Express your opinion about immigration laws and quotas. Should they exist?

▶ 4. Describe what the U.S. would be like if, after the colonists declared their independence from England, no more immigrants had been allowed to enter the U.S.

▶ 5. What might America have missed had the following immigrants not been allowed to enter the U.S.: John Astor, Irving Berlin, Andrew Carnegie, Walter Gropius, Meyer Guggenheim, Joseph Pulitzer, David Sarnoff.

▶ 6. Have your child recite the poem inscribed on the pedestal of the Statue of Liberty. Ask your child to reflect on the meaning of these words.

Pronoun Blunders

Three errors are often made when using pronouns.
Follow the rules below to avoid these errors.

Do not use an object pronoun as the subject of a sentence.
Incorrect: Us are playing hockey.
Correct: We are playing hockey.

Do not add extra pronouns that duplicate the subject.
Incorrect: Bonnie, she has won the tennis match.
Correct: Bonnie has won the tennis match.

In a sentence with a compound subject, it is incorrect to
put the pronoun **I** before the noun.
Incorrect: I and Sheila will attend the game.
Correct: Sheila and I will attend the game.

Rewrite each sentence correctly on the line below.

1. I and Mr. James were planning the school Sports Day. _____

_____

2. Mrs. Shawn and Mrs. Thompson they volunteered to help Mr. Thompson and me
with the concession stand. _____

_____

3. I and Mrs. Thompson will also prepare the food. _____

_____

4. Bob, he will make arrangements for all the sports equipment. _____

_____

5. We had challenged them the eighth graders to a game. _____

_____

6. Us were forming a relay team. _____

_____

7. John will time we in the races. _____

_____

8. John, he has been involved in many races. _____

_____

114

Learn at Home, Grade 6

Reflexive Pronouns

Reflexive pronouns reflect the action of the verb back to the subject.

Myself, yourself, herself, himself, itself, ourselves, yourselves and themselves are reflexive pronouns.

Examples: Roger made **himself** a model of the space shuttle.
The shuttle landed **itself**, using only gravity to pull it down.

Complete each sentence with the appropriate reflexive pronoun.

1. The Davenport children congratulated _____ on the good spot they found.

2. We sure found_____ a good viewpoint from which to watch the shuttle landing.

3. David imagined_____ trying to maneuver in a space shuttle that was hurtling toward earth.

4. "I told_____ that I will become a commander someday," Earl said.

5. Deborah enjoyed _____ at the shuttle launch.

6. "You could train _____ for space travel if you built a model simulator," David's parents suggested.

Write the reflexive pronoun from the box that matches each subject listed below.

1. Peter _____

2. The dog _____

3. Gwen _____

4. Monica and I _____

5. Heather and Kimberly _____

6. You and Carolyn _____

7. I _____

8. You _____

myself
yourself
himself
yourselves
themselves
itself
herself
ourselves

Learn at Home, Grade 6

Pursuing Pronouns

A **personal pronoun** takes the place of one or more nouns. An **interrogative pronoun** introduces a question. A **relative pronoun** introduces a group of words that acts as an adjective.

Examples: I am excited about the track meet today. (personal pronoun)

What event does Bill plan to enter? (interrogative pronoun)

The track meet, **which** we went to last week, was an exciting event. (relative pronoun)

Write **personal**, **interrogative** or **relative** in the blank to identify each pronoun.

1. **Which** sprinting race is your favorite?_____

2. **We** both like the same type of running shoes. _____

3. The high jump is a challenge **that** I would like to take on. _____

4. **Who** would like to warm up with me?_____

5. A boy **whom** I knew won the track meet. _____

6. **You** are a natural when it comes to long-distance running. _____

7. Is it true that **she** would like to join our running club?_____

8. **Whose** house should the team go to for the end-of-the-year party?

_____

Complete each sentence with a pronoun.

1. I tried to find my shoes _____ were lost. (relative)

2. _____ told us it won't be a problem for them to run today. (personal)

3. The boy _____ won the race is a great runner. (relative)

4. _____ would like to be our fourth runner in the relay race? (interrogative)

Learn at Home, Grade 6

Write each spelling word next to either its antonym or its synonym. Use a thesaurus if necessary.

beast
beneath
breathe
defeat
disease
eavesdrop
freak
greasy
increase
lease
leave
meager
plead
release
repeat
scream
weave
wreath

1. _____ ample
2. _____ hold
3. _____ above
4. _____ victory
5. _____ health
6. _____ arrive
7. _____ decrease

1. _____ oddity
2. _____ animal
3. _____ braid
4. _____ rent
5. _____ overhear
6. _____ slick
7. _____ garland
8. _____ inhale
9. _____ beg
10. _____ yell
11. _____ say again

List four more words that contain the long **e** sound of **ea**. **Write** either an antonym or a synonym for each word. Label each one **A** (antonym) or **S** (synonym).

New Word	A/S
_____ _____	_____
_____ _____	_____
_____ _____	_____
_____ _____	_____

Mr. Quotient's Class Divides

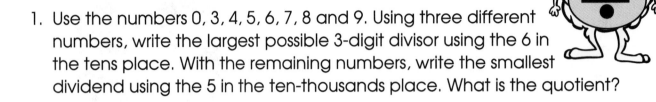

Mr. Quotient's class was studying division. Help them solve the following problems.

1. Use the numbers 0, 3, 4, 5, 6, 7, 8 and 9. Using three different numbers, write the largest possible 3-digit divisor using the 6 in the tens place. With the remaining numbers, write the smallest dividend using the 5 in the ten-thousands place. What is the quotient?

   _____

2. There were 3,192 people in attendance at the football game. There were 45 bleacher rows in the stadium. If 84 people could sit in each bleacher row, did everyone have a seat?

   _____

3. There were 1,848 candy bars available for the candy sale. There were 154 students ready to sell them. To keep sales equal, how many candy bars should be put in each salesperson's box?

   _____

4. Marathon Mike worked 7,272 problems in 36 weeks. How many did he average each week?

   _____

5. Mr. Quotient's class collected a total of 972 leaves for a science project. There were 27 students in the class. What was the average number each student collected?

   _____

6. Shanna wrote 144 Spanish vocabulary words during the months of April and May. How many words, on average, did she write each week during those months?

   _____

Extension: 96,785,642 ÷ 24 ÷ 35 ÷ 3 = _____

Learn at Home, Grade 6

Freezing Hot Water

Some people say that hot water freezes faster than cold water. What do you think? Could this be possible? Doesn't water have to get colder before it can freeze? If so, it would make more sense to start with very cold water when you want to make ice. But did you know that between the periods of a hockey game the ice is resurfaced with hot water? Could it be that hot water does freeze faster than cold water under certain conditions? Let's find out!

State the Problem:
Write a question that asks what you want to find out from your investigation.

Form a Hypothesis:
What do you think your scientific investigation will prove? Make a smart guess. Write a sentence that states what you think the answer to your question will be.

Plan the Procedure:
1. Before a scientist begins experimenting, he/she usually does some research on the topic to find what other scientists have learned. This information is used to plan the procedure for the experiment. Finding the answer to the following questions will help you understand water and how it "behaves":

   a. What is a water molecule?   b. What are the three forms (states) of water?
   c. At what temperature does each form of water change into a new form?

2. Here is an example of how you could do the experiment. Take two identical ice cube trays and fill them to the same level with water, one with hot, the other with cold. Use a thermometer to record the water temperature. Place the trays in the freezer and check them at 5 minute intervals. Note which one has ice crystals forming first.

   When designing a test for your hypothesis, it is very important that you control all the variables. For example, use the same kind of container for each trial and put the container in the same spot in the freezer each time.

3. Write a step-by-step description of your experiment.
4. Make a detailed list of materials.

	Language Skills	**Spelling**	**Reading**
Monday	Have your child choose a topic, make a plan for writing, then begin work on a rough draft.	Pretest your child on these spelling words: beige freight protein caffeine heifer receipt conceit height receive conceive leisure seizure foreign neither skein forfeit perceive weight Correct the pretest, add personalized words and make two copies of this week's study list.	Teach your child to preview a book to determine if it interests him/her. Previewing may include reading the inside flap of the book's jacket, the table of contents and/or the first page. Give your child two books by the same author to preview. Discuss your child's first impressions of the two books. Have him/her select one of the books to read this week.
Tuesday	**Prepositions:** Review *prepositional phrases*. *See* Language Skills, Week 11, number 1. Discuss how prepositions, adverbs and the infinitive forms of verbs are sometimes confused. *See* Language Skills, Week 11, number 2. Have your child complete **Preposition, Adverb or Verb?** (p. 124).	Study this week's spelling words. Have your child complete **Missing Freight** (p. 126).	Discuss the current reading book in a conference.
Wednesday	Continue your discussion of prepositions and prepositional phrases. Have your child complete **Prepositional Phrases** (p. 125).	Have your child use each of this week's spelling words correctly in a sentence.	**Compare and Contrast:** Discuss different methods of comparing and contrasting. Have your child compare two books using a Venn diagram. *See* Reading, Week 11, number 1.
Thursday	**Participles:** Introduce your child to the *present* and *past participle*. *See* Language Skills, Week 11, number 3. Have your child write eight sentences containing present participles and eight sentences containing past participles.	Have your child study this week's spelling words.	Have your child compare two books using a chart or pair of lists. *See* Reading, Week 11, number 2. Discuss the advantages and disadvantages of the list format versus the Venn diagram. Which method of comparison does your child prefer? Why? Have your child complete **What's the Difference?** (p. 127).
Friday	Have your child gather his/her best or favorite stories, articles, art and poetry from this school year. Help him/her compile them into a literary magazine. Make copies of the completed magazine and send to friends and family members. *See* **Publishing Your Child's Work**. (p 5).	Give your child the final spelling test. Have your child record pretest and final test words in his/her word bank.	Hold a reading conference. With your child, discuss the types of books he/she likes to read. Choose other books of a similar type for future reading assignments.

Learn at Home, Grade 6

Math	**Science**	**Social Studies**
Division A remainder can be written as a fraction. Teach your child how to write the remainder as a fractional part of the quotient. *See* Math, Week 11, number 1. Have your child complete the division problems provided, writing the remainders as fractions. *See* Math, Week 11, number 2.	**Elements** What is an element? Explain to your child that matter is made up of basic elements. *See* Science, Week 11, number 1. Have your child separate a mixture of candy, nuts and raisins into the three elements. Then, have him/her make a graph of the elements. The graph should show how many of each element was found in a given quantity of the mixture.	**Turn of the Century** The turn of the century was a time of great expansion for the U.S. Many immigrants continued to settle in the U.S. The U.S. sought land to colonize and annex. The U.S. began to produce enough goods to begin exporting to other countries. Have your child write about what it means to be a world power. Why was the U.S. interested in other countries?
Give your child a series of quotients with remainders. Have your child write a division problem that will result in each quotient. **Examples:** 3 R1 10 ÷ 3 5 R4 299 ÷ 59	Have your child separate a mixture of sand and rice. What is the easiest method for separating? Can you think of another method? Do you need some other tools?	The Spanish-American War occurred in 1898. Have your child add this date to the time line. Have your child read about the war and define related terms. *See* Social Studies, Week 11, number 1.
Following the correct order of operations, your child would normally multiply and divide from left to right before adding and subtracting from left to right. For the purpose of today and tomorrow's activities, however, your child must disregard the rules of order and simply work from left to right. Have your child complete **Missing Signs** (p. 128).	Introduce your child to the periodic table of the elements found in any encyclopedia. There are 109 basic elements which make up all matter.	Provide your child with six essay topics related to the Spanish-American War. *See* Social Studies, Week 11, number 2. Have your child write an essay on one of the topics.
Have your child complete **A Number Challenge** (p. 129).	Introduce the term *atom* and teach your child about the parts of an atom. Discuss the structure of an atom. *See* Science, Week 11, number 2. Have your child build models of atoms using jelly beans or marshmallows. *See* Science, Week 11, number 3.	Write facts about the tenures of Presidents McKinley and T. Roosevelt on index cards and attach the cards on the time line.
Challenge your child to come up with number pairs for given clues. *See* Math, Week 11, number 3.	Have your child read about the work of Dmitri Mendeleev. Discuss how his work led to the creation of the periodic table. Have your child study the arrangement of the elements on the periodic table. *See* Science, Week 11, number 4.	Arrange for your child to perform a community service. Have your child write in his/her Social Studies Journal.

TEACHING SUGGESTIONS AND ACTIVITIES

LANGUAGE SKILLS (Prepositions/Participles)

▶ 1. Brainstorm a list of prepositional phrases (under the couch, to the store, in the box). Have your child underline the noun or pronoun at the end of each prepositional phrase. Explain that the noun or pronoun is the *object* of the prepositional phrase.

▶ 2. Write sentences in which the word *to* is used as part of a prepositional phrase or as part of an infinitive. Have your child identify the difference.

We went *to the sale* yesterday.　　　　　He was talking *to my uncle*.

Sam sold candy *to raise* money.　　　　He planned *to buy* a bike with the money he made.

▶ 3. A participle is a verb that can also act as an adjective. The present participle ends in *ing*. The past participle usually ends in *ed*.

The *snoring* man makes a lot of noise. (present adjective)　　　The man is *snoring*. (verb)

The *struck* bird fell to the ground. (past adjective)　　　The bird struck the window. (verb)

READING (Compare and Contrast)

▶ 1. Draw a Venn diagram, a pair of intersecting circles used for comparisons. Write the name of one book over the left circle and the name of the other book over the right circle. Discuss how the books are alike. Have your child write the similarities in the part of the diagram where the circles overlap and write ways each book is unique in the corresponding circles.

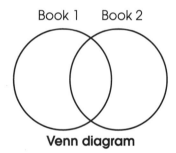

Venn diagram

▶ 2. Have your child choose two books to compare—one book that he/she liked and one book that he/she did not like. Have him/her draw a line down the middle of a page and write the name of one book at the top of each column. Ask your child to list what he/she liked and disliked about each book. Discuss your child's list and come to a conclusion about what kind of books your child likes to read.

MATH (Division)

▶ 1. Have your child solve the division problem 125 ÷ 60. The answer is 2 R5. The remainder can be written as a fractional part of the quotient by placing it over the divisor. The answer becomes $2^5/_{60}$ or $2^1/_{12}$.

▶ 2. Copy the following division problems (and others) for your child to solve. Have him/her write the remainders as fractions.

$45 ÷ 6 \ (7^1/_2)$　　　　$82 ÷ 9 \ (9^1/_9)$　　　　$135 ÷ 10 \ (13^1/_2)$

$72 ÷ 7 \ (10^2/_7)$　　　$39 ÷ 6 \ (6^1/_2)$　　　$245 ÷ 12 \ (20^5/_{12})$

▶ 3. Read the following clues, one at a time. Have your child try to guess the number pair described in each clue. The answers are given in parentheses.

a. What pair of numbers has a sum of 9 and a quotient of 2? (6 and 3)

b. What pair of numbers has a difference of 3 and a quotient of 4? (1 and 4)

c. What pair of numbers has a sum of 12 and a quotient of 2? (8 and 4)

d. What pair of numbers has a difference of 2 and a quotient of 2? (4 and 2)

e. What pair of numbers has a product of 50 and a quotient of 2? (5 and 10)

f. What pair of numbers has a product of 72 and a quotient of 2? (6 and 12)

g. What pair of numbers has a product of 24 and a quotient of 6? (2 and 12)

h. What pair of numbers has a difference of 21 and a quotient of 8? (24 and 3)

i. What pair of numbers has a sum of 24 and a quotient of 3? (6 and 18)

　　　　　　　　　　　　　　　　　Learn at Home, Grade 6

SCIENCE (Elements)

▶ 1. It is difficult to show your child examples of things that are made up of single elements. Most things are mixtures, or combinations of two or more elements. Even something as basic as water is made up of two elements: hydrogen and oxygen. Help your child understand that elements are the building blocks that make up matter. This week, provide your child with different mixtures and ask him/her to separate the mixtures by logical methods. Methods may be as simple as sorting or using a strainer or as complicated as using heat and evaporation to bring out dissolved substances.

▶ 2. An *atom* is the smallest particle of an element that can exist and still retain the element's properties. Atoms are so small that millions could be placed on the tip of a straight pin. Every atom in a given element contains the same arrangement of *protons, neutrons* and *electrons. Protons* are positively charged particles found in the nucleus. *Neutrons* are neutral particles also found in the nucleus. *Electrons* are negatively charged particles found in rings or shells around the nucleus. Each shell can hold a certain number of electrons. (See an encyclopedia for more information on electron shells.)

▶ 3. Help your child make a large model of an atom. Draw a 3-inch circle on white paper to represent the nucleus of the atom. Use three colors of marshmallows or jelly beans to represent the three types of particles found within an atom. The candies representing protons and neutrons should be placed in the nucleus; the candies representing electrons should be placed in rings around the nucleus. Have your child build several different atoms. The makeup of some common atoms is given here.

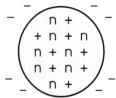

oxygen atom: 8 protons (+), 8 neutrons (n), 8 electrons (–)

nitrogen: 7 protons, 7 neutrons, 7 electrons

helium: 2 protons, 2 neutrons, 2 electrons

sodium: 11 protons, 12 neutrons, 11 electrons

fluorine: 9 protons, 10 neutrons, 9 electrons

▶ 4. The 109 elements on the periodic table are arranged in rows by *atomic number.* Each horizontal row is called a *period.* Elements are also arranged vertically in *groups* with similar characteristics. Those groups will be studied in Week 13.

SOCIAL STUDIES (Turn of the Century)

▶ 1. Have your child define each of the following terms as they relate to the Spanish-American War: *rebels, insurrection, yellow journalism, oppression, U.S.S. Maine, Battle of Manila Bay, Rough Riders, Theodore Roosevelt, Santiago, armistice, Treaty of Paris, anti-imperialism.*

▶ 2. Allow your child to choose from the following essay questions on the Spanish-American War. Have him/her write a short, factual essay in response to the question.

Discuss why the *U.S.S. Maine* was in Cuba and the controversy surrounding its destruction. Include information about and samples of "yellow journalism."

Point out where the main battles of the war were fought. Explain why the battles were on opposite sides of the world.

Discuss the causes of the war and its outcomes.

Define imperialism. Discuss whether or not it was ethical to go to war.

Make a time line of the Spanish-American War beginning with the explosion of the **Maine** and ending with the signing of the Treaty of Paris.

Explain why the Panama Canal was built.

Preposition, Adverb or Verb?

Don't confuse prepositions with adverbs or with phrases made of **to** plus a verb.

Examples: All the students went **to** the zoo. (preposition)
We really wanted **to** go. (verb part)
We started getting excited **before** the trip. (preposition)
Have you gone to the zoo **before**? (adverb)

Identify each **bold** word as a preposition, adverb or verb part.

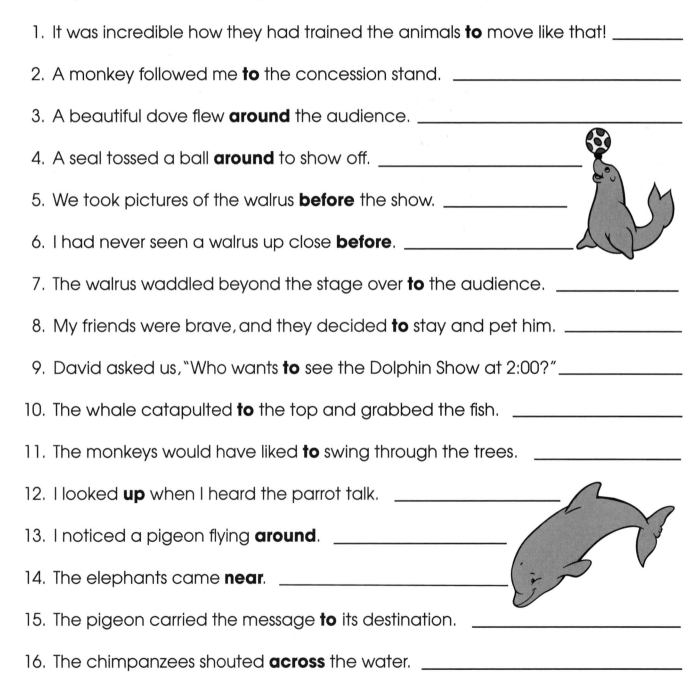

1. It was incredible how they had trained the animals **to** move like that! _____

2. A monkey followed me **to** the concession stand. _____

3. A beautiful dove flew **around** the audience. _____

4. A seal tossed a ball **around** to show off. _____

5. We took pictures of the walrus **before** the show. _____

6. I had never seen a walrus up close **before**. _____

7. The walrus waddled beyond the stage over **to** the audience. _____

8. My friends were brave, and they decided **to** stay and pet him. _____

9. David asked us, "Who wants **to** see the Dolphin Show at 2:00?" _____

10. The whale catapulted **to** the top and grabbed the fish. _____

11. The monkeys would have liked **to** swing through the trees. _____

12. I looked **up** when I heard the parrot talk. _____

13. I noticed a pigeon flying **around**. _____

14. The elephants came **near**. _____

15. The pigeon carried the message **to** its destination. _____

16. The chimpanzees shouted **across** the water. _____

Learn at Home, Grade 6

Prepositional Phrases

A **prepositional phrase** is a group of words that begins with a preposition and ends with a noun or pronoun. It can act as an adjective or adverb.

Examples: Pineapple is also grown **outside of Hawaii**. (adverb)
The sandwiches **with the peanut butter** were the best ones. (adjective)
We ate the peanut butter sandwiches **at night**. (adverb)

Underline the prepositional phrase in each sentence.

1. Peanuts are enjoyed around the world.

2. Peanuts are native to South America.

3. Peanut pods develop beneath the ground.

4. The pegs, which are the pod stems, push their way under the soil.

5. Peanuts are part of the legume family.

6. Most peanuts are grown in Africa and Asia.

Tell whether each prepositional phrase acts as an **adjective** or an **adverb**.

1. Wait until choir practice is over to eat peanut butter. _____

2. Peanut butter on a spoon is a delicious and quick snack. _____

3. Have you ever enjoyed celery with peanut butter and raisins? _____

4. Try your peanut butter sandwich with cold milk. _____

5. I love peanut butter on toast. _____

6. I enjoy eating peanuts at a ball game. _____

Missing Freight

Add vowels to each set of consonants to spell words from the list.

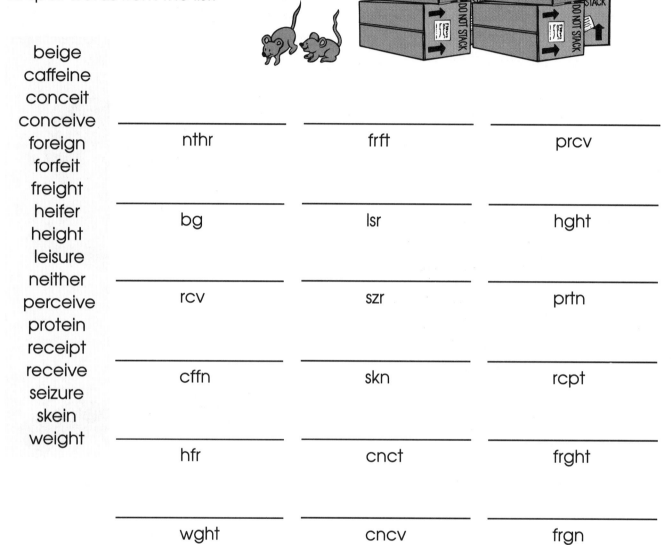

beige
caffeine
conceit
conceive
foreign
forfeit
freight
heifer
height
leisure
neither
perceive
protein
receipt
receive
seizure
skein
weight

nthr	frft	prcv
bg	lsr	hght
rcv	szr	prtn
cffn	skn	rcpt
hfr	cnct	frght
wght	cncv	frgn

Choose six spelling words to divide into syllables.

1. _____ 2. _____

3. _____ 4. _____

5. _____ 6. _____

Learn at Home, Grade 6

What's the Difference?

One day, David and Donald were discussing alligators. David insisted that alligators and crocodiles were the same animal but that people called them by different names. Donald insisted, however, that the two animals were entirely different reptiles. Kim walked up just in time to save the boys from further squabbling. Kim, who had lived in Florida for ten years, could settle this one.

She told David that alligators and crocodiles are separate reptiles. She told them that although they are similar looking and are both called crocodilians, they are very different. Both have a long, low, cigar-shaped body, short legs and a long, powerful tail to help them swim. But most crocodiles have a pointed snout instead of a round one like the alligator's. She also pointed out that while both have tough hides, long snouts and sharp teeth to grasp their prey, the crocodile is only about two-thirds as heavy as an American alligator of the same length and can therefore move much more quickly. David and Donald were impressed with Kim's knowledge.

Kim also told the boys another way to tell the two reptiles apart. She said that both have an extra long lower fourth tooth. This tooth fits into a pit in the alligator's upper jaw, while in the crocodile, it fits into a groove in the side of the upper jaw and shows when the crocodile's mouth is closed. David and Donald thanked Kim for the information, looked at each other sheepishly and walked away laughing.

Match:

crocodile   fourth tooth shows when mouth is shut

round snout

called crocodilian

alligator   fourth tooth is in a pocket in upper jaw

pointed snout

Write three ways alligators and crocodiles are alike and three ways they are different.

Alike	Different
_____	_____
_____	_____
_____	_____

Name two other animals that are sometimes thought to be the same.

_____   _____

Missing Signs

Fill in the circles with +, −, x, or ÷ to make the problem true.

3 ◯ 3 ◯ 3 ⟶ 9

3 ◯ 3 ◯ 3 ⟶ 3

3 ◯ 3 ◯ 3 ⟶ 2

3 ◯ 3 ◯ 3 ⟶ 4

3 ◯ 3 ◯ 3 ⟶ 12

3 ◯ 3 ◯ 3 ⟶ 18

3 ◯ 3 ◯ 3 ⟶ 3

3 ◯ 3 ◯ 3 ⟶ 6

3 ◯ 3 ◯ 3 ⟶ 0

3 ◯ 3 ◯ 3 ⟶ 27

5 ◯ 5 ◯ 5 ⟶ 50

5 ◯ 5 ◯ 5 ⟶ 5

5 ◯ 5 ◯ 5 ⟶ 30

5 ◯ 5 ◯ 5 ⟶ 2

5 ◯ 5 ◯ 5 ⟶ 15

5 ◯ 5 ◯ 5 ⟶ 20

5 ◯ 5 ◯ 5 ⟶ 6

5 ◯ 5 ◯ 5 ⟶ 125

5 ◯ 5 ◯ 5 ⟶ 0

5 ◯ 5 ◯ 5 ⟶ 5

A Number Challenge

Fill in the blanks to make each problem true. To check your work, start at the left and do each operation in order to get the given answer.

1. __ + __ − __ = 2

2. __ − __ ÷ __ = 3

3. __ + __ ÷ __ = 4

4. __ × __ − __ = 5

5. __ − __ × __ = 6

6. __ × __ ÷ __ = 3

7. __ ÷ __ + __ = 4

8. __ ÷ __ − __ = 5

9. __ ÷ __ × __ = 6

10. __ × __ + __ = 7

11. __ ÷ __ + __ = 12

12. __ ÷ __ − __ = 15

13. __ ÷ __ × __ = 20

14. __ × __ ÷ __ = 8

15. __ + __ × __ = 24

129

Language Skills	**Spelling**	**Reading**
Monday Have your child choose a topic, make a plan for writing, then begin work on a rough draft.	Pretest your child on these spelling words: achieve kerchief shield ancient mischief shriek believe niece siege brief piece thief field pierce wield hosiery retrieve yield Correct the pretest, add personalized words and make two copies of this week's study list.	Introduce this week's reading selection. Suggestion: *The Phantom Tollbooth* by Norton Juster.
Tuesday **Direct and Indirect Objects:** A direct object is a noun or pronoun that comes after the action verb in a sentence. A direct object tells who or what receives the action of the verb. Give your child several sentences containing direct objects. Have him/her identify the verb phrase in each sentence and circle the direct object. *See* Language Skills, Week 12, number 1.	Study this week's spelling words. Have your child complete **The Mischievous Thief** (p. 135).	Discuss the current reading book in a conference. Focus on idioms.
Wednesday An *indirect object* is a noun or pronoun that tells to whom or for whom the action of the verb is done. Give your child several sentences containing indirect objects. Have him/her circle the indirect object in each sentence. *See* Language Skills, Week 12, number 2.	Have your child use each of this week's spelling words correctly in a sentence.	**Main Idea:** Review the concept of main idea. Have your child complete **Beth Is Sick** (p. 136).
Thursday Work with your child to make a proofreading checklist. Make a list of things your child should look for when proofreading his/her own writing. Have your child apply this list to the story he/she is writing this week.	Have your child study this week's spelling words.	Discuss the main idea of each chapter read so far in the current reading book. *See* Reading, Week 12, numbers 1 and 2.
Friday Review pronoun/antecedent agreement and run-on sentences. Have your child complete **Penguins Keeping Warm** (p. 134).	Give your child the final spelling test. Have your child record pretest and final test words in his/her word bank.	Hold a reading conference. Have your child predict the outcome of the book or discuss the ending.

Learn at Home, Grade 6

Math	Science	Social Studies
Division Teach your child the following terms: *mean, mode, median* and *range*. *See* Math, Week 12, numbers 1–4. Create four simple charts or graphs that present information such as test scores or movie running times. Ask your child to find the mean, mode, median and range for each chart, rounding his/her answers to the nearest hundredth.	**Elements** Each element has a one- or two-letter abbreviation called a *symbol*. While some symbols are easy to recognize (Ne for neon), others are more puzzling (Na for sodium or K for potassium). Have your child research the origins of some of these unusual symbols. Have your child use the symbols to write words or sentences. **Example:** PoPCoRn.	**Panama Canal** One result of the Spanish-American War was the decision to build a passage from the Atlantic Ocean to the Pacific Ocean. The Panama Canal passes through Central America, thus eliminating the need to travel all the way around the tip of South America. Have your child draw a detailed map of the Panama Canal and of the trip around South America that the canal replaces.
Guide your child through an activity in organizing and analyzing data. Have your child complete **Statistical Experiments** (p. 137). Then, have your child collect, organize, analyze and report data on a topic of his/her choice.	Have your child identify different elements that were named for people, places and planets. *See* Science, Week 12, number 1.	Have your child do research, then draw a diagram showing how the locks and the canal move ships from one ocean to the other. *See* Social Studies, Week 12, number 1.
Given the area and the length of one side of a rectangle, your child should be able to determine its width. Draw and label the following rectangles. Have your child find the width of each one. length = 5 cm area = 20 cm^2 length = 7 cm area = 42 cm^2 length = 6 cm area = 12 cm^2 length = 18 cm area = 72 cm^2 length = 9 cm area = 54 cm^2	Explain the significance of the numbers on the periodic table of the elements. The atomic number and atomic mass signify the number of protons, neutrons and electrons in an element. *See* Science, Week 12, number 2. Create math problems for your child to solve using the atomic mass and weight of different elements. *See* Science, Week 12, number 3.	Have your child read, then write, about the building of the canal. Ask him/her to include information about the many obstacles encountered during construction, such as disease, engineering, money and politics.
The missing length of a prism can be found given the volume and two of the dimensions. Volume = length x width x depth. Draw and label the following rectangular prisms. Have your child find the depth of each one. vol. = 125 cm^3 l = 5 cm w = 5 cm vol. = 180 cm^3 l = 3 cm w = 12 cm vol. = 640 cm^3 l = 8 cm w = 8 cm vol. = 144 cm^3 l = 2 cm w = 8 cm	Have your child refer to the atomic numbers on the periodic table to solve a puzzle. Have your child complete **Chemical Magic Square** (p. 139).	Discuss the political disputes regarding U.S. ownership of the Panama Canal Zone. *See* Social Studies, Week 12, number 2. Who does your child think should own the zone?
Review U.S. Customary units of measurement. Show your child how to convert one unit to another unit. Have your child complete **Weight and Capacity** (p. 138).	Discuss where elements can be found in, on or around Earth. Help your child do some research and make a chart identifying where common elements are most often found. *See* Science, Week 12, number 4.	Arrange for your child to perform a community service. Have your child write in his/her Social Studies Journal.

131

TEACHING SUGGESTIONS AND ACTIVITIES

LANGUAGE SKILLS (Direct and Indirect Objects)

▶ 1. Copy the following sentences onto the chalkboard. The direct objects are underlined. Have your child identify the verb phrase in each sentence, then circle each direct object.

At some time, everyone has received an important or interesting <u>letter</u> in the mail. The postal system carries vast <u>amounts</u> of correspondence every day. It may surprise <u>you</u> to know how old this idea is.

In 3000 B.C., runners carried <u>messages</u> for their rulers. The runners memorized <u>them</u> before leaving. The first Roman emperor, Caesar Augustus, created an efficient postal <u>system</u>. He built <u>roads</u> for his messengers. The smooth roads helped <u>them</u> run faster. King Edward IV of England set up a <u>series</u> of post houses. At first, these handled only official <u>mail</u>. Later, ordinary citizens could use <u>them</u>. Charles II of Great Britain started <u>the London Penny Post</u> in 1683. A person could mail a <u>letter</u> to anywhere in London for a penny. Rowland Hill envisioned the <u>envelope</u>. He also suggested <u>stamps</u> with glue. Britain issued the first postage <u>stamps</u> on May 6, 1840. The world has been using postage <u>stamps</u> ever since. Our efficient postal system helps <u>us</u> each and every day.

▶ 2. Have your child look for the action verbs in the following sentences. The indirect objects are underlined. Copy these sentences without underlining. Have your child circle the indirect object in each sentence.

The sun sends <u>the earth</u> a tremendous amount of energy every hour.

The sun provides <u>plants</u> life-giving energy.

A process called photosynthesis gives <u>plants</u> the ability to convert that energy.

Green plants provide <u>animals</u> energy for growth and function.

Solar energy offers <u>us</u> weather variations around the world.

The winds provide <u>people</u> energy to power some machines.

Eclipses of the sun give <u>scientists</u> opportunities to study the sun's corona.

The sun's infrared rays give <u>sunbathers</u> their sunburns.

The sun's energy gives <u>milk</u> its Vitamin D.

Prolonged exposure to the sun can give <u>people</u> health problems.

READING (Main Idea)

▶ 1. The main ideas in a book may be implied rather than stated. Ask your child to reflect on the messages that the characters are communicating. Could your child also benefit from the lessons the book's characters are learning? Each chapter may have one or more main ideas. One chapter's main idea may be to teach the reader about the character's background. Another chapter's main idea may be to introduce a problem. Discuss the main ideas as your child reads.

▶ 2. The main idea of a paragraph is often stated in the first sentence. Choose several paragraphs from the current reading book. Have your child read each paragraph carefully, then state the main idea. Have your child identify which paragraphs state the main idea in the first sentence.

MATH (Division)

▶ 1. *Mean* is another term for average. It is found by adding all the numbers in a situation and dividing by the number of occurrences. **Example:** One week, Eunice returned 7 bottles to the recycling station. Another week, she returned 8 bottles, and a third week, she returned 9 bottles. The average is calculated by adding the three occurrences and dividing by 3. The average number of bottles Eunice returned in a week was 8.

▶ 2. When a list of numbers is arranged in numerical order, the *median* is the middle number.
Example: 32°, 36°, 38°, <u>40°</u>, 41°, 45°, 46°

Learn at Home, Grade 6

When there are an even number of occurrences, the median is found by taking the average of the two middle numbers. In the following example, the median is 39.5°.

Example: 32°, 36°, 38°, <u>39°</u>, <u>40°</u>, 41°, 45°, 46°

▶ 3. The number that occurs most frequently is called the *mode*.

Example: 32°, <u>34°</u>, <u>34°</u>, 33°, <u>34°</u>, 36°, 30°

▶ 4. The *range* is the difference between the greatest and the least possibility.

Example: 32°, 36°, 38°, 40°, 41°, 45°, 46°
The range is 46° – 32° or 14°.

SCIENCE (Elements)

▶ 1. Have your child study the periodic table by looking for elements named for:

planets—uranium, neptunium, plutonium

people—nobelium, mendelevium, fermium, curium, lawrencium

places—francium, europium, californium, berkelium, americium, polonium

Have your child read about Nobel, Fermi, the Curies and E. O. Lawrence to find out why these scientists were honored by having elements named for them.

▶ 2. The *atomic number* of an element is the number of protons found in the nucleus. The number of electrons in a neutral atom of that element will also be the same. For example, carbon's atomic number is 6—it has 6 protons in its nucleus and 6 electrons around the nucleus. The *atomic mass* of an atom is the total number of protons and neutrons in the nucleus. For example, carbon's atomic mass is 12. The nucleus of the atom contains 6 protons and 6 neutrons. By subtracting the atomic number from the atomic mass of an atom, the number of neutrons can be determined. Refer to the periodic table to find the atomic number and atomic mass of given atoms.

How many neutrons are in an atom of Ne?
atomic mass = 20   atomic number = 10   20 – 10 = ___ neutrons

How many neutrons are in an atom of Sr?
atomic mass = 88   atomic number = 38   88 – 38 = ___ neutrons

▶ 3. Give your child the following problems and/or similar ones. Have him/her refer to the periodic table to solve the problems.

How many neutrons are in an atom of Ca?   How many neutrons are in an atom of Cl?

How many neutrons are in an atom of U?   How many neutrons are in an atom of Pb?

▶ 4. Chemical elements are found throughout the solar system. Most elements occur naturally in or on the earth. Some elements are manufactured and others are created in nuclear reactors or in nuclear explosions. Using reference materials, have your child discover where the following elements are located most abundantly.

gold	silver	lead	copper	aluminum	tungsten
uranium	tin	mercury	bromine	iron	cobalt
titanium	chromium	nickel	zinc	radium	platinum

SOCIAL STUDIES (Panama Canal)

▶ 1. Have your child draw a side view of the Panama Canal, labeled with details such as length, depth and time required at each station along the way. The canal is about 50 miles (80 kilometers) long. It takes a ship about 8 hours to travel from one ocean to the other. Have your child take an imaginary ship through the canal beginning at Limón Bay. Have your child take the ship through the Gatun Locks and up 85 feet, through Gatun Lake and the narrow Gaillard Cut, then back down through the Pedro Miguel and Miraflores Locks. Finally, have your child bring the ship through the Bay of Panama into the Pacific Ocean.

▶ 2. Have your child read about the agreement between the U.S. and Panama to give the U.S. control of the Panama Canal Zone. How much did the U.S. pay for this privilege? How long was the agreement meant to last? How did the Panamanians feel about the deal?

Skill Lessons

Read the paragraphs about penguins. Make sure all pronouns and their antecedents agree. Correct run-on sentences.

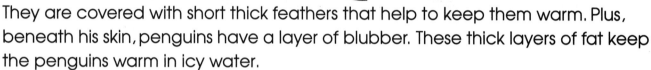

   Penguins are unusual birds found in Antarctica and other southern locations. They spend a lot of time in the icy ocean waters, they do not get cold. They are covered with short thick feathers that help to keep them warm. Plus, beneath his skin, penguins have a layer of blubber. These thick layers of fat keep the penguins warm in icy water.

   Baby penguins, called chicks, do not have as much insulation as its parents have they do not yet have blubber or waterproof feathers to keep it warm and dry. The chicks' fluffy down feathers plus their parents' body heat keep it safe from the cold. A small penguin may huddle under the warm body of an adult, and sometimes the adults form a tight circle around a group of several chicks and eventually the little penguins will be able to survive on his own.

Complete the article by adding a final paragraph.

_____

_____

_____

_____

_____

_____

_____

_____

The Mischievous Thief

achieve
ancient
believe
brief
field
hosiery
kerchief
mischief
niece
piece
pierce
retrieve
shield
shriek
siege
thief
wield
yield

Use the code to retrieve the stolen words. Crack the code by assigning a number to each letter of the alphabet.
Example: A = 1, B = 2

$\overline{1}$ $\overline{14}$ $\overline{3}$ $\overline{9}$ $\overline{5}$ $\overline{14}$ $\overline{20}$ $\overline{16}$ $\overline{9}$ $\overline{5}$ $\overline{18}$ $\overline{3}$ $\overline{5}$

$\overline{6}$ $\overline{9}$ $\overline{5}$ $\overline{12}$ $\overline{4}$ $\overline{25}$ $\overline{9}$ $\overline{5}$ $\overline{12}$ $\overline{4}$

$\overline{20}$ $\overline{8}$ $\overline{9}$ $\overline{5}$ $\overline{6}$ $\overline{19}$ $\overline{8}$ $\overline{18}$ $\overline{9}$ $\overline{5}$ $\overline{11}$

$\overline{14}$ $\overline{9}$ $\overline{5}$ $\overline{3}$ $\overline{5}$ $\overline{1}$ $\overline{3}$ $\overline{8}$ $\overline{9}$ $\overline{5}$ $\overline{22}$ $\overline{5}$

$\overline{2}$ $\overline{5}$ $\overline{12}$ $\overline{9}$ $\overline{5}$ $\overline{22}$ $\overline{5}$ $\overline{23}$ $\overline{9}$ $\overline{5}$ $\overline{12}$ $\overline{4}$

$\overline{19}$ $\overline{9}$ $\overline{5}$ $\overline{7}$ $\overline{5}$ $\overline{19}$ $\overline{8}$ $\overline{9}$ $\overline{5}$ $\overline{12}$ $\overline{4}$

$\overline{2}$ $\overline{18}$ $\overline{9}$ $\overline{5}$ $\overline{6}$ $\overline{8}$ $\overline{15}$ $\overline{19}$ $\overline{9}$ $\overline{5}$ $\overline{18}$ $\overline{25}$

$\overline{16}$ $\overline{9}$ $\overline{5}$ $\overline{3}$ $\overline{5}$ $\overline{11}$ $\overline{5}$ $\overline{18}$ $\overline{3}$ $\overline{8}$ $\overline{9}$ $\overline{5}$ $\overline{6}$

$\overline{13}$ $\overline{9}$ $\overline{19}$ $\overline{3}$ $\overline{8}$ $\overline{9}$ $\overline{5}$ $\overline{6}$

$\overline{18}$ $\overline{5}$ $\overline{20}$ $\overline{18}$ $\overline{9}$ $\overline{5}$ $\overline{22}$ $\overline{5}$

135

Beth Is Sick

Poor Beth is sick, and she doesn't know why. She felt great yesterday, but this morning she woke up with a headache, a fever and a horrible sore throat. Beth is disappointed because today is the day her class is going to the new science museum. Why did she have to be sick on a field trip day? How did she get ill so quickly?

Beth and Kim talk on the phone about Beth's situation for twenty minutes. Because they planned to be field trip partners, Kim is really sad Beth isn't going to school today. Kim tells Beth she probably got sick because she didn't wear a jacket to school yesterday, and it was a cold day. She tells Beth that if your body gets cold, you catch germs more easily. Beth tells Kim that is silly. She believes Kim has a virus.

Beth remembers learning about viruses in science class. Mr. Fridley told them that viruses are noncellular structures that can only be seen through an electron microscope, which magnifies them thousands of times. On its own, a virus is a lifeless particle that can't reproduce, but when a virus enters a living cell, it starts reproducing and can sometimes harm the host cell. Viruses that harm host cells cause disease like chicken pox, the flu and colds. Mr. Fridley told them that shaking hands with or being sneezed or coughed on by an infected person may infect you with the virus. Beth believes that she became infected from someone since lots of people are sick at this time of year. Kim promises Beth a full report on the science museum.

Underline the main idea of the story.

Beth has a headache, fever and a sore throat.
Beth and Kim try to discover why Beth is sick.
Viruses cause diseases.
Mr. Fridley taught them about viruses.

Check the correct answers.

Viruses...
☐ can't be seen through an ordinary light microscope.
☐ pass easily from one person to another.
☐ are thousands of times bigger than regular cells.
☐ enter living cells and start reproducing.

What are some ways to avoid viruses?_____

_____

_____

Learn at Home, Grade 6

Statistical Experiments

Statistical experiments involve collecting, organizing and analyzing data.
Ms. Botanical's class is interested in growing a flower garden for the whole school
to enjoy. To collect data on flower preferences, they surveyed all 435 students in
the school. They noted the results below.

Favorite Flowers

Types of Flowers	Number of Votes
Black-eyed Susans	57
Petunias	63
Irises	32
Tulips	78
Hollyhocks	7
Daffodils	53
Daisies	84

Organize the data:

List the flowers in order from the most popular to the least. _____
_____
_____

Analyze the data:

1. Based on these data, which five flowers should the students plant?_____

   _____

2. Which flower should definitely not be planted? _____

3. Do the number of votes justify planting a garden? Why or why not? _____

   _____

4. What is the mean? _____

5. What is the mode? _____

6. What is the median? _____

7. What is the range? _____

Learn at Home, Grade 6

Weight and Capacity

Weight

1 pound (lb.) = 16 ounces (oz.)

1 ton (T.) = 2,000 pounds

Capacity

1 cup (c.) = 8 fluid ounces (fl. oz.)

1 pint (pt.) = 2 cups

1 quart (qt.) = 2 pints

1 gallon (gal.) = 4 quarts

Example 2

To change from a smaller unit to a larger unit, divide.

176 fl. oz. = _____ c.

8 fl. oz. = 1 c.
176 ÷ 8 = 22
176 fl. oz. = 22 c.

Example 1

To change from a larger unit to a smaller unit, multiply.

5 T. = _____ lb.

1 T. = 2,000 lb.
5 x 2,000 = 10,000
5 T. = 10,000 lb.

Example 3

Express remainders in terms of the original unit.
25 c. = 12 pt. 1 c.

25 c. = _____ pt.
2 c. = 1 pt.
25 ÷ 2 = 12 R1

Complete.

1. 16 pt. = _____ qt.

2. 12 gal. = _____ qt.

3. 5 lb. = _____ oz.

4. 150 oz. = ___ lb. ___ oz.

5. 5 gal. 3 qt. = _____ qt.

6. 2 lb. 3 oz. = _____ oz.

Compare using >, <, =.

7. 1 gal. [ ] 6 qt.

8. 560 oz. [ ] 35 lb.

9. 15 pt. [ ] 25 c.

Learn at Home, Grade 6

Chemical Magic Square

Use the Periodic Table to help you complete this activity. Read the clues concerning the elements in the boxes below. **Write** the correct atomic number in the box. Add the numbers across, down and diagonally to produce a magic square.

What is your answer? _____

This element is located directly above lithium. _____	This element is located to the left of sulfur. _____	This element is located directly below carbon. _____	This element is located directly above magnesium. _____	_____
This element is located to the right of sodium. _____	This element is located to the left of nitrogen. _____	This element is located directly above phosphorus. _____	This element is located directly above chlorine. _____	_____
This element is located to the left of fluorine. _____	This element is located below helium. _____	This element is located directly above potassium. _____	This element is located directly above aluminum. _____	_____
This element is located to the left of silicon. _____	This element is located directly below hydrogen. _____	This element is located directly above neon. _____	This element is located to the left of chlorine. _____	_____
_____ _____		_____	_____	_____

	Language Skills	**Spelling**	**Reading**
Monday	Have your child choose a topic, make a plan for writing, then begin work on a rough draft.	Pretest your child on these spelling words: applause daughter nautical assault exhaust pauper audience fraud restaurant automobile laundry sauna autumn naughty slaughter caulk nausea trauma Correct the pretest, add personalized words and make two copies of this week's study list.	Choose a nonfiction book for this week's reading selection. Introduce the book today.
Tuesday	**Conjunctions:** *Conjunctions* join words, groups of words or entire sentences. Some common conjunctions are *and, but* and *or*. Write several sentences that contain conjunctions. Leave a space where each conjunction should be. Have your child choose the best conjunction to complete each sentence. *See* Language Skills, Week 13, number 1 for sample sentences.	Study this week's spelling words. Have your child complete **Automobile Exhaust** (p. 145).	Discuss the current reading book in a conference. Focus on reasons for reading.
Wednesday	Teach your child to use correct punctuation when joining clauses or sentences. Two complete sentences are joined with a comma and a conjunction. Subordinating conjunctions do not always require a comma. *See* Language Skills, Week 13, number 2. Have your child write ten sentences that contain conjunctions. Have him/her focus on correct punctuation.	Have your child use each of this week's spelling words correctly in a sentence.	**Taking Notes:** With your child, discuss reasons for taking notes. *See* Reading, Week 13, number 1. With your child, brainstorm situations in which a person might want to take notes. Ask your child to jot notes as he/she reads this week's book to remember specific facts about the subject.
Thursday	**Interjections:** Review *interjections*. An interjection expresses a feeling and has no grammatical relation to the rest of the sentence in which it appears. Interjections may express happiness, surprise, anger, disappointment, joy or danger. Have your child cite interjections that might express each of these feelings. Have your child complete **Interjections** (p. 144).	Have your child study this week's spelling words.	Teach your child to reflect on the purpose for taking notes before starting to read or research. *See* Reading, Week 13, number 2. Teach your child to organize his/her note-taking so that it is orderly and easy to follow.
Friday	Introduce the proper use of direct address in a sentence. *See* Language Skills, Week 13, number 3. Have your child generate a list of writing situations in which it would be appropriate to use direct address. Have your child include examples for each situation.	Give your child the final spelling test. Have your child record pretest and final test words in his/her word bank.	Hold a reading conference in which you determine a project for your child to complete using the information gathered this week.

Learn at Home, Grade 6

Math	Science	Social Studies
Problem Solving With your child, discuss problem-solving strategies, such as looking for clue words to determine the required operation or drawing a picture or chart to help illustrate the problem. Sometimes a problem can be solved by extending a pattern. Have your child complete **Multiply or Divide?** (p. 146).	**Metals and Nonmetals** Study the groups found on the periodic table this week. *See* Science, Week 13, number 1. The element iodine is used to test for the presence of starch in foods. Have your child complete **Testing for Starch** (p. 149). **Note: Pure iodine is poisonous if swallowed.** Buy tincture of iodine at a drug store and supervise your child during his/her independent investigation.	**Twentieth Century** Have your child read about Presidents Taft and Wilson. Have him/her write three facts about each president on index cards. Add them to the time line.
Generate 6–8 situational problems for your child to solve using multiplication and division. Center the problems around a common theme, such as travel times or distances. **Example:** It is 3 times as far from Minneapolis to New Orleans as it is from Minneapolis to Chicago. The distance from Minneapolis to New Orleans is 1,215 miles. How many miles is it from Minneapolis to Chicago?	Most elements are metals. *See* Science, Week 13, number 2. Have your child locate the two groups of nonmetals on the right side of the periodic table. Explain that all metals share some basic characteristics: They lose electrons in chemical reactions; they are shiny; they are good conductors; they can be bent or stretched; and they can be hammered into thin sheets. Compare metals and nonmetals.	The twentieth century has been a time of great change. Read about the changing roles of women during this century—especially the suffrage movement. Have your child create a collage depicting what he/she believes are the roles of women today.
Continue to give your child practice with problem solving. Have your child complete **Shifty Sam's "Rip-Off" Record Shop** (p. 147).	Look at nutrition labels from cereals, breads and meats. Have your child identify the metals listed (sodium, potassium, calcium and iron). Explain that a healthy diet includes 10 milligrams of iron each day. Have your child find out the iron content of different foods. Discuss the consequences of an iron-poor diet. Help your child find iron filings in cereal. *See* Science, Week 13, number 3.	**World War I:** Introduce World War I (WWI). WWI was labeled "the war to end all wars." It was also known as the "Great War." Discuss the reasons for these names. *See* Social Studies, Week 13. Have your child read about the development of the airplane from the first one flown by the Wright brothers to those used by the military in WWI. Have your child write about or draw pictures of the changes.
Review concepts related to division. Then, test your child's understanding of division. Have your child complete **Division Review** (p. 148).	Have your child keep track of his/her diet for one day. Then, ask your child to look up the amount of iron on labels and in a nutrition resource. Have your child calculate the milligrams of iron in his/her diet for one day.	Help your child understand the concept of *allies*. WWI was a war of alliances. It was another way of saying, "My friends and I are stronger than you and your friends." Discuss how this concept caused the war to be more widespread than it needed to be. Have your child list or show on a map the different alliances formed during WWI. Have your child indicate the allied powers, the central powers and the neutral nations.
Teach your child how to use different functions on the calculator. *See* Math, Week 13, number 1.	Have your child look up and define the term *radioactivity*. Then, have your child name the elements that are radioactive.	Arrange for your child to perform a community service. Have your child write in his/her Social Studies Journal.

TEACHING SUGGESTIONS AND ACTIVITIES

LANGUAGE SKILLS (Conjunctions/Interjections)

▷ 1. Here are some examples for you to follow:

Saturn has rings _____ moons surrounding it.

Saturn is a small light as seen from Earth _____ is a giant in space.

▷ 2. Subordinating conjunctions include *since, while, as, when, after, before, whether, although, if* and *because*. These conjunctions are used to join a dependent clause to an independent clause. When a sentence begins with a subordinate conjunction, use a comma to separate the clauses. If the dependent clause follows an independent clause, no comma is used.

After Harvey finished his chores, he went to play with his friends.

Harvey went to play with his friends **after** he finished his chores.

▷ 3. Stating the name of the person being spoken to or addressed is called direct address. The direct address is always followed by a comma. **Examples:** Ted, this is for you. Poor thing, let me help you.

READING (Taking Notes)

▷ 1. A *note* is a brief written record used to aid the memory. People take notes in many different situations. Usually a note is a list or a phrase; it is rarely a complete, punctuated sentence. Notes are taken for the note-taker. As long as the note-taker can understand the notes, the format is not important.

▷ 2. Teach your child to think about the purpose of note-taking before starting to read. Read the following paragraph aloud to your child without any introduction. Have your child take notes.

Mrs. Johnson was about to go to the grocery store to buy supplies for dinner. She planned on preparing fish with lemon, peas and potatoes for the main course and apple pie for dessert. She discovered she needed a lemon, apples, potatoes and brown sugar. She asked if anyone else needed anything from the store. Mr. Johnson asked her to pick up some orange juice and crackers. Their son, Josh, asked her to buy cookies.

After you finish reading, ask your child what Mrs. Johnson needed to buy at the store. Without an introduction, your child may not have taken very careful notes, or he/she may have written too much. Discuss the need for knowing the purpose before reading. Then, tell your child to take notes while you read a second paragraph. Explain to your child that the purpose this time is to find out how much money Charlene spent.

Charlene met her friends for lunch. She ordered a hamburger, fries and a soda. Her lunch cost two dollars and fifty-nine cents. After lunch, Charlene and her friends went ice-skating. Skating cost a dollar. Charlene had to pay an additional fifty cents to rent skates. While skating, she bought a cup of hot cocoa for thirty cents. After skating, Charlene and her friends stopped at a video-game store. Charlene spent sixty-five cents playing games.

After your child has calculated the money spent, discuss how it was easier to take notes when the purpose was clear. Relate this to taking notes while reading. It is important to reflect on your purpose before you start to read. Ask questions about the topic you are studying. Attempt to find answers to the questions as you read and take notes.

MATH (Problem Solving)

▷ 1. Teach your child to use the memory function on a calculator. The memory function works well when multiplying and adding in the same problem. Imagine you are adding up prices at the grocery store. You have purchased 3 loaves of bread at $1.59 each, 5 boxes of sandwich bags at $0.89 each and 3 quarts of milk at $1.39 each. First, total the bread by multiplying 3 x $1.59. Type *3 x 1.59 =*, then add the results to memory by typing *M+*. Next, total the sandwich bags by typing *5 x .89 = M+*. (This will add $4.45 to the amount currently in memory.) Finally, total the milk by typing *3 x 1.39 = M+*. (This will add $4.17 to the amount currently in memory.) To find the total, press the MR or MRC key, which recalls the amount in memory. In this case, the display will be 13.39. The total cost of the groceries is $13.39. Use the *clear* or *MC* (memory clear) button to work on the next problem.

Learn at Home, Grade 6

SCIENCE (Metals and Nonmetals)

▶ 1. Refer to the periodic table of the elements and point out that there are groups of elements that possess similar properties. If you look at the chart in an encyclopedia, you will find the groups color-coded. Introduce your child to the following groups of elements: alkali metals, alkaline earth metals, nonmetals and noble gases. Name examples from each group. Have your child name places where these elements are commonly found (e.g., noble gases—neon is found in many store signs).

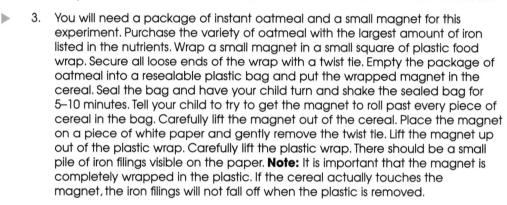

▶ 2. Introduce the study of metallic elements by displaying samples of nails, copper wire, aluminum foil, tools, coins, silverware, buttons, paper clips and jewelry. What are the similarities among the different metals? What are some other metals you can find in your home? Have your child identify some of the common metals on the periodic table of the elements, then name some common uses of metals.

▶ 3. You will need a package of instant oatmeal and a small magnet for this experiment. Purchase the variety of oatmeal with the largest amount of iron listed in the nutrients. Wrap a small magnet in a small square of plastic food wrap. Secure all loose ends of the wrap with a twist tie. Empty the package of oatmeal into a resealable plastic bag and put the wrapped magnet in the cereal. Seal the bag and have your child turn and shake the sealed bag for 5–10 minutes. Tell your child to try to get the magnet to roll past every piece of cereal in the bag. Carefully lift the magnet out of the cereal. Place the magnet on a piece of white paper and gently remove the twist tie. Lift the magnet up out of the plastic wrap. Carefully lift the plastic wrap. There should be a small pile of iron filings visible on the paper. **Note:** It is important that the magnet is completely wrapped in the plastic. If the cereal actually touches the magnet, the iron filings will not fall off when the plastic is removed.

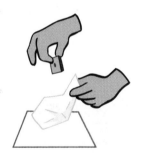

SOCIAL STUDIES (World War I)

BACKGROUND

World War I brought great changes around the world. It was called the "war to end all wars," but the harsh peace conditions imposed on Germany at the end of the war actually played a key role in setting the stage for World War II. Instead of providing a lasting peace, World War I became a prelude for the unprecedented destruction caused by Hitler, Mussolini and Hirohito. WWI was war on a scale never before witnessed. The sheer cost in loss of human lives was staggering. Total losses for the entire war include about 10 million troops. It is estimated that the number of civilian dead exceeded that number. This war also signaled the introduction of many weapons still used in modern warfare. These twentieth-century weapons include the airplane, the tank, the submarine, the machine gun, the hand grenade, poison gas and long-range artillery.

Interjections

An **interjection** that shows strong feeling is followed by an exclamation point. The next word begins with a capital letter.

Example: Quiet! He's not finished yet.

An **interjection** that shows mild feeling is followed by a comma. The next word is not capitalized.

Example: Oh, is that correct?

Rewrite the sentences to show strong feeling. Punctuate and capitalize properly.

1. hurrah we won the game.

   _____

2. whew that was a close one.

   _____

Rewrite the sentences on the lines. Punctuate and capitalize properly.

1. yes you may go to the movies.

   _____

2. well we're glad you're finally here.

   _____

Rewrite the sentences below correctly.

1. hush you don't want to upset her.

   _____

2. well we're glad you came to the meeting.

   _____

3. quiet you'll wake up everyone.

   _____

144

Learn at Home, Grade 6

Complete the word associations using the spelling words.

applause	1. prince and _____
assault	2. _____ and ship
audience	3. crisis and _____
automobile	4. _____ and soap
autumn	5. _____ and fall
caulk	6. entertainer and _____
daughter	7. _____ and spa
exhaust	8. _____ and deceit
fraud	9. cheering and _____
laundry	10. _____ and fumes
naughty	11. _____ and transportation
nausea	12. son and _____
nautical	13. _____ and nice
pauper	14. _____ and seal
restaurant	15. kill and _____
sauna	16. _____ and battery
slaughter	17. _____ and diner
trauma	18. upset stomach and _____

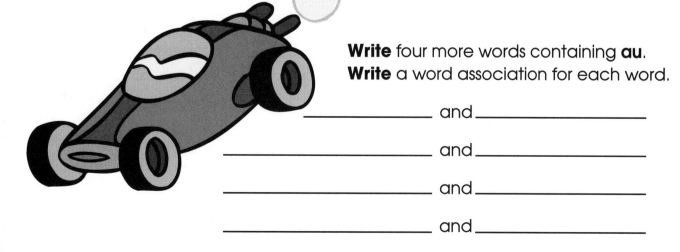

Write four more words containing **au**.
Write a word association for each word.

_____ and _____

_____ and _____

_____ and _____

_____ and _____

Multiply or Divide?

These key words will help you know
when to multiply and when to divide.

Multiplication key words: **in all, altogether,
times** and **each**

Division key words: **per, each**

Circle the key words and **solve** the story problems.

1. There are 9 classrooms at the vocational school. The average number of students per classroom is 27 students. How many students altogether are there in the school? _____	2. Thirty-five students are studying auto mechanics. Three times that many are studying business. How many students are studying business? _____
3. The semester is 16 weeks long. Students attend class 5 days a week. How many days in all must a student attend class each semester? _____	4. In one class of 27 students, each student used $30.00 worth of materials. Altogether, how much did materials cost this class? _____
5. Lunch cost each student $11.50 for a 5-day week. How much does each lunch cost? _____	6. The average student drives a total of 8 miles per day to attend classes. How many miles in all does a student drive during the 80-day semester? _____

Learn at Home, Grade 6

Shifty Sam's "Rip-Off" Record Shop

Shifty Sam sells the latest rock releases along with some oldies. You have to keep a close eye on Sam, or you may get ripped off.

Solve the problems on another sheet of paper. **Write** your answers in the spaces provided.

① The Ear Splitters' latest release, regularly $8.98, is on sale at 5 CDs for $46.95. How much more or less would you pay at the sale price for all 5 CDs?	
② The Funky Monkeys' new CD went fast. Sam made $4,540.90 on 455 copies. The correct price should be $7.99. How much did Sam charge for each CD? How much extra did he charge?	
③ Sam made $4.59 profit on each copy of the 323 CDs he sold by the Brainbangers. He is supposed to make only $3.29 profit on each one. How much extra did he make on the 323 CDs?	
④ Your aunt wanted to buy some CDs by Hart N. Soule which regularly sell for $3.67 each. Sam offered to sell her a dozen CDs for $44.00. How much will she save by buying 12 CDs?	
⑤ You wanted 180 copies of Hits of the 1940s to use as Frisbees. Each record cost $.79. Sam gave you $47.80 in change from $200. How much did he cheat you?	
⑥ Sam sold 7,000 copies of Golden Oldies for $3.99 each. He made a $2.00 profit on each record. How much money did he get for all 7,000 copies? How much profit did he earn?	
⑦ Sam charged $1.79 more for each copy of the Dippers' new CD than he was supposed to. His price was $7.89, and he sold 3,500 copies. How much extra money did he get?	
⑧ Sam sold 4,328 copies of Country Classics at $4.99 each. His profit was $1.45 on each one. How much money did he get in all? How much profit did he earn?	

Division Review

Divide.

1.

$32\overline{)6,543}$

2.

$69\overline{)112,346}$

3.

$9\overline{)876}$

4. How many hours are in 255 minutes?

5. How many weeks are there in 90 days?

6. Find the missing length.

| area = 153 m² | 9m |

7. $17x = 272$

   $x =$ _____

8. Write the remainder as a fraction.

   $27\overline{)6,925}$

9. A chicken farm produced 7,256 eggs each day. How many egg cartons are needed each day? (A carton holds one dozen eggs.)

148

Learn at Home, Grade 6

Testing for Starch

Starch is found in many foods and plants. Iodine is an indicator of starch. It turns blue-black when placed on a substance containing starch. **Safety Note: Iodine can be dangerous. Do not taste, spill or misuse it in any way.** Place a drop of iodine on each of the substances listed in the chart. Record the results. The first one is done for you.

Substance	Color of Iodine	Starch: Yes or No
white bread	blue-black	yes
brown bread		
dry cereal		
brown leaf		
popped popcorn		
oatmeal		
orange peel		
lemon peel		
liquid starch		
newspaper		
paper towel		
tissue		
water		
alcohol		
dish soap		
cloth		

Language Skills	**Spelling**	**Reading**
Monday **Writing Letters** Review the basic parts of a friendly letter. *See* Language Skills, Week 14, number 1. Have your child look in a writing handbook to read more about writing letters. Have your child write a rough draft of a letter to a friend, using a standard friendly letter format. Have your child address the envelope correctly and send the finished letter.	Pretest your child on these spelling words: diabetes diagram diaper diabolic dialect diaphragm diacritical dialogue diaries diadem dialysis diathermy diagnosis diameter diatomic diagonal diamond diatribe Correct the pretest, add personalized words and make two copies of this week's study list.	Introduce this week's reading selection or continue with the book from last week.
Tuesday Compare the format of a standard business letter with that of a friendly letter. *See* Language Skills, Week 14, number 2. Have your child draw a diagram or complete a chart comparing the purpose and format of a friendly letter and a business letter.	Study this week's spelling words. Have your child complete **Diamonds Are a Girl's Best Friend** (p. 154).	Discuss the current reading book in a conference. Focus on story elements (characters, setting, conflict, mood or tone, plot, resolution and theme).
Wednesday Have your child plan and write a business letter to request information for a research topic. Have him/her edit and revise the letter before writing it neatly in the final format. Then, have him/her address the envelope and send the letter.	Have your child use each of this week's spelling words correctly in a sentence.	**Application of Concepts:** Assign a project that will require your child to apply a concept from the reading to a new situation. For example, have your child make a mobile or model to illustrate events or concepts from the story. Or, have your child role-play or dramatize a climactic event.
Thursday Have your child plan and write a business letter to express an opinion on an environmental or a political issue. Have him/her edit and revise the letter before writing it neatly in the final format. Then, have your child address the envelope and send the letter.	Have your child study this week's spelling words.	Have your child write in his/her Reading Journal about a personal experience that is similar to an event in the reading.
Friday Have your child plan and write a business letter to praise or thank someone for a service or a performance of some kind. Have him/her edit and revise the letter before writing it neatly in the final format. Then, have your child address the envelope and send the letter.	Give your child the final spelling test. Have your child record pretest and final test words in his/her word bank.	Hold a reading conference. Ask your child to reread parts of the story that were emotionally charged. Have him/her read with expression. Discuss.

Learn at Home, Grade 6

Math	**Science**	**Social Studies**
Mixed Operations Teach your child the proper order of operations to solve problems that involve more than one operation. *See* Math, Week 14, number 1. Have your child complete **Equations** (p. 155).	**Chemical Compounds** Introduce chemical compounds. A *chemical compound* is a substance in which two or more elements have combined in a chemical reaction. **Examples:** Table salt (NaCl) is a combination of sodium (Na) and chlorine (Cl). Carbonated water (H_2CO) is hydrogen, carbon and oxygen. With your child, find other examples of chemical compounds.	**World War I** Help your child check out books on WWI from the library (recommendations: *The First World War* by John D. Clare, *World War I* by Gail Stewart). Look at magazines from the time period to learn what was going on in the United States as the war was beginning in Europe. Have your child write about the causes for the war in Europe and explain why the U.S. got involved.
Give your child a series of numbers. Have him/her use the four operations ($+$, $-$, x, $\div$) to arrive at a given solution. Your child may rearrange the numbers and add parentheses as needed to ensure that the order of operation rules are followed. Some problems may have more than one solution. **Examples:** $$3 \quad 3 \quad 3 \quad 3 \quad = 30$$ $$6 \quad 6 \quad 6 \quad 6 \quad = 13$$ $$5 \quad 4 \quad 1 \quad 4 \quad = 28$$	The smallest unit of a chemical compound is a *molecule*. A water molecule is made up of two hydrogen atoms and one oxygen atom. The chemical symbol for water is H_2O. Have your child make candy models of molecules, using gumdrops or colored marshmallows as elements. Provide toothpicks for holding the molecules together. *See* Science, Week 14, number 1.	Have your child look in a dictionary or appropriate resource to define the following terms related to WWI: *ace, allies, bayonet, booby trap, cavalry, central powers, dogfight, doughboy, line (military), nationalism, neutral, no man's land, parapet, propaganda, reparation, international waters, U-boat, trench, Western Front, trench foot.*
Model a puzzle that uses order of operations and familiar numbers to solve equations. *See* Math, Week 14, number 2 for sample problems. Have your child create his/her own order of operations games and puzzles.	Have your child read about the chemical compound sugar in reference books and in other materials. Have your child make a bar graph showing per capita sugar consumption each year in several countries. Data are provided in Science, Week 14, number 2.	Help your child select a project (or two) related to WWI. Your child may wish to choose a person or a battle to research and report on. See Social Studies, Week 14, numbers 1–7 for other project ideas. Give your child a copy of **Chronology of Events** (p. 157) as an overview and time line of events of the war.
Have your child complete **Games** (p. 156).	Have your child read about some of the following chemical compounds in reference materials: aspirin, salt, starch, alcohol, ammonia, baking soda, methane, gasoline, dry ice, carbon monoxide, wax, ether, propane, lye, formaldehyde, hydrochloric acid, formic acid, lime and chalk.	Allow time for your child to continue working on his/her WWI project.
Have your child write situational problems that use mixed operations and order of operations.	Have your child create "Twenty Questions" riddles about common chemical compounds. *See* Science, Week 14, number 3.	Arrange for your child to perform a community service. Have your child write in his/her Social Studies Journal.

LANGUAGE SKILLS (Writing Letters)

▶ 1. A friendly letter includes five basic parts: *heading, greeting, body, closing* and *signature*. In the standard format, the heading, closing and signature start at the center of the page. The greeting and body are left aligned. Paragraphs are usually indented. The heading includes the address of the person sending the letter and the date. See Letter A below.

▶ 2. A business letter includes six basic parts: *heading, inside address, greeting, body, closing* and *signature*. In the full-block style, all six parts are left-aligned on the page. Paragraphs are not indented. The heading includes the address of the person sending the letter and the date. The inside address includes the title and address of the person to whom the letter is being sent. Note that the greeting is followed by a colon rather than a comma. Also note that the signature is printed and typed. See Letter B below.

Letter A

123 First Street
Anytown, MA 12345
March 15, 2003

Dear Sam,

    The body of your letter is single-spaced and contains a personal message.
    Each paragraph is indented and there is no extra return (space) between paragraphs.

Sincerely,

Brian

Letter B

123 First Street
Anytown, MA 12345
March 15, 2003

Director of Tourists
9876 Oceanside Lane
Surf City, CA 91008

Dear Director:

The body of your letter is single-spaced and contains a polite, formal message.

The paragraphs are not indented. There is an extra return between paragraphs.

Sincerely,

Brian Johnson

Brian Johnson

MATH (Mixed Operations)

▶ 1. Have your child memorize the following rules regarding the order of operations to solve problems that mix the four operations.

    a. Perform all work in parentheses first.

    b. Perform all multiplication and division from left to right.

    c. Then, perform all addition and subtraction from left to right.

Example:

$$80 - 4 + 3 \times 6 - 2 \times (2 + 3) =$$
$$80 - 4 + 3 \times 6 - 2 \times (5) =$$ *First complete work in parentheses.*
$$80 - 4 + (18) - 2 \times 5 =$$ *Multiply and divide.*
$$80 - 4 + 18 - (10) =$$
$$(76) + 18 - (10) =$$ *Add and subtract.*
$$94 - 10 = 84$$

▶ 2. Have your child replace each variable with the number established in the clue, then follow the order of operations to solve the problem.

Problem: $(a + b) \times c =$
Clues:
a = the number of stripes on the U.S. flag
b = the number of wheels on a tricycle
c = the number of people in a set of twins
The answer is $(13 + 3) \times 2 = 32$.

Problem: $(d - e) \times f =$
Clues:
d = the age you must be to vote in the U.S.
e = the number in a baker's dozen
f = the number of days in a week
The answer is $(18 - 13) \times 7 = 35$.

     Learn at Home, Grade 6

SCIENCE (Chemical Compounds)

▶ 1. Have your child use the following color code for the elements:

oxygen (O): red   bromine (Br): orange   sulfur (S): yellow   carbon (C): black
nitrogen (N): blue   iodine (I): purple   chlorine (Cl): green   hydrogen (H): white

Have your child build the following molecules:

water (H_2O)   hydrogen peroxide (H_2O_2)
carbon dioxide (CO_2)   sulfur dioxide (SO_2)
carbon monoxide (CO)   ammonia (NH_4)
hydrogen iodide (HI)   bromobenzene (C_6H_5Br)
hydrogen chloride (HCl)   methane (CH_4)
hydrogen sulfide (H_2S)   carbon tetrachloride (CCl_4)

▶ 2. The following is a list of sugar consumption in *kg per person*.

Australia (53.12)	Iceland (43.13)	Netherlands (45.85)	Switzerland (40.86)
Canada (40.86)	Ireland (45.40)	New Zealand (56.30)	United States (44.95)
Denmark (49.03)	Israel (56.30)	Sweden (43.58)	United Kingdom (47.22)

▶ 3. Have your child compose a riddle about a common chemical compound. Use the following as an example.

What Compound Am I?

(1) I am used to preserve meats.
(2) I was once used for bartering.
(3) The word *salary* comes from my name.
(4) I am found in underground mines.
(5) I am found in the oceans.
(6) I have cubic crystals.
(7) I am white in color.
(8) I am used in many foods.
(9) I am made of two elements.
(10) One element has the atomic number 11.
(11) One element has the atomic number 17.
(12) I am spread on icy roads and sidewalks to melt the ice.
(13) I absorb moisture quickly.
(14) My atoms are held together by ionic bonding.
(15) I produce a bright yellow flame when burned.
(16) I conduct electricity when dissolved in water.
(17) I will corrode many metals.
(18) I am used in blocks for animals to lick.
(19) I form a mineral called halite.
(20) I am found in large amounts in a lake in Utah.

Answer: sodium chloride, or salt

SOCIAL STUDIES (World War I)

▶ 1. Have your child read *War Game* by Michael Foreman and write a book report.

▶ 2. Have your child make a poster enticing people to enlist or encouraging people to buy U.S. war bonds.

▶ 3. Have your child write several imaginary diary entries as if he/she were an 18-year-old soldier going off to war. Have him/her continue the journal as he/she imagines the soldier in the trenches hearing the sound of shell fire and seeing the wounded being brought back on stretchers.

▶ 4. Have your child write about the treaties that made up the Peace of Paris: Treaty of Versailles, Treaty of Saint Germain, Treaty of Trianon, Treaty of Sevres and Treaty of Neuilly.

▶ 5. Have your child write a newspaper article about the flu pandemic of 1918. Who was affected? What were the symptoms? Where did it originate? When did it begin and end? How did people try to prevent the spread of the flu?

▶ 6. Write about what life was like back home during the war. Have him/her search and report on the work of women, victory gardens, war bonds and the temperance movement.

▶ 7. Have your child draw examples of the new technology first used in WWI.

153

diabetes
diabolic
diacritical
diadem
diagnosis
diagonal
diagram
dialect
dialogue
dialysis
diameter
diamond
diaper
diaphragm
diaries
diathermy
diatomic
diatribe

Fill in the blanks with the correct missing letters to complete the spelling words.

dia __ __ __ __   dia __ __ __ __

dia __ __ __ __ __ __ __ __

dia __ __ __   dia __ __ __ __ __ __

dia __ __ __ __   dia __ __ __ __ __

dia __ __ __ __   dia __ __ __ __ __ __

dia __ __ __ __ __   dia __ __ __ __ __

dia __ __ __ __   dia __ __ __

dia __ __ __ __ __ __

dia __ __ __ __ __

dia __ __ __ __ __ __

dia __ __ __ __ __

dia __ __ __ __ __

Choose one of the spelling words. Do some research on it. Then, **write** a paragraph (5 or 6 sentences) telling what you learned about the word.

_____

_____

_____

_____

_____

_____

Learn at Home, Grade 6

Equations

Solve the equations on another sheet of paper. **Write** your answers here.

1. $5 + 6 - 4 =$

2. $(3 \times 4) \div 3 =$

3. $(32 \div 8) + 3 =$

4. $(40 \div 8) - 2 =$

5. $6 + (8 \times 3) =$

6. $14 + 12 - 6 =$

7. $(2 \times 9) + 4 =$

8. $(8 \times 8) + 6 =$

9. $6 + (6 \div 6) =$

10. $45 \div (5 \times 3) =$

11. $9 + 7 - 10 =$

12. $(15 \times 2) \div 3 =$

13. $(3 \times 7) - 1 =$

14. $(18 \div 9) \times 8 =$

15. $(36 \div 9) + 8 =$

16. $(21 \div 7) + 6 =$

17. $7 + 8 - 8 =$

18. $9 + 6 - 12 =$

19. $12 + 7 - 8 =$

20. $(56 \div 8) + 4 =$

21. $(64 \div 8) + 5 =$

22. $14 + (2 \times 8) =$

23. $(7 + 9) \div 2 =$

24. $(15 \div 3) \times 2 =$

25. $(5 + 3) \times 3 =$

26. $15 - 7 + 3 =$

27. $(3 + 7) \times (10 \div 2) =$

28. $6 + (8 \div 2) =$

29. $3 \times (5 + 6) =$

30. $15 + (3 \times 2) =$

31. $14 - (8 - 2) - 1 =$

32. $16 - (10 - 4) =$

33. $(14 + 6) \div 5 =$

34. $(3 + 2) \times (4 + 6) =$

35. $12 \times (3 + 2) =$

36. $6 \times (4 + 5) =$

37. $3 + 6 \times 2 + 5 =$

38. $8 + (4 \times 5) =$

39. $(6 \times 8) + 2 =$

40. $30 + (16 \times 2) =$

41. $3 \times (9 + 2) =$

42. $52 - (5 + 3) =$

43. $(64 \div 8) \times 3 =$

44. $25 - (3 + 8) =$

45. $21 \div (3 + 4) =$

Games

1. Choose any 2-digit number. Multiply the tens digit by 5. Add 7. Now, double this number. Add the ones digit of the original number. Now subtract 14. The answer is the original number.

2. Choose any 3-digit number. Multiply the hundreds digit by 2. Add 3. Now, multiply by 5. Add 7. Add the tens digit. Multiply by 2. Add 3. Multiply by 5. Add the ones digit. Now, subtract 235. The answer is the original number.

3. Fold a sheet of paper so that there are 16 squares and each crease can fold either way. Number the squares from 1 to 16 as shown in the diagram below. Now, fold the paper into a one-by-one square any way you like. Using scissors, trim the four edges so that there are sixteen separate squares. Without flipping any of the squares, lay them out on a desk or table. Add the numbers facing upward. Their total is 68.

1	2	3	4
5	6	7	8
9	10	11	12
13	14	15	16

4. One week (Sunday through Saturday) there is a birthday party every day. No two children are invited to the same party. Find out the day that each child attends a party.

   Hint: Use a chart with days of the week across and children's names down the side.

   a. Lisa and Pat don't go to a party on a Friday or a Saturday.
   b. Pat and Alice don't go on a Tuesday, but Sandy does.
   c. Jennifer goes to a party on Wednesday.
   d. Jim goes to a party the day after Jennifer.
   e. Lisa goes to a party the day before Pat.
   f. Paul goes to a party on a Saturday.

Learn at Home, Grade 6

Chronology of Events

1914

June 28 — Archduke Francis Ferdinand is assassinated in Sarajevo, Bosnia

July 28 — Austria-Hungary declares war on Serbia

August 3 — Germany invades Belgium

August 10 — Fighting begins on the Eastern Front with the invasion of Russia by Austria-Hungary

September 9 — Germans retreat north to Soissons as the Battle of the Marne ends

December 25 — First Zeppelin bombs England

1915

February 18 — German naval blockade of England begins

April 22 — Second Battle of Ypres begins with the first major gas attack by the Germans

April 25 — Allied troops land on the Gallipoli Peninsula

May 7 — German submarine sinks the *Lusitania* passenger ship

May 23 — Italian Front develops with Italy's declaration of war on Austria-Hungary

August 5 — Germans take Warsaw

December 8 — British defeated by the Turks; they evacuate the Gallipoli Peninsula

1916

February 21 — Germans begin the Battle of Verdun

April 21 — German cruiser and submarine attempt to land arms in Ireland

May 31 — British and German fleets fight in the Battle of Jutland

July 1 — Allies begin the Battle of the Somme

December 15 — French victory at Verdun

1917

February 1 — Germans resume unrestricted submarine warfare

March 3 — Germans secretly transport Lenin (pre-revolution) from Switzerland to Russia

March 8 — Russian Revolution begins with workers' strikes

March 15 — Russian government overthrown and Czar Nicholas II resigns

April 6 — United States declares war on Germany

June 24 — American troops start landing in France

December 15 — Russia signs an armistice with Germany; fighting ends on the Eastern Front

1918

January 8 — President Wilson presents his Fourteen Points for a comprehensive peace

February 10 — Russia announces its withdrawal from the war

March 21 — Germany launches the first of its final three offensives on the Western Front

August 6 — End of Second Battle of the Marne

August 7 — German sailors mutiny at Wilhelmshaven

August 30 — Germans retreat in Flanders

September 26 — Allies initiate their last offensive on the Western Front

October 5 — First peace note sent by Germans to President Wilson

November 11 — Germany signs armistice; World War I ends

	Language Skills	**Spelling**	**Reading**
Monday	**Creative Writing** "Elephants never forget" is an old saying. What is one thing that your child will never forget? Could it be a vacation or a birthday party? Maybe it was a special gift he/she received or the time he/she broke an arm. Have your child choose a topic, then write about it.	Pretest your child on these spelling words: example extend extinguish exchange extent extol exercise exterior extract expense exterminate extraordinary expert external extravagant explore extinct extreme Correct the pretest, add personalized words and make two copies of this week's study list.	**Comprehension** Introduce this week's reading selection. Suggestion: *Island of the Blue Dolphins* by Scott O'Dell. *See* Reading, Week 15 for a list of discussion topics related to the book.
Tuesday	"Give me a hand" is a request for assistance. It is an American expression that dates back to colonial days when neighbors helped neighbors with barn raisings and other difficult tasks. Have your child describe a time when someone gave him/her a helping hand or when your child helped out someone else. How did it make your child feel?	Study this week's spelling words. Have your child complete **Extra Extraordinary** (p. 162).	Discuss the current reading book in a conference. Focus on setting and characterization.
Wednesday	Everyone likes to "pig out" occasionally on junk food. Have your child describe his/her favorite "pig out" foods and where and when he/she indulges in them.	Have your child use each of this week's spelling words correctly in a sentence.	Have your child choose one scene from the story to rewrite from the perspective of the main character. Ask your child to consider what he/she would have done in the main character's situation.
Thursday	Everyone, both young and old, likes to laugh. Cartoons, comic strips, jokes, amusing stories, sitcoms and funny incidents are just some of the things that can prompt laughter. Have your child describe in writing something that makes him/her laugh.	Have your child study this week's spelling words.	Have your child write descriptive paragraphs about spring and winter on the island.
Friday	Ask your child to imagine he/she has been chosen by NASA to journey to Earth's twin planet. The twin planet is just like Earth—it has the same landforms, vegetation and animals—but it is uninhabited by humans. Your child will live there alone for 1 year. Food, shelter and clothing will be provided, and your child will be allowed to bring only five things. What would your child bring and why?	Give your child the final spelling test. Have your child record pretest and final test words in his/her word bank.	Hold a reading conference. Discuss the actual events on which this week's story is based. See the author's note in the book. Have your child complete a book project.

158

Learn at Home, Grade 6

Math	**Science**	**Social Studies**
Decimal Fractions Review how to estimate addition problems by rounding decimal fractions to the nearest whole number. When rounding to a whole number, look at the number directly to the right of the decimal point. If that number is 5 or greater, round up; if that number is less than 5, round down. Give your child ten addition problems with decimals to estimate by rounding.	**Salt** Help your child make homemade ice cream. *See* Science, Week 15, number 1. Put the ingredients in a small, resealable plastic bag. Place the bag inside a larger resealable bag. Add crushed ice and $1/4$ cup of salt to the large bag. Seal the large bag. Have your child put on mittens and shake and roll the bags until the ice-cream ingredients freeze (about 20 minutes).	**World War I** Allow time for your child to continue working on his/her WWI project from last week.
Review how to add decimal fractions. 1. Line up the decimal points. 2. Add zeros to keep position, if necessary. 3. Bring the decimal point down to the solution. 4. Add, carrying when needed. Have your child complete **Swiss Sentences** (p. 163).	Discuss why you added salt to the ice in the outer bag when you made ice cream yesterday. Salt lowers the freezing point of water, causing ice to melt. In the process of melting, ice pulls heat from its surroundings. So, as the salt melted the ice in the bag, heat was absorbed from the ice-cream ingredients, causing them to freeze.	Allow time for your child to continue working on his/her WWI project. Have your child write a bibliography of the resources used in the project.
The metric system of measurement is easy to learn because it is in base ten. The units are converted by moving decimal points. Discuss the names of metric units and their relationships to each other. *See* Math, Week 15, numbers 1 and 2. Have your child complete several metric conversions. Use the given problems or write your own. *See* Math, Week 15, number 3.	Discuss the use of salt on icy roads. *See* Science, Week 15, number 2. Have your child read the information and complete the experiments on **Salt and Ice** (p. 165).	Allow time for your child to continue working on his/her WWI project. Have your child make a final copy of the project to present.
Review how to estimate subtraction problems by rounding decimal fractions to the nearest whole number. Have your child estimate the subtraction problems provided in Math, Week 15, number 4.	Discuss the results of yesterday's experiments. *See* Science, Week 15, number 3.	Have your child read the Fourteen Points proposed by President Wilson. Discuss how these points influenced the peace treaties. *See* Social Studies, Week 15, numbers 1 and 2.
Review how to subtract decimal fractions. 1. Line up the decimal points. 2. Add zeros to keep position, if necessary. 3. Bring the decimal point down to the solution. 4. Subtract, borrowing when needed. Have your child complete **Robin Hood's Loot** (p. 164).	Discuss the sodium content of different foods. Have your child do research to find out how much salt is acceptable in a person's daily diet. Have your child calculate how much salt he/she ingests in a day. How does this compare to the recommended intake? If necessary, have your child write a proposal for how he/she can reduce his/her own salt intake.	Arrange for your child to perform a community service. Have your child write in his/her Social Studies Journal.

TEACHING SUGGESTIONS AND ACTIVITIES

READING (Comprehension)

Chapter 1: Why did the Indians have two names?

Chapter 2: Do you believe that Chowig should have shared the white bass with the Aleuts? Explain.

Chapter 4: How did the Indians know the Aleuts were about to leave?

Chapter 5: What did Kimke plan to do to preserve the tribe? Was it a good idea?

Chapter 7: Did Karana make a wise decision by returning to the island with her brother?

Chapter 8: How did Ramo die?

Chapter 9: What skills were important for survival on the island?

Chapter 11: How did Karana feel when she returned to the island?

Chapter 12: To what was Karana referring when she said, "Everything I wanted was there at hand"?

Chapter 14: How was Karana's daily life affected by her injured leg?

Chapter 15: Why did Karana decide to save the dog?

Chapter 16: Why did Karana decide she needed the canoe?

Chapter 17: Why did Rontu return to Karana after a brief time back in the wild?

Chapter 19: Do you think Karana should have captured the young birds?

Chapter 20: How did Karana protect her food supply?

Chapter 21: How did Karana feel before and after meeting Tutok?

Chapter 23: How did the wounded otter respond to Karana's help?

Chapter 24: Why did Karana decide she would kill no more animals?

Chapter 25: How was Karana affected by Rontu's death?

Chapter 27: What effects did the tidal wave and earthquake have on Karana and the animals?

Chapter 28: How did Karana feel as the ship sailed away?

Chapter 29: How did the men prepare Karana for leaving the island? Do you think she enjoyed her life on the mainland? Explain.

MATH (Decimal Fractions)

▶ 1. The gram (weight or mass), liter (liquid) and meter (length) constitute the basic units of measurement in the metric system. Smaller units are identified by the prefixes *deci, centi* and *milli*. Larger units are identified by the prefixes *deca, hecto* and *kilo*. Have your child observe a meterstick carefully to analyze the system. One meter is divided into 10 decimeters (also known as 0.1 of a meter). The meter is further divided into 100 centimeters and 1,000 millimeters.

▶ 2. To change to a smaller unit in the metric system, multiply by 10 for each box you move to the right. Move the decimal point one place to the right for each box.

Example: Decimeters to millimeters is two boxes to the right. Multiply by 100.
$$2.3 \times 100 = 230 \qquad 2.3 \text{ dm} = 230 \text{ mm}$$

To change to a larger unit in the metric system, divide by 10 for each box you move to the left. Move the decimal point one place to the left for each box.

Example: Decimeters to hectometers is three boxes to the left. Divide by 1,000.
$$5 \div 1,000 = 0.005 \qquad 5 \text{ dm} = 0.005 \text{ hm}$$

km	hm	da	mm	dm	cm	mm
1,000 m	100 m	10 m	1 m	0.1 m	0.01m	0.001m
thousands	hundreds	tens	ones	tenths	hundredths	thousandths

kilometer (km)
hectometer (hm)
dekameter (dam)
meter (m)
decimeter (dm)
centimeter (cm)
millimeter (mm)

Learn at Home, Grade 6

3. Give your child the following problems (and/or others) to solve. Have him/her use the chart in #2 to make the conversions.

80 km = ____ dm	16 mm = ____ dm	12.1 m = ____ mm	253 mm = ____ cm
7.1 hm = ____ cm	4.6 dam = ____ dm	0.01 hm = ____ mm	623 cm = ____ m
5.32 hm = ____ m	0.01 dm = ____ km	9 cm = ____ dam	2,340,000 mm = ____ km

4. Write the following problems on the chalkboard. Have your child estimate the difference in each problem. Have him/her round to the nearest whole number, tenth or hundredth, then subtract.

84.9 − 21.736	9.365 − 2.844	811.56 − 378.53	53.499 − 2.356
9.157 − 4.51	762.1 − 445.9	79.12 − 33.6	314.23 − 278.5

SCIENCE (Salt)

1. Your child may choose to make chocolate ice cream, fruit-flavored ice cream, frozen yogurt or sorbet. Have your child gather the appropriate ingredients from the choices below.

   a. Mix a half cup of milk with a tablespoon of sugar and your favorite fruit.

   b. Mix a half cup of milk with chocolate syrup to taste.

   c. Mix a half cup of yogurt with a tablespoon of sugar and your favorite fruit.

   d. Use a half cup of juice to make a sorbet.

2. Ask your child why salt is sprinkled on streets and sidewalks when they are icy. Explain that the freezing point of water is lowered by adding salt. Antifreeze works the same way: antifreeze is added to the water in a car radiator to lower its freezing point during extremely cold weather. When salt is sprinkled on an icy sidewalk or street, it lowers the freezing point of the water, so the ice melts.

3. The results of Part 2 of yesterday's (**Salt and Ice** pg. 165) experiment with salt and ice may seem to contradict Part 1. Your child should have observed that the ice cube in the plain water melted most quickly, while the ice cube in the saltiest water melted more slowly. This was due to the fact that the addition of salt to the water increased its density, which, in turn, made the molecules in the water slow down. Traveling more slowly, the molecules in the salty water didn't collide as often or as energetically as the molecules in the plain water. Being struck less energetically, the bonds of the ice crystals held together longest in the saltiest water.

SOCIAL STUDIES (World War I)

1. World War I ended when Germany agreed to an armistice on November 11, 1918. Then, the process of writing a lasting peace treaty began. The basis for the treaty negotiations was President Wilson's Fourteen Points. Wilson's Fourteen Points outlined his vision of a lasting international peace. They were designed to bolster the Allies' morale as well as assure the Central Powers of fair treatment after the war was over. Have your child find a copy or summary of Wilson's Fourteen Points in an encyclopedia or other resource. Discuss the significance of each of the points. Which points relate directly to the causes of the war? Ask your child to explain why the U.S. was the only nation at the peace table wanting nothing for itself.

2. Have your child choose one of Wilson's Fourteen Points to consider more carefully. Have your child explain in writing why that particular point was important in establishing lasting world peace.

Extra Extraordinary

example
exchange
exercise
expense
expert
explore
extend
extent
exterior
exterminate
external
extinct
extinguish
extol
extract
extraordinary
extravagant
extreme

Complete the puzzle using the spelling words. Use each word once. One word has been filled in for you.

E＿ ＿ ＿ ＿ ＿ ＿

＿ X＿ ＿ ＿ ＿ ＿

＿ ＿ T＿ ＿ ＿ ＿ ＿

＿ ＿ ＿ ＿ R＿ ＿ ＿

＿ ＿ ＿ ＿ ＿ ＿ ＿ ＿ A＿ ＿

E＿ ＿ ＿ ＿ ＿ ＿

＿ X ＿ ＿ ＿ ＿

＿ ＿ T＿ ＿ ＿ ＿

＿ ＿ ＿ R＿ ＿ ＿

＿ ＿ A＿ ＿ ＿ ＿

＿ ＿ ＿ O＿

＿ ＿ ＿ ＿ ＿ R＿

＿ ＿ ＿ ＿ ＿ D

＿ ＿ ＿ I ＿ ＿ ＿ ＿ ＿

＿ ＿ ＿ ＿ N＿ ＿

＿ ＿ ＿ ＿ ＿ A＿ ＿

＿ ＿ ＿ ＿ R＿

E X T R A O R D I N A R Y

Use your own words to create a puzzle. Each word should link with another.

Example:

```
              H
              A
    S H E E P  P
    U         P
    G         Y
    A
    R
```

Learn at Home, Grade 6

Swiss Sentences

Complete these cheesy number sentences.

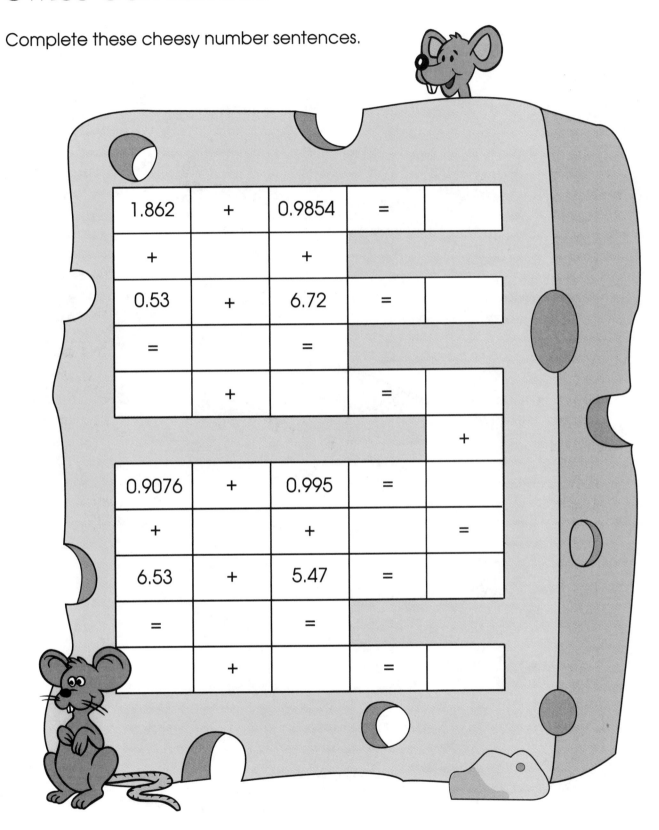

1.862	+	0.9854	=	
+		+		
0.53	+	6.72	=	
=		=		
	+		=	

				+
0.9076	+	0.995	=	
+		+		=
6.53	+	5.47	=	
=		=		
	+		=	

Robin Hood's Loot

As you know, Robin Hood stole from the rich and gave to the poor. Follow his stealing and giving path to figure out how much he has left for himself at the end.

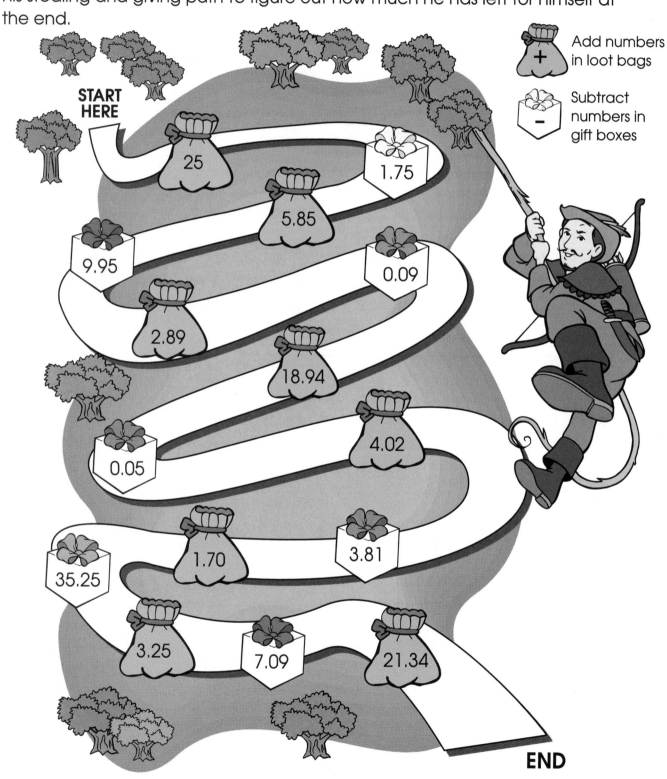

Add numbers in loot bags

Subtract numbers in gift boxes

START HERE

25

1.75

5.85

9.95

0.09

2.89

18.94

0.05

4.02

35.25

1.70

3.81

3.25

7.09

21.34

END

Learn at Home, Grade 6

Salt and Ice

Adding solute to a liquid creates a solution. This solution will be denser than the liquid water by itself. The denser a solution is, the more slowly molecules in it will move. Imagine trying to swim in a swimming pool full of pudding, which is much denser than water. It would be harder for you to move quickly in the denser medium, just as it is more difficult for molecules. The denser a solution is, the colder it has to be before the solution will freeze.

Part 1

Fill a bowl or a glass with water almost to the top, and float an ice cube in it. Set an unlighted wooden match across the top of the ice cube. Make sure that some of the match hangs off the edge of the ice cube. Sprinkle salt lightly over it. Wait approximately 2 minutes. Then, try to lift the match upward.

What happened? _____

_____

Why do you think this happened? _____

_____

Part 2

Fill three glasses half-full with water, each having the same temperature. Put a little piece of masking tape on each one and label them #1, #2 and #3. Leave #1 as plain tap water. Add 1 teaspoon of salt to #2 and stir. Add 1 tablespoon of salt to #3 and stir. Next, place an ice cube in each glass. Add the cubes to the three glasses at the exact same time, and do not stir. Time how long it takes for the ice cube in each glass to melt. Record your data on the chart below.

Sample	Time to Melt (seconds)
#1	
#2	
#3	

	Language Skills	**Spelling**	**Reading**
Monday	Have your child choose a topic, make a plan for writing, then begin work on a rough draft.	Pretest your child on these spelling words: adapt admire advance address admit advantage adequate admonish advent adhere adopt adventure adjective adorn advice adjust adult advise Correct the pretest, add personalized words and make two copies of this week's study list.	Introduce this week's reading selection or continue with the book from last week.
Tuesday	**Punctuation:** Discuss various uses of the *colon*. Refer to a writing handbook, if necessary. *See* Language Skills, Week 16, number 1. Have your child complete **Colons and Lists** (p. 170).	Study this week's spelling words. Have your child complete **Classified Ads** (p. 171).	Discuss the current reading book in a conference. Focus on vocabulary.
Wednesday	Have your child write five sentences that contain lists, using colons and other punctuation correctly. The following are some possible topics for the sentences: circus animals, clothing, entertainment, cars and apples.	Have your child use each of this week's spelling words correctly in a sentence.	**Library Resources:** Familiarize your child with other resource materials, such as almanacs and *The Guinness Book of World Records.* Generate (or have your child generate) twelve questions regarding world records. **Example:** *How tall is/was the tallest human being on record?* Then, have your child look in *The Guinness Book of World Records* to find the answers.
Thursday	Explain that colons are also used when writing play dialogue. *See* Language Skills, Week 16, number 2. Have your child write a dialogue between two people. Then, have him/her convert the dialogue into a short play or skit. Have your child write out the script, using colons after the characters' names and including any appropriate stage directions. Act out the completed scene with your child.	Have your child study this week's spelling words.	Discuss the concept of a biographical dictionary. Have your child read one at the library or check one out and read it at home. Ask your child to describe how the book is organized and what types of information it contains. Have your child find two people who have similar backgrounds or fields of study. Then, have your child compare and contrast the two in a paragraph.
Friday	Refer to a writing handbook and review rules for capitalization and commas. Give your child several sentences with errors in capitalization and use of commas. Have your child read each sentence carefully and mark any necessary changes. Have him/her rewrite the sentences correctly.	Give your child the final spelling test. Have your child record pretest and final test words in his/her word bank.	Hold a reading conference in which you discuss the sequence of events in this week's story.

Learn at Home, Grade 6

Math	**Science**	**Social Studies**
Decimal Fractions Help your child explore a practical application of adding and subtracting decimal fractions: balancing a checkbook. Create a realistic scenario (owning a business) in which your child must keep track of deposits and withdrawals. Have your child design checks for his/her business, then keep track of at least fifteen transactions related to the account.	**Acids and Bases** *Acids* and *bases* are two categories of chemical compounds. Discuss acids with your child today. Have your child read about some common acids and their uses. *See* Science, Week 16, number 1.	**Roaring Twenties** The United States experienced a period of growth and prosperity following World War I. Have your child read about some of the fads and fascinations of the 1920s. *See* Social Studies, Week 16, numbers 1 and 2. Have your child list some of the changes in the country that made the 1920s "roaring."
Give your child additional practice subtracting decimal fractions. Have your child complete **Charting the Weather** (p. 172).	Discuss bases with your child today. Explain the relationship between bases and acids. Have your child read about some common bases and their uses. *See* Science, Week 16, number 2. Have your child read about how pioneer families made soap from animal fats and potash.	Some of the biggest changes in the country after the war were related to women. Have your child read about the changing roles of women in the 1920s. *See* Social Studies, Week 16, number 3. Have your child describe ways in which women had become more independent in the years during and following the war.
Review metric conversions. Focus on centimeters, meters and millimeters. Gather 10 or 12 facts about the sizes of different lizards. **Examples:** A common iguana is 200 cm long. Use these facts to generate fifteen situational problems. **Example:** *How many meters long is a common iguana?* The problems should require your child to make metric conversions and to add and subtract decimals.	Introduce the use of chemical indicators for identifying acids and bases. *See* Science, Week 16, number 3. Have your child complete **Acids and Bases** (p. 173). He/she will need red and blue litmus paper to perform the experiment.	Read about the music popular in the 1920s. Have your child research and write about a famous jazz musician from that period.
Teach your child to estimate before multiplying decimals. Estimating first will help your child decide if he/she has solved the problem correctly. *See* Math, Week 16, number 1. Have your child estimate these costs: 5 basketballs at $48.98 each 15 books at $6.89 each 8 pencils at $0.39 each 7 sheets of stickers at $1.23 each	Vinegar and other acids react with baking soda. Help your child conduct an experiment in which he/she dilutes vinegar and observes its reaction with baking soda. *See* Science, Week 16, number 4.	During the 1920s, people had more leisure time to enjoy organized sports and more people participated in sports. Sports heroes from the 1920s include Babe Ruth and Lou Gehrig. Have your child choose a sport. Have your child write about it as though he/she were reporting on a specific game for a radio broadcast.
Review how to multiply decimal fractions. *See* Math, Week 16, number 2. Give your child ten problems that involve multiplying decimal fractions. *See* Math, Week 16, number 3. Have your child estimate each product before multiplying, then compare the estimates with the actual products.	Have your child read about glue in several reference materials. Teach him/her how to make a simple glue from skim milk, vinegar and baking soda. *See* Science, Week 16, number 5.	Arrange for your child to perform a community service. Have your child write in his/her Social Studies Journal.

Learn at Home, Grade 6

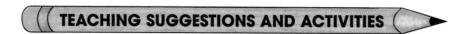

TEACHING SUGGESTIONS AND ACTIVITIES

LANGUAGE SKILLS (Punctuation)

▶ 1. Review the most common uses of the colon.

A colon is used between the hour and minutes when time is displayed in digital format.

A colon is used after the salutation in a business letter.

A colon is used to introduce a list or series of things, especially after the words "as follows" or "the following."

Example: I will need the following ingredients for the pie: flour, butter, eggs and apples.

A colon is not used if the series is preceded by an expression such as "for example," "namely," "for instance" or "that is." Such expressions are set off with commas.

Example: I will need several things for the pie, namely, flour, butter, eggs and apples.

▶ 2. A colon is used after the speaker's name in play directions. Quotation marks are not used. Stage directions are inserted between the speaker's name and the colon and are put in parentheses and italics.

MATH (Decimal Fractions)

▶ 1. When estimating decimal products, round to a whole number to make the multiplication easy.

Example: Your neighbor asked you to baby-sit for 4.75 hours at a rate of $3.25 per hour. How much will you earn? Estimate the answer first. Do the multiplication mentally by rounding to the nearest whole numbers. Think of 4.75 as 5; think of $3.25 as 3. You would make approximately $15 baby-sitting. (actual answer = $15.44)

▶ 2. When multiplying decimal fractions, you do not need to line up the decimal points as with addition and subtraction. After multiplying, count the total number of places after the decimals in the factors. There should be the same number of places following the decimal point in the product.

▶ 3. Have your child copy the following ten problems onto lined paper. Have him/her estimate, then solve, each problem. Your child may check his/her answers using a calculator.

36.5 x 8.4	516.24 x 0.3	3.614 x 0.57	516.4 x 0.04	462.3 x 7.1
742.01 x 3.4	0.316 x 1.7	486.1 x 5.6	56.01 x 0.8	20.147 x 3.8

SCIENCE (Acids and Bases)

▶ 1. *Acids* have special properties: They taste sour; they conduct electricity; they can be corrosive; and they react with bases to form salts. Explain that some acids are weak (vinegar) and some are strong (sulfuric). Some common acids are found in citrus fruits, aspirin, eyewashes, detergents and insects. Acids are used to etch glass and metals, to clean cement and bricks, in cooking and in swimming pools. Have your child read about acids, including their origins and their uses.

Review some common acids and where they are found:

acetic acid (vinegar)

carbonic acid (carbonated beverages)

hydrochloric acid (gastric juices in stomach)

nitric acid (fertilizers and explosives)

sulfuric acid (car batteries)

▶ 2. *Bases* also have special properties: They have a bitter taste; they are slippery; they can be corrosive; they conduct electricity; and they react with acids to form salts. Explain that some bases are weak (aluminum hydroxide) and some are strong (sodium hydroxide). Just like strong acids, strong bases will burn the skin. Have your child read about bases, including their origins and their uses.

Learn at Home, Grade 6

Review some of the common bases and where they are found:

ammonium hydroxide (household ammonia)

aluminum hydroxide (deodorants)

calcium hydroxide (mortar and plaster)

magnesium hydroxide (antacid)

sodium hydroxide (drain cleaner, production of soap)

3. Ask whether your child has ever tested or observed someone testing the water in a swimming pool before adding chemicals. That ph test is an indicator for acids and bases. The indicator changes colors in the presence of an acid or base. The strength of an acid or base can be determined by the color of the test results.

4. *You will need:* 5 clear plastic cups, water, vinegar, baking soda, paper towels and a measuring teaspoon

   Directions:

   a. Label the five cups A, B, C, D and E.

   b. Add 1 tsp. of water and 1 tsp. of vinegar to cup A.

   c. Add 1 tsp. of water and 5 tsp. of vinegar to cup B.

   d. Add 1 tsp. of water and 10 tsp. of vinegar to cup C.

   e. Add 1 tsp. of water and 15 tsp. of vinegar to cup D.

   f. Add 1 tsp. of water and 20 tsp. of vinegar to cup E.

   g. Place cups A, B, C, D and E on paper towels.

   h. Dump one teaspoon of baking soda into each cup.

   i. Observe the reactions—speed and volume—in each cup. Record your observations on a chart.

   Discuss your child's observations. Have your child find the answers to the following questions: *What gas was produced in each reaction? Why are baking soda and sour milk used in many recipes? Why is a paste of baking soda sometimes used on insect bites?*

5. *You will need:* skim milk, vinegar, baking soda, water, a metric measuring cup, a measuring tablespoon, a small jar with a lid, a popsicle stick and cooking oil

   Directions:

   a. Heat 450 mL of skim milk and 5 Tbs. vinegar in a pan. Stir mixture while heating until curdling begins.

   b. Remove from heat and continue to stir.

   c. After cooling, pour off the liquid (whey).

   d. Place the remaining curds in a small jar. Add 60 mL water and 1 Tbs. baking soda. Stir with the popsicle stick until thoroughly mixed. Add a few drops of cooking oil and stir.

   e. Place the lid on the jar. The glue will remain moist until you need it in an activity.

SOCIAL STUDIES (Roaring Twenties)

1. Have your child write the names of Presidents Harding, Coolidge and Hoover and their years in office on index cards. Then, have your child write at least three things that happened during each man's administration and place the card on the time line.

2. The years after WWI were prosperous and happy ones. These years were called the Roaring Twenties. Have your child read about the 1920s and define the following terms: *bootlegging, Charleston, flappers, prohibition, speakeasy* and *suffrage.*

3. With the passing of the Nineteenth Amendment in 1920, women finally earned the right to vote. Many women at this time began to join the workforce and went to college as well. Electricity in homes provided women with time-saving devices, such as washing machines and vacuum cleaners. Women's dress styles changed along with forms of entertainment.

Colons and Lists

Use a **colon** when writing a list of items if "follows" or "the following" is used in the introduction and the list of items immediately follows. Commas (and sometimes semicolons) are used to separate the items in the list.

Example: The clown was wearing **the following:**
striped pants, a polka-dot shirt, floppy shoes and baggy socks.

Do not use a colon if the list of items is introduced by such words as "namely," "for instance," "for example" or "that is." Instead, set off the phrase with commas.

Example: A clown could wear, **for example**, striped pants, a polka-dot shirt, floppy shoes and baggy socks.

There are eight different outfits that could be made from the clothes listed.
Fill in the blanks and correctly punctuate the eight different lists.

Ties (striped, paisley)   Shirts (white, blue)   Pants (khaki, gray)

1. John could wear the following a striped tie white shirt and khaki pants.

2. He could also wear for instance a striped tie _____ shirt and khaki pants.

3. John could wear the outfit as follows a paisley tie white shirt and khaki pants.

4. He might try wearing for example a _____ tie blue shirt and khaki pants.

5. He could try namely a striped tie white shirt and gray pants.

6. Otherwise, he might try as follows a striped tie _____ shirt and gray pants.

7. He could outfit himself in the following a paisley tie white shirt and _____ pants.

8. John could choose a last choice as follows a paisley tie _____ shirt and gray pants.

Learn at Home, Grade 6

Classified Ads

adapt
address
adequate
adhere
adjective
adjust
admire
admit
admonish
adopt
adorn
adult
advance
advantage
advent
adventure
advice
advise

Write each spelling word under the proper category (noun, verb or adjective). Some words can act as more than one part of speech.

Noun
1. _____
2. _____
3. _____
4. _____
5. _____
6. _____
7. _____
8. _____

Verb
1. _____
2. _____
3. _____
4. _____
5. _____
6. _____
7. _____
8. _____
9. _____
10. _____
11. _____

Adjective
1. _____
2. _____

Write a brief classified ad for a newspaper using at least five spelling words.
Example: Adults wanted. Please adopt my pet mouse. Mice adapt easily to new surroundings. My mom admonished and advised me to give him up.

_____
_____
_____
_____
_____

Charting the Weather

For four months, the students in Ms. Forecaster's class charted the sunny, partly sunny and cloudy days. The following chart shows their findings to the nearest tenth.

MONTH	SUNNY	PARTLY SUNNY	CLOUDY
October	13.4	12.8	4.8
November	7	13.1	9.9
December	6.3	11	13.7
January	8.4	16.7	5.9

1. How many more sunny days did January have than December?   _____

2. In November, how many more cloudy days were there than sunny days?   _____

3. How many more partly sunny days were there than sunny days in January?   _____

4. What is the difference in days between the month with the most cloudy days and the month that had the fewest cloudy days?   _____

5. Which month had the most sunny days? How many more sunny days did it have than the month with the second most? Which month came in second?   _____

6. Which month had the most cloudy days? Which month had the fewest cloudy days? How many total cloudy days were there in these four months?   _____

Extension: Find the total number of sunny, partly sunny and cloudy days in these four months. Then, find the average number of days for each type of weather.

Learn at Home, Grade 6

Acids and Bases

Acids and bases are chemical compounds. Some of these compounds are strong and abrasive. Many are used as cleaning agents. Litmus paper is an indicator. Indicators are affected when acid or base is present in a substance. Blue litmus paper turns red when dipped in an acid. Red litmus paper turns blue when dipped in a base.

Use blue and red litmus paper to test each one of the substances on the chart. Record the results by writing the color the paper turns when dipped and whether the substance is an acid or a base. The first one is done for you.

Substance	Blue Litmus	Red Litmus	Acid, Base or Neither
lemon juice	red	red	acid
vinegar			
ammonia			
orange juice			
tea			
milk			
baking soda and water			
cleanser and water			
water			
vinegar and salt			
grapefruit juice			
antacid pills and water			
cola			

	Language Skills	**Spelling**	**Reading**
Monday	**Punctuation** A *semicolon* is used to join two independent clauses that are closely related. An independent clause is a group of words that could stand as a complete sentence by itself. **Example:** Rob bought a new bat; the old bat was in bad shape. Have your child join related sentences using a semicolon. Have your child complete **Semicolon** (p. 178).	Pretest your child on these spelling words: probe project propel produce prolong proportion profane promise propose profound promote prosper progress pronoun protein prohibit pronounce provoke Correct the pretest, add personalized words and make two copies of this week's study list.	Introduce this week's reading selection or continue with the book from last week.
Tuesday	Review other uses of the semicolon. *See* Language Skills, Week 17, numbers 1 and 2. Have your child write five original sentences using semicolons.	Study this week's spelling words. Have your child complete **You're a Pro!** (p. 179).	Discuss the current reading book in a conference. Focus on predicting outcomes.
Wednesday	*Quotation marks* set off the exact words of the speaker. The speaker's first word begins with a capital letter. *See* Language Skills, Week 17, numbers 3 and 4 for more on punctuation with quotation marks. Write several sentences containing dialogue on the chalkboard. Omit all punctuation and capitalization. Have your child add correct punctuation and capitalize letters where necessary.	Have your child use each of this week's spelling words correctly in a sentence.	**Inference:** To infer is to interpret meaning from given information. Ask your child to make inferences about characters in this week's book. Discuss the clues that led to your child's conclusions. Have your child use inference to write a profile of one character. Ask your child to describe the character, where he/she lives, his/her greatest achievement, favorite food, occupation and hobbies.
Thursday	Have your child write a short story that contains a lot of dialogue. Once your child has written a draft of the story, have him/her go back through and check his/her use of quotation marks and other punctuation.	Have your child study this week's spelling words.	Read an article to your child. When you are finished reading, ask questions that will require your child to infer information from the article. *See* Reading, Week 17.
Friday	Review the use of apostrophes in contractions and possessives. Then, explain that apostrophes can also be used to form plurals of letters and numbers (6's, W's) and to take the place of omitted letters and numbers ('99 for 1999 or misbehavin' for misbehaving). Have your child scan a book or magazine for apostrophes. Have your child describe the function of each apostrophe found.	Give your child the final spelling test. Have your child record pretest and final test words in his/her word bank.	Hold a reading conference. Discuss your child's earlier predictions and compare with the actual outcomes.

Learn at Home, Grade 6

Math	**Science**	**Social Studies**
Decimal Fractions Use situational problems to show your child the practical applications of multiplying decimals. Discuss other situations in which it may be necessary to multiply decimals. Have your child complete **Comparison** (p. 180).	**Chemical Reactions** Introduce your child to the concept of a chemical reaction. Signals that a chemical reaction has occurred include a change in color (indicators, ripening of fruits), the production of heat or light (striking a match, burning a candle) or the production of a gas (antacid in water, baking soda and vinegar) or solid (vinegar in skim milk). *See* Science, Week 17, number 1.	**Great Depression** Introduce the Great Depression and explain what it was. *See* Social Studies, Week 17. The depression was initiated by the fall of the stock market. For over 10 years, many Americans were hungry, jobless and homeless. Have your child research and write about President Hoover's actions during the depression.
Help your child discover a pattern in multiplying decimal fractions by 10. Give your child several problems to solve (e.g., 1.25 x 10). Your child will soon see that to multiply a decimal fraction by 10, he/she simply has to move the decimal point one place to the right. Extend the pattern to multiplying by other powers of ten, such as 100 and 1,000.	Rusting metal is the evidence of a chemical reaction we see every day. Tools, bridges, poles, outdoor furniture, statues and structures must be painted and/or treated to prevent rusting and corrosion. Moisture and other gases in the air react with metals and cause them to tarnish or corrode. Have your child conduct an experiment on the rusting of iron. *See* Science, Week 17, number 2.	Discuss the many causes of the Great Depression, including the stock market crash, bank failures, uneven distribution of wealth and the farm depression.
Teach your child to estimate before dividing decimals. To estimate a division problem, round the dividend and the divisor to whole numbers, then divide. Estimating first will help your child decide if he/she has divided correctly. If the whole number estimates both end in zero, cancel the zeros to make the division even easier. Give your child several division problems with decimal fractions to estimate.	With your child, review the ice and salt experiment from Week 15. Then, have your child conduct an experiment with aluminum foil. *See* Science, Week 17, number 3.	Have your child read about Roosevelt's New Deal programs that provided jobs to out-of-work Americans. Have your child add Franklin Roosevelt's terms as president to the time line. Have him/her read about Roosevelt's terms in office and write about some of his greatest accomplishments as president.
Geometry: The *circumference* of a circle is the distance around its outer edge. To find the circumference of a circle, multiply its diameter by a special number called *pi*, represented by the symbol π and equaling approximately 3.14. Introduce your child to the formula for finding the circumference of a circle: $C = \pi \times d$ (circumference equals pi times diameter). Have your child complete **Circumference of Circles** (p. 181).	Have your child conduct an experiment with household ammonia and vinegar. *See* Science, Week 17, number 4.	Help your child prepare a project related to the Great Depression. Arrange for your child to interview a person who remembers 1929 and the years of hardship that followed or have your child paint a picture of a "Hooverville." *See* Social Studies, Week 17, numbers 1–4 for more project ideas.
The *area* of a circle can be found using the formula $A = \pi \times r^2$ ($\pi \approx 3.14$, r = radius). Have your child use a ruler and a compass to draw six circles with radii of 2 in., 2.5 in., 6 cm, 6.8 cm, 3.5 cm and 5.2 cm. Have your child calculate the area of each circle. **Example:** The circle with a radius of 2 inches has an area of 12.56 in.^{2} 3.14 x (2 x 2) = 12.56	Have your child conduct a simple experiment with fresh fruit and preservatives. Have your child take a bite out of an apple and place the piece on a paper towel. Cut a second piece of the apple with a knife and place it on a paper towel. Cut a third piece with a knife, dip it in fruit freshener solution and place on a paper towel. Have your child observe the apple pieces during the day. What happens?	Arrange for your child to perform a community service. Have your child write in his/her Social Studies Journal.

TEACHING SUGGESTIONS AND ACTIVITIES

LANGUAGE SKILLS (Punctuation)

▶ 1. A *semicolon* is used instead of a comma in a compound sentence when one clause contains commas in a series.
Example: I bought ice cream, peanut butter, jelly and bread; but I forgot the eggs.

▶ 2. Semicolons are also used to separate items in a series when the items contain commas.
Example: On our trip to California, we swam, snorkeled and surfed in the ocean; hiked through redwood forests; saw the sights at Disneyland and drove past the beautiful homes in Los Angeles.

▶ 3. When the speaker is named first, the comma comes before the opening quotation mark.
Example: The man at the store said, "This is the last day of the sock sale."

When the speaker is named last, the comma comes immediately before the closing quotation mark.
Example: "Then, I had better buy all the socks you have left," the customer replied.

When the speaker is named in the middle of the quotation, commas are used to separate it.
Example: "If you prefer," said the salesman, "I can ring these up while you keep looking."

▶ 4. A *question mark* or *exclamation point* comes before the closing quotation mark when the punctuation is part of the direct quote.
Example: Look at the beautiful sunset!" called Fran.

A question mark or exclamation point comes after the closing quotation mark when the punctuation is not part of the direct quote.
Example: Did you see the sign that read "Do not feed the animals"?

READING (Inference)

Ask your child to listen carefully as you read the following article. Follow up the article with the questions below.

The whole town of Greenville is nervous. There has been so much rain lately that the people are afraid their town will be flooded. Greenville hasn't flooded since 1988 when there was so much rain that Otter River overflowed its banks. Many people's homes and businesses were destroyed by all the water. Those businesses that were spared were still shut down for several weeks. The city of Greenville was virtually shut down! Now there is a chance that the same thing might happen again.

Floods can be very damaging. The common causes of river floods are too much rain and/or the sudden melting of large amounts of snow or ice. Under these conditions, rivers may receive more than ten times as much water as their beds can hold.

It has been an unusually wet spring. The Otter River is already approaching its capacity and more rain is on the way. The weather forecast predicted 6 more inches of rain over the next two days. That is more rain than the city usually gets in three months during this time of year. Everyone is concerned. Fortunately, the city of Greenville built a levee after the flood of 1988. The people of Greenville are hoping that the levee will hold the water back.

▶ 1. If Greenville gets more rain, which of the following things could happen?

The levee could break.	The library could float away.
The students could go boating.	The city could move.
Homes could be lost.	The levee could hold the water back.
Businesses could be lost.	The river could empty.

▶ 2. In what ways could the effects of the rain be devastating?

SCIENCE (Chemical Reactions)

▶ 1. Begin your study of chemical reactions with a simple demonstration. Drop an antacid tablet into a glass of water. Have your child observe and describe the change that takes place. The evidence that this is a chemical reaction is the production of a gas (effervescence). Chemical changes take place when food is

176

Learn at Home, Grade 6

eaten, when metals are refined, when materials burn, when metals corrode and when fireworks shoot off.

▶ 2. Help your child conduct an experiment on the rusting of iron.

You will need: steel wool, water, vinegar, 4 plastic cups and cooking oil

Directions: Label the cups: A, B, C and D.
   a. Tear off a small piece of steel wool, roll into a ball and place in cup A.
   b. Tear off a second piece of steel wool, roll into a ball, dip in water and place in cup B.
   c. Tear off a third piece of steel wool, roll into a ball, dip in vinegar and place in cup C.
   d. Tear off a fourth piece of steel wool, roll into a ball, dip in cooking oil and place in cup D.
   e. Record your observations of the four cups over a period of several days.

Discuss the results. How did the steel wool react differently to each substance? In which cup(s) did you observe a chemical reaction? How could you tell?

▶ 3. Help your child conduct an experiment with aluminum foil and several salts.

You will need: aluminum foil, copper sulfate, water, table salt, a clear plastic cup, a popsicle stick and a plastic teaspoon.

Directions: Add about one-half cup water to the plastic cup. Add several teaspoons of table salt (sodium chloride) to the water and stir. Add several teaspoons of copper sulfate to the water and stir. **Safety Note: Wash hands thoroughly if they come in contact with the copper sulfate.** Tear off several small pieces of aluminum foil, roll into tiny balls and place in the cup of salt solution. Observe changes over the next 5 minutes. Set the cup aside and observe again after several hours. Discuss the changes that occur.

▶ 4. Help your child conduct an experiment in which an acid is used to neutralize a base.

You will need: clear household ammonia, vinegar, phenolphthalein indicator, water, clear plastic cups, a popsicle stick and an eyedropper.

Directions: Fill one plastic cup about half-full with water. Pour some ammonia into a second cup. Using the eyedropper, add 20 drops of the ammonia to the water. Be sure to use only clear, non-sudsing ammonia. Stir with the popsicle stick. Add 5 drops of the phenolphthalein indicator. Record the color that appears in the ammonia solution. Pour some vinegar into a third cup. Wash the eyedropper thoroughly under running water to clean out the ammonia. Add the vinegar, drop by drop, to the ammonia solution. Stir with the stick after each drop. Count the number of drops of vinegar needed to cause the pink color to disappear completely. You may repeat the experiment by adding more or less than 20 drops of ammonia to the water.

Why was the phenolphthalein added to the ammonia or the base?

At what point can you say that the vinegar had neutralized the base?

Predict what would happen if a drop of ammonia were added to the solution at that point.

Why are bases used in antacid tablets for upset stomachs?

SOCIAL STUDIES (Great Depression)

BACKGROUND
The Great Depression stands as the worst economic disaster in U.S. history. Lasting for over a decade, it affected every type of business and industry. At the height of the depression, unemployment rose to nearly 13 million, and America became a nation of bread lines and soup kitchens. Only massive federal programs initiated by President Roosevelt's New Deal prevented the depression from becoming worse. Even then, the economy did not fully recover until the start of World War II.

Have your child choose from the following project ideas.

▶ 1. Write a paragraph of what a person standing in a bread line might be thinking and/or feeling.

▶ 2. Write a front-page headline for a newspaper printed on Tuesday, October 30, 1929.

▶ 3. Discuss what jobs today are safe from layoffs. Look in the paper to see what businesses are laying off employees. What might these jobless people do to continue to support their families?

▶ 4. Many songs were written during the depression that told about the hard times. "Brother, Can You Spare a Dime?" is just one example. Help your child find the lyrics and melody of the song. Have your child read the lyrics carefully (and listen to a recording, if possible), then write an analysis of the song's meaning.

Semicolon

A **semicolon** is used to join two independent clauses that are closely related if a conjunction is not used. An **independent clause** is a group of words that could stand as a complete sentence by itself.

Examples:

The boys were in trouble; they were late for dinner.

(These sentences are closely related. The second explains the first.)

It was the third of September.
The boys were in trouble.

(These sentences aren't closely related. Write them as two separate sentences.)

Read each pair of sentences. **Rewrite** those that could be joined by a semicolon.

1. The tiny hummingbird builds a small nest. Its jelly bean-sized eggs fit nicely into it.

_____

2. Some birds build with unusual materials. You may find string or ribbon woven into a nest. _____

_____

3. A nest's location can tell you a bird's diet. Most birds live near their food supply.

_____

4. A gull's nest is on the shore. Gulls eat fish and other kinds of seafood.

_____

5. A woodpecker lives in a hole in a tree. It eats insects that live in trees.

_____

6. Some birds take over old nests. Purple martins live in birdhouses.

_____

7. A woodpecker makes a hole to live in and later moves out. An elf owl moves right into it. _____

_____

8. A swan builds a nest among the reeds. The reeds help hide the nest from the swan's enemies. _____

_____

Learn at Home, Grade 6

You're a Pro

1. probe
2. produce
3. profane
4. promise
5. profound
6. progress
7. prohibit
8. project
9. prolong
10. promote
11. pronoun
12. pronounce
13. propel
14. proportion
15. propose
16. prosper
17. protein
18. provoke

Complete the magic square. **Write** the number of each spelling word in the lettered square that corresponds to its definition. Two of the words will not be used.

A. create; vegetables
B. to stop
C. stir up; make angry
D. speak clearly; articulate
E. stick out; a plan
F. deep and intense
G. a replacement for a noun
H. suggest

I. move forward
J. an essential part of diet
K. growth; to improve
L. blaphemous
M. have good fortune
N. to raise to a higher level
O. agreement to do something
P. to lengthen

A	B	C	D
E	F	G	H
I	J	K	L
M	N	O	P

Check your work by adding each row and then each column of numbers. If all the sums are the same, you have matched correctly.

Write the two words that were not included in the square.

1. _____   2. _____

Write the six words that can be used either as nouns or as verbs.

1. _____   2. _____

3. _____   4. _____

5. _____   6. _____

Comparison

Mr. Bigfoot's class was comparing numbers by multiplying decimals. Round your answer to the nearest hundredth.

1. Andy's shoe is 10.4 inches long. Tony's is 1.2 times as long. How long is Tony's shoe?

_____

2. Alicia can jump 24.8 inches. Jill can jump 1.05 times as high. How high can Jill jump?

_____

3. The paper basket holds 288 sheets of paper. It is 0.25 full. How many sheets of paper are in it?

_____

4. Misha's dog weighs 98.5 pounds. Tom's dog weighs 1.25 times as much. How much does Tom's dog weigh?

_____

5. The area of Mr. Bigfoot's classroom is 981.75 square feet. The gym is 4.50 times as large. What is the area of the gym?

_____

6. The box holds 48 pencils. It was 0.75 full. How many more pencils would fit in the box?

_____

7. Amy is 5.250 feet tall. The ceiling is 2.075 times Amy's height. How tall is the ceiling?

_____

Extension: Place the decimal point in the underlined number.

1. 213.05 x 2.3 = 49 0 0 1 5   2. 4.87 x 0 4 6 = 2.2402   3. 6 0 1 x 0.08 = 4.808

Learn at Home, Grade 6

Circumference of Circles

Circumference is the distance around a circle.

$C = \pi \times d$
π (pi) $\approx$ 3.14 or $\frac{22}{7}$ ($\approx$ means approximately
d = diameter equals to)
Use $\pi \approx$ 3.14 and round to the nearest one.

Example 1:
$C = \pi \times d$
$C \approx 3.14 \times 8.6$
$C \approx 27.004$ km
$C \approx 27$ km

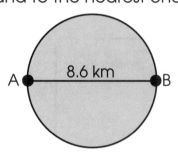

A ● —— 8.6 km —— ● B

Example 2:
The radius of the circle is 16 mm.
Diameter is twice the radius.
So, d = 16 x 2 = 32
$C \approx 3.14 \times 32$
$C \approx 100.48$ mm
$C \approx 100$ mm

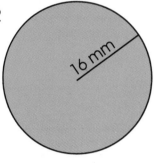

16 mm

Example 3:
Find the perimeter of the figure.
Circumference of the
circle $\approx 3.14 \times 3 \approx 9.42$ m

$9.42 + 11 + 11 = 31.42$ m

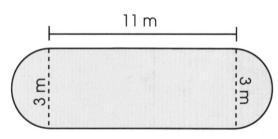

11 m

3 m   3 m

Find the circumference of each circle. Use $\pi \approx$ 3.14 and round to the nearest one.

1.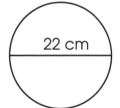
22 cm

2.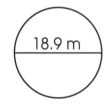
18.9 m

3. 7.6 km

4. 3.9 dam

Find the perimeter of each figure.

5.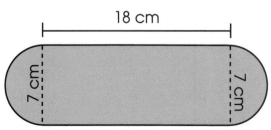
18 cm

7 cm   7 cm

6.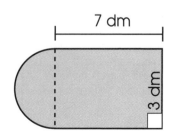
7 dm

3 dm

	Language Skills	**Spelling**	**Reading**
Monday	Have your child choose a topic, make a plan for writing, then begin work on a rough draft.	Select words from the past 8 weeks for this week's pretest. Correct the pretest, add personalized words and make two copies of this week's study list.	Introduce this week's reading selection or continue with the book from last week.
Tuesday	**Using a Dictionary:** List ten vocabulary words that are unfamiliar to your child. Have your child look up the words in a dictionary and write a paraphrased definition for each.	Have your child categorize spelling words from the past 8 weeks by vowel sound and spelling.	Discuss the current reading book in a conference. Focus on the plot and the changing excitement level.
Wednesday	Discuss the fact that a word may have more than one meaning. Also review the concept of a *synonym*. Have your child complete **This Is So Fine** (p. 186).	Have your child look up spelling words in the dictionary. Have him/her write the proper pronunciation(s) of each word on the index cards in the word bank.	**Cause and Effect:** Teach your child to find cause and effect relationships in a story. Have your child read the story, **Wherefore Art Thou?** (p. 187) and write five cause-and-effect statements.
Thursday	Play a game to familiarize your child with dictionary language. Choose a word from the dictionary that is unfamiliar to you. Make up your own definition of the word, imitating the style of a dictionary entry. Read your definition and the dictionary definition aloud. Your child earns points by guessing which is the correct definition. You earn points by fooling your child. Switch roles and repeat with other words.	Help your child make a code for the letters of the alphabet. Encode the review spelling words. Have your child decode the words. Have your child use the code to encode other spelling words from the past 8 weeks.	Have your child write five cause-and-effect statements about this week's reading book.
Friday	Review the uses of the hyphen. *Hyphens* are used in the number words twenty-one through ninety-nine. They are used in some compound words. Hyphens are also used when a word must be divided in text. Check the dictionary to determine where a hyphen may be placed in a word. Have your child write hyphenated words correctly. *See* Language Skills, Week 18, numbers 1 and 2.	Give your child the final spelling test.	Hold a reading conference in which you ask questions and challenge your child to think critically about the concepts in the book.

Learn at Home, Grade 6

Math	**Science**	**Social Studies**
Decimal Fractions Help your child discover a pattern in dividing decimal fractions by 10. Give your child several problems to solve (e.g., 12.5 ÷ 10). Your child will soon see that to divide a decimal fraction by 10, he/she simply has to move the decimal point one place to the left. Extend the pattern to dividing by other powers of 10, including 100 and 1,000.	**Mixtures and Solutions** Explain the difference between a mixture and a solution. A *mixture* consists of two or more substances that are not combined chemically. A *solution* is a mixture in which the substances cannot be separated by mechanical means. Show your child examples of each. Then, guide your child in a simple exploration of mixtures and solution. *See* Science, Week 18, numbers 1 and 2.	**Great Depression** Discuss whether or not Hoover was to blame for the depression. Discuss why people voted for Roosevelt in the 1932 election. Have your child compare Presidents Hoover and Roosevelt. How did their philosophies of government differ?
Provide practice for your child in dividing decimal fractions. Have your child estimate the quotient before dividing, then compare the estimate with the actual quotient. *See* Math, Week 18, number 1. Have your child complete ten problems dividing decimals. *See* Math, Week 18, number 2.	Explain to your child that solutions can also be solids or gases. Have your child conduct an experiment with salt, food coloring and water. *See* Science, Week 18, number 3.	Discuss what effect the depression may have had on children and young people.
Use situational problems to show your child the practical applications of dividing decimals. Discuss other situations in which it may be necessary to divide decimals. Have your child complete **Shopping for Soccer Supplies** (p. 188).	Sometimes when two or more liquids are mixed together, they separate. These liquids are *immiscible*—that is, they will not mix completely and permanently with each other. Oil and water are two such liquids. *See* Science, Week 18, number 4. Have your child complete **Oil and Water Emulsions** (p. 190).	Have your child read about how the International Apple Growers' Association provided apples to the jobless. *See* Social Studies, Week 18, number 1. Discuss why people would choose to sell apples on the street when they could get a free meal at a soup kitchen. Have your child set up a chart to record the profit or loss for a week of apple sales. *See* Social Studies, Week 18, number 2.
Explain that when a divisor has a decimal point, your child must shift the decimal to the right in both the divisor and the dividend. In effect, the child must multiply both numbers by 10, 100 or 1,000. *See* Math, Week 18, number 3. Give your child ten or twelve division problems in which the divisor is a decimal fraction. Observe your child's approach as he/she solves the problems on the chalkboard.	Have your child complete **Ocean in a Bottle Emulsions** (p. 191).	Because the depression brought people's spirits down, they sought diversions to brighten their days. Read about the most popular forms of entertainment during the depression years. *See* Social Studies, Week 18, number 3. Have your child compare entertainment of the 1930s to entertainment today.
Give your child more practice dividing with a decimal fraction in the divisor. Have your child complete **Dividing by a Decimal** (p. 189).	Review the chemistry concepts, terms and experiments from the past 8 weeks. *See* Science, Week 18, number 5. Have your child draw a picture of a chemist in his/her Science Log. Have your child write a paragraph describing what he/she thinks is the work of a chemist. Have your child compare today's picture and paragraph with those created in Week 10. What has your child learned?	Arrange for your child to perform a community service. Have your child write in his/her Social Studies Journal.

TEACHING SUGGESTIONS AND ACTIVITIES

LANGUAGE SKILLS (Using a Dictionary)

▷ 1. Write the following compound words on the chalkboard. Tell your child to look up each word in a dictionary and rewrite the word correctly.

oil well	forty seven	pent up	saber toothed
coal mine	twenty nine	old time	safe conduct
letter perfect	band wagon	dining room	out of date
seventy three	soft soap	gas station	once over
safety-pin	soft spoken	mother of pearl	box seat

▷ 2. Write the following divided words on the chalkboard. Some are divided correctly. Have your child rewrite those words that are not divided correctly.

fin-	pad-	mist-	ho-	fan-	sing-	ir-	vet-	musk-	list-
ish	ding	rust	mage	ciful	le	on	o	et	en

MATH (Decimal Fractions)

▷ 1. When dividing decimal fractions, always put the quotient's decimal point directly above the dividend's decimal point. Zeros can always be added to the end of decimal fractions without changing the value of the decimal fraction. There are no remainders in decimal division—continue to add zeros to the dividend and divide until there is no remainder.

▷ 2. Have your child copy the following ten problems on lined paper, then solve. Have him/her continue to add zeros to the dividend until there is no remainder. If the problem continues, have your child round the quotient to the nearest hundred thousandth.

36.5 ÷ 8	516.24 ÷ 5	3.614 ÷ 7	516.375 ÷ 45	462.3 ÷ 20
742.01 ÷ 34	0.3145 ÷ 17	486.1 ÷ 5	56.01 ÷ 8	20.14 ÷ 38

▷ 3. Your child must shift the decimal point in order to divide with a whole number divisor. Dividing by a decimal divisor is not allowed! Therefore, when a divisor is a decimal fraction, the decimal point must be shifted to the right until there are no more decimal places. The decimal point in the dividend must be moved the same number of places.

SCIENCE (Mixtures and Solutions)

▷ 1. Have your child examine several examples of mixtures.

    a. Sprinkle some salt and pepper together on a sheet of paper. Have your child examine this mixture with a magnifying glass in order to see the two different substances.

    b. Collect a scoop of dirt from outside, pour it on a sheet of paper and have your child examine it with a magnifying glass. Ask your child to describe the many materials found in the dirt.

    c. Make a fruit salad or green salad. Have your child identify the different fruits or vegetables in the salad.

    d. Pour out a small scoop of powdered chocolate or fruit drink mix onto a sheet of paper. Have your child examine it with a magnifying glass. Ask your child to describe the different substances in the drink mix.

▷ 2. Have your child examine several examples of solutions.

    a. Add a teaspoon of instant, sweetened tea to a glass of water and stir. Have your child describe the liquid solution after stirring. Can the individual particles of tea or sugar be seen? Tasted? Do they settle to the bottom of the glass after several minutes?

    b. Add a teaspoon of powdered fruit drink mix to a glass of water and stir. Have your child describe the liquid solution after stirring. Can the individual particles of the drink mix be seen? Do they settle to the bottom of the glass after several minutes?

Learn at Home, Grade 6

▶ 3. Help your child conduct an experiment with salt solutions.

You will need: 3 small jars with lids (baby food jars), 6 clear plastic cups, table salt, food coloring (red, blue and yellow), a plastic teaspoon, water, a large glass jar

Directions:

  a. Add 3 teaspoons of salt to each jar. Add 5 drops of red food coloring to the first jar, 5 drops of blue food coloring to the second jar and 5 drops of yellow food coloring to the third jar. Screw the lids on the three jars and shake thoroughly. What happens to the salt crystals?

  b. Fill three of the plastic cups about half-full with water. Add the red salt to the first cup of water and stir. Describe the salt solution. (Not all of the salt may dissolve.) Add the blue salt to the second cup of water. Rinse the plastic spoon and stir this solution. Add the yellow salt to the third cup of water. Rinse the plastic spoon and stir this solution.

  c. Pour some of the red solution into an empty plastic cup. Add some of the blue solution and stir. What is the color change?

  d. Pour some of the red solution into an empty plastic cup. Add some of the yellow solution and stir. What is the color change?

  e. Pour some of the blue solution into an empty plastic cup. Add some of the yellow solution and stir. What is the color change?

  f. Predict the final color if all six of the solutions are mixed. Pour all six solutions into a large glass jar. Was your prediction correct?

▶ 4. When an oil-and-water solution is shaken or stirred, some momentary mixing occurs, but the oil quickly gathers back on top of the water. Soap and other detergents have a unique molecular structure in which one end of the molecule is polar and the other end is nonpolar. This structure allows the soap to *emulsify* a solution. The emulsifying process breaks up the oil concentration in a solution and suspends the oil molecules throughout the water. Mixing occurs because the polar ends of the soap molecules mix with the polar molecules of water, and the nonpolar ends of the soap molecules are attracted to the nonpolar oil molecules. Soap and other detergents are effective cleaning agents because of their ability to emulsify grease and oil and because they break the surface tension of water.

▶ 5. Use some of the following discussion questions to review your study of chemistry:

Why is the study and knowledge of chemistry important in our world?

What new products do we have today because of developments in chemistry?

How is chemistry used in life science, medicine, geology, nutrition, energy and fuels, synthetic fibers, plastics and the environment?

What are some problems associated with chemicals, their storage and their disposal?

What are some of the common chemicals used in the classroom or home?

SOCIAL STUDIES (Great Depression)

▶ 1. In the fall of 1930, the International Apple Growers' Association, in an attempt to boost sagging sales, began to sell boxes of apples on credit to the jobless to peddle on the nation's streets. An energetic person who worked 12 long hours and sold his/her entire box might make a handsome profit of as much as $1.70 a day!

▶ 2. Men and women could get a box of 72 apples on credit. At the end of the day, they paid $1.75 for the box of apples. Each apple sold for 5 cents. A bundle of paper bags to put the apples in cost 10 cents. In addition, the peddler may have had to pay 10 cents for subway fare. Have your child make a chart to show how much a person could make selling one box of apples each day for a week.

▶ 3. Some 27 million households had radios, and listening to radio constituted the main leisure activity for some families. They listened to radio dramas, news, sports and Roosevelt's fireside chats. Going to the movies was also popular. A double feature cost only a dime. The films were generally lighthearted and avoided topics that reminded people of their everyday concerns. The craze of assembling jigsaw puzzles originated during the depression years. And carryovers from the 1920s included dance marathons and flagpole sitting.

This Is So Fine

Rewrite each sentence below, replacing the word **fine** with one of the synonyms given. Since the synonyms have slight differences in meaning, be careful to choose the correct one.

Fine: clear, delicate, elegant, small, sharp, subtle

1. The queen wore a **fine** gown encrusted with jewels.

   _____

   _____

2. I wash this blouse by hand because of its **fine** lace collar.

   _____

   _____

3. The sand in an hourglass must be very **fine** to trickle as it does.

   _____

   _____

4. We need **fine** weather for sailing.

   _____

   _____

5. Dad used a whetstone to put a **fine** edge on the knife.

   _____

   _____

6. Sometimes there is a **fine** line between innocence and guilt.

   _____

   _____

Learn at Home, Grade 6

Wherefore Art Thou?

Madeline loves to play detective. She loves exploring, searching for clues and unraveling mysteries.

One morning, Mrs. Candy Gramme, the English teacher, introduced Shakespeare to Madeline's class. She had removed her earrings to demonstrate medieval helmet gear. During her presentation, she noticed that one of her earrings was missing. She could not have removed them more than 5 minutes earlier. Now, helmet off and hair a frazzle, Mrs. Gramme was bewildered.

She asked the class to read Act Three, Scene One, while she searched for her jewelry. Mrs. Gramme peered intently around her desk, kneeling on all fours. Madeline, never one to sit still very long, quietly rose from her seat and walked stealthily toward the front. As she passed Sean, she accidentally stepped on his toe. Sean squelched a scream as he woke from his mid-morning nap.

"What are you doing?" he croaked in his typically raspy whisper.

"If you get me in trouble, I'll squeeze your pinky," Madeline threatened.

Sean immediately stilled.

Madeline stood quietly behind her teacher whose back was to the class. Madeline leaned over, glancing left and right, searching for the red earring. Wait! What was that under the desk?

"There it is!" Madeline shouted. Mrs. Gramme was so startled at the sound of

Madeline's voice that she backed into Rosemary Ann Thyme's desk. Rosemary, who had been leaning back in her chair, fell over, sending her copy of *Hamlet* sailing to the tiled floor. Single sheets of Shakespeare scattered in outrageous fortune.

Madeline was still pointing under Mrs. Gramme's desk. Yes, indeed, a red shape was there, but it was not an earring. As the sheets of paper were settling, a mouse, holding a red candy wrapper, ran into the primitive radiator system.

"Oh," said Madeline disappointedly.

"Madeline," said Mrs. Gramme with remarkable patience, "would you rather be a student or a permanent fixture in the principal's office?"

"To be, or not to be: that is the question," pondered Madeline.

Shopping for Soccer Supplies

The soccer team members needed to buy their own shin guards, socks, shoes and shorts. A couple of the players volunteered to do some comparative shopping to find the store with the best deal. Use their chart to answer the questions below.

SPORTS CORNER		**JOE'S SOCCER**
Socks. . . . . 3 pairs for $9.30		Socks. . . . . .2 pairs for $6.84
Shoes. . . . . 2 pairs for $48.24		Shoes. . . . . .3 pairs for $84.15
Shin Guards. . . . . 4 pairs for $32.48		Shin Guards. . . . . 5 pairs for $35.70
Shorts. . . . . 5 pairs for $60.30		Shorts. . . . . .4 pairs for $36.36

1. Which store had the better price for socks? _____

   How much less were they per pair? _____

2. Which store had the better price for shin guards? _____

   How much would you save per pair? _____

3. How much would one pair of shoes and socks cost at Joe's Soccer? _____

   How much at Sports Corner? _____

4. Which store had the better price for shorts? _____

   How much less were they per pair? _____

5. Total the price per pair for each item at each store. If you could shop at only one store, which one would give you the best overall deal? _____

   How much would you save? _____

Learn at Home, Grade 6

Dividing by Decimals

What kind of problems will these decimal glasses help you solve? Solve the problems. Then, **write** them in descending order (from greatest to least) beneath the blanks at the bottom of the page. **Write** each matching letter above the number to solve the riddle.

S $2.1\overline{)8.4}$ = 21. $\overline{)84.}$

V $0.36\overline{)1.872}$

O $1.24\overline{)0.4712}$

N $8\overline{)1.12}$

D $0.3\overline{)17.7}$

I $6\overline{)126.}$

I $.082\overline{)0.3772}$

— $7.4\overline{)103.6}$

I $5.5\overline{)3.025}$

___ ___ ___ ___ ___ ___ ___ ___ ___ ___

Oil and Water Emulsions

Investigation

Fill a clear glass jar about half-full with water. Add several drops of food coloring. Describe what happens._____

_____

Add about 1 inch of oil to the top of the water. Does the oil stay at the top of the jar?_____

Add several drops of food coloring to the top of the oil. What happens to the food coloring? _____

Use an eyedropper to poke a hole in the oil near the food coloring. What happens?_____

Put the lid on the jar. Shake the jar for 1 minute. Wait 1 minute. Is the oil on top? Is oil heavier or lighter than water?_____

_____

Emulsions

Let your jar of oil and water settle for a few minutes. Add a different color of food coloring to the top of the oil. Fill an eyedropper with liquid soap. Drop this soap right on the food coloring. Do this several times. What happens to the food coloring? _____

_____

Shake the jar several times. Observe the results. What happens to the oil? _____

_____

Let the jar stand undisturbed for a few minutes. What happens to the oil? _____

_____

Learn at Home, Grade 6

Ocean in a Bottle Emulsions

Investigation

• Fill a glass jar about half-full with water. Add several drops of food coloring to the water. Use blue, blue-green or blue-red food coloring, depending on the color you want the ocean to be. Add oil to the jar until it is about 3/4 full. Tighten the lid and turn the jar on its side. Do you see the ocean effect? _____

Emulsions

• Stand the jar upright. Add 8 eye droppers full of liquid dish soap to the jar. What happens?_____
_____

• Shake the jar vigorously. What happens?_____
_____

• Shake the jar vigorously again, then place it in a bag filled with ice cubes. How many minutes does it take for the oil to completely return to the top?_____

• After the oil and water have separated, shake the jar again vigorously. Place the jar in a pan of warm water, near a warm radiator or in the hot sun. How many minutes does it take this time for the oil to return completely to the top? _____

Extending the Concept

• Place a spoonful of mayonnaise in one small plastic cup and a spoonful of margarine in another small plastic cup. Fill a third plastic cup half-full with milk. Set each of these in a pan of warm water, in the hot sun or near (but not touching) a warm radiator. Wait 1 hour. Describe what happens to each of these substances.

_____

_____

_____

• How are these substances like oil and water?_____
_____

_____

	Language Skills	Spelling	Reading
Monday	Have your child choose a topic, make a plan for writing and begin working on a rough draft.	Pretest your child on these spelling words: precaution — premature — prescribe precise — premeditate — preserve predict — premium — presume prefer — prepare — prevail prefix — prepay — prevent prehistoric — preschool — previous Have your child correct the pretest. Add personalized words and make two copies of this week's study list.	**Comprehension** Introduce this week's reading selection. Suggestion: *Shiloh* by Phyllis Reynolds Naylor. *See* Reading, Week 19, numbers 1–8 for cross-curricular activity suggestions to accompany your study of the book.
Tuesday	**Sentences:** Review the four sentence types: *declarative, imperative, interrogative* and *exclamatory*. Discuss the appropriate final punctuation for each. Then, have your child write four sentences on a single subject. **Examples:** *Wolves hunt in packs.* *Watch out for the wolf!* *What do wolves eat?* *Wow! That wolf is beautiful!*	Review this week's spelling words. Have your child complete **Predictable Prefixes** (p. 196).	Discuss this week's reading in a conference. Focus on point of view. From what or whose point of view is the story written? Discuss why the author chose to tell the story from that perspective.
Wednesday	Choose a topic of interest to your child. Write 8–10 sentences on that topic on the chalkboard, omitting final punctuation. Have your child fill in periods, exclamation points and question marks as needed. Have your child identify each sentence by type. Then, have your child rewrite each sentence as a different type. **Example:** That ant is amazing! *Isn't that ant amazing?*	Have your child use each of this week's spelling words correctly in a sentence.	The Prestons did not always use correct grammar. Have your child scan the book to locate examples of poor grammar. Then, have your child rewrite each sentence using correct grammar.
Thursday	Review *simple* and *compound sentences*. *See* Language Skills, Week 19, numbers 1 and 2. Write a variety of sentences on the chalkboard. Ask your child to state whether each sentence is simple or compound. Have your child underline the subjects once and the verbs twice, adding commas where needed.	Have your child study this week's spelling words.	Review the use of similes. A *simile* compares two things using the words *like* or *as*. **Example:** He shot out of bed *like* a rocket. Discuss the meaning of similes from the book. Have your child complete **Shiloh** (p. 197).
Friday	Have your child write simple and compound sentences using given groups of subjects and verbs. *See* Language Skills, Week 19, number 3.	Give your child the final spelling test. Have your child record pretest and final test words in his/her word bank.	Hold a reading conference to discuss the ending of the book.

192

Learn at Home, Grade 6

Math	Science	Social Studies
Decimal Fractions Have your child use centimeter graph paper to draw models of decimal fractions. Let a 10 x 10 square box represent one whole. A row of ten squares represents 0.1. The decimal fraction 0.75 would be illustrated by shading 75 squares. Have your child draw the following decimal fractions: 0.3 0.42 0.90 1.05 0.65 0.4 0.08 2.31	**Light** Introduce the concept of light energy. *See* Science, Week 19. Display the following items: flashlight, candle, magnifying lens, camera, microscope, prism, light bulb and eyeglasses. Ask your child to explain how each of these objects is related to the study of light. *Why is light energy so important to life on Earth? Could we exist without it?* *See* Science, Week 19, numbers 1 and 2.	**World War II** Begin a discussion of World War II. *See* Social Studies, Week 19. Discuss what was happening in other parts of the world while America was dealing with the Great Depression. *See* Social Studies, Week 19, number 1. Have your child make a glossary of WWII vocabulary. *See* Social Studies, Week 19, number 2.

Review metric units of measure. *See* Math, Week 19.
Have your child calculate masses equivalent to the following:
    40 g   3,000 g   720 g
    82 g   350 g   4 g
Then, have your child calculate equivalent volumes and distances using liters and meters as base units.
	Ask your child to name some natural (fireflies, fish, lightning, the sun and stars, volcanic eruptions, Northern Lights) and some artificial (bulbs, burning fuels or candle, fireworks) sources of light. Using old magazines and newspapers, have your child make a poster of the forms of light energy. Provide scissors, glue and poster board. Have your child add pictures to the poster as you discuss other forms of light energy.	Obtain books and articles about WWII for your child to read. Since there is so much information available on this war, break your discussions into smaller units of study.
		Have your child read about the causes of the war. What was the position of the U.S. at the beginning of the war?

Review decimal fractions as covered so far this year in preparation for tomorrow's quiz. Encourage your child to ask questions.	When light hits an object, one of three things can happen: it can pass through, it can bounce off or it can be absorbed. Introduce the terms *opaque, translucent* and *transparent*. *See* Science, Week 19, number 3. Have your child make a chart to show how different objects respond to light. The chart should name the object and tell whether it is opaque, translucent or transparent.	Have your child read about the economic situation in Germany after World War I. Discuss Germany's inflation and unemployment and its role in World War II. *See* Social Studies, Week 19, number 3 for discussion topics.
Quiz your child on his/her understanding of decimal fractions. Have your child complete **Decimal Test** (p. 198).	Use reference materials to explain to your child how the human eye works. Have your child draw and label a diagram of the human eye.	Have your child read about and discuss the rise of Mussolini and fascism. *See* Social Studies, Week 19, number 4 for discussion topics.
Reteach any concepts missed on the test.	Have your child make a pinhole camera to model the behavior of the human eye. Have your child complete **Pinhole Camera** (p. 199).	Arrange for your child to perform a community service. Have your child write in his/her Social Studies Journal.

TEACHING SUGGESTIONS AND ACTIVITIES

LANGUAGE SKILLS (Sentences)

▶ 1. A simple sentence contains a subject and a predicate and expresses a single thought.
   Example: John dropped the ball.

   A simple sentence may contain a compound subject.
   Example: John and Bill raced for the ball.

   A simple sentence may contain a compound predicate.
   Example: John fell on and recovered the ball.

   A simple sentence may contain a compound subject and a compound predicate.
   Example: John and Bill brought and used two baseballs.

▶ 2. A compound sentence contains two simple sentences joined by a conjunction, such as *and, but, or* or *nor.* A comma is used before the conjunction.
   Examples: The rain poured from the clouds, and the porch got wet.
   A strong wind knocked over our flower pots, but nothing was broken.

▶ 3. Write several groups of subjects and verbs on the chalkboard. After each group, write the word *simple* or *compound* in parentheses. Have your child use the group of words to write the type of sentence indicated.

   squirrel, chipmunk, scampered (simple)   tigers, blue jays, played (simple)
   horse, trotted, elephant, lumbered (compound) mother, cooked, washed, she (compound)
   Margaret, rode, Janet, walked (compound)   hats, swirled, twisted (simple)
   yesterday, today, was, is (compound)   ducks, geese, swam (simple)

READING (Comprehension)

Have your child complete some or all of the following activities as he/she reads *Shiloh* this week. If you have chosen a different book to read this week, adapt the activities to the setting, characters and events in that book.

▶ 1. Have your child locate West Virginia on a map. Have him/her read about the state in an encyclopedia.

▶ 2. Have your child look up information on a hermit crab. Does a hermit crab make a good pet?

▶ 3. Have your child explain the difference between needs and wants to a family like the Prestons.

▶ 4. Think about what would you do and say if you discovered he/she were hiding a dog? Have your child role-play the situation with another person.

▶ 5. Have your child brainstorm a list of ways that children can earn money.

▶ 6. Have your child make a drawing of Judd's trailer and garden.

▶ 7. Have your child write a new ending: How would the story have been different if Judd had not shot the deer?

▶ 8. Have your child discuss the irony in the fact that hunting (something Marty hated) helped Marty win Shiloh.

MATH (Decimal Fractions)

The metric system is a base-ten system. The basic unit of mass is the gram. A gram weighs about the same as a small paper clip. To find the equivalent mass in milligrams, multiply by 1,000. A paper clip has a mass of 1,000 mg. To find the equivalent mass in kilograms, divide by 1,000. A paper clip has a mass of 0.001 kg. Reproduce the chart below for your child. Give your child measurements in grams to convert into other units. The pattern and prefixes are the same for meters and liters.

Larger units			Base	Smaller units		
kilo-	hecta-	deca-	gram	deci-	centi-	milli-
÷ 1,000	÷ 100	÷ 10	x 1	x 10	x 100	x 1,000

Learn at Home, Grade 6

SCIENCE (Light)

BACKGROUND

Light energy from natural and artificial sources provides many benefits to people. The study of light includes the human eye and its parts, mirrors, lenses, colors and optical instruments. Many professions in medicine, astronomy, biology, theater and art depend on light energy. Provide plenty of resources on light for your child's reference.

▶ 1. Visible light is just one of the forms of radiation associated with light energy. Other forms include x rays, ultraviolet rays and infrared rays. Have your child read about some of the early theories about light by Socrates, Pythagoras, Newton, Huygens and Einstein.

▶ 2. Add appropriate light vocabulary to the spelling lessons over the next few weeks.

light energy	refraction	primary colors	visible light
fluorescent	mirror	prism	translucent
incandescent	opaque	radiation	transparent
lens	pigments	reflection	electromagnetic spectrum

▶ 3. Gather objects made of paper, wood, metal, plastic and glass. Shine a flashlight on a piece of wood and ask your child to describe the result. Repeat with a mirror and clear glass. Discuss the terms *opaque, trancent* and *transparent*. Have your child aim the flashlight at the other materials and classify each one as opaque, translucent or transparent. Then, ask your child to name other objects or that fit each category.

SOCIAL STUDIES (World War II)

BACKGROUND

After the terrible cost of World War I, no one believed Germany would be willing to risk another war. However, the harsh conditions inflicted on Germany by the terms of the Treaty of Versailles created a fertile environment for radical politicians. Adolf Hitler soon rose to power and swiftly marshaled the resources of the entire nation for military conquest.

▶ 1. Other countries across the world were suffering economically at the same time America was. The people of Italy, Germany and Japan turned to dictators promising economic prosperity. The Germans turned to Adolf Hitler. The Italians followed Benito Mussolini. The Japanese formed a military dictatorship. Germany, Italy and Japan became aggressive in their goals for territorial expansion. Lenin led a revolution in Russia. Stalin became the country's dictator after Lenin's death, enforcing a new form of government called *communism*.

▶ 2. Have your child make a glossary of World War II vocabulary in his/her Social Studies Journal. The glossary should include the following words:

anti-Semitism	blitzkrieg	communism	Holocaust	nationalism
autarchy	D-Day	fascism	isolationism	Nazism
Axis powers	dictator	Gestapo	kamikaze	U-boats

▶ 3. Help your child research the economic situation in Germany prior to World War II. Discuss your child's findings.

What impact does inflation have on a national economy?

How did Germany's inflation affect imports and exports?

How does inflation affect savings accounts?

Why did Hitler blame the poor economy on a Jewish conspiracy?

Why is a nation's economy often better during wartime than peacetime?

▶ 4. Help your child research the rise of Mussolini and fascism. Discuss your child's findings.

What conditions led to the rise of Mussolini?

How does fascism differ from democracy?

Why did totalitarian states try to control the media and schools and to eliminate all forms of criticism?

Why do totalitarian states depend on secret police?

Complete the puzzle using the spelling words.
Use each word once.

precaution	prepare
precise	prepay
predict	preschool
prefer	prescribe
prefix	preserve
prehistoric	presume
premature	prevail
premeditate	prevent
premium	previous

```
P _ _ _ _ _ _ _
_ _ _ _ _ R _
_ _ E _ _ _
_ _ D _ _ _
_ _ _ _ I _ _
_ _ _ _ C _ _ _ _
_ _ _ _ _ _ _ T
_ _ _ _ _ A _ _ _
_ _ _ _ _ _ _ B _
_ _ _ _ _ _ _ L
_ _ E _ _ _ _ _ _ _
P _ _ _ _ _ _ _ _ _
_ _ _ _ _ R _ _
_ _ _ _ _ _ _ _ E _
_ _ _ F _ _ _
_ _ _ _ I _ _
_ _ _ _ _ X
_ _ _ _ _ _ _ E
```

PREDICTABLE PREFIXES

Change the meaning of two words from the list by adding a different prefix.

1. _____   2. _____

Learn at Home, Grade 6

Shiloh

A **simile** is a comparison using the words **like** or **as**. **Underline** the similes in these sentences. **Write** another simile with the same or nearly the same meaning.

1. My dream leaks out like water in a paper bag.

   _____

2. I hold Shiloh as careful as I carry Becky when she's asleep.

   _____

3. I'm as happy as a flea on a dog.

   _____

4. Keeping Shiloh a secret is like having a bomb waiting to go off.

   _____

5. I'm as tense as a cricket at night.

   _____

6. Ma hums to Shiloh like he's a baby in a cradle.

   _____

Complete these sentences with a simile of your own.

7. Shiloh looked at Dara Lynn like _____.

8. Doc Murphy was as gentle as _____ with Shiloh.

9. Judd trying to be nice was like _____.

10. The Prestons were happy as _____ to have Shiloh.

Decimal Test

1. 0.45 + 0.96 + 0.52 = _____

2. 26.3 − 4.8 = _____

3. Use > or < to compare each pair of numbers.

     5.01 ____5.003   6.15 ____6.015   3.05 ____5.03

4. Write sixty-one hundredths in numeral form. _____

5. 35.1 + 475.11 + 0.54 + 0.3 + 15 = _____

6. 81 − 0.04 = _____

7. Round 27.553 to the nearest tenth. _____

8. Round 62.814 to the nearest hundredth. _____

9. Round 5.06921 to the nearest hundredth. _____

10. Write 0.07 in words. _____

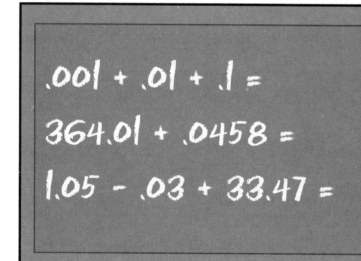

$$.001 + .01 + .1 =$$
$$364.01 + .0458 =$$
$$1.05 - .03 + 33.47 =$$

11. 16 x 0.18 = _____   15. 25.6 x 0.11 = _____

12. 0.504 ÷ 12 = _____   16. 22.1 + 0.008 = _____

13. 63 x 0.5 = _____   17. 3.65 ÷ 20 = _____

14. 90 − 10.50 = _____   18. 2.64 ÷ 5 = _____

Learn at Home, Grade 6

Pinhole Camera

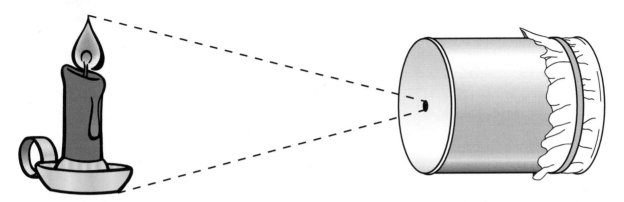

Use a large can that has a very small hole in the center of one end and that is open at the other end. Stretch one sheet of tissue paper over the open end and rubber band it in place. In a darkened room, hold the small opening about 6 inches (10 cm) away from a lighted candle. **As always, be careful when dealing with fire.** Line up the small opening with the candle flame. Hold the end covered with tissue towards you and look at the tissue. You should be able to see the back of an image projected onto the tissue showing through from the inside of the can. Move the can slightly forward and back to focus the image.

Observations
What do you see projected onto the tissue? _____

_____

Is there anything unusual about the image? _____

_____

Facts to Know
The pinhole camera you have just made models how an image is formed in the human eye. Light enters the eye through a small opening called the pupil and projects an image against the retina on the back of the eyeball. The image is upside down when it reaches the retina, but the brain automatically reverses it so we perceive the image as upright.

Draw lines connecting the parts of the pinhole camera with the corresponding parts of the eye.

retina   small opening

pupil   tissue

Learn at Home, Grade 6

	Language Skills	Spelling	Reading
Monday	Have your child choose a topic, make a plan for writing and begin working on a rough draft.	Pretest your child on these spelling words: percent perish persevere percussion permanent persist perfume permit personality perhaps peroxide perspire peril perpendicular persuade period perplex perturb Have your child correct the pretest. Add personalized words and make two copies of this week's study list.	Introduce the new reading selection or continue with the book from last week.
Tuesday	**Sentences:** Encourage your child to vary the types of sentences in order to make a paragraph more interesting. Write several pairs of simple sentences on the chalkboard. Have your child combine the sentences by adding key words. **Example:** The dog ran after the cat. The dog barked. *The dog barked as it ran after the cat.*	Review this week's spelling words. Have your child complete **Perplexing Personalities** (p. 206).	Discuss the current reading book in a conference. Focus on identifying the conflict in the story.

Wednesday	A complex sentence contains one independent clause and one or more dependent clauses. A dependent clause cannot stand on its own as a sentence. Have your child complete **Sentences: Simple, Compound and Complex** (p. 204).	Have your child use each of this week's spelling words correctly in a sentence.	Learning to use resources in the library takes practice. Make a list of ten questions for your child to answer using library resources. Have your child first identify the appropriate resource to use, then look to find the answer. Some sample questions:
			    What is the definition of *sleuth*?
			    Who was Sir Arthur Conan Doyle?
			    Are there any private investigators in your hometown?

Thursday	Have your child complete **"Variety Is the Spice of Life"** (p. 205).	Have your child study this week's spelling words.	**Problem Solving:** Teach your child strategies for solving problems. Have your child read a scenario, then follow four problem-solving steps to generate a solution to the problem. *See* Reading, Week 20, numbers 1 and 2.
Friday	Teach your child to use interesting verbs in order to create a more vivid picture in his/her writing. **Example:** *Patty <u>raced</u> home after school to see Grandma.* This sentence creates a better mental picture than the following: *Patty <u>ran</u> home after school to see Grandma.* Have your child substitute verbs to create more descriptive sentences. *See* Language Skills, Week 20.	Give your child the final spelling test. Have your child record pretest and final test words in his/her word bank.	Hold a reading conference. Ask your child to evaluate the actions of the characters in the book.

Learn at Home, Grade 6

Math	Science	Social Studies
Fractions Review the concept of fractions. Ask your child to draw some simple models of fractions. Assess whether the concept needs reteaching. If so, use physical models and drawings to help your child understand the concept of parts of a whole. *See* Math, Week 20, number 1. Name several fractions for your child to draw or build using a model.	**Reflection** Introduce the terms *reflection* and *refraction*. Demonstrate examples of each. *See* Science, Week 20, number 1.	**World War II** Have your child read about the Japanese surprise attack on Pearl Harbor. Have your child read newspaper accounts from December 7, 1941. Have your child draw a map of Hawaii, indicating where the attack took place. Have him/her label the map with other relevant information.
Use a model to teach your child about equivalent fractions. *See* Math, Week 20, number 2. Have your child draw a picture model of the following fractions: $1/3$, $3/4$, $2/3$, $11/12$, $5/6$. Ask your child to draw a line to connect the equivalent fractions.	Encourage your child to explore *plane*, *convex* and *concave* mirrors. Gather the following objects: a flashlight, flat and curved shiny pot lids, flat mirrors, aluminum foil, a car hubcap, a shiny metal spoon and a metal can. *See* Science, Week 20, numbers 2–4. Have your child make a chart of the objects and classify them as plane, convex or concave mirrors.	Have your child read about some of the key battles of WWII. Discuss. Have your child draw and color a map showing the key battles of WWII. As your child reads about different battles and invasions, have him/her label the countries involved. Your child should make a color key for the map. For example, have your child color the Axis countries brown, the Allies blue and occupied countries yellow.
Teach your child how to find equivalent fractions using multiplication or division. To find equivalent fractions, multiply or divide the numerator and denominator by the same number. In effect, you are multiplying (or dividing) the fraction by one ($4/4 = 1$), which does not change the value. *See* Math, Week 20, number 3. Give your child ten fractions. Have him/her name three equivalent fractions for each.	Help your child conduct an experiment to explore reflection and diffraction. Your child will need a flashlight, a protractor, a mirror and a flat surface to work on. *See also* Science, Week 20, number 5. Have your child complete **Light Waves** (p. 208).	Have your child read about the battles of Iwo Jima and Okinawa. Discuss. Study a map of Japan with your child. Have him/her find the islands of Iwo Jima and Okinawa. Ask your child to answer the following questions in his/her Social Studies Journal: *What was the cost in American and Japanese lives? What is a kamikaze? Do you think the battles were necessary?*
Teach your child to simplify a fraction to its lowest terms. To simplify a fraction, divide the numerator and denominator by the same number. To simplify to lowest terms, find the GCF (*greatest common factor*) of the numerator and denominator. *See* Math, Week 20, number 4. Have your child complete **Tall Trivia** (p. 207).	Help your child explore the use of mirrors in a periscope. Have your child complete **Making a Periscope** (p. 209).	Have your child read about the use of the atom bomb on Hiroshima and Nagasaki. Discuss the key figures involved in the decision to use the bomb and the events leading up to the ultimate launch of the bombs. Have your child write about whether future wars will involve the use of nuclear weapons.
To convert a mixed number to an improper fraction, multiply the whole number by the denominator and add the numerator. Write this sum over the denominator. **Example:** $4^3/4 = \dfrac{4 \times 4 + 3}{4} = \dfrac{19}{4}$ or $(4 = {}^{16}/4)$ ${}^{16}/4 + {}^3/4 = {}^{19}/4$ Write mixed numbers and corresponding improper fractions on the chalkboard. Have your child match the equivalent numbers.	Have your child use a prism to refract light. The denser the material, the more light it will bend. Glass is more dense than air, so the light bends as it passes through the prism. Each of the colors in the spectrum bends a different amount so you can see the different colors.	Arrange for your child to perform a community service. Have your child write in his/her Social Studies Journal.

TEACHING SUGGESTIONS AND ACTIVITIES

LANGUAGE SKILLS (Sentences)

Copy the following sentences on the chalkboard. Have your child rewrite each sentence, replacing the verb with another, more descriptive verb.

The bee went past my ear.   Miss Jones said what to study for the test.

Thunder sounded in the distance.   The children went down the hill like a herd of elephants.

We made beaded jewelry.   Mother put butter on the bread.

Brooke loved chocolate candy.   The skaters skated around the rink.

READING (Problem Solving)

▶ 1. Copy the following scenario for your child to read.

Four friends had been sailing for two hours before they spied a group of uninhabited mountain islands in the large sea. The small rig hit a boulder and sprung a leak about 500 feet from the shore of the smallest island. The island appeared to be about a half mile wide and a mile long and contained plenty of lush vegetation. The four friends swam ashore, leaving the boat behind with everything on it. One friend rescued a plastic bag of sandwiches wrapped in foil. Tired and frightened, the friends gathered to take stock of their situation. They looked upward toward the clear sky and bright sun and noticed birds circling overhead. One of the friends spied footprints in the sand.

▶ 2. Have your child follow these problem-solving steps to help the friends through this troublesome time.

  a. State some conclusions from the information provided in the paragraph.

  b. Ask some questions to obtain more information.

  c. What prior knowledge would be helpful in this situation?

  d. State some sensible things to do.

MATH (Fractions)

▶ 1. Find ways for your child to use fractions in everyday activities such as cooking, drawing, telling time or measuring with a ruler. Stress that a fraction is not a static size; its size depends on the size of the whole. For example, $\frac{1}{2}$ of a candy bar is not the same size as $\frac{1}{2}$ of a wedding cake.

▶ 2. Equivalent fractions name the same model in different ways. Shade $\frac{1}{2}$ of a rectangle. Draw a line in the rectangle so the shaded part looks like $\frac{2}{4}$. The shaded area hasn't changed in relation to the whole, so $\frac{1}{2}$ and $\frac{2}{4}$ are equivalent fractions. Draw two more lines in the figure so the fraction looks like $\frac{4}{8}$.

▶ 3. To find equivalent fractions, multiply or divide the numerator and denominator by the same number.

$$\frac{1}{2} \times \frac{4}{4} = \frac{4}{8} \qquad \frac{4}{8} \div \frac{2}{2} = \frac{2}{4}$$

To find an equivalent fraction with a given denominator, find out what number was multiplied or divided to get that denominator. Then, multiply or divide the numerator by the same number.

$$\frac{2}{3} \times \frac{?}{?} = \frac{}{9} \qquad \frac{2}{3} \times \frac{3}{3} = \frac{6}{9}$$

▶ 4. As an alternative to finding the GCF, use any number that is a common factor of the numerator and denominator. Divide and find a common factor for the resulting fraction. Repeat until the fraction is in simplest terms.

$$\frac{84}{96} \div \frac{2}{2} = \frac{42}{48} \div \frac{3}{3} = \frac{14}{16} \div \frac{2}{2} = \frac{7}{8}$$

Learn at Home, Grade 6

SCIENCE (Reflection)

▶ 1. *Reflection* occurs when light waves bounce off an object. Using a small flashlight, demonstrate the reflection of light from a mirror or shiny metal surface. *Refraction* occurs when light waves bend. Place a pencil upright in a glass half-full of water and have your child describe the effect. The pencil appears to be broken, because you are viewing part of the pencil out of the water and part of the pencil underwater. The speed of the light entering the denser water is slowed, and the image is refracted.

▶ 2. Have your child examine his/her reflection in the inside of the spoon and then the outside of the spoon. Have your child describe the images. Then, have your child view his/her image in a flat mirror and describe the image. A mirror can be any surface or material which reflects light. The flat mirror is also called a *plane* mirror. The inside of the spoon is called a *concave* mirror, and the outside of the spoon is called a *convex* mirror.

▶ 3. Have your child view his/her image in the hubcap, the inside and outside of flat and curved pot lids, a piece of aluminum foil and the outside of a shiny metal can. Ask your child to classify each object as a plane, concave or convex mirror.

▶ 4. Use the following questions to spark discussion or for your child to answer in his/her Science Log:

Have you ever seen a large convex mirror mounted in the ceiling or corner of a store?

What is the purpose of the mirror?

What types of mirrors are found on or in a car?

What does a concave mirror do to a reflected image?

What does a convex mirror do to a reflected image?

What does a plane mirror do to a reflected image?

What types of mirrors are used in reflecting telescopes?

▶ 5. *Reflection* occurs when a wave strikes an object and bounces back. If a wave hits a smooth surface at an angle, the wave will be reflected in the opposite direction but at an equal angle. The angle of incidence (where the light wave strikes) is equal to the the angle of reflection (where the light wave bounces back).

Diffraction is the bending of waves around sharp edges. A light wave spreads slightly when it travels through a small opening. The edges of the index cards should appear slightly fuzzy.

Sentences

Simple, Compound and Complex

A simple sentence has a complete subject and predicate.
Example: The little brown rabbit hopped all around the yard.

A compound sentence has two or more simple sentences joined together.
Example: Patrick tried to pick the rabbit up, but it quickly hopped away.

A complex sentence contains one independent clause and one or more dependent clauses.
Example: After several tries, Patrick finally caught the frightened rabbit.

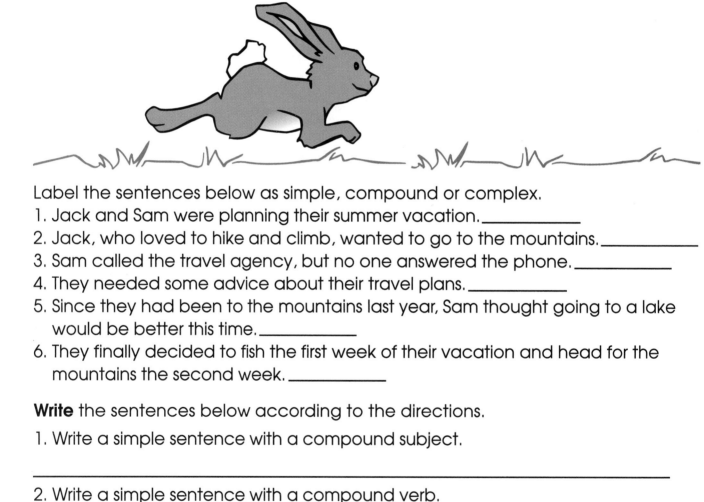

Label the sentences below as simple, compound or complex.
1. Jack and Sam were planning their summer vacation._____
2. Jack, who loved to hike and climb, wanted to go to the mountains._____
3. Sam called the travel agency, but no one answered the phone._____
4. They needed some advice about their travel plans._____
5. Since they had been to the mountains last year, Sam thought going to a lake would be better this time._____
6. They finally decided to fish the first week of their vacation and head for the mountains the second week. _____

Write the sentences below according to the directions.

1. Write a simple sentence with a compound subject.

_____

2. Write a simple sentence with a compound verb.

_____

3. Write a compound sentence using and as the conjunction.

_____

4. Write a complex sentence using the subordinating conjunction after.

_____

Learn at Home, Grade 6

"Variety Is the Spice of Life"

Writing is more interesting when sentences are written in different ways. Sentences may be short or long, begin with phrases or clauses or change their order.

Rewrite the paragraphs below. Divide some sentences and combine others. Vary their beginnings.

My sister broke her leg playing soccer. She was playing center. She was in a tournament. She tripped over the ball when she tried to trap the ball and fell to the ground immediately. An ambulance came and an ambulance had on its siren and she went away in the ambulance.

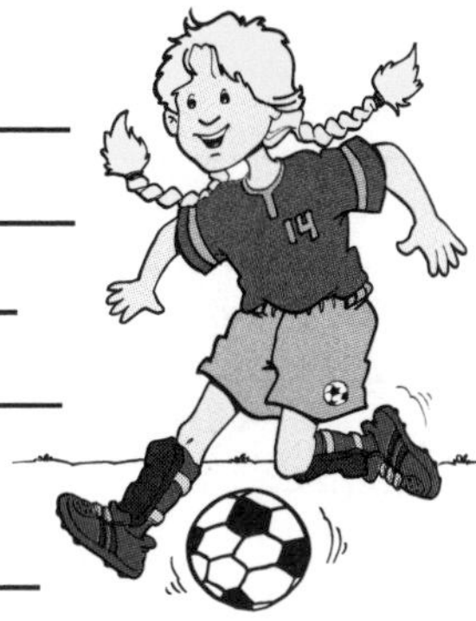

The school year was about to begin. I had to get ready for it. Mother took me to the store. I had to get a notebook. I had to get paper. I had to get pens with blue ink and pencils with erasers. I saw my friends at the store. They were getting ready for school too.

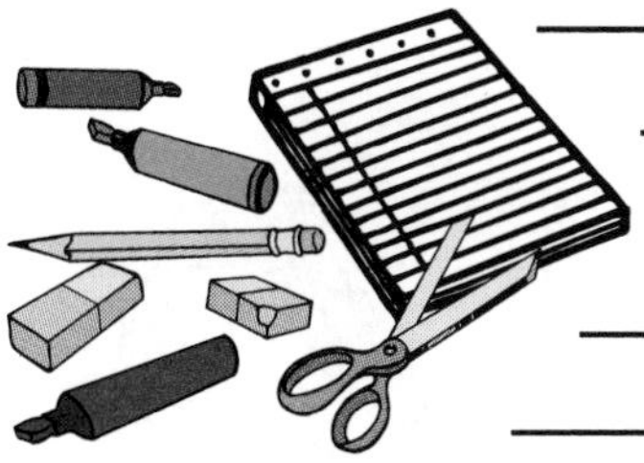

Jamie's mother got a new car. It was a good-looking one. The car was bright red and it had a sun roof and it had a stereo and it could go fast. It had four speeds. Jamie could not give anyone a lift there were only two seats. Jamie was not old enough to drive. He sat in the seat next to his mom.

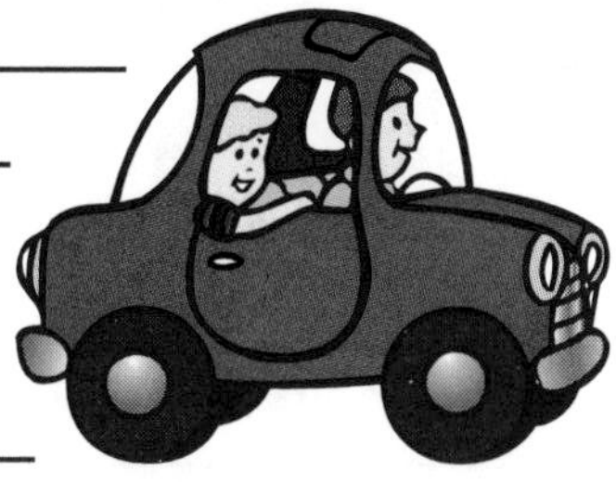

Perplexing Personalities

Divide each spelling word into syllables and **underline** the syllable that is stressed. Refer to a dictionary if necessary.

percent	perhaps	perish	peroxide	persevere	perspire
percussion	peril	permanent	perpendicular	persist	persuade
perfume	period	permit	perplex	personality	perturb

1. _____

2. _____

3. _____

4. _____

5. _____

6. _____

7. _____

8. _____

9. _____

10. _____

11. _____

12. _____

13. _____

14. _____

15. _____

16. _____

17. _____

18. _____

Write a paragraph using as many spelling words as possible. Add your own words beginning with **per**.

_____

_____

_____

_____

_____

Learn at Home, Grade 6

Tall Trivia

The Empire State Building, a famous building in New York City, has 102 floors. Find out how many stairs it has by shading in the boxes that contain correctly reduced fractions.

$\frac{10}{12}=\frac{5}{6}$	$\frac{12}{43}=\frac{2}{7}$	$\frac{20}{48}=\frac{5}{12}$	$\frac{2}{10}=\frac{1}{5}$	$\frac{9}{72}=\frac{1}{8}$	$\frac{40}{49}=\frac{6}{7}$	$\frac{5}{10}=\frac{1}{2}$	$\frac{45}{64}=\frac{7}{10}$	$\frac{3}{42}=\frac{5}{16}$	$\frac{29}{63}=\frac{3}{7}$	$\frac{6}{9}=\frac{2}{3}$	$\frac{9}{24}=\frac{3}{8}$	$\frac{3}{18}=\frac{1}{6}$
$\frac{5}{20}=\frac{1}{4}$	$\frac{4}{50}=\frac{1}{10}$	$\frac{21}{30}=\frac{7}{10}$	$\frac{4}{15}=\frac{2}{7}$	$\frac{24}{30}=\frac{4}{5}$	$\frac{5}{33}=\frac{2}{11}$	$\frac{14}{22}=\frac{7}{11}$	$\frac{19}{63}=\frac{4}{15}$	$\frac{16}{50}=\frac{9}{25}$	$\frac{18}{56}=\frac{2}{6}$	$\frac{4}{20}=\frac{1}{5}$	$\frac{5}{65}=\frac{1}{12}$	$\frac{20}{65}=\frac{4}{13}$
$\frac{8}{28}=\frac{2}{7}$	$\frac{40}{56}=\frac{5}{8}$	$\frac{8}{16}=\frac{1}{2}$	$\frac{3}{21}=\frac{1}{7}$	$\frac{6}{8}=\frac{3}{4}$	$\frac{26}{52}=\frac{6}{13}$	$\frac{5}{15}=\frac{1}{3}$	$\frac{40}{52}=\frac{5}{6}$	$\frac{27}{43}=\frac{5}{8}$	$\frac{31}{42}=\frac{3}{4}$	$\frac{10}{25}=\frac{2}{5}$	$\frac{3}{40}=\frac{1}{15}$	$\frac{14}{70}=\frac{1}{5}$
$\frac{15}{27}=\frac{5}{9}$	$\frac{18}{100}=\frac{3}{20}$	$\frac{14}{21}=\frac{2}{3}$	$\frac{6}{22}=\frac{3}{10}$	$\frac{18}{20}=\frac{9}{10}$	$\frac{29}{60}=\frac{9}{20}$	$\frac{25}{70}=\frac{5}{14}$	$\frac{5}{50}=\frac{1}{10}$	$\frac{10}{40}=\frac{1}{4}$	$\frac{38}{59}=\frac{2}{3}$	$\frac{35}{45}=\frac{7}{9}$	$\frac{7}{63}=\frac{2}{21}$	$\frac{6}{30}=\frac{1}{5}$
$\frac{7}{70}=\frac{1}{10}$	$\frac{12}{30}=\frac{4}{15}$	$\frac{42}{49}=\frac{6}{7}$	$\frac{16}{25}=\frac{4}{5}$	$\frac{12}{27}=\frac{4}{9}$	$\frac{27}{100}=\frac{13}{15}$	$\frac{16}{36}=\frac{4}{9}$	$\frac{5}{44}=\frac{1}{8}$	$\frac{14}{21}=\frac{2}{3}$	$\frac{28}{36}=\frac{4}{5}$	$\frac{7}{28}=\frac{1}{4}$	$\frac{18}{56}=\frac{1}{3}$	$\frac{6}{15}=\frac{2}{5}$
$\frac{6}{10}=\frac{3}{5}$	$\frac{25}{50}=\frac{5}{12}$	$\frac{25}{30}=\frac{5}{6}$	$\frac{24}{64}=\frac{3}{8}$	$\frac{6}{33}=\frac{2}{11}$	$\frac{19}{28}=\frac{3}{4}$	$\frac{36}{40}=\frac{9}{10}$	$\frac{14}{22}=\frac{7}{11}$	$\frac{3}{18}=\frac{1}{6}$	$\frac{45}{80}=\frac{3}{10}$	$\frac{9}{18}=\frac{1}{2}$	$\frac{18}{90}=\frac{1}{5}$	$\frac{26}{40}=\frac{13}{20}$

Every year, there is a race to the top of the Empire State Building. In 1993, the winner got to the top in 10 minutes, 18 seconds. How many stairs did the winner go up per second, rounded to the nearest whole number?

_____

Light Waves

You will need: a flashlight, a protractor, a mirror, black construction paper and a sheet of white paper

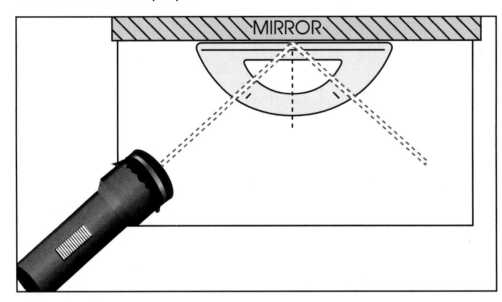

Angle of Incidence ($\angle i$)	Angle of Reflection ($\angle r$)
15°	
40°	
55°	

Observing Reflection

Set up your materials as shown above. Once the protractor is in place, mark two points on either side of the 90° mark and connect that line all the way to the base of the mirror. Replace the protractor so that the 90° mark sits on this line. This will make it easier to judge the angles of the light.

Cut a $\frac{1}{4}$ in. slit in the black paper and tape it over the front of the flashlight. Shine the flashlight in at the angles listed in the chart above and find the degree readings for the angle of the light reflected. (This is called the angle of incidence.) Subtract that number from 90° to determine the angle of reflection.

Observing Diffraction

Take two index cards and hold them very close together in front of a window. Look carefully at the edges of the cards that are close together. What do you notice about them? _____

_____

Making a Hypothesis

What generalization can you make about the angles of incidence and reflection when a wave strikes a smooth surface? _____

_____

What happens to waves when they travel through narrow slits? _____

_____

Learn at Home, Grade 6

Making a Periscope

Light travels in a straight line. Mirrors reflect light in a straight line. The slanted mirrors in a periscope allow the user to see above a normal field of view.

You will need: a shoebox, poster board, tape, scissors, glue, 2 small mirrors

Making the Periscope

Stand your box vertically. Take the lid off and cut a 1-inch-square hole on one side near the top. Cut another hole on the other side near the bottom of the box. Fold a long narrow piece of poster board into thirds. Overlap and tape two of the folded sides to make a triangle. Trim the triangle so that it will fit into the bottom of the box opposite the top hole. Use tape or glue to attach both triangles. Attach one mirror onto the slanting side of the bottom triangle and the other mirror onto the top triangle. Make sure each mirror slants at the same angle and that both mirrors face into the box. Place the lid back on your box.

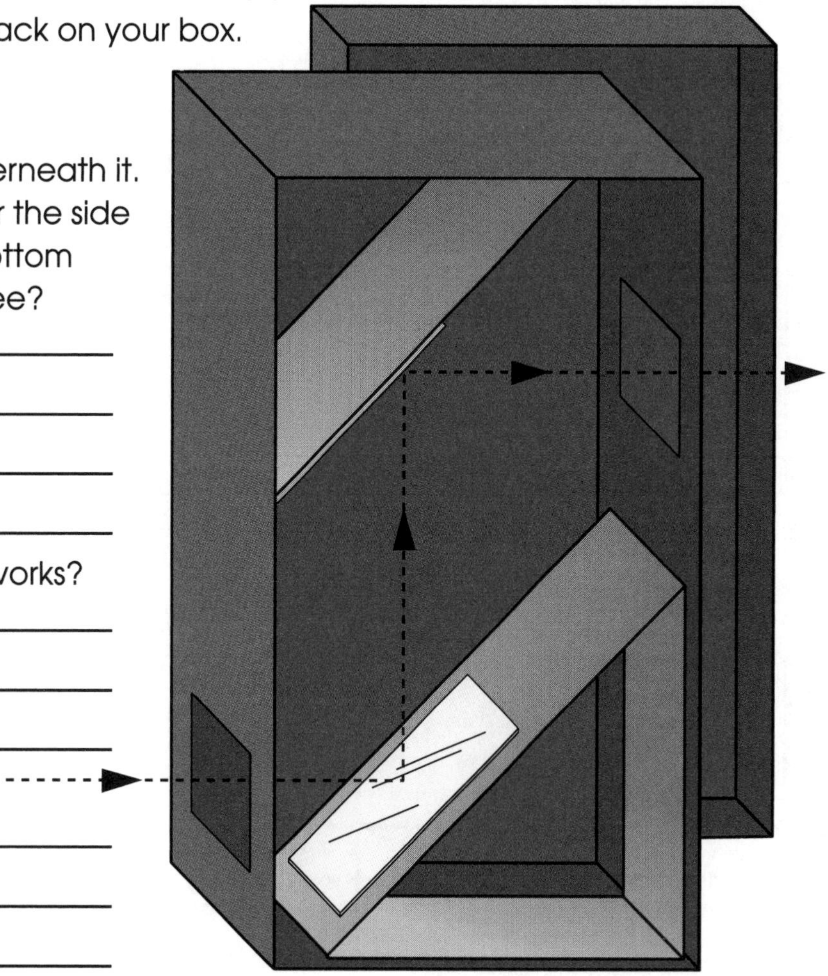

Using the Periscope

Kneel beside your desk or sit underneath it. Hold the tip of the periscope over the side of your desk. Look through the bottom hole at the mirror. What do you see?

_____

_____

_____

_____

Why do you think the periscope works?

_____

_____

_____

What do the mirrors do?

_____

_____

_____

Modifying the Investigation

Change the angle of your triangles. Does this change what you see?

_____

Learn at Home, Grade 6

	Language Skills	**Spelling**	**Reading**
Monday	Have your child choose a topic, make a plan for writing and begin working on a rough draft.	Pretest your child on these spelling words: interact interject intersect intercept intermission interstate interchange internal interval intercom interpret intervene interest interrogative interview interfere interrupt intertwine Have your child correct the pretest. Add personalized words and make two copies of this week's study list.	Introduce this week's reading selection or continue with the book from last week.
Tuesday	**Diagramming Sentences:** With your child, discuss the purpose of diagramming sentences. *See* Language Skills, Week 21. Teach your child to diagram simple sentences on a single horizontal line, separating the subject and verb with a vertical line. Articles are placed on a diagonal line beneath the nouns they modify. *See* Language Skills, Week 21, numbers 1 and 2.	Review this week's spelling words. Have your child complete **Intercepting the Ball** (p. 216).	Discuss the current reading book in a conference. Focus today on the Reading Journal.
Wednesday	Teach your child to diagram sentences with compound subjects. The two subjects are written on parallel horizontal lines, joined by *and*, and connected to the horizontal line containing the predicate. *See* Language Skills, Week 21, numbers 3 and 4.	Have your child use each of this week's spelling words correctly in a sentence.	**Reading for Understanding:** Some information in a book may not be stated outright. In these cases, information must be *inferred*. Teach your child to read carefully, reflecting on the information presented, and recognize inferred meanings. Have your child complete **What Do You Think?** (p. 217).
Thursday	Teach your child to diagram sentences with compound predicates. The two verbs are written on parallel horizontal lines, joined by *and*, and connected to the horizontal line containing the subject. *See* Language Skills, Week 21, numbers 5 and 6. Have your child complete **Dizzying Diagrams** (p. 214).	Have your child study this week's spelling words.	Choose a passage or chapter from this week's book to discuss in detail. Ask your child to evaluate the reading in his/her Reading Journal. Evaluation may include criticizing or justifying an action, debating an issue or recommending a change.
Friday	Teach your child to diagram sentences with adjectives and adverbs. Just like articles, adjectives are written on diagonal lines beneath the nouns they modify. Adverbs are written on diagonal lines beneath the verbs they modify. Have your child complete **Adjective and Adverb Modifiers** (p. 215).	Give your child the final spelling test. Have your child record pretest and final test words in his/her word bank.	Respond to your child's journal entry by proposing a different view or bringing up contradictory information. Challenge your child to think more deeply about the topic. Have your child write an imaginary editorial on a topic related to one raised in the book. Encourage your child to express his/her views clearly and support his/her arguments.

Learn at Home, Grade 6

Math	**Science**	**Social Studies**
Fractions Fractions can be written as decimals by dividing the numerator by the denominator. Decimals can be written as fractions by writing the number as it is read, then reducing it. *See* Math, Week 21, numbers 1 and 2. Based on today's lesson, explain how a whole number can be written as a fraction. **Example:** $4 = {}^{16}/_4$	**Light Spectrum** The electromagnetic spectrum shows waves ranging from short gamma rays to long radio waves. Visible light is a small band in the middle of the spectrum. *See* Science, Week 21, number 1.	**World War II** Spend several days reading about and discussing the Holocaust. Rent the movie *Schindler's List* and watch it over the next several days. Discuss the story and try to answer any questions your child may have.
To convert an improper fraction to a mixed number, divide the numerator by the denominator. Write the remainder over the divisor. **Example:** ${}^{13}/_3 = 13 \div 3 = 4^1/_3$ Have your child write the following improper fractions as mixed numbers: ${}^{37}/_7 \qquad {}^{3}/_2 \qquad {}^{127}/_5 \qquad {}^{59}/_{12}$ ${}^{154}/_5 \qquad {}^{133}/_8 \qquad {}^{51}/_8 \qquad {}^{100}/_3$	Use a prism to project the visible spectrum of colors. Introduce your child to the mnemonic device *ROY G BIV. See* Science, Week 21, number 2.	Have your child read about the Holocaust in an encyclopedia. Then, have your child read a nonfictional account of the time in a book such as *The Diary of a Young Girl* by Anne Frank or *The Holocaust: A History of Courage and Resistance* by Bea Stadtler. Discuss the reading with your child.
Review multiplication of fractions. *See* Math, Week 21, number 3. Have your child draw models of the following multiplication problems: $\frac{1}{2} \times \frac{3}{4} \qquad \frac{5}{6} \times \frac{2}{3}$	Explain to your child that the colors we see are wavelengths of light reflected off an object. Hold up a sheet of red construction paper. Explain that when light hits the paper, all wavelengths are absorbed by the paper except red. White light is a mixture of the seven colors of the spectrum. When all the colors are blended, they produce white. Have your child make a color wheel using **The Spectrum Color Wheel** (p. 219).	Make sure your child is familiar with vocabulary related to the Holocaust. Your child should know and understand these terms: *anti-Semitism, Aryan, concentration camp, crematorium, death camp, deportation, genocide, Gestapo, ghetto, Holocaust, Juden, Nazi, prejudice, racism, scapegoat, swastika, yellow star.* *See also* Social Studies, Week 21, numbers 1 and 2.
If possible, cancel numbers when multiplying fractions. This is done by dividing a numerator and a denominator by their GCF. Cancelling will make the multiplication easier and the resulting product will be in simpler terms. **Example:** $\frac{2\cancel{8}}{11} \times \frac{3}{\cancel{4}_1} = \frac{6}{11}$ Give your child ten multiplication problems with fractions for practice.	Arrange a trip to a printing press to observe the printing process. Observe the mixing of the three primary colors (red, yellow and blue—also called magenta, yellow and cyan) to create colorful pages. Have your child write about the process of applying three colors to create all the colors necessary for printing.	After WWII, much of Europe lay in ruins. Most nations had no money to rebuild. The U.S. provided loans and grants to individual nations to help rebuild towns and cities. Ask your child to explain why he/she thinks the U.S. chose to help rebuild Europe.
When multiplying fractions by a whole number, place a one as a denominator under the whole number. Multiply as usual. **Example:** $4 \times \frac{2}{3} = \frac{4}{1} \times \frac{2}{3} = \frac{8}{3}$ Have your child complete **Soccer Fractions** (p. 218).	Have your child create a painting with tempera paints using only the three primary colors. Encourage the child to mix and blend the colors to make new colors.	Arrange for your child to perform a community service. Have your child write in his/her Social Studies Journal.

TEACHING SUGGESTIONS AND ACTIVITIES

LANGUAGE SKILLS (Diagramming Sentences)

BACKGROUND
Diagramming is a tool that can be used to further your child's understanding of the structure of the English language. A diagrammed sentence is a visual demonstration of the structural relationships among elements within the sentence.

▶ 1. Simple sentences containing a single subject and a single verb can be diagrammed using a single horizontal line bisected by a vertical line. The vertical line separates the subject from the verb. The articles *a, an* and *the* are adjectives and are placed on a diagonal line beneath the nouns they modify.

Trees sway.

Trees | sway

The birds can sing.

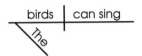

▶ 2. Give your child the following sentences. Have him/her underline the subjects once and the verbs twice, then diagram each sentence.

a. Dogs run.

b. Cats climb.

c. The fish swim.

d. Snakes slide.

e. A duck quacks.

f. The salamanders slither.

g. Dinosaurs rumble.

h. Badgers burrow.

i. The hyena yelps.

▶ 3. Sentences containing compound subjects require two parallel lines joined by diagonal lines to the horizontal line containing the verb. Note how the conjunction is written on a dotted line connecting the subjects.

Allison and Thomas won.

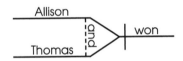

The boy and girl laughed.

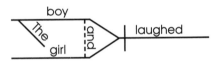

▶ 4. Give your child the following sentences. Have him/her underline the subjects once and the verbs twice, then diagram each sentence.

a. The soldiers and the civilians fled.

b. The shells and grenades exploded.

c. A fighter and a bomber collided.

d. The battle and the war were lost.

e. The horse and rider fell.

f. The castle and the parapet were taken.

g. General Grant and General Lee met.

h. The general and the officers surrendered.

▶ 5. Sentences containing compound verbs require two parallel lines joined by diagonal lines to the horizontal line containing the subject. Note how the conjunction(s) is/are written on a dotted line connecting the verbs.

March came and went.

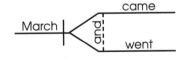

The audience will either cheer or boo.

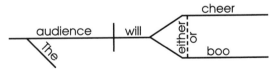

▶ 6. Give your child the following sentences. Have him/her underline the subjects once and the verbs twice, then diagram each sentence.

a. She swung and missed.

b. Kenisha and Riva ate and drank.

c. Frederick either plays or watches.

d. A dog can growl and whimper.

e. John and Gwen will listen and decide.

f. The crowd clapped and cheered.

g. The nomads packed and fled.

h. The hen and the rooster watched and waited.

Learn at Home, Grade 6

MATH (Fractions)

▶ 1. Fractions can be written as decimals by dividing the numerator by the denominator.

Examples: $^3/_4 = 0.75$

$$\begin{array}{r} 0.75 \\ 4\overline{)3.00} \\ \underline{-2\,8} \\ 20 \\ \underline{-20} \\ 0 \end{array}$$

$6\,^7/_8 = 6.875$

$$\begin{array}{r} 0.875 \\ 8\overline{)7.000} \\ \underline{-6\,4} \\ 60 \\ \underline{-56} \\ 40 \\ \underline{-40} \\ 0 \end{array}$$

Have your child write the following fractions as decimals: $^3/_{20}$ $3\,^7/_{10}$ $^4/_{25}$ $8\,^5/_8$ $^2/_5$ $2\,^{15}/_{16}$

▶ 2. Decimals can be written as fractions by reading the decimal, writing it out as read and reducing.

Examples: 0.55
Read as fifty-five hundredths
Write as $^{55}/_{100}$
Reduce to $^{11}/_{20}$

3.17
Read as three and seventeen hundredths
Write as $3\,^{17}/_{100}$
Already in lowest terms

Have your child write the following decimals as fractions: 0.642   8.7   0.64   3.16   0.85   1.625

▶ 3. To multiply fractions, simply multiply the numerators to find the numerator and multiply the denominators to find the denominator.

Examples: $^1/_3 \times ^2/_5 = ^2/_{15}$ $^7/_9 \times ^3/_8 = ^{21}/_{72}$

To help explain this, read the "x" as "of."
Then, $^1/_2 \times ^1/_2 = ^1/_4$ reads $^1/_2$ of $^1/_2 = ^1/_4$.
Demonstrate the concept visually with the diagram at right.

$\dfrac{1}{2}$ $\dfrac{1}{2}$ of $\dfrac{1}{2}$ = $\dfrac{1}{4}$

SCIENCE (Light Spectrum)

▶ 1. Explain that visible light is a small part of the total band of energy waves called the *electromagnetic spectrum*. Find a diagram of the electromagnetic spectrum in an encyclopedia. *Gamma rays* have the greatest amount of energy and shortest wavelengths. *Radio waves* have the least amount of energy and longest wavelengths. Ask whether the child knows any special uses for ultraviolet light, infrared light, radio waves or x rays.

▶ 2. *ROY G BIV* is a mnemonic device used to remember the order of the colors in the spectrum: *red, orange, yellow, green, blue, indigo, violet*. Have your child project a spectrum of light onto the ceiling using a simple technique. Fill a clear glass jar with water and lean a small rectangular mirror inside the jar. Shine a flashlight onto the mirror, and a spectrum will be projected onto the wall or ceiling. Try adjusting the angle of the flashlight to get the best results. Explain that the red end of the spectrum has the longest wavelengths and the least energy, and the violet end of the spectrum has the shortest wavelengths and the most energy.

SOCIAL STUDIES (World War II)

▶ 1. Disease ran rampant among the prisoners in concentration camps. Have your child read about the following diseases: *cholera, diphtheria, dysentery, smallpox, scarlet fever, tuberculosis* and *typhus*. Have your child make a chart showing each disease and indicating its definition, causes, symptoms and prevention.

▶ 2. Have your child read about recent examples of human rights violations. In what parts of the world do these violations continue? Compare the current examples with the Holocaust. Discuss some of the international organizations whose mission it is to put an end to such violations, such as Amnesty International.

Dizzying Diagrams

Read the following sentences. **Underline** the subjects once and the verbs twice. On the line after each sentence, **write** whether the subjects and predicates are simple or compound. Then, diagram the sentences correctly below.

1. The baby laughs and smiles. (S)_____

   (P)_____

2. A bear hibernates. (S)_____

   (P)_____

3. The brother and sister argue. (S)_____

   (P)_____

4. The wind and rain howled and blew. (S)_____

   (P)_____

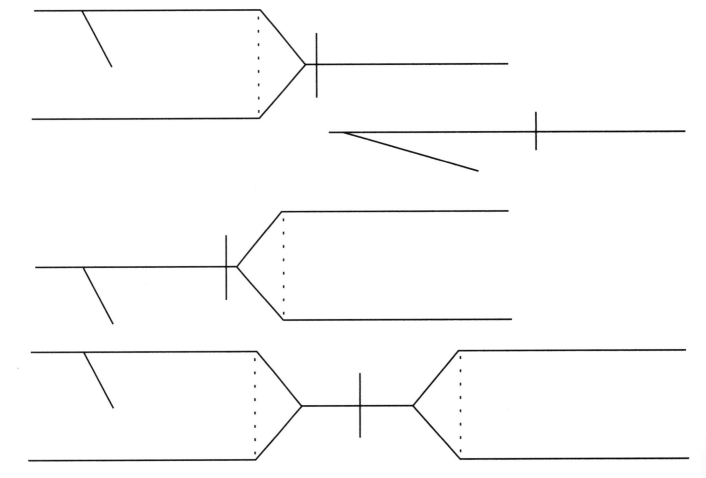

Learn at Home, Grade 6

Adjective and Adverb Modifiers

An adjective is placed on a diagonal line beneath the noun it modifies.

Examples: The red fish swam.

A blue dolphin leapt and splashed.

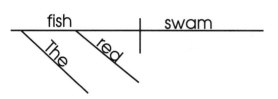

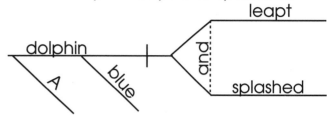

An adverb is placed on a diagonal line beneath the verb it modifies. If the adverb modifies an adjective or another adverb, it is placed on a line parallel to the word it modifies and connected to it by a line.

Examples: Rainy weather occurs often here.   The car drove very quickly.

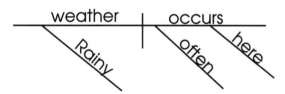

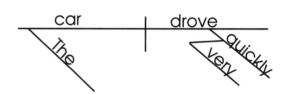

Read the following sentences. **Underline** the adjectives and **circle** the adverbs. Then, diagram the sentences on other sheet of paper.

1. The blue-green water sparkled.

2. Huge waves crashed loudly.

3. The little plovers scurried away.

4. The hot sun shone brightly.

Create sentences to fit these diagrams. **Write out** each sentence on another sheet of paper before writing it in the diagram.

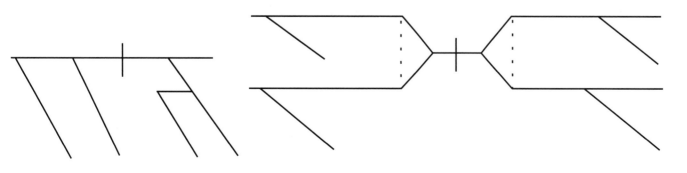

Learn at Home, Grade 6

Intercepting the Ball

Write each spelling word in the category in which it belongs. Some words fit into more than one category.

interact
intercept
interchange
intercom
interest
interfere
interject
intermission
internal
interpret
interrogative
interrupt
intersect
interstate
interval
intervene
interview
intertwine

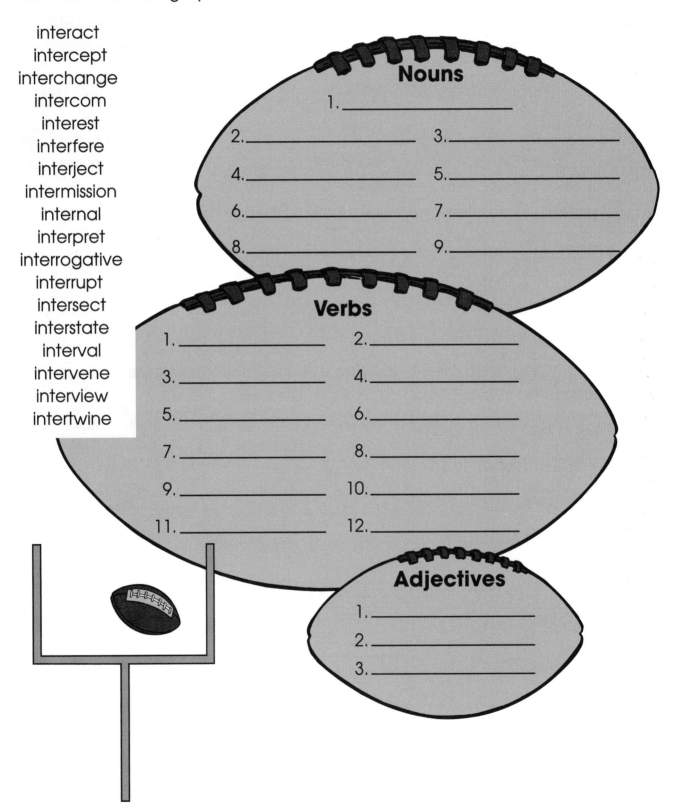

Nouns

1. _____
2. _____ 3. _____
4. _____ 5. _____
6. _____ 7. _____
8. _____ 9. _____

Verbs

1. _____ 2. _____
3. _____ 4. _____
5. _____ 6. _____
7. _____ 8. _____
9. _____ 10. _____
11. _____ 12. _____

Adjectives

1. _____
2. _____
3. _____

Learn at Home, Grade 6

What Do You Think?

Read each sentence. **Write** two sentences explaining what could have caused each event to happen.

1. The bird ceased its singing in the forest.

    a. _____

    b. _____

2. Tim came home crying. His backpack was open.

    a. _____

    b. _____

3. Five hundred people laughed at Lana as she stood in the bright light.

    a. _____

    b. _____

4. The saddled horse galloped onto the track without a jockey.

    a. _____

    b. _____

5. Pam sat soaking wet on the bench with her friends.

    a. _____

    b. _____

6. Martin stared with mouth agape at his teacher, Mr. Lancaster.

    a. _____

    b. _____

Soccer Fractions

Soccer is a popular sport at Forestview Middle School.

1. There are 30 students in one seventh-grade classroom.
    If $\frac{1}{3}$ of them play soccer, how many play soccer?   _____

2. One-sixth of 24 soccer players are girls. How many boys
    are on the team?   _____

3. The coach ordered 48 uniforms for the seventh-grade
    team. The sizes varied. Two-thirds of the uniforms were
    large sizes. How many were large sizes?   _____

4. Eighty-four people came to watch one game.
    Six-eighths of the spectators were parents. How many
    were parents?   _____

5. Thirty-two candy bars were sold at the first game. Two-
    eighths of them were with almonds. How many almond
    bars were sold?   _____

6. One sixth-grade team played 10 games. Three-fifths of
    the games were played at home. How many were
    away games?   _____

7. The eighth graders won eight of their games. One-fourth
    of the games were won by only two points. How many
    were won by two points?   _____

8. Out of the 486 students at Forestview Middle School,
    $\frac{1}{3}$ of them play soccer. How many of the students
    do not play soccer?   _____

Extension: Each game is 90 minutes long. Eleven players per team are on the
field at one time. If each of the 24 players on a team must play for an equal
fraction of the time, how long will each team member play?

Learn at Home, Grade 6

The Spectrum Color Wheel

White light is made up of seven colors of the spectrum: red, orange, yellow, green, blue, indigo and violet. You can see these colors in a rainbow or when light passes through a glass prism.

You will need: a compass, a piece of white poster board, a short nail or screw, a hand drill

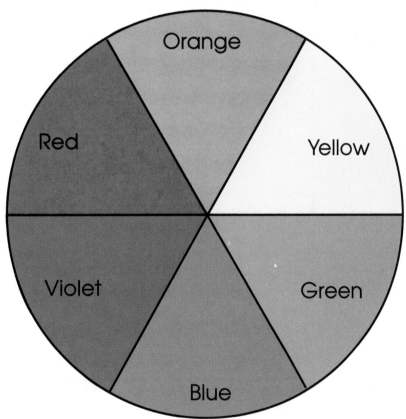

Making a Color Wheel

Set your compass at a radius of 2 inches. Draw a circle on the poster board and mark a point on the circle. Keep your compass setting the same and draw six arcs around the circle. Make a point where each arc crosses the circle. Next, draw lines from each point to the center of the circle. Color each section in this order: red, orange, yellow, green, blue and violet. Cut out the circle.

Turning the Color Wheel

Have an adult help you press a short nail or screw through the center of the color wheel. Place the nail in the bit of a small hand drill. Lock it tightly in place. Turn on the drill and watch the color wheel spin. What happens? _____

_____

219

	Language Skills	Spelling	Reading
Monday	Have your child choose a topic, make a plan for writing and begin working on a rough draft.	Pretest your child on these spelling words: infect · inspire · instruct inflate · install · insult inform · instant · intense injury · instead · intent insecure · instinct · intrude insist · institute · invade Have your child correct the pretest. Add personalized words and make two copies of this week's study list.	**Story Elements** Introduce this week's reading selection. Suggestion: *From the Mixed-Up Files of Mrs. Basil E. Frankweiler* by E. L. Konigsburg. Discuss the elements of a story. Use a serial comic strip to review the elements. *See* Reading, Week 22, number 1.
Tuesday	**Diagramming Sentences:** Teach your child to diagram sentences with appositives. An *appositive* is a phrase set off by commas that explains a nearby noun or noun phrase. In diagramming, appositives are written in parentheses following the words they explain. Have your child complete **Appositives** (p. 224).	Review this week's spelling words. Have your child complete **Inflated Inner Tubes** (p. 228).	Discuss the current reading book in a conference. Focus on identifying the conflict and predicting outcomes.
Wednesday	Teach your child to diagram sentences with prepositional phrases. *Prepositional phrases* that act like adjectives are written on diagonal lines beneath the nouns they modify. *Prepositional phrases* that act like adverbs are written on diagonal lines beneath the verbs they modify. Have your child complete **Adjective Prepositional Phrases** (p. 225).	Have your child use each of this week's spelling words correctly in a sentence.	Teach your child to plot the elements of a story on a line graph to track the excitement level. The climax of the story should be the highest point on the graph. *See* Reading, Week 22, number 2.
Thursday	Teach your child to diagram sentences with direct objects. A *direct object* receives the action of the verb. The direct object is placed on the horizontal line after the subject and verb. It is separated from the verb by a vertical line that does not cross below the horizontal line. Have your child complete **Direct Objects** (p. 226).	Have your child study this week's spelling words.	Discuss fact and opinion. Can your child recognize the difference? *See* Reading, Week 22, number 3. Have your child complete **You Be the Judge** (p. 229).
Friday	Teach your child to diagram sentences with indirect objects. An *indirect object* names the person to whom or for whom something is done. The indirect object is placed on a horizontal line parallel to the verb. Modifiers of the indirect object are placed on diagonal lines beneath it. Have your child complete **Indirect Objects** (p. 227).	Give your child the final spelling test. Have your child record pretest and final test words in his/her word bank.	Hold a reading conference to discuss the outcome(s) of the story. Was your child surprised by the ending? Have your child rewrite the ending of the story as he/she would have written it.

Learn at Home, Grade 6

Math	Science	Social Studies
Fractions Teach your child to estimate the products of mixed numbers before multiplying. Then, show your child the procedure for multiplying mixed numbers. *See* Math, Week 22, numbers 1 and 2. Write eight to ten word problems involving multiplication of fractions for your child to solve. *See* Math, Week 22, number 3 for some sample problems.	**Lenses** Allow your child to explore convex and concave lenses. Demonstrate their effects on light. *See* Science, Week 22, numbers 1 and 2.	**The Postwar Period** Discuss the period of American prosperity that immediately followed WWII. *See* Social Studies, Week 22. Discuss events that reached outside of the U.S., such as the formation of an organization called the U.N. and the beginnings of the Cold War. *See* Social Studies, Week 22, numbers 1–4.
Have your child find fractions in designs. Have your child complete **Designing Fractions** (p. 230).	Have your child conduct a simple experiment using a drop of water as a lens. *See* Science, Week 22, number 3.	After WWII, the U.S. tried to avoid the mistakes made after WWI. Have your child compare American attitudes and policies after World War I with those after World War II. Ask your child six questions. *See* Social Studies, Week 22, number 5. Have your child make a list of points for each war, then use those points to construct a short compare-and-contrast essay.
Teach your child the formula for finding the area of a triangle: multiply the length of the base by the height of the triangle, then multiply that number by one-half. **Note:** The height of the triangle is not always the length of a side. area = $\frac{1}{2}$ (b x h) Have your child complete **I'm Hungry!** (p. 231).	Have your child read about nearsightedness, farsightedness and astigmatism. Have your child research how lenses are used to correct these vision problems.	Discuss people who had the greatest influence in the years following WWII. Consider four categories of people: *politicians, entertainers, innovators* and *leaders*. Have your child choose one personality from each category to research. Have him/her explain how the person fits into that particular category and describe the impact that person had on American society.
Generate problems that combine measurement and fractions for your child to solve. **Example:** *Kyle and Traci measured 18 $\frac{5}{6}$ yards from their house to the bus stop. How many feet is that? How many inches?*	Have your child read about professions related to vision and the eyes. What is the distinction between an optometrist and an ophthalmologist?	The Korean War brought the U.S. overseas again just 5 years after the end of WWII. Discuss the involvement of the United Nations and American troops in this battle. Have your child add the Korean War to the time line. Have him/her research the war and write details on an index card.
Use today to catch up and review the material on fractions covered so far. Encourage your child to ask questions if he/she has any. Discuss any difficulties your child may be having with certain concepts.	If possible, arrange a trip to an optical lab where lenses are made, a science lab where an electron microscope is used, an observatory where telescopes are used, a science lab where different types of microscopes are used or a nature trail where binoculars are used.	Arrange for your child to perform a community service. Have your child write in his/her Social Studies Journal.

TEACHING SUGGESTIONS AND ACTIVITIES

READING (Story Elements)

▶ 1. For several days in a row, cut a serial comic strip from the newspaper. Cut the frames apart and put them in an envelope. Have your child arrange the frames in sequential order. When the frames are arranged, discuss the story elements: characters, setting, problem(s), climax and solution(s).

▶ 2. Have your child keep a record of the events in the story as they unfold. Have your child make a line graph. The horizontal axis will show events from the story, and the vertical axis will list level of excitement. See the illustration at right for an example. As the story unfolds, have your child place the events on the graph and plot the level of excitement in pencil. As your child reads, he/she may adjust the excitement levels of the previous events. The completed graph will trace the story's plot.

▶ 3. A *fact* is something that is known to be true or that can be measured or counted. An *opinion* is a belief or view held by a person and not necessarily based on fact. Give examples of facts and opinions. Have your child identify whether each statement is a fact or an opinion. Discuss clue words that help identify the statement.

Examples:

The temperature is below freezing.

It's like the North Pole outside.

It appears that someone took my money.

I am missing fifteen dollars from my purse.

There seems to be a delay.

The bus is an hour late.

My vegetables are the best in town.

My tomatoes won first prize at the garden show.

MATH (Fractions)

▶ 1. To estimate the product of two mixed fractions, round each fraction to the nearest whole number. Decide if each fraction is less than or greater than $1/2$. If the fraction is greater than $1/2$, round to the next whole number. If the fraction is less than $1/2$, the whole number stays the same.

Example: Estimate the product of $5^7/10 \times 2^3/10$

　　　Round $5^7/10$
　　　Since $7/10$ is greater than $1/2$, round up to 6.
　　　Round $2^3/10$
　　　Since $3/10$ is less than $1/2$, round down to 2.
　　　$6 \times 2 = 12$

Hint: If you are not sure whether a fraction is greater than or less than $1/2$, multiply the numerator by 2. If the product is greater than the denominator, the fraction is greater than $1/2$. If the product is less than the denominator, the fraction is less than $1/2$.

▶ 2. If one factor in a multiplication problem is a fraction, then all factors must be fractions. If any of the factors is a mixed number, it must be converted into an improper fraction.

▶ 3. Generate eight to ten word problems involving multiplication of fractions for your child to solve. Center the problems around a common theme.

Examples:

　a. Jenna sold $7^1/2$ flats of strawberries at the farmer's market. Michael sold $2^2/3$ times that many. How many flats of strawberries did Michael sell?

　b. Kari bought a $8^1/4$-ounce jar of honey at the market. Hugh bought a jar that was $3/4$ that size. How many ounces of honey did Hugh buy?

　c. Gregor sold $12^3/5$ pounds of organic potatoes. Jonah, who owns a small restaurant, bought $10^1/2$ times as many potatoes. How many potatoes did Jonah buy?

Learn at Home, Grade 6

d. Gwen sold 17 heads of lettuce. Each weighed approximately $2^4/_9$ pounds. How many pounds of lettuce did Gwen sell all together?

SCIENCE (Lenses)

▶ 1. Display a variety of convex and concave lenses (a magnifying glass, binoculars, a telescope, eyeglasses, a paperweight, a camera). Have your child look at the same object through a magnifying lens, binoculars, telescope or eyeglasses. Ask your child to describe how the object looks with and without the lens. Then, have your child hold a magnifying glass or eyeglass lens in front of a flashlight and describe the light's projection. Go outside and have your child project the sunlight onto a sidewalk or a piece of cardboard with a magnifying glass.

▶ 2. A convex lens is thicker in the center than on the edges. Light can be projected through this type of lens for use in motion-picture projectors. A concave lens is thinner in the center than on the edges and cannot be used to project light onto an object. Concave lenses are used to correct nearsighted vision.

▶ 3. Place a drop of water on the glossy cover of a magazine so that the droplet is over some letters or numbers. Examine the shape of the droplet to determine whether it is a convex or concave lens. Look through the droplet of water to see how it magnifies the print underneath.

SOCIAL STUDIES (The Postwar Period)

BACKGROUND
Between 1945 and the early 1960s, there were plenty of jobs to go around. The United States was producing a fascinating variety of goods for people who had done without during wartime shortages. Government-backed loans made it possible for a young married couple to buy a new home with a down payment of only a few hundred dollars. Exciting new cars rolled off the assembly line and into the family garage. America's factories were making all kinds of labor-saving devices for homes and farms. Medical science produced thousands of new medical products, such as the anti-polio vaccine. Never before in history had so many people enjoyed so much prosperity. People were too busy concentrating on getting ahead to care about world affairs.

▶ 1. Immediately after the war, the U.S. and other countries established a group called the United Nations (UN) dedicated to keeping world peace. Have your child look in a recent newspaper for information on what the UN is currently discussing and debating.

▶ 2. The Cold War began after WWII when the Soviet Union used military force to install communist governments in eastern European countries. This action generated fear that the Soviet Union would try to communize western Europe as well. Have your child explain the term *Cold War.*

▶ 3. Provide information on the Cold War for your child's reference. Have him/her define the following vocabulary words related to the Cold War:

Berlin Blockade	capitalism	compromise	neutral country
Berlin Wall	Cold War	Imperialism	occupation zones
bloc	communism	Iron Curtain	satellites

▶ 4. The use of the atom bomb in Japan during WWII ushered in the nuclear age. Both superpowers (the United States and the Soviet Union) in the Cold War built up an arsenal of nuclear weapons. Fortunately, none were ever fired.

▶ 5. Ask your child the following six questions. Have him/her respond to each question twice: once for the years immediately after WWI and once for the years immediately after WWII.

> *How did Congress and the rest of the country prepare for returning veterans?*
> *What was the United States' attitude toward European nations?*
> *What was the relationship between labor unions and the changing economy?*
> *What changes happened in terms of population growth and shifts?*
> *What was the attitude of the American republic toward foreign relations?*
> *What attitudes and situations prevailed in the area of race relations?*

Appositives
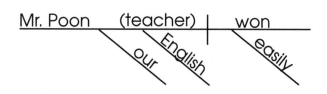

An **appositive** is placed in parentheses following the word it identifies or explains. Any words that modify the appositive should be placed on diagonal lines directly beneath it.

Examples:

Mr. Poon, our English teacher, won easily.

Venice, a famous Italian city, was conquered that year.

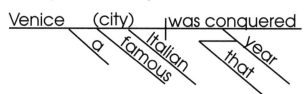

Read the following sentences. **Underline** the appositives once and their modifiers twice. Then, diagram the sentences on another sheet of paper.

1. Kerri, my older sister, left immediately.

2. His car, a vintage roadster, crashed.

3. The senator, a Democrat, voted today.

4. That man, the village chief, will command.

5. Baseball, my favorite sport, ended yesterday.

6. The dog, a huge shepherd, jumped up.

Create sentences to fit the diagrams below. **Write out** each sentence before writing it in the diagram.

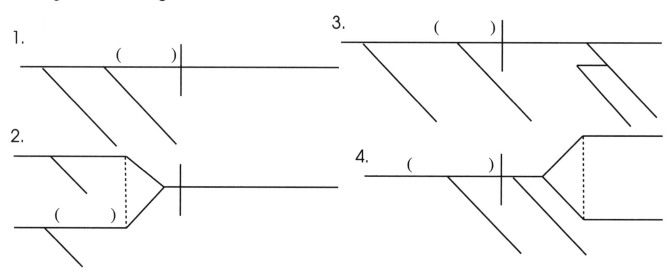

Learn at Home, Grade 6

Adjective Prepositional Phrases

Adjective prepositional phrases are placed beneath the nouns they modify. The preposition is placed on a slanted line and its object is placed on a horizontal line connected to it. Modifiers of the object of the preposition are placed on slanted lines beneath the object.

Examples:

The puppy in the shop window jumped up.

The novel by Hemingway was finally located.

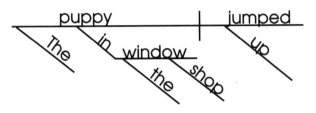
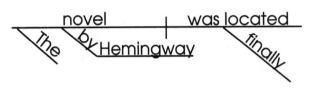

Read the following sentences. **Underline** the prepositions once and their objects twice. Then, diagram the sentences on another sheet of paper.

1. My friend with the broken arm is leaving.

2. The drugstore in town burned last night.

3. The musical with the best choreography will win.

4. A man in a red jumpsuit and a woman in a yellow dress ran away.

5. The music on the radio is disrupting.

6. The doctors in the hospital are working very hard.

Create sentences to fit the diagrams. **Write out** each sentence before writing it in the diagram.

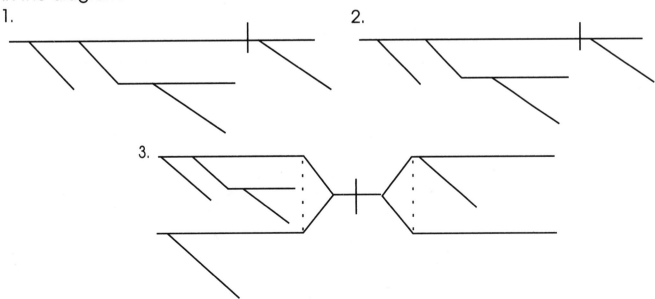

Direct Objects

A **direct object** is placed on the same horizontal line as the subject and the verb. It is separated from the verb by a short vertical line which does not cross the horizontal line. Modifiers of the direct object are placed on diagonal lines directly beneath it.

Examples:

The men tracked a bear.

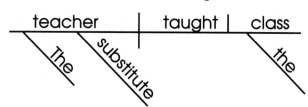

The substitute teacher taught the class.

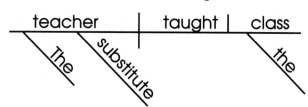

Read the following sentences. **Underline** the verbs once and the direct objects twice. Then, diagram the sentences on another sheet of paper.

1. The Polar Bears won the championship.

2. Darcy answered the teacher's question.

3. The salesclerk in the men's department sold every pink shirt in stock.

4. Marcel received a check and other gifts.

5. The three networks sent their best reporters to the scene.

6. A good student will read a newspaper every day.

Create sentences to fit the diagrams. **Write out** each sentence before writing it in the diagram.

1.

3.

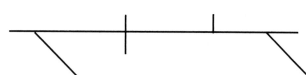

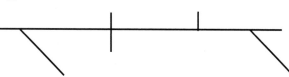

2.

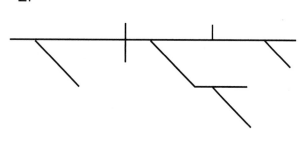

4.

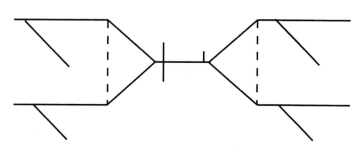

Learn at Home, Grade 6

Indirect Objects

An **indirect object** is always placed below the verb on a line parallel to the verb and connected to it by a diagonal line. Modifiers of the indirect object are placed on slanted diagonal lines directly beneath it.

Examples: I gave them a sheet of paper.

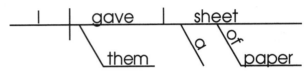

You should write your friend a letter.

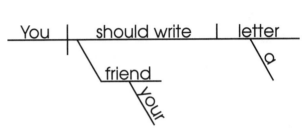

Read the following sentences. **Underline** the verbs once, the direct objects twice and the indirect objects three times. Then, diagram the sentences on another sheet of paper.

1. She gives me a headache.
2. Paul told them the bad news.
3. The director taught the choir a new song.
4. He gave Sharon a symbol of his love.
5. I sent Barbara a postcard from France.
6. The star goalie left his sister two tickets at the gate.

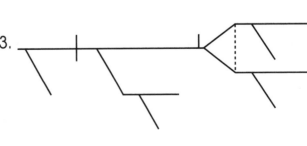

Create sentences to fit the diagrams. **Write out** each sentence before writing it in the diagram.

1.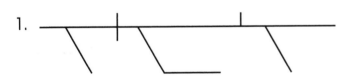

2.

3.

Inflated Inner Tubes

Inflate the inner tubes by adding the missing vowels to each word.

infect
inflate
inform
injury
insecure
insist
inspire
install
instant
instead
instinct
institute
instruct
insult
intense
intent
intrude
invade

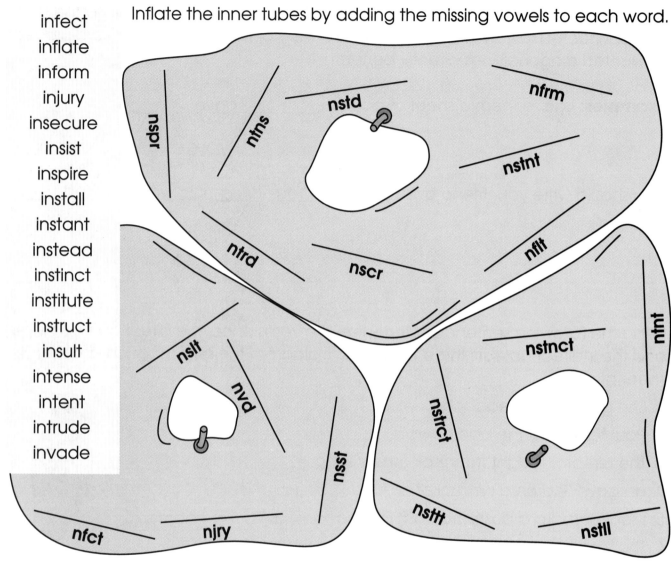

Write a short definition for five of the spelling words.

1. _____

2. _____

3. _____

4. _____

5. _____

Learn at Home, Grade 6

You Be The Judge

The lawyer is asking the witnesses many questions. Some of the answers are facts, some are opinions. The judge will only accept facts. Read each question and answer. Check fact or opinion next to each answer. If you checked fact, write a second answer that is an opinion. If you checked opinion, write a second answer that is a fact.

FACT OPINION?

☐ **fact**	1. **question:**	Mr. Wallace, what was the stranger wearing?
☐ **opinion**	**answer:**	He was wearing a blue coat, red scarf, black slacks and black shoes.

☐ **fact**	2. **question:**	Mr. Henry, what did you hear from your window?
☐ **opinion**	**answer:**	I heard a sound that must have been the intruder breaking in.

☐ **fact**	3. **question:**	Ms. Harris, what time did you notice the broken lock?
☐ **opinion**	**answer:**	It was 10:15 p.m., just as I arrived home.

☐ **fact**	4. **question:**	Mrs. Patterson, do you know the owner of the stolen painting?
☐ **opinion**	**answer:**	He is the nicest boss I have ever worked for.

☐ **fact**	5. **question:**	Mr. Samuels, was the painting insured?
☐ **opinion**	**answer:**	Yes, the painting was insured for ten thousand dollars.

☐ **fact**	6. **question:**	Miss Ryan, did you see the defendant take the painting?
☐ **opinion**	**answer:**	Of course he took it! It had to be him.

Designing Fractions

Mr. Artsy's class was studying design. He drew the following design for the students to study.

Find what fraction each pattern is of the whole square.

1. ▨ = ___   2. ▦ = ___   3. ▦ = ___   4. ▤ = ___

5. ▨ = ___   6. ◉ = ___   7. ▨ = ___   8. ◪ = ___

9. ⬤ = ___   10. ▤ = ___   11. ◆ = ___   12. ◎ = ___

Extension: Make your own design in a square. Look at the patterns and list what fraction of the whole each pattern represents.

Learn at Home, Grade 6

I'm Hungry!

Help Gerry the Giraffe get to the tree by shading in the path that contains the correct areas. Then, find the correct areas for the ones that are wrong.
Remember: area = $\frac{1}{2}$ (b x h)

Learn at Home, Grade 6

© 1999 Tribune Education. All Rights Reserved.

	Language Skills	**Spelling**	**Reading**
Monday	Have your child choose a topic, make a plan for writing and begin working on a rough draft.	Pretest your child on these spelling words: auction digestion operation champion election opinion collection location portion companion mention position competition occupation region cushion onion religion Have your child correct the pretest. Add personalized words and make two copies of this week's study list.	Introduce the new reading selection or continue with the book from last week.
Tuesday	**Writing Paragraphs:** What is a paragraph? Discuss the purpose of a paragraph and what makes a good paragraph. *See* Language Skills, Week 23.	Review this week's spelling words. Have your child complete **Alphabetizing Champion** (p. 236).	Discuss the current reading book in a conference. Focus on plot. Have your child explain what has happened in the story so far.
Wednesday	Have your child write a topic sentence for each topic listed below. Each topic sentence should express an opinion or feeling about the topic. Save the topic sentences for later lessons. homesick saving energy a nightmare leftovers made in America sick in bed cats as pets hot breezes a safe environment rising smoke	Have your child use each of this week's spelling words correctly in a sentence.	**Summarizing:** Review the skill of summarizing. Ask your child to recall a familiar children's story, such as *Little Red Riding Hood,* and tell you what the story is about. Point out that his/her response is a "summary." A story summary is a brief description of the problem and events in a story. A summary may also include an evaluation or opinion. Have your child write a summary of one chapter from the book he/she is reading.
Thursday	Have your child choose one of the topic sentences written yesterday. Ask your child to fill out a paragraph by writing sentences that contain details to support the topic sentence.	Have your child study this week's spelling words.	Newspaper articles often state in the first paragraph what you can expect to read in the rest of the article. Read several newspaper articles with your child and summarize and discuss what the articles are about. Have your child read a newspaper article on a topic of interest. Have your child write a summary of the article.
Friday	Have your child write an ending sentence for the paragraph that restates the topic sentence or reminds the reader of the point of the paragraph. The final sentence should be strong and interesting. Encourage your child to use humor or descriptive language when appropriate.	Give your child the final spelling test. Have your child record pretest and final test words in his/her word bank.	Hold a reading conference. Have your child choose and read aloud passages from the book that create strong visual images in the mind of the reader.

Learn at Home, Grade 6

Math	Science	Social Studies
Division of Fractions Teach your child how to divide fractions. *See* Math, Week 23, numbers 1 and 2. Have your child complete **Dividing Fractions** (p. 237).	**Light** Explain the difference between incandescent and fluorescent light bulbs. *See* Science, Week 23, number 1. Have your child count the number of incandescent and fluorescent lights in your house. Have your child plot the information on a bar graph to compare the two. Discuss the difference in energy costs between the two types of bulbs.	**The Protest Years** The 1960 and 1970s saw many protests. *See* Social Studies, Week 23. The biggest social issue of the 1960s was civil rights. Discuss the rights that have been won over the years. Review the **Synopsis of Civil Rights Acts** (p. 241) with your child. Have your child write an example of someone acting under the authority of each act. *See also* Social Studies, Week 23, number 1.
Discuss practical situations in which you would need to divide fractions. Have your child complete **Art Show** (p. 238).	Your child may already be familiar with a strobe light, which creates the illusion that something is moving differently than it is. Have your child imitate the effects of a strobe light with a stroboscope. Have your child complete **Stroboscope** (p. 240).	Add presidents from the 1960s and early 1970s to the time line. Have your child write the names of Presidents John Kennedy, Lyndon Johnson, Richard Nixon and Gerald Ford on index cards followed by their years in office. Have your child read about each president, then write at least three things that happened during each one's administration on the backs of the index cards. Attach the cards to the time line.
Provide your child with situational problems to solve using division of fractions. *See* Math, Week 23, number 3.	Demonstrate the science of chromatography, or the separation of colors. *See* Science, Week 23, number 2. Have your child repeat the chromatography experiment, testing different variables. For the first round of tests, have your child vary the paper; for the second round, the liquid solvent; for the third round, the source of pigment. *See* Science, Week 23, number 3.	Have your child locate Vietnam on a map. Have him/her read about the Vietnam War. *See* Social Studies, Week 23, number 2. Discuss. Add the dates of the war (1957–1975) and U.S. involvement to the time line. Look at political cartoons from this period. Discuss the symbolism of the hawk and dove. Have your child draw a political cartoon (one that might have appeared at the time of the war) to comment on the Vietnam War.
Continue to discuss and practice division with fractions. Have your child complete **Invert and Multiply** (p. 239).	Demonstrate the spectrum of light using soap bubbles. Buy some bubble solution with a wand and have your child blow bubbles in the sunlight. Observe the colors that appear on the bubbles. The bubbles refract light much like raindrops refract light to produce rainbows. *See* Science, Week 23, number 4.	Ask your child to contemplate what he/she has learned about the protest years. Have your child write a poem using couplets beginning with the following phrases: I used to think . . . But now I know . . .
Show your child how to change fractions and mixed numbers to percents. Divide the numerator by the denominator. Move the decimal two places to the right before adding the percent sign. **Example:** $\dfrac{9}{10}$ $9 \div 10 = 0.9$ Move the decimal: 90.0 Add the percent sign: 90%	Have your child write a poem, story or riddle about light. Encourage your child to include vocabulary and concepts discussed in his/her writing.	Arrange for your child to perform a community service. Have your child write in his/her Social Studies Journal.

TEACHING SUGGESTIONS AND ACTIVITIES

LANGUAGE SKILLS (Writing Paragraphs)

A good paragraph should focus on one topic and contain a strong beginning, middle and end. The beginning of a paragraph is often the topic sentence. A *topic sentence* should grab the reader's attention and state what the paragraph is about. The best topic sentence states an opinion or feeling about the topic. This sets the stage for the rest of the paragraph to support this feeling or opinion. The middle of the paragraph includes details and supports the topic sentence. The end of the paragraph follows all the details and restates the topic sentence or reminds the reader of the point of the paragraph.

MATH (Division of Fractions)

▶ 1. To divide fractions, simply invert and multiply. In other words, multiply the first fraction by the *reciprocal* (or inversion) of the second fraction. Read the following scenario to teach the concept of reciprocal fraction.

James has 12 ounces of soda in a can. He wants to divide it evenly among himself and two friends. James has to figure out how many ounces to give each of them. James can divide 12 ounces by 3 to find that each person will get 4 ounces. But with what James knows about fractions, he can also multiply 12 by $^1/_3$ to get the same answer. One-third is the reciprocal of 3.

The reciprocal is found by inverting the fraction. Have your child find the reciprocal of a variety of numbers, including whole numbers, fractions and mixed numbers.
What is the reciprocal of . . .

$^2/_3$ ($^3/_2$) $2^1/_6 = {}^{13}/_6$ ($^6/_{13}$) 5 ($^1/_5$)

▶ 2. To divide fractions, multiply the first fraction by the reciprocal of the second fraction.
Example: $^4/_5 \div {}^2/_6 = {}^4/_5 \times {}^6/_2 = {}^{24}/_{10} = {}^{12}/_5 = 2^2/_5$

▶ 3. Copy or read aloud the following situational problems for your child to solve.

 a. Dottie fixed $^2/_3$ of the box of flapjack mix for breakfast. Each flapjack consisted of $^1/_8$ of the batter that she mixed. How many delicious flapjacks was she able to make using these portions?

 b. There was $^2/_3$ of the huge king salmon in the refrigerator at Andy's house ready to be served. If the family ate $^5/_{10}$ of this at each meal, how many meals will it take to finish this delicious fish?

 c. There is $^5/_9$ of the red watermelon left to enjoy. If Jerry's family cuts up and eats $^4/_8$ of it at a time, how many times will it take the family to finish it?

 d. Doug still needs to clean $^1/_3$ of the pool before he can go on his trip to the mountains. If he cleans $^5/_8$ of this amount in 1 hour, how many hours will it take for him to complete this task?

 e. Lowell has $^5/_9$ of a quart of orange juice to share with his friends on a field trip. If each friend gets $^1/_4$ of a quart, how many friends get orange juice on the trip?

SCIENCE (Light)

▶ 1. Observe the inner workings of a clear incandescent light bulb and a fluorescent light bulb. Explain the differences between these two types of bulbs and the light that they produce.

The incandescent light is produced by heat. Have your child imagine a burning candle—the candle produces both heat and light. Ask your child to name some other devices that produce both heat and light (toaster, oven coils, burning charcoal, the sun). Put the incandescent light bulb in a lamp and observe the filament in the bulb when it is turned on.

Fluorescent light is produced when ultraviolet rays strike phosphors inside a bulb. The fluorescent bulb or tube is filled with gas. The inside of the bulb is coated with phosphors, chemicals that glow when ultraviolet radiation is present. Fluorescent light is much cooler than incandescent light and uses much less electrical energy. If you have a fluorescent light, have your child observe and feel the lighted bulb.

Learn at Home, Grade 6

2. Use a water-soluble black marking pen to make a large dot on a paper coffee filter. Have your child use an eyedropper to add drops of water to the black dot and observe the changes for a few minutes. The colors that are part of the black pigment should begin to separate. Ask your child to describe the order of colors observed after a few minutes and how this order is similar to the color spectrum studied earlier.

3. For the paper, your child could use a paper towel, a tissue, a sheet of newsprint or an index card. The liquid solvent could be water, ammonia, rubbing alcohol, vinegar or a soft drink. The pigment could come from paint, flower or leaf stains, ink or food coloring.

4. Help your child conduct a second experiment with bubbles. Cover a table or desk with a sheet of plastic (a garbage bag works well). Pour a small amount of liquid detergent solution onto the center of the plastic. Have your child hold a drinking straw straight down in the solution and blow gently until a bubble appears. As the child continues to blow, the bubble will get much larger. Have your child describe the colors in the bubble. Use different liquid detergents to determine which brand produces the largest or the most colorful bubbles.

SOCIAL STUDIES (The Protest Years)

BACKGROUND

The 1960s and early 1970s were disturbing and disorderly times in the United States. It was a period of both great idealism and great upheaval. One president was assassinated, another declined to run again because of opposition to an undeclared war and a third, facing impeachment, resigned.

Thousands of boycotts, demonstrations, sit-ins and marches occurred during this period as various advocates came on the scene and began to exert influence. Each of these advocates had a particular message and means of delivery. Just as Martin Luther King, Jr., became the symbol of civil rights agitation, Ralph Nader emerged as the defender of American consumers against defective and unsafe products. Bob Dylan, with his folk songs, expressed the hopes and angers of his generation. Women such as Gloria Steinem and Shirley Chisholm held up the hope for equal opportunity for women.

Another reason for protest was the Vietnam War. Peace advocates viewed U.S. involvement in the war as immoral and an improper use of human and economic resources. Supporters believed the war was necessary to stop the spread of communism in Asia.

1. Read aloud each situation below. Have your child tell which civil rights act is demonstrated.

    Valerie had not been allowed to vote before, so she got help registering. (1960)

    The doors were open to everyone who wanted to see the movie. (1964)

    My father realized that the government was using an incorrect middle name for him. (1974)

    The architect of the new building made sure all passageways were wide enough for a wheelchair to pass through. (1990)

2. Have your child try to answer the questions below as he/she reads about the Vietnam War.

    What were the reasons for U.S. involvement in the war?

    What countries fought in the war? Do you think all the parties who fought should have been involved? Give reasons for your opinions.

    Was America's security at risk in any way?

    Identify the "hawks" and "doves."

religion
region
portion
collection
competition
companion
onion
champion
cushion
opinion
auction
occupation
election
operation
location
mention
digestion
position

Write each spelling word in the correct category and in alphabetical order.

two-syllable words

_____

_____

_____

_____

_____

_____

four-syllable words

_____

_____

_____

three-syllable words

_____

_____

_____

_____

_____

_____

_____

Learn at Home, Grade 6

Dividing Fractions

$6 \div \frac{1}{4}$

Step 1: Write both numbers as fractions. $\frac{6}{1} \div \frac{1}{4}$

Step 2: Invert the second fraction and multiply. $\frac{6}{1} \times \frac{4}{1}$

Step 3: Reduce. $\frac{24}{1} = 24$

Solve each problem.

1. $7 \div \frac{1}{3}$

2. $8 \div \frac{1}{2}$

3. $16 \div \frac{1}{3}$

4. $6 \div \frac{1}{2}$

5. $5 \div \frac{1}{6}$

6. $18 \div \frac{1}{7}$

7. $8 \div \frac{1}{5}$

8. $7 \div \frac{1}{9}$

9. $15 \div \frac{1}{6}$

Art Show

Ms. Creative had her students busy preparing for the year-end art show.

1. Kelly needed to finish seven paintings for the show. If she painted $\frac{1}{3}$ of a painting each session, how many sessions would it take her to finish all seven? _____

2. Fong's responsibility was to glaze six pieces of pottery. He was able to complete $\frac{1}{4}$ of a pot's glaze in one class. How many classes will it take him to glaze all six pieces? _____

3. Karen needed to have nine black-and-white sketches finished for the show. If she finished about $\frac{2}{4}$ of one in each class, how many classes would it take Karen to finish all nine? _____

4. Two sculptures were needed to highlight the entrance of the exhibit. One-sixteenth of each sculpture was completed in each art class. How many classes will it take to complete both sculptures? _____

5. The students took a sheet of art paper that was $\frac{8}{9}$ of a yard long to make a mural. Once the mural was complete it needed to be cut into sections, each $\frac{2}{18}$ of a yard long. How many pieces will there be? _____

6. A painted carousel horse was the hit of the show. Three-tenths was painted each day. How many days did it take to finish? _____

Extension:

Divide by $\frac{2}{4}$	
$\frac{3}{8}$	a.
5	b.
$\frac{10}{6}$	c.

Divide by $\frac{1}{3}$	
4	a.
$\frac{3}{8}$	b.
$\frac{8}{10}$	c.

Learn at Home, Grade 6

Invert and Multiply

Solve the problems. Reduce
your answers to lowest terms.

1. $\dfrac{1}{5} \div 3$

2. $\dfrac{5}{7} \div 15$

3. $\dfrac{7}{8} \div 21$

4. $\dfrac{3}{5} \div 12$

5. $\dfrac{3}{7} \div 6$

6. $\dfrac{3}{8} \div 6$

7. $\dfrac{5}{7} \div 10$

8. $\dfrac{5}{6} \div 15$

9. $\dfrac{7}{10} \div 2$

10. $\dfrac{7}{8} \div 14$

11. $\dfrac{7}{9} \div 7$

12. $\dfrac{1}{4} \div 3$

Stroboscope

You will need: a 6-inch square piece of poster board, a straight pin, a pencil with an eraser

Making a Stroboscope

Cut out the pattern shown below. Place the pattern on a piece of poster board and **cut it out** carefully. Push a pin through the center of the disk, then into the eraser of a pencil.

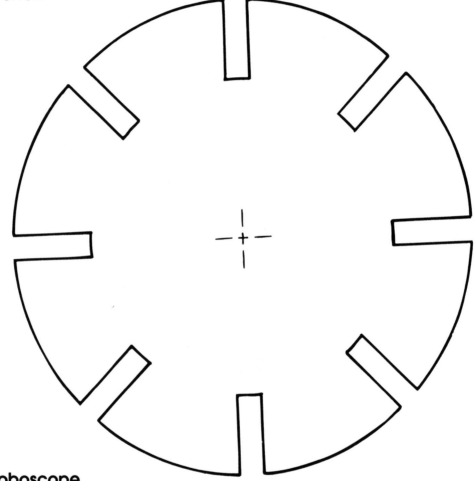

Using the Stroboscope

Hold the stroboscope in front of one eye. Look at a rotating object such as a fan while you spin the disk. What does it look like? _____

Making and Testing Hypotheses

What would happen if the fan were moving faster? _____
_____

Look into a mirror and spin the scope. What happens? _____
_____

Design another stroboscope with a disk of another size. Try more or fewer notches.

Learn at Home, Grade 6

Synopsis of Civil Rights Acts

1957 — **Civil Rights Act of 1957**
Set up Commission on Civil Rights to investigate civil rights violations. Creates Civil Rights Division in Department of Justice to enforce federal civil rights laws and regulations.

1960 — **Civil Rights Act of 1960**
Provides referees to help African Americans register to vote.

1964 — **Civil Rights Act of 1964**
Orders businesses that serve people to do so regardless of race, color, religion or national origin. Bars discrimination by employers and unions. Establishes Equal Employment Opportunity Commission to enforce fair employment policies. Cuts off federal funding for any program or activity which allows racial discrimination.

1968 — **Civil Rights Act of 1968**
Ends discrimination in sale or rental of housing.

1974 — **Privacy Act**
Makes it possible for U.S. residents to check themselves in government files and request correction.
Right of Privacy Law
Recognizes a person's right not to have pictures used for advertising without permission.

1990 — **Americans With Disabilities Act**
Protects handicapped people from discrimination by private employers. Requires that buildings and mass transportation be accessible to disabled people. Orders phone companies to provide devices to people with speech and hearing disorders so they can make and receive calls.

1991 — **Civil Rights Act of 1991**
Makes winning job discrimination suits easier for workers. Employer must prove that his/her hiring or promotion practices are necessary to his/her business. Gives victims the right to sue for monetary damages in cases of intentional job discrimination based on sex, religion, national origin or disability.

	Language Skills	**Spelling**	**Reading**
Monday	**Writing Paragraphs** Have your child choose a topic, make a plan for writing and begin working on a rough draft. Encourage your child to practice writing strong paragraphs.	Pretest your child on these spelling words: chemical medical surgical classical musical technical comical optical theatrical cylindrical practical tropical electrical radical typical identical skeptical vertical Have your child correct the pretest. Add personalized words and make two copies of this week's study list.	Introduce this week's reading selection or continue with the book from last week.
Tuesday	Find an example of a well-written, strong paragraph from a book. Copy each sentence on a separate index card. Scramble the cards. Have your child arrange the sentences to form a paragraph. Discuss the clues that helped your child order the paragraph.	Review this week's spelling words. Have your child complete **Chemical Reaction** (p. 246).	**Vocabulary:** With your child, discuss this week's reading book in a conference. Focus on vocabulary. Ask your child to write down unfamiliar words from the reading. Have your child guess at their meanings based on context, then look up the definitions in a dictionary. How accurate were your child's guesses?
Wednesday	Look at several models of good paragraphs and discuss the elements of a strong paragraph. *See* Language Skills, Week 24, number 1.	Have your child use each of this week's spelling words correctly in a sentence.	Ask your child to look up the word *etymology* and write a definition in his/her own words. Then, discuss the meaning of the word *etymology* and explore word origins as indicated in the dictionary. *See* Reading, Week 24, number 1.
Thursday	Have your child choose one of the topic sentences generated on Wednesday, Week 23. Brainstorm a list of feelings, adjectives and adverbs associated with the topic. Have your child write a descriptive paragraph incorporating several words from the list. *See* Language Skills, Week 24, number 2.	Have your child study this week's spelling words.	Look through a dictionary with your child to find words with origins in Latin, Spanish or French. Many English words have origins in other languages. Introduce your child to common English words that have origins in other languages. Have your child use these words in sentences. *See* Reading, Week 24, number 2.

Friday	Have your child write a topic sentence and two supporting sentences about each of the following subjects:
	    a trip to the dentist
	    a scary dream
	    holiday times
	    shopping for a gift
	    favorite season
		Give your child the final spelling test. Have your child record pretest and final test words in his/her word bank.	Hold a reading conference with your child. Discuss the meaning of new words in context.
			Have your child complete **Do You Speak Spanish?** (p. 247).

Learn at Home, Grade 6

Math	Science	Social Studies
Fractions How can you tell which of two fractions is larger without drawing a picture? Ask your child to come up with a procedure for comparing fractions. If your child has difficulty, remind him/her that if the denominators are the same, it is easy to compare fractions. *See* Math, Week 24, number 1.	**Sound** *Sound* is caused by *vibrations*. *See* Science, Week 24. Ask your child to tell you where the vibration is when we use our voices. Ask your child to touch his/her throat while speaking or singing. Then, have him/her whisper and then mouth some words. Have your child describe the difference in the vibrations felt on the throat. *See* Science, Week 24, number 1.	**The Protest Years** President Kennedy brought youth to the White House when he took office in 1961. He brought many changes to America in an effort many called the *New Frontier*. Among his goals was putting a man on the moon before 1970. Have your child research and list the accomplishments in space from the time that NASA was created to the time that Neil Armstrong and Edwin Aldrin stepped foot on the moon.
To keep fractions in simplest terms when choosing a common denominator, use the *least common multiple*. *See* Math, Week 24, number 2.	Have your child make a poster showing the many sources of sound using pictures from old magazines, newspapers, ads and catalogs. Have your child group the pictures into categories (artificial sounds, musical instruments, sounds of nature) and label them. Other poster themes might include *Early Uses of Sound, Communications Through Sound, History of Sound, Noise Pollution*.	The women's movement made great strides in the 1970s. The ERA had a tremendous influence on women in America. Career opportunities and equal pay for women improved. *See* Social Studies, Week 24, number 1. Have your child write a letter expressing his/her opinion as to whether or not the ERA should be ratified.
Adding fractions is simple when the denominators are the same. Simply add the numerators and keep the same denominator. When there are mixed numbers involved, add the whole numbers, then the fractions. Have your child complete **Egyptian Math** (p. 248).	Sound is made by vibration. Changing the tightness of a vibrating string changes the character of the sound. *See* Science, Week 24, number 2. An *oscilloscope* is an instrument that can detect the variation in frequency and pitch of sound vibrations. Help your child make a simple oscilloscope. *See* Science, Week 24, number 3.	Discuss the rising concern about pollution and conservation. *See* Social Studies, Week 24, number 2. Discuss the oil crisis of the 1970s. What impact did it have? How did it change people's attitudes toward cars and driving?
When adding fractions with unlike denominators, find equivalent fractions for one or both fractions so the denominators are the same. Find the *least common multiple* of the denominators and make equivalent fractions, then add. Have your child complete **Adding Unlike Fractions** (p. 249).	Study how the human ear works to admit sound vibrations. Have your child read about the different parts of the ear and their functions. Have your child draw and label a diagram of the inner ear. Discuss hearing impairments and what causes them.	Have your child add presidents from the late 1970s to the present to the time line. Have your child write the names of Presidents Jimmy Carter, Ronald Reagan, George Bush, Bill Clinton and any succeeding presidents on index cards followed by their years in office. On the back of each card, have your child list at least three things that happened during each president's administration. Then, have your child attach the cards to the time line.
When adding mixed numbers, add the whole numbers first, then the fractions. Generate fifteen to twenty addition problems with fractions and mixed numbers. Have your child solve the problems, reducing his/her answers to lowest terms.	Have your child design and create a stringed instrument that produces at least four different notes.	Arrange for your child to perform a community service. Have your child write in his/her Social Studies Journal.

TEACHING SUGGESTIONS AND ACTIVITIES

LANGUAGE SKILLS (Writing Paragraphs)

▶ 1. Look through a variety of books and magazines and select strong paragraphs for your child to read. Have your child read each paragraph, identify the main idea and describe the purpose of the supporting sentences (to describe, explain, compare or persuade).

▶ 2. Sometimes it is helpful to make an outline before writing a paragraph.

Topic Sentence: I could tell that my mom had been baking.

    I. There were several clues.

        A. Aroma of cinnamon

        B. Warmth from the oven

        C. My mouth started watering

    II. I ran to the kitchen.

Ending Sentence: My mom makes the best cinnamon raisin cookies in town.

Final Paragraph:

I could tell that my mom had been baking. When I opened the door to the house, I felt a rush of warmth from the oven's heat. The aroma of cinnamon met me at the door, and my mouth started watering in anticipation. When I ran to the kitchen, I saw my favorite cookies cooling on the rack. My mom makes the best cinnamon raisin cookies in town.

READING (Vocabulary)

▶ 1. Ask your child to think of last names that are also common nouns, such as Baker, Smith, Tanner and Snow. Discuss the origin of names. Sometimes people took on names that indicated their profession. Sometimes inventions are named after the people who invented them. Have your child look up the following words in the dictionary. Ask the child to write two meanings for each word.

    limerick   Rugby   Ford   Chateaubriand

    Chesterfield   sandwich   Panama   Tony

▶ 2. Review the dictionary symbols (abbreviations) that indicate word origins. Write the following words, or words of your own, on the chalkboard.

    boulevard   chapeau   digit   lariat   menu   mustache

    oleander   poncho   robot   siesta   taco   valet

Tell your child to copy the words on a sheet of writing paper, leaving about five lines between them. After each word, have your child write the origin of the word in parentheses. Then, have your child write the definition of the word and use the word correctly in a sentence.

MATH (Fractions)

▶ 1. It may be hard for your child to tell which fraction is larger: $^5/_6$ or $^{11}/_{12}$. The best way to compare fractions is to find a common denominator. In this case, the common denominator would be 12. Multiply the numerator and denominator by 2, and $^5/_6$ becomes $^{10}/_{12}$. Now it is easy to see that $^{11}/_{12}$ is larger than $^5/_6$. When the denominators are the same, comparing these fractions is the same as comparing 10 apples and 11 apples.

▶ 2. The *least common multiple* (LCM) is found by listing all the multiples of both denominators and identifying the smallest multiple both numbers have in common.

Example: What is the least common multiple of the following denominators?

    $\dfrac{5}{6}$ and $\dfrac{13}{15}$ **6:** 6, 12, 18, 24, <u>30</u>, 36

                   15: 15, <u>30</u>, 45, 60

Which fraction is larger? $\dfrac{25}{30}$ $\dfrac{26}{30}$

Learn at Home, Grade 6

SCIENCE (Sound)

BACKGROUND
Sounds are caused by *vibrations*. There are many kinds of sounds including natural, artificial, soft, loud, pleasant, unpleasant, warning, musical, voice, geological, weather, chemical and animal. Sound vibrations reach your eardrums, and messages are sent to your brain to be interpreted. Sounds vary in pitch and loudness. Musical instruments produce sounds through string, wind or percussional vibrations. Instruments such as microphones, megaphones and hearing aids help people to hear sounds better.

▶ 1. Add sound-related vocabulary to the weekly spelling lists as the terms are discussed.

acoustics	decibel	loudness	music	resonance	trough
amplitude	frequency	medium	noise	reverberation	vibration
crest	hertz	megaphone	pitch	timbre	wavelength

▶ 2. Have your child touch his/her throat and make humming sounds. Then, have him/her make some low growls and high screeches and feel the changes in the vibrations on the throat and describe the differences. Stretch a rubber band between your hands and have your child pluck the band as you stretch it tighter and tighter. Ask your child to describe the different sounds produced. The rubber band is similar to the vocal cords in the throat. Different qualities of sound are produced as the vocal cords become tighter or more relaxed. Ask your child to recall a time when he/she was hoarse. What happened to his/her voice? Have your child think of other situations in which vibrations are changed by the tightness of strings or bands of different materials.

▶ 3. Use a can opener to cut a tin can open at both ends. Be careful of any sharp edges. Cover one end of the can with a piece of balloon pulled taut like a drum. Hold it in place with a tight rubber band.

Cut a small piece of thick, reflective plastic (or a piece of mirror). Use rubber cement or glue to stick the plastic to the balloon as shown in the illustration. Be sure not to attach the plastic exactly to the center.

Stand near a strong beam of sunlight coming through a window (or use a flashlight). Hold the oscilloscope so that the sunlight reflects off the plastic like a mirror onto a wall. Sing into the mouth of the can. Watch the wall. Patterns of lines, loops, curves or other shapes should be visible.

SOCIAL STUDIES (The Protest Years)

▶ 1. Have your child read about the *Equal Rights Amendment* (ERA). What does it state? In 1972, Congress passed the ERA. It did not become law, however, because the amendment was not ratified by enough states. Discuss the current state of women's rights. *Are men and women viewed as equals today in the workplace and at home? Support your answer.*

▶ 2. Pollution and conservation became hot issues in the 1970s. Have your child complete one or more of the activities listed below.

    a. Read a newspaper article about pollution or conservation. Write a summary of the article and express an opinion.

    b. Research the development of conservation as a movement. Make a time line of events starting in the early 1900s.

    c. List what your family does to help improve the environment.

    d. Read about antipollution laws passed by the federal government. Do you think pollution should be controlled at the federal or local level? Support your answer.

Chemical Reaction

chemical
classical
comical
cylindrical
electrical
identical
medical
musical
optical
practical
radical
skeptical
surgical
technical
theatrical
tropical
typical
vertical

Rewrite the adjectives from the spelling list and add a noun to make a short phrase.
Example: *political — political reaction*

1._____
2._____
3._____
4._____
5._____
6._____
7._____
8._____
9._____
10._____
11._____
12._____
13._____
14._____
15._____
16._____
17._____
18._____

Write a quatrain (a poem with four rhyming lines).
Try to end each line using a spelling word.

Example: **Me**
Usually I like to be practical,
But sometimes I'd rather be radical.
Occasionally I feel kind of musical,
But the results are often quite comical.

_____
_____
_____
_____

Learn at Home, Grade 6

Do You Speak Spanish?

Read the story. Then, use context clues to translate the **bold** Spanish words into English.

doll	sun	parrot	bookstore	chair
lake	eat	glass	brother	cool
house	mother	teacher	grandpa	good
door	swim	table	school	sick
money	garden	pretty	windows	hot

The **sol** _____ in the sky was shining brightly that day. In our **escuela**

_____, my **maestra** _____ needed to open all **ventanas**

_____ to cool the air. I wished we could leave the building to **nadar**

_____ at the **lago** _____ nearby.

To avoid the heat of my walk to my **casa** _____, I stopped at a

líbreria _____. It felt **bueno** _____ indoors, so I sat and read some

of the colorful and **lindo** _____ magazines. My **silla** _____ was

very hard to sit on so I left. But the weather was **caliente** _____!

At home I stayed in our shaded flower **jardin** _____ so I might feel

the **fresco** _____ breeze. My brother brought me a **vaso** _____

of juice and set it on a **mesa** _____ nearby. I felt **enferma** _____

from the heat.

At suppertime my **abuelo** _____ came for a visit. He knocked at

the **puerta** _____ even though he comes every evening to **comer**

_____. Today, he had **dinero** _____ to buy me a **muneca**

_____ for my collection. He bought my **hermano** _____ a

volleyball. For my **mamá** _____ he bought a **loro** _____ that

talks and squawks too much!

Learn at Home, Grade 6

Egyptian Math

Help build the pyramid by adding the fractions.
Reduce each to its lowest term.

Use the following rule:

$$a + b = c$$

$$\frac{4}{15} \qquad \frac{8}{15} \qquad \frac{1}{15} \qquad \frac{2}{15} \qquad \frac{7}{15}$$

Learn at Home, Grade 6

Adding Unlike Fractions

Example: $\dfrac{4}{5}$ + $\dfrac{1}{4}$

$$\dfrac{4}{5} + \dfrac{1}{4} = \dfrac{4(x4)}{5(x4)} + \dfrac{1(x5)}{4(x5)} = \overset{\text{add}}{\dfrac{16 \longleftrightarrow 5}{20 \longleftrightarrow 20}} = \dfrac{21}{20} = 1\dfrac{1}{20}$$

$\overset{}{\underset{\text{same}}{}}$

5, 10, 15, 20

4, 8, 12, 16, 20

Steps:

1. Find the LCM of both denominators (20).
2. Multiply the numerator and denominator of each fraction by a number to arrive at the LCM.
3. Add numerators.
4. Denominators stay the same.
5. Write improper fractions as mixed numbers.
6. Reduce to lowest terms.

Remember: Since you are multiplying both numerator and denominator by the same number, you are just multiplying the fraction by 1 ($\dfrac{4}{4}$ = 1, $\dfrac{5}{5}$ = 1).

Add.

1. $\dfrac{2}{3}$ + $\dfrac{1}{5}$

2. $\dfrac{3}{4}$ + $\dfrac{1}{6}$

3. $\dfrac{7}{8}$ + $\dfrac{5}{6}$

4. $\dfrac{1}{2}$ + $\dfrac{8}{9}$

5. $\dfrac{11}{12}$ + $\dfrac{1}{4}$

6. $\dfrac{3}{10}$ + $\dfrac{1}{5}$

7. $\dfrac{3}{4}$ + $\dfrac{2}{5}$

8. $\dfrac{5}{8}$ + $\dfrac{9}{10}$

9. $\dfrac{1}{5}$ + $\dfrac{7}{15}$

Language Skills	**Spelling**	**Reading**
Monday — **Writing Paragraphs** Have your child choose a topic, make a plan for writing and begin working on a rough draft. Encourage your child to continue practicing writing strong paragraphs.	Pretest your child on these spelling words: aggravate, appreciate, circulate, enunciate, estimate, fascinate, graduate, hesitate, immigrate, liberate, migrate, narrate, navigate, participate, populate, rotate, terminate, translate. Have your child correct the pretest. Add personalized words and make two copies of this week's study list.	Introduce this week's reading selection. Suggestion: *The Secret Garden* by Frances Hodgson Burnett. **Note:** If you choose to read *The Secret Garden* this week, evaluate your child's comprehension daily. The vocabulary and dialects in the book may be unfamiliar to your child.
Tuesday — Give your child several paragraphs to read and analyze. Use well-written paragraphs found in books and magazines. Alter the paragraphs so there are sentences that do not support the topic sentence, or change the topic sentence so that it does not state the main idea of the paragraph. Have your child improve the paragraphs by crossing out sentences that do not belong or rewriting misfit topic sentences.	Review this week's spelling words. Have your child complete **Migration Fascination** (p. 254).	Discuss the current reading book in a conference. Focus on character analysis.
Wednesday — Have your child plan a paragraph using an outline, concept map or list. Have your child follow these steps to write a good paragraph: Choose a subject. List details about the subject. Write a topic sentence expressing the main idea. Use the details to write support sentences. Write a strong wrap-up sentence. Have your child plan and write a paragraph about a recent event.	Have your child use each of this week's spelling words correctly in a sentence.	Draw a Venn diagram with three circles. Write the names Mary, Dickson and Colin in the circles. Have your child use the diagram to compare and contrast the three characters. Encourage your child to consider physical appearance, behavior, interests and living conditions.
Thursday — Have your child plan and write a persuasive paragraph. The paragraph should present a convincing argument supported by details.	Have your child study this week's spelling words.	**Prefixes/Root Words:** Study prefixes and root words that come from Greek and Latin. *See* Reading, Week 25, numbers 1 and 2. Discuss analogies. Encourage your child to look for similarities and relationships between things. Have your child complete **Sing Is to Song as . . .** (p. 255).
Friday — Have your child plan and write a paragraph that gives directions. The paragraph should present the information clearly and in an order that makes sense.	Give your child the final spelling test. Have your child record pretest and final test words in his/her word bank.	Hold a reading conference. Discuss the ways in which the characters in the story have changed.

Learn at Home, Grade 6

Math	Science	Social Studies
Subtraction of Fractions Subtraction of fractions is simple when the denominators are the same. Simply subtract the numerators and keep the same denominator. Subtracting one-half from three-halves is the same as subtracting one ball from three balls. Give your child twenty subtraction problems with fractions (same denominators) to solve. Review your child's work.	**Sound** Have your child read about and define the term *wavelength*. Demonstrate wavelength using a long rope. *See* Science, Week 25, number 1. *Frequency* is the number of crests or troughs of a sound wave that pass a given point in 1 second. Use the rope to demonstrate how the waves can be made to go faster or slower.	**Moving Toward the Future** Have your child create a time line showing U.S. involvement in world events since the end of the Cold War. Have your child consider American involvement over the years in the following countries: China, the former Soviet Union, Iraq, Iran, Egypt, Israel, Kuwait, the former Yugoslavia, Nicaragua and El Salvador.
Teach your child how to subtract fractions from whole numbers. *See* Math, Week 25, number 1. Have your child complete **Fractions** (p. 256).	Have your child read about and define the terms *pitch*. Pitch is directly related to frequency. The higher the frequency, the higher the pitch. If possible, obtain some tuning forks to demonstrate different pitches. Have your child name things that emit sounds at a high pitch and things that emit sounds at a low pitch. Discuss *amplitude*. *See* Science, Week 25, number 2.	"If we do not learn about the mistakes of the past, we are doomed to repeat them." Ask your child to consider some of the issues confronting society today to see if he/she can find any historical precedents for them. *How did we respond in the past? How should we respond now? How can the past affect the future?* Have your child write an essay about what we as a nation have learned that will help us meet the unknown challenges of the future.
When subtracting fractions with unlike denominators, find equivalent fractions for one or both fractions so the denominators are the same. Find the *least common multiple* of the denominators and make equivalent fractions, then subtract. Have your child complete **Fraction Frenzy** (p. 257).	Have your child read about and define the term *decibel*. Look at a chart showing the decibel levels of common sounds. *See* Science, Week 25, number 3. Generate some problems that require your child to use information from the decibel chart. **Examples:** *How many decibels louder is a power saw than a purring cat? How many times louder is a conversation than a whisper?*	Find a newspaper article that covers a current issue that has implications for the future. Possible topics include homelessness, violence, substance abuse, child abuse, social security, gun control, education and illegal immigration. Ask your child to read the article carefully, then reflect on the information it presents. Pose questions that require your child to find connections between the current issue and past events. *See* Social Studies, Week 25, number 1.
When subtracting mixed numbers, you may need to borrow from the whole number before subtracting. When the fractions have the same denominators, subtract the whole numbers and then the fractions. *See* Math, Week 25, number 2. Have your child complete **Subtracting Unlike Mixed Numbers** (p. 258).	Gather twelve film canisters or plastic eggs for a simple experiment. Place a small object (tack, pea, cotton ball, rice, paper clip, washer, die, marble, etc.) inside each container and label with a number from 1 to 12. Have your child shake the containers and place them in order from softest to loudest. Have your child note the order on paper and guess what each object is before looking inside the containers.	Help your child make a "Hallway of History." Allow your child to develop and draw an image that will help him/her remember the eras of U.S. history. *See* Social Studies, Week 25, number 2.
Estimating sums or differences with fractions is an important skill. It has many practical applications, and it can be used as a self-check to make sure an addition or subtraction answer is reasonable. *See* Math, Week 25, number 3. Have your child complete **Fun Facts** (p. 259).	Have your child write about noise. Let your child decide the format—a poem, an article, a letter to an editor, a riddle. If there is time, have your child illustrate the piece as well.	Arrange for your child to perform a community service. Have your child write in his/her Social Studies Journal.

TEACHING SUGGESTIONS AND ACTIVITIES

READING (Prefixes/Root Words)

▶ 1. Study some prefixes and root words derived from Latin and Greek words. Here is a list to get you started:

anti (against)	bio (life)	graph (write)	octa (eight)	scope (see)
auto (self)	centi (hundred)	mega (large)	phone (sound)	tele (at a distance)
biblio (book)	ex (away from)	micro (small)	photo (light)	tri (three)

▶ 2. Have your child combine some of the root words and prefixes to form words, such as *bibliography, megaphone, microscope* and *photograph*. Then, use the prefixes to form other words, such as *antisocial, expanse, biology, photosynthesis* and *triathlon,* and have your child write the definitions.

MATH (Subtraction of Fractions)

▶ 1. Start with models. Have your child show you five wholes. Ask your child to take away one-half of one whole. Write the same problem on paper. Have your child "borrow" one whole from the five and make it a fraction with a like denominator ($^2/_2$). Then, your child can subtract the fractions.

Example: $5 - ^1/_2$ (Think of 5 as $4^2/_2$) $= 4^2/_2 - ^1/_2 = 4^1/_2$

▶ 2. Use the following problem to demonstrate borrowing from a whole number:

Ling has $2^1/_4$ cups of cooking oil. She used $1^3/_4$ cups in a recipe and wants to figure out how much oil she has left. How can Ling subtract $^3/_4$ cup from $^1/_4$ cup? How much oil does she have left?

To solve this problem, borrow from the ones place of the first fraction.

a. Borrow 1 cup from $2^1/_4$ cups.
b. Write the 1 cup as a fraction. (1 cup is equivalent to $^4/_4$ of a cup.)
c. Add the $^4/_4$ to the first fraction ($^4/_4 + 1^1/_4 = 1^5/_4$).
d. Subtract the second mixed number from the first (altered) mixed number. $1^5/_4 - 1^3/_4$.
e. The answer is $^2/_4$ or $^1/_2$.

▶ 3. Estimating sums or differences involves the same process as estimating products. Decide if each fraction is less than or greater than $^1/_2$. If the fraction is $^1/_2$ or greater, round to the next whole number. If the fraction is less than $^1/_2$, the whole number stays the same. Add or subtract the whole numbers to obtain the estimate.

Hint: If you are not sure whether a fraction is greater than or less than $^1/_2$, multiply the numerator by 2. If this product is greater than the denominator, the fraction is greater than $^1/_2$. If this product is less than the denominator, the fraction is less than $^1/_2$.

SCIENCE (Sound)

▶ 1. Sound waves are measured by their wavelength. A *wavelength* is the distance between a point on one sound wave to the same point on the next wave. Demonstrate waves with a long rope. Have the child hold one end of the rope. Take the other end and swing the rope in an up and down motion to produce a wave effect. Have your child make a sketch of this wave. The highest point on the wave is called the *crest;* the lowest point of the wave is called the *trough.* The distance between one crest and the next crest or between one trough and the next trough is the wavelength.

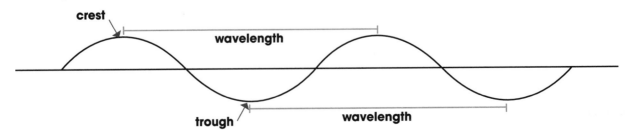

Learn at Home, Grade 6

2. The *amplitude* of a sound wave is the height. Have your child make a soft whispering sound, then a loud yell. The loud yell takes more energy and has a higher amplitude than the soft sound. People who work around loud noises, such as airplanes, machinery, traffic or explosive detonations, wear special ear protection. If possible, borrow some of these ear protectors from a factory or airline worker for your child to examine. With the ear protectors in place, turn on some music to a very high volume and have your child describe the effect. Obtain materials from your doctor on the effects of prolonged exposure to loud noise or music.

3. Explain that the volume of a sound is measured in units called decibels (dB). The following chart lists some decibel readings for common events.

0 dB	threshold of audibility	70–80 dB	street traffic
20 dB	whisper	75 dB	vacuum cleaner
25 dB	purring cat	100 dB	power saw
30 dB	very soft music	110 dB	thunder
40–50 dB	average residence	140 dB	threshold of pain
60 dB	conversation	140–170 dB	jet plane taking off

SOCIAL STUDIES (Moving Toward the Future)

1. Once he/she has read the article, have your child answer the following questions:

   What is the topic of your article?

   What basic issue is involved?

   What might be some solutions to the problem?

   Describe a similar situation from the past.

   What was the outcome?

   Could there have been a better solution?

2. Using the sketch at right as a guide, have your child create an image of a hallway on a piece of poster board. Each room should represent a different era in U.S. history. Have your child label the rooms, adding any applicable notes, then think of an icon to help remember each room. The icon should represent a key moment or event from that particular era and trigger recognition for the child.

   Example: a confederate flag to represent the Civil War period. Have your child sketch an appropriate icon at the entrance to each room.

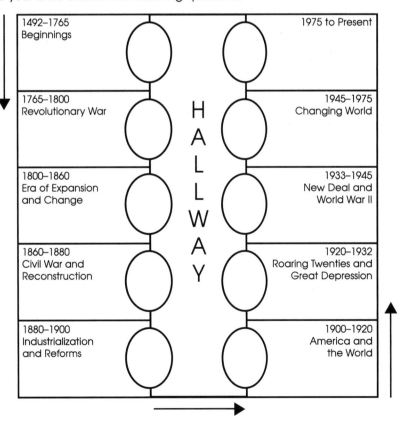

Migration Fascination

aggravate
appreciate
circulate
enunciate
estimate
fascinate
graduate
hesitate
immigrate
liberate
migrate
narrate
navigate
participate
populate
rotate
terminate
translate

Drop the final **e** and add the suffix **tion** to change each verb to a noun form. Then, make word associations by writing the noun form next to a word in the numbered column. The first one is done for you.

1. a sharing   <u>participation</u>

2. boats   _____

3. gifts   _____

4. blood   _____

5. birds   _____

6. slave   _____

7. senior   _____

8. tire   _____

9. entering   _____

10. cost   _____

11. Spanish   _____

12. a play   _____

13. problem   _____

14. words   _____

15. interest   _____

16. final   _____

17. people   _____

18. pausing   _____

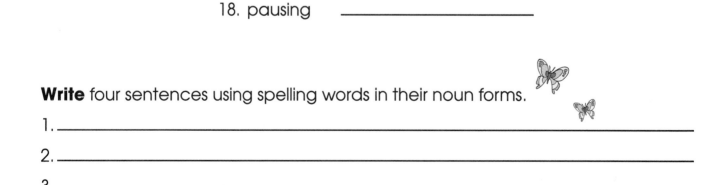

Write four sentences using spelling words in their noun forms.

1. _____

2. _____

3. _____

4. _____

Learn at Home, Grade 6

Sing Is to Song as . . .

Complete each phrase.

1. Glue is to sticking as pencil is to _____.

2. Son is to mother as daughter is to _____.

3. Country is to continent as city is to _____.

4. 5 is to 15 a 4 is to _____.

5. Garage is to car as library is to _____.

6. Victoria is to lake as Pacific is to _____.

7. Hot is to steam as cold is to _____.

8. Weak is to strong as good is to _____.

9. Skin is to human as _____ are to fish.

10. 2 is to bicycle as 3 is to _____.

11. Clipper is to sail as _____ is to paddle.

12. Drama is to act as ballet is to _____.

13. *Adiós* is to Spanish as *au revoir* is to _____.

14. Pilot is to aircraft as nurse is to _____.

15. Damascus is to Syria as Tokyo is to _____.

16. Moo is to herd as _____ is to flock.

17. Lion is to pride as wolf is to _____.

18. Racket is to tennis as club is to _____.

Fractions

Subtract. Reduce your answers to lowest terms and **write** them here. The first one has been done for you.

1. $5 \quad 4\frac{4}{4}$
   $-\frac{3}{4} \quad -\frac{3}{4}$
   $\overline{} \quad 4\frac{1}{4}$

2. 8
   $-\frac{7}{8}$

3. 4
   $-\frac{3}{6}$

4. 10
   $-\frac{3}{8}$

5. 14
   $-\frac{2}{5}$

6. 11
   $-\frac{7}{9}$

7. 4
   $-\frac{3}{5}$

8. 7
   $-\frac{5}{8}$

9. 6
   $-\frac{2}{4}$

10. 12
    $-\frac{3}{6}$

11. 9
    $-\frac{5}{8}$

12. 3
    $-\frac{6}{10}$

13. 7
    $-\frac{3}{4}$

14. 40
    $-\frac{3}{7}$

15. 5
    $-\frac{2}{3}$

16. 8
    $-\frac{5}{9}$

17. 11
    $-\frac{6}{12}$

18. 4
    $-\frac{3}{8}$

19. 6
    $-\frac{5}{7}$

20. 9
    $-\frac{3}{4}$

21. 12
    $-\frac{5}{9}$

22. 4
    $-\frac{6}{11}$

23. 7
    $-\frac{5}{10}$

24. 32
    $-\frac{5}{7}$

25. 25
    $-\frac{3}{4}$

26. 20
    $-\frac{5}{8}$

27. 5
    $-\frac{3}{6}$

28. 8
    $-\frac{2}{5}$

Learn at Home, Grade 6

Fraction Frenzy

Subtract. Reduce your answers to lowest terms and **write** them here.

1. $\dfrac{3}{8}$
    $-\dfrac{1}{4}$

2. $\dfrac{2}{5}$
    $-\dfrac{2}{15}$

3. $\dfrac{3}{4}$
    $-\dfrac{1}{12}$

4. $\dfrac{5}{6}$
    $-\dfrac{1}{3}$

5. $\dfrac{3}{5}$
    $-\dfrac{2}{10}$

6. $\dfrac{6}{7}$
    $-\dfrac{3}{14}$

7. $\dfrac{5}{8}$
    $-\dfrac{5}{16}$

8. $\dfrac{7}{10}$
    $-\dfrac{2}{20}$

9. $\dfrac{2}{4}$
    $-\dfrac{1}{12}$

10. $\dfrac{5}{15}$
    $-\dfrac{1}{5}$

11. $\dfrac{7}{16}$
    $-\dfrac{2}{8}$

12. $\dfrac{4}{9}$
    $-\dfrac{1}{3}$

13. $\dfrac{5}{7}$
    $-\dfrac{2}{14}$

14. $\dfrac{9}{10}$
    $-\dfrac{2}{5}$

15. $\dfrac{2}{3}$
    $-\dfrac{1}{9}$

16. $\dfrac{5}{8}$
    $-\dfrac{1}{4}$

17. $\dfrac{2}{4}$
    $-\dfrac{1}{2}$

18. $\dfrac{3}{6}$
    $-\dfrac{1}{3}$

19. $\dfrac{1}{2}$
    $-\dfrac{2}{8}$

20. $\dfrac{8}{9}$
    $-\dfrac{3}{18}$

21. $\dfrac{6}{8}$
    $-\dfrac{2}{16}$

22. $\dfrac{3}{4}$
    $-\dfrac{5}{16}$

23. $\dfrac{7}{16}$
    $-\dfrac{3}{8}$

24. $\dfrac{5}{6}$
    $-\dfrac{2}{18}$

25. $\dfrac{7}{21}$
    $-\dfrac{1}{7}$

26. $\dfrac{8}{24}$
    $-\dfrac{2}{12}$

27. $\dfrac{5}{6}$
    $-\dfrac{3}{16}$

28. $\dfrac{7}{10}$
    $-\dfrac{1}{5}$

Subtracting Unlike Mixed Numbers

Example: $41\frac{2}{8} - 20\frac{2}{3}$

$$41\frac{2}{8} - 20\frac{2}{3} = 41\frac{2(\times 3)}{8(\times 3)} - 20\frac{2(\times 8)}{3(\times 8)} = 41\frac{6}{24} - 20\frac{16}{24} = 40\frac{30}{24} - 20\frac{16}{24} =$$

subtract

same

8, 16, (24)

3, 6, 9, 12, 15, 18, 21, (24)

$$20\frac{14}{24} = 20\frac{7}{12}$$

Steps:
1. Find the LCM of both denominators (24).
2. Multiply the numerator and denominator of each fraction by a number to arrive at the LCM.
3. When regrouping, borrow a whole number and write the fraction as an improper fraction.
4. Subtract whole numbers.
5. Subtract numerators.
6. Denominators stay the same.
7. Reduce your answer to lowest terms.

Subtract.

1. $24\frac{2}{9} - 11\frac{2}{3}$

2. $86\frac{1}{5} - 72\frac{7}{10}$

3. $44\frac{3}{8} - 26\frac{5}{6}$

4. $19\frac{1}{4} - 12\frac{2}{3}$

5. $17\frac{4}{5} - 8\frac{1}{4}$

6. $50\frac{2}{9} - 26\frac{1}{2}$

7. $10\frac{1}{2} - 3\frac{2}{3}$

8. $12\frac{1}{5} - 7\frac{2}{3}$

9. $28\frac{5}{12} - 11\frac{2}{3}$

Learn at Home, Grade 6

Fun Facts

The World Trade Center towers in New York are so large and tall that each tower has its own. . .

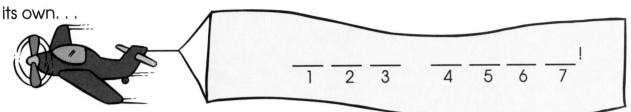

$$\underline{}\ \underline{}\ \underline{}\quad \underline{}\ \underline{}\ \underline{}\ \underline{}\ !$$
$$1\quad 2\quad 3\qquad 4\quad 5\quad 6\quad 7$$

To find the answer, follow the directions below.

Put an O above number 5 if the estimated difference between $13\frac{1}{3}$ and $5\frac{3}{7}$ is 8.

Put an A above number 6 if the estimated difference between $21\frac{5}{6}$ and $9\frac{4}{9}$ is 12.

Put an R above number 4 if the estimated difference between $16\frac{9}{20}$ and $13\frac{11}{15}$ is 3.

Put a B above number 1 if the estimated difference between $8\frac{3}{5}$ and $3\frac{7}{12}$ is 6.

Put a C above number 4 if the estimated difference between $25\frac{7}{20}$ and $13\frac{7}{12}$ is 11.

Put an E above number 7 if the estimated difference between $32\frac{7}{15}$ and $14\frac{9}{16}$ is 17.

Put a D above number 3 if the estimated difference between $18\frac{1}{3}$ and $15\frac{4}{13}$ is 2.

Put an I above number 2 if the estimated difference between $19\frac{7}{10}$ and $9\frac{6}{11}$ is 10.

Put a P above number 3 if the estimated difference between $58\frac{5}{12}$ and $42\frac{3}{10}$ is 16.

Put a D above number 6 if the estimated difference between $30\frac{13}{20}$ and $19\frac{7}{18}$ is 12.

Put an L above number 1 if the estimated difference between $11\frac{5}{7}$ and $5\frac{2}{5}$ is 6.

Put a Z above number 1 if the estimated difference between $16\frac{3}{8}$ and $9\frac{3}{7}$ is 7.

	Language Skills	**Spelling**	**Reading**
Monday	**Writing Paragraphs** Have your child choose a topic, make a plan for writing and begin working on a rough draft. Encourage your child to continue practicing writing strong paragraphs.	Pretest your child on these spelling words: atrocious　ferocious　precious conscious　furious　serious curious　generous　spacious delicious　gracious　suspicious disastrous　luscious　vicious enormous　malicious　vivacious Have your child correct the pretest. Add personalized words and make two copies of this week's study list.	Introduce this week's reading selection or continue with the book from last week.
Tuesday	An *essay* or *composition* is made up of several paragraphs. Each paragraph stands on its own but contributes to the essay as a whole. *See* Language Skills, Week 26, number 1. Have your child write a biographical essay about a famous person or about someone he/she knows. *See* Language Skills, Week 26, number 2.	Review this week's spelling words. Have your child complete **Malicious Monsters** (p. 264).	Discuss the current reading book in a conference. Focus on the author's purpose for writing this piece. Discuss why the author might have written this particular book—to entertain, to teach a lesson, etc.
Wednesday	Have your child write an essay about a familiar animal. The essay should begin with a strong introductory paragraph expressing why the animal was chosen. The body of the essay should have at least two paragraphs filled with details and information about the animal. The final paragraph should not introduce new information but restate key points from the essay and bring the essay to a close.	Have your child use each of this week's spelling words correctly in a sentence.	**Outlining:** Review the format for outlining. Have your child choose an interesting article from an encyclopedia that contains an outline. Have your child read the outline first, then read the article and compare to the outline. Have your child read a second article that is short but still includes an outline. Have your child outline the article, then compare his/her outline with the published outline.
Thursday	Writing strong beginning and ending paragraphs is challenging. Have your child read beginning and ending paragraphs from magazine articles and books. Discuss what makes them good paragraphs. Have your child choose a story that he/she wrote this year. Ask your child to revise the beginning and ending paragraphs.	Have your child study this week's spelling words.	Discuss the practical uses for outlines. An outline is an organized format for taking notes—build the outline as you read a text, then refer to it later to recall information. An outline can help you study for a test. An outline is also ideal for organizing thoughts before writing a paper or a speech. Have your child refer to the outline created yesterday, then summarize the article in his/her own words.
Friday	In an essay, each paragraph has its own topic sentence. Begin a new paragraph when the emphasis of the essay changes. Copy an interesting article or essay as one long paragraph. Have your child read the article carefully. Then, ask your child to divide the piece into paragraphs. Show your child how to use the paragraph sign (¶) to show where a new paragraph should begin.	Give your child the final spelling test. Have your child record pretest and final test words in his/her word bank.	Hold a reading conference to monitor your child's understanding of the reading.

Learn at Home, Grade 6

Math	Science	Social Studies
Fractions Discuss practical applications for subtracting fractions. Have your child write one or two situational problems, then solve them. Have your child complete **Research Time** (p. 265).	**Sound** Sound waves travel at different speeds through different mediums. *See* Science, Week 26, numbers 1 and 2. Have your child make a simple stethoscope out of a cardboard paper towel tube.	**Latitude and Longitude** The world is often divided into hemispheres: northern and southern, or eastern and western. Review the locations of the four hemispheres. Have your child complete **Hemispheres** (p. 268).
Provide practice problems for your child using all four operations and fractions. *See* Math, Week 26, number 1.	Explore the use of a megaphone as an amplifier of sound. Have your child make his/her own megaphone to perform a simple experiment. *See* Science, Week 26, number 3.	The lines on a globe help pinpoint the locations of places in the world. Review *lines of latitude* and *longitude*. *See* Social Studies, Week 26, numbers 1 and 2. Give your child practice naming lines of latitude and longitude on a globe. Point to a place on the globe and have the child name the location by latitude and longitude.
Review the procedure for converting fractions to decimals: simply divide the numerator by the denominator. Give your child several fractions to convert into decimals. *See* Math, Week 26, number 2 for sample problems.	Just as light can be reflected, so can sound. Discuss the reflection of sound and the meaning of the term *acoustics*. *See* Science, Week 26, number 4. Have your child conduct a simple experiment to find the best insulating material to mask the sound of a ticking clock inside a shoe box.	Teach your child to estimate latitude and longitude when describing a location between the labeled lines. *See* Social Studies, Week 26, number 3. Have your child complete **Plotting North American Cities** (p. 269).
Use today to review fraction concepts learned so far. Let your child catch up on any assignments as well.	Explore musical instruments with your child. Show your child real instruments, if you have access to any. If you do not have any instruments of your own, take your child to visit a music store. Study families of instruments and countries of origin of unusual instruments.	Name cities for your child to locate on a globe. *See* Social Studies, Week 26, number 4. Have your child find the approximate location of his/her hometown on a globe. Have your child trace around the globe to find other cities located on the same parallel. How do the climates of the cities compare? Then, have your child find other cities located on the same meridian. How do these climates compare?
Test your child's understanding of fractions. Have your child complete **Fraction Test** (p. 266). Reteach any skills missed on the test, if necessary.	Have your child build a simple instrument called a panpipe. Have your child complete **Panpipes** (p. 267).	Arrange for your child to perform a community service. Have your child write in his/her Social Studies Journal.

TEACHING SUGGESTIONS AND ACTIVITIES

LANGUAGE SKILLS (Writing Paragraphs)

▶ 1. The paragraphs in an essay work together to tell about the main idea or topic, but each paragraph should still have its own topic sentence and supporting sentences. In an essay, the first paragraph and final paragraph grab the reader's attention and state the main idea. In multiple-paragraph writing, the first paragraph generally introduces the topic. The middle paragraphs provide information and details. The final paragraph restates the topic, ties everything together and states a conclusion.

▶ 2. Have your child plan out the essay before writing by listing the main topic or topic sentence of each paragraph. The first paragraph of the essay should introduce the subject and explain why your child chose to write about him/her. The second paragraph could describe early accomplishments. The third paragraph could describe later accomplishments. The fourth paragraph should summarize and wrap up the essay.

MATH (Fractions)

▶ 1. Give your child ten situational problems to solve. Center the problems around a common theme, such as desserts. Here are some sample problems:

   a. Myra ate $^1/_4$ of her mother's famous key lime pie. Her brother Nick ate $^1/_3$ of the pie. How much of the pie did Myra and Nick eat altogether?

   b. Mr. Michaels sold $^5/_8$ of his 48 loaves of banana bread at the bake sale. How many loaves did he sell?

   c. Judy bought 36 doughnuts for brunch. She and her friends ate $^5/_6$ of the doughnuts. How many doughnuts were left over after brunch?

   d. Karl had $^2/_3$ of his birthday cake left. He invited some friends over after school, and they ate $^5/_8$ of the remaining cake. How much of the whole cake did they eat?

▶ 2. Give your child 35–40 fractions and mixed numbers to convert into decimals. Have your child round his/her answers to the nearest thousandth. Here are some sample numbers to get you started:

$\frac{1}{2}$	$\frac{2}{5}$	$\frac{8}{9}$	$\frac{3}{4}$	$\frac{1}{8}$	$\frac{4}{9}$	$\frac{13}{20}$	$\frac{5}{8}$
$\frac{7}{40}$	$4\frac{4}{5}$	$3\frac{2}{6}$	$6\frac{1}{3}$	$42\frac{1}{3}$	$1\frac{2}{9}$	$\frac{39}{40}$	$17\frac{3}{5}$
$\frac{14}{15}$	$32\frac{1}{8}$	$\frac{3}{50}$	$8\frac{1}{5}$	$2\frac{1}{4}$	$\frac{7}{12}$	$\frac{6}{25}$	$5\frac{21}{30}$
$\frac{16}{33}$	$\frac{2}{15}$	$\frac{3}{13}$	$4\frac{2}{7}$	$\frac{6}{17}$	$\frac{23}{25}$	$\frac{3}{11}$	$82\frac{3}{8}$

SCIENCE (Sound)

▶ 1. Sound waves can travel through solids, liquids or gases. Ask your child to recall swimming underwater in a pool and hearing the sounds around the pool. Explain that sounds travel much faster through solids than through liquids and much faster through liquids than through gases. Place a ticking clock on a table. Ask your child to listen to the sound by placing his/her ear on the same table. Then, have your child lift his/her head and listen again. Your child should observe that the ticking was louder when the sound traveled through the solid table than when it traveled through the air.

▶ 2. Have your child name some objects or devices used to increase the intensity of sound waves (amplifiers, microphones, megaphones, hearing aids, etc.). Explain that materials can also be used to muffle or decrease the intensity of sound waves, such as insulation, carpet, foam and fabrics. Acoustical tiles and materials are used in sound and recording studios, concert halls, radio and television stations and factories to absorb or soften sounds.

Learn at Home, Grade 6

3. Show your child a picture of someone using a megaphone and discuss the purpose of the megaphone. Next, have your child make a simple megaphone from a piece of poster board. Ask your child to stand in the corner of the room opposite from you. Speak softly without using the megaphone and then through the megaphone. Ask your child to describe the difference in your voice's audibility. Discuss the following questions:

When would you need to use a simple megaphone?

How could the megaphone also be used as a hearing device?

What part of a tuba, trumpet, trombone or bugle is similar to a megaphone? How?

4. An echo is a *reflection* of sound. Ask your child why he/she thinks a sound echoes off walls or the sides of a deep canyon. Explain that the echo or reflection of sound is called *reverberation*. In a large auditorium, materials are used on the stage and throughout the auditorium to control the reverberations of the sounds produced on stage. The expressions "the acoustics are poor" and "the acoustics are good" are used to describe how the sounds are controlled through the design of a building or the materials used. Some modern auditoriums have movable panels that can be adjusted to achieve the desired acoustic effect.

SOCIAL STUDIES (Latitude and Longitude)

1. The lines that stretch from the North Pole to the South Pole are called *lines of longitude*, or *meridians*. The lines of longitude tell how far east or west of the *prime meridian* (0°) a location is. The *prime meridian* is the imaginary line that passes through Greenwich, England. All lines of longitude are measured from the prime meridian in *degrees*. Everything west of the prime meridian is labeled *W* for west, and everything east of the prime meridian is labeled *E* for east.

2. The lines that go around the globe from east to west are called *lines of latitude*, or *parallels*. The lines of latitude tell how far north or south of the *equator* (0°) a location is. All lines of latitude are measured from the equator in *degrees*. Everything north of the equator is labeled *N* for north, and everything south of the equator is labeled *S* for south.

3. If there is not a labeled line of longitude going through a designated place, the map reader must note the nearest lines of longitude. Look between the meridians 70° W and 80° W. Trace your finger and count, "71°, 72°, 73°, 74°, 75°, 76°," etc. Teach your child to estimate the number of degrees to describe the location of a site between labeled lines of latitude or longitude.

4. Write some of the following cities on the chalkboard. Have your child name the latitude and longitude for each. Remind your child to indicate both the number of degrees and whether it is east or west of the prime meridian and north or south of the equator.

Los Angeles, U.S.A.	London, England	Wellington, New Zealand
Tokyo, Japan	Bangkok, Thailand	Santiago, Chile
Nairobi, Kenya	Teheran, Iran	Paris, France
Cairo, Egypt	Shanghai, China	Glasgow, Scotland
Baghdad, Iraq	Madrid, Spain	La Paz, Bolivia
Canberra, Australia	Prague, Czech Republic	Reykjavik, Iceland
Athens, Greece	Helsinki, Finland	Oslo, Norway
Quito, Ecuador	Karachi, Pakistan	Lisbon, Portugal

Malicious Monsters

atrocious
conscious
curious
delicious
disastrous
enormous
ferocious
furious
generous
gracious
luscious
malicious
precious
serious
spacious
suspicious
vicious
vivacious

Use an adjective from the spelling list to describe each noun below. Both adjective and noun will begin with the same letter.

Adjective	Noun
Example:	
1. _precious_	princess
2. _____	cat
3. _____	limes
4. _____	sunroom
5. _____	villain
6. _____	Frankenstein
7. _____	gift
8. _____	dessert
9. _____	elephant
10. _____	situation
11. _____	felines
12. _____	violinist
13. _____	commitment
14. _____	act
15. _____	demonstration
16. _____	secret agent
17. _____	gestures
18. _____	mischief

Use four of the adjective/noun phrases above to create an interesting sentence that makes sense. **Underline** each phrase.

Example: Six ferocious felines and one curious cat sat in the senator's spacious sunroom eating delicious dessert.

_____

_____

_____

Learn at Home, Grade 6

Research Time

Mr. Write-A-Lot assigned research papers to his class. He divided the class into two groups. One person from each group was responsible for each part of the research process.

1. Marisha and John each found several books on their subjects. It took Marisha $2\frac{1}{2}$ hours to skim through her stack of books, and it took John $1\frac{3}{4}$ hours to look through his. How much longer did it take Marisha? _____

2. Neal and Geraldo were working on note cards. Neal was able to complete his in $48\frac{4}{6}$ minutes, and it took Geraldo $51\frac{3}{8}$ minutes to finish his. How much longer did Geraldo take?_____

3. Bobby and Gordon found it difficult to write outlines. It took Bobby $38\frac{2}{3}$ minutes and Gordon $36\frac{3}{4}$ minutes. How many more minutes did it take Bobby?_____

4. Anita finished the first draft of her report in $48\frac{1}{2}$ minutes, while it took Pablo $51\frac{3}{8}$ minutes to write his. How much longer did it take Pablo?_____

5. The final draft of their reports went smoothly for Katie and Laura. Katie zipped hers off in $18\frac{3}{4}$ minutes, and Laura's took $21\frac{1}{8}$ minutes. How much longer did Laura's final draft take? _____

6. Find out how long it took Marisha, Geraldo, Bobby, Anita and Katie altogether. Then, find out how long it took John, Neal, Gordon, Pablo and Laura. Find the difference between the two groups' times. _____

Extension: Subtract $2\frac{7}{8}$ from . . .

a. 4

b. $5\frac{1}{8}$

c. $8\frac{7}{8}$

d. $6\frac{3}{8}$

e. $7\frac{5}{8}$

f. $9\frac{6}{8}$

Fraction Test

1. $\dfrac{1}{6} + \dfrac{4}{6} =$

2. $4\dfrac{1}{12} + 3\dfrac{2}{12} =$

3. $18\dfrac{1}{3} + 12\dfrac{1}{3} =$

4. $19\dfrac{1}{5} + 4\dfrac{2}{3} =$

5. $37 - \dfrac{3}{11} =$

6. $\dfrac{4}{5} - \dfrac{1}{4} =$

7. $\dfrac{4}{5} \times \dfrac{3}{8} =$

8. $\dfrac{5}{6} \times 15 =$

9. $4\dfrac{1}{4} \times \dfrac{2}{5} =$

10. $3\dfrac{1}{2} \times 2\dfrac{1}{3} =$

11. $7 \times \dfrac{3}{5} =$

12. $\dfrac{3}{7} \div \dfrac{4}{5} =$

13. $\dfrac{2}{3} \div 9 =$

14. $2\dfrac{6}{7} \div \dfrac{5}{14} =$

15. $\dfrac{1}{2} \div \dfrac{1}{3} =$

16. $7\dfrac{1}{3} \div 2\dfrac{2}{6} =$

17. Write $\dfrac{3}{5}$ as a decimal. _____

18. Leroy got $\dfrac{7}{8}$ of his 24 homework problems correct. How many did he correct? _____

19. Jean gave $\dfrac{3}{16}$ of her allowance to her sister and $\dfrac{1}{8}$ of her allowance to her brother. How much of her allowance did she give away? _____

20. Jack and Jill had a canteen full of 5 quarts of grape juice. They drank $3\dfrac{5}{9}$ quarts. How much was left? _____

Learn at Home, Grade 6

Panpipes

Sound is produced by **vibrations**. A column of air will vibrate when you blow across it. A short column of air will have a high pitch. A long column of air will have a low pitch.

Making the Panpipes

Take five pieces of tubing that are the following lengths: 6 inches, 5 inches, 4 inches, 3 inches and 2 inches. Lay the tubes in a row, arranging them from longest to shortest, about 1 inch apart. With the tops even, tape them together.

 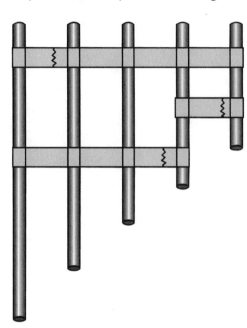

Playing the Panpipes

Blow across the top of each tube, like a flute player. Listen to the sounds. Which tube has the highest pitch?

_____

Blow across the tubes again going first in one direction, then in the other. Describe the sound.

_____

What do you think makes the pitch change?

_____

What would happen if you added and blew on a tube that is 1 inch longer than the longest tube already on your pipes?

_____

Hemispheres

The earth is a sphere. When the earth is cut in half along a vertical or horizontal axis, hemispheres are created. The **equator** divides the earth into the **Northern Hemisphere** and the **Southern Hemisphere**. The **prime meridian**, which runs from the North Pole to the South Pole, divides the earth into the **Eastern Hemisphere** and the **Western Hemisphere**.

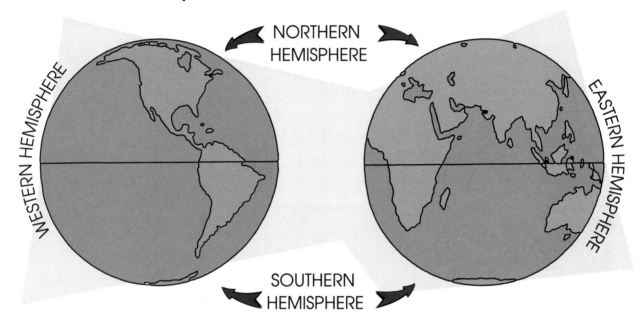

Study the illustration of the hemispheres. Then, read the following country names. Decide in which two hemispheres (Eastern or Western, and Northern or Southern) each is located.

Example: The United States lies in the Northern and Western Hemispheres.

Use a more detailed globe or map to find the exact locations of the countries.

1. Australia _____

2. India _____

3. Japan _____

4. Italy _____

5. Argentina _____

6. Ethiopia _____

7. South Africa _____

8. Mexico _____

9. China _____

10. Canada _____

11. Israel _____

12. Chile _____

13. Iraq _____

14. Peru _____

Learn at Home, Grade 6

Plotting North American Cities

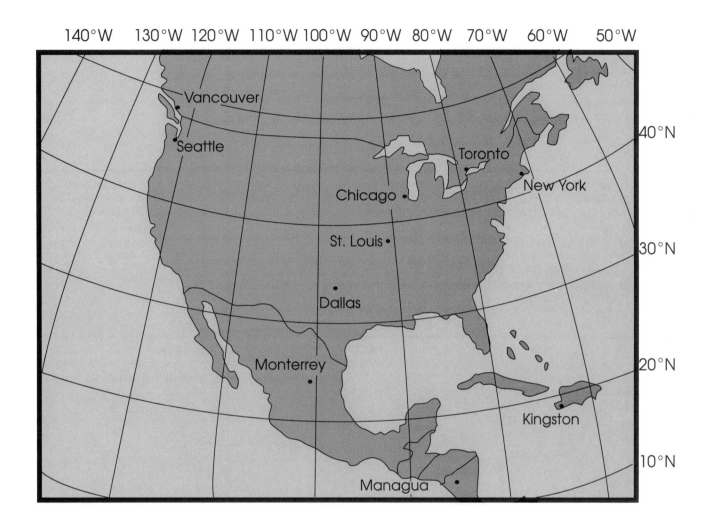

Determine the approximate coordinates of the North American cities on the map above. **Write** the coordinates for each city in the blanks below.

	Latitude	Longitude		Latitude	Longitude
1. Seattle	_____	_____	2. St. Louis	_____	_____
3. Kingston	_____	_____	4. Toronto	_____	_____
5. Dallas	_____	_____	6. New York	_____	_____
7. Vancouver	_____	_____	8. Monterrey	_____	_____
9. Managua	_____	_____	10. Chicago	_____	_____

	Language Skills	**Spelling**	**Reading**
Monday	**Writing Paragraphs** Have your child choose a topic, make a plan for writing and begin working on a rough draft. Encourage your child to continue practicing writing strong paragraphs.	Select words from the past 8 weeks for this week's pretest. Have your child correct the pretest and make a list of any misspelled words. Have your child study the list this week.	Choose a nonfiction book as this week's reading selection. Introduce the book.
Tuesday	Descriptive writing is a way of "painting a picture with words." Some words describe how things look; others describe how things feel. Read several groups of descriptive phrases to your child. Ask him/her to guess what each group of words describes. Then, have your child write a descriptive paragraph about one of those topics. *See* Language Skills, Week 27, number 1.	Have your child use spelling words from the past 8 weeks to write tongue twisters.	Discuss the current reading book in a conference. Focus on purpose for reading. Why does your child think he/she is reading this particular book?
Wednesday	Discuss the editorial section of the newspaper. Have your child look at articles and letters on the editorial page as models of persuasive writing. Have your child choose a topic and write a persuasive essay. *See* Language Skills, Week 27, number 2.	Have your child write words from the past 8 weeks using colorful paint or markers.	**Outlining:** Help your child develop an outline based on this week's nonfiction book. *See* Reading, Week 27, number 1.
Thursday	Today, discuss explanatory writing. An *explanatory composition* states reasons for supporting an opinion. The opinion is stated in the topic sentence, the reasons for supporting it are discussed in the middle paragraphs and a conclusion is drawn in the final paragraph. Have your child write an explanatory composition based on given topic sentences. *See* Language Skills, Week 27, number 3.	Have your child look up the spelling words in the dictionary. Then, have your child write a sentence (on the index card) for each word in his/her word bank.	Take an existing outline and mix up the order of the headings and subheadings. Have your child arrange the headings in a meaningful order. *See* Reading, Week 27, number 2.
Friday	An expository paragraph may explain a fact or idea, give directions or define a term. Help your child select a narrow topic about which to write an expository paragraph. Encourage your child to choose a topic related to a current unit of study, such as sound, geography or rivers. The child may need to do some additional research before writing the paragraph.	Give your child the final spelling test.	Hold a reading conference to check your child's comprehension of the reading. Ask pointed questions to determine your child's level of understanding.

Learn at Home, Grade 6

Math	**Science**	**Social Studies**
Ratios and Percents Discuss the meaning of *ratio*. *See* Math, Week 27, numbers 1 and 2. *What is the ratio of females to males in your family?* Have your child compare that ratio to a friend's family. Discuss the value of using ratios. Have your child complete **Hhhmm?** (p. 274).	**Sound** Discuss the sounds of nature, such as wind, waves and thunder. What causes the sound in each case? (vibration) Explain how to calculate the distance of a thunderstorm by counting the time elapsed (in seconds) between the lightning and thunder, then dividing by 5. (Light travels faster than sound.) This gives you the distance in miles. *See* Science, Week 27, numbers 1 and 2.	**Latitude and Longitude** Answer questions about latitude and longitude. *See* Social Studies, Week 27, number 1.
Explain how to create equal ratios by multiplying or dividing each term by the same number. *See* Math, Week 27, number 3. Have your child complete the equal ratio problems in Math, Week 27, number 4.	Play recordings of common sounds in nature or make sounds in the classroom while your child shuts his/her eyes. Ask your child to identify the different sounds.	**Rivers:** Discuss why pioneers often settled along waterways. Water is important for drinking, cooking, cleaning and transportation. On a map of the U.S., have your child find a major river and count the number of major cities that lie along its banks. Have your child complete **River System** (p. 276).
Discuss the relationship between percentages and ratios. *Percent* is actually a number out of 100. Therefore, 25% is the same as the ratio 25:100. To convert a percent to a fraction, place the percent number over 100 and simplify to lowest terms. **Example:** $35\% = \dfrac{35}{100} = \dfrac{7}{20}$ Have your child convert several different percents to fractions.	Visit a radio or television station or a musical concert. Have your child prepare questions prior to the visit and write a summary or report after the visit.	Refer to a world map to locate important rivers of the world. Help your child identify where each begins and into what body of water each flows. Have your child refer to an atlas, encyclopedia or almanac to learn about ten important rivers, then make a chart to present the information. *See* Social Studies, Week 27, number 2.
To change fractions to percents, divide the numerator by the denominator. Then, move the decimal point two places to the right. Add the percent sign. *See* Math, Week 27, number 5 for an explanation of changing mixed numbers to percents. Have your child complete **Percents** (p. 275).	Have your child research deafness, hearing impairment, diseases of the ear and hearing aid technology. Introduce your child to Helen Keller and her achievements. Help your child learn to form some basic words using American Sign Language.	Have your child complete **River Cities** (p. 277).
Give your child practice comparing fractions, decimals and percents. Create a three-column, ten-row chart with the headings *Fraction, Decimal* and *Percent*. In each row, write a number in only one of the columns. Your child must find the other two forms for each number. **Example:** 0.05 Your child must find the fraction ($\frac{5}{100} = \frac{1}{20}$) and the percent (5%).	Have your child make a concept map to review concepts learned in the unit on sound. Have your child write the word *sound* in the center of a sheet of paper, then write related areas of study on radiating arms around the word. Around each area of study, have your child add details about that particular area.	Arrange for your child to perform a community service. Have your child write in his/her Social Studies Journal.

```
◁══ TEACHING SUGGESTIONS AND ACTIVITIES ══▷
```

LANGUAGE SKILLS (Writing Paragraphs)

▶ 1. Read aloud the following groups of descriptive phrases. Have your child guess what each group describes.

crowd cheering, the loud "crack" of a bat, the smell of hot dogs

rising dust, bending trees, dark clouds

shaky knees, fast heartbeat, sick feeling in stomach

water splashing, sand between the toes, colorful shells

Have your child write a descriptive paragraph about one of these topics.

▶ 2. When a person wants to persuade others of a certain opinion, he/she must state the opinion clearly and back it up with strong arguments or evidence. It is important to understand the topic fully in order to write a well-organized and persuasive piece.

Give your child a list of common proverbs, such as those listed here. Have your child write a persuasive essay about one of the proverbs, arguing that it is indeed true or that it is completely false.

Look before you leap.   You can't tell a book by its cover.

A dog is a man's best friend.   He who hesitates is lost.

▶ 3. Have your child write an explanatory composition around the following topic sentences. Have your child write a good paragraph with supporting sentences for each topic sentence. The completed paragraphs will comprise a composition.

Chewing gum is not allowed in school.

Chewing gum in class is disruptive.

People are careless about where they put their chewed gum.

It can be dangerous to chew gum while participating in strenuous sports.

The chewing gum rule was not made because teachers were mean, but because they care.

READING (Outlining)

▶ 1. Select a passage from this week's nonfiction book for your child to read. Once your child has finished the passage, discuss the reading. Help your child organize the information in the format of an outline.

▶ 2. The title of the following scrambled outline is "Dogs." Have your child arrange the headings to create a meaningful outline. Hint: There are three main topics.

Reasons for training	Grooming	Breeds	Brush teeth	Shots
Medical	Retrievers	Exercise	Setters	Guard dogs
Good manners	General care	Hunting game	Feeding	Spaniels
Guide dogs	Terriers	Wash and cut		

MATH (Ratios and Percents)

▶ 1. A ratio compares two or more quantities. Ratios may describe a variety of relationships. A recipe may use ratios. For example, 2 parts flour to 1 part water can be written as the ratio 2:1. A ratio may also describe probability. There may be a 4:1 chance that you will pull a blue sock out of a drawer of blue and white socks. Ratios may also explain rates such as the number of miles your car travels on a gallon of gasoline. A ratio may also compare quantities. For example, if an animal shelter receives 3 dogs for every 4 cats . . .

the ratio of dogs to cats is 3:4.   the ratio of dogs to animals is 3:7.

the ratio of cats to dogs is 4:3.   the ratio of cats to animals is 4:7.

▶ 2. Ratios may be written three (or more) ways: 3:4, 3 to 4, or $^3/_4$. Look for ratios used around the house, in the community and in the media. Make note of the various words used in the comparisons (to, for, per, etc.).

Learn at Home, Grade 6

▶ 3. Ratios name relationships, not specific numbers. If you look in your sock drawer and closet, you may discover that the ratio of pairs of socks to pairs of shoes is 5:2. That does not mean you necessarily have two pairs of shoes. Using the ratio, you can plot different numbers into an equation and come up with some different options. The equation is the same as for finding equivalent fractions. Write the ratio like a fraction. If you have 6 pairs of shoes, how many pairs of socks do you have?

socks $\dfrac{5}{2}$ x $\dfrac{3}{3}$ = $\dfrac{?}{6}$ The answer is 15 socks. 15:6 is an equal ratio to 5:2.
shoes

▶ 4. Copy or read aloud the following ratio problems for your child to solve.

     a. A baseball player has a ratio of 4 hits for every 10 times at bat. Using that ratio, how many hits would he have if he went to bat 20 times? 5 times? How many times at bat would he need to get 16 hits? 30 hits?

     b. The farmers' market sells apples at a cost of 5 for $1.00. How many apples can you buy for $6.00? How much does it cost to buy 20 apples? What is the cost for 1 apple?

     c. An airplane travels at 550 miles per hour. If the plane flies for 4 hours, how far has it gone? How long will it take to fly 3,025 miles?

     d. On vacation, a family drives at an average of 90 km per hour. At this rate, how long will it take to drive to the next stop 315 km away? How far will they travel every minute?

     e. A train travels 195 miles every 3 hours. How many miles per hour is the train traveling?

▶ 5. Mixed numbers can be converted into percents two ways:

     a. Change the mixed number to an improper fraction, then divide.

         Example: $4\,{}^2/_3 = {}^{14}/_3$
                $14 \div 3 = 4.6666$ or 467%

     b. Or, multiply the whole number by 100% and add the percent calculated by the fraction.

         Example: $4\,{}^2/_3$
                $4 \times 100\% = 400\%$
                ${}^2/_3 = .6666$ or 67%
                $400\% + 67\% = 467\%$

SCIENCE (Sound)

Give your child problems to solve using this simple formula. Here are two sample problems.

▶ 1. How far away is a storm if the time between the lightning and thunder is . . .

     a. 25 seconds?   b. 40 seconds?   c. 5 seconds?   d. 1 minute?

▶ 2. If a thunderstorm is 15 miles away, how much time should elapse between a streak of lightning and a rumble of thunder?

SOCIAL STUDIES (Latitude and Longitude)

▶ 1. Have your child find the answers to the following questions. Provide any necessary resources.

     Some lines of latitude have special names. What are they and where are they located?

     What country spans the greatest number of degrees of longitude?

     What country reaches the highest degree of south latitude?

     Where do all lines of longitude come together?

     Over what land and water bodies is the Arctic Circle drawn?

     What are the approximate coordinates of your hometown?

▶ 2. Have your child read about these important rivers: Amazon, Colorado, Danube, Ganges, Niger, Mississippi, Nile, Rhine, Volga and Yangtze. Have your child make a chart to present the information he/she has learned, including the location and length of each river, as well as where (lake, ocean) the river ultimately ends.

Hhhmm?

Find the answer to the riddle below by solving the following ratios. Put the corresponding problem letter above each answer below. When you have answered the riddle, **write** each ratio two other ways, then find two equivalent ratios for each one.

E. tennis shoes to sandals _____
N. bare feet to men's dress shoes _____
S. high heels to tennis shoes _____
E. sandals to bare feet _____
E. men's dress shoes to high heels _____
A. high heels to sandals _____
T. bare feet to tennis shoes _____
A. high heels to bare feet _____
D. tennis shoes to men's dress shoes _____
H. men's dress shoes to sandals _____
H. bare feet to sandals _____
R. sandals to high heels _____
H. tennis shoes to high heels _____
D. sandals to tennis shoes _____
T. men's dress shoes to tennis shoes _____
H. tennis shoes to bare feet _____
L. high heels to men's dress shoes _____
A. men's dress shoes to bare feet _____
A. bare feet to high heels _____
H. sandals to men's dress shoes _____

What do the four H's stand for in the 4-H Club?

___ ___ ___ ___,   ___ ___ ___ ___ ___,
3:5 6:5 2:5 3:1   5:6 3:6 1:5 6:2 5:3

___ ___ ___ ___ ___ ___,   ___ ___ ___ ___ ___
1:6 1:2 5:2 2:1 1:3 6:1   3:2 2:6 5:1 6:3 2:3

Learn at Home, Grade 6

Percents

Convert these proper fractions and mixed numbers into percents. Show your work on another sheet of paper. **Write** your answers here.

1. $\dfrac{37}{100} =$

2. $\dfrac{3}{100} =$

3. $\dfrac{65}{100} =$

4. $\dfrac{49}{100} =$

5. $\dfrac{1}{4} =$

6. $\dfrac{12}{100} =$

7. $\dfrac{11}{50} =$

8. $\dfrac{71}{100} =$

9. $4\dfrac{1}{2} =$

10. $3\dfrac{1}{4} =$

11. $1\dfrac{3}{4} =$

12. $\dfrac{2}{5} =$

13. $\dfrac{3}{10} =$

14. $\dfrac{63}{100} =$

15. $\dfrac{1}{20} =$

16. $\dfrac{1}{5} =$

17. $\dfrac{17}{20} =$

18. $\dfrac{57}{100} =$

19. $\dfrac{3}{5} =$

20. $\dfrac{1}{25} =$

21. $\dfrac{7}{10} =$

22. $5\dfrac{1}{4} =$

23. $\dfrac{37}{50} =$

24. $\dfrac{23}{100} =$

25. $\dfrac{1}{2} =$

26. $\dfrac{9}{10} =$

27. $\dfrac{81}{100} =$

28. $\dfrac{39}{100} =$

29. $3\dfrac{3}{4} =$

30. $\dfrac{73}{100} =$

31. $\dfrac{7}{20} =$

32. $9\dfrac{1}{2} =$

33. $\dfrac{4}{5} =$

34. $\dfrac{1}{10} =$

35. $\dfrac{13}{20} =$

36. $\dfrac{91}{100} =$

37. $\dfrac{51}{100} =$

38. $5\dfrac{1}{4} =$

39. $\dfrac{11}{100} =$

40. $\dfrac{3}{20} =$

River System

The river systems of the world provide people with transportation, energy and fertile soil, as well as water for drinking, washing and irrigation. The terms below are used to describe a river system. Learn the meanings of these terms, then label the parts of the river on the illustration.

flood plain	delta	mouth
tributary	rapids	swamp
lake	levee	source

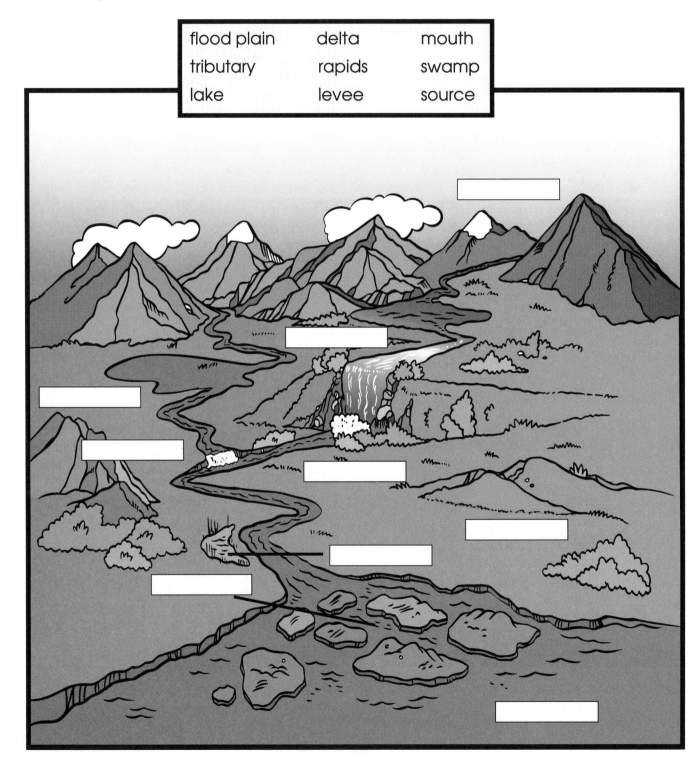

Learn at Home, Grade 6

River Cities

Many of the world's great cities began as small towns and settlements along major rivers. Communities near water were easily accessible. Water was readily available for drinking, cooking, washing, irrigation and obtaining food. Use an atlas, almanac or encyclopedia to help you complete the chart.

River	City	Country	Continent
Mississippi			
	New York		
	Rome		
Nile			
	London		
	Buenos Aires		
Seine			
	Shanghai		

	Language Skills	**Spelling**	**Reading**
Monday	Have your child write a review about a fiction book that he/she read recently. *See* Language Skills, Week 28, number 1.	Pretest your child on the following words: authorize hypnotize pasteurize burglarize idolize patronize capsize immunize plagiarize characterize memorize recognize emphasize modernize summarize harmonize organize terrorize Have your child correct the pretest. Add personalized words and make two copies of this week's study list.	Introduce this week's reading selection.
Tuesday	**Writing a Narrative:** Teach your child the elements of a narrative. *See* Language Skills, Week 28, number 2. Have your child write a narrative about a personal experience that was enjoyable, funny, frightening or unusual.	Review this week's spelling words. Have your child complete **Organize or Capsize** (p. 282).	**Comprehension:** Discuss the current reading book in a conference. Focus on reading comprehension. Ask pointed questions to test your child's understanding of the text.
Wednesday	Discuss perspective. *Perspective* is the point of view from which a story is told. Review the meaning of first, second and third person. Have your child rewrite the narrative from yesterday in the third person.	Have your child use each of this week's spelling words correctly in a sentence.	With your child, discuss the need to draw conclusions from a text while reading. Give your child a list of facts and conclusions. Have him/her determine which conclusion is correct. *See* Reading, Week 28, numbers 1–3 for examples.
Thursday	Newspaper articles are very often narratives. Discuss the 5 W's of a news article. Provide your child with a list of facts and ask him/her to write a news article about them. *See* Language Skills, Week 28, number 3. Have your child use his/her imagination to fill in details for the facts provided. Have your child write a narrative about the event in the third person.	Have your child study this week's spelling words.	Stress the importance of reading carefully so as not to misinterpret information. Have your child complete **Timely Words** (p. 283).
Friday	Show your child a picture that tells a story. Have your child write four paragraphs about the picture: one descriptive, one persuasive, one narrative and one expository.	Give your child the final spelling test. Have your child record pretest and final test words in his/her word bank.	Hold a conference to discuss the current reading book.

Learn at Home, Grade 6

Math	**Science**	**Social Studies**
Percents Discuss practical applications of percentages. To find the percentage of a given number, convert the percentage back to a decimal and multiply by the given number. **Example:** Find 20% of 45. 45 x .20 = 9.00 20% of 45 is 9 Have your child complete **Percentages** (p. 284).	**Ecology** With your child, discuss the meaning of the term *ecology*. *See* Science, Week 28. Ecology is the study of the interrelationships of organisms and the environment. Have your child define *environment*. Have your child complete **Enlightening Information** (p. 285).	**Western Hemisphere** Study the regions of North America. *See* Social Studies, Week 28, number 1. Give your child a copy of **North and Central America** (p. 286). Have him/her color-code the political regions of North and Central America and create a key.
Teach your child about savings accounts and earning interest. If your child doesn't have a savings account at a bank, help him/her open one. Write several situational problems related to interest for your child to solve. See Math, Week 28 for sample problems.	Have your child write a description of his/her environment. Since your child may be a part of more than one environment, ask him/her to choose the environment in which he/she spends the most time. What are the *biotic* and *abiotic factors* in your child's environment?	With your child, study a physical map of North America. Ask him/her questions about North America's location, size, regions and land formations. Have your child name lines of latitude and longitude; locate rivers, mountains and oceans; name borders and other features. Give your child a second copy of **North and Central America** (p. 286). Have him/her label at least ten physical features on the map.
Take your child to a store where they are offering 25% or 30% discounts off original prices. Have your child calculate the sale prices of a variety of items. To find the sale price, have your child calculate the discount (e.g., 25% of $32 is $8), then subtract the discount from the original price (e.g., $32 – $8 = $24).	Have your child make a glossary of ecology-related terms in his/her Science Log. *See* Science, Week 28, number 1.	Have your child study the political regions of South America. *See* Social Studies, Week 28, number 2. Give your child a copy of **South America** (p. 287). Have him/her color-code the political regions of South America and create a key.
Your child has already learned how to calculate the percentage of a number. Now, challenge him/her to figure out what percentage one number is to another. **Example:** 5 is ____% of 25 (20%) Give your child several problems like this one to solve.	**Soil:** Introduce your child to the study of *soil*, one of the earth's most important land resources. Collect samples of *clay, loam, sand* and *humus*. Ask your child to observe each soil sample with a magnifying glass and look for color, smell, texture and components of the soils. Soils may be mixtures of many materials, both inorganic and organic. *See* Science, Week 28, number 2.	With your child, study a physical map of South America. Ask him/her questions about South America's location, size, regions and land formations. Have your child name lines of latitude and longitude; locate rivers, mountains and oceans; name borders and other features. Give your child a second copy of **South America** (p. 287). Have your child label at least ten physical features on the map.
Teach your child to estimate percentages. This has its most practical applications when estimating sales tax or the appropriate amount to tip. Think in terms of 10% when estimating. Finding 10% is easy—simply move the decimal point to the left one place. Estimate other percentages by thinking about how they relate to 10%. For example, 10% of $15.29 is about $1.50, so 20% would be about $3.00.	Help your child compose a letter to a state or local soil conservation service, requesting information about the soils of your state or area.	Arrange for your child to perform a community service. Have your child write in his/her Social Studies Journal.

TEACHING SUGGESTIONS AND ACTIVITIES

LANGUAGE SKILLS (Writing a Narrative)

▶ 1. Show your child examples of book reviews from newspapers or magazines. Most book reviews include a summary of the plot (characters, setting, problem), as well as opinions and recommendations. The reviewer points out what is most interesting or least enjoyable about a book. The reviewer may try to persuade others to read (or not to read) the book.

▶ 2. A narrative tells about an event or experience. The narrative gives usually covers details in the order in which they occurred.

▶ 3. Provide your child with facts about a news event (real or imagined). Here is a list of facts related to one event. Use these facts or make up your own.

Who: Mr. Dakota Rainier	What: killed a fly with his garlic breath
Where: Gilroy, California	When: on Labor Day
Why: unintentional	How: ate 5 whole loaves of garlic bread

READING (Comprehension)

Give your child a list of facts and conclusions like those listed here. Ask him/her to check the correct conclusion, then write another plausible conclusion for each fact.

▶ 1. Only one person is known to have even been hit by a meteorite.

Meteorites usually fall in forests, lakes or hills.

The chances of being hit by a meteorite are almost zero.

▶ 2. A "jiffy" is defined as one hundred thousand billion billionths of a second.

A jiffy is an incredibly short period of time.

A jiffy is enough time for a quick phone call.

▶ 3. Killer bees have been responsible for killing almost three hundred people in Brazil since 1957.

Killer bees are especially threatening to people in Brazil.

Killer bees pose a worldwide threat to people.

MATH (Percents)

▶ 1. Samantha deposited $12.35 into her savings account. She earns 8% interest monthly.

Figure how much Samantha would earn in interest at the end of one month.

What would her savings balance be at the beginning of her second month?

▶ 2. Jeremy decided he would borrow $225.00 for a new mountain bike. His interest rate on the 3-year loan was 18% per year. How much would he pay in interest for this loan?

SCIENCE (Ecology/Soil)

BACKGROUND

Ecology is an area of worldwide concern, as we struggle to protect our water, air, animals and plants. Since ecology encompasses a wide range of topics, you may wish to focus your study on one or two areas of special interest. Find out what your child is most interested in—endangered plants and animals, conservation, communities in nature (forest communities, ocean communities, desert communities, grassland communities), ground water supply, rainforests, pollution, recycling—and concentrate your lessons on those topics.

Learn at Home, Grade 6

▷ 1. Add ecology terms to the weekly spelling lists. Have your child add a glossary of ecology terms to his/her Science Log, using the following words to get started. Encourage your child to add new words as he/she encounters them in your study of ecology.

population	acid rain	endangered	habitat
pollution	interdependent	biodiversity	environment
ecology	litter	toxic	soil
community	extinct	nutrients	biotic
crop rotation	forest management	organic farming	waste management
ecosystem	greenhouse effect	pesticide	wildlife reserve

▷ 2. Have your child refer to resources to answer some of the following questions about soil.

What is soil?

What is topsoil?

Why is soil important to all organisms?

Which sample seems richest in organic material?

Which sample seems to be the heaviest?

Which sample seems to be the lightest?

Which sample has the smallest particles?

Which sample has the largest particles?

What is the value of a mixture of soils?

Which soil would be found in a garden?

Which soil would be found on a beach?

Which soil would make a good foundation for a house?

SOCIAL STUDIES (Western Hemisphere)

▷ 1. North America may be subdivided in a number of different ways. It may be divided into *Anglo-America* and *Latin America*. Some divide the continent agriculturally (the *Corn Belt*, the *Columbia Basin*, the *Wheat Region*). Some may divide the continent into the *North, New England,* the *Gulf* and the *Pacific*. The political divisions include Canada, United States, Mexico, Central America and the Caribbean Islands.

▷ 2. South America is divided into twelve countries and two dependencies. There are three major land regions: the *Andes Mountains,* the *Central Plains* and the *Eastern Highlands.* The continent of South America forms part of Latin America which includes Mexico, Central America and the West Indies.

Organize or Capsize

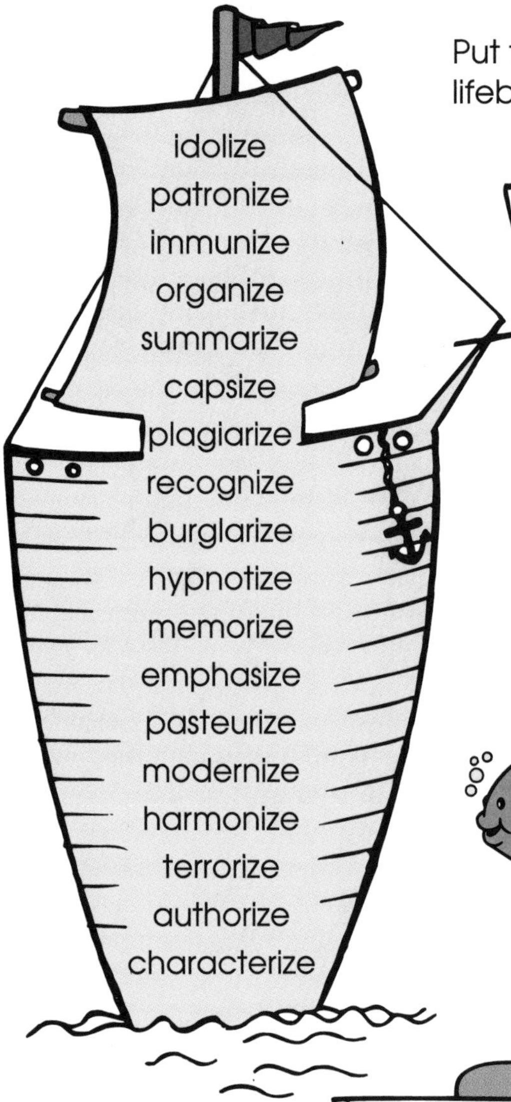

Put the spelling words in alphabetical order in the lifeboats before the ship capsizes.

idolize
patronize
immunize
organize
summarize
capsize
plagiarize
recognize
burglarize
hypnotize
memorize
emphasize
pasteurize
modernize
harmonize
terrorize
authorize
characterize

1. _____ 2. _____
3. _____ 4. _____
5. _____ 6. _____

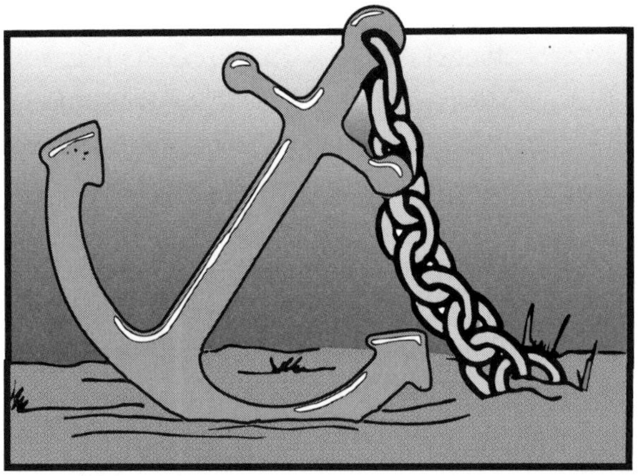

7. _____ 8. _____
9. _____ 10. _____
11. _____ 12. _____

13. _____ 14. _____
15. _____ 16. _____
17. _____ 18. _____

Learn at Home, Grade 6

Timely Words

Read each sentence. **Circle** the two words
that tell when something happens. **Write**
each circled word on the correct line to
show which word would come before or
after the other word in time.

1. Mike hopes to someday visit Washington D.C., but meanwhile he reads books
   about the capital city.
   before _____ **after** _____

2. Some of the tourists left immediately for the airport while others planned to
   leave later in the day.
   before _____ **after** _____

3. Although John has put off mowing the yard for now, he knows he must
   eventually get it done.
   before _____ **after** _____

4. Kim said she would have arrived sooner, but she waited for a phone call that
   finally came.
   before _____ **after** _____

5. Tom wanted to appear earlier in the play, but his character did not appear
   until the last scene.
   before _____ **after** _____

6. The photographer said that Sally would have her picture taken first, but that
   Kevin would be next.
   before _____ **after** _____

Circle the word that would come before the other word. Use the circled word in
a sentence.

1. immediately - later: _____

_____

2. earlier - last: _____

_____

Percentages

Sally and Gabriel wrote percentage problems for extra credit. Once you have solved their problems, make up some of your own on another sheet of paper.

1. There were 400 students in the school. If 38% of the students were boys, how many boys were there? _____

2. Out of the 345 sheets of construction paper in Mrs. Rainbow's class, 20% were red and 40% were blue. How many sheets were red? _____
    How many sheets were blue? _____

3. Only 19% of the 400 students ate the cafeteria food on Monday. How many students purchased cafeteria food Monday? _____

4. 25% of 76 band members can play a clarinet.
    How many can play a clarinet? _____

5. 35 trees were planted around the school. 60% were maples. How many of the trees planted were maple? _____

6. The local pizza parlor gave the eighth-grade class a 25% discount on pizzas they purchased to sell at the football game. Each pizza originally cost $12.00. How much did the eighth graders pay per pizza? _____
    If they purchased 12 pizzas, how much did they save together? _____

7. They saw these signs at the sports shop nearby. Figure each sale price.

Sale!
15% off
All In-Line Skates!
Regularly
$97.00

25% Savings
All Mitts!
Regularly
$24.00

Huge Savings!
20% off
All Bicycles
Regularly
$132.00

_____   _____   _____

Learn at Home, Grade 6

Enlightening Information

An **environment** includes all living and nonliving things with which an organism interacts. These living and nonliving things are **interdependent**, that is, they depend on one another. The living things in an environment (plants, animals) are called **biotic factors**, and the nonliving things (soil, light, temperature) are called **abiotic factors**. **Ecology** is the study of the relationships and interactions of living things with one another and their environment.

Living things inhabit many different environments. A group of organisms living and interacting with each other in their nonliving environment is called an **ecosystem**. The different organisms that live together in an ecosystem are called a **community**. Within a community, each kind of living thing (i.e., frogs) makes up a **population**.

Study the picture. Follow the directions.

1. Label two biotic factors and two abiotic factors in the picture.

2. Explain the relationships among the living things in the pictured environment.

3. Label the type of ecosystem pictured.

4. Circle all the members of the community.

5. Explain how the organisms in this environment are dependent upon one another.

6. List the different kinds of populations that live in the environment.

Learn at Home, Grade 6

Learn at Home, Grade 6

	Language Skills	Spelling	Reading
Monday	**Story Elements** The setting of a story is often established from the outset. Many times the setting is indirectly described by clues given here and there. Read the beginning paragraphs of a novel until your child can describe the setting. Discuss the words and images that communicated the setting.	Pretest your child on the following words: archery, greenery, refinery celery, grocery, robbery cemetery, hatchery, slippery drapery, machinery, stationery embroidery, misery, surgery fiery, mockery, trickery Have your child correct the pretest. Add personalized words and make two copies of this week's study list.	Introduce this week's reading selection or continue with the book from last week.
Tuesday	Read sentences aloud to your child. Have your child describe the setting in each. Discuss the key words and phrases that helped your child determine the setting. Then, have your child write a paragraph about one of those settings. *See* Language Skills, Week 29, number 1.	Review this week's spelling words. Have your child complete **Cemetery Epitaphs** (p. 292).	Discuss the current reading book in a conference. Focus on descriptive passages.
Wednesday	The characters in a story are usually established early on. The author generally introduces much more than just the characters' names, including what they look like and how they act. *See* Language Skills, Week 29, number 2.	Have your child use each of this week's spelling words correctly in a sentence.	**Character Analysis:** Ask your child to compare the characters and setting in this week's book to the characters and setting in a similar book. Have your child make a chart listing the similarities and differences.
Thursday	Write the following character descriptions across the top of the chalkboard: *monster, young child, old man, clown*. Under each character named, have your child list words and actions to help develop the character. Then, have your child write a paragraph about one of the characters, using the details listed.	Have your child study this week's spelling words.	Have your child imagine, then write, a conversation with a character from the current reading book.
Friday	Discuss the plot of a story. *See* Language Skills, Week 29, number 3.	Give your child the final spelling test. Have your child record pretest and final test words in his/her word bank.	Hold a reading conference to evaluate the choices made in the book. Discuss whether the characters made wise choices. Did the author make wise choices?

Learn at Home, Grade 6

Math	Science	Social Studies
Percents Have your child solve situational problems with mixed operations and percents. *See* Math, Week 29, number 1.	**Soil** Have your child collect soil samples from three different locations. Have him/her put the samples in plastic bags, label each with the date and location and bring them inside to study. *See* Science, Week 29, number 1.	With your child, define and discuss the meaning of *climate*. Have your child read about the climates of North America, Central America and South America in an encyclopedia. Have your child compare a location in North America, with a location in South and Central America. Have the child indicate on a map where all three places are located, then describe the three places and their climates.
Banks sometimes offer *compound interest* on a savings account. With compound interest, the interest earned in one period is added to the principal for the next period. Ask your child to imagine that he/she put $200 in a savings account that earns 5% interest compounded yearly. Have your child make a chart and calculate how much he/she will earn over 10 years if he/she does not add to the principal.	Introduce the concept of *soil management*. Discuss and describe the attributes of healthy soil. *See* Science, Week 29, number 2. Have your child read about *composting* as a way to create richer soil. Help your child start a compost pile near your home. *See* Science, Week 29, number 3.	**Canada:** Have your child describe the physical borders and exact location of Canada. Encourage your child to use names of oceans, lines of latitude and longitude, measurements and proximity to other landmarks to describe its location. *See* Social Studies, Week 29 for background information on this unit of study.
Discuss the difference between similar figures and congruent figures. *Similar figures* are same in shape but different in size. *Congruent figures* are identical in both shape and size. *See* Math, Week 29, number 2. Have your child make a design made of similar and congruent figures. Have your child draw each figure carefully. Encourage your child to be creative.	Have your child read about the Dust Bowl of the Great Plains states. *See* Science, Week 29, number 4. Have your child write a story about living conditions in the Dust Bowl.	Give your child a copy of **Canada** (p. 293). Have your child label the map with the names of Canada's provinces and territories, along with their capitals. Then, have him/her label the important rivers and bodies of water that lie in and around Canada. *See* Social Studies, Week 29, number 1.
Have your child locate lines of symmetry on a variety of shapes. A *line of symmetry* divides a figure into two parts that are exactly the same or congruent. Some figures may have more than one line of symmetry, while others have none.	**Biomes:** Have your child read about the *rainforest* biome. Give your child an atlas or globe to locate rainforests throughout the world. What kinds of plants and animals are found there? Discuss the type of soil found in the rainforest. How is it different from the soil found in your area? Help your child conduct a simple experiment with soil. *See* Science, Week 29, number 5.	Give your child a second copy of **Canada** (p. 293). Have him/her color-code the map to show the major land regions and create a key. *See* Social Studies, Week 29, number 2. Then, have your child label at least ten physical features.
Use today to review any material your child finds difficult or for your child to complete unfinished work.	Have your child read about the *temperate forest* biome. What plants and animals are found there? Where are the world's temperate forests located?	Arrange for your child to perform a community service. Have your child write in his/her Social Studies Journal.

TEACHING SUGGESTIONS AND ACTIVITIES

LANGUAGE SKILLS (Story Elements)

▶ 1. Read aloud the following sentences. Have your child describe the setting of each.

The dog wagged his tail as he cleaned the crumbs from under the table.

Sally wrapped herself in another blanket and continued to watch the scary movie alone in the dark.

The town clock chimed eleven times. The band began to play and lead a parade welcoming the hero home.

Have your child select one of the above settings and write a paragraph about it. Your child should describe what the place looked like, what sounds could be heard and how the character felt.

▶ 2. An author needs to develop characters so they are believable—even in make-believe stories. Read aloud the two descriptions of Penny that follow. Ask your child which paragraph gives a clearer image of the character.

Penny was baby-sitting for the Johnsons' little girl, Lori, for the first time. Penny looked friendly. Lori brought out her dolls and began to play on the floor next to Penny.

Penny arrived early at the Johnsons' because it was her first time baby-sitting for their little girl, Lori. She wanted to get to know Lori a little before the Johnsons left for the evening. Five-year-old Lori looked at Penny carefully. Penny was smiling at her. Penny's long hair was pulled back in a pony tail with a pink ribbon, and her smile seemed to make even her freckles sparkle. Lori asked Penny to play dolls with her.

Discuss why the second paragraph creates a clearer image of Penny. Developing a character involves creating a feeling of what sort of person the character is. Adjectives are not the only way to describe a person. A picture of a character may also be developed through his/her actions.

▶ 3. The plot of a story involves characters who interact and try to solve a problem. Have your child read each of the problems below and tell one way each might be solved.

The sixth-graders were riding the bus on their way home from a field trip to Chicago. Suddenly, they heard a loud noise, and the driver brought the bus to a stop. The driver stepped out of the bus for a minute. When she returned, she announced to the students that the bus had a flat tire.

Daryl's new puppy loved to chew. Daryl bought her bones and chew toys, but the puppy only liked to chew shoes—Dad's shoes!

Holly and Tad were sailing their little boat close to shore when a strong wind came up suddenly. Everyone on the beach saw their boat turn over.

MATH (Percents)

▶ 1. Have your child solve the following situational problems.

a. A waitress served three tables with total bills of $62.90, $38.45 and $24.85. If each table left a 15% tip, how much in tips will the waitress earn? What is the average tip?

b. Another waiter served dinner to two parties. The first party had a bill of $382.50. The second party had a bill of half that amount. If each group left a 15% tip, how much did the waiter earn?

c. At one table of 12 diners, 5 people ordered the shrimp dinner at $12.95 each. Four people ordered the lasagna at $9.95 each. Three people ordered chicken for $8.50 each. What was the total bill (do not apply taxes)? What tip should they leave?

▶ 2. The angles of similar figures are identical, and their sides are proportional in length. If you compare the lengths of the similar sides of the two figures, each pair of similar sides will have the same ratio. The angles and sides of congruent figures are identical.

SCIENCE (Soil/Biomes)

▶ 1. Have your child spread each soil sample on a separate sheet of white paper to examine with a magnifying glass. Have your child note his/her findings, then return the samples to the plastic bags. Next, have your child

290

weigh each soil sample, recording the date and weight of each. Instruct your child to leave each bag open for a few days, then weigh each sample again. Is there a difference in weight? Why?

▶ 2. Sometimes soil must be managed to keep it healthy for supporting living organisms. Farmers who plant in the same soil year after year are in danger of robbing their soil of nutrients. Experts in *soil management* instruct farmers in techniques for improving the quality of soil. Have your child read about soil nutrients, crop rotation, irrigation and the use of pesticides. Discuss the concept of organic gardening or farming.

▶ 3. To start a compost pile, you need a little bedding of leaves and grass clippings in a partly sunny location. Add food waste in small amounts and stir into the bedding. Too much food waste can start to smell or attract unwanted animals. Have your child keep a journal of the dates and types of materials added to the compost. Add water periodically if the compost is too dry. When the food waste has decomposed and the compost looks like rich, black dirt, add the natural fertilizer to a garden plot or potted plants.

▶ 4. In the 1930s, wind storms blew away the topsoil in the southern Great Plains. The topsoil had become loose and dry because the native grasslands had been overgrazed and replaced with wheatlands. Wheat did not protect the ground against wind. A drought in the early 1930s only increased the destructive power of the strong winds. Eventually, the topsoil was blown away, and new crops could not be grown. The barren land eroded further and dust storms drove people from the land.

▶ 5. The floor of a rainforest is covered with fallen leaves. But beneath that layer of leaves lies a very unusual soil. Rainforest soil is formed when rainwater breaks down rocks. The soil in the rainforest is many yards thick and made mostly of clay and a sticky material that resists erosion. Many of the nutrients, however, have been washed away by rains, leaving much of the rainforest soil infertile.

Help your child conduct a simple experiment to explore how different types of soil are affected by water.

You will need: $^1/_2$ cup each of three types of soil (clay, sand and topsoil), three plastic sandwich bags, three 10-oz. plastic cups, rubber bands, toothpicks, a measuring cup, masking tape and water

Directions:

   a. Put the soils in a warm dry place. Let them dry overnight.

   b. Use a toothpick to make ten small holes in the bottom of each plastic bag.

   c. Put each soil in a separate plastic bag.

   d. Set each bag in a plastic cup, folding the top of the bag over the edge of the cup. Hold the bags in place with rubber bands. Label the cups by type of soil.

   e. Predict: What do you think will happen when you add water to each soil?

   f. Pour $^1/_2$ cup of water into each bag. Wait 15 minutes. Answer the following questions.

      1) Which soil held the most water?

      2) How is that soil different from the others?

      3) What can you tell about rainforest soil?

SOCIAL STUDIES (Canada)

BACKGROUND

For the remainder of the year, your child will study individual countries in North America, Central America and South America. Help your child gather resources for research activities, including nonfiction books, encyclopedias, an atlas, primary sources, videos, newspapers and magazines. Activities are suggested in the lesson plans, but you may choose to have your child do a more in-depth study of a few states, provinces or countries.

▶ 1. Have your child label the bodies of water that surround Canada, as well as the major bodies of water found within its borders: the Great Lakes, St. Lawrence River, Hudson Bay, Nelson River, Lake Winnipeg, Mackenzie River, Great Bear Lake, Great Slave Lake, Columbia River, Yukon River, Fraser River.

▶ 2. Canada has eight major land regions: the Pacific Ranges and Lowlands, the Rocky Mountains, the Arctic Islands, the Interior Plains, the Canadian Shield, the Hudson Bay Lowlands, the St. Lawrence Lowlands and the Appalachian Region.

Cemetery Epitaphs

Use a spelling word to complete each word group.

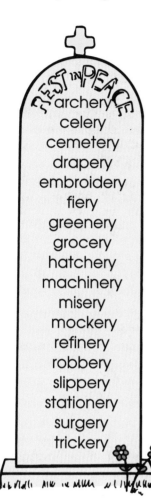

archery
celery
cemetery
drapery
embroidery
fiery
greenery
grocery
hatchery
machinery
misery
mockery
refinery
robbery
slippery
stationery
surgery
trickery

1. graveyard, burial place, _____

2. industrial, purifier, _____

3. operation, medical procedure, _____

4. slick, shifting, _____

5. blazing, glowing, _____

6. stalk, vegetable, _____

7. theft, stealing, _____

8. curtains, covering, _____

9. pain, sorrow, _____

10. handiwork, sewing, _____

11. grass, plants, _____

12. notepad, envelopes, _____

13. bow shooting, sport, _____

14. engines, power tools, _____

15. insult, false appearance _____

16. prank, joke, _____

17. foodstuffs, store, _____

18. incubator, brooder, _____

Write an epitaph (a tombstone inscription) for a tombstone you might find in a cemetery. The epitaph may be wacky, creepy or sentimental. Try to use several words from the list.

Example: Here lies George who ate too much celery. He simply couldn't resist any kind of greenery, and the surgery didn't help. I am sad to say that he died in misery.

Learn at Home, Grade 6

	Language Skills	**Spelling**	**Reading**
Monday	**Story Elements** Have your child use part of the **Story Organizer** (p. 19) to plan a story before writing it. Have your child map out the setting, characters, problem, events and solution to the story. Once your child has decided on these elements, think of five related vocabulary words. Write these words on the activity sheet for your child to define. Have your child write the story.	Pretest your child on the following words: amplify fortify notify beautify glorify qualify certify horrify rectify clarify identify simplify dignify justify solidify falsify magnify verify Have your child correct the pretest. Add personalized words and make two copies of this week's study list.	Introduce this week's reading selection. Suggestion: *The Sign of the Beaver* by Elizabeth George Speare.
Tuesday	A *narrative story* is like a narrative paragraph, only longer. A narrative story is made up of a series of paragraphs that tell about a sequence of events in order. A story is generally narrated in the first or third person. Show your child an interesting picture from a magazine or book. Have him/her imagine a story based on the picture, then tell the story in writing.	Review this week's spelling words. Have your child complete **Magnify the Situation** (p. 298).	Discuss the current reading book in a conference. Focus on the meaning of the book's title.
Wednesday	Encourage your child to include conversation in a story to make it more realistic. Review the proper use of quotation marks. *See* Language Skills, Week 30, number 1. Have your child write a sequel to yesterday's story (using the same characters but a different problem) that includes passages of dialogue.	Have your child use each of this week's spelling words correctly in a sentence.	**Mood:** Discuss *mood* (or tone) as an element of a story. An author can establish a mood through sensory images and the use of symbolism. A story's mood may be dark, light, funny, happy, sad, adventurous or mysterious. Find passages that set a specific mood. Have your child read the passages, define the mood and discuss the words that help establish that mood.
Thursday	Discuss the meaning of the term *composition*. Compare it to a narrative. *See* Language Skills, Week 30, number 2.	Have your child study this week's spelling words.	Have your child choose a mood for a story, then list words that would help establish that mood. Repeat with other moods. Then, have your child choose one of the moods and use the list of related words to write a paragraph. Encourage your child to choose his/her words carefully when writing the paragraph.
Friday	Have your child write a composition on a familiar topic.	Give your child the final spelling test. Have your child record pretest and final test words in his/her word bank.	Hold a reading conference. Discuss how to find the meaning of new words by looking for clues in context. Have your child complete **The Sign of the Beaver** (p. 299).

Learn at Home, Grade 6

Math	**Science**	**Social Studies**
Proportion Teach your child how to determine if two ratios are equivalent. *Equivalent ratios* are in *proportion*. *See* Math, Week 30, number 1. Have your child complete **Sam the Squirrel** (p. 300).	**Biomes** A forest is a rich resource for plants, animals and humans. Discuss the many benefits of forests to different kinds of organisms. *See* Science, Week 30, number 1. Have your child complete **From Field to Forest** (p. 302).	**Canada** Have your child read about and look at maps of plant and animal life in Canada. *See* Social Studies, Week 30, number 1.
Give your child a proportion with a missing value. Teach your child to find the value of an unknown variable using cross products. *See* Math, Week 30, number 2. Have your child complete **Proportions** (p. 301).	With your child, discuss the abundance of life that can be found on a rotting log in a forest. Have your child complete **Life on a Rotting Log** (p. 303).	Have your child read about Canadian history (including French and English involvement) up to the time of the American Revolution. Have your child complete an activity related to the history of Canada. *See* Social Studies, Week 30, numbers 2–4. Have your child complete **Speaking Canadian** (p. 304).
Using graph paper, draw a geometric shape whose sides are all a whole number of units in length. Have your child calculate the perimeter and area of the shape. Then, have your child draw a similar figure with a given ratio. **Example:** *Draw a rectangle that is one-fourth the size of the original.* Repeat with several other shapes and proportions. *See* Math, Week 30, number 3.	Have your child read about the *grassland* biome. What plants and animals are found there? What is the difference between a *steppe* and a *prairie*? Have your child draw a prairie food web. Ask your child to write a paragraph explaining what would happen to the other plants and animals if there were a decrease in the population of one plant or animal.	With your child, discuss Canada's population. About 75% of the Canadian population lives near the border between Canada and the U.S. About 77% of the population resides in urban areas. Have your child complete **Which Is Which?** (p. 305).
Find a simple object in the room. Ask your child to measure the object carefully and draw a scale model of the object. Have your child make a scale to accompany the drawing that tells the relative size of the object.	Discuss the impact of new housing and city developments on animal and plant habitats. Introduce the term *wetlands*. *See* Science, Week 30, number 2. Have your child read "The Great Debate." *See* Science, Week 30, number 3. Ask your child to make two lists of arguments—one for and one against the building of the new Riverton Ball Park.	Canada is rich in natural resources. Have your child read about important Canadian resources and industries. *See* Social Studies, Week 30, number 5. Have your child write a brief report on one Canadian province or territory. *See* Social Studies, Week 30, number 6.
Teach your child to determine actual distances represented on a map by using the scale that accompanies the map.	Have your child read about the *freshwater pond* biome. What plants and animals are found there? Have your child make a list of animals that live on the surface of the pond, those that live mid-depth and a those that live on the bottom of the pond. Have your child study a drop of pond water under a microscope and identify what he/she sees.	Arrange for your child to perform a community service. Have your child write in his/her Social Studies Journal.

Learn at Home, Grade 6

TEACHING SUGGESTIONS AND ACTIVITIES

LANGUAGE SKILLS (Story Elements)

▷ 1. Use quotation marks only around the exact words that a character speaks. Use a comma to separate the quotation from the speaker.

Examples: Mom said, "Thank you for your help."
"You are welcome," replied Gary.

Each time a new person talks, indent and begin a new paragraph.

▷ 2. Planning a composition is similar to planning a story. The paragraphs in a composition work together to develop or explain an idea rather than a plot. Follow these steps before writing a composition:

a. Choose a topic (a trip, cars, sports, music, friends, plants, a building, animals, food, movies).

b. Narrow the topic so it can be covered in five or six paragraphs. For example, if *plants* were the topic, narrow it down to a specific type of plant, its living conditions or its uses

c. Brainstorm details about the narrowed topic.

d. Group the details into categories. Label the main idea for each group of details.

e. Write the composition: write an introductory paragraph, middle paragraphs and a final paragraph. The topic sentence for the introductory paragraph should state the main idea of the composition; each topic sentence for the middle paragraphs should state the main idea for one group of details.

MATH (Proportion)

▷ 1. Use equal ratios or cross products to test for proportion. In a proportion, cross products are equal.

Equal Ratios

$$\frac{8}{10} \frac{(\div 2)}{(\div 2)} \frac{4}{5}$$

Cross Products

$$\frac{8}{10} \times \frac{4}{5} \qquad 8 \times 5 = 10 \times 4$$

▷ 2. Use cross multiplication to solve for an unknown value in a proportion or set of equal ratios.

Example:

$$\frac{6}{8} = \frac{12}{r}$$

$12 \times 8 = 96$
So $6r = 96$
$r = 16$

▷ 3. A scale is the ratio between a reproduction and the actual. Scales are commonly seen on maps and models. Usually a scale gives the copy's measurement first, then the actual, as in 1 inch = 5 miles. In this case, every inch represents 5 miles.

To practice using scales, draw a simple figure on a sheet of graph paper. Then, decide on an appropriate scale, such as 1 square to 3 squares. Have your child use this scale to draw a larger version of the original figure. For every 1 square on the original, use 3 squares to draw the copy.

SCIENCE (Biomes)

▷ 1. Forests are homes to many plants and animals; they provide them with food and shelter. Forests are also important resources for humans. Many everyday products come from the forest, including paper and maple syrup. Forests also provide beautiful places for nature walks and can even help prevent flooding. Have your child read about these and the many other benefits of forests to humans.

▷ 2. When new developments such as parks, zoos, shopping centers, schools, highways, golf courses, amusement parks, landfills and housing are proposed for a city, a planning board or commission must review the plans and environmental issues before granting rezoning or building permits. Citizens of the city may appear at meetings to take part in the discussions and decisions. One major concern in this country is the draining and use of wetlands for expansion of farms, highways and housing developments. Some people view wetlands as useless swamps. Environmentalists try to educate people about the value of wetlands. Wetlands provide

Learn at Home, Grade 6

homes for many plants and animals. They also act like a sponge to protect areas from flooding. Have your child read about the other values of wetlands. What kinds of plants and animals inhabit wetlands?

▶ 3. **The Great Debate**
Downtown Riverton neighbors 300 acres of wetlands. This area of marshes and ponds is home to hundreds of species of plants and animals. A group of citizens from the city of Riverton wants to build a new baseball stadium on this land. Riverton has never had a professional baseball team, nor has it ever had any professional sports teams. Riverton is a large city of almost 750,000 people, and marshes are the only open land available near downtown. Some citizens would like to save the wetlands and build the ball park elsewhere, possibly in the suburbs. What do you think? What do you want to happen to the wetlands?

SOCIAL STUDIES (Canada)

▶ 1. Have your child make an alphabetical list of Canada's varied plant and animal life. After each entry, have your child list one fact about the particular plant or animal. Ask your child to draw pictures of the plants and animals where they can be found on the map **Canada** (p. 293).

▶ 2. Have your child make a time line of Canadian history beginning in 1497. Ask your child to include the names of explorers, settlements and events that involved the British and French in Canada up to the time of the American Revolution.

▶ 3. Have your child draw a picture of a native Canadian trading with a Frenchman.

▶ 4. Have your child list reasons for French/English rivalry.

▶ 5. Canada leads in the production of newsprint, and it ranks as a leader in the production of hydroelectric power. Other important industries and resources are listed below.

Agriculture: beef cattle, canola, chickens, eggs, hogs, milk and wheat

Fishing: cod, lobster and salmon

Forestry: fir, pine and spruce

Manufacturing: aluminum, chemicals, electrical equipment, fabricated metal products, food products, motor vehicles and parts, paper products, petroleum products, steel and wood products

Mining: coal, copper, gold, iron ore, natural gas, petroleum, uranium and zinc

Exports: fish, metals, natural gas, newsprint, petroleum, wheat and wood

▶ 6. Have your child include the following information in his/her report:

capital	population
area	natural resources
bordering provinces/territories/U.S. states	chief agricultural products
interesting places to visit	major industries
brief history	map

Magnify the Situation

Unscramble the letters to find the spelling word (verb) that goes with each clue (direct object). The first one has been done for you.

	verb	**direct object**

amplify
beautify
certify
clarify
dignify
falsify
fortify
glorify
horrify
identify
justify
magnify
notify
qualify
rectify
simplify
solidify
verify

1. (piifmyls) _____simplify_____ the problem
2. (abyfieut) _____ a city park
3. (ulyfaiq) _____ your answer
4. (iyrfroh) _____ your teacher
5. (fyidosli) _____ the liquid
6. (ffsliay) _____ the document
7. (yvfrie) _____ your identiity
8. (ynifot) _____ the authorities
9. (pfliaym) _____ the sound
10. (ifyustj) _____ your actions
11. (lrofgiy) _____ a hero
12. (cfteryi) _____ the situation
13. (cfyrail) _____ your question
14. (yfftroi) _____ the walls
15. (iafymng) _____ the cells
16. (fnditeiy) _____ the criminal
17. (ngifydi) _____ the procedure
18. (itrecyf) _____ the check

My name is Sam Sneed. It is my job to clarify the evidence,verify the facts, indentify the murderer, and notify the authorities. I do not intend to glorify but I am the best in my field. In order to qualify for this position I had to study very hard for many years. All the hard work paid off. I am now certified and have a very satisfying position as a _____ .

Learn at Home, Grade 6

The Sign of the Beaver

Read the following sentences. Based on context, write a definition for each **bold** word. Then, look up the definitions and **circle** yes if you were correct. If you were not correct, change your answer.

1. ". . . when his rage died down, that he felt a **prickle** of fear."

   Prickle means _____ yes

2. ". . . he saw the sunlight glinted through the **chinks** on the roof."

   Chinks means _____ yes

3. " . . . but he thought he'd rather have the **pesky** insects himself."

   Pesky means _____ yes

4. "Matt sat **pondering** the strange idea."

   Pondering means _____ yes

5. "He strutted and pranced in ridiculous **contortions** . . ."

   Contortions means _____ yes

6. "Now **wampum** no good to pay for gun."

   Wampum means _____ yes

7. "**Warily**, he made his way through the brush."

   Warily means _____ yes

8. "The brown eyes looked up at the Indian boy with **admiration**."

   Admiration means _____ yes

9. " . . . they **wielded** their bats with no heed to each other's heads. . ."

   Wielded means _____ yes

10. "Matt forced himself to eat **sparingly** of these things."

    Sparingly means _____ yes

Sam the Squirrel

Help Sam get the acorns to the tree by shading in the path containing the correct proportions.

Learn at Home, Grade 6

Proportions

Solve the problems. **Write** your answers here.

1. $\dfrac{2}{4} = \dfrac{n}{8}$

    $n =$

2. $\dfrac{3}{x} = \dfrac{9}{15}$

    $x =$

3. $\dfrac{n}{20} = \dfrac{5}{4}$

    $n =$

4. $\dfrac{5}{6} = \dfrac{30}{n}$

    $n =$

5. $\dfrac{27}{n} = \dfrac{9}{10}$

    $n =$

6. $\dfrac{3}{14} = \dfrac{n}{42}$

    $n =$

7. $\dfrac{2}{n} = \dfrac{24}{72}$

    $n =$

8. $\dfrac{3}{9} = \dfrac{x}{54}$

    $x =$

9. $\dfrac{3}{7} = \dfrac{x}{42}$

    $x =$

10. $\dfrac{6}{12} = \dfrac{12}{n}$

    $n =$

11. $\dfrac{7}{8} = \dfrac{42}{x}$

    $x =$

12. $\dfrac{3}{8} = \dfrac{n}{48}$

    $n =$

13. $\dfrac{12}{13} = \dfrac{24}{x}$

    $x =$

14. $\dfrac{7}{9} = \dfrac{21}{n}$

    $n =$

15. $\dfrac{7}{4} = \dfrac{x}{28}$

    $x =$

16. $\dfrac{n}{30} = \dfrac{5}{3}$

    $n =$

17. $\dfrac{5}{40} = \dfrac{2}{m}$

    $m =$

18. $\dfrac{6}{2} = \dfrac{t}{20}$

    $t =$

19. $\dfrac{3}{9} = \dfrac{x}{15}$

    $x =$

20. $\dfrac{6}{n} = \dfrac{4}{8}$

    $n =$

21. $\dfrac{7}{4} = \dfrac{49}{y}$

    $y =$

22. $\dfrac{6}{8} = \dfrac{n}{48}$

    $n =$

23. $\dfrac{y}{15} = \dfrac{1}{3}$

    $y =$

24. $\dfrac{40}{120} = \dfrac{4}{n}$

    $n =$

25. $\dfrac{9}{3} = \dfrac{27}{y}$

    $y =$

26. $\dfrac{14}{6} = \dfrac{n}{3}$

    $n =$

27. $\dfrac{12}{3} = \dfrac{12}{n}$

    $n =$

28. $\dfrac{24}{8} = \dfrac{}{m}$

    $m =$

29. $\dfrac{25}{6} = \dfrac{75}{n}$

    $n =$

30. $\dfrac{3}{12} = \dfrac{x}{48}$

    $x =$

31. $\dfrac{5}{25} = \dfrac{t}{20}$

    $t =$

32. $\dfrac{n}{55} = \dfrac{2}{11}$

    $n =$

From Field to Forest

Through a series of changes, an abandoned farmer's field can develop into a climax forest. These changes take an orderly pattern called **succession**.
Read the description of each step in the succession of an abandoned farmer's field in the southeastern United States.

Farmer's Abandoned Field
Ten years after Farmer Brown quit working his farm, small pine seedlings began to grow in the abandoned field along with low-growing shrubs, grasses and herbs. List some animals that would live in this habitat.

_____

_____

_____

Pine Forest
Twenty-five years have passed, and the pines have grown tall and mature. Young oak trees start to grow beneath the pines. List some animals that would live in this habitat.

_____

_____

_____

Oak-Pine Forest
The oak trees reach for the sun between the old pine trees. Many older pines die, and young oaks begin to replace them. List some animals that would live in this habitat.

_____

_____

_____

Oak Climax Forest
The large oaks dominate the forest. Young oaks grow in the understory, but young pines cannot grow in the shade of the oaks. List some animals that would live in this habitat.

_____

_____

_____

Learn at Home, Grade 6

Life on a Rotting Log

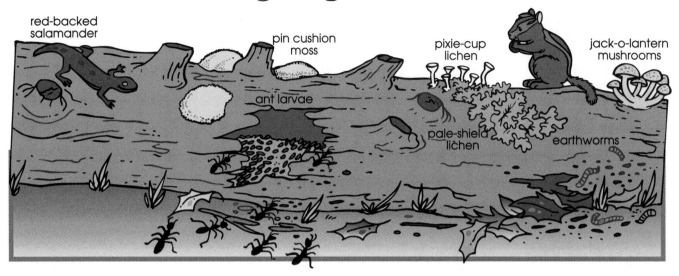

red-backed salamander

pin cushion moss

pixie-cup lichen

jack-o-lantern mushrooms

ant larvae

pale-shield lichen

earthworms

The forest community is not limited to animals and plants that live in or near living trees. As the succession of the forest continues, many trees will die and fall to the ground. The actions of plants, animals, bacteria, lichens and weather help break the dead log down and return its components to the forest soil.

1. List the different kinds of plant life that are found on the rotting log. _____
_____

2. How do the small plants help the log decay? _____
_____

3. How do the plants benefit from the log? _____
_____

4. What kinds of small animals are found in or on the rotting log? _____
_____

5. How do these animals help the log decay? _____
_____

The lichen found on the rotting log is an interesting type of plant. It is actually made up of two organisms living together in symbiosis. What two organisms form a lichen? What does each of these organisms need to live? How do the organisms help each other? _____
_____
_____
_____

Learn at Home, Grade 6

Speaking Canadian

Use the word box to complete the puzzle and discover the name of a company given the rights to a huge tract of land in northern Canada in 1570.

constable	hydro	mukluk	zed
curling	char	metis	reveillon
coureurs de bois	loyalists	Lower Canada	wapiti
Quebecois	Eskimo	Canada Day	Micmac	Klondike

1. Trout-like fish
2. Animal-skin boot
3. Letter z (for those who haven't watched Sesame Street)
4. Indian word meaning eaters of raw meat
5. Quebec's French-speaking citizens
6. Area once famed for its gold
7. Police officer
8. French traders not licensed to gather furs
9. Name once given to French-speaking Canada

10. Colonists loyal to Britain during the American Revolution, many of whom fled to Nova Scotia
11. Game in which heavy stones are slid toward a target
12. _____ electricity
13. Descendants of French settlers and their Indian wives
14. elk
15. Indian tribe from Eastern Canada
16. Quebec feast which follows the Christmas Midnight Mass
17. Canada's birthday

Learn at Home, Grade 6

Which Is Which?

Use the charts to answer the questions.

Population Distribution Chart

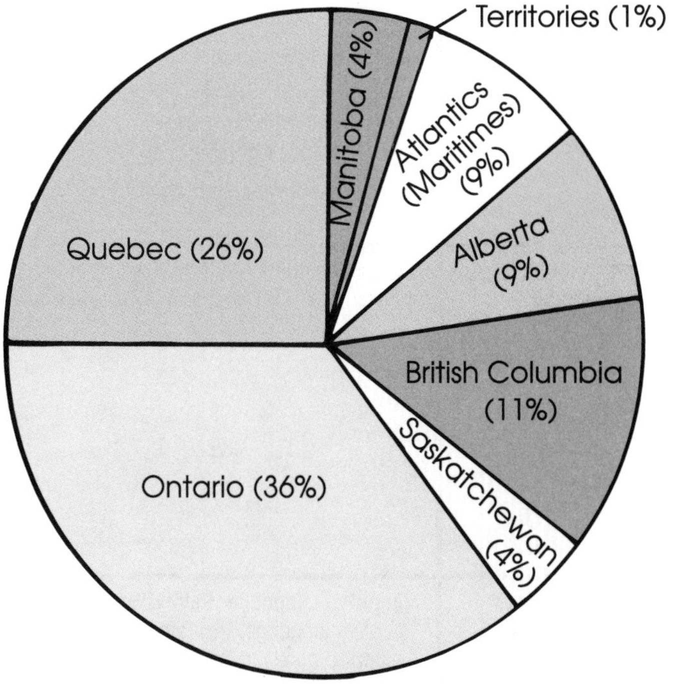

Territories (1%)
Manitoba (4%)
Atlantics (Maritimes) (9%)
Quebec (26%)
Alberta (9%)
British Columbia (11%)
Ontario (36%)
Saskatchewan (4%)

Area Distribution Chart

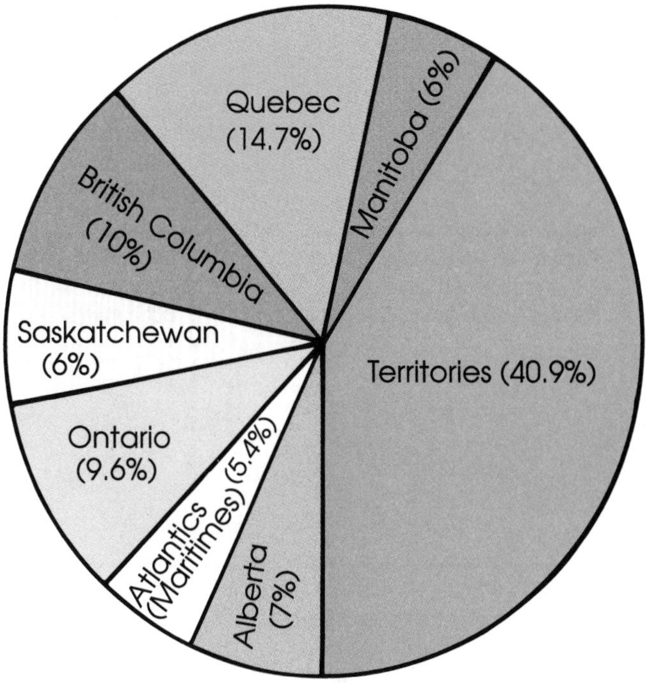

Quebec (14.7%)
Manitoba (6%)
British Columbia (10%)
Saskatchewan (6%)
Territories (40.9%)
Ontario (9.6%)
Atlantics (Maritimes) (5.4%)
Alberta (7%)

1. Which province has a population about the same as that of the Atlantic (Maritime) provinces? _____

2. Which two provinces have similar populations? _____

3. Which province is the largest in area? _____

4. Which province has population and area percentages nearly alike? _____

5. Which lands take up more than 40% of the area of Canada? _____

6. Which province has a larger population, Alberta or Ontario? _____

7. Which province is smaller, Saskatchewan or British Columbia? _____

8. Which takes up less area, Alberta or the Atlantic (Maritime) Provinces? _____

9. Which two provinces together make up more than 60% of Canada's population? _____

10. Which province has the greatest population density? _____

	Language Skills	Spelling	Reading
Monday	Help your child write an information report using notes. *See* Language Skills, Week 31, number 1.	Pretest your child on the following words: banquet hatchet quiet blanket helmet racket bonnet interpret scarlet cabinet jacket skillet corset magnet velvet faucet packet violet Have your child correct the pretest. Add personalized words and make two copies of this week's study list.	Introduce this week's reading selection or continue with the book from last week.
Tuesday	**Poetry:** Compare poetry to prose. Discuss the difference and have your child make a chart or write a paragraph comparing the two.	Review this week's spelling words. Have your child complete **Cleaning Cabinets** (p. 310).	Discuss the current reading book in a conference. Focus on the Reading Journal.
Wednesday	Poetry is very concise, but it may contain grand concepts, create vivid images and evoke strong feelings. Poetry uses *rhyme, rhythm, alliteration, metaphor, hyperbole* and *creativity* to present ideas. Poetry can be fun to listen to and read. Have your child write a definition of poetry. Challenge your child by asking him/her to write the definition using poetic language.	Have your child use each of this week's spelling words correctly in a sentence.	**Figurative Language:** Review types of figurative language, including *simile, metaphor, personification* and *idiom. See* Reading, Week 31, numbers 1–4. Have your child complete **Up a Tree** (p. 311).
Thursday	Introduce your child to two common rhyming patterns used in poetry. *See* Language Skills, Week 31, number 2. Have your child find poems containing these rhyming patterns.	Have your child study this week's spelling words.	Ask your child to look through magazines, books and newspapers to find three examples of each of the four types of figurative language. Have your child copy each figure of speech and identify it by type (simile, metaphor, personification, idiom).
Friday	Take turns with your child reading aloud poems from a book of poetry. Discuss the rhythm of the poems. Tap out rhythms as you read.	Give your child the final spelling test. Have your child record pretest and final test words in his/her word bank.	Hold a reading conference. Discuss passages in the current book that contain figurative language.

Learn at Home, Grade 6

Math	Science	Social Studies
Scale Have your child use a scale to convert actual distances to distances on a map. Provide your child with a list of actual distances, such as kilometers to the grocery store, kilometers to the zoo or kilometers to Grandma's house. Ask your child to calculate what each distance would be on a map which uses a scale of 1 cm = 3 km.	**Endangered Animals** Introduce and explain the terms *endangered* and *extinct*. *See* Science, Week 31, number 1.	**Mexico** Have your child describe in writing the exact location of Mexico, using names of oceans, lines of latitude and longitude, measurements and proximity to other landmarks.
Have your child draw his/her bedroom and its furnishings using the scale 1 in. = 1 ft.	Have your child choose two or three endangered animals to research this week. Ask your child to research where they live, why they are endangered, their habits and other interesting facts. Have your child present the information in a report, a poster or a diorama. *See* Science, Week 31, number 2 for a partial list of endangered animals.	Give your child a copy of **Mexico** (p. 315). Have your child draw the boundaries and label the states of Mexico, as well as important rivers and bodies of water.
Use today to review or catch up on ratios, proportions, percents, similar shapes, symmetry and scale.	Allow time for your child to continue his/her research on endangered animals.	Have your child read about the history of Mexico and choose from the related activities. *See* Social Studies, Week 31, numbers 1–5.
Test your child's understanding of ratios. Have your child complete **Ratio Test** (p. 312). Reteach any skills missed on the test, if necessary.	Allow time for your child to continue his/her research on endangered animals. Have your child complete **Animal Math** (p. 313).	Have your child read about Mexico City and choose from the related activities. *See* Social Studies, Week 31, numbers 6–8.
Give your child some brainteasers to solve. *See* Math, Week 31, number 1.	Allow time for your child to continue his/her research on endangered animals. Have your child complete **Animal Magic** (p. 314).	Arrange for your child to perform a community service. Have your child write in his/her Social Studies Journal.

TEACHING SUGGESTIONS AND ACTIVITIES

LANGUAGE SKILLS (Poetry)

▶ 1. When writing a report, it may be necessary to get information from reference books. If that is the case, take notes from the sources. Review with your child some techniques for taking notes in his/her own words. Below are some notes taken about mammals. These notes are well-organized and in an outline format. Have your child write a report from this information.

Characteristics of mammals
Warm-blooded
Backbones
Covered with hair
Live young
Brain more complex than other animals

Location and size
All continents and climates
Some adapt to only one environment, others to several
Some small, some large
Larger mammals need more land to live on

Adaptations
Teeth (tusks, tiny teeth)
Kind of feet, reasons for different kinds (use, travel)
Some hibernate

▶ 2. Here are two common rhyming patterns used in poetry.

Examples:

Mary let the cat in,	(a)	The peacock is a king on high,	(a)
Rescued from the cold.	(b)	His cloak is spread out in the sky.	(a)
With fur matted and thin,	(a)	In his throne, he looks so proud,	(b)
It purrs its thanks, loud and bold.	(b)	He holds his head up in a cloud.	(b)

READING (Figurative Language)

▶ 1. A *simile* compares two unlike things using the words *like* or *as*.

Examples: Katie's dog ran like lightning after my cat.
I'm hungry as a horse.
The children sat as quiet as mice waiting for the movie to start.

▶ 2. A *metaphor* compares two unlike things by stating that one thing is the other.

Examples: Molly is a living doll for cleaning up the kitchen.
The sailboats were ghosts riding on the water.
The sunrise was a purple, orange and pink painting.

▶ 3. *Personification* lends human qualities to or animates nonhuman objects.

Examples: The gust of wind swept the barn off its foundation.
An open door welcomed us to the party.
The forbidding fence warned us not to trespass.

▶ 4. An *idiom* is an expression that has come to have a meaning other than its literal meaning.

Examples: Robert was down in the dumps when he got his grades.
The class was in hot water when they didn't settle down after recess.
He certainly pulled the wool over my eyes.

Learn at Home, Grade 6

MATH (Brainteasers)

▶ 1. Copy the following brainteasers for your child. Your child must draw each figure without lifting the pencil from the page and without tracing any line more than once. There may be more than one solution for some figures.

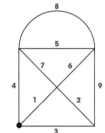 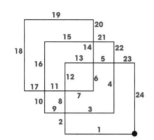 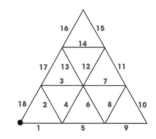 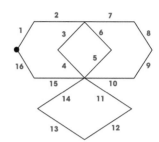

SCIENCE (Endangered Animals)

▶ 1. Plant and animal populations may decrease for natural reasons (fire, drought, floods, ice, climatic changes, disease) or as a result of human activity, such as destruction of habitat or chemical pollution. When a plant or animal population becomes so small that it may completely disappear from Earth, it is called an *endangered species*. When the species of plant or animal has disappeared from Earth, it is said to be *extinct*. Some endangered animals include the orangutan, bald eagle, Florida manatee and whooping crane. Some extinct animals include the saber-toothed tiger, mastodon, giant ground sloth, dodo bird and the dinosaurs.

▶ 2. Below is a partial list of the world's endangered animals.

African forest elephant	black rhinoceros	jaguar	prairie dog
American crocodile	California condor	leatherback sea turtle	pronghorn
Arabian oryx	cheetah	maned wolf	red kangaroo
Asian elephant	chinook salmon	marine otter	sea lion
Asiatic lion	Florida manatee	mountain gorilla	snow leopard
aye-aye	Galapagos turtle	northern spotted owl	whooping crane
Bactrian camel	giant panda	northern white rhinoceros	yak
bald eagle	grizzly bear	ocelot	

SOCIAL STUDIES (Mexico)

▶ 1. Create a model of an ancient Aztec temple.

▶ 2. Identify the areas of the ancient Mayan and Aztec civilizations on a map of Mexico and Central America.

▶ 3. Read about the construction of the pyramids built in ancient Mexico. Describe the symbolism.

▶ 4. Draw a picture of the Mexican flag and explain the significance of the colors and the coat of arms.

▶ 5. Look at pictures of the pottery and clay figures of the Mayans and Aztecs. Copy the style to create your own clay figures.

▶ 6. Read about the following men and their roles in Mexico's history: Maximilian, Hernando Cortés, Porfirio Díaz and Moctezuma (or Montezuma) II. Write a summary of each man's importance to Mexico City.

▶ 7. Write about some of the popular cultural events in Mexico City. What is housed in the National Museum of Anthropology? What can you see at the Palacio de Bellas Artes? Who are Diego Rivera and Freida Khalo?

▶ 8. Mexico City is built over the former Aztec capital of Tenochtitlán. Research and draw an illustration of the former capital or write about the invasion of the Spanish.

Cleaning Cabinets

Unscramble the groups of letters in the kitchen cabinets to form words from the word list.

banquet
blanket
bonnet
cabinet
corset
faucet
hatchet
helmet
interpret
jacket
magnet
packet
quiet
racket
scarlet
skillet
velvet
violet

gmenta	tnnboe	ttehach
_____	_____	_____
oietvl	catejk	theelm
_____	_____	_____
quenbat	tracke	caefut
_____	_____	_____
tellisk	vetlev	baicnet
_____	_____	_____
taselrc	cakept	tablenk
_____	_____	_____
treetprin	tiuqe	trosce
_____	_____	_____

Identify the number of syllables in five spelling words. Then, **write** a synonym and antonym for each.

	syllables	synonym	antonym
_____	_____	_____	_____
_____	_____	_____	_____
_____	_____	_____	_____
_____	_____	_____	_____
_____	_____	_____	_____

310

Up a Tree

Match these expressions with their meanings.

_____ all the personality of wallpaper paste   a. without question

_____ a piece of my mind   b. consider clearly

_____ running amok   c. becoming wild

_____ beyond a shadow of a doubt   d. gather up great quantities

_____ think straight   e. a very bland disposition

_____ ace in the hole   f. strong opinion

_____ shop like a bear about to hibernate   g. from a bad situation to a
                                                        worse one

_____ out of the frying pan and into the fire   h. special advantage

Write two sentences using the above expressions.
Example: When my teacher asked me to give the answer, I couldn't think straight.

1. _____

2. _____

Ratio Test

1. A basketball player makes 7 free throws out of every 12 thrown.

   a. **Write** a ratio of the free throws made to the number thrown. _____

   b. **Write** a ratio of the free throws taken to the number missed. _____

   c. With this same ratio, how many free throws would the player make out of 24 throws? _____

2. **Write** the following percents as fractions in reduced form:

   12% _____   260% _____

3. **Write** the following fractions as percents:

   $\frac{15}{100}$ = _____ $\frac{1}{4}$ = _____ $2\frac{2}{5}$ = _____

4. **Write** the following percents as decimals:

   68% = _____   1% = _____

5. **Write** the following decimals as percents:

   0.18 = _____   0.05 = _____   3.24 = _____

6. Find 15% of 40. _____

7. Find 4% of 20. _____

8. Two hundred fifty people attended the fiesta. Of the fiesta guests, 52% were female. How many guests were female? _____

9. The quarterback completed 8 out of 25 passes. What percentage of passes were completed? _____

10. Are the following ratios in proportion?

   $\frac{3}{8} = \frac{27}{72}$ _____ $\frac{1}{7} = \frac{3}{20}$ _____

11. Solve for x in the following proportions:

   $\frac{18}{3} = \frac{x}{2}$ $\frac{6}{x} = \frac{24}{12}$

   $x =$ _____ $x =$ _____

Learn at Home, Grade 6

Animal Math

This chart lists some of the body statistics of fifteen endangered animals. Use these measurements to solve the problems below.

Animal	Height	Weight	Length
Mountain gorilla	6 feet	450 pounds	
Brown hyena	25 inches	70 pounds	3 feet
Black rhinoceros	5.5 feet	4,000 pounds	12 feet
Cheetah	2.5 feet	100 pounds	5 feet
Leopard	2 feet	150 pounds	4.5 feet
Spectacled bear	2.5 feet	300 pounds	5 feet
Giant armadillo		100 pounds	4 feet
Vicuna	2.5 feet	100 pounds	
Central American tapir	3.5 feet	500 pounds	8 feet
Black-footed ferret		1.5 pounds	20 inches
Siberian tiger	38 inches	600 pounds	6 feet
Orangutan	4.5 feet	200 pounds	
Giant panda		300 pounds	6 feet
Polar bear		1,600 pounds	8 feet
Yak	5.5 feet	1,200 pounds	

1. What is the total height of a mountain gorilla, a vicuna and a yak? _____
2. What is the total weight of a leopard, a cheetah and a polar bear? _____
3. What is the total weight of a giant panda and a giant armadillo? _____
4. Add the lengths of a black rhinoceros, a spectacled bear and a Siberian tiger. _____
5. Add the heights of two leopards, three yaks and four orangutans. _____
6. Subtract the height of a vicuna from the height of a cheetah. _____
7. Multiply the height of a Central American tapir by the height of a mountain gorilla. _____
8. Add the heights of a brown hyena and a Siberian tiger. _____
9. Add the weights of all the animals. _____
10. For the animals whose lengths are given, arrange the lengths of the animals from longest to shortest on another sheet of paper.

Animal Magic

Read the animal name in Column A. Choose the correct description from Column B. **Write** the number of the answer in the Magic Square below. The first one has been done for you.

Column A

A. grizzly bear
B. koala
C. peregrine falcon
D. California condor
E. black-footed ferret
F. cheetah
G. orangutan
H. giant panda
I. Florida manatee
J. kit fox
K. blue whale
L. whooping crane
M. red wolf
N. green sea turtle
O. brown hyena
P. jaguar

Column B

1. large bear of the American grasslands
2. lives on dry grasslands of South Africa
3. the most valuable reptile in the world
4. largest soaring bird of North America
5. the tallest American bird
6. the fastest animal on land
7. the only great ape outside Africa
8. large aquatic seal-like animal
9. large black and white mammal of China
10. small, fast mammal; nocturnal predator
11. largest animal in the world
12. member of the weasel family
13. has interbred with coyotes in some areas
14. also called a duck hawk; size of a crow
15. eats leaves of the eucalyptus tree
16. know as "el tigre" in Spanish

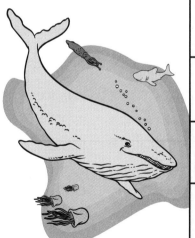

A 1	B	C	D
E	F	G	H
I	J	K	L
M	N	O	P

Add the numbers across, down and diagonally. What answer do you get? _____

Why do you think this is called a magic square? _____

_____

Learn at Home, Grade 6

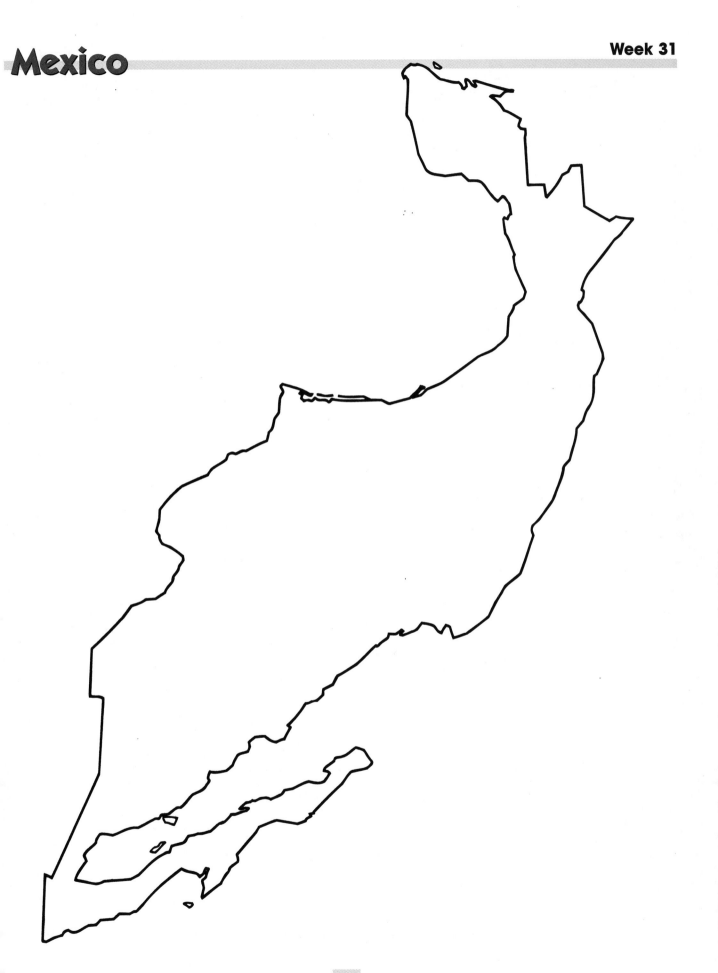

	Language Skills	**Spelling**	**Reading**
Monday	**Poetry** Discuss strategies for writing poetry. Walk your child through the process. *See* Language Skills, Week 32, number 1. Have your child follow this process to write a rhyming poem.	Pretest your child on the following words: admit edit orbit bandit emit profit benefit exhibit prohibit commit habit solicit credit inherit spirit debit limit visit Have your child correct the pretest. Add personalized words and make two copies of this week's study list.	**Biography** Choose a biography for this week's reading selection. There are many interesting biographies written by Jean Fritz that are appropriate for the sixth-grade level. Introduce the subject of the book today.
Tuesday	Review similes. Ask your child to look for similes in poetry. Have your child write a poem where each line is a different simile about the same subject. *See* Language Skills, Week 32, number 2.	Review this week's spelling words. Have your child complete **Going into Orbit** (p. 320).	Discuss the current reading book in a conference. Have your child use other resources to research the life of the subject of the biography.
Wednesday	Encourage your child to use similes in poetry to create vivid images. *See* Language Skills, Week 32, number 3.	Have your child use each of this week's spelling words correctly in a sentence.	Have your child take notes in chronological order as he/she reads the biography. Once finished with the book, have your child make a time line of the person's life. This is just another way of taking notes.
Thursday	Review metaphors. Discuss the use of metaphors in poetry. Read some poems to your child that contain metaphors. *See* Language Skills, Week 32, number 4. Have your child write a poem containing at least one metaphor.	Have your child study this week's spelling words.	Have your child write a summary of the biography based on the information contained in the time line.
Friday	Discuss other literary techniques often used in poetry: *assonance, consonance* and *onomatopoeia. See* Language Skills, Week 32, number 5. Have your child experiment with these techniques by writing short poems of two or four lines each.	Give your child the final spelling test. Have your child record pretest and final test words in his/her word bank.	Hold a reading conference. Discuss the format of a biography.

     Learn at Home, Grade 6

Math	Science	Social Studies
Statistics Review the procedures for finding mean, median, mode and range. *See* Math, Week 32, number 1. Give your child lists of numbers gathered from a newspaper or magazine. Have your child find the mean, median, mode and range for each group of numbers.	**Endangered Plants** Have your child read about endangered plants. *What threatens plant species today?* *See* Science, Week 32, number 1.	**Mexico** Prior to the 1940s, Mexico's economy was based on agriculture and mining. Today, tourism is extremely important to Mexico's economy. Have your child read about important resources and industries in Mexico. *See* Social Studies, Week 32, number 1.
Graphing: Review how to graph ordered pairs on a coordinate graph. Have your child complete **Browser** (p. 321).	If possible, arrange a trip to a local zoo or botanical garden and view some of the endangered animals and plants. Have your child write about two of the plants seen there. *See* Science, Week 32, number 2.	Have your child write a brief report on one of Mexico's states. *See* Social Studies, Week 32, number 2.
Have your child draw a simple picture on a sheet of graph paper. Once the drawing is complete, have your child draw and number the horizontal and vertical axes outside of the image. Following the example of yesterday's activity, have your child create a list of ordered pairs that could lead someone to draw the picture.	Introduce and explain the term *biodiversity*. Our planet has a rich diversity of species that makes it a beautiful and interesting environment. Have your child read about how biodiversity is important to the survival of the planet.	**Central America:** Refer to a map of Central America and discuss important borders and cities. Give your child a copy of **Central America Political Map** (p. 323). Have your child label each country and its capital, noting the capital's coordinates on the chart. Then, have your child color each country a different color and label the Pacific Ocean, the Caribbean Sea, the Gulf of Panama and the Panama Canal.
Have your child create an index to a map. The index should list features and locations in alphabetical order and identify the coordinates with an ordered pair. *See* Math, Week 32, number 2.	Ask your child to research the plants that do well in your area. Based on this information, have your child plan a small outdoor garden for your yard, patio, window box or roof. Guide your child in preparing the soil, planting the seeds or seedlings and caring for the plants. Have your child keep a record of how he/she cares for the plants in his/her Science Log and record any growth.	The countries of Central America have unique terrain, diverse populations and different lifestyles. Guide your child in researching the countries individually. Your child may want to take a different approach with each country. Have your child research and present information on the country of Belize. *See* Social Studies, Week 32, number 3.
Have your child complete **Graphs** (p. 322). Discuss the topics on the completed activity sheet.	Some people rely on herbal medicines and remedies. Have your child read about herbs and their many uses. If possible, have your child prepare questions and interview someone who grows or uses herbs.	Have your child research and present information on the country of El Salvador. *See* Social Studies, Week 32, number 3. Arrange for your child to perform a community service. Have your child write in his/her Social Studies Journal.

TEACHING SUGGESTIONS AND ACTIVITIES

LANGUAGE SKILLS (Poetry)

▶ 1. Encourage your child to follow this process when writing poetry:
   a. Select a subject.
   b. Think about the subject. Picture it in your head.
   c. Write down ideas, feelings and descriptions of the subject.
   d. Decide on a form for the poem.
   e. Write a first draft.
   f. Revise. Adjust the rhyme and/or rhythm of the poem.
   g. Write a final draft.

▶ 2. Write the beginning of a simile on the chalkboard. Have your child complete it several different ways.
   Example: The puppy is like . . .
   The puppy is like a warm ball of fur.
   The puppy is like yellow cotton.
   The puppy is as wild as a bear cub.

   The result is a poem. Have your child create poems around other similes: I feel like . . .
   The sun is as . . .

▶ 3. Show your child how a simile may start a line of poetry. Write some examples on the board and discuss.

   Like a lion roaring in my ear, the train rushed by with its whistle blowing.
   Like the middle of the night, the room was silent.

   Write other similes that might start a line of poetry. Have your child finish the lines.

   Like cool summer breezes,   Like a snake crawling up my leg,
   Like a blow on the head,   Like walking on hot pavement,

▶ 4. Metaphors are often used in poetry because they create a strong feeling or image.
   Examples: *The boy was a bullet racing across the field.*
   My sister was a parrot who copied everything I said.
   My ten-year-old cousin Trisha is a gourmet cook.
   My grandmother is an angel.

▶ 5. *Assonance* is the repetition of vowel sounds. (Sandy sat at that laundromat last Saturday.)
   Consonance is the repetition of consonant sounds. (Sally sells seashells by the seashore.)
   Onomatopoeia is the use of a word whose sound makes you think of its meaning. (buzz, splash, hiss)

MATH (Statistics/Graphing)

▶ 1. *Mean* is the average. It is found by dividing the sum of all possibilities by the number of possibilities. When the possibilities are arranged in numerical order, the middle number is called the *median*. The *mode* is the number that occurs most often. The *range* is the difference between the greatest and least possibility.

▶ 2. Maps are often placed over a grid that helps the mapreader locate things more easily. The index of cities, landmarks or businesses refers to the coordinates of the grid. Have your child create an index to a map (use a map that is relevant to your child) by listing locations in alphabetical order and identifying ordered pairs. If the map does not already have an x and y axis, have your child add them.

Learn at Home, Grade 6

SCIENCE (Endangered Plants)

▶ 1. Use the following questions to guide your child's research on endangered plants:

Why might you be asked not to pick the wildflowers in a park or along a nature trail?

How has the loss of bamboo forests affected the giant panda?

Why does the deforestation of a tropical rainforest affect the many species of plants?

Why would the giant redwood forests be difficult to replace?

How does a forest fire affect the plants in a given area?

How have industrial chemicals and wastes destroyed plants in certain areas?

What was the potato famine of Ireland and what were the effects?

▶ 2. Discussion or research topic: What is the role of zoos and wildlife centers in the effort of preservation of species?

SOCIAL STUDIES (Mexico/Central America)

▶ 1. Mexico is the world's primary source of silver. Other important industries and resources are listed below.

Agriculture: beef cattle, coffee, corn, milk and wheat

Fishing: anchovies, oysters, sardines, shrimp and tuna

Manufacturing: iron and steel, motor vehicles and processed foods

Mining: iron ore, natural gas and petroleum

Exports: coffee, petroleum, motor vehicles and engines

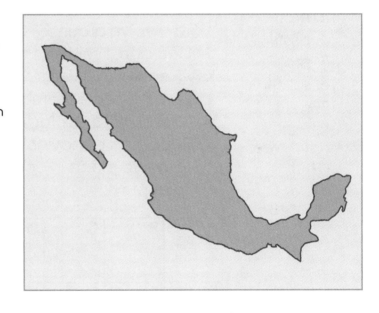

▶ 2. Have your child include the following information in his/her report:

capital

population

area

natural resources

bordering provinces/territories/U.S. states

chief agricultural products

interesting places to visit

major industries

brief history

map

▶ 3. As your child studies the countries of Central America, have him/her consider population, physical features, history, ethnic make-up, industry, agriculture, natural resources, foods, culture, economy, language, tourism and politics. Have your child choose a different area of focus for each country and a unique way in which to present the data. Each presentation may take one of the following forms:

map	report	diorama	drawing	essay
poster	interview	comic strip	poem	slide show
graph	time line	demonstration	model	puppet show

Going Into Orbit

1. admit
2. bandit
3. benefit
4. commit
5. credit
6. debit
7. edit
8. emit
9. exhibit
10. habit
11. inherit
12. limit
13. orbit
14. profit
15. prohibit
16. solicit
17. spirit
18. visit

Complete the magic square by writing the number of the word from the list in the lettered square that corresponds to its definition. One of the words will not be used.

Definitions

A. Robber or outlaw
B. To correct or revise
C. Go to see; stay as a guest
D. To restrict; boundary
E. To send forth or to give off
F. Asset; acknowledgment; recognition
G. To receive property after another dies
H. To forbid
I. To revolve around
J. Courage; liveliness
K. A record of debt; to charge with a debt
L. To serve or be useful to
M. To seek or to ask for
N. Repeated behavior, often involuntary
O. To do; to place in confinement
P. To display

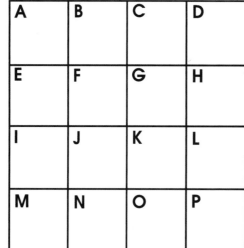

A	B	C	D
E	F	G	H
I	J	K	L
M	N	O	P

____ ____ ____ ____

Check your magic square by adding each row and then each column of numbers. If all the sums are the same, you have matched correctly.

Learn at Home, Grade 6

Browser

Graph the ordered pairs in each group. Number each dot. Connect each point with the next point using a straight line. Do not connect the last point in one group with the first point in another group. The first one is done for you.

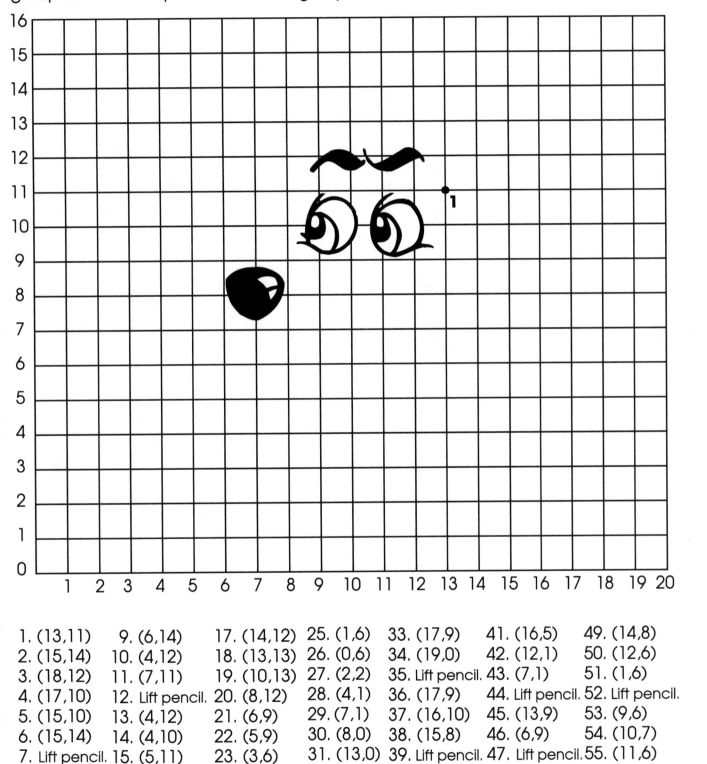

1. (13,11)	9. (6,14)	17. (14,12)	25. (1,6)	33. (17,9)	41. (16,5)	49. (14,8)
2. (15,14)	10. (4,12)	18. (13,13)	26. (0,6)	34. (19,0)	42. (12,1)	50. (12,6)
3. (18,12)	11. (7,11)	19. (10,13)	27. (2,2)	35. Lift pencil.	43. (7,1)	51. (1,6)
4. (17,10)	12. Lift pencil.	20. (8,12)	28. (4,1)	36. (17,9)	44. Lift pencil.	52. Lift pencil.
5. (15,10)	13. (4,12)	21. (6,9)	29. (7,1)	37. (16,10)	45. (13,9)	53. (9,6)
6. (15,14)	14. (4,10)	22. (5,9)	30. (8,0)	38. (15,8)	46. (6,9)	54. (10,7)
7. Lift pencil.	15. (5,11)	23. (3,6)	31. (13,0)	39. Lift pencil.	47. Lift pencil.	55. (11,6)
8. (8,12)	16. Lift pencil.	24. (2,7)	32. (17,5)	40. (16,8)	48. (14,7.5)	

Graphs

Graphs have a vertical axis and a horizontal axis. The axes are labeled to show what is being compared.

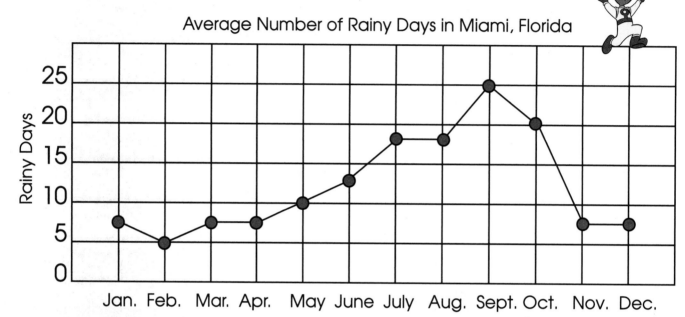

Average Number of Rainy Days in Miami, Florida

Use the data plotted on the graph to **answer** the following questions.

1. What is the title of the graph?

_____

2. How is the vertical axis labeled?

_____

3. What is contained in the horizontal axis?

_____

4. Which month had the greatest number of rainy days?

_____

5. Which two-month period shows the greatest change in the number of rainy days?

_____

6. Which month was the driest?

_____

Use the graph to **fill in** the blanks below.

7. range:_____   8. mean:_____   9. median _____   10. mode: _____

Learn at Home, Grade 6

Central America

Political Map

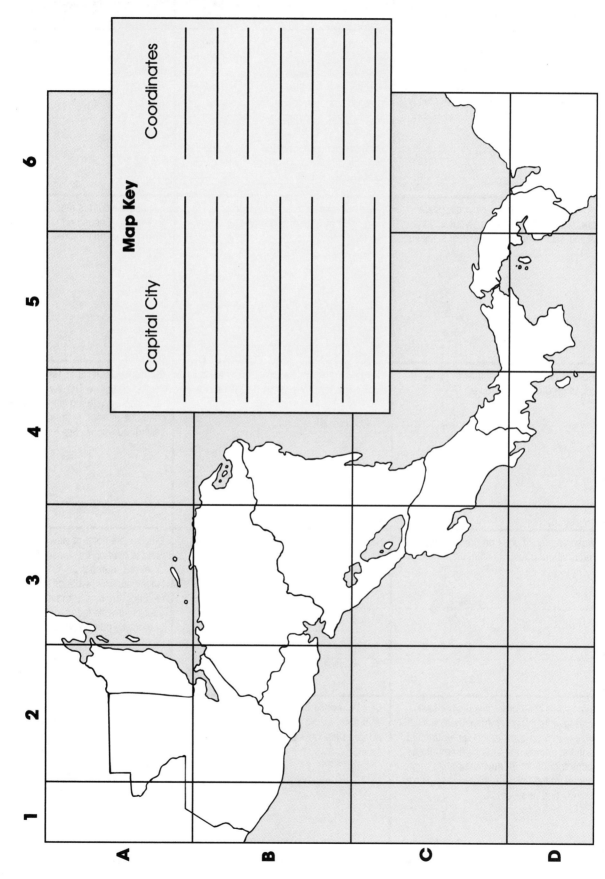

Map Key

Capital City

Coordinates

6

5

4

3

2

1

A B C D

Learn at Home, Grade 6

	Language Skills	Spelling	Reading
Monday	**Poetry** Continue to study poetry this week. Review several types of poetry with your child. *See* Language Skills, Week 33, numbers 1–6. Have your child write several *haiku* today on favorite natural subjects.	Pretest your child on the following words: author dictator monitor bachelor director orator collector editor professor conductor emperor protector conqueror inspector sculptor creator instructor senator Have your child correct the pretest. Add personalized words and make two copies of this week's study list.	Introduce this week's reading selection. Suggestion: *I, Houdini* by Lynne Reid Banks.
Tuesday	Have your child write a *cinquain* poem and a *quatrain* poem. Help your child watch the rhyme and number of syllables.	Review this week's spelling words. Have your child complete **Investigator Hector** (p. 328).	Discuss the current reading book in a conference. Focus on the distinction between fact and fantasy.
Wednesday	Have your child write a *limerick* today about an unusual character.	Have your child use each of this week's spelling words correctly in a sentence.	**Reference Materials:** Take your child to your local library. Review the different reference materials available. Have your child use different resources to answer several questions. *See* Reading, Week 33, number 1.
Thursday	Have your child write an *acrostic* poem today about a favorite animal.	Have your child study this week's spelling words.	Discuss the point of view in the book your child is reading this week. *See* Reading, Week 33, number 2. Have your child write an adventure featuring the book's main character. Have your child write the story from the main character's point of view.
Friday	Have your child assemble his/her best and favorite poems from the past few weeks into an anthology. Help your child edit the poems and arrange them into a book format. Then, have your child make copies of the finished anthology to give to friends and relatives.	Give your child the final spelling test. Have your child record pretest and final test words in his/her word bank.	Hold a reading conference. Discuss the "exceptional talents" of the book's main character. Then, discuss your child's own exceptional talents.

Learn at Home, Grade 6

Math	Science	Social Studies
Graphing Review the parts of a *line graph*. *See* Math, Week 33, number 1. A line graph shows change over time. Have your child complete **Double Line Graphs** (p. 329). Then, have your child make a double line graph to show morning and evening temperatures over the course of 7 days.	**Acid Rain** Discuss the meaning of the term *acid rain*, as well as its causes and effects. *See* Science, Week 33. Over the course of this week, your child will conduct an experiment on acid rain. The goal of the experiment is to determine how the strength of acid will affect the growth of a plant. Have your child state the problem in his/her Science Log. *See* Science, Week 33, number 1.	**Central America** Have your child research and present information on the country of Honduras. *See* Social Studies, Week 32, number 3.
Review the parts of a *bar graph*. A bar graph compares two or more quantities. *See* Math, Week 33, number 2. Have your child make a bar graph using the following information, then write three statements describing the data. **Title:** Heights of Garden Flowers **Data:** daisy – 3 ft. 6 in. yarrow – 2 ft. hollyhock – 6 ft. peony – 3 ft. coneflower – 3 ft.	Help your child form a hypothesis and record it in his/her Science Log. *See* Science, Week 33, number 2.	Have your child research and present information on the country of Panama. *See* Social Studies, Week 32, number 3.
Explain to your child that a *double bar graph* can show a comparison between two sets of data. Have your child complete **Double Bar Graphs** (p. 330).	Help your child plan the procedure for his/her acid rain experiment. Have him/her record the plan in his/her Science Log. *See* Science, Week 33, number 3.	Have your child research and present information on the country of Costa Rica. *See* Social Studies, Week 32, number 3.
A *circle graph* (or *pie chart*) is used when a whole is divided into parts. It is often used to demonstrate percentages. Have your child complete **Circle Graphs** (p. 331).	Have your child begin the experiment according to his/her plan. Remind your child to measure the acid water carefully and to water the plants according to the schedule laid out in the plan. Have your child measure the plants and record the data accurately on the chart. If he/she notices anything unusual about the plants, have him/her record the observations along with the other data.	Have your child research and present information on the country of Guatemala. *See* Social Studies, Week 32, number 3.
Have your child draw a circle graph to illustrate how he/she spends or saves money each month.	After several days (sometime in the next week or two), have your child analyze the data and draw a conclusion. Have your child write a report explaining what he/she has learned about the effects of acid rain on the growth of plants.	Have your child research and present information on the country of Nicaragua. *See* Social Studies, Week 32, number 3. Arrange for your child to perform a community service. Have your child write in his/her Social Studies Journal.

TEACHING SUGGESTIONS AND ACTIVITIES

LANGUAGE SKILLS (Poetry)

There are many different types of poetry—a poem can take almost any form. Read a variety of poetry with your child. Discuss the styles of your child's favorite poets and review the types of poems described below.

▶ 1. *Haiku* is traditionally about a topic in nature and is made up of three lines: the first and third lines have five syllables and the second line has seven syllables.

▶ 2. A *cinquain* is made up of five lines, each with a given number of syllables or words.

syllables: 2, 4, 6, 8, 2   words: 1, 2, 3, 4, 1

▶ 3. Each verse of a *quatrain* contains four lines with one of the following rhyming schemes:

a, a, a, a   a, a, b, b   a, b, a, b   a, b, b, a

▶ 4. A *limerick* is a humorous five-line poem that often begins, "There was a ____ from ____." Lines one, two and five rhyme; lines three and four rhyme and are shorter.

▶ 5. The subject of an *acrostic* poem is written vertically. Each letter in the word is used to begin a line of the poem.

▶ 6. Poems written in *free verse* have no rhyme or notable rhythm. These poems often use figurative language to create vivid images.

READING (Reference Materials)

▶ 1. Give your child the following questions to research. Have your child write the answer to each question and list where (in what type of resource book) he/she found the information.

What is the approximate latitude and longitude of Mexico City?

Who fought in the Battle of the Little Bighorn and who won?

What did General Ulysses S. Grant say when General Robert E. Lee surrendered to him at the Appomattox Courthouse?

What was unique about Helen Keller and who was her teacher?

What is the second highest point in Asia?

Who built the Great Wall of China?

What is a "nonentity"?

Who was president of the United States when Panama and the U.S. signed a treaty agreeing to the construction of a canal connecting the Atlantic and Pacific Oceans?

How many square feet are in an acre?

What are three synonyms for the word "startled"?

What artist painted the ceiling of the Sistine Chapel?

What kind of weather is the northeastern part of the United States currently experiencing?

▶ 2. *Point of view* is the angle from which a story is told.

A *first-person* point of view means the author or one of the characters is telling the story. The narrator uses the pronouns *I* and *me* to tell the story.

A *third-person* point of view means someone outside the story is telling it. The third person will be either limited (cannot see into the characters' minds) or omniscient (outside the story but knows what's in the minds of the characters).

Learn at Home, Grade 6

MATH (Graphing)

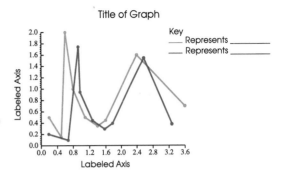

Title of Graph

Key
___ Represents _____
___ Represents _____

Labeled Axis

Labeled Axis

▶ 1. A line graph must contain the following elements:
  a. A title that clearly explains the subject of the graph
  b. Clearly labeled axes, numbers beginning at 0
  c. A legend, or key, to show what the different lines mean
  d. Specific points plotted on the graph
  e. Points connected with a line

▶ 2. A bar graph must contain the following elements:
  a. A title that clearly explains the subject of the graph
  b. Clearly labeled axes, numbers beginning at 0
  c. Shaded rectangular bars spanning from zero to the quantity represented

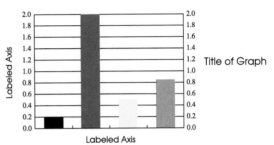

Labeled Axis

Title of Graph

Labeled Axis

SCIENCE (Acid Rain)

BACKGROUND
Rain, snow and other kinds of precipitation that are polluted by acids are called *acid rain*. Acid rain has polluted our rivers, streams and lakes, causing many fish to die. Scientists also believe that acid rain affects how plants grow.

▶ 1. This experiment will involve using different strengths of acids and recording their effects on plant growth. Have your child write a question that asks what he/she wants to learn from the experiment.

▶ 2. Before beginning the experiment, ask your child to form a *hypothesis*, or prediction, of what the results will be. What kind of effect will watering a plant with "acid rain" have on its growth? Will the "acid rain" make the plant grow taller and stronger, or shorter and weaker?

▶ 3. One of the best ways to begin this project is to find information at the library about acids and acid rain. **Working with acids can be very dangerous. Review safety rules.** Be sure your child has read about different kinds of acids, the strengths of acids, how to measure the pH of an acid and how to handle acids.

  a. Have your child grow several plants in both the control and the experimental groups. The control plants should get regular water, not acid water.

  b. Have your child write a step-by-step description of the experiment, including a list of materials, the types of acid to be used, the kinds of plants to be used, how often he/she will water the plants, how much he/she will water the plants and how he/she will measure the plants' growth. Your child should also list controlled variables, such as the amount of sunlight, type of soil and temperature.

  c. Have your child make a chart to record data. The chart should include headings such as *Plant, Water pH Level, Amount of Water/Day, Height on Day 1, Height on Day 2*, etc.

Investigator Hector

author
bachelor
collector
conductor
conqueror
creator
dictator
director
editor
emperor
inspector
instructor
monitor
orator
professor
protector
sculptor
senator

Investigator Hector must investigate several people. Read the clues to identify each person's occupation. **Write** the correct spelling word in the blank.

Clues

1. Arnie Andrew, acclaimed novelist _____
2. Darla Day, direction giver _____
3. Olive Oyle, opinionated speaker _____
4. Ernie Egoist, empire ruler _____
5. Clint Corn, card accumulator _____
6. Irene Ink, intelligent informer _____
7. Edgar Edge, eager reviser _____
8. Dastardly D., dreaded tyrant _____
9. Carl Carr, cartoon designer _____
10. Sue Smit, sincere Congresswoman _____
11. Sam Son, serious carver _____
12. Brad Bad, bearded single _____
13. Pete Pane, prominent teacher _____
14. Ivan Ize, investigative examiner _____
15. Casey Clark, choirmaster _____
16. Maggie May, money overseer _____
17. Conrad Carp, courageous victor _____
18. Prince Paul, powerful defender _____

Write a short definition for five spelling words.

1. _____

2. _____

3. _____

4. _____

5. _____

Double Line Graphs

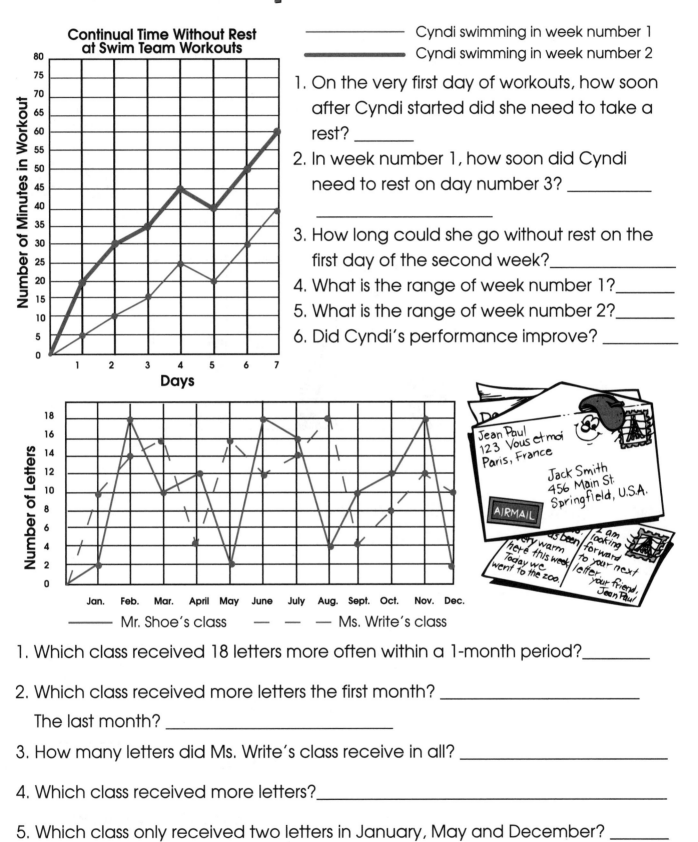

Continual Time Without Rest at Swim Team Workouts

Number of Minutes in Workout

Days

——————— Cyndi swimming in week number 1

━━━━━━━ Cyndi swimming in week number 2

1. On the very first day of workouts, how soon after Cyndi started did she need to take a rest? _____

2. In week number 1, how soon did Cyndi need to rest on day number 3? _____

   _____

3. How long could she go without rest on the first day of the second week?_____

4. What is the range of week number 1?_____

5. What is the range of week number 2?_____

6. Did Cyndi's performance improve? _____

Number of Letters

Jan. Feb. Mar. April May June July Aug. Sept. Oct. Nov. Dec.

——————— Mr. Shoe's class   — — — Ms. Write's class

1. Which class received 18 letters more often within a 1-month period?_____

2. Which class received more letters the first month? _____

   The last month? _____

3. How many letters did Ms. Write's class receive in all? _____

4. Which class received more letters?_____

5. Which class only received two letters in January, May and December? _____

_____

Double Bar Graphs

Double bar graphs allow the comparison of two sets of data. The following double bar graph compares the growth of two states. (Population figures are rounded to the nearest half million.)

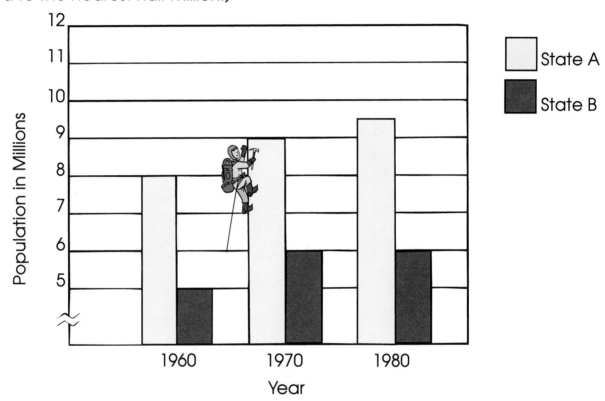

Use the graph to **answer** the following questions.

1. What was the population of State A in 1960?

_____

2. What was the population of State B in 1960?

_____

3. Which state experienced greater growth in population from 1970 to 1980?

_____

4. What was the growth of State A from 1960 to 1970?

_____

5. What was State B's population gain from 1960 to 1970?

_____

6. Which state had greater population growth from 1960 to 1980? What was it?

_____

Learn at Home, Grade 6

Circle Graphs

Circle graphs are best to use when a total amount has been divided into parts. Each part illustrates a portion of the whole.

Examples:

Favorite Soda Flavors

Cola	40%
Root Beer	30%
Lemon Lime	30%

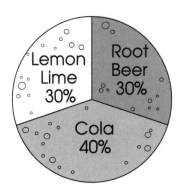

Use the following information to complete the circle graphs.

1. Birthplaces of the first ten U.S. presidents:

Virginia	60%
Massachusetts	20%
New York	10%
South Carolina	10%

2. Recyclables collected on Ecology Day:

paper	50%
aluminum cans	15%
plastic	15%
rubber	10%
glass	10%

3. Pizza preferences:

cheese	30%
cheese and pepperoni	20%
cheese and mushroom	10%
the works	40%

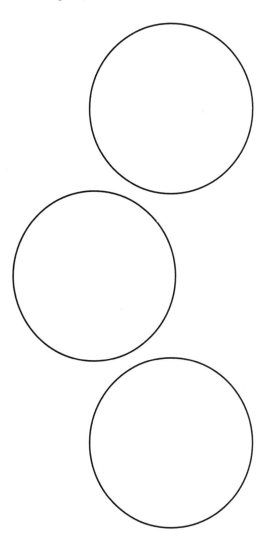

	Language Skills	**Spelling**	**Reading**
Monday	Have your child write about an autobiographical incident. The piece should have a clear beginning, middle and end. Encourage your child to express what he/she learned from the incident and include humor, if appropriate.	Pretest your child on the following words: adhesive fugitive offensive creative impressive persuasive defensive impulsive positive expensive motive relative explosive native repulsive expressive negative sensitive Have your child correct the pretest. Add personalized words and make two copies of this week's study list.	**Poetry** Select poetry anthologies for this week's reading lessons. Introduce the books today.
Tuesday	**Public Speaking:** With your child, brainstorm reasons for speaking in public. Discuss good presentation habits. *See* Language Skills, Week 34, number 1. Have your child present the paper he/she wrote yesterday. Encourage him/her to use the presentation skills discussed today.	Review this week's spelling words. Have your child complete **Creative Native** (p. 336).	Discuss the poems your child is reading in a conference.
Wednesday	Teach your child how to introduce someone properly. *See* Language Skills, Week 34, number 2. Have your child practice making introductions.	Have your child use each of this week's spelling words correctly in a sentence.	Review some of the different types of poetry and show examples of each. *See* Reading, Week 34, number 1.
Thursday	Teach your child how to give a demonstration speech. A *demonstration speech* includes verbal instructions and visual modeling of a procedure. Have your child prepare and deliver a demonstration speech on a familiar topic.	Have your child study this week's spelling words.	Read aloud a poem for your child to interpret. *See* Reading, Week 34, number 2.
Friday	Discuss some possible issues and audiences for a persuasive speech. Help your child arrange to deliver a speech to an actual audience. Suggested audiences include township board, library board, school board or city council.	Give your child the final spelling test. Have your child record pretest and final test words in his/her word bank.	Hold a reading conference. Have your child practice reading poems aloud.

Math	Science	Social Studies
Graphing Have your child convert data into percentages, then degrees of a circle to create a circle graph. *See* Math, Week 34, number 1.	**Recycling** With your child, discuss the importance of recycling. Teach your child the three *R's—reduce, reuse* and *recycle. See* Science, Week 34, number 1.	**South America** What percentage of South America's population resides in each country? Have your child make a circle graph that depicts the percentage of the population of each country as compared to the total population of the continent. *See* Social Studies, Week 34, number 1.
Have your child make a circle graph to represent the colors found in a bag of candy. Have your child tally the number of each color on a chart, then calculate the percentages of each color to make the circle graph. Finally, have your child write three statements about the data he/she collected.	Help your child find out what items can be recycled in your community. Then, have him/her make a poster that will remind you and your family to set aside those items rather than throwing them in the trash.	The countries of South America have unique terrain, diverse populations and different lifestyles. Guide your child in researching the countries individually. For each country, your child may take a different approach. *See* Social Studies, Week 34, number 2. Have your child research and present information on the country of Argentina.
Use today to review and catch up on work related to statistics and graphing.	Collect cans, bottles, straws, foam containers, cups, wrappers, boxes, rubber bands, wire, bottle caps, magazines and other disposable materials. Let your child select several of these objects to use to create a sculpture or collage.	Have your child read about Simón Bolívar. *See* Social Studies, Week 34, number 3. Have your child research and present information on the country of Bolivia. *See* Social Studies, Week 34, number 2.
Test your child's understanding of statistics. Have your child complete **Statistics Test** (p. 337). Reteach any skills missed on the test, if necessary.	Have your child write a proposal of ways your family can reduce and reuse materials. *See* Science, Week 34, number 2.	Have your child research and present information on the country of Brazil. *See* Social Studies, Week 34, number 2.
Probability: Discuss the meaning of *probability. See* Math, Week 34, number 2. Ask your child to imagine that the letters of the word *probability* are put into a bag. Have your child determine the probability of picking each letter.	Have your child read about landfills and the problems associated with creating and maintaining them. Have your child draw a diagram showing a side view of a landfill. Ask your child to explain how a landfill differs from a dump.	Have your child research and present information on the country of Chile. *See* Social Studies, Week 34, number 2. Arrange for your child to perform a community service. Have your child write in his/her Social Studies Journal.

TEACHING SUGGESTIONS AND ACTIVITIES

LANGUAGE SKILLS (Public Speaking)

▶ 1. When speaking in public, keep in mind the following points:

Know your subject. First, gather information and write it in abbreviated form. Then, write an introduction. Follow with details about the subject.

Practice. Read what you are going to say from notes. Repeat the speech several times until you are well acquainted with the sequence and wording. Deliver the speech while looking in a mirror. Tape record yourself speaking and listen.

Stand tall and look at your audience.

Speak distinctly and loud enough for the audience to hear you clearly.

Speak with appropriate expression. Use your notes only as a reminder. Avoid "filler" words like "uh" or "um."

▶ 2. Teach your child appropriate language for introducing two people who do not know each other. Teach your child to use the names of both people and to give some information that will help them understand the other's relationship to you. The italicized words in the example below explain the relationship of each person to the speaker. Using just a name will mean little to the two people you are introducing.

Example: "Dr. Bouchard, I'd like you to meet *my friend* Maggie. Maggie, this is *my doctor* who is also *my aunt's neighbor.*"

READING (Poetry)

▶ 1. Discuss what poetry is. With your child, brainstorm a list of different types of poetry (rhyming, free verse, limerick, cinquain, haiku, ballad, shape, etc.). Also discuss some of the literary devices commonly used in poetry, such as *rhyme, rhythm, alliteration, repetition, onomatopoeia* and *visual arrangement* of words.

▶ 2. Read aloud one verse at a time of a multi-verse poem, such as "Late Butterflies" by Howard Nemerov. Do not tell your child the title of the poem during the first reading. Discuss your child's interpretation after each verse. Read the poem a second time. This time, tell your child the title and read the poem in its entirety. If your child visualizes the poem any differently, ask him/her to describe the difference. Have your child fold a sheet of paper into six sections (or the number of verses) and illustrate each verse in order.

MATH (Graphing)

▶ 1. Have your child complete the chart using the given data from a bake sale held at the library. Then, have your child make a circle graph showing percentages based on this information.

Goods Sold	Number of Items	Percent	Degrees of the Circle
Cupcakes	30		
Layer Cakes	15		
Brownies	35		
Carrot Cakes	20		
Oatmeal Cookies	100		
Chocolate Chip Cookies	150		

▶ 2. *Probability* is the likelihood that a particular event will occur. Probability is expressed as a ratio in fraction form. A *probability ratio* compares the number of favorable outcomes to the total number of possible outcomes.

Example: What is the probability of a coin landing heads up on one toss? There are two sides to the coin so there are two possible outcomes to the toss. There is one favorable outcome—heads. The probability is 1 out of 2 or $^1/_2$.

Learn at Home, Grade 6

SCIENCE (Recycling)

▶ 1. With your child, brainstorm a list of objects and materials that can be reused, such as cardboard boxes, plastic spray bottles, glass containers, paper bags, plastic cups and clothing. Then, list objects and materials that can be recycled, such as newspapers, paper, cardboard boxes, plastic bottles and glass jars. Discuss ways in which your child can help reduce his/her own consumption of nonrenewable resources.

▶ 2. *Reduce:* We have become a "disposable" society. We throw away paper and plastic plates, cups, silverware, disposable diapers, paper towels, plastic garbage bags, products that come with excessive packaging and more. Be careful when you shop!

   Reduce: We often throw away broken things that could be repaired. How many times have you tossed out a toy or article of clothing because it was easier to buy a new one than to repair it?

   Reuse: We can reuse lots of things. Use both sides of a sheet of paper. Empty containers can be used for storage. Scraps and other throwaways make wonderful art materials.

   Reuse: Sometimes our trash can be someone else's treasure. Take your unwanted items to a homeless shelter or to a social service organization. Just make sure your items are not *too* well used.

SOCIAL STUDIES (South America)

▶ 1. Refer to a current encyclopedia for population information. Have your child calculate the total population of South America by adding the population figures from the twelve countries and two dependencies. Then, have your child calculate what percentage each country's population is of the total.

▶ 2. As your child studies the countries of South America, have him/her consider population, physical features, history, ethnic make-up, industry, agriculture, natural resources, foods, culture, economy, language, tourism and politics. Have your child choose a different area of focus for each country and a unique way in which to present the data. Each presentation may take one of the following forms:

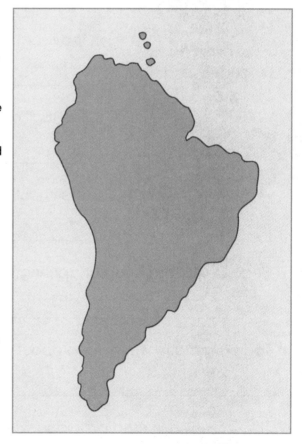

map	report	diorama
drawing	essay	poster
interview	comic strip	poem
slide show	graph	puppet show
time line	model	demonstration

▶ 3. Simón Bolívar is often called the "George Washington of South America." Have your child read to find out whether the two men could have known each other. Have your child imagine what advice Bolívar might have asked of Washington and what advice Washington might have given. Discuss whether or not "George Washington of South America" is an appropriate nickname for Bolívar. Ask your child to explain why or why not.

Creative Native

adhesive
creative
defensive
expensive
explosive
expressive
fugitive
impressive
impulsive
motive
native
negative
offensive
persuasive
positive
relative
repulsive
sensitive

Circle the two incorrect words in each sentence.
Write the correct spelling word in the blanks.

1. The detective tried to find a motion for the repulsion murder.

   _____ , _____

2. Susie is very expression and persuaded when she speaks.

   _____ , _____

3. My related wore an expenses leather coat to the mall.

   _____ , _____

4. The team used an impression defensely strategy in the game.

   _____ , _____

5. The fugition was a nation of Canada.

   _____ , _____

6. The impulsed child destroyed his creator artwork.

   _____ , _____

7. Because my skin is sensory, pulling the adhesion tape hurt.

   _____ , _____

8. Today, in math, we learned about position and negated numbers.

   _____ , _____

9. The offensly unit used exploded weapons to defeat its foe.

   _____ , _____

Learn at Home, Grade 6

Statistics Test

Create a line, circle or bar graph from the information given.

1. Kids' favorite foods:

Fast Food	Sweets	Fruit	Chips
100	220	85	95

2. Miles traveled by a salesman in 1 week:

Monday	Tuesday	Wednesday	Thursday	Friday
250	75	167	101	87

3. Amount of homework per night for each grade:

1st Grade	2nd Grade	3rd Grade	4th Grade	5th Grade	6th Grade
1/2 hr.	1 hr.	2 hr.	2 hr.	3 hr.	3 1/2 hr

4. Weather in Anytown:

Type	Autumn	Winter
Sunny	18	30
Rainy	3	10
Cloudy	6	20
Snowy	3	10

	Language Skills	Spelling	Reading
Monday	**Research Report** Discuss the procedure for organizing and writing a research report. *See* Language Skills, Week 35, number 1. Help your child choose a topic for a report and begin the research process.	Pretest your child on the following words: ability majority possibility community minority prosperity curiosity oddity quantity generosity opportunity security immunity personality simplicity longevity popularity validity Have your child correct the pretest. Add personalized words and make two copies of this week's study list.	Introduce this week's reading selection. Suggestion: *Old Possum's Book of Practical Cats* by T. S. Eliot.
Tuesday	Review how to *skim*, use an index and locate resources on a given topic. Help your child locate information on his/her topic in a variety of resources.	Review this week's spelling words. Have your child complete **Personality Plus** (p. 342).	**Characterization:** Discuss the current reading book in a conference. Focus on characterization.
Wednesday	Teach your child how to take complete notes without copying the text word for word. Write only the main ideas and exact facts that relate to the topic of the report. It is important to write notes legibly, but grammar is not an issue. Use abbreviations, write numerals and draw sketches when helpful. Introduce the concept of *plagiarism*. *See* Language Skills, Week 35, number 2.	Have your child use each of this week's spelling words correctly in a sentence.	Read aloud several poems for your child. Have him/her draw a picture based on the description in each poem.
Thursday	*Lectures* and *interviews* are two other types of sources that can be useful in researching a topic. Teach your child how to take notes from an oral presentation. *See* Language Skills, Week 35, number 3.	Have your child study this week's spelling words.	Play the music from the Broadway musical "Cats" by Andrew Lloyd Webber. Ask your child to listen for familiar lyrics.
Friday	Have your child continue to take notes from a variety of resources for the research report. Then, have your child organize his/her notes into a logical sequence.	Give your child the final spelling test. Have your child record pretest and final test words in his/her word bank.	Hold a reading conference. Have your child compare Eliot's book and Webber's music.

Learn at Home, Grade 6

Math	**Science**	**Social Studies**

Probability
A canister contains 200 jelly beans—75 cherry, 36 lime, 44 grape and 45 orange. What is the probability of choosing the given flavors?
 	
   grape   orange
   cherry   grape or lime
   orange or cherry   lime
   lemon   grape or cherry
See Math, Week 35, number 1.
	Pollution
	Define the term *pollution*. Pollution is a problem in many ecosystems. Air and water are two common types of pollution. Ask your child to name other types of pollution. Discuss the damage caused by pollution. Have your child list and describe substances that pollute the air and water. *See* Science, Week 35, number 1.
		South America
		Have your child research and present information on the country of Columbia. *See* Social Studies, Week 34, number 2.

Probability is a comparison of the number of favorable outcomes with the total possible outcomes. How do you determine the total possible outcomes of a compound event? *See* Math, Week 35, number 2. Have your child complete **Tree Diagrams and Compound Events** (p. 343).	Help your child conduct an experiment to find out if there is pollution in your area. Have your child cut 3" x 5" rectangles of adhesive shelf paper. Tape the shelf paper, sticky side out, to index cards. Punch a hole in each card and hang the cards by a piece of string in various locations in and around your house. After several weeks, examine the cards. Which locations proved to have the most pollutants in the air?	Have your child research and present information on the country of Ecuador. *See* Social Studies, Week 34, number 2.
Making tree diagrams can be cumbersome work, especially when there are many possible outcomes. Teach your child how to use multiplication to achieve the same results. *See* Math, Week 35, number 3.	The word *ozone* has more than one meaning. Ozone is created naturally in the earth's stratosphere; it blocks out the harmful ultraviolet rays from the sun. This is considered "good" ozone. Have your child read about the "bad" ozone. *See* Science, Week 35, number 2. Ask your child to design a car that does not run on gas and does not produce hydrocarbons.	Have your child research and present information on the country of Guyana. *See* Social Studies, Week 34, number 2.
Integers: Introduce your child to *integers* in a realistic situation. *See* Math, Week 35, number 4. Draw a number line to illustrate to your child the relationship between negative and positive integers.	Have your child write a haiku about an aspect of ecology. **Example:** Brown chirping insect, Munching on the wet, green grass, Watching out for frogs.	Have your child research and present information on the country of Paraguay. *See* Social Studies, Week 34, number 2.
**Make a large number line on the floor (with shelf paper) or sidewalk (with sidewalk chalk). Plot zero in the center, positive numbers to the right of zero and negative numbers to the left. Play a game in which you tell your child to walk on the number line in positive and negative directions. *See* Math, Week 35, number 5.	Help your child make a list of hazardous chemicals found in your home. Have him/her find out how to dispose of these chemicals properly. What alternatives are there to using these chemicals?	Have your child research and present information on the country of Peru. *See* Social Studies, Week 34, number 2. Arrange for your child to perform a community service. Have your child write in his/her Social Studies Journal.

TEACHING SUGGESTIONS AND ACTIVITIES

LANGUAGE SKILLS (Research Report)

▶ 1. Before your child begins working on the research report, review some organizational steps. It may be helpful to make a chart of these steps for your child's reference.

   a. Select a topic.

   b. Gather reference materials and narrow the topic.

   c. Make a list of questions about the narrow topic. Write each question on an index card.

   d. Using the reference materials, find answers to the questions and write them on the cards. Note the source of the information for use in the bibliography.

   e. If two sources present conflicting information, look at a third source to confirm one or the other.

   f. Organize the note cards in a logical sequence.

   g. Write an outline.

   h. Write a rough draft.

   i. Revise and edit the report.

   j. Write a final draft.

▶ 2. *Plagiarism* is the act of passing off another's words or ideas as your own. Do not copy words exactly from a resource without quoting or otherwise acknowledging the author.

   You may wish to quote an author if you . . .

   a. want to lend authority to your words.

   b. think the author has expressed an idea so well that you want to repeat it in your report.

▶ 3. Taking notes on a lecture or interview is difficult, since the information is said only once. Teach your child to listen carefully, filtering the information and jotting down only the important points and interesting facts. Remind your child that "correctness" is not an issue and that using abbreviations and numbers is acceptable. Give your child practice taking notes in a lecture situation. Read the following passage while your child takes notes. After the reading, discuss your child's notes. Point out any strengths and areas that need improvment.

   Alaska covers more territory than any of the fifty United States yet ranks forty-ninth in population. There is so much land that it would be possible to give one square mile to every person in the state. Alaska also contains the United States' highest point and the northernmost city. Mount McKinley is 20,320 feet high. Barrow, Alaska, is almost at the top of the world.

   California, by contrast, ranks third in state land size, with about 160,000 square miles, and first in population, with nearly 30,000,000. The population density of California is 188 persons per square mile. That is 188 times more dense than Alaska's population density. California does hold some record-breaking geographic statistics. It contains the lowest point, Death Valley, and the highest mountain in the forty-eight contiguous states, Mount Whitney.

MATH (Probability/Integers)

▶ 1. Probability ranges from 0 (an impossible occurrence) to 1 (an event that is certain to occur). Add together the probabilities of choosing grape, orange, cherry and lime jelly beans. The total should be 1, since it is certain that you will choose one of those flavors.

   Answers:

grape	$44/200$	orange	$45/200$
cherry	$75/200$	grape or lime	$80/200$
orange or cherry	$120/200$	lime	$36/200$
lemon	$0/200$	grape or cherry	$119/200$

   Imagine that someone eats all of the cherry-flavored jelly beans. Discuss what happens to the probability of choosing each of the remaining flavors. (The probability increases for the other flavors.)

Learn at Home, Grade 6

▶ 2. If you toss one coin, there are only two possible outcomes: heads and tails. If you toss a penny and a nickel, the possible outcomes increase. To find out the possible outcomes, you can draw a *tree diagram*. First, list all the possibilities with one coin (heads and tails). Then, next to each possibility, list all the possible outcomes of the other coin.

Penny Outcomes   **Nickel Outcomes**

head ——————————— head   There are four possible outcomes:
                      tail   1.   penny head, nickel head
                                     2.   penny head, nickel tail
tail ——————————— head   3.   penny tail, nickel head
                      tail   4.   penny tail, nickel tail

Out of four possible outcomes, what is the probability that you will get a penny head and a nickel head? ($^1/_4$) What is the probability that you will get two heads? ($^1/_4$) What is the probability that you will get one head and one tail? ($^2/_4$ or $^1/_2$)

▶ 3. In a compound event, multiply the possible outcomes of each event to determine the total possible outcomes.

   Example: If you roll three dice at once, what is the total number of ways the dice could land? Each die has 6 possible outcomes. Multiply 6 x 6 x 6 to get the total possible outcomes. The total is 216.

   Ask your child to determine the number of possible outcomes in the following scenario:

   A car dealership offers 32 different models of vehicles. Each model offers a choice of 8 interior colors, 8 exterior colors and the option of automatic or manual transmission. Use multiplication to determine how many combinations are possible. *Answer: 32 x 8 x 8 x 2 = 4,096 possibilities.*

▶ 4. Integers include all positive whole numbers, all negative whole numbers and zero. The opposite of 3 is – 3 as evidenced in the following equation: 3 + – 3 = 0. Both numbers are an equal distance from zero on a number line. It may be confusing to talk about negative numbers. There are many real situations in which your child may explore integers. A checkbook has credits and debits—the debits are negative numbers. Think of a football field with the center line as zero and the positive and negative yards on either side. Think of the surface of the water as zero and talk about diving below the water as a negative number and rising above the water as positive. A thermometer is also a natural tool for exploring integers. Think of your child's interests, and have him/her practice adding positive and negative integers in a realistic scenario.

▶ 5. Have your child stand on the number line at zero. Then, say an addition sentence for him/her to demonstrate by walking on the number line.

   Example: 6 + – 7 = ___
   Your child walks six steps to the right, then seven steps to the left. This will bring the child to – 1.

   Here are some other problems to get you started:

6 + – 5 =	2 + 5 =	– 3 + –5 =	– 3 + 5 =
1 + – 2 =	– 8 + 2 =	– 3 + –2 =	– 4 + 8 =
3 + – 2 + 5 + – 7 + 1 =		– 2 + 4 + –1 + 5 =	

SCIENCE (Pollution)

▶ 1. Some of the substances that pollute air and water include household and garden chemicals, insecticides, herbicides, smoke, exhaust from motor vehicles, trash, industrial wastes, mining wastes, oil spills, acid rain and chemical spills.

▶ 2. Ozone can also be a toxic gas called *smog*. Smog is an air pollutant that hovers close above the earth's surface and affects the air we breathe. Smog can irritate our eyes, burn our throats and cause damage to our forests and crops. The main chemical reaction that creates ozone occurs when we mix three main ingredients: 1) the two main components of air, nitrogen and oxygen, in high temperatures form *nitrogen oxides*; 2) *hydrocarbons*, which come from the exhaust tailpipes of cars and trucks; and 3) *sunlight*.

Personality Plus

community
validity
immunity
majority
minority
ability
quantity
personality
opportunity
generosity
curiosity
popularity
oddity
simplicity
security
prosperity
longevity
possibility

Complete each phrase with a spelling word. The words will appear in alphabetical order.

1. Don't waste your __ __ __ __ __ __ __ .

2. I live in a __ __ __ __ __ __ __ __ __ .

3. __ __ __ __ __ __ __ __ __ killed the cat.

4. The wealthy man's __ __ __ __ __ __ __ __ __ helped those less fortunate.

5. John has an __ __ __ __ __ __ __ __ to the measles.

6. __ __ __ __ __ __ __ __ __ runs in the family.

7. __ __ __ __ __ __ __ __ rules!

8. The rest of you are in the __ __ __ __ __ __ __ __ .

9. Mr. Smith's strange collection was an __ __ __ __ __ __ .

10. This is your big __ __ __ __ __ __ __ __ __ __ __ .

11. Marie has a charming __ __ __ __ __ __ __ __ __ __ __ .

12. Who will win the __ __ __ __ __ __ __ __ __ __ contest?

13. The __ __ __ __ __ __ __ __ __ __ __ __ always exists.

14. Good fortune brings __ __ __ __ __ __ __ __ __ .

15. It is sold in a large __ __ __ __ __ __ __ __ .

16. There is __ __ __ __ __ __ __ __ in numbers.

17. Life is made easier by __ __ __ __ __ __ __ __ __ __ .

18. The __ __ __ __ __ __ __ __ of her test scores was confirmed by the teacher.

Learn at Home, Grade 6

Tree Diagrams & Compound Events

Mary's family is looking at new cars. They have narrowed it down to the following choices. The tree diagram below shows the possible outcomes.

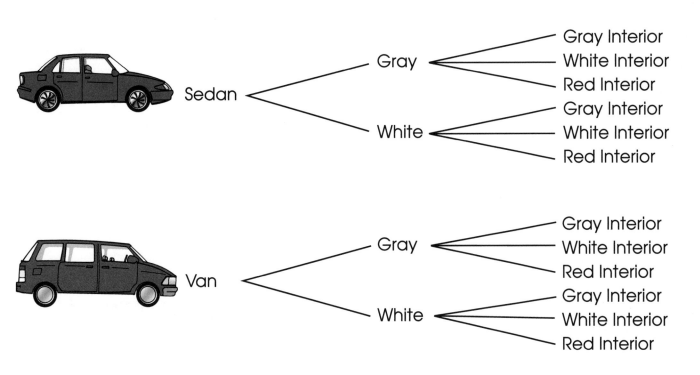

1. The compound event described above
   has how many possible outcomes?   _____

2. What is the probability that Mary's family
   will select a gray sedan with a black interior?   _____

3. What is the probability that they will select
   a gray van?   _____

4. What is the probability that they will select
   a white van with a red interior?   _____

Extension: On another sheet of paper, show a different way to figure the number of possible outcomes in this compound event without drawing a tree diagram.

	Language Skills	**Spelling**	**Reading**
Monday	**Research Report** Have your child write a rough draft of his/her report. The report should include facts learned from the research. Remind your child to use quotation marks and give credit to the author when copying material directly from a text.	Select words from the past 8 weeks for this week's pretest. Have your child correct the pretest and make a list of any misspelled words. Have your child study the list this week.	**Review of Reading** Introduce this week's reading selection or continue with the book from last week.
Tuesday	Read through the rough draft of the report with your child. Discuss. Offer some constructive criticism. Review proofreading marks. *See* Language Skills, Week 36, number 1. Have your child proofread and revise the rough draft.	Ask your child to find spelling words from the past 8 weeks that contain identifiable root words. Have your child list each spelling word and its root word.	Discuss the current reading book in a conference. Focus on the author's style.
Wednesday	Teach your child how to make a bibliography. *See* Language Skills, Week 36, number 2. Refer to a writing handbook or other resource for appropriate bibliography format for books, encyclopedias,magazines, newspapers, videos and interviews. Have your child make a bibliography of sources for the report.	Give your child clues that will lead him/her to guess a spelling word. Clues may include hints as to the word's meaning, origin, number of syllables, root words or affixes.	With your child, brainstorm a list of different types of stories, such as action, biography, fable, myth, tragedy, novel and folktale. Discuss elements of a story that make reading interesting, such as dialogue, mood, tempo and descriptive passages. Have your child complete a copy of **Story Organizer** (p. 19) for this week's book.
Thursday	Have your child do a final proofread and make a final copy of the research report.	Have your child make a crossword puzzle using spelling words from the past 8 weeks. Have your child use definitions as clues.	Have your child make a chart of the books he/she has read this year. Ask your child to make up headings for the chart to communicate what he/she has learned about literature this year. Possible headings include *title, author, genre, rating, mood, characterization, conflict, solution, best scene, lesson learned* and *recommendation*.
Friday	Have your child gather his/her best and favorite writing and artwork from this year. Help your child publish his/her work in a literary magazine. Make copies of the magazine for friends and relatives.	Give your child the final spelling test.	Hold a final reading conference. Help your child make a list of books to read over the summer.

Learn at Home, Grade 6

Math	**Science**	**Social Studies**
Integers Make a desk-size number line with positive and negative integers for your child's reference. Discuss strategies for adding positive and negative integers. Work through several problems together with your child. *See* Math, Week 36, number 1. Have your child complete the top half of **Integers** (p. 348).	**Ecology** The greenhouse effect theory holds that the temperature of the earth is gradually increasing and will soon alter the ecology of the earth. *See* Science, Week 36, number 1. Ask your child: *What do you think the effects on the ecology of the earth will be if the temperature continues to increase?*	Have your child research and present information on the country of Suriname. *See* Social Studies, Week 34, number 2.
Have your child complete situational problems that involve reading a thermometer. *See* Math, Week 36, number 2.	Help your child build a terrarium to simulate the greenhouse effect. *See* Science, Week 36, number 2.	Have your child research and present information on the country of Uruguay. *See* Social Studies, Week 34, number 2.
Subtraction with integers can be tricky. Explain that to subtract an integer, you must add its opposite. **Example:** In the problem 4 – -6, add the opposite of -6 which is +6. Rewrite the equation as 4 + +6 = 10. The difference is 10. Try it on a number line. The difference between +4 and –6 is 10. Give your child other subtraction problems to solve. *See* Math, Week 36, number 3.	Have your child interview an ecologist about his/her work. Help your child prepare questions prior to the interview about the necessary training for such a job, a typical day and what makes the job interesting. *See* Science, Week 36, number 3.	Have your child research and present information on the country of Venezuela. *See* Social Studies, Week 34, number 2.
Have your child complete the bottom half of **Integers** (p. 348). Review math skills covered this year.	Ask your child to imagine life on earth 1,000 years into the future. It will be quite different from life today. *If a group of future scientists uncovered one of our landfills, what could they learn about us? What do you think they would think of us?*	Review your study of the Western Hemisphere. Have your child complete **Mapping Mania** (pgs. 350–351).
Test your child's understanding of math concepts covered this year. Have your child complete **Overview Test** (p. 349). Reteach any skills missed on the test, if necessary.	Review concepts from the unit on ecology. Have your child write a paragraph summarizing what he/she has learned about ecology. Then, have your child write a second paragraph describing a practice he/she will change based on this learning.	Have your child evaluate his/her experience with community service. What has the child learned?

TEACHING SUGGESTIONS AND ACTIVITIES

LANGUAGE SKILLS (Research Report)

▷ 1. Teach your child how to use the following proofreader's marks:

<u>b</u>
‗ Use a capital letter   ⌐ Indent

⊙ Insert a period   ¶ Start a new paragraph

/\. Insert a comma   \/ \/ Insert quotation marks

/\ Insert   \/ Insert an apostrophe

ℬ Use a lower-case letter   ℰ Delete

▷ 2. A bibliography is a list of books or articles used in the report. The bibliography provides information about the resources so the reader can see where the writer of the report got his/her information. Each entry in the bibliography includes the title, author, publisher, location of publisher and date published. Some include page numbers or volume numbers.

MATH (Integers)

▷ 1. Give your child the following problems to solve. Discuss strategies as your child solves the problems.

$4 + -5 =$	$6 + -8 =$	$-3 + -4 =$	$8 + 9 =$
$-4 + 8 =$	$3 + -9 =$	$13 + -14 =$	$-8 + 0 =$
$-24 + 14 =$	$-3 + 15 =$	$-16 + 16 =$	$-2 + 12 =$

▷ 2. Have your child complete the following situational problems by adding and subtracting integers.

   a. In the morning, the thermometer registered –3°F. It later rose 8°, then dropped 6° by the end of the day. What was the temperature at the end of the day? (–1°F)

   b. The next day was much warmer. It started at 12°F. It later rose 8°, then dropped 6° by the end of the day. What was the temperature at the end of the day? (14°F)

   c. The storm was responsible for a very low temperature the following morning. It was –12°F, then it dropped 8° more, rose 15°, then dropped again 4°. What was the final temperature? (–9°F)

   d. The thermometer registered 28°F on Thursday morning. It quickly dropped 5°, then rose 15°, then dropped another 4°. The day ended with the temperature rising another 8°. What was the temperature at the end of the day? (42°F)

   e. Friday's temperature started at 16°F. It then dropped 3°, rose 21°, dropped 6°, then rose 4°. What was the ending temperature? (32°F)

▷ 3. Give your child the following problems to solve. Discuss strategies as your child works the problems.

$10 - (-2) =$	$7 - (-4) =$	$-6 - 8 =$	$8 - (-9) =$
$-18 - 9 =$	$-5 - (-8) =$	$15 - 20 =$	$-32 - (-10) =$
$83 - (-21) =$	$25 - (-5) =$	$21 - 40 =$	$-3 - (-3) =$

Learn at Home, Grade 6

SCIENCE (Ecology)

▶ 1. Ask your child to describe the temperature inside a closed car that has been sitting a long time in the sun during the summer. Explain that the heat rays that enter the car are trapped inside the car by the glass. The temperature increases inside the car. This is similar to the *greenhouse effect.* The atmosphere naturally traps heat and keeps the earth warm. However, since the increased use of fossil fuels has increased the amount of carbon dioxide in the atmosphere, the temperature of the earth has increased. We help prevent the addition of carbon dioxide and other gases to our atmosphere by reducing the amount of fossil fuels we use and by reducing the clear cutting of forests.

▶ 2. Place several inches of soil in the bottom of an aquarium. Plant small plants in the soil and water them lightly. Place a thermometer inside and cover the aquarium with plastic wrap. Set the aquarium in direct sunlight. Have your child observe the *terrarium* over a period of several weeks and record the temperature changes during this period. How do the plants react? Simulate the greenhouse effect by shining a heat lamp into the aquarium on the side opposite of the sun. Observe the plants over several days to see how they react.

▶ 3. Arrange for your child to interview one of the following people about his/her vocation or hobby as it relates to the field of ecology.

ecologist	wildlife manager	agriculture agent
soil conservationist	gardener	game and fish representative
park ranger	marine biologist	someone who works at an aquarium
fishing enthusiast	horticulturist	someone who raises earthworms

Integers

Solve the problems. **Write** your answers here.

1. $-12 + 1 =$

2. $-7 + 9 =$

3. $-2 + 10 =$

4. $-14 + 7 =$

5. $-12 + 12 =$

6. $-14 + 3 =$

7. $-10 + -10 =$

8. $-5 + 0 =$

9. $-12 + -11 =$

10. $-6 + 9 =$

11. $-8 + 12 =$

12. $-1 + 12 =$

13. $-15 + -10 =$

14. $-2 + 8 =$

15. $-30 + 2 =$

16. $-4 + 5 =$

17. $10 - (-14) =$

18. $-14 - (-7) =$

19. $10 - (-3) =$

20. $-10 - 6 =$

21. $-5 - (-5) =$

22. $-8 - (-9) =$

23. $-30 - (-8) =$

24. $-14 - 9 =$

25. $-16 - (-4) =$

26. $20 - 30 =$

27. $-10 - 4 =$

348

Overview Test

1. **Write** 7,245,208.07 in words. _____

_____

2. Round 3,657.189 . . .

    to the nearest hundredth. _____

    to the nearest whole number. _____

3. $d \times 14 = 56$

    $d =$ _____

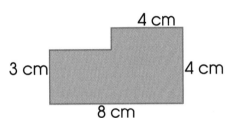

4. What is the perimeter? _____

    What is the area? _____

5. $\begin{array}{r} 792 \\ \times\ 34 \\ \hline \end{array}$

6. $2^5 =$ _____

7. $23\overline{)653}$

8. 50 hours =

    _____days

    _____hours

9. $15 + 3 \times 2 =$ _____

10. $\begin{array}{r} 0.148 \\ \times\ 0.7 \\ \hline \end{array}$

11. $2.6\overline{)15.47}$

12. $\dfrac{3}{5} \times \dfrac{10}{18} =$

13. $2\dfrac{1}{2} \div \dfrac{1}{2} =$

14. $2\dfrac{5}{8} + \dfrac{3}{4} =$

15. $17 - 5\dfrac{1}{2} =$

16. 15% of 20 = _____

17. 14 is _____% of 20

18. $\dfrac{5}{40} = \dfrac{2}{m}$

    $m =$ _____

19. $-6 + 9 =$ _____

20. $14 - (-12) =$ _____

Mapping Mania

Refer to a map of Canada and the United States to complete the following.

1. A group of islands close to each other is called an archipelago. Name the archipelago that extends southwest from Alaska. _____

2. What state is made up of an archipelago? _____

3. Why are Texas, Louisiana, Mississippi, Alabama and Florida known as the Gulf states? _____

4. The Great Lakes hold $\frac{1}{5}$ of all surface freshwater in the world. Name the American states and Canadian province that border these lakes. _____
_____

5. What Canadian province retains its French heritage and language? _____

6. Name the Canadian Maritime Provinces. _____
_____

7. Name the oceans that border Canada. _____

8. Name the American state that borders two oceans. _____
Name the oceans. _____

9. Name the state made up of two peninsulas. _____

10. Name the three major mountain chains found in North America. _____
_____

11. Locate a map with time zones. Find the number of time zones within the contiguous United States. _____ Name them. _____
_____

12. Name the states that have the Mississippi River as a border. _____
_____

Challenge!
There is one place in North America where you could get into a boat at one state capital, sail to the nearby capital of a Canadian province and continue along the coast to another state capital. Name the three capitals. _____
_____

Learn at Home, Grade 6

Refer to a map of Central America and South America to complete the following.

1. Name the large peninsula in Mexico that separates the Gulf of Mexico from the Caribbean._____

2. Name the four nations that still have possessions in the Caribbean region.

_____

3. Which Central American country is not officially Spanish speaking? (It was formerly British Honduras.)_____

4. In 1949, this Central American country abolished its army. Today, it is one of the most stable countries in Latin America. Its president won a Nobel Peace Prize in 1987 for working to end fighting in Central America. It lies west of Panama and south of Nicaragua. Identify the country. _____

5. Name the countries that border the Gulf of Mexico._____

_____

6. Which South American countries lie on the equator?_____

_____

7. Does any South American country lie completely outside the tropics? If so, which one?_____

8. Name the cape at the southern tip of South America. _____

9. Name three countries in South America where Spanish is not the official language.

_____

10. In 1935, one of the great scientists in history, Charles Darwin, spent a month in the Galápagos Islands, part of Ecuador. His visit was the inspiration for the theory of natural selection that revolutionized science. Give the absolute and relative locations of the Galápagos._____

_____

11. Name the only country in South America without a coastline. _____

Seeing Double

accept
accurate
arrange
ballot
commit
common
different
install
necessary
occasion
opposite
quarrel
really
recess
support
surround
terrible
tomorrow

Add letters to the double consonants to spell the words on the list and complete each short phrase.

1. **ba llot** box
2. **co** mm **it** a crime
3. **te rr ible** day
4. **a** cc **ept** it
5. **insta** ll a program
6. **rea** ll **y** nice
7. **rece** ss time
8. **a** rr **ange** neatly
9. special **o** cc **asion**
10. **co** mm **on** name
11. **su pport** group
12. lover's **quarrel**
13. **di fferent** choice
14. **su rr ound** sound
15. **o** pp **osite** end
16. **a** cc **urate** count
17. **nece** ss **ary** work
18. a new **to mo rr ow**

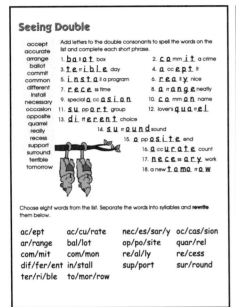

Choose eight words from the list. Separate the words into syllables and **rewrite** them below.

ac/ept	ac/cu/rate	nec/es/sar/y	oc/cas/sion
ar/range	bal/lot	op/po/site	quar/rel
com/mit	com/mon	re/al/ly	re/cess
dif/fer/ent	in/stall	sup/port	sur/round
ter/ri/ble	to/mor/row		

page 18

Story Organizer

Author _____ Date _____

Title _____

Vocabulary	Definitions
_____	_____
_____	_____
_____	_____
_____	_____

Setting: _____

Answers will vary.

Characters: _____

Problem: _____

Events: _____

_____

_____

Solution: _____

_____

Did you enjoy this story? 1 2 3 4 5 6
Not   Very
at all   much!

page 19

Down the Ladder

Follow the directions to get to the bottom of the ladder.
Start with this number.

4,351,614,926

Add 4,000,000 to the number.	4,355,614,926
Subtract 40,000 from the number.	4,355,574,926
Decrease the number by 4,000.	4,355,570,926
Increase the number by 3,000,000.	4,358,570,926
Increase it by 5,000,000.	4,363,570,926
Subtract 10 from the number.	4,363,570,916
Subtract 40,000 from the number.	4,363,530,916
Add 30,000 to the number.	4,363,560,916
Increase the number by 2,000.	4,363,562,916

YOU MADE IT TO THE BOTTOM!

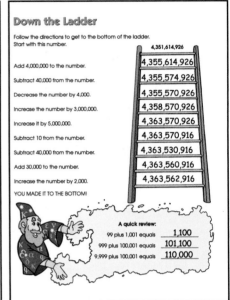

A quick review:
99 plus 1,001 equals **1,100**
999 plus 100,001 equals **101,100**
9,999 plus 100,001 equals **110,000**

page 20

Anticipation Guide

Read each statement and **circle** true or false in the left column. **Read** from a variety of resources to check the accuracy of your answers. Then, **circle** true or false in the right column as you prove or disprove statements. On another sheet of paper, **rewrite** each false statement as a true statement.

True ??? ??? False

Before Reading   **After Reading**

Answers will vary.

		After Reading
true false	1. The pituitary gland controls development and body growth.	(true) false
true false	2. Hormones are substances produced by an organism which regulates its growth and development.	true (false)
true false	3. A healthy body is able to protect itself from disease.	(true) false
true false	4. Mucus is a good substance to have in your nose.	(true) false
true false	5. Your skull has cavities.	(true) false
true false	6. An adult skeleton has 206 bones.	true (false)
true false	7. Enzymes in the stomach help digest food.	true (false)
true false	8. Blood contains plasma, blood cells and platelets.	true (false)
true false	9. The brain is made up of two hemispheres.	(true) false
true false	10. Blood traveling from the heart is full of oxygen.	(true) false
true false	11. The nervous system contains the brain, spinal cord and nerves.	true (false)
true false	12. Muscles need oxygen when they are active.	(true) false

page 21

The Supportive System

The bones are the body's supportive system. They are usually divided into two major groups—bones of the middle (skull, backbone and ribs) and bones of the arms and legs (including the shoulder and hip bones). When you were born, your skeleton was made of soft bones called **cartilage**. As you grew, most of that cartilage turned into bone. However, all people still have some cartilage in their bodies. Our noses and our ears are cartilage, and there are pads of cartilage between sections of the backbone that acts as cushions.

Bones do more than just support the body. The center of the bone, called **bone marrow**, makes new blood cells for our body. Bones are also a storage house for important minerals like calcium and phosphorous.

Answer the questions below. Use a science book or an encyclopedia if necessary.

Answers may include:
1. What are the main functions of the skeletal system?
   The skeleton supports the body.
   The skeleton protects internal organs.
   Bone marrow produces new blood cells.
   Bones store important minerals.
2. What is the largest bone in your body? **the femur**
3. What is the smallest bone in your body? **the stapes, or stirrup**
4. What do bones first develop as? **cartilage**
5. What does bone marrow do? **produces blood cells**
6. Do all bones have real bone marrow? **no**
7. What is the outer layer of a bone called? **compact bone**
8. Where two bones meet is called a **joint**

Fascinating Fact! Did you know that a giraffe has the same number of vertebrae in its neck as you?

page 23

Earthshaking Adventure

Locate each spelling word in the word search. Words can be found up, down, forward and backward.

anywhere	copyright	earthquake
earthshaking	farewell	gentleman
headache	however	landslide
lifeguard	lifetime	mantelpiece
meanwhile	nighttime	otherwise
skewbald	skinflint	throughout

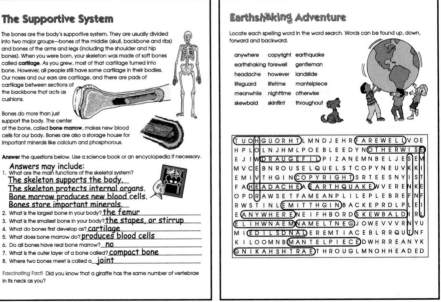

page 28

Learn at Home, Grade 6

What Time?

1. Mary was out of bed at 6:30 a.m. She had lunch 6 hours later. What time did Mary have lunch?

6 hours **Ahead** = **12:30** p.m.

2. Mary returned from school at 4:00 p.m. Mary had left for school 8½ hours earlier. What time did Mary leave for school?

8½ hours **Back** = **7:30** a.m.

3. Mary ate breakfast at 7:00 a.m. and ate dinner 11 hours later. What time did she eat dinner?

11 hours **Ahead** = **6:00 P.M.**

4. Mary started her homework at 7:30 p.m. and studied for 3½ hours. What time did Mary stop studying?

3½ hours **Ahead** = **11:00 P.M.**

5. On Saturday, Mary baby-sat for a neighbor's child. The parents returned at 3:00 p.m. They had been gone 5 hours. At what time did Mary start baby-sitting?

5 hours **Back** = **10:00 A.M.**

6. Mary's party started at 8:00 p.m. and was over 2½ hours later. Mary spent 1½ hours cleaning up after the last guest left. What time was Mary through cleaning?

4 hours **Ahead** = **12:00 A.M.**

7. Mary's math class starts at 2:30 p.m. Her music class starts 4½ hours earlier. What time does Mary's music class start?

4½ hours **Back** = **10:00 A.M.**

8. School is out at 3:00 p.m. Baseball practice lasts 2 hours, and then the team takes ½ hour to shower and get dressed. What time does the team leave school?

2½ hours **Ahead** = **5:30 P.M.**

page 29

Thermometers

Write each temperature in degrees Celsius (°C).

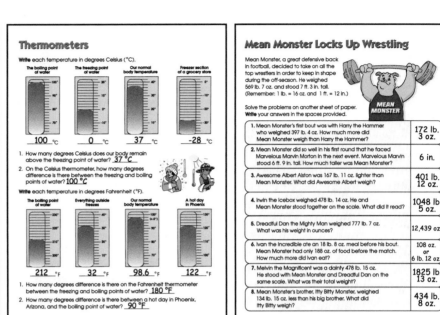

The boiling point of water **100** °C   The freezing point of water **0** °C   Our normal body temperature **37** °C   Freezer section of a grocery store **-28** °C

1. How many degrees Celsius does our body remain above the freezing point of water? **37 °C**
2. On the Celsius thermometer, how many degrees difference is there between the freezing and boiling points of water? **100 °C**

Write each temperature in degrees Fahrenheit (°F).

The boiling point of water **212** °F   Everything outside freezes **32** °F   Our normal body temperature **98.6** °F   A hot day in Phoenix **122** °F

1. How many degrees difference is there on the Fahrenheit thermometer between the freezing and boiling points of water? **180 °F**
2. How many degrees difference is there between a hot day in Phoenix, Arizona, and the boiling point of water? **90 °F**

page 30

Mean Monster Locks Up Wrestling

Mean Monster, a great defensive back in football, decided to take on all the top wrestlers in order to keep in shape during the off-season. He weighed 569 lb. 7 oz. and stood 7 ft. 3 in. tall. (Remember: 1 lb. = 16 oz. and 1 ft. = 12 in.)

Solve the problems on another sheet of paper. **Write** your answers in the spaces provided.

1. Mean Monster's first bout was with Harry the Hammer who weighed 397 lb. 4 oz. How much more did Mean Monster weigh than Harry the Hammer?	172 lb. 3 oz.
2. Mean Monster did so well in his first round that he faced Marvelous Marvin Morton in the next event. Marvelous Marvin stood 6 ft. 9 in. tall. How much taller was Mean Monster?	6 in.
3. Awesome Albert Alston was 167 lb. 11 oz. lighter than Mean Monster. What did Awesome Albert weigh?	401 lb. 12 oz.
4. Irwin the Icebox weighed 478 lb. 14 oz. He and Mean Monster stood together on the scale. What did it read?	1048 lb. 5 oz.
5. Dreadful Dan the Mighty Man weighed 777 lb. 7 oz. What was his weight in ounces?	12,439 oz.
6. Ivan the Incredible ate an 18 lb. 8 oz. meal before his bout. Mean Monster had only 188 oz. of food before the match. How much more did Ivan eat?	108 oz. or 6 lb. 12 oz.
7. Melvin the Magnificent was a dainty 478 lb. 15 oz. He stood with Mean Monster and Dreadful Dan on the same scale. What was their total weight?	1825 lb. 13 oz.
8. Mean Monster's brother, Itty Bitty Monster, weighed 134 lb. 15 oz. less than his big brother. What did Itty Bitty weigh?	434 lb. 8 oz.

page 31

Count Them

Count some of the bones in your body. Use a science book or an encyclopedia to help you **answer** the questions below.

Some answers will vary.

1. How many cavities are there in your head? **3** What are they for? **eye and air passages in nose**
2. How many bones do you feel in your upper arm? **1** How many are there? In your lower arm? **2** How many are there? How many bones are in your arms (counting your hands)? **30 each**
3. How many bones can you feel that form one palm of your hand? These are called **metacarpals** How many are there? **5**
4. How many bones do you feel in the fingers and thumb of one of your hands? How many are there? **14** These are called **phalanges** Which finger has fewer bones than the others? **thumb**
5. How many pairs of ribs do you count? How many are there? **12** How many pairs are attached to the sternum? **7**
6. How many bones do you feel in one of your legs? How many are there? **4**
7. The skeleton makes up about 18% of the body's weight. How much do you weigh? How much do your bones weigh?
8. What is the longest single bone in your body? **femur** This bone accounts for ¼ of your height. About how long is this bone?
9. An adult human skeleton has 206 bones. There are 26 vertebrae. What percentage of the body's bones comprise the backbone? **12.62%**
10. How many bones do you have altogether in your hands? **54 (27 ea)** What other part of your body has the same number of bones? **feet**

Fascinating Fact! Did you know babies are born with about 350 separate bones?

page 32

Meeting Places

The place two bones meet is called a **joint**. Joints allow us to bend, twist and turn our bodies. The human body has several different types of joints. Each allows a different kind of movement. Read the descriptions below. Then, **write** examples of the joints below each description.

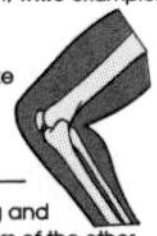

Hinge Joints — These joints can only move in one direction, like a door hinge. One bone works against another. Movement is back and forth on one plane. **Examples:**

knees, elbows

Ball-and-Socket Joints — These joints provide us with swinging and rotating movements. Make a fist with one hand. Cup the fingers of the other. Put your fist inside the cupped hand. You can turn your fist (the ball) in any direction within your cupped hand (the socket). **Examples:**

hips, shoulders

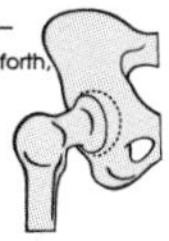

Saddle Joints — These joints move in two directions, back and forth, up and down in rotation. **Examples:**

fingers, toes

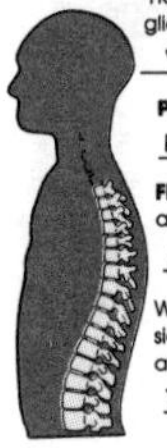

Sliding Joints — In a sliding joint, several bones next to one another bend together in limited gliding motion. **Examples:**

vertebrae

Pivot Joints — These joints give us a rotating motion. **Examples:**

neck, wrist

Fixed Joints — With these types of joints, bones are fused together and permit no movement. **Examples:**

skull, pelvis

What part of your body can move forward, backward, side to side and around on top of a vertical axis and is not one of the above?

the head

page 33

Verb Tense

The **present tense** tells what is happening now.
Example: Jamie runs today in the big race.
The **past tense** tells about an action which happened in the past.
Example: Jamie ran in the preliminary race yesterday.
The **future tense** tells about an action which will occur in the future. It is formed by using the helping verb will with the present tense of the verb.
Example: Jamie will run in the Olympics someday.

Underline the verb in each sentence. Tell whether the verb is in the present tense, past tense or future tense.

1. Thousands of years ago, the Chinese used more than one name. **past**
2. Today, the Chinese still give their children three names. **present**
3. Family names, or last names, came about in various ways. **past**
4. These names will remain for centuries into the future. **future**
5. Some writers use "pseudonyms," or fictitious names. **present**
6. Eric Blair wrote under the assumed name George Orwell. **past**
7. Immigrants will introduce new names to the United States. **future**
8. Some people use nicknames instead of their legal names. **present**

Fill in the chart below.

Verb	Present Tense	Past Tense	Future Tense
see	see, sees	saw	will see
hide	hide, hides	hid	will hide
swim	swim, swims	swam	will swim
catch	catch, catches	caught	will catch
leave	leave, leaves	left	will leave
run	run, runs	ran	will run
throw	throw, throws	threw	will throw

page 38

Answer Key

Mussel With Muscle

Write the correct homophone from the spelling words under each picture.
Write the matching homophone below it.

cymbal	symbol	hangar	hanger	muscle
mussel	pare	pear	pause	paws
plain	plane	principal	principle	tacks
tax	waist	waste		

cymbal / symbol

tacks / tax

plane / plain

waist / waste

muscle / mussel

hanger / hangar

paws / pause

principal / principle

pair / pear

page 39

The Right Stuff

Circle the resource book you would use to find . . .

1. A recipe for baking homemade bread.
   encyclopedia (cookbook) The Life of a Beaver

2. A description of how beavers make dams.
   almanac (The Life of a Beaver) The Guinness Book of World Records

3. A map of the United Kingdom.
   thesaurus (world atlas) The Guinness Book of World Records

4. The ingredients for Turkish delight.
   The Life of a Beaver   world atlas   (cookbook)

5. Information about the author, C. S. Lewis.
   almanac (encyclopedia) Guidebook for Art Instructors

6. The name of the world's most massive dam.
   (The Guinness Book of World Records) dictionary   thesaurus

7. The oldest words in the English language.
   almanac   atlas   (The Guinness Book of World Records)

8. Another word for "trouble."
   (thesaurus) atlas   cookbook

9. Why a beaver slaps its tail.
   dictionary (The Life of a Beaver) atlas

10. The pronunciation of "courtier."
    The Hobbit (dictionary) almanac

11. What camphor is used for.
    (dictionary) The Life of a Beaver thesaurus

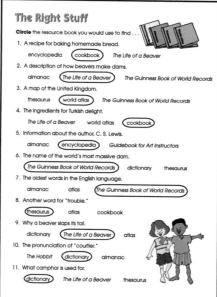

page 40

What's the Idea?

Circle the sentence that best expresses the main idea of each paragraph.

1. Edmund began to question whether or not the lion in the Queen's courtyard was alive. The large creature looked as if it were about to pounce on a dwarf. But it did not move. Then Edmund noticed the snow on the lion's head and back. Only a statue would be covered like that!
   - The statue is snow-covered.
   - (Edmund wonders if the lion is alive.)
   - The lion is ready to jump.

2. The resting party of children and beavers heard the sound of jingling bells. Mr. Beaver dashed out of his hiding place and soon called the others to join him. He could hardly contain himself with excitement. Father Christmas here!
   - Mr. Beaver is a brave animal. • The group hears a jingling sound.
   - (Father Christmas has come to Narnia.)

3. Poor Edmund! Because he came to the Queen, he expected her to reward him gratefully with Turkish delight. After all, he had traveled so far and had suffered miserably in the cold. When the Queen finally commanded that he receive food and drink, the cruel dwarf brought Edmund a bowl of water and a hunk of dry bread.
   - (Edmund is not rewarded as he expects.) • Edmund receives bread and
   - The young boy suffered from the cold.   water.

4. Peter knew he must rescue Susan from the wolf. When the wolf charged, Susan climbed up a nearby tree. The wolf's snapping and snarling mouth was inches away. When Peter looked more closely, he realized that his sister was about to faint. Rushing in with his sword, Peter slashed at the beast.
   - Peter kills the wolf. • The wolf snarls at Susan.
   - (Peter realizes he must save his sister.)

Choose one of the following sentences as your main idea and **write** a paragraph.

1. The Queen demands that Edmund be returned to her.
2. Aslan's army loses the Queen and her dwarf.
3. Father Christmas gives gifts to the beavers and the three children.

Paragraphs will vary.

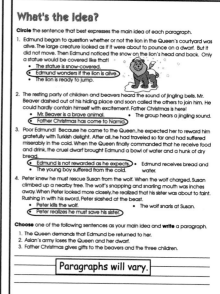

page 41

Metric Units of Length

1 cm = 10 mm

Hint: If it's 0.5 or greater, round up to the next cm. If it's less than 0.5, round down.
Complete each conversion.

30 mm = **3** cm   8.5 cm = **85** mm   50 mm = **5** cm
80 mm = **8** cm   38 mm = **3.8** cm   5.9 cm = **59** mm
14.2 cm = **142** mm   4.7 cm = **47** mm   900 mm = **90** cm

Measure each section of the rocket to the nearest millimeter.
A = **17** mm
B = **29** mm
C = **11** mm
D = **20** mm
E = **43** mm
F = **21** mm
G = **78** mm

Measure each section of the hot air balloon to the nearest half centimeter.
A = **4** cm
B = **1.5** cm
C = **7** cm
D = **2** cm
E = **1** cm
F = **4.5** cm

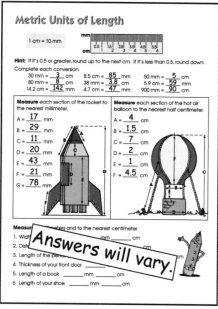

Measure ... meters and to the nearest centimeter.
1. Width ... mm ... cm
2. Dist...
3. Length of the pen...
4. Thickness of your front door ___
5. Length of a book ___ mm ___ cm
6. Length of your shoe ___ mm ___ cm

Answers will vary.

page 42

Units of Capacity

Complete each equation so that it equals 1 gallon.

1. 3 qt. + **1** qt. = 1 gal.
2. 4 c. + 2 pt. + **2** qt. = 1 gal.
3. 2 c. + 1 pt. + **3** qt. = 1 gal.
4. 3 qt. + 2 c. + **2** c. = 1 gal.

1 pt. = 2 c.   1 qt. = 2 pt.   1 gal. = 4 qt.

5. 2 pt. + **2** qt. + 1 qt. = 1 gal.
6. 6 c. + **2** c. + 2 qt. = 1 gal.

Match each equivalent capacity.

= 1 c.   = 1 pt.   = 1 qt.   = 1/2 gal.   = 1 gal.

1. a.
2. d.
3. b.
4. c.

a.
b.
c.
d.

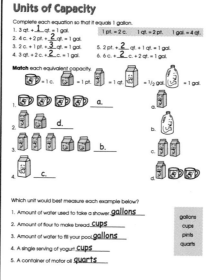

Which unit would best measure each example below?

1. Amount of water used to take a shower **gallons**
2. Amount of flour to make bread **cups**
3. Amount of water to fill your pool **gallons**
4. A single serving of yogurt **cups**
5. A container of motor oil **quarts**

gallons
cups
pints
quarts

page 43

The Body's Communication System

Your body's **central nervous system** is made up of two parts: the **brain** and the **spinal cord**. The rest of the system consists of nerves coming from the brain and the spinal cord. These nerves are called **sensory nerve cells** and **motor nerve cells**. A stimulus causes your sensory nerve cells to carry messages from your skin and sense organs to your brain.

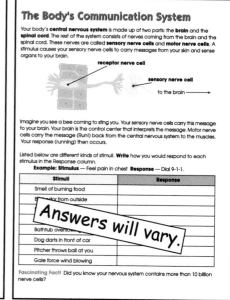

receptor nerve cell
sensory nerve cell
to the brain →

Imagine you see a bee coming to sting you. Your sensory nerve cells carry this message to your brain. Your brain is the control center that interprets the message. Motor nerve cells carry the message (Run!) back from the central nervous system to the muscles. Your response (running) then occurs.

Listed below are different kinds of stimuli. **Write** how you would respond to each stimulus in the Response column.
Example: Stimulus — Feel pain in chest **Response** — Dial 9-1-1.

Stimuli	Response
Smell of burning food	
... dog from outside	
Bathtub overflow...	Answers will vary.
Dog darts in front of car	
Pitcher throws ball at you	
Gale force wind blowing	

Fascinating Fact! Did you know your nervous system contains more than 10 billion nerve cells?

page 44

Learn at Home, Grade 6

Think Fast

While riding your bike down the street, a car suddenly pulls out in front of you. Your eyes send a message to your brain. Your brain sends a message to your muscles to apply the brakes. How long did it take you to stop? This time is called your **reaction time**.

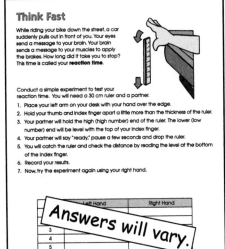

Conduct a simple experiment to test your reaction time. You will need a 30 cm ruler and a partner.

1. Place your left arm on your desk with your hand over the edge.
2. Hold your thumb and index finger apart a little more than the thickness of the ruler.
3. Your partner will hold the high (high number) end of the ruler. The lower (low number) end will be level with the top of your index finger.
4. Your partner will say "ready," pause a few seconds and drop the ruler.
5. You will catch the ruler and check the distance by reading the level at the bottom of the index finger.
6. Record your results.
7. Now, try the experiment again using your right hand.

	Left Hand	Right Hand
3		
4	*Answers will vary.*	
5		

Average: _____

Which hand had the fastest reaction time? ____

page 45

Linking or Helping Verbs

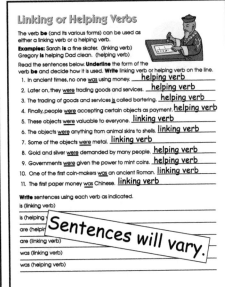

The verb **be** (and its various forms) can be used as either a linking verb or a helping verb.

Examples: Sarah **is** a fine skater. (linking verb)
Gregory **is** helping Dad clean. (helping verb)

Read the sentences below. **Underline** the form of the verb **be** and decide how it is used. **Write** linking verb or helping verb on the line.

1. In ancient times, no one <u>was</u> using money. __helping verb__
2. Later on, they <u>were</u> trading goods and services. __helping verb__
3. The trading of goods and services <u>is</u> called bartering. __helping verb__
4. Finally, people <u>were</u> accepting certain objects as payment. __helping verb__
5. These objects <u>were</u> valuable to everyone. __linking verb__
6. The objects <u>were</u> anything from animal skins to shells. __linking verb__
7. Some of the objects <u>were</u> metal. __linking verb__
8. Gold and silver <u>were</u> demanded by many people. __helping verb__
9. Governments <u>were</u> given the power to mint coins. __helping verb__
10. One of the first coin-makers <u>was</u> an ancient Roman. __linking verb__
11. The first paper money <u>was</u> Chinese. __linking verb__

Write sentences using each verb as indicated.

is (linking verb)

is (helping *Sentences will vary.*

are (helping

are (linking verb)

was (linking verb)

was (helping verb)

page 50

Present a Present

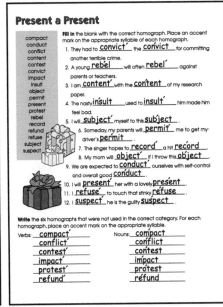

compact
conduct
conflict
content
contest
convict
impact
insult
object
permit
present
protest
rebel
record
refund
refuse
subject
suspect

Fill in the blank with the correct homograph. Place an accent mark on the appropriate syllable of each homograph.

1. They had to __convict´__ the __con´vict__ for committing another terrible crime.
2. A young __rebel´__ will often __rebel´__ against parents or teachers.
3. I am __content´__ with the __con´tent__ of my research paper.
4. The nasty __in´sult__ used to __insult´__ him made him feel bad.
5. I will __subject´__ myself to this __sub´ject__ .
6. Someday, my parents will __permit´__ me to get my driver's __per´mit__ .
7. The singer hopes to __record´__ a hit __rec´ord__ .
8. My mom will __object´__ if I throw this __ob´ject__ .
9. We are expected to __conduct´__ ourselves with self-control and overall good __con´duct__ .
10. I will __present´__ her with a lovely __pres´ent__ .
11. I __refuse´__ to touch that stinky __ref´use__ .
12. I __suspect´__ he is the guilty __sus´pect__ .

Write the six homographs that were not used in the correct category. For each homograph, place an accent mark on the appropriate syllable.

Verbs:	Nouns:
__compact´__	__com´pact__
__conflict´__	__con´flict__
__contest´__	__con´test__
__impact´__	__im´pact__
__protest´__	__pro´test__
__refund´__	__re´fund__

page 51

Geometric Figures

Example	Description	Symbol	Read
Point	A point is an end of a line segment (an exact location in space).	A	point A
Line	A line is a collection of points in a straight path that extends in two directions without end.	$\overleftrightarrow{DE}$	line DE
Line Segment	A line segment is part of a line with two endpoints.	$\overline{RS}$	segment RS
Ray	A ray is part of a line having only one endpoint.	$\overrightarrow{BC}$	ray BC
Angle	An angle is two rays having a common endpoint.	$\angle CDE$	angle CDE
Plane	A plane is an endless flat surface.	plane STU	plane STU

Use the figure to **write** the symbol for each.

1. 1 ray ____
2. a plane ____
3. 3 points ____ *Answers will vary.*
4. 2 lines ____
5. 3 angles ____
6. 3 line segments ____

page 52

What Am I?

To find the answers to the two riddles below, find the answer that matches each figure and **write** the figure's corresponding letter above it.

What is the most prevalent form of life on Earth?

I N S E C T S
$\overrightarrow{AB}$ $\overline{AB}$ $\overleftrightarrow{MN}$ $\overline{NM}$ Point G · Point C · Plane A

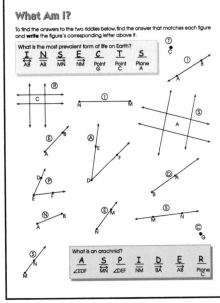

What is an arachnid?

A S P I D E R
$\angle EDF$ $\overleftrightarrow{MN}$ $\angle DEF$ $\overline{NM}$ $\overrightarrow{BA}$ $\overline{AB}$ Plane C

page 53

Classifying Triangles

The sum of the angles in any triangle is 180°.

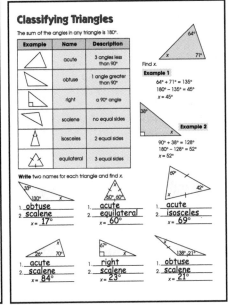

Example	Name	Description
	acute	3 angles less than 90°
	obtuse	1 angle greater than 90°
	right	a 90° angle
	scalene	no equal sides
	isosceles	2 equal sides
	equilateral	3 equal sides

Find x.

Example 1
64° + 71° = 135°
180° – 135° = 45°
x = 45°

Example 2
90° + 38° = 128°
180° – 128° = 52°
x = 52°

Write two names for each triangle and find x.

1. obtuse
2. scalene
   x = 17°

1. acute
2. equilateral
   x = 60°

1. acute
2. isosceles
   x = 69°

1. acute
2. scalene
   x = 84°

1. right
2. scalene
   x = 23°

1. obtuse
2. scalene
   x = 21°

page 54

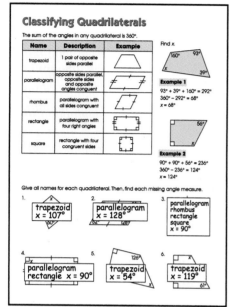

Classifying Quadrilaterals

The sum of the angles in any quadrilateral is 360°.

Name	Description	Example
trapezoid	1 pair of opposite sides parallel	
parallelogram	opposite sides parallel, opposite sides and opposite angles congruent	
rhombus	parallelogram with all sides congruent	
rectangle	parallelogram with four right angles	
square	rectangle with four congruent sides	

Find x.

Example 1
93° + 39° + 160° = 292°
360° – 292° = 68°
x = 68°

Example 2
90° + 90° + 56° = 236°
360° – 236° = 124°
x = 124°

Give all names for each quadrilateral. Then, find each missing angle measure.

1. trapezoid x = 107°
2. parallelogram x = 128°
3. parallelogram rhombus rectangle square x = 90°
4. parallelogram rectangle x = 90°
5. trapezoid x = 54°
6. trapezoid x = 119°

page 55

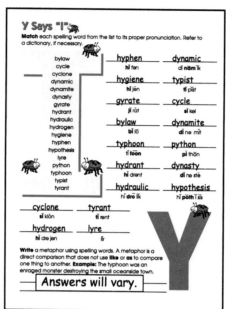

Y Says "I"

Match each spelling word from the list to its proper pronunciation. Refer to a dictionary, if necessary.

bylaw
cycle
cyclone
dynamic
dynamite
dynasty
gyrate
hydrant
hydraulic
hydrogen
hygiene
hyphen
hypothesis
lyre
python
typhoon
typist
tyrant

hyphen — hī fen
dynamic — dī năm ĭk
hygiene — hī jēn
typist — tī pĭst
gyrate — jī rāt
cycle — sī kel
bylaw — bī lô
dynamite — dī ne mīt
typhoon — tī fōōn
python — pī thŏn
hydrant — hī drent
dynasty — dī ne stē
hydraulic — hī drô lĭk
hypothesis — hī pŏth ĭ sĭs
cyclone — sī klōn
tyrant — tī rent
hydrogen — hī dre jen
lyre — līr

Write a metaphor using spelling words. A metaphor is a direct comparison that does not use **like** or **as** to compare one thing to another. **Example:** The typhoon was an enraged monster destroying the small oceanside town.

Answers will vary.

page 60

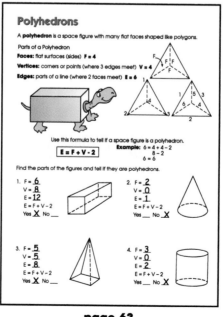

Summer Daze

Write the number of the definition that applies to each **bold** word.

3 1. When Mr. Wong works, he never **putters** around.

2 2. Mabel would **cop** the prize as the best stickball player in the sixth grade.

2 3. The two small girls will **stalk** the tiger swallowtail very carefully.

3 4. The **cop** smiled as Shirley humbly scurried by.

1 5. I would wear gloves if I wished to climb that **spruce** in the forest.

2 6. Shirley imagined spiders **stalking** her in the furnace room.

1 7. She never considered that she might **cop** fruit from the market.

3 8. Will the students **spruce** up the playground before they leave for the summer?

2 9. The **putter** missed the ninth hole by a mile.

1 10. Shirley discovered that she liked celery **stalks** very much.

Glossary

stalk 1) a plant stem 2) to stealthily pursue one's prey 3) to walk with a slow, stiff stride

putter 1) a golf club used on the green 2) a golfer who putts 3) to work slowly

cop 1) to steal 2) to capture 3) a police officer

spruce 1) an evergreen tree 2) the wood from this tree 3) to make neat

page 61

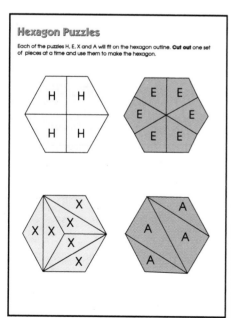

Hexagon Puzzles

Each of the puzzles H, E, X and A will fit on the hexagon outline. **Cut out** one set of pieces at a time and use them to make the hexagon.

page 62

Polyhedrons

A **polyhedron** is a space figure with many flat faces shaped like polygons.

Parts of a Polyhedron
Faces: flat surfaces (sides) F = 4
Vertices: corners or points (where 3 edges meet) V = 4
Edges: parts of a line (where 2 faces meet) E = 6

Use this formula to tell if a space figure is a polyhedron.
$$E = F + V - 2$$

Example: 6 = 4 + 4 – 2
8 – 2
6 = 6

Find the parts of the figures and tell if they are polyhedrons.

1. F = 6
V = 8
E = 12
E = F + V – 2
Yes X No __

2. F = 2
V = 0
E = 1
E = F + V – 2
Yes __ No X

3. F = 5
V = 5
E = 8
E = F + V – 2
Yes X No __

4. F = 3
V = 0
E = 2
E = F + V – 2
Yes __ No X

page 63

The Circulatory System I

Read the information below. **Underline** the two main functions and the main organ of the circulatory system. Then, answer the questions.

The circulatory system is responsible for transporting materials throughout the body and for regulating body temperature.

The heart is vital to the circulatory system. It pumps blood to all parts of the body. The blood then carries nutrients and other important materials to the cells. Blood also carries waste products away from cells to disposal sites like the liver, lungs and kidneys.

The circulatory system also acts as a temperature control for the body. Warmer blood from the center of the body is brought to the surface to be cooled. On a cold day, the blood vessels contract very little allowing little blood to flow through. This is why skin might appear pale, or even blue. However, in hot weather, blood vessels widen and more blood is able to flow through them to increase the loss of heat. Thus, your skin looks pinker and feels warmer.

1. What are the two main functions of the circulatory system? transporting materials throughout the body and regulating body temperature

2. The blood carries important nutrients to the cells

3. Blood carries waste products away from cells and to the liver lungs and kidneys

4. Warmer blood is brought from the center of the body to the surface of the body to be cooled.

5. In cold weather, why does your skin appear pale, or even blue? Blood vessels contract, allowing little blood to flow through.

A "Hearty" Experiment
You will need: a tennis ball and a watch with a second hand. Hold the tennis ball in your stronger hand and give it a hard squeeze. This is about the strength it takes your heart muscle to contract to pump one beat. Squeeze the ball as hard as you can and release it 70 times in 1 min.
Record how you Answers will vary.
Conclusion:

page 64

Learn at Home, Grade 6

The Circulatory System II

There are two circulatory systems in the human body. Each begins and ends in the heart. The larger system is called the **systemic circulatory system**. It branches out to all parts of the body with oxygenated blood and returns to the heart with "bad blood." The smaller system is called the **pulmonary circulatory system**. It is much shorter because it travels only to the lungs and back to the heart with oxygenated blood.

Blood vessels that carry blood to the heart are called **veins**. Those that carry it away are called **arteries**. Blood from the systemic circulatory system flows from the **superior and interior vena cavas** into the **right atrium**, then into the **right ventricle** and out through the **pulmonary arteries** to the lungs. At the same time, blood from the lungs enters the atrium from pulmonary veins, drops into the **left ventricle**, is pumped into the body's largest artery, called the **aorta**, then flows into blood vessels that carry it to various parts of the body.

Follow the directions below.
1. **Color** the systemic circulatory system red.
2. **Color** the pulmonary circulatory system grey.
3. **Draw** blue arrows to show the flow of the systemic circulatory system.
4. **Draw** black arrows to show the flow of the pulmonary circulatory system.
5. **Label** the parts of the circulatory system listed in the box. If a number in parentheses follows a part, label it that many times.

aorta
superior and inferior vena cava
right and left atriums
right and left ventricles
pulmonary veins (2)
arteries leading from aorta
pulmonary arteries (2)

Labels: aorta, arteries from aorta, superior vena cava, pulmonary artery, pulmonary artery, pulmonary veins, right atrium, inferior vena cava, right ventricle, left ventricle, pulmonary veins, left atrium

page 65

Agreement of Subject and Verb

A **singular subject** takes a singular verb.
Example: Bill washes the dishes.

A **plural subject** takes a plural verb.
Example: They watch television.

A **compound subject** connected by **and** takes a plural verb.
Example: Mary and Bill read books.

For a **compound subject** connected by **either/or** or **neither/nor**, the verb agrees with the subject closer to it.
Examples: Either my aunt or my uncle takes us to games. Neither my grandfather nor my grandmothers are over 85 years old.

A **singular indefinite pronoun** as the subject takes a singular verb (anybody, anyone, everybody, everyone, no one, somebody, someone, something).
Example: Everyone enjoys games.

Write the correct present-tense form of each verb on the line.

1. Everyone __enjoys__ wearing interesting hats. (enjoy)
2. Many people __wear__ hats for various activities. (wear)
3. One factory __makes__ only felt hats. (make)
4. Either bamboo grass or the leaves of a pine tree __make__ wonderful straw hats. (make)
5. Factories __produce__ straw hats, too. (produce)
6. Somebody __braids__ the straw material. (braid)
7. Either machines or a worker __bleaches__ the braided material. (bleach)
8. Chemicals and gelatins __stiffen__ straw hats. (stiffen)
9. Ironing __finishes__ the hat-making process. (finish)

page 70

Tony's Tuxedo

banjo
buffalo
echo
halo
mosquito
patio
portfolio
ratio
rodeo
silo
soprano
stereo
studio
tobacco
tomato
tornado
tuxedo
zero

Write the spelling words in the correct category. The first one is done for you.

Two-Syllable Words
ban·jo
ec·ho
ha·lo
si·lo
ze·ro
rat·i·o

Three-Syllable Words
to·bac·co
ro·de·o
to·ma·to
mos·qui·to
so·pra·no
ste·re·o
tux·e·do
buf·fa·lo
tor·na·do
stu·di·o
pat·i·o

Four-Syllable Word
port·fo·li·o

Alliteration is a poetic device that groups words together with the same initial sound. **Write** a sentence using alliteration that includes at least two of your spelling words.
Example: Tony the tourist tried to tuck in his untidy tuxedo during a terrible tornado in town.

Answers will vary.

page 71

Perimeter

Perimeter is the distance around an area. Find the perimeter of each figure.

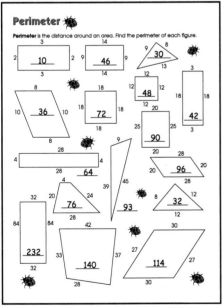

page 72

Area

Area is the number of square units contained in a surface. Find the area of each outlined shape by counting units.

Hint: $\frac{1}{2}$ of 4   Hint: $\frac{1}{2}$ of 10

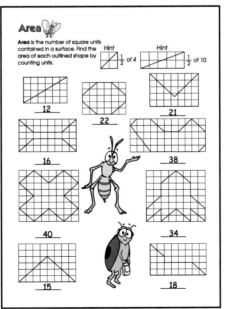

page 73

Volume

Volume is the measure of the inside of a figure. Find the volume. Count the boxes.

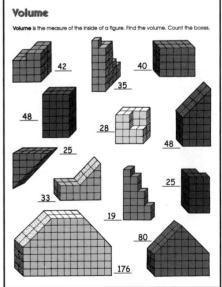

42, 40, 35, 48, 28, 48, 25, 25, 33, 19, 80, 176

page 74

Volume of Prisms

Volume is measured in cubic units.
Volume of a nonrectangular prism
= base area • height

Volume of a rectangular prism
= l • w • h

$V = b \cdot h$
$V = (\frac{1}{2} \cdot 4 \cdot 6) \cdot 12$
$V = 144 \text{ in}^3$

$V = 8 \cdot 5 \cdot 3$
$V = 120 \text{ m}^3$

Find the volume of each prism

1. 1050 cm^3
4. 343 in.^3
7. 18 ft.^3

2. 12.768 ft.^3
5. $1\frac{1}{5} \text{ cm}^3$
8. 60 mm^3

3. 50 m^3
6. 120 in.^3

page 75

The Digestive/Urinary System

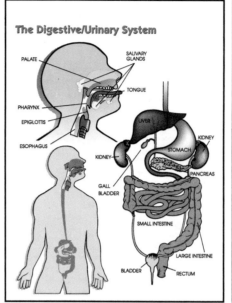

PALATE, SALIVARY GLANDS, TONGUE, PHARYNX, EPIGLOTTIS, LIVER, ESOPHAGUS, KIDNEY, STOMACH, KIDNEY, PANCREAS, GALL BLADDER, SMALL INTESTINE, LARGE INTESTINE, BLADDER, RECTUM

page 76

Traveling the Alimentary Canal

After you take a bite of food, it travels along a path through the human body called the **alimentary canal**, or the digestive tract. The canal, as it is shown here, is not how it actually is inside the body. Inside your body, it is folded back and forth so that it fits.

Fill in the missing words in the paragraph below. Use the words in the Word Box. You might also need a science book or an encyclopedia to help you.

Food and water enter the alimentary canal by way of the __mouth__. Digestion of food begins here where it is __chewed__ and broken into smaller pieces. Digestive enzymes, produced by __salivary glands__, help to break down food further before it is swallowed and passed through the __esophagus__ into the __stomach__. In the stomach, the food is mixed with __enzymes__ and digestive juices in a churning motion. As the food is digested, it changes into a thick liquid called __chyme__. The chyme passes into the __small intestine__ in small amounts. The __pancreas__ produces pancreatic juices, and the __liver__ produces __bile__ which is stored in the __gall bladder__. These are released into the small intestine as needed to work with intestinal juices and chyme and contractions made by the intestine's walls to move the chyme along. The digested food is absorbed by tiny __blood__ and lymph vessels in the __walls__ of the small intestine and carried through the __circulatory__ system to feed the body. Small amounts of water and minerals are removed from undigested food matter, and this and waste food products are stored in the __large intestine__. This waste becomes a solid, brown material called __feces__ which is finally eliminated through the __rectum__.

salivary glands	enzymes	large intestine	chyme
pancreas	mouth	small intestine	esophagus
rectum	stomach	gall bladder	feces
circulatory	chewed	blood	walls
liver	bile		

Fascinating Fact! Did you know that during your lifetime, your digestive system may process between 60,000 and 100,000 pounds of food?

page 77

Comparing With Adjectives

The **comparative** form of an adjective is used to compare two nouns. It is formed in two ways: by adding the suffix **er** to the adjective or by using the words **more** or **less** with the adjective.

Examples:

David is a **faster** runner than Thomas.
David is **more** diligent at track practice than Thomas.

The **superlative** form of an adjective is used to compare three or more nouns. It is also formed in two ways: by adding the suffix **est** to the adjective or by using the words **most** or **least** with the adjective.

Examples:

David is the **fastest** runner on the track team.
David is the **most** diligent worker on the track team.

Circle the adjective of comparison in each of the following sentences. On the line, **write** if the adjective is written using the comparative form or the superlative form.

1. Central High has the (shortest) basketball team in the league. __superlative__

2. One of their (most skillful) plays is to pass the ball through their opponents' legs. __superlative__

3. Central wins a lot of games because the team's players are (more clever) dribblers than the opposing players. __comparative__

4. The opposing team is (dizzier) because Central dribbles circles around them. __comparative__

5. The (toughest) game of the year was against South High. __superlative__

6. Central's captain won the game with the (fanciest) shot of the game. __superlative__

page 82

Desert Merchant

clergy
clerk
concern
derby
desert
dessert
error
fern
fertilizer
intern
merchant
mercury
referee
reserve
serpent
sherbet
temperature
thermostat

Write a spelling word to complete each phrase. Be sure to **write** the possessive form when it's required.

Possessive Nouns

1. __mercant's__ merchandise
2. __mercury's__ chemical symbol
3. __referee's__ decision
4. __thermostat's__ temperature
5. __serpent's__ scales
6. __intern's__ patients
7. __clergy's__ church
8. __clerk's__ store
9. __desert's__ sand

Nouns

10. man's felt __derby__
11. patio's potted __fern__
12. Susie's orange __sherbert__
13. gas tank's __reserve__
14. diner's delicious __dessert__
15. mathematician's __error__
16. farmer's __fertilizer__
17. Carol's constant __concern__
18. sick child's __temperature__

Use the nouns from the list to form possessives in a few sentences.

Sentences will vary.

page 83

Understanding Rembrandt

Answer the questions below from your reading of Rembrandt.

True or False
Rembrandt . . .

__T__ was one of the greatest artists of all time.
__F__ was born on July 15, 1606, in Florence, Italy.
__T__ began painting at an early age.
__F__ traveled to Amsterdam at the age of fifteen to study architecture.

Check and write:
Rembrandt used ☐ soft ☑ bright colors and __glossy__ paints.

Underline:
In 1634, Rembrandt married . . .
a wealthy and educated girl named Saskia.
a poor girl from Amsterdam named Saskia.

Check and write:
Although Rembrandt was successful as an artist,
☑ tragedy ☐ good fortune began to strike his family.

Three of his __4__ children died at a very early age.

In 1642, ☐ Rembrandt's father died. ☑ Rembrandt's wife died.

Rembrandt's sadness caused him to use ☑ darker ☐ lighter colors.

Check, circle and write:
Rembrandt died on October 4, ☑ 1669. ☐ 1700.

Rembrandt's most famous painting was called __The Night Watch__

Rembrandt's works included:

☑ paintings ☑ drawings ☑ etchings ☑ self-portraits

page 85

Learn at Home, Grade 6

Multiplication

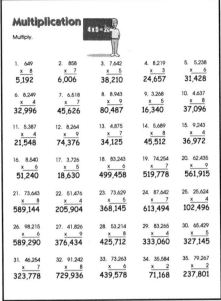

Multiply.

1. 649 × 8 = **5,192**	2. 858 × 7 = **6,006**	3. 7,642 × 5 = **38,210**	4. 8,219 × 3 = **24,657**	5. 5,238 × 6 = **31,428**
6. 8,249 × 4 = **32,996**	7. 6,518 × 7 = **45,626**	8. 8,943 × 9 = **80,487**	9. 3,268 × 5 = **16,340**	10. 4,637 × 8 = **37,096**
11. 5,387 × 4 = **21,548**	12. 8,264 × 9 = **74,376**	13. 4,875 × 7 = **34,125**	14. 5,689 × 8 = **45,512**	15. 9,243 × 4 = **36,972**
16. 8,540 × 6 = **51,240**	17. 3,726 × 5 = **18,630**	18. 83,243 × 6 = **499,458**	19. 74,254 × 7 = **519,778**	20. 62,435 × 9 = **561,915**
21. 73,643 × 8 = **589,144**	22. 51,476 × 4 = **205,904**	23. 73,629 × 5 = **368,145**	24. 87,642 × 7 = **613,494**	25. 25,624 × 4 = **102,496**
26. 98,215 × 6 = **589,290**	27. 41,826 × 9 = **376,434**	28. 53,214 × 8 = **425,712**	29. 83,265 × 4 = **333,060**	30. 65,429 × 5 = **327,145**
31. 46,254 × 7 = **323,778**	32. 91,242 × 8 = **729,936**	33. 73,263 × 6 = **439,578**	34. 35,584 × 2 = **71,168**	35. 79,267 × 2 = **237,801**

page 86

The Stock Market

Choose a stock to follow for the next 4 weeks. **Fill in** the information about your stock in the box below. Then, track the information you find in the newspaper on the chart.

Name of stock _____
Information will vary.
Total cost _____

Answers will vary.

Date	High	Low	Close	Net Change		Date	High	Low	Close	Net Change

After 4 weeks, complete the following analysis of your stock's performance.

1. What was the highest price per share during the past 4 weeks? _____
2. At that price, what would have been the total value of your stock? _____
3. If you had sold your shares that day, what would have been your profit or loss? _____
4. What was the lowest price per share during the past 4 weeks? _____
5. At that price, what would have been the total value of your stock? _____
6. If you had sold your shares that day, what would have been your profit or loss? _____

page 87

This, That, These, Those

The adjectives **this** and **that** are singular. The adjectives **these** and **those** are plural. **This** and **these** refer to things that are nearby. **That** and **those** refer to things that are farther away.

Examples: This elevator we are riding is called a "lift" in England.
Those apartments across the street are called "flats."

Use **this** and **that** correctly in the sentences below.
1. **This** cookie I have in my hand is called a "biscuit" in England.
2. **That** car trunk over there is called a "boot."
3. **This** parking lot is called a "car park."
4. **That** vacation we took last year would be called a "holiday."
5. **That** box of French fries Monica has is called "chips."
6. **That** can of fruit on the shelf is called a "bottle" of fruit.

Use **these** and **those** correctly in the sentences below.
1. **Those** dollars she is handing you are the English form of currency called "pounds."
2. Isn't it interesting how **those** baby carriages across the street are called "prams"?
3. **Those** bathrooms we just passed are called "loos."
4. **Those** 7 gallons of gas you purchased at the last gas station would be called "petrol" in England.
5. All **Those** soccer games you had fun playing in would be called "football games."
6. **These** differences show that even though people in both countries speak English, we are separate and unique in our own language.

page 92

Proper Nouns and Adjectives

Proper nouns and **adjectives** always begin with a capital letter.

Examples: Mount Rainier
the Sahara Desert (**the** is usually not capitalized)
the English language
Italians

Underline each geographical name that should be capitalized.

<u>australia</u> is the smallest continent on Earth. The western half of this continent is dominated by the <u>great sandy desert</u>, the <u>gibson desert</u> and the <u>great victoria desert</u>. Two mountain ranges, the <u>macdonnell range</u> and the <u>musgrave range</u>, are located in this area. The great dividing range is a long mountain chain that runs along <u>australia</u>'s eastern coastline. Surrounding this small continent are the <u>indian ocean</u>, the <u>timor sea</u>, the <u>arafura sea</u>, the <u>coral sea</u> and the <u>pacific ocean</u>. You may have read about the <u>great barrier reef</u>, which lies between its northeast shoreline and the <u>coral sea</u>.

<u>australia</u> is divided into six main areas: <u>western australia</u>, <u>south australia</u>, the <u>northern territory</u>, <u>queensland</u>, <u>new south wales</u> and <u>victoria</u>. The capital of <u>australia</u> is <u>canberra</u>, which is located in <u>new south wales</u>. Its highest point is <u>mt. kosciusko</u>, which is southwest of <u>canberra</u>. Two large lakes, <u>lake eyre</u> and <u>lake torrens</u>, lie in <u>south australia</u>. The <u>darling</u>, <u>warrego</u> and <u>murray</u> rivers flow through the southeast corner. Much of <u>australia</u>'s land is used for grazing sheep and cattle.

Underline each word that should be capitalized.
1. <u>americans</u> and the <u>english</u> speak the <u>english</u> language.
2. <u>english</u> is a <u>germanic</u> language, as are <u>german</u> and <u>dutch</u>.
3. <u>swedish</u>, <u>norwegian</u> and <u>danish</u> are also <u>germanic</u> languages.
4. <u>italian</u> and <u>spanish</u> are two romance languages.
5. The <u>romance</u> languages come from <u>latin</u>, the language of all <u>romans</u>.
6. The languages of the <u>russians</u>, <u>poles</u>, <u>czechs</u> and <u>slavs</u> have a common origin.
7. Many <u>africans</u> speak <u>hebrew</u> and <u>arabic</u>.
8. The language of <u>indians</u> and <u>pakistanis</u> is hindustani.
9. Many <u>american</u> students study <u>french</u> and <u>german</u>.
10. <u>spanish</u> and <u>latin</u> are also often studied.

page 93

Scrambled Eggs

Word list:
breakfast, breath, cleanse, dread, feather, health, heavy, instead, leather, meant, spread, sweat, thread, threat, tread, wealth, weapon, weather

Unscramble each group of letters to spell a word from the list.

trlehae	**leather**	hhetal	**health**	
lwehat	**wealth**	tnmea	**meant**	
tsewa	**sweat**	dhtrae	**thread**	
rddae	**dread**	tterah	**threat**	
ayveh	**heavy**	eteharw	**weather**	
dtare	**tread**	oanwpe	**weapon**	
tekarbasf	**breakfast**	sdatnei	**instead**	
dsarpe	**spread**	cesenal	**cleanse**	
herfate	**feather**	ebhatr	**breath**	

Which sound does **ea** make in each word? **short e**

Write two other words that have the **ea** combination and make the short **e** sound.
1. _____

A **couplet** is a two-line poem that rhymes (two sets of two) using at least four words from the list.

Example:
When my butt... ...read.
But I wa... ...le gum instead.
This unfor... ...now fills me with dread.
Before Mo... ...es me, to my room I will tread.

Answers will vary.

page 94

A Land of Many Peoples

The Iroquois were a group of tribes joined together by a common language. Their enemies, the Algonquin, were several tribes of another language group.

Listed below are the names of some Native American tribes and the states that claim them. Remember that Native Americans often moved from state to state.

Write each tribe's name in or by its state name on the map. Then, **color** each state the correct color. The colors symbolize common language groups.

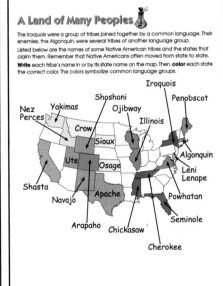

Nez Perces, Yakimas, Shoshoni, Ojibway, Iroquois, Penobscot, Crow, Sioux, Illinois, Algonquin, Ute, Osage, Leni Lenape, Shasta, Navajo, Apache, Powhatan, Arapaho, Chickasaw, Seminole, Cherokee

page 95

Many Times Over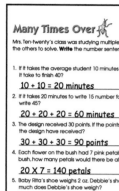

Mrs. Ten-twenty's class was studying multiples. Each student wrote a problem for the others to solve. **Write** the number sentence and answer for each problem.

1. If it takes the average student 10 minutes to finish 20 problems, how long would it take to finish 40?

   10 + 10 = 20 minutes

2. If it takes 20 minutes to write 15 number facts, how long would it take to write 45?

   20 + 20 + 20 = 60 minutes

3. The design received 30 points. If the points were tripled, how many points would the design have received?

   30 + 30 + 30 = 90 points

4. Each flower on the bush had 7 pink petals. If there were 20 flowers on the bush, how many petals would there be altogether?

   20 X 7 = 140 petals

5. Baby Rita's shoe weighs 2 oz. Debbie's shoe weighs 10 times as much. How much does Debbie's shoe weigh?

   10 X 2 = 20 oz.

6. Tyrone kept a bug collection in 10 boxes that each held 20 different kinds of bugs. Nikki had 30 boxes of 20 bugs each. How many bugs did they have altogether?

   (10 X 20) + (30 X 20) = 200 + 600 = 800 bugs

7. Barbara was making glitter stars for her wizard costume. If it took her 36 minutes to make 16 stars, how long would it take her to make 40 more stars?

   36 + 36 + 18 = 90 minutes

8. The boy scouts were making model cars. Each model car had 62 parts. If they made 8 model cars, how many total parts would there be?

   8 X 62 = 496 parts

page 96

Millions Mysteries

Follow the clues to **fill in** the mystery numbers.

4 , 8 7 6 9 5 3

1. Use the numbers 3 to 9. Each is used only once.
2. The ones, tens and hundreds are odd numbers.
3. The hundred thousands, ten thousands and thousands are in backwards counting order.
4. There are 3 times as many hundreds as ones.
5. There are 2 times as many hundred thousands as millions.

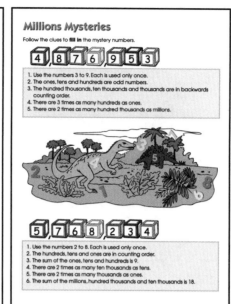

5 7 6 8 2 3 4

1. Use the numbers 2 to 8. Each is used only once.
2. The hundreds, tens and ones are in counting order.
3. The sum of the ones, tens and hundreds is 9.
4. There are 2 times as many ten thousands as tens.
5. There are 2 times as many thousands as ones.
6. The sum of the millions, hundred thousands and ten thousands is 18.

page 97

Multiplication

1. 467 × 35 = 16,345	2. 538 × 47 = 25,286	3. 393 × 82 = 32,226	4. 304 × 529 = 160,816	5. 246 × 824 = 202,704
6. 146 × 532 = 77,672	7. 308 × 236 = 72,688	8. 326 × 92 = 29,992	9. 735 × 45 = 33,075	10. 268 × 39 = 10,452
			11. 486 × 513 = 249,318	12. 314 × 249 = 78,186

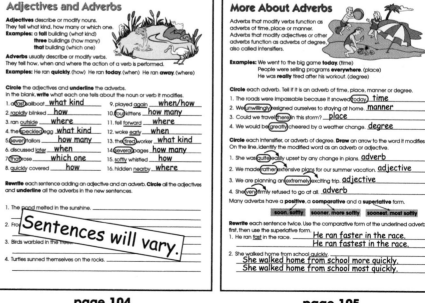

page 98

Problem Solving

Mr. Solve-it's class measured the school and the school grounds when solving problems dealing with area, perimeter and volume.

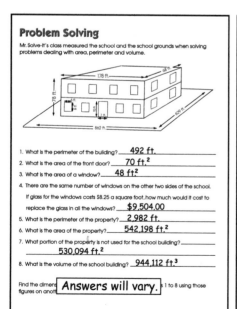

178 ft.   68 ft.
78 ft.   650 ft.
862 ft.

1. What is the perimeter of the building? **492 ft.**
2. What is the area of the front door? **70 ft.²**
3. What is the area of a window? **48 ft²**
4. There are the same number of windows on the other two sides of the school.

   If glass for the windows costs $8.25 a square foot, how much would it cost to replace the glass in all the windows? **$9,504.00**
5. What is the perimeter of the property? **2,982 ft.**
6. What is the area of the property? **542,198 ft.²**
7. What portion of the property is not used for the school building? **530,094 ft.²**
8. What is the volume of the school building? **944,112 ft.³**

Find the dimens **Answers will vary.** 1 to 8 using those figures on anoth

page 99

Adjectives and Adverbs

Adjectives describe or modify nouns. They tell what kind, how many or which one.
Examples: a **tall** building (what kind)
three buildings (how many)
that building (which one)

Adverbs usually describe or modify verbs. They tell how, when and where the action of a verb is performed.
Examples: He ran **quickly**. (how) He ran **today**. (when) He ran **away**. (where)

Circle the adjectives and **underline** the adverbs. In the blank, **write** what each one tells about the noun or verb it modifies.

1. a (fast) sailboat **what kind**
2. rapidly blinked **how**
3. ran outside **where**
4. the (speckled) egg **what kind**
5. (seven) tailors **how many**
6. discussed later **when**
7. (that) rose **which one**
8. quickly covered **how**
9. played again **when/how**
10. (four) kittens **how many**
11. fell forward **where**
12. woke early **when**
13. the (tired) worker **what kind**
14. (several) pages **how many**
15. softly whistled **how**
16. hidden nearby **where**

Rewrite each sentence adding an adjective and an adverb. **Circle** all the adjectives and **underline** all the adverbs in the new sentences.

1. The pond melted in the sunshine. _____
2. Fro **Sentences will vary.**
3. Birds warbled in the trees. _____
4. Turtles sunned themselves on the rocks. _____

page 104

More About Adverbs

Adverbs that modify verbs function as adverbs of time, place or manner. Adverbs that modify adjectives or other adverbs function as adverbs of degree, also called intensifiers.

Examples: We went to the big game **today**. (time)
People were selling programs **everywhere**. (place)
He was **really** tired after his workout. (degree)

Circle each adverb. Tell if it is an adverb of time, place, manner or degree.

1. The roads were impassable because it snowed (today.) **time**
2. We (unwillingly) resigned ourselves to staying at home. **manner**
3. Could we travel (here) in this storm? **place**
4. We would be (greatly) cheered by a weather change. **degree**

Circle each intensifier, or adverb of degree. **Draw** an arrow to the word it modifies. On the line, identify the modified word as an adverb or adjective.

1. She was (quite) really upset by any change in plans. **adverb**
2. We made (rather) extensive plans for our summer vacation. **adjective**
3. We are planning an (extremely) exciting trip. **adjective**
4. She (very) firmly refused to go at all. **adverb**

Many adverbs have a **positive**, a **comparative** and a **superlative** form.

soon, softly	sooner, more softly	soonest, most softly

Rewrite each sentence twice. Use the comparative form of the underlined adverb first, then use the superlative form.

1. He ran fast in the race. **He ran faster in the race.**
   He ran fastest in the race.
2. She walked home from school quickly. **She walked home from school more quickly.**
   She walked home from school most quickly.

page 105

Learn at Home, Grade 6

Confusing Adjectives and Adverbs

Good, bad, sure and real are adjectives. They modify nouns.
Examples: That was a **good** dinner. He made a **bad** choice.

Badly, surely and really are adverbs.
They modify verbs, adjectives and other adverbs.
Examples: He ran **badly**. He **really** wanted to go.

Better, worse, best and worst are adjectives if they modify nouns. They are adverbs if they modify verbs, adverbs or adjectives.
Examples: That's my **best** work. (adjective)
He sang **best** last night. (adverb)

Well is an adjective if it refers to health.
Well is an adverb if it tells how something is done.
Examples: She feels **well** today. (adjective)
He rode the horse **well**. (adverb)

Circle the correct word in parentheses. On the line, **write** whether it is an adverb or adjective. Then, **underline** the word(s) in the sentence it modifies.

1. Tim was (sure) surely) he could go to the museum. __adjective__
2. He wanted to go with his friends (bad/badly). __adverb__
3. He (sure/surely) could finish his work before noon. __adverb__
4. Susan had done a (good) well) job of convincing him to try. __adjective__
5. Tim thought he could manage (good/better) with a schedule. __adverb__
6. He could make (better) well) time if he was organized. __adjective__
7. His list of chores was (worse) bad) than he thought. __adjective__
8. Tim first cleaned up his room (real/really) well. __adverb__
9. He just had to see the (real/really) dinosaur fossil. __adjective__
10. Tim felt (well) good) and whistled as he worked. __adjective__
11. He always worked (best) good) under pressure. __adverb__
12. It turned out to be a (real/really) pleasure to help. __adjective__

page 106

Keep Behavin'

It was time for another of Mr. Fridley's science classes on behaviors. This time, the class was going to discuss learned behaviors. Mr. Fridley explained that learned behaviors are behaviors that change as a result of experience.

First, Mr. Fridley explained learning by association. This type of learning connects a stimulus with a particular response. He asked if anyone could give him an example. Lee suggested that when the bell rings at the end of class, the students put away their pens and pick up their books. Mr. Fridley congratulated Lee on his answer and said that the students learned to associate the stimulus of the bell with the response of leaving class.

There are several kinds of learning by association. One results in a conditioned response—a desired response to an unusual stimulus. Mr. Fridley reminded them of Ivan Pavlov's experiments with dogs. In the experiments, Pavlov found that dogs salivated when they smelled meat. Pavlov began ringing a bell every time he was about to give meat to a dog. In time, the dog salivated when the bell rang, whether or not there was any meat. Pavlov had trained the dogs to respond to the bell instead of the food.

Another kind of learning by association involves teaching animals to act in a certain way by rewarding them for their behavior. This is called positive reinforcement and may be as simple as a rat pressing a lever to get food. This type of learning, however, may also involve a complex series of tasks.

Match:

conditioned response — study hard—get a good grade
positive reinforcement — hear siren—panic

Underline:
Both types of learning by association involve . . .
a stimulus. a learned association.
a response. experiments.

Circle:
If a squirrel learns to climb into a bird feeder to obtain food, it has learned by . . .

conditioned response. unconditioned response.
(positive reinforcement.) negative reinforcement.

Write:
Write examples of something you have learned by conditioned response and something you have learned by positive... | Answers will vary.

page 107

Even Distribution

Some students in Ms. Statistic's class used their own experiences to study the distributive property.

1. Marcus bought three sets of baseball cards each time he went to the store. The first week, he went to the store twice. The second week, he went once. The third week, he went four times. How many sets of cards did he buy during the three weeks? __3 (2 + 1 + 4) = 21 sets__

2. Jessie found six seashells and three sand dollars on her first visit to the beach. With the same luck, how many shells and sand dollars would she find in three visits? __3 (6 + 3) = 27 seashells and sandollars__

3. Alicia saved $.30 out of her allowance for several weeks so that she could buy a bottle of nail polish for $1.79. How many weeks did she need to save $.30? __6 weeks__

4. Kim hit one single, one double and two home runs in her first softball game this season. If she could continue at this rate, how many home runs, singles and doubles would she have after six games?
__1 × 6 = 6 singles   1 × 6 = 6 doubles__
__2 × 6 = 18 home runs__

5. Each person in the class was given two sheets of green construction paper, one sheet of brown and three sheets of orange. There are 27 students in the class. How many sheets of colored paper did Ms. Statistic need?
__27 (2 + 1 + 3) = 162 sheets__

6. Tony, a novice runner, ran $\frac{1}{2}$ mile on his first try, $1\frac{1}{4}$ miles on his second try and 2 miles on his third try. How far would he run in 2 weeks if he ran the same distances the next week?
__2 ($\frac{1}{2}$ + $1\frac{1}{4}$ + 2) = $7\frac{1}{2}$ miles__

Extension: Design an art project. Figure how much of each type of material you will need.

page 108

Nine-Week Test

1. **Write** the number 3,512,978 in words.
__three million, five hundred twelve__
__thousand, nine hundred seventy-eight__

2. Subtract the following from the number 2,846,238:
   4,000 __2,842,238__
   20,000 __2,826,238__
   600,000 __2,246,238__

3. Round 38.462 ... to the nearest tenth. __38.5__
   to the nearest ten. __40__
   to the nearest hundredth. __38.46__

4. **Draw** a triangle on another sheet of paper with the following specifications:
   $\overline{AB}$ is perpendicular to $\overline{AC}$.
   $\overline{AB}$ is 10 cm.
   ∠ACB is 45°

5. Name the type of triangle. __right isosceles triangle__

6. Calculate the area. If $\overline{BC}$ is 14cm, what is the perimeter?
   area __50 cm²__
   perimeter __34 cm__

7. Multiply.

78	48	362	40,286
× 3	× 12	× 38	× 245
234	576	13,756	9,870,070

8. **Write** 6⁴ in factor form and standard form. __6 × 6 × 6 × 6__   __1,296__

page 109

Pronoun Blunders

Three errors are often made when using pronouns. Follow the rules below to avoid these errors.
Do not use an object pronoun as the subject of a sentence.
   Incorrect: **Us** are playing hockey.
   Correct: **We** are playing hockey.
Do not add extra pronouns that duplicate the subject.
   Incorrect: Bonnie, she has won the tennis match.
   Correct: Bonnie has won the tennis match.
In a sentence with a compound subject, it is incorrect to put the pronoun I before the noun.
   Incorrect: I and Sheila will attend the game.
   Correct: Sheila and I will attend the game.

Rewrite each sentence correctly on the line below.

1. I and Mr. James were planning the school Sports Day. __Mr. James and I__ __were planning the school Sports Day.__

2. Mrs. Shawn and Mrs. Thompson they volunteered to help Mr. Thompson and me with the concession stand. __Mrs. Shawn and Mrs. Thompson voluteered__ __to help Mr. Thompson and me with the concession stand.__

3. I and Mrs. Thompson will also prepare the food. __Mrs. Thompson and__ __I will also prepare the food.__

4. Bob, he will make arrangements for all the sports equipment. __Bob will__ __make arrangements for all the sports equipment.__

5. We had challenged them the eighth graders to a game. __We had__ __challenged the eighth graders to a game.__

6. Us were forming a relay team. __We were forming a relay team.__

7. John will time we in the races. __John will time us in the races.__

8. John, he has been involved in many races. __John has been involved__ __in many races.__

page 114

Reflexive Pronouns

Reflexive pronouns reflect the action of the verb back to the subject.

Myself, yourself, herself, himself, itself, ourselves, yourselves and themselves are reflexive pronouns.

Examples: Roger made **himself** a model of the space shuttle.
The shuttle landed **itself**, using only gravity to pull it down.

Complete each sentence with the appropriate reflexive pronoun.

1. The Davenport children congratulated __themselves__ on the good spot they found.
2. We sure found __ourselves__ a good viewpoint from which to watch the shuttle landing.
3. David imagined __himself__ trying to maneuver in a space shuttle that was hurtling toward earth.
4. "I told __myself__ that I will become a commander someday," Earl said.
5. Deborah enjoyed __herself__ at the shuttle launch.
6. "You could train __yourself__ for space travel if you built a model simulator," David's parents suggested.

Write the reflexive pronoun from the box that matches each subject listed below.

1. Peter __himself__
2. The dog __itself__
3. Gwen __herself__
4. Monica and I __ourselves__
5. Heather and Kimberly __themselves__
6. You and Carolyn __yourselves__
7. I __myself__
8. You __yourself__

myself
yourself
himself
yourselves
themselves
itself
herself
ourselves

page 115

Pursuing Pronouns

A **personal pronoun** takes the place of one or more nouns. An **interrogative pronoun** introduces a question. A **relative pronoun** introduces a group of words that acts as an adjective.

Examples: I am excited about the track meet today.
(personal pronoun)

What event does Bill plan to enter?
(interrogative pronoun)

The track meet, **which** we went to last week, was an exciting event. (relative pronoun)

Write **personal**, **interrogative** or **relative** in the blank to identify each pronoun.

1. **Which** sprinting race is your favorite? _interrogative_
2. **We** both like the same type of running shoes. _personal_
3. The high jump is a challenge **that** I would like to take on. _relative_
4. **Who** would like to warm up with me? _interrogative_
5. A boy **whom** I knew won the track meet. _relative_
6. **You** are a natural when it comes to long-distance running. _personal_
7. Is it true that **she** would like to join our running club? _personal_
8. **Whose** house should the team go to for the end-of-the-year party? _interrogative_

Complete each sentence with a pronoun.

1. I tried to find my shoes _that_ were lost. (relative)
2. _They_ told us it won't be a problem for them to run today. (personal)
3. The boy _who_ won the race is a great runner. (relative)
4. _Who_ would like to be our fourth runner in the relay race? (interrogative)

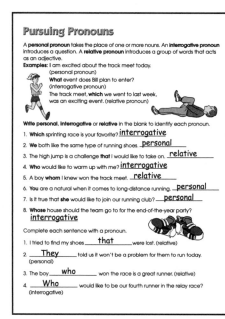

page 116

Easygoing

beast
beneath
breathe
defeat
disease
eavesdrop
freak
greasy
increase
lease
leave
meager
plead
release
repeat
scream
weave
wreath

Write each spelling word next to either its antonym or its synonym. Use a thesaurus if necessary.

1. _meager_ — ample
2. _release_ — hold
3. _beneath_ — above
4. _defeat_ — victory
5. _disease_ — health
6. _leave_ — arrive
7. _increase_ — decrease

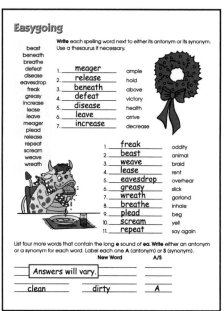

1. _freak_ — oddity
2. _beast_ — animal
3. _weave_ — braid
4. _lease_ — rent
5. _eavesdrop_ — overhear
6. _greasy_ — slick
7. _wreath_ — garland
8. _breathe_ — inhale
9. _plead_ — beg
10. _scream_ — yell
11. _repeat_ — say again

List four more words that contain the long **e** sound of **ea**. **Write** either an antonym or a synonym for each word. Label each one **A** (antonym) or **S** (synonym).

New Word		A/S
Answers will vary.		
clean	dirty	A

page 117

Mr. Quotient's Class Divides

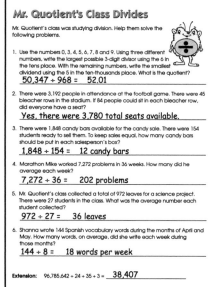

Mr. Quotient's class was studying division. Help them solve the following problems.

1. Use the numbers 0, 3, 4, 5, 6, 7, 8 and 9. Using three different numbers, write the largest possible 3-digit divisor using the 6 in the tens place. With the remaining numbers, write the smallest dividend using the 5 in the ten-thousands place. What is the quotient?
   50,347 ÷ 968 = _52.01_

2. There were 3,192 people in attendance at the football game. There were 45 bleacher rows in the stadium. If 84 people could sit in each bleacher row, did everyone have a seat?
   Yes, there were 3,780 total seats available.

3. There were 1,848 candy bars available for the candy sale. There were 154 students ready to sell them. To keep sales equal, how many candy bars should be put in each salesperson's box?
   1,848 ÷ 154 = _12 candy bars_

4. Marathon Mike worked 7,272 problems in 36 weeks. How many did he average each week?
   7,272 ÷ 36 = _202 problems_

5. Mr. Quotient's class collected a total of 972 leaves for a science project. There were 27 students in the class. What was the average number each student collected?
   972 ÷ 27 = _36 leaves_

6. Shanna wrote 144 Spanish vocabulary words during the months of April and May. How many words, on average, did she write each week during those months?
   144 ÷ 8 = _18 words per week_

Extension: 96,785,642 ÷ 24 + 35 ÷ 3 = _38,407_

page 118

Preposition, Adverb or Verb?

Don't confuse prepositions with adverbs or with phrases made of **to** plus a verb.

Examples: All the students went **to** the zoo. (preposition)
We really wanted **to** go. (verb part)
We started getting excited **before** the trip. (preposition)
Have you gone to the zoo **before**? (adverb)

Identify each **bold** word as a preposition, adverb or verb part.

1. It was incredible how they had trained the animals **to** move like that! _verb part_
2. A monkey followed me **to** the concession stand. _preposition_
3. A beautiful dove flew **around** the audience. _preposition_
4. A seal tossed a ball **around** to show off. _adverb_
5. We took pictures of the walrus **before** the show. _preposition_
6. I had never seen a walrus up close **before**. _adverb_
7. The walrus waddled beyond the stage over **to** the audience. _preposition_
8. My friends were brave, and they decided **to** stay and pet him. _verb part_
9. David asked us, "Who wants **to** see the Dolphin Show at 2:00?" _verb part_
10. The whale catapulted **to** the top and grabbed the fish. _preposition_
11. The monkeys would have liked **to** swing through the trees. _verb part_
12. I looked **up** when I heard the parrot talk. _adverb_
13. I noticed a pigeon flying **around**. _adverb_
14. The elephants came **near**. _adverb_
15. The pigeon carried the message **to** its destination. _preposition_
16. The chimpanzees shouted **across** the water. _preposition_

page 124

Prepositional Phrases

A **prepositional phrase** is a group of words that begins with a preposition and ends with a noun or pronoun. It can act as an adjective or adverb.

Examples: Pineapple is also grown **outside of Hawaii**. (adverb)
The sandwiches **with the peanut butter** were the best ones. (adjective)
We ate the peanut butter sandwiches **at night**. (adverb)

Underline the prepositional phrase in each sentence.

1. Peanuts are enjoyed <u>around the world</u>.
2. Peanuts are native <u>to South America</u>.
3. Peanut pods develop <u>beneath the ground</u>.
4. The pegs, which are the pod stems, push their way <u>under the soil</u>.
5. Peanuts are part <u>of the legume family</u>.
6. Most peanuts are grown <u>in Africa and Asia</u>.

Tell whether each prepositional phrase acts as an **adjective** or an **adverb**.

1. Wait until choir practice is over to eat peanut butter. _adverb_
2. Peanut butter on a spoon is a delicious and quick snack. _adjective_
3. Have you ever enjoyed celery with peanut butter and raisins? _adjective_
4. Try your peanut butter sandwich with cold milk. _adverb_
5. I love peanut butter on toast. _adjective_
6. I enjoy eating peanuts at a ball game. _adverb_

page 125

Missing Freight

Add vowels to each set of consonants to spell words from the list.

beige
caffeine
conceit
conceive
foreign
forfeit
freight
heifer
height
leisure
neither
perceive
protein
receipt
receive
seizure
skein
weight

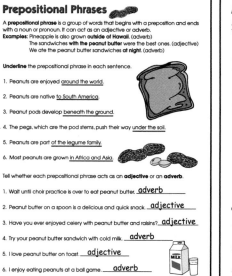

neither nthr	_forfeit_ frft	_perceive_ prcv
beige bg	_leisure_ lsr	_height_ hght
receive rcv	_seizure_ szr	_protein_ prtn
caffeine cffn	_skein_ skn	_receipt_ rcpt
heifer hfr	_conceit_ cnct	_freight_ frght
weight wght	_conceive_ cncv	_foreign_ frgn

Choose six spelling words to divide into syllables.

1. _____ 2. pro · tein
3. _Answers will vary._
5. _____ 6. _____

page 126

Learn at Home, Grade 6

What's the Difference?

One day, David and Donald were discussing alligators. David insisted that alligators and crocodiles were the same animal but that people called them by different names. Donald insisted, however, that the two animals were entirely different reptiles. Kim walked up just in time to save the boys from further squabbling. Kim, who had lived in Florida for ten years, could settle this one.

She told David that alligators and crocodiles are separate reptiles. She told them that although they are similar looking and are both called crocodilians, they are very different. Both have a long, low, cigar-shaped body, short legs and a long, powerful tail to help them swim. But most crocodiles have a pointed snout instead of a round one like the alligator's. She also pointed out that while both have tough hides, long snouts and sharp teeth to grasp their prey, the crocodile is only about two-thirds as heavy as an American alligator of the same length and can therefore move much more quickly. David and Donald were impressed with Kim's knowledge.

Kim also told the boys another way to tell the two reptiles apart. She said that both have an extra long lower fourth tooth. This tooth fits into a pit in the alligator's upper jaw, while in the crocodile, it fits into a groove in the side of the upper jaw and shows when the crocodile's mouth is closed. David and Donald thanked Kim for the information, looked at each other sheepishly and walked away laughing.

Match:

crocodile — fourth tooth shows when mouth is shut
— round snout
— called crocodilian
alligator — fourth tooth is in a pocket in upper jaw
— pointed snout

Write three wo[rds] ... ys they are different. **Answers may include:**

Alike	Different
tough hide	alligators have round snout, crocodiles have pointed
short legs	crocodiles are lighter
long, powerful tail	crocodiles are faster

Name two other animals that are sometimes thought to be the same.
Answers will vary. toad frog

page 127

Missing Signs

Fill in the circles with +, −, x, or ÷ to make the problem true.

3 + 3 + 3 → 9
3 + 3 x 3 → 18
3 x 3 ÷ 3 → 3
3 ÷ 3 ÷ 3 → 3
3 + 3 − 3 → 2
3 x 3 − 3 → 6
3 + 3 + 3 → 4
3 − 3 x 3 → 0
3 x 3 + 3 → 12
3 x 3 x 3 → 27

5 + 5 x 5 → 50
5 x 5 − 5 → 20
5 ÷ 5 x 5 → 5
5 ÷ 5 + 5 → 6
5 x 5 + 5 → 30
5 x 5 x 5 → 125
5 + 5 ÷ 5 → 2
5 − 5 x 5 → 0
5 + 5 + 5 → 15
5 ÷ 5 ÷ 5 → 5

page 128

A Number Challenge

Fill in the blanks to make each problem true. To check your work, start at the left and do each operation in order to get the given answer.

1. __ + __ − __ = 2
2. __ − __ + __ = 3
3. __ + __ + __ = 4
4. = 15
5. __ − __ x = 20
6. __ x __ + __ = 3
7. __ + __ + __ = 4
8. __ + __ − __ = 5
9. __ + __ x __ = 6
10. __ x __ + __ = 7
11. __ + __ + __ = 12
14. __ x __ + __ = 8
15. __ + __ x __ = 24

Answers will vary.

page 129

Skill Lessons

Read the paragraphs about penguins. Make sure all pronouns and their antecedents agree. Correct run-on sentences.

Penguins are unusual birds found in Antarctica and other southern locations. They spend a lot of time in the icy ocean waters, yet they do not get cold. They are covered with short thick feathers that help to keep them warm. Plus, beneath their skin, penguins have a layer of blubber. These thick layers of fat keep the penguins warm in icy water.

Baby penguins, called chicks, do not have as much insulation as their parents have. They do not yet have blubber or waterproof feathers to keep them warm and dry. The chicks' fluffy down feathers plus their parents' body heat keep them safe from the cold. A small penguin may huddle under the warm body of an adult, and sometimes the adults form a tight circle around a group of several chicks and eventually the little penguins will be able to survive on their own.

Complete the article by adding a final paragraph.

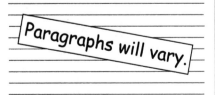

Paragraphs will vary.

page 134

The Mischievous Thief

achieve
ancient
believe
brief
field
hosiery
kerchief
mischief
niece
piece
pierce
retrieve
shield
shriek
siege
thief
wield
yield

Use the code to retrieve the stolen words. Crack the code by assigning a number to each letter of the alphabet.
Example: A = 1, B = 2

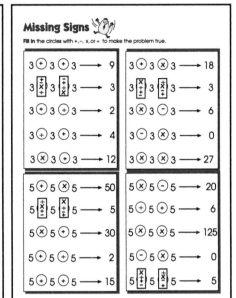

a n c i e n t — 1 14 3 9 5 14 20
p i e r c e — 16 9 5 18 3 5
f i e l d — 6 9 5 12 4
y i e l d — 25 9 5 12 4
t h i e f — 20 8 9 5 6
s h r i e k — 19 8 18 9 5 11
n i e c e — 14 9 5 3 5
a c h i e v e — 1 3 8 9 5 22 5
b e l i e v e — 2 5 12 9 5 22 5
w i e l d — 23 9 5 12 4
s i e g e — 19 9 5 7 5
s h i e l d — 19 8 9 5 12 4
b r i e f — 2 18 9 5 6
h o s i e r y — 8 15 19 9 5 18 25
p i e c e — 16 9 5 3 5
k e r c h i e f — 11 5 18 3 8 9 5 6
m i s c h i e f — 13 9 19 3 8 9 5 6
r e t r i e v e — 18 5 20 18 9 5 22 5

page 135

Beth Is Sick

Poor Beth is sick, and she doesn't know why. She felt great yesterday, but this morning she woke up with a headache, a fever and a horrible sore throat. Beth is disappointed because today is the day her class is going to the new science museum. Why did she have to be sick on a field trip day? How did she get ill so quickly?

Beth and Kim talk on the phone about Beth's situation for twenty minutes. Because they planned to be field trip partners, Kim is really sad Beth isn't going to school today. Kim tells Beth she probably got sick because she didn't wear a jacket to school yesterday, and it was a cold day. She tells Beth that if your body gets cold, you catch germs more easily. Beth tells Kim she is silly. She believes Kim has a virus.

Beth remembers learning about viruses in science class. Mr. Fridley told them that viruses are noncellular structures that can only be seen through an electron microscope, which magnifies them thousands of times. On its own, a virus is a lifeless particle that can't reproduce, but when a virus enters a living cell, it starts reproducing and can sometimes harm the host cell. Viruses that harm host cells cause disease like chicken pox, the flu and colds. Mr. Fridley told them that shaking hands with or being sneezed or coughed on by an infected person may infect you with the virus. Beth believes that she became infected from someone since lots of people are sick at this time of year. Kim promises Beth a full report on the science museum.

Underline the main idea of the story.
Beth has a headache, fever and a sore throat.
Beth and Kim try to discover why Beth is sick.
Viruses cause diseases.
Mr. Fridley taught them about viruses.

Check the correct answers.

Viruses...
☑ can't be seen through an ordinary light microscope.
☑ pass easily from one person to another.
☐ are thousands of times bigger than regular cells.
☑ enter living cells and start reproducing.

What are some
Answers will vary.

page 136

Statistical Experiments

Statistical experiments involve collecting, organizing and analyzing data. Ms. Botanical's class is interested in growing a flower garden for the whole school to enjoy. To collect data on flower preferences, they surveyed all 435 students in the school. They noted the results below.

Favorite Flowers

Types of Flowers	Number of Votes
Black-eyed Susans	57
Petunias	63
Irises	32
Tulips	78
Hollyhocks	7
Daffodils	53
Daisies	84

Organize the data:
List the flowers in order from the most popular to the least.
daisies, tulips, petunias, black-eyed Susans, daffodils, irisis, hollyhocks

Analyze the data:
1. Based on these data, which five flowers should the students plant? **daisies, tulips, petunias, black-eyed Susans and daffodils**
2. Which flower should definitely not be planted? **hollyhocks**
3. Do the number of votes justify planting a garden? Why or why not? **Yes. A majority of students have demonstrated their interest by participating in the survey.**
4. What is the mean? **53.43**
5. What is the mode? **no mode**
6. What is the median? **57**
7. What is the range? **77**

page 137

Weight and Capacity

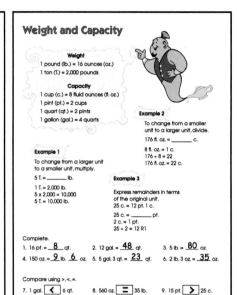

Weight
1 pound (lb.) = 16 ounces (oz.)
1 ton (T.) = 2,000 pounds

Capacity
1 cup (c.) = 8 fluid ounces (fl. oz.)
1 pint (pt.) = 2 cups
1 quart (qt.) = 2 pints
1 gallon (gal.) = 4 quarts

Example 1
To change from a larger unit to a smaller unit, multiply.
5 T. = _____ lb.

1 T. = 2,000 lb.
5 × 2,000 = 10,000
5 T. = 10,000 lb.

Example 2
To change from a smaller unit to a larger unit, divide.
176 fl. oz. = _____ c.

8 fl. oz. = 1 c.
176 ÷ 8 = 22
176 fl. oz. = 22 c.

Example 3
Express remainders in terms of the original unit.
25 c. = 12 pt. 1 c.

25 c. = _____ pt.
2 c. = 1 pt.
25 ÷ 2 = 12 R1

Complete.
1. 16 pt. = **8** qt.   2. 12 gal. = **48** qt.   3. 5 lb. = **80** oz.
4. 150 oz. = **9** lb. **6** oz.   5. 5 gal. 3 qt. = **23** qt.   6. 2 lb. 3 oz. = **35** oz.

Compare using >, <, =.
7. 1 gal. **<** 6 qt.   8. 560 oz. **=** 35 lb.   9. 15 pt. **>** 25 c.

page 138

Chemical Magic Square

Use the Periodic Table to help you complete this activity. Read the clues concerning the elements in the boxes below. **Write** the correct atomic number in the box. Add the numbers across, down and diagonally to produce a magic square.

What is your answer? **34**

This element is located directly above lithium.	This element is located to the left of sulfur.	This element is located directly below carbon.	This element is located directly above magnesium.	
1	15	14	4	34
This element is located to the right of sodium.	This element is located to the left of nitrogen.	This element is located directly above phosphorus.	This element is located directly above chlorine.	
12	6	7	9	34
This element is located to the left of fluorine.	This element is located below helium.	This element is located directly above potassium.	This element is located directly above aluminum.	
8	10	11	5	34
This element is located to the left of silicon.	This element is located directly below hydrogen.	This element is located directly above neon.	This element is located to the left of chlorine.	
13	3	2	16	34
34	34	34	34	34

34 34   34   34   34   34

page 139

Interjections

An **interjection** that shows strong feeling is followed by an exclamation point. The next word begins with a capital letter.
Example: Quiet! He's not finished yet.
An **interjection** that shows mild feeling is followed by a comma. The next word is not capitalized.
Example: Oh, is that correct?

Rewrite the sentences to show strong feeling. Punctuate and capitalize properly.

1. hurrah we won the game.
   Hurrah! We won the game.
2. whew that was a close one.
   Whew! That was a close one.

Rewrite the sentences on the lines. Punctuate and capitalize properly.

1. yes you may go to the movies.
   Yes, you may go to the movies.
2. well we're glad you're finally here.
   Well, we're glad you're finally here.

Rewrite the sentences below correctly.

1. hush you don't want to upset her.
   Hush! You don't want to upset her.
2. well we're glad you came to the meeting.
   Well, we're glad you came to the meeting.
3. quiet you'll wake up everyone.
   Quiet! You'll wake up everyone.

page 144

Automobile Exhaust

Complete the word associations using the spelling words.

applause
assault
audience
automobile
autumn
caulk
daughter
exhaust
fraud
laundry
naughty
nausea
nautical
pauper
restaurant
sauna
slaughter
trauma

1. prince and **pauper**
2. **nautical** and ship
3. crisis and **trauma**
4. **laundry** and soap
5. **autumn** and fall
6. entertainer and **audience**
7. **sauna** and spa
8. **fraud** and deceit
9. cheering and **applause**
10. **exhaust** and fumes
11. **automobile** and transportation
12. son and **daughter**
13. **naughty** and nice
14. **caulk** and seal
15. kill and **slaughter**
16. **assault** and battery
17. **restaurant** and diner
18. upset stomach and **nausea**

Write four more words containing **au**.
Write a meaningful sentence for each word.

Answers will vary.

_____ and _____
auction and **sale**
_____ and _____

page 145

Multiply or Divide?

These key words will help you know when to multiply and when to divide.
Multiplication key words: **in all, altogether, times** and **each**
Division key words: **per, each**

Circle the key words and **solve** the story problems.

1. There are 9 classrooms at the vocational school. The average number of students per classroom is 27 students. How many students (altogether) are there in the school?
   27
   × 9
   243 students   243

2. Thirty-five students are studying auto mechanics. Three (times) that many students are studying business. How many students are studying business?
   35
   × 3
   105 students   105

3. The semester is 16 weeks long. Students attend class 5 days a week. How many days (in all) must a student attend class each semester?
   16
   × 5
   80 days   80

4. In one class of 27 students (each) student used $30.00 worth of materials (Altogether) how much did materials cost this class?
   27
   × 30
   $810.00   810

5. Lunch cost each student $11.50 for a 5-day week. How much does (each) lunch cost?
   $11.50 ÷ 5 = $2.30
   $2.30

6. The average student drives a total of 8 miles per day to attend classes. How many miles (in all) does a student drive during the 80-day semester?
   80
   × 8
   640 miles   640

page 146

Learn at Home, Grade 6

Shifty Sam's "Rip-Off" Record Shop

Shifty Sam sells the latest rock releases along with some oldies. You have to keep a close eye on Sam, or you may get ripped off.

Solve the problems on another sheet of paper. **Write** your answers in the spaces provided.

1. The Ear Splitters' latest release, regularly $8.98, is on sale at 5 CDs for $46.95. How much more or less would you pay at the sale price for all 5 CDs? — **$2.05 more**

2. The Funky Monkeys' new CD went fast. Sam made $4,540.90 on 455 copies. The correct price should be $7.99. How much did Sam charge for each CD? How much extra did he charge? — **$9.98 each $1.99 extra**

3. Sam made $4.59 profit on each copy of the 323 CDs he sold by the Brainbangers. He is supposed to make only $3.29 profit on each one. How much extra did he make on the 323 CDs? — **$419.90 extra**

4. Your aunt wanted to buy some CDs by Hart N. Soule which regularly sell for $3.67 each. Sam offered to sell her a dozen CDs for $44.00. How much will she save by buying 12 CDs? — **She will save $.04**

5. You wanted 180 copies of Hits of the 1940s to use as Frisbees. Each record cost $.79. Sam gave you $47.80 in change from $200. How much did he cheat you? — **$10.00**

6. Sam sold 7,000 copies of Golden Oldies for $3.99 each. He made a $2.00 profit on each record. How much money did he get for all 7,000 copies? How much profit did he earn? — **$27,930.00 for all $14,000.00 profit**

7. Sam charged $1.79 more for each copy of the Dippers' new CD than he was supposed to. His price was $7.89, and he sold 3,500 copies. How much extra money did he get? — **$6,265.00 extra**

8. Sam sold 4,328 copies of Country Classics at $4.99 each. His profit was $1.45 on each one. How much money did he get in all? How much profit did he earn? — **$21,596.72 total $6,275.60 profit**

page 147

Division Review

Divide.

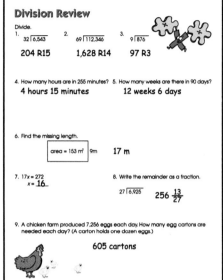

1. $32\overline{)6,543}$ — **204 R15**

2. $69\overline{)112,346}$ — **1,628 R14**

3. $9\overline{)876}$ — **97 R3**

4. How many hours are in 255 minutes? — **4 hours 15 minutes**

5. How many weeks are there in 90 days? — **12 weeks 6 days**

6. Find the missing length.

area = 153 m² | 9m | **17 m**

7. $17x = 272$ $x =$ **16**

8. Write the remainder as a fraction.

$27\overline{)6,925}$ — **$256\frac{13}{27}$**

9. A chicken farm produced 7,256 eggs each day. How many egg cartons are needed each day? (A carton holds one dozen eggs.)

605 cartons

page 148

Testing for Starch

Starch is found in many foods and plants. Iodine is an indicator of starch. It turns blue-black when placed on a substance containing starch. **Safety Note: Iodine can be dangerous. Do not taste, spill or misuse it in any way.** Place a drop of iodine on each of the substances listed in the chart. Record the results. The first one is done for you.

Substance	Color of Iodine	Starch: Yes or No
white bread	blue-black	yes
brown bread	blue-black	yes
dry cereal	blue-black	yes
brown leaf	blue-black	yes
popped popcorn	blue-black	yes
oatmeal	blue-black	yes
orange peel	brown	no
lemon peel	brown	no
liquid starch	blue-black	yes
newspaper	brown	no
paper towel	brown	no
tissue	brown	no
water	brown	no
alcohol	brown	no
dish soap	brown	no
cloth	brown	no

page 149

Diamonds Are a Girl's Best Friend

diabetes
diabolic
diacritical
diadem
diagnosis
diagonal
diagram
dialect
dialogue
dialysis
diameter
diamond
diaper
diaphragm
diaries
diathermy
diatomic
diatribe

Fill in the blanks with the correct missing letters to complete the spelling words.

Answers may vary.

dia**gram** dia**lect**
dia**critical**
dia**dem** dia**gnosis**
dia**betes** dia**bolic**
dia**mond** dia**logue**
dia**meter** dia**lysis**
dia**ries** dia**per**
dia**phragm**
dia**gonal**
dia**thermy**
dia**tomic**
dia**tribe**

Choose one of the spelling words. Do some research on it. Then, **write** a paragraph (5 or 6 sentences) telling what you learned about the word.

Answers may vary.

page 154

Equations

Solve the equations on another sheet of paper. **Write** your answers here.

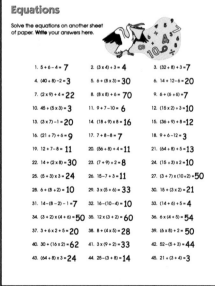

1. 5 + 6 − 4 = **7**
2. (3 × 4) + 3 = **4**
3. (32 + 8) + 3 = **7**
4. (40 + 8) − 2 = **3**
5. 6 + (8 × 3) = **30**
6. 14 + 12 − 6 = **20**
7. (2 × 9) + 4 = **22**
8. (8 × 8) + 6 = **70**
9. 6 + (6 + 6) = **7**
10. 45 + (5 × 3) = **3**
11. 9 + 7 − 10 = **6**
12. (15 × 2) + 3 = **10**
13. (3 × 7) − 1 = **20**
14. (18 + 9) × 8 = **16**
15. (36 + 9) + 8 = **12**
16. (21 + 7) + 6 = **9**
17. 7 + 8 − 8 = **7**
18. 9 + 6 − 12 = **3**
19. 12 + 7 − 8 = **11**
20. (56 + 8) + 4 = **11**
21. (64 + 8) + 5 = **13**
22. 14 + (2 × 8) = **30**
23. (7 + 9) + 2 = **8**
24. (15 + 3) × 2 = **10**
25. (5 + 3) × 3 = **24**
26. 15 − 7 + 3 = **11**
27. (3 + 7) × (10 + 2) = **50**
28. 6 + (8 + 2) = **10**
29. 3 × (5 + 6) = **33**
30. 15 + (3 × 2) = **21**
31. 14 − (8 − 2) − 1 = **7**
32. 16 − (10 − 4) = **10**
33. (14 + 6) + 5 = **4**
34. (3 + 2) × (4 + 6) = **50**
35. 12 × (3 + 2) = **60**
36. 6 × (4 + 5) = **54**
37. 3 + 6 × 2 + 5 = **20**
38. 8 + (4 × 5) = **28**
39. (6 × 8) + 2 = **50**
40. 30 + (16 × 2) = **62**
41. 3 × (9 + 2) = **33**
42. 52 − (5 + 3) = **44**
43. (64 + 8) × 3 = **24**
44. 25 − (3 + 8) = **14**
45. 21 + (3 + 4) = **3**

page 155

Games

4. One week (Sunday through Saturday) there is a birthday party every day. No two children are invited to the same party. Find out the day that each child attends a party.

Hint: Use a chart with days of the week across and children's names down the side.

a. Lisa and Pat don't go to a party on a Friday or a Saturday.
b. Pat and Alice don't go on a Tuesday, but Sandy does.
c. Jennifer goes to a party on Wednesday.
d. Jim goes to a party the day after Jennifer.
e. Lisa goes to a party the day before Pat.
f. Paul goes to a party on a Saturday.

Sunday	— Lisa
Monday	— Pat
Tuesday	— Sandy
Wednesday	— Jennifer
Thursday	— Jim
Friday	— Lisa
Saturday	— Paul

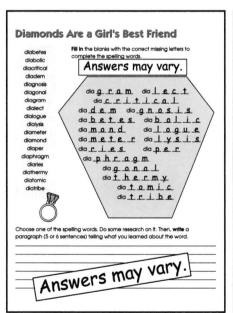

page 156

Extra Extraordinary

Complete the puzzle using the spelling words. Use each word once. One word has been filled in for you.

Answers may vary.

example
expense
expert
explore
extend
extent
exterior
exterminate
external
extinct
extinguish
extol
extract
extraordinary
extravagant
extreme

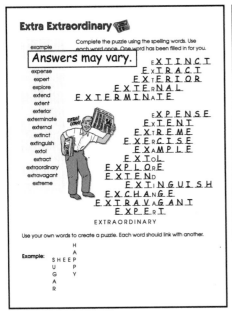

E X T I N C T
E X T R A C T
E X T E R I O R
E X T E R N A L
E X T E R M I N A T E
E X P E N S E
E X T E N T
E X T R E M E
E X E R C I S E
E X A M P L E
E X T O L
E X P L O R E
E X T E N D
E X T I N G U I S H
E X C H A N G E
E X T R A V A G A N T
E X P E R T
E X T R A O R D I N A R Y

Use your own words to create a puzzle. Each word should link with another.

Example:
H
A
S H E E P
U P P
G Y
A
R

page 162

Swiss Sentences

Complete these cheesy number sentences.

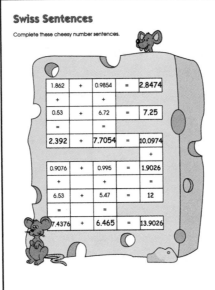

1.862	+	0.9854	=	2.8474
+		+		
0.53	+	6.72	=	7.25
=		=		
2.392	+	7.7054	=	10.0974
				+
0.9076	+	0.995	=	1.9026
+		+		
6.53	+	5.47	=	12
=		=		
7.4376	+	6.465	=	13.9026

page 163

Robin Hood's Loot

As you know, Robin Hood stole from the rich and gave to the poor. Follow his stealing and giving path to figure out how much he has left for himself at the end.

Add numbers in loot bags

Subtract numbers in gift boxes

START HERE

25   1.75
5.85
9.95   0.09
2.89
18.94
0.05   4.02
35.25
1.70   3.81
3.25   7.09   21.34

He has **$25.00** at the end.

END

page 164

Salt and Ice

Adding solute to a liquid creates a solution. This solution will be denser than the liquid water by itself. The denser a solution is, the more slowly molecules in it will move. Imagine trying to swim in a swimming pool full of pudding, which is much denser than water. It would be harder for you to move quickly in the denser medium, just as it is more difficult for molecules. The denser the solution is, the colder it has to be before the solution will freeze.

Part 1
Fill a bowl or a glass with water almost to the top, and float an ice cube in it. Set an unlighted wooden match across the top of the ice cube. Make sure that some of the match hangs off the edge of the ice cube. Sprinkle salt lightly over it. Wait approximately 2 minutes. Then, try to lift the match up.

What happened?

Answers will vary.

Why do

Part 2
Fill three glasses half-full with water, each having the same temperature. Put a little piece of masking tape on each one and label them #1, #2 and #3. Leave #1 as plain tap water. Add 1 teaspoon of salt to #2 and stir. Add 1 tablespoon of salt to #3 and stir. Next, place an ice cube in each glass. Add the cubes to the three glasses at the exact same time, and do not stir. Time how long it takes for the ice cube in each glass to melt. Record your data on the chart below.

| Sample | Time to Melt (sec..) |
| #1 | |

Data will vary.

page 165

Colons and Lists

Use a **colon** when writing a list of items if "follows" or "the following" is used in the introduction and the list of items immediately follows. Commas (and sometimes semicolons) are used to separate the items in the list.

Example: The clown was wearing **the following:**
striped pants, a polka-dot shirt, floppy shoes and baggy socks.

Do not use a colon if the list of items is introduced by such words as "namely," "for instance," "for example" or "that is." Instead, set off the phrase with commas.

Example: A clown could wear, **for example,** striped pants, a polka-dot shirt, floppy shoes and baggy socks.

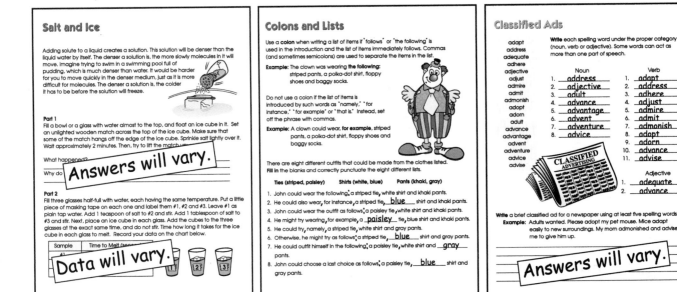

There are eight different outfits that could be made from the clothes listed. **Fill in** the blanks and correctly punctuate the eight different lists.

Ties (striped, paisley)   Shirts (white, blue)   Pants (khaki, gray)

1. John could wear the following: a striped tie, white shirt and khaki pants.
2. He could also wear, for instance, a striped tie, **blue** shirt and khaki pants.
3. John could wear the outfit as follows: a paisley tie, white shirt and khaki pants.
4. He might try wearing, for example, a **paisley** tie, blue shirt and khaki pants.
5. He could try, namely, a striped tie, white shirt and gray pants.
6. Otherwise, he might try as follows: a striped tie, **blue** shirt and gray pants.
7. He could outfit himself in the following: a paisley tie, white shirt and **gray** pants.
8. John could choose a last choice as follows: a paisley tie, **blue** shirt and gray pants.

page 170

Classified Ads

adapt
address
adequate
adhere
adjective
adjust
admire
admit
admonish
adopt
adorn
adult
advance
advantage
advent
adventure
advice
advise

Write each spelling word under the proper category (noun, verb or adjective). Some words can act as more than one part of speech.

Noun		Verb
1. **address**	1.	**adapt**
2. **adjective**	2.	**address**
3. **adult**	3.	**adhere**
4. **advance**	4.	**adjust**
5. **advantage**	5.	**admire**
6. **advent**	6.	**admit**
7. **adventure**	7.	**admonish**
8. **advice**	8.	**adopt**
	9.	**adorn**
	10.	**advance**
	11.	**advise**

Adjective
1. **adequate**
2. **advance**

Write a brief classified ad for a newspaper using at least five spelling words.
Example: Adults wanted. Please adopt my pet mouse. Mice adapt easily to new surroundings. My mom admonished and advised me to give him up.

Answers will vary.

page 171

Learn at Home, Grade 6

Charting the Weather

For four months, the students in Ms. Forecaster's class charted the sunny, partly sunny and cloudy days. The following chart shows their findings to the nearest tenth.

1. How many more sunny days did January have than December? **2.1 days**

2. In November, how many more cloudy days were there than sunny days? **2.9 days**

3. How many more partly sunny days were there than sunny days in January? **8.3 days**

4. What is the difference in days between the month with the most cloudy days and the month that had the fewest cloudy days? **8.9 days**

5. Which month had the most sunny days? How many more sunny days did it have than the month with the second most? Which month came in second? **October/5 days January**

6. Which month had the most cloudy days? Which month had the fewest cloudy days? How many total cloudy days were there in these four months? **December/October 34.3 days**

Extension: Find the total number of sunny, partly sunny and cloudy days in these four months. Then, find the average number of days for each type of weather.

Sunny: 35.1 days
Partly Sunny: 53.6 days
Cloudy: 34.3 days

Averages
Sunny: 8.8 days
Partly Sunny: 13.4 days
Cloudy: 8.6 days

page 172

Acids and Bases

Acids and **bases** are chemical compounds. Some of these compounds are strong and abrasive. Many are used as cleaning agents. Litmus paper is an indicator. Indicators are affected when acid or base is present in a substance. Blue litmus paper turns red when dipped in an acid. Red litmus paper turns blue when dipped in a base.

Use blue and red litmus paper to test each one of the substances on the chart. Record the results by writing the color the paper turns when dipped and whether the substance is an acid or a base. The first one is done for you.

Substance	Blue Litmus	Red Litmus	Acid, Base or Neither
lemon juice	red	red	acid
vinegar	red	red	acid
ammonia	blue	blue	base
orange juice	red	red	acid
tea	red	red	acid
milk	blue	red	neither
baking soda and water	blue	blue	base
cleanser and water	blue	blue	base
water	blue	red	neither (b)
vinegar and salt	red	red	acid
grapefruit juice	red	red	acid
antacid pills and water	blue	blue	base
cola	blue	red	neither (a)

page 173

Semicolon

A **semicolon** is used to join two independent clauses that are closely related if a conjunction is not used. An **independent clause** is a group of words that could stand as a complete sentence by itself.

Read each pair of sentences. **Rewrite** those that could be joined by a semicolon.

1. The tiny hummingbird builds a small nest. Its jelly bean-sized eggs fit nicely into it. **The tiny hummingbird builds a small nest; its jelly bean-sized eggs fit nicely into it.**

2. Some birds build with unusual materials. You may find string or ribbon woven into a nest. **Some birds build with unusual materials; you may find string or ribbon woven into a nest.**

3. A nest's location can tell you a bird s diet. Most birds live near their food supply. **A nest's location can tell you a bird's diet; most birds live near their food supply.**

4. A gull's nest is on the shore. Gulls eat fish and other kinds of seafood. **A gull's nest is on the shore; gulls eat fish and other kinds of seafood.**

5. A woodpecker lives in a hole in a tree. It eats insects that live in trees. **A woodpecker lives in a hole in a tree; it eats insects that live in trees.**

6. Some birds take over old nests. Purple martins live in birdhouses. **These sentences are not closely related.**

7. A woodpecker makes a hole to live in and later moves out. An elf owl moves right into it. **A woodpecker makes a hole to live in and later moves out; an elf owl moves right into it.**

8. A swan builds a nest among the reeds. The reeds help hide the nest from the swan's enemies. **A swan builds a nest among the reeds; the reeds help hide the nest from the swan's enemies.**

page 178

You're a Pro

1. probe
2. produce
3. profane
4. promise
5. profound
6. progress
7. prohibit
8. project
9. prolong
10. promote
11. pronoun
12. pronounce
13. propel
14. proportion
15. prosper
16. protein
17. protein
18. provoke

Complete the magic square. **Write** the number of each spelling word in the lettered square that corresponds to its definition. Two of the words will not be used.

A. create; vegetables
B. to stop
C. stir up; make angry
D. speak clearly; articulate
E. stick out; a plan
F. deep and intense
G. a replacement for a noun
H. suggest
I. move forward
J. an essential part of diet
K. growth; to improve
L. blaphemous
M. have good fortune
N. to raise to a higher level
O. agreement to do something
P. to lengthen

A 2	B 7	C 8	D 12
E 8	F 5	G 11	H 15
I 13	J 17	K 6	L 3
M 16	N 10	O 4	P 9

Check your work by adding each row and then each column of numbers. If all the sums are the same, you have matched correctly.

Write the two words that were not included in the square.
1. **probe** 2. **proportion**

Write the six words that can be used either as nouns or as verbs.
1. **probe** 2. **produce**
3. **promise** 4. **progress**
5. **project** 6. **proportion**

page 179

Comparison

Mr. Bigfoot's class was comparing numbers by multiplying decimals. Round your answer to the nearest hundreth.

1. Andy's shoe is 10.4 inches long. Tony's is 1.2 times as long. How long is Tony's shoe? **12.48 inches**

2. Alicia can jump 24.8 inches. Jill can jump 1.05 times as high. How high can Jill jump? **26.04 inches**

3. The paper basket holds 288 sheets of paper. It is 0.25 full. How many sheets of paper are in it? **72 sheets**

4. Misha's dog weighs 98.5 pounds. Tom's dog weighs 1.25 times as much. How much does Tom's dog weigh? **123.13 pounds**

5. The area of Mr. Bigfoot's classroom is 981.75 square feet. The gym is 4.50 times as large. What is the area of the gym? **4,417.88 square feet**

6. The box holds 48 pencils. It was 0.75 full. How many more pencils would fit in the box? **12 pencils**

7. Amy is 5.250 feet tall. The ceiling is 2.075 times Amy's height. How tall is the ceiling? **10.89 feet**

Extension: Place the decimal point in the underlined number.

1. 213.05 x 2.3 = **490.015**   2. 4.87 x **0.46** = 2.2402   3. **60.1** x 0.08 = 4.808

page 180

Circumference of Circles

Circumference is the distance around a circle.

C = π x d
π (pi) = 3.14 or $\frac{22}{7}$ (≈ means approximately
d = diameter   equals to)
Use π ≈ 3.14 and round to the nearest one.

Example 1:
C = π x d
C = 3.14 x 8.6
C = 27.004 km
C ≈ 27 km

(circle labeled A — 8.6 km — B)

Example 2:
The radius of the circle is 16 mm.
Diameter is twice the radius.
So, d = 16 x 2 = 32
C = 3.14 x 32
C = 100.48 mm
C ≈ 100 mm

(circle labeled 16 mm)

Example 3:
Find the perimeter of the figure.
Circumference of the circle = 3.14 x 3 = 9.42 m
9.42 + 11 + 11 = 31.42 m

(figure: 11 m, 3 m)

Find the circumference of each circle. Use π ≈ 3.14 and round to the nearest one.

1. (22 cm) **69 cm**   2. (18.9 m) **59 m**   3. (7.6 km) **48 km**   4. (24 dam) **48 km**

Find the perimeter of each figure.

5. (18 cm, 7 cm) **57.98 cm**   6. (7 dm, 3 dm) **21.71 dm**

page 181

This Is So Fine

Rewrite each sentence below, replacing the word **fine** with one of the synonyms given. Since the synonyms have slight differences in meaning, be careful to choose the correct one.

Fine: clear, delicate, elegant, small, sharp, subtle

1. The queen wore a **fine** gown encrusted with jewels.
   The queen wore an elegant gown encrusted with jewels.

2. I wash this blouse by hand because of its **fine** lace collar.
   I wash this blouse by hand because of its delicate lace collar.

3. The sand in an hourglass must be very **fine** to trickle as it does.
   The sand in an hourglass must be very small to trickle as it does.

4. We need **fine** weather for sailing.
   We need clear weather for sailing.

5. Dad used a whetstone to put a **fine** edge on the knife.
   Dad used a whetstone to put a sharp edge on the knife.

6. Sometimes there is a **fine** line between innocence and guilt.
   Sometimes there is a subtle line between innocence and guilt.

page 186

Shopping for Soccer Supplies

The soccer team members needed to buy their own shin guards, socks, shoes and shorts. A couple of the players volunteered to do some comparative shopping to find the store with the best deal. Use their chart to answer the questions below.

SPORTS CORNER	
Socks	3 pairs for $9.30
Shoes	2 pairs for $48.24
Shin Guards	4 pairs for $32.48
Shorts	5 pairs for $60.30

JOE'S SOCCER	
Socks	2 pairs for $6.84
Shoes	3 pairs for $84.15
Shin Guards	5 pairs for $35.70
Shorts	4 pairs for $36.36

1. Which store had the better price for socks?   Sports Corner
   How much less were they per pair? $0.32

2. Which store had the better price for shin guards?   Joe's Soccer
   How much would you save per pair? $0.98

3. How much would one pair of shoes and socks cost at Joe's Soccer? $31.47
   How much at Sports Corner? $27.22

4. Which store had the better price for shorts?   Joe's Soccer
   How much less were they per pair? $2.97 less

5. Total the price per pair for each item at each store. If you could shop at only one store, which one would give you the best overall deal?   Sports Corner
   How much would you save? $0.30

page 187

Dividing by Decimals

What kind of problems will these decimal glasses help you solve? Solve the problems. Then, **write** them in descending order (from greatest to least) beneath the blanks at the bottom of the page. **Write** each matching letter above the number to solve to the riddle.

S 2.1$\overline{)8.4}$ = 21.$\overline{)84.}$ → 4

V 0.36$\overline{)1.872}$ → 5.2

O 1.24$\overline{)0.4712}$ → 0.38

N 8$\overline{)1.12}$ → 0.14

D 0.3$\overline{)17.7}$ → 59

I 6$\overline{)126.}$ → 21

I .082$\overline{)0.3772}$ → 4.6

— 7.4$\overline{)103.6}$ → 14

I 5.5$\overline{)3.025}$ → 0.55

D I — V I S I O N

page 189

Oil and Water Emulsions

Investigation
Fill a clear glass jar about half-full with water. Add several drops of food coloring. Describe what happens.

Add about 1 inch of oil to the top of the water. Does the oil stay at the top of the jar?

Add several drops of food coloring to the top of the oil. What happens to the food coloring?

Use an eyedropper to poke a hole in the oil near the food coloring.
What happens?
Put the lid on the jar and shake it for 1 minute. Wait 1 minute. Is the oil on top? Is oil head?

Emulsions
Let your jar of oil and water settle for a few.
Add a different color of food coloring to the top of the oil. Fill an eyedropper with liquid soap. Drop this soap right on the food coloring. Do this several times. What happens to the food coloring?

Shake the jar several times. Observe the results. What happens to the oil?

Let the jar stand undisturbed for a few minutes. What happens to the oil?

Answers will vary.

page 190

Ocean in a Bottle Emulsions

Investigation
• Fill a glass jar about half-full with water. Add several drops of food coloring to the water. Use blue, blue-green or blue-red food coloring, depending on the color you want the ocean to be. Add oil to the jar until it is about 3/4 full. Tighten the lid and turn the jar on its side. Do you see the ocean effect?

Emulsions
• Stand the jar upright. Add 8 eye droppers full of liquid dish soap to the jar. What happens?
• Shake the jar vigorously. What happens?
• Shake the jar and place it in a bag filled with water. What happens to the oil?
• After the oil and water separate, shake again vigorously. Place the jar near a warm radiator or in the hot sun. How many minutes does it take this time for the oil to return completely to the top?

Extending the Concept
• Place a spoonful of mayonnaise in one small plastic cup and a spoonful of margarine in another small plastic cup. Fill a third plastic cup half-full with milk. Set each of these in a pan of warm water, in the hot sun or near (but not touching) a warm radiator. Wait 1 hour. Describe what happens to each of these substances.

• How are these substances like oil and water?

Answers will vary.

page 191

Predictable Prefixes

Complete the puzzle using the spelling words. Use each word once.

precaution · precise · predict · prefer · prefix · prehistoric · premature · premeditate · premium

prepare · prepay · preschool · prescribe · preserve · presume · prevail · prevent · previous

P R E V I O U S
P R E P A R E
P R E P A Y
P R E D I C T
P R E C I S E
P R E S C H O O L
P R E V E N T
P R E M A T U R E
P R E S C R I B E
P R E V A I L
P R E H I S T O R I C
P R E C A U T I O N
P R E S E R V E
P R E M E D I T A T E
P R E F E R
P R E M I U M
P R E F I X
P R E S U M E

PREDICTABLE PREFIXES

Change the meaning of two words from the list by adding a different prefix.
1. Answers will vary.   2. Infer

page 196

Learn at Home, Grade 6

Shiloh

A **simile** is a comparison using the words **like** or **as**. **Underline** the similes in these sentences. **Write** another simile with the same or nearly the same meaning.

1. My dream leaks out like water in a paper bag.
   Answers will vary.
2. I hold Shiloh as careful as I carry Becky when she s asleep.
3. I'm as happy as a flea on a dog.
4. Keeping Shiloh a secret is like having a bomb waiting to go off.
5. I'm as tense as a cricket at night.
6. Ma hums to Shiloh like he's a baby in a cradle.

Complete these sentences with a simile of your own.

7. Shiloh looked _____ like _____
8. Doc Murphy wa— [Answers will vary.] with Shiloh.
9. Judd trying to be nice was like _____
10. The Prestons were happy as _____ to have Shiloh.

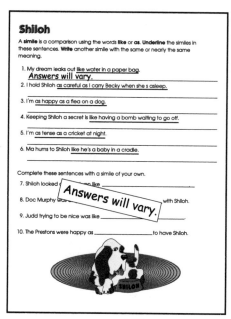

page 197

Decimal Test

1. 0.45 + 0.96 + 0.52 = __1.93__
2. 26.3 − 4.8 = __21.5__
3. Use > or < to compare each pair of numbers.

   5.01 _>_ 5.003   6.15 _>_ 6.015   3.05 _<_ 5.03
4. Write sixty-one hundredths in numeral form. __0.61__
5. 35.1 + 475.11 + 0.54 + 0.3 + 15 = __526.05__
6. 81 − 0.04 = __80.96__
7. Round 27.553 to the nearest tenth. __27.6__
8. Round 62.814 to the nearest hundredth. __62.81__
9. Round 5.06921 to the nearest hundredth. __5.07__
10. Write 0.07 in words. __seven hundredths__

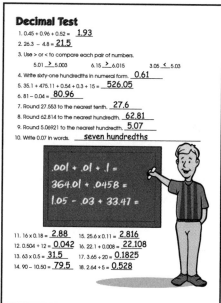

.001 + .01 + .1 =

364.01 + .0458 =

1.05 − .03 + 33.47 =

11. 16 × 0.18 = __2.88__   15. 25.6 × 0.11 = __2.816__
12. 0.504 ÷ 12 = __0.042__   16. 22.1 ÷ 0.008 = __22.108__
13. 63 × 0.5 = __31.5__   17. 3.65 ÷ 20 = __0.1825__
14. 90 − 10.50 = __79.5__   18. 2.64 ÷ 5 = __0.528__

page 198

Pinhole Camera

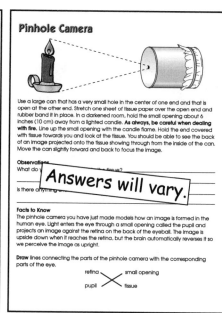

Use a large can that has a very small hole in the center of one end and that is open at the other end. Stretch one sheet of tissue paper over the open end and rubber band it in place. In a darkened room, hold the small opening about 6 inches (10 cm) away from a lighted candle. **As always, be careful when dealing with fire.** Line up the small opening with the candle flame. Hold the end covered with tissue towards you and look at the tissue. You should be able to see the back of an image projected onto the tissue showing through from the inside of the can. Move the can slightly forward and back to focus the image.

Observations
What do ___ **Answers will vary.**
Is there anything _____

Facts to Know
The pinhole camera you have just made models how an image is formed in the human eye. Light enters the eye through a small opening called the pupil and projects an image against the retina on the back of the eyeball. The image is upside down when it reaches the retina, but the brain automatically reverses it so we perceive the image as upright.

Draw lines connecting the parts of the pinhole camera with the corresponding parts of the eye.

retina ╳ small opening
pupil   tissue

page 199

Sentences
Simple, Compound and Complex

A **simple** sentence has a complete subject and predicate.
Example: The little brown rabbit hopped all around the yard.

A **compound** sentence has two or more simple sentences joined together.
Example: Patrick tried to pick the rabbit up, but it quickly hopped away.

A **complex** sentence contains one independent clause and one or more dependent clauses.
Example: After several tries, Patrick finally caught the frightened rabbit.

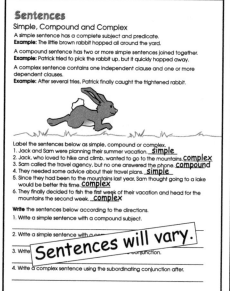

Label the sentences below as simple, compound or complex.

1. Jack and Sam were planning their summer vacation. __simple__
2. Jack, who loved to hike and climb, wanted to go to the mountains. __complex__
3. Sam called the travel agency, but no one answered the phone. __compound__
4. They needed some advice about their travel plans. __simple__
5. Since they had been to the mountains last year, Sam thought going to a lake would be better this time. __complex__
6. They finally decided to fish the first week of their vacation and head for the mountains the second week. __complex__

Write the sentences below according to the directions.

1. Write a simple sentence with a compound subject.
2. Write a simple sentence with a co— **Sentences will vary.**
3. Write _____ conjunction.
4. Write a complex sentence using the subordinating conjunction after.

page 204

"Variety Is the Spice of Life"

Writing is more interesting when sentences are written in different ways. Sentences may be short or long, begin with phrases or clauses or change their order.

Rewrite the paragraphs below. Divide some sentences and combine others. Vary their beginnings.

My sister broke her leg playing soccer. She was playing center. She was in a tournament. She tripped over the ball when she tried to trap the ball and fell to the ground immediately. An ambulance came and an ambulance had on its siren and she went away in the ambulance.

The school year was about to begin. I had to get rea— ___ e to the store. I had to get a notebook. I had to get pe— nk and pencils with erasers. I saw my friends ____ school too.

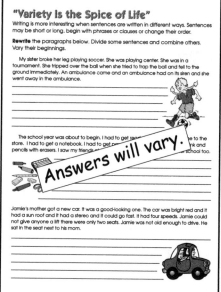

Answers will vary.

Jamie's mother got a new car. It was a good-looking one. The car was bright red and it had a sun roof and it had a stereo and it could go fast. It had four speeds. Jamie could not give anyone a lift there were only two seats. Jamie was not old enough to drive. He sat in the seat next to his mom.

page 205

Perplexing Personalities

Divide each spelling word into syllables and **underline** the syllable that is stressed. Refer to a dictionary if necessary.

percent   perhaps   perish   peroxide   persevere   perspire
percussion   peril   permanent   perpendicular   persist   persuade
perfume   period   permit   perplex   personality   perturb

1. __per cent__
2. __per cus sion__
3. __per fume or per fume__
4. __per haps__
5. __per il__
6. __pe ri od__
7. __per ish__
8. __per ma nent__
9. __per mit or per mit__
10. __per ox ide__
11. __per pen dic u lar__
12. __per plex__
13. __per se vere__
14. __per sist__
15. __per son al i ty__
16. __per spire__
17. __per suade__
18. __per turb__

Write a paragraph using as many spelling words as possible. Add your own words beginning with **per**.

Answers will vary.

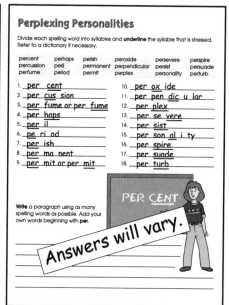

PER CENT

page 206

Tall Trivia

The Empire State Building, a famous building in New York City, has 102 floors. Find out how many stairs it has by shading in the boxes that contain correctly reduced fractions.

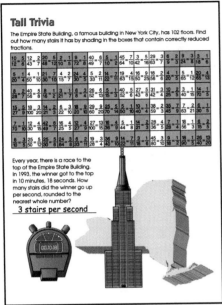

Every year, there is a race to the top of the Empire State Building. In 1993, the winner got to the top in 10 minutes, 18 seconds. How many stairs did the winner go up per second, rounded to the nearest whole number?

3 stairs per second

Light Waves

You will need: a flashlight, a protractor, a mirror, black construction paper and a sheet of white paper

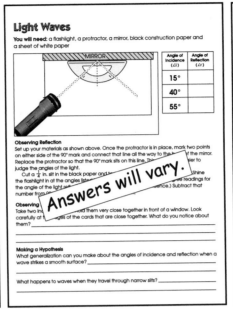

	Angle of Incidence (∠I)	Angle of Reflection (∠r)
	15°	
	40°	
	55°	

Observing Reflection
Set up your materials as shown above. Once the protractor is in place, mark two points on either side of the 90° mark and connect that line all the way to the edge of the mirror. Replace the protractor so that the 90° mark sits on this line. This will make it easier to judge the angles of the light.

Cut a ¼ in. slit in the black paper and ... Shine the flashlight in at the angles listed ... readings for the angle of the light ... ence.) Subtract that number from ...

Observing
Take two in... old them very close together in front of a window. Look carefully at ... ges of the cards that are close together. What do you notice about them? _____

Making a Hypothesis
What generalization can you make about the angles of incidence and reflection when a wave strikes a smooth surface? _____

What happens to waves when they travel through narrow slits? _____

Answers will vary.

Making a Periscope

Light travels in a straight line. Mirrors reflect light in a straight line. The slanted mirrors in a periscope allow the user to see above a normal field of view.
You will need: a shoebox, poster board, tape, scissors, glue, 2 small mirrors

Making the Periscope
Stand your box vertically. Take the lid off and cut a 1-inch-square hole on one side near the top. Cut another hole on the other side near the bottom of the box. Fold a long narrow piece of poster board into thirds. Overlap and tape two of the folded sides to make a triangle. Trim the triangle so that it will fit into the bottom of the box opposite the top hole. Use tape or glue to attach both triangles. Attach one mirror onto the slanting side of the bottom triangle and the other mirror onto the top triangle. Make sure each mirror slants at the same angle and that both mirrors face into the box. Place the lid back on your box.

Using the Periscope
Kneel beside your desk or sit underneath it. Hold the tip of the periscope over the side of your desk. Look through the bottom hole at the mirror. What do you ...

Why do you think the periscope works? _____

What do the mirrors do? _____

Answers will vary.

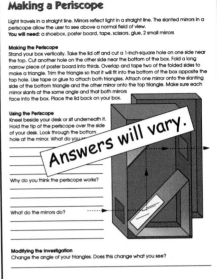

Modifying the Investigation
Change the angle of your triangles. Does this change what you see? _____

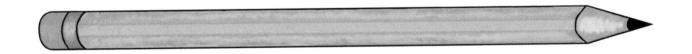

Dizzying Diagrams

Read the following sentences. **Underline** the subjects once and the verbs twice. On the line after each sentence, **write** whether the subject and predicate are simple or compound. Then, diagram the sentences correctly below.

1. The baby laughs and smiles. (S) **simple**
   (P) **compound**
2. A bear hibernates. (S) **simple**
   (P) **simple**
3. The brother and sister argue. (S) **compound**
   (P) **simple**
4. The wind and rain howled and blew. (S) **compound**
   (P) **compound**

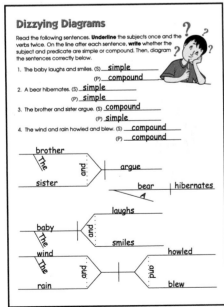

Adjective and Adverb Modifiers

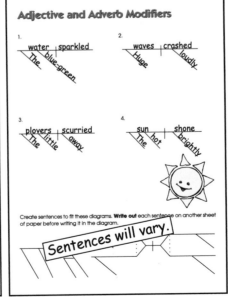

Create sentences to fit these diagrams. **Write out** each sentence on another sheet of paper before writing it in the diagram.

Sentences will vary.

Intercepting the Ball

Write each spelling word in the category in which it belongs. Some words fit into more than one category.

interact
intercept
interchange
intercom
interest
interfere
interject
intermission
internal
interpret
interrogative
interrupt
intersect
interstate
interval
intervene
interview
intertwine

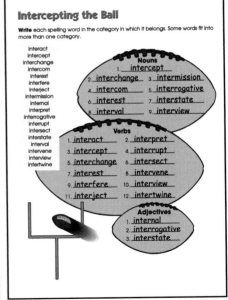

Nouns
1. intercept 2. interchange 3. intermission
4. intercom 5. interrogative 6. interest
7. interstate 8. interval 9. interview

Verbs
1. interact 2. interpret 3. intercept 4. interrupt
5. interchange 6. intersect 7. interest 8. intervene
9. interfere 10. interview 11. interject 12. intertwine

Adjectives
1. internal 2. interrogative 3. interstate

370

What Do You Think?

Read each sentence. **Write** two sentences explaining what could have caused each event to happen.

1. The bird ceased its singing in the forest.
   a. A predator was nearby.
   b. _____

2. Tim came home crying. His backpack was open.
   a. _____
   b. _____

3. Five hundred people laughed at Lana as she stood in the bright light.
   a. _____
   b. _____

4. The saddled horse galloped ___ a jockey.
   a. _____
   b. _____

5. Pam sat ___ on the bench with her friends.
   a. _____
   b. _____

6. Martin stared with mouth agape at his teacher, Mr. Lancaster.
   a. _____
   b. _____

Answers will vary.

page 217

Soccer Fractions

Soccer is a popular sport at Forestview Middle School.

1. There are 30 students in one seventh-grade classroom. If $\frac{1}{3}$ of them play soccer, how many play soccer? **10 students**

2. One-sixth of 24 soccer players are girls. How many boys are on the team? **20 boys**

3. The coach ordered 48 uniforms for the seventh-grade team. The sizes varied. Two-thirds of the uniforms were large sizes. How many were large sizes? **32 large uniforms**

4. Eighty-four people came to watch one game. Six-eighths of the spectators were parents. How many were parents? **63 parents**

5. Thirty-two candy bars were sold at the first game. Two-eighths of them were with almonds. How many almond bars were sold? **8 almond bars**

6. One sixth-grade team played 10 games. Three-fifths of the games were played at home. How many were away games? **4 away games**

7. The eighth graders won eight of their games. One-fourth of the games were won by only two points. How many were won by two points? **2 games**

8. Out of the 486 students at Forestview Middle School, $\frac{1}{3}$ of them play soccer. How many of the students do not play soccer? **324 students**

Extension: Each game is 90 minutes long. Eleven players per team are on the field at one time. If each of the 24 players on a team must play for an equal fraction of the time, how long will each team member play? **41.25 minutes**

page 218

The Spectrum Color Wheel

White light is made up of seven colors of the spectrum: red, orange, yellow, green, blue, indigo and violet. You can see these colors in a rainbow or when light passes through a glass prism.

You will need: a compass, a piece of white poster board, a short nail or screw, a hand drill

Answers will vary.

Making a Color Wheel
Set your compass at a radius of 2 inches. Draw a circle on the poster board and mark a point on the circle. Keep your compass setting the same and draw six arcs around the circle. Make a point where each arc crosses the circle. Next, draw lines from each point to the center of the circle. Color each section in this order: red, orange, yellow, green, blue and violet. Cut out the circle.

Turning the Color Wheel
Have an adult help you press a short nail or screw through the center of the color wheel. Place the nail in the bit of a small hand drill. Lock it tightly in place. Turn on the drill and watch the color wheel spin. What happens? _____

page 219

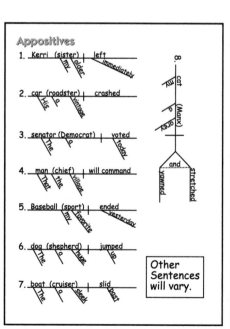

Appositives

1. Kerri (sister) left
2. car (roadster) crashed
3. senator (Democrat) voted
4. man (chief) will command
5. Baseball (sport) ended
6. dog (shepherd) jumped
7. boat (cruiser) slid

Other Sentences will vary.

page 224

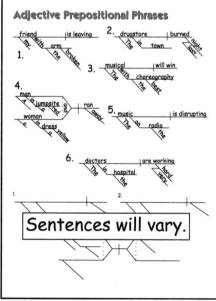

Adjective Prepositional Phrases

1.
2.
3.
4.
5.
6.

Sentences will vary.

page 225

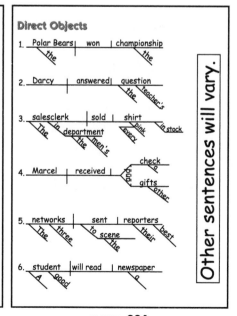

Direct Objects

1. Polar Bears won championship
2. Darcy answered question
3. salesclerk sold shirt
4. Marcel received check gifts
5. networks sent reporters
6. student will read newspaper

Other sentences will vary.

page 226

Indirect Objects

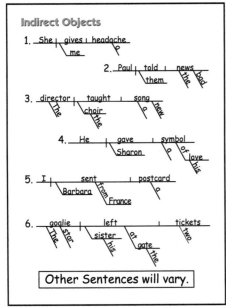

1. She gives me headache
2. Paul told them the bad news
3. The director taught the choir new song
4. He gave Sharon symbol of his love
5. I sent Barbara postcard from France
6. The star goalie left his sister two tickets at the gate

Other Sentences will vary.

page 227

Inflated Inner Tubes

Infect
inflate
inform
injury
insecure
insist
inspire
install
instant
instead
instinct
institute
instruct
insult
intense
intent
intrude
invade

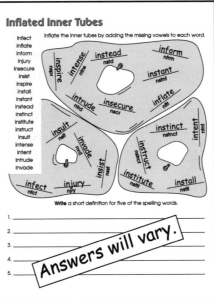

Inflate the inner tubes by adding the missing vowels to each word.

instead — nstd
inform — nfrm
intense — ntns
inspire — nscr
instant — nstnt
intrude — ntrd
insecure — nscr
inflate — nflt
insult — nsl
invade — nvd
instinct — nstnct
instruct — nstrct
intent — ntnt
insist — nsst
institute — nsttt
install — nstll
infect — nfct
injury — njry

Write a short definition for five of the spelling words.

1. ____
2. ____
3. ____
4. ____
5. ____

Answers will vary.

page 228

You Be The Judge

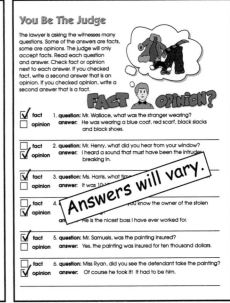

The lawyer is asking the witnesses many questions. Some of the answers are facts, some are opinions. The judge will only accept facts. Read each question and answer. Check fact or opinion next to each answer. If you checked fact, write a second answer that is an opinion. If you checked opinion, write a second answer that is a fact.

FACT OPINION?

☑ fact ☐ opinion 1. **question:** Mr. Wallace, what was the stranger wearing?
answer: He was wearing a blue coat, red scarf, black slacks and black shoes.

☐ fact ☑ opinion 2. **question:** Mr. Henry, what did you hear from your window?
answer: I heard a sound that must have been the intruder breaking in.

☑ fact ☐ opinion 3. **question:** Ms. Harris, what time...
answer: It was 10...

☐ fact ☑ opinion 4. **question:** ...you know the owner of the stolen...
answer: He is the nicest boss I have ever worked for.

☑ fact ☐ opinion 5. **question:** Mr. Samuels, was the painting insured?
answer: Yes, the painting was insured for ten thousand dollars.

☐ fact ☑ opinion 6. **question:** Miss Ryan, did you see the defendant take the painting?
answer: Of course he took it! It had to be him.

Answers will vary.

page 229

Designing Fractions

Mr. Artsy's class was studying design. He drew the following design for the students to study.

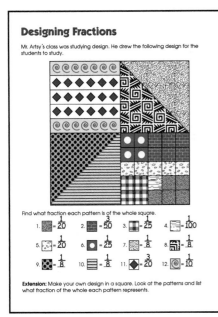

Find what fraction each pattern is of the whole square.

1. $= \frac{3}{20}$
2. $= \frac{3}{50}$
3. $= \frac{1}{25}$
4. $= \frac{1}{100}$
5. $= \frac{1}{20}$
6. $= \frac{1}{25}$
7. $= \frac{1}{8}$
8. $= \frac{1}{8}$
9. $= \frac{1}{8}$
10. $= \frac{1}{8}$
11. $= \frac{3}{20}$
12. $= \frac{1}{10}$

Extension: Make your own design in a square. Look at the patterns and list what fraction of the whole each pattern represents.

page 230

I'm Hungry!

Help Gerry the Giraffe get to the tree by shading in the path that contains the correct areas. Then, find the correct areas for the ones that are wrong.
Remember: area = $\frac{1}{2}$(b x h)

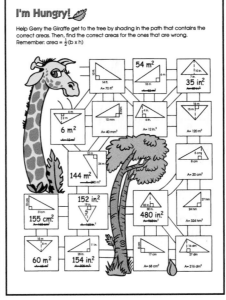

54 m²
35 in²
A= 70 ft²
6 m²
A= 40 mm²
A= 12 in²
A= 120 m²
144 m²
A= 20 cm²
152 in²
480 in²
155 cm²
A= 324 hm²
60 m²
154 in²
A= 68 cm²
A= 216 dm²

page 231

Alphabetizing Champion

religion
region
portion
collection
competition
companion
onion
champion
cushion
opinion
auction
occupation
election
operation
location
mention
digestion
position

Write each spelling word in the correct category and in alphabetical order.

two-syllable words
auction
cushion
mention
onion
portion
region

four-syllable words
competition
occupation
operation

three-syllable words
champion
collection
companion
digestion
election
location
opinion
position
religion

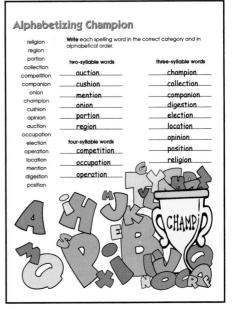

page 236

Learn at Home, Grade 6

Dividing Fractions

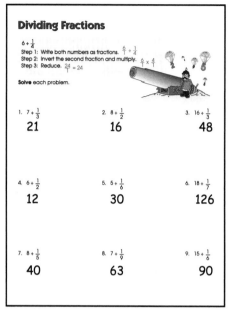

$6 \div \frac{1}{4}$

Step 1: Write both numbers as fractions. $\frac{6}{1} \div \frac{1}{4}$
Step 2: Invert the second fraction and multiply. $\frac{6}{1} \times \frac{4}{1}$
Step 3: Reduce. $\frac{24}{1} = 24$

Solve each problem.

1. $7 \div \frac{1}{3}$
   21

2. $8 \div \frac{1}{2}$
   16

3. $16 \div \frac{1}{3}$
   48

4. $6 \div \frac{1}{2}$
   12

5. $5 \div \frac{1}{6}$
   30

6. $18 \div \frac{1}{7}$
   126

7. $8 \div \frac{1}{5}$
   40

8. $7 \div \frac{1}{9}$
   63

9. $15 \div \frac{1}{6}$
   90

page 237

Art Show

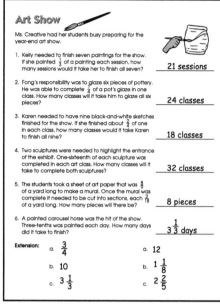

Ms. Creative had her students busy preparing for the year-end art show.

1. Kelly needed to finish seven paintings for the show. If she painted $\frac{1}{3}$ of a painting each session, how many sessions would it take her to finish all seven?
   21 sessions

2. Fong's responsibility was to glaze six pieces of pottery. He was able to complete $\frac{1}{4}$ of a pot's glaze in one class. How many classes will it take him to glaze all six pieces?
   24 classes

3. Karen needed to have nine black-and-white sketches finished for the show. If she finished about $\frac{1}{2}$ of one in each class, how many classes would it take Karen to finish all nine?
   18 classes

4. Two sculptures were needed to highlight the entrance of the exhibit. One-sixteenth of each sculpture was completed in each art class. How many classes will it take to complete both sculptures?
   32 classes

5. The students took a sheet of art paper that was $\frac{8}{9}$ of a yard long to make a mural. Once the mural was complete it needed to be cut into sections, each $\frac{1}{9}$ of a yard long. How many pieces will there be?
   8 pieces

6. A painted carousel horse was the hit of the show. Three-tenths was painted each day. How many days did it take to finish?
   $3\frac{1}{3}$ days

Extension:
a. $\frac{3}{4}$
b. 10
c. $3\frac{1}{3}$

a. 12
b. $1\frac{1}{8}$
c. $2\frac{2}{5}$

page 238

Invert and Multiply

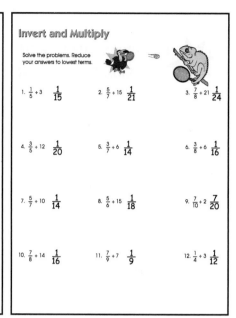

Solve the problems. Reduce your answers to lowest terms.

1. $\frac{1}{5} \div 3$ $\frac{1}{15}$

2. $\frac{5}{7} \div 15$ $\frac{1}{21}$

3. $\frac{7}{8} \div 21$ $\frac{1}{24}$

4. $\frac{3}{5} \div 12$ $\frac{1}{20}$

5. $\frac{3}{7} \div 6$ $\frac{1}{14}$

6. $\frac{3}{8} \div 6$ $\frac{1}{16}$

7. $\frac{5}{7} \div 10$ $\frac{1}{14}$

8. $\frac{5}{6} \div 15$ $\frac{1}{18}$

9. $\frac{7}{10} \div 2$ $\frac{7}{20}$

10. $\frac{7}{8} \div 14$ $\frac{1}{16}$

11. $\frac{7}{9} \div 7$ $\frac{1}{9}$

12. $\frac{1}{4} \div 3$ $\frac{1}{12}$

page 239

Stroboscope

You will need: a 6-inch square piece of poster board, a straight pin, a pencil with an eraser

Making a Stroboscope
Cut out the pattern shown below. Place the pattern on a piece of poster board and cut it out carefully. Push a pin through the center of the disk, then into the eraser of a pencil.

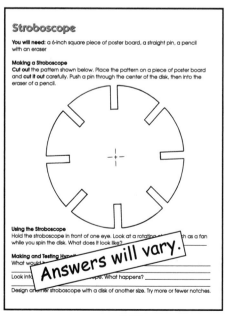

Using the Stroboscope
Hold the stroboscope in front of one eye. Look at a rotating object such as a fan while you spin the disk. What does it look like?

Making and Testing Hypotheses
What would _____

Look into _____ope. What happens? _____

Design another stroboscope with a disk of another size. Try more or fewer notches.

Answers will vary.

page 240

Chemical Reaction

chemical	
classical	
comical	
cylindrical	
electrical	
identical	
medical	
musical	
optical	
practical	
radical	
skeptical	
surgical	
technical	
theatrical	
tropical	
typical	
vertical	

Rewrite the adjectives from the spelling list and add a noun to make a short phrase.
Example: *political — political reaction*

1. chemical reaction
2. classical music
3. comical story
4. cylindrical shape
5. electrical tape
6. identical twins
7. medical breakthrough
8. musical instrument
9. optical nerve
10. practical advice
11. radical surgery
12. skeptical look
13. surgical gloves
14. technical jargon
15. theatrical gesture
16. tropical breeze
17. typical day
18. vertical drop

Write a quatrain (a poem with four rhyming lines). Try to end each line using a spelling word.

Example: **Me**
Usually _____
_____
_____ are often quite comical.

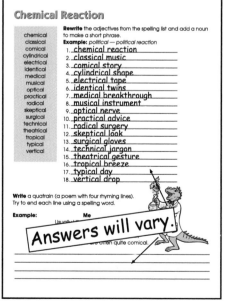

Answers will vary.

page 246

Do You Speak Spanish?

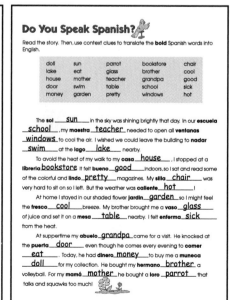

Read the story. Then, use context clues to translate the **bold** Spanish words into English.

doll	sun	parrot	bookstore	chair
lake	eat	glass	brother	cool
house	mother	teacher	grandpa	good
door	swim	table	school	sick
money	garden	pretty	windows	hot

The **sol** ___sun___ in the sky was shining brightly that day. In our **escuela** ___school___, my **maestra** ___teacher___ needed to open all **ventanas** ___windows___ to cool the air. I wished we could leave the building to **nadar** ___swim___ at the **lago** ___lake___ nearby.

To avoid the heat of my walk to my **casa** ___house___, I stopped at a **libreria** ___bookstore___. It felt **bueno** ___good___ indoors, so I sat and read some of the colorful and **lindo** ___pretty___ magazines. My **silla** ___chair___ was very hard to sit on so I left. But the weather was **caliente** ___hot___!

At home I stayed in our shaded flower **jardin** ___garden___ so I might feel the **fresco** ___cool___ breeze. My brother brought me a **vaso** ___glass___ of juice and set it on a **mesa** ___table___ nearby. I felt **enferma** ___sick___ from the heat.

At suppertime my **abuelo** ___grandpa___ came for a visit. He knocked at the **puerta** ___door___ even though he comes every evening to **comer** ___eat___. Today, he had **dinero** ___money___ to buy me a **muneca** ___doll___ for my collection. He bought my **hermano** ___brother___ a volleyball. For my **mamá** ___mother___ he bought a **loro** ___parrot___ that talks and squawks too much!

page 247

Egyptian Math

Help build the pyramid by adding the fractions.
Reduce each to its lowest term.

Use the following rule:

$a + b = c$

	$3\frac{3}{4}$	
$2\frac{1}{5}$		$1\frac{3}{5}$
$\frac{7}{5}$	$\frac{4}{5}$	$\frac{4}{5}$
$\frac{4}{5}$	$\frac{3}{5}$	$\frac{1}{5}$	$\frac{3}{5}$
$\frac{4}{15}$	$\frac{8}{15}$	$\frac{1}{15}$	$\frac{2}{15}$	$\frac{7}{15}$

page 248

Adding Unlike Fractions

Example: $\frac{4}{5} + \frac{1}{4}$

$$\frac{4}{5} + \frac{1}{4} = \frac{4(x4)}{5(x4)} + \frac{1(x5)}{4(x5)} = \frac{16}{20} + \frac{5}{20} = \frac{21}{20} = 1\frac{1}{20}$$

5, 10, 15, 20
4, 8, 12, 16, 20

Steps:
1. Find the LCM of both denominators (20).
2. Multiply the numerator and denominator of each fraction by a number to arrive at the LCM.
3. Add numerators.
4. Denominators stay the same.
5. Write improper fractions as mixed numbers.
6. Reduce to lowest terms.

Remember: Since you are multiplying both numerator and denominator by the same number, you are just multiplying the fraction by 1 ($\frac{4}{4} = 1$, $\frac{5}{5} = 1$).

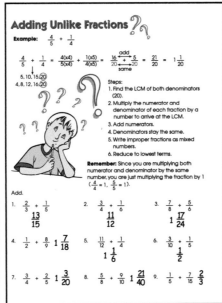

Add.

1. $\frac{2}{3} + \frac{1}{5}$ $\frac{13}{15}$

2. $\frac{3}{4} + \frac{1}{6}$ $\frac{11}{12}$

3. $\frac{7}{8} + \frac{5}{6}$ $1\frac{17}{24}$

4. $\frac{1}{2} + \frac{8}{9}$ $1\frac{7}{18}$

5. $\frac{11}{12} + \frac{1}{4}$ $1\frac{1}{6}$

6. $\frac{3}{10} + \frac{1}{5}$ $\frac{1}{2}$

7. $\frac{3}{4} + \frac{2}{5}$ $1\frac{3}{20}$

8. $\frac{5}{8} + \frac{9}{10}$ $1\frac{21}{40}$

9. $\frac{1}{5} + \frac{7}{15}$ $\frac{2}{3}$

page 249

Migration Fascination

Drop the final e and add the suffix **tion** to change each verb to a noun form. Then, make word associations by writing the noun form next to a word in the numbered column. The first one is done for you.

aggravate
appreciate
circulate
enunciate
estimate
fascinate
graduate
hesitate
immigrate
liberate
migrate
narrate
navigate
participate
populate
rotate
terminate
translate

1. a sharing — participation
2. boats — navigation
3. gifts — appreciation
4. blood — circulation
5. birds — migration
6. slave — liberation
7. senior — graduation
8. tire — rotation
9. entering — immigration
10. cost — estimation
11. Spanish — translation
12. a play — narration
13. problem — aggravation
14. words — enunciation
15. interest — fascination
16. final — termination
17. people — population
18. pausing — hesitation

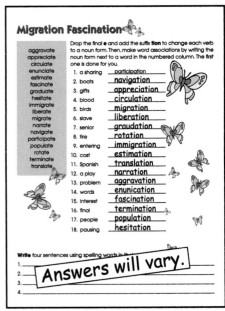

Write four sentences using spelling words in the

1.
2. Answers will vary.
3.
4.

page 254

Sing Is to Song, as . . .

Complete each phrase.   Answers may vary.

1. Glue is to sticking as pencil is to _writing_.
2. Son is to mother as daughter is to _father_.
3. Country is to continent as city is to _state_.
4. 5 is to 15 a 4 is to _12_.
5. Garage is to car as library is to _book_.
6. Victoria is to lake as Pacific is to _ocean_.
7. Hot is to steam as cold is to _ice_.
8. Weak is to strong as good is to _bad_.
9. Skin is to human as _scales_ are to fish.
10. 2 is to bicycle as 3 is to _tricycle_.
11. Clipper is to sail as _canoe_ is to paddle.
12. Drama is to act as ballet is to _dance_.
13. Adiós is to Spanish as au revoir is to _French_.
14. Pilot is to aircraft as nurse is to _hospital_.
15. Damascus is to Syria as Tokyo is to _Japan_.
16. Moo is to herd as _honk_ is to flock.
17. Lion is to pride as wolf is to _pack_.
18. Racket is to tennis as club is to _golf_.

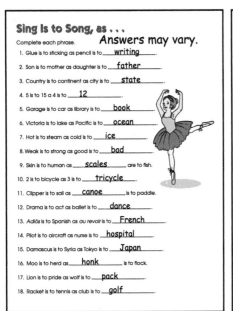

page 255

Fractions

Subtract. Reduce your answers to lowest terms and **write** them here. The first one has been done for you.

1. $5 \quad 4\frac{4}{4}$ $- \frac{3}{4}$ $4\frac{1}{4}$

2. $8 - \frac{7}{8}$ $7\frac{1}{8}$

3. $4 - \frac{3}{6}$ $3\frac{3}{6} = 3\frac{1}{2}$

4. $10 - \frac{3}{8}$ $9\frac{5}{8}$

5. $14 - \frac{2}{5}$ $13\frac{3}{5}$

6. $11 - \frac{7}{8}$ $10\frac{1}{8}$

7. $4 - \frac{3}{5}$ $3\frac{2}{5}$

8. $7 - \frac{3}{8}$ $6\frac{5}{8}$

9. $6 - \frac{1}{2}$ $5\frac{1}{2} = 5\frac{1}{2}$

10. $12 - \frac{1}{2}$ $11\frac{1}{2} = 11\frac{1}{2}$

11. $9 - \frac{5}{8}$ $8\frac{3}{8}$

12. $3 - \frac{3}{5}$ $2\frac{2}{5} = 2\frac{2}{5}$

13. $7 - \frac{3}{4}$ $6\frac{1}{4}$

14. $40 - \frac{3}{7}$ $39\frac{4}{7}$

15. $5 - \frac{2}{3}$ $4\frac{1}{3}$

16. $8 - \frac{5}{9}$ $7\frac{4}{9}$

17. $11 - \frac{6}{12}$ $10\frac{6}{12} = 10\frac{1}{2}$

18. $4 - \frac{5}{8}$ $3\frac{3}{8}$

19. $6 - \frac{2}{7}$ $5\frac{5}{7}$

20. $9 - \frac{3}{4}$ $8\frac{1}{4}$

21. $12 - \frac{5}{9}$ $11\frac{4}{9}$

22. $4 - \frac{11}{...}$ $3\frac{6}{11}$

23. $7 - \frac{5}{10}$ $6\frac{5}{10} = 6\frac{1}{2}$

24. $32 - \frac{5}{7}$ $31\frac{2}{7}$

25. $25 - \frac{3}{4}$ $24\frac{1}{4}$

26. $20 - \frac{5}{8}$ $19\frac{3}{8}$

27. $5 - \frac{3}{6}$ $4\frac{3}{6} = 4\frac{1}{2}$

28. $8 - \frac{2}{5}$ $7\frac{3}{5}$

page 256

Fraction Frenzy

Subtract. Reduce your answers to lowest terms and **write** them here.

1. $\frac{3}{8} - \frac{1}{8}$ $\frac{2}{8} = \frac{1}{4}$

2. $\frac{2}{5} - \frac{1}{3}$ $\frac{4}{15}$

3. $\frac{3}{4} - \frac{1}{12}$ $\frac{8}{12} = \frac{2}{3}$

4. $\frac{5}{6} - \frac{1}{2}$ $\frac{2}{6} = \frac{1}{3}$

5. $\frac{3}{5} - \frac{1}{3}$ $\frac{2}{...}$

6. $\frac{4}{7} - \frac{3}{14}$ $\frac{5}{14}$

7. $\frac{5}{8} - \frac{1}{16}$ $\frac{9}{16}$

8. $\frac{7}{10} - \frac{1}{4}$ $\frac{9}{20} = \frac{3}{...}$

9. $\frac{2}{3} - \frac{1}{4}$ $\frac{5}{12}$

10. $\frac{5}{6} - \frac{2}{15}$ $\frac{...}{15}$

11. $\frac{7}{8} - \frac{3}{16}$ $\frac{...}{16}$

12. $\frac{4}{9} - \frac{1}{...}$ $\frac{...}{9}$

13. $\frac{5}{7} - \frac{1}{14}$ $\frac{8}{14} = \frac{4}{7}$

14. $\frac{9}{10} - \frac{2}{...}$ $\frac{5}{10} = \frac{1}{2}$

15. $\frac{7}{8} - \frac{3}{...}$ $\frac{...}{...}$

16. $\frac{5}{6} - \frac{1}{8}$ $\frac{...}{...}$

17. $\frac{3}{4} - \frac{1}{...}$ $\frac{0}{...}$

18. $\frac{3}{8} - \frac{1}{...}$ $\frac{...}{6}$

19. $\frac{1}{2} - \frac{...}{8}$ $\frac{...}{8} = \frac{1}{4}$

20. $\frac{5}{6} - \frac{...}{...}$ $\frac{...}{18}$

21. $\frac{5}{8} - \frac{...}{...}$ $\frac{...}{16} = \frac{...}{...}$

22. $\frac{3}{4} - \frac{...}{16}$ $\frac{...}{16}$

23. $\frac{7}{10} - \frac{...}{...}$ $\frac{...}{...}$

24. $\frac{5}{6} - \frac{...}{...}$ $\frac{...}{18}$

25. $\frac{7}{...} - \frac{...}{...}$ $\frac{4}{21}$

26. $\frac{8}{...} - \frac{...}{...}$ $\frac{...}{24} = \frac{1}{6}$

27. $\frac{5}{...} - \frac{...}{...}$ $\frac{31}{48}$

28. $\frac{7}{10} - \frac{...}{...}$ $\frac{5}{10} = \frac{1}{2}$

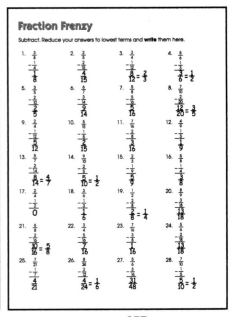

page 257

Learn at Home, Grade 6

Subtracting Unlike Mixed Numbers

Example: $41\frac{2}{8} - 20\frac{2}{3}$

$41\frac{2}{8} - 20\frac{2}{3} = 41\frac{2(3)}{8(3)} - 20\frac{2(8)}{3(8)} = 41\frac{6}{24} - 20\frac{16}{24} = 40\frac{30}{24} - 20\frac{16}{24}$

8, 16 (24)

3, 6, 9, 12, 15, 18, 21 (24)

$20\frac{14}{24} = 20\frac{7}{12}$

Steps:
1. Find the LCM of both denominators (24).
2. Multiply the numerator and denominator of each fraction by a number to arrive at the LCM.
3. When regrouping, borrow a whole number and write the fraction as an improper fraction.
4. Subtract whole numbers.
5. Subtract numerators.
6. Denominators stay the same.
7. Reduce your answer to lowest terms.

Subtract.

1. $24\frac{2}{3} - 11\frac{2}{3}$ $12\frac{5}{9}$

2. $86\frac{1}{5} - 72\frac{7}{10}$ $13\frac{5}{10} = 13\frac{1}{2}$

3. $44\frac{3}{8} - 26\frac{5}{6}$ $17\frac{13}{24}$

4. $19\frac{1}{4} - 12\frac{2}{3}$ $6\frac{7}{12}$

5. $17\frac{4}{5} - 8\frac{1}{4}$ $9\frac{11}{20}$

6. $50\frac{2}{9} - 26\frac{1}{2}$ $23\frac{13}{18}$

7. $10\frac{1}{2} - 3\frac{2}{3}$ $6\frac{5}{6}$

8. $12\frac{1}{5} - 7\frac{2}{3}$ $4\frac{8}{15}$

9. $28\frac{5}{12} - 11\frac{2}{3}$ $16\frac{9}{12} = 16\frac{3}{4}$

page 258

Fun Facts

The World Trade Center towers in New York are so large and tall that each tower has its own . . .

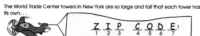

Z I P   C O D E !
1 2 3   4 5 6 7

To find the answer, follow the directions below.

Put an O above number 5 if the estimated difference between $13\frac{1}{3}$ and $5\frac{3}{7}$ is 8.

Put an A above number 6 if the estimated difference between $21\frac{5}{6}$ and $9\frac{4}{9}$ is 12.

Put an R above number 4 if the estimated difference between $16\frac{5}{20}$ and $13\frac{11}{18}$ is 3.

Put a B above number 1 if the estimated difference between $8\frac{1}{2}$ and $3\frac{1}{12}$ is 6.

Put a C above number 4 if the estimated difference between $25\frac{7}{20}$ and $13\frac{7}{12}$ is 11.

Put an E above number 7 if the estimated difference between $32\frac{7}{8}$ and $14\frac{2}{10}$ is 17.

Put a D above number 3 if the estimated difference between $18\frac{1}{3}$ and $15\frac{4}{5}$ is 2.

Put an I above number 2 if the estimated difference between $19\frac{7}{20}$ and $9\frac{4}{11}$ is 10.

Put a P above number 3 if the estimated difference between $58\frac{5}{9}$ and $42\frac{3}{10}$ is 16.

Put a D above number 6 if the estimated difference between $30\frac{13}{20}$ and $19\frac{7}{18}$ is 12.

Put an L above number 1 if the estimated difference between $11\frac{5}{9}$ and $5\frac{2}{13}$ is 6.

Put a Z above number 1 if the estimated difference between $16\frac{4}{9}$ and $9\frac{2}{7}$ is 7.

page 259

Malicious Monsters

Use an adjective from the spelling list to describe each noun below. Both adjective and noun will begin with the same letter.

#	Adjective	Noun
	Example:	
1.	precious	princess
2.	curious	cat
3.	luscious	limes
4.	spacious	sunroom
5.	vicious	villain
6.	furious	Frankenstein
7.	generous	gift
8.	delicious	dessert
9.	enormous	elephant
10.	serious	situation
11.	ferocious	felines
12.	vivacious	violinist
13.	conscious	commitment
14.	atrocious	act
15.	disastrous	demonstration
16.	suspicious	secret agent
17.	gracious	gestures
18.	malicious	mischief

Use four of the adjective/noun phrases above to create an interesting sentence that makes sense. **Underline** each phrase.

Example: Six ferocious felines and one ... acious sunroom e... Answers will vary.

page 264

Research Time

Mr. Write-A-Lot assigned research papers to his class. He divided the class into two groups. One person from each group was responsible for each part of the research process.

1. Marisha and John each found several books on their subjects. It took Marisha $2\frac{1}{2}$ hours to skim through her stack of books, and it took John $1\frac{3}{4}$ hours to look through his. How much longer did it take Marisha? $\frac{3}{4}$ hour longer

2. Neal and Geraldo were working on note cards. Neal was able to complete his in $48\frac{5}{6}$ minutes, and it took Geraldo $51\frac{3}{8}$ minutes to finish his. How much longer did Geraldo take? $2\frac{17}{24}$ minutes longer

3. Bobby and Gordon found it difficult to write outlines. It took Bobby $38\frac{2}{3}$ minutes and Gordon $36\frac{3}{4}$ minutes. How many more minutes did it take Bobby? $1\frac{11}{12}$ more minutes

4. Anita finished the first draft of her report in $48\frac{1}{2}$ minutes, while it took Pablo $51\frac{3}{8}$ minutes to write his. How much longer did it take Pablo? $2\frac{7}{8}$ minutes longer

5. The final draft of their reports went smoothly for Katie and Laura. Katie zipped hers off in $18\frac{3}{4}$ minutes, and Laura's took $21\frac{1}{8}$ minutes. How much longer did Laura's final draft take? $2\frac{3}{8}$ minutes longer

6. Find out how long it took Marisha, Geraldo, Bobby, Anita and Katie altogether. Then, find out how long it took John, Neal, Gordon, Pablo and Laura. Find the difference between the two groups' times. $307\frac{7}{24}$ minutes $262\frac{11}{12}$ minutes $44\frac{3}{8}$ minutes

Extension: Subtract $2\frac{7}{8}$ from . . .

a. $1\frac{1}{8}$ d. $3\frac{1}{2}$

b. $2\frac{1}{4}$ e. $4\frac{6}{8} = 4\frac{3}{4}$

c. 6   f. $6\frac{7}{8}$

page 265

Fraction Test

1. $\frac{1}{6} + \frac{4}{6} = \frac{5}{6}$

2. $4\frac{1}{12} + 3\frac{2}{3} = 7\frac{3}{12} = 7\frac{1}{4}$

3. $18\frac{1}{3} + 12\frac{1}{3} = 30\frac{3}{3} = 31$

4. $19\frac{1}{5} + 4\frac{2}{3} = 23\frac{13}{15}$

5. $37 - \frac{3}{11} = 36\frac{8}{11}$

6. $\frac{4}{5} - \frac{1}{4} = \frac{11}{20}$

7. $\frac{4}{5} \times \frac{3}{8} = \frac{3}{10}$

8. $\frac{5}{6} \times 15 = 12\frac{1}{2}$

9. $\frac{1}{4} \times \frac{2}{5} = \frac{1}{10} = 1\frac{7}{10}$

10. $3\frac{1}{2} \times 2\frac{1}{3} = 8\frac{1}{6}$

11. $7 \times \frac{3}{5} = 1\frac{4}{5}$

12. $\frac{3}{7} + \frac{4}{5} = \frac{15}{28}$

13. $\frac{2}{3} \div 9 = \frac{2}{27}$

14. $2\frac{6}{7} + \frac{5}{14} = 8$

15. $\frac{1}{2} + \frac{1}{3} = \frac{3}{2} = 1\frac{1}{2}$

16. $7\frac{1}{3} + 2\frac{2}{8} = 3\frac{1}{7}$

17. Write $\frac{3}{5}$ as a decimal.   0.6

18. Leroy got $\frac{7}{8}$ of his 24 homework problems correct. How many did he correct?   21

19. Jean gave $\frac{3}{10}$ of her allowance to her sister and $\frac{1}{8}$ of her allowance to her brother. How much of her allowance did she give away? $\frac{5}{16}$

20. Jack and Jill had a canteen full of 5 quarts of grape juice. They drank $3\frac{5}{8}$ quarts. How much was left? $1\frac{4}{9}$ quarts

page 266

Panpipes

Sound is produced by **vibrations**. A column of air will vibrate when you blow across it. A short column of air will have a high pitch. A long column of air will have a low pitch.

Making the Panpipes

Take five pieces of tubing that are the following lengths: 6 inches, 5 inches, 4 inches, 3 inches and 2 inches. Lay the tubes in a row, arranging them from longest to shortest, about 1 inch apart. With the tops even, tape them together.

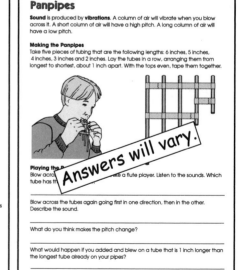

Playing the ... Answers will vary. ... ke a flute player. Listen to the sounds. Which tube has th...

Blow across the tubes again going first in one direction, then in the other. Describe the sound.

What do you think makes the pitch change?

What would happen if you added and blew on a tube that is 1 inch longer than the longest tube already on your pipes?

page 267

Hemispheres

The earth is a sphere. When the earth is cut in half along a vertical or horizontal axis, hemispheres are created. The **equator** divides the earth into the **Northern Hemisphere** and the **Southern Hemisphere**. The prime meridian, which runs from the North Pole to the South Pole, divides the earth into the **Eastern Hemisphere** and the **Western Hemisphere**.

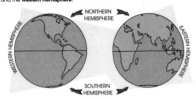

NORTHERN HEMISPHERE

WESTERN HEMISPHERE

EASTERN HEMISPHERE

SOUTHERN HEMISPHERE

Study the illustration of the hemispheres. Then, read the following country names. Decide in which two hemispheres (Eastern or Western, and Northern or Southern) each is located.
Example: The United States lies in the Northern and Western Hemispheres.
Use a more detailed globe or map to find the exact locations of the countries.

1. Australia __Eastern / Southern__   2. India __Eastern / Northern__
3. Japan __Eastern / Northern__   4. Italy __Eastern / Northern__
5. Argentina __Western / Southern__   6. Ethiopia __Eastern / Northern__
7. South Africa __Eastern / Southern__   8. Mexico __Western / Northern__
9. China __Eastern / Northern__   10. Canada __Western / Northern__
11. Israel __Eastern / Northern__   12. Chile __Western / Southern__
13. Iraq __Eastern / Northern__   14. Peru __Western / Southern__

page 268

Plotting North American Cities

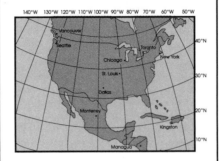

Determine the approximate coordinates of the North American cities on the map above. **Write** the coordinates for each city in the blanks below.

		Latitude	Longitude			Latitude	Longitude
1.	Seattle	46°N	122°W	2. St. Louis	38°N	91°W
3.	Kingston	18°N	74°W	4. Toronto	44°N	79°W
5.	Dallas	33°N	98°W	6. New York	42°N	71°W
7.	Vancouver	48°N	123°W	8. Monterrey	24°N	101°W
9.	Managua	13°N	86°W	10. Chicago	42°N	88°W

page 269

Hhhmm?

Find the answer to the riddle below by solving the following ratios. Put the corresponding problem letter above each answer below. When you have answered the riddle, **write** each ratio two other ways, then find two equivalent ratios for each one.

E. tennis shoes to sandals __3:6__
N. bare feet to men's dress shoes __5:1__
S. high heels to tennis shoes __2:3__
E. sandals to bare feet __6:5__
E. men's dress shoes to high heels __1:2__
A. high heels to sandals __2:6__
T. bare feet to tennis shoes __5:3__
A. high heels to bare feet __2:5__
D. tennis shoes to men's dress shoes __3:1__
H. men's dress shoes to sandals __1:6__
H. bare feet to sandals __5:6__
R. sandals to high heels __6:2__
H. tennis shoes to high heels __3:2__
D. sandals to tennis shoes __6:3__
T. men's dress shoes to tennis shoes __1:3__
H. tennis shoes to bare feet __3:5__
L. high heels to men's dress shoes __2:1__
A. men's dress shoes to bare feet __1:5__
A. bare feet to high heels __5:2__
H. sandals to men's dress shoes __6:1__

What do the four H's stand for in the 4-H Club?

H E A D   H E A R T
3:5 6:5 2:5 3:1   5:6 3:6 1:5 6:2 5:3

H E A L T H   H A N D S
1:6 1:2 5:2 2:1 1:3 6:1   3:2 2:6 5:1 6:3 2:3

page 274

Percents

Convert these proper fractions and mixed numbers into percents. Show your work on another sheet of paper. **Write** your answers here.

1. $\frac{37}{100}$ = 37%   2. $\frac{3}{100}$ = 3%   3. $\frac{65}{100}$ = 65%   4. $\frac{49}{100}$ = 49%   5. $\frac{1}{4}$ = 25%

6. $\frac{12}{100}$ = 12%   7. $\frac{11}{50}$ = 22%   8. $\frac{71}{100}$ = 71%   9. $4\frac{1}{2}$ = 450%   10. $3\frac{1}{4}$ = 325%

11. $1\frac{3}{4}$ = 175%   12. $\frac{2}{5}$ = 40%   13. $\frac{3}{10}$ = 30%   14. $\frac{63}{100}$ = 63%   15. $\frac{1}{20}$ = 5%

16. $\frac{1}{5}$ = 20%   17. $\frac{17}{20}$ = 85%   18. $\frac{57}{100}$ = 57%   19. $\frac{3}{5}$ = 60%   20. $\frac{1}{25}$ = 4%

21. $\frac{7}{10}$ = 70%   22. $5\frac{1}{4}$ = 525%   23. $\frac{37}{50}$ = 74%   24. $\frac{23}{100}$ = 23%   25. $\frac{1}{2}$ = 50%

26. $\frac{9}{10}$ = 90%   27. $\frac{81}{100}$ = 81%   28. $\frac{39}{100}$ = 39%   29. $3\frac{3}{4}$ = 375%   30. $\frac{73}{100}$ = 73%

31. $\frac{7}{20}$ = 35%   32. $9\frac{1}{2}$ = 950%   33. $\frac{4}{5}$ = 80%   34. $\frac{1}{10}$ = 10%   35. $\frac{13}{20}$ = 65%

36. $\frac{91}{100}$ = 91%   37. $\frac{51}{100}$ = 51%   38. $5\frac{1}{4}$ = 525%   39. $\frac{11}{100}$ = 11%   40. $\frac{3}{20}$ = 15%

page 275

River System

The river systems of the world provide people with transportation, energy and fertile soil, as well as water for drinking, washing and irrigation. The terms below are used to describe a river system. Learn the meanings of these terms, then label the parts of the river on the illustration.

flood plain   delta   mouth
tributary   rapids   swamp
lake   levee   source

source

rapids

lake

tributary

flood plain

levee

delta

swamp

mouth

page 276

River Cities

Many of the world's great cities began as small towns and settlements along major rivers. Communities near water were easily accessible. Water was readily available for drinking, cooking, washing, irrigation and obtaining food. Use an atlas, almanac or encyclopedia to help you complete the chart.

River	City	Country	Continent
Mississippi	St. Louis	U.S.A	North America
Hudson	New York	U.S.A	North America
Tiber	Rome	Italy	Europe
Nile	Cairo	Egypt	Africa
Thames	London	England	Europe
Rio la Plata	Buenos Aires	Argentina	South America
Seine	Paris	France	Europe
Yangtze	Shanghai	China	Asia

page 277

Learn at Home, Grade 6

Organize or Capsize

Put the spelling words in alphabetical order in the lifeboats before the ship capsizes.

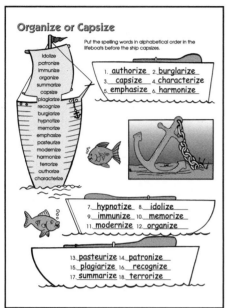

Idolize
patronize
immunize
organize
summarize
capsize
plagiarize
recognize
burglarize
hypnotize
memorize
emphasize
pasteurize
modernize
harmonize
terrorize
authorize
characterize

1. authorize 2. burglarize
3. capsize 4. characterize
5. emphasize 6. harmonize

7. hypnotize 8. idolize
9. immunize 10. memorize
11. modernize 12. organize

13. pasteurize 14. patronize
15. plagiarize 16. recognize
17. summarize 18. terrorize

page 282

Timely Words

Read each sentence. **Circle** the two words that tell when something happens. **Write** each circled word on the correct line to show which word would come before or after the other word in time.

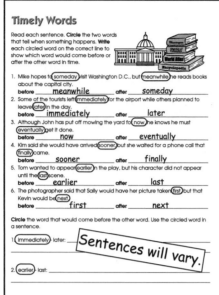

1. Mike hopes to (someday) visit Washington D.C., but (meanwhile) he reads books about the capital city.
   before __meanwhile__ after __someday__
2. Some of the tourists left (immediately) for the airport while others planned to leave (later) in the day.
   before __immediately__ after __later__
3. Although John has put off mowing the yard for (now,) he knows he must (eventually) get it done.
   before __now__ after __eventually__
4. Kim said she would have arrived (sooner,) but she waited for a phone call that (finally) came.
   before __sooner__ after __finally__
5. Tom wanted to appear (earlier) in the play, but his character did not appear until the (last) scene.
   before __earlier__ after __last__
6. The photographer said that Sally would have her picture taken (first,) but that Kevin would be (next.)
   before __first__ after __next__

Circle the word that would come before the other word. Use the circled word in a sentence.

1. (immediately) later: ___Sentences will vary.___

2. (earlier) last: _____

page 283

Percentages

Sally and Gabriel wrote percentage problems for extra credit. Once you have solved their problems, make up some of your own on another sheet of paper.

1. There were 400 students in the school. If 38% of the students were boys, how many boys were there? __152 boys__
2. Out of the 345 sheets of construction paper in Mrs. Rainbow's class, 20% were red and 40% were blue. How many sheets were red? __69 red__
   How many sheets were blue? __138 blue__
3. Only 19% of the 400 students ate the cafeteria food on Monday. How many students purchased cafeteria food Monday? __76 students__
4. 25% of 76 band members can play a clarinet. How many can play a clarinet? __19 band members__
5. 35 trees were planted around the school. 60% were maples. How many of the trees planted were maple? __21 maples__
6. The local pizza parlor gave the eighth-grade class a 25% discount on pizzas they purchased to sell at the football game. Each pizza originally cost $12.00. How much did the eighth graders pay per pizza? __$9.00__
   If they purchased 12 pizzas, how much did they save together? __$36.00__
7. They saw these signs at the sports shop nearby. Figure each sale price.

Sale! 15% off All In-Line Skates! Regularly $97.00

25% Savings All Mitts! Regularly $24.00

Huge Savings! 20% off All Bicycles Regularly $132.00

$82.45 $18.00 $105.60

page 284

Enlightening Information

An **environment** includes all living and nonliving things with which an organism interacts. These living and nonliving things are **interdependent**, that is, they depend on one another. The living things in an environment (plants, animals) are called **biotic factors**, and the nonliving things (soil, light, temperature) are called **abiotic factors**. **Ecology** is the study of the relationships and interactions of living things with one another and their environment.

Living things inhabit many different environments. A group of organisms living and interacting with each other in their nonliving environment is called an **ecosystem**. The different organisms that live together in an ecosystem are called a **community**. Within a community, each kind of living thing (i.e., frogs) makes up a **population**.

Study the picture. Follow the directions.
1. Label two biotic factors and two abiotic factors in the picture.
   abiotic: sun, sky, water, rock
   biotic: butterfly, dragonfly, fish, turtle, cattails
   snails, frogs, bugs
2. Explain the relationships among the living things in the pictured environment.
   The living things in the picture depend on each other
   for food,
3. Label the type of ecosystem pictured.
   Pond
4. Circle all the members of the community.
   Circle all the living things—plants and animals.
5. Explain how the organisms in this environment are dependent upon one another.
   Frogs eat insects; insects eat plants; plants grow in
   water; fish live in water; etc.
6. List the different kinds of populations that live in the environment.
   frogs, fish, turtles, dragonflies, butterflies, etc.

page 285

Cemetery Epitaphs

Use a spelling word to complete each word group.

archery
celery
cemetery
drapery
embroidery
fiery
greenery
grocery
hatchery
machinery
misery
mockery
refinery
robbery
slippery
stationary
surgery
trickery

1. graveyard, burial place, __cemetery__
2. industrial, purifier, __refinery__
3. operation, medical procedure, __surgery__
4. slick, shifting, __slippery__
5. blazing, glowing, __fiery__
6. stalk, vegetable, __celery__
7. theft, stealing, __robbery__
8. curtains, covering, __drapery__
9. pain, sorrow, __misery__
10. handiwork, sewing, __embroidery__
11. grass, plants, __greenery__
12. notepad, envelopes, __stationary__
13. bow shooting, sport, __archery__
14. engines, power tools, __machinery__
15. insult, false appearance, __mockery__
16. prank, joke, __trickery__
17. foodstuffs, store, __grocery__
18. incubator, brooder, __hatchery__

Write an epitaph (a tombstone inscription) for a tombstone you might find in a cemetery. The epitaph may be wacky, creepy or sentimental. Try to use several words from the list.
Example: Here lies George who ate too much celery. He simply couldn't resist any kind of greenery, and the surgery didn't help. I am sad to say that he died in misery.

page 292

Magnify the Situation

Unscramble the letters to find the spelling word (verb) that goes with each clue (direct object). The first one has been done for you.

		verb	direct object
amplify	1. (plifmyls)	simplify	the problem
beautify	2. (abyfleut)	beautify	a city park
certify	3. (ulyfalq)	qualify	your answer
clarify	4. (iyrfroh)	horrify	your teacher
dignify	5. (fyldosll)	solidify	the liquid
falsify	6. (ffsllay)	falsify	the document
fortify	7. (yvfrle)	verify	your identity
glorify	8. (ynifot)	notify	the authorities
horrify	9. (pflaaym)	amplify	the sound
identify	10. (ifyustf)	justify	your actions
justify	11. (irofgly)	glorify	a hero
magnify	12. (cffteryf)	rectify	the situation
notify	13. (cfyrall)	clarify	your question
qualify	14. (yfttrol)	fortify	the walls
rectify	15. (iafymrng)	magnify	the cells
simplify	16. (fndltely)	identify	the criminal
solidify	17. (ngifydl)	dignify	the procedure
verify	18. (ltrecyf)	certify	the check

My name is Sam Sneed. It is my job to clarify the evidence, verify the facts, indentify the murderer, and notify the authorities. I do not intend to glorify but I am the best in my field. In order to qualify for this position I had to study very hard for many years. All the hard work paid off. I am now certified and have a very satisfying position as a __detective__.

page 298

The Sign of the Beaver

Read the following sentences. Based on context, write a definition for each **bold** word. Then, look up the definitions and **circle** yes if you were correct. If you were not correct, change your answer.

Answers will vary.

1. ". . . when his rage died down, that he felt a **prickle** of fear."
Prickle means _____ yes

2. ". . . he saw the sunlight glinted through the **chinks** on the roof."
Chinks means _____ yes

3. ". . . but he ~~ought~~ he'd rather have the **pesky** insects himself."
Pesky m~~_____~~ yes

4. "Matt _____"
Pondering me~~_____~~ yes

5. "He strutted and pranced _____"
Contortions means _____ yes

6. "Now **wampum** no good to pay for gun."
Wampum means _____ yes

7. "**Warily**, he made his way through the brush."
Warily means _____ yes

8. "The brown eyes looked up at the Indian boy with **admiration**."
Admiration means _____ yes

9. ". . . they **wielded** their bats with no heed to each other's heads. . ."
Wielded means _____ yes

10. "Matt forced himself to eat **sparingly** of these things."
Sparingly means _____ yes

page 299

Sam the Squirrel

Help Sam get the acorns to the tree by shading in the path containing the correct proportions.

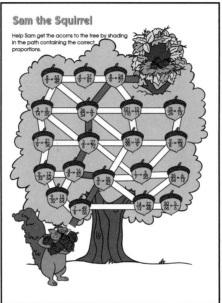

page 300

Proportions

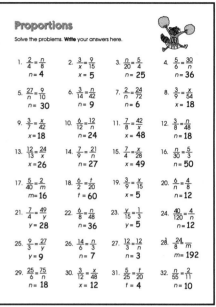

Solve the problems. **Write** your answers here.

1. $\frac{2}{4} = \frac{n}{8}$
$n = 4$

2. $\frac{3}{x} = \frac{9}{15}$
$x = 5$

3. $\frac{n}{20} = \frac{5}{4}$
$n = 25$

4. $\frac{5}{6} = \frac{30}{n}$
$n = 36$

5. $\frac{27}{n} = \frac{9}{10}$
$n = 30$

6. $\frac{3}{14} = \frac{n}{42}$
$n = 9$

7. $\frac{2}{n} = \frac{24}{72}$
$n = 6$

8. $\frac{3}{9} = \frac{x}{54}$
$x = 18$

9. $\frac{3}{7} = \frac{x}{42}$
$x = 18$

10. $\frac{6}{12} = \frac{12}{n}$
$n = 24$

11. $\frac{7}{8} = \frac{42}{x}$
$x = 48$

12. $\frac{3}{8} = \frac{n}{48}$
$n = 18$

13. $\frac{12}{13} = \frac{24}{x}$
$x = 26$

14. $\frac{7}{9} = \frac{21}{n}$
$n = 27$

15. $\frac{7}{4} = \frac{x}{28}$
$x = 49$

16. $\frac{n}{30} = \frac{5}{3}$
$n = 50$

17. $\frac{5}{40} = \frac{2}{m}$
$m = 16$

18. $\frac{6}{2} = \frac{t}{20}$
$t = 60$

19. $\frac{3}{9} = \frac{5}{15}$
$x = 5$

20. $\frac{6}{n} = \frac{4}{8}$
$n = 12$

21. $\frac{7}{4} = \frac{49}{y}$
$y = 28$

22. $\frac{6}{8} = \frac{n}{48}$
$n = 36$

23. $\frac{y}{15} = \frac{1}{3}$
$y = 5$

24. $\frac{40}{120} = \frac{4}{n}$
$n = 12$

25. $\frac{9}{3} = \frac{27}{y}$
$y = 9$

26. $\frac{14}{6} = \frac{n}{3}$
$n = 7$

27. $\frac{12}{3} = \frac{12}{n}$
$n = 3$

28. $\frac{24}{m}$
$m = 192$

29. $\frac{25}{6} = \frac{75}{n}$
$n = 18$

30. $\frac{3}{12} = \frac{x}{48}$
$x = 12$

31. $\frac{5}{25} = \frac{t}{20}$
$t = 4$

32. $\frac{n}{55} = \frac{2}{11}$
$n = 10$

page 301

From Field to Forest

Through a series of changes, an abandoned farmer's field can develop into a climax forest. These changes take an orderly pattern called **succession**. Read the description of each step in the succession of an abandoned farmer's field in the southeastern United States.

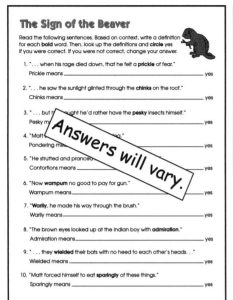

Farmer's Abandoned Field
Ten years after Farmer Brown quit working his farm, small pine seedlings began to grow in the aband~~_____~~ field along low-growi~~_____~~ shrubs, g~~_____~~ and herbs. List some animals that would live in this habitat.

Pine Forest
Twenty-five years have passed, and the pines have grown tall and mature. Young oak tree seedlings start to grow beneath the ~~_____~~ List some animals ~~_____~~ would live in this habitat.

Oak-Pine Forest!
The oak trees reach for the sun between the old pine trees. Many older pines die, and young oaks begin to replace them.

Oak Climax Forest
The large oaks dominate the forest. Young oaks grow in the understory, but young pines cannot grow in the shade of the oaks. List some animals that would live in this habitat.

Answers will vary.

page 302

Life on a Rotting Log

red-backed salamander · pin cushion moss · plate-cup lichen · jack-o-lantern mushrooms · ant larvae · pole-shield lichen · earthworms

The forest community is not limited to animals and plants that live in or near living trees. As the succession of the forest continues, many trees will die and fall to the ground. The actions of plants, animals, bacteria, lichens and weather help break the dead log down and return its components to the forest soil.

1. List the different kinds of plant life that are found on the rotting log. **lichen, moss, mushrooms**
2. How do the small plants help the log decay? **The roots create open spaces in the log.**
3. How do the plants benefit from the log? **The log offers plants a source of food, protection and a place to grow**
4. What kinds of small animals are found in or on the rotting log? **salamander, ants, earthworms, chipmunk**
5. How do these animals help the log decay? **They eat and chew on the log.**

The lichen found on the rotting log is an interesting type of plant. It is actually made up of two organisms living together in symbiosis. What two organisms form a lichen? What does each of these organisms need to live? How do the organisms help each other? **A lichen is made up of an algae and a fungus. The algae makes food by means of photosynthesis. The fungus absorbs the water that the algae needs to live.**

page 303

Speaking Canadian

Use the word box to complete the puzzle and discover the name of a company given the rights to a huge tract of land in northern Canada in 1570.

constable	hydro	mukluk	zed
curling	metis	revellion	revellion
coureur de bois	loyalists	Lower Canada	wapiti
Quebecois	Eskimo	Canada Day	Micmac	Klondike

1. Trout-like fish
2. Animal-skin boot
3. Letter z (for those who haven't watched Sesame Street)
4. Indian word meaning eaters of raw meat
5. Quebec's French-speaking citizens
6. Area once famed for its gold
7. Police officer
8. French traders not licensed to gather furs
9. Name once given to French-speaking Canada
10. Colonists loyal to Britain during the American Revolution, many of whom fled to Nova Scotia
11. Game in which heavy stones are slid toward a target
12. _____ electricity
13. Descendants of French settlers and their Indian wives
14. elk
15. Indian tribe from Eastern Canada
16. Quebec feast which follows the Christmas Midnight Mass
17. Canada's birthday

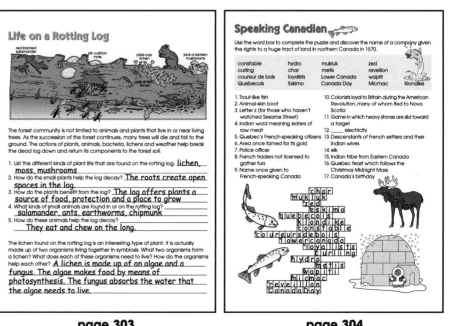

page 304

Learn at Home, Grade 6

Which Is Which?

Use the charts to answer the questions.

Population Distribution Chart

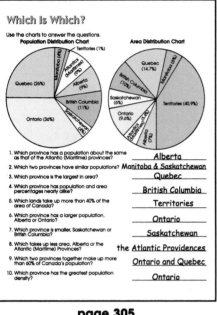

Area Distribution Chart

1. Which province has a population about the same as that of the Atlantic (Maritime) provinces? **Alberta**
2. Which two provinces have similar populations? **Manitoba & Saskatchewan**
3. Which province is the largest in area? **Quebec**
4. Which province has population and area percentages nearly alike? **British Columbia**
5. Which lands take up more than 40% of the area of Canada? **Territories**
6. Which province has a larger population, Alberta or Ontario? **Ontario**
7. Which province is smaller, Saskatchewan or British Columbia? **Saskatchewan**
8. Which takes up less area, Alberta or the Atlantic (Maritime) Provinces? **the Atlantic Providences**
9. Which two provinces together make up more than 60% of Canada's population? **Ontario and Quebec**
10. Which province has the greatest population density? **Ontario**

page 305

Cleaning Cabinets

Unscramble the groups of letters in the kitchen cabinets to form words from the word list.

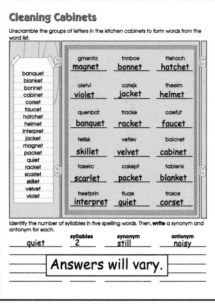

Word list:
banquet, blanket, bonnet, cabinet, corset, faucet, hatchet, helmet, interpret, jacket, magnet, packet, quiet, racket, scarlet, skillet, velvet, violet

gmenta **magnet**	tnnboe **bonnet**	ttehach **hatchet**
oletvl **violet**	catejk **jacket**	theelm **helmet**
quenbat **banquet**	tracke **racket**	caefut **faucet**
tellisk **skillet**	vetlev **velvet**	balcnet **cabinet**
taseirc **scarlet**	cakept **packet**	tablenk **blanket**
treetprin **interpret**	tiuqe **quiet**	trosce **corset**

Identify the number of syllables in five spelling words. Then, **write** a synonym and antonym for each.

| | syllables | synonym | antonym |
| quiet | 2 | still | noisy |

Answers will vary.

page 310

Up a Tree

Match these expressions with their meanings.

- **e** all the personality of wallpaper paste — a. without question
- **f** a piece of my mind — b. consider clearly
- **c** running amok — c. becoming wild
- **a** beyond a shadow of a doubt — d. gather up great quantities
- **b** think straight — e. a very bland disposition
- **h** ace in the hole — f. strong opinion
- **d** shop like a bear about to hibernate — g. from a bad situation to a worse one
- **g** out of the frying pan and into the fire — h. special advantage

Write two sentences using the above expressions.
Example: When my teacher asked me to give the answer, I couldn't think straight.

1.
2.

Sentences will vary.

page 311

Ratio Test

1. A basketball player makes 7 free throws out of every 12 thrown.
   a. **Write** a ratio of the free throws made to the number thrown. **7:12**
   b. **Write** a ratio of the free throws taken to the number missed. **12:5**
   c. With this same ratio, how many free throws would the player make out of 24 throws? **14 free throws**

2. **Write** the following percents as fractions in reduced form:
   $12\% = \frac{12}{100} = \frac{3}{25}$ $260\% = 2\frac{6}{10} = 2\frac{3}{5}$

3. **Write** the following fractions as percents:
   $\frac{15}{100} = $ **15%** $\frac{1}{4} = $ **25%** $2\frac{2}{5} = $ **240%**

4. **Write** the following percents as decimals:
   $68\% = $ **0.68** $1\% = $ **0.01**

5. **Write** the following decimals as percents:
   $0.18 = $ **18%** $0.05 = $ **5%** $3.24 = $ **324%**

6. Find 15% of 40. **6**
7. Find 4% of 20. **0.8**
8. Two hundred fifty people attended the fiesta. Of the fiesta guests, 52% were female. How many guests were female? **130 female guests**
9. The quarterback completed 8 out of 25 passes. What percentage of passes were completed? **32%**
10. Are the following ratios in proportion?
    $\frac{3}{8} = \frac{27}{72}$ **yes** $\frac{1}{7} = \frac{3}{28}$ **no**
11. Solve for x in the following proportions:
    $\frac{8}{3} = \frac{x}{2}$ $\frac{6}{x} = \frac{24}{12}$
    $x = $ **12** $x = $ **3**

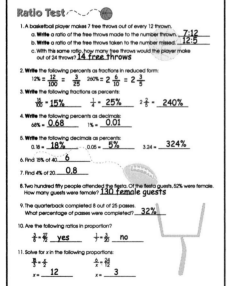

page 312

Animal Math

This chart lists some of the body statistics of fifteen endangered animals. Use these measurements to solve the problems below.

Animal	Height	Weight	Length
Mountain gorilla	6 feet	450 pounds	
Brown hyena	25 inches	70 pounds	3 feet
Black rhinoceros	5.5 feet	4,000 pounds	12 feet
Cheetah	2.5 feet	100 pounds	5 feet
Leopard	2 feet	150 pounds	4.5 feet
Spectacled bear	2.5 feet	300 pounds	5 feet
Giant armadillo		100 pounds	4 feet
Vicuna	2.5 feet	100 pounds	
Central American tapir	3.5 feet	500 pounds	8 feet
Black-footed ferret		1.5 pounds	20 inches
Siberian tiger	38 inches	600 pounds	6 feet
Orangutan	4.5 feet	200 pounds	
Giant panda		300 pounds	6 feet
Polar bear		1,600 pounds	8 feet
Yak	5.5 feet	1,200 pounds	

1. What is the total height of a mountain gorilla, a vicuna and a yak? **14 ft.**
2. What is the total weight of a leopard, a cheetah and a polar bear? **1,850 lb.**
3. What is the total weight of a giant panda and a giant armadillo? **400 lb.**
4. Add the lengths of a black rhinoceros, a spectacled bear and a Siberian tiger. **23 ft.**
5. Add the heights of two leopards, three yaks and four orangutans. **38.5 ft.**
6. Subtract the height of a vicuna from the height of a cheetah. **0 ft.**
7. Multiply the height of a Central American tapir by the height of a mountain gorilla. **21 ft.**
8. Add the heights of a brown hyena and a Siberian tiger. **63 ft.**
9. Add the weights of all the animals. **9,671.5 lb.**
10. **rhinoceros, tapir, polar bear, tiger, panda, cheetah, spectacled bear, leopard, armadillo, hyena, ferret**

page 313

Animal Magic

Read the animal name in Column A. Choose the correct description from Column B. **Write** the number of the answer in the Magic Square below. The first one has been done for you.

Column A
A. grizzly bear
B. koala
C. peregrine falcon
D. California condor
E. black-footed ferret
F. cheetah
G. orangutan
H. giant panda
I. Florida manatee
J. kit fox
K. blue whale
L. whooping crane
M. red wolf
N. green sea turtle
O. brown hyena
P. jaguar

Column B
1. large bear of the American grasslands
2. lives on dry grasslands of South Africa
3. the most valuable reptile in the world
4. largest soaring bird of North America
5. the tallest American bird
6. the fastest animal on land
7. the only great ape outside Africa
8. large aquatic seal-like animal
9. large black and white mammal of China
10. small, fast mammal; nocturnal predator
11. largest animal in the world
12. member of the weasel family
13. has interbred with coyotes in some areas
14. also called a duck hawk; size of a crow
15. eats leaves of the eucalyptus tree
16. know as "el tigre " in Spanish

A 1	B 15	C 14	D 4
E 12	F 6	G 7	H 9
I 8	J 10	K 11	L 5
M 13	N 3	O 2	P 16

Add the numbers across, down and diagonally. What answer do you get? **34**

Why do you think this is called a magic square? **Every row, column and diagonal adds up to 34.**

page 314

Going Into Orbit

1. admit
2. bandit
3. benefit
4. commit
5. credit
6. debit
7. edit
8. emit
9. exhibit
10. habit
11. inherit
12. limit
13. orbit
14. profit
15. prohibit
16. solicit
17. spirit
18. visit

Complete the magic square by writing the number of the word from the list in the lettered square that corresponds to its definition. One of the words will not be used.

Definitions

A. Robber or outlaw
B. To correct or revise
C. Go to see; stay as a guest
D. To restrict; boundary
E. To send forth or to give off
F. Asset; acknowledgment; recognition
G. To receive property after another dies
H. To forbid
I. To revolve around
J. Courage; liveliness
K. A record of debt; to charge with a debt
L. To serve or be useful to
M. To seek or to ask for
N. Repeated behavior, often involuntary
O. To do; to place in confinement
P. To display

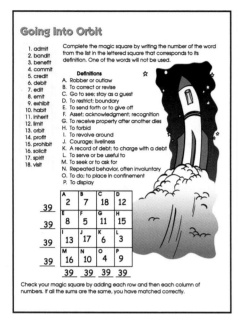

	A 2	B 7	C 18	D 12
39	E 8	F 5	G 11	H 15
39	I 13	J 17	K 6	L 1
39	M 16	N 10	O 4	P 9
39	39	39	39	39

Check your magic square by adding each row and then each column of numbers. If all the sums are the same, you have matched correctly.

page 320

Browser

Graph the ordered pairs in each group. Number each dot. Connect each point with the next point using a straight line. Do not connect the last point in one group with the first point in another group. The first one is done for you.

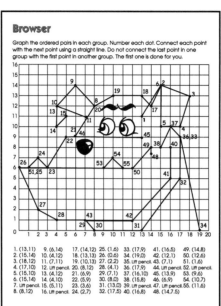

1. (13,11)
2. (15,14)
3. (18,12)
4. (17,10)
5. (15,10)
6. (15,14)
7. Lift pencil.
8. (8,12)
9. (6,14)
10. (4,12)
11. (7,11)
12. Lift pencil.
13. (4,12)
14. (4,10)
15. (5,11)
16. Lift pencil.
17. (14,12)
18. (13,13)
19. (10,13)
20. (8,12)
21. (6,9)
22. (5,9)
23. (3,6)
24. (2,7)
25. (1,6)
26. (0,6)
27. (2,2)
28. (4,1)
29. (7,1)
30. (8,0)
31. (13,0)
32. (17,5)
33. (17,9)
34. (12,1)
35. Lift pencil.
36. (17,9)
37. (16,10)
38. (15,8)
39. Lift pencil.
40. (16,8)
41. (16,5)
42. (7,1)
43. (7,1)
44. Lift pencil.
45. (13,9)
46. (6,9)
47. Lift pencil.
48. (14,7.5)
49. (14,8)
50. (12,6)
51. (1,6)
52. Lift pencil.
53. (9,6)
54. (10,7)
55. (11,6)

page 321

Graphs

Graphs have a vertical axis and a horizontal axis. The axes are labeled to show what is being compared.

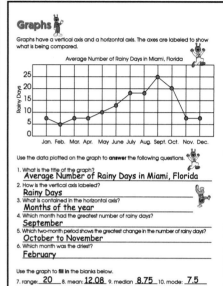

Use the data plotted on the graph to **answer** the following questions.

1. What is the title of the graph?
   Average Number of Rainy Days in Miami, Florida
2. How is the vertical axis labeled?
   Rainy Days
3. What is contained in the horizontal axis?
   Months of the year
4. Which month had the greatest number of rainy days?
   September
5. Which two-month period shows the greatest change in the number of rainy days?
   October to November
6. Which month was the driest?
   February

Use the graph to **fill in** the blanks below.

7. range: **20** 8. mean: **12.08** 9. median **8.75** 10. mode: **7.5**

page 322

Central America

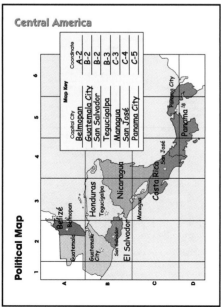

	Coordinate
	A-2
	B-2
	B-2
	C-3
	C-4
	C-5

Map Key
Capital City
Belmopan
Guatemala City
San Salvador
Tegucigalpa
Managua
San José
Panama City

Political Map

page 323

Investigator Hector

author
bachelor
collector
conductor
conqueror
creator
dictator
director
editor
emperor
inspector
instructor
monitor
orator
professor
protector
sculptor
senator

Investigator Hector must investigate several people. Read the clues to identify each person's occupation. **Write** the correct spelling word in the blank.

Clues

1. Arnie Andrew, acclaimed novelist **author**
2. Darla Day, direction giver **director**
3. Olive Oyle, opinionated speaker **orator**
4. Ernie Egoist, empire ruler **emperor**
5. Clint Corn, card accumulator **collector**
6. Irene Ink, intelligent informer **instructor**
7. Edgar Edge, eager reviser **editor**
8. Dastardly D., dreaded tyrant **dictator**
9. Carl Carr, cartoon designer **creator**
10. Sue Smit, sincere Congresswoman **senator**
11. Sam Son, serious carver **sculptor**
12. Brad Bad, bearded single **bachelor**
13. Pete Pane, prominent teacher **professor**
14. Ivan Ize, investigative examiner **inspector**
15. Casey Clark, choirmaster **conductor**
16. Maggie May, money overseer **monitor**
17. Conrad Carp, courageous victor **conquerer**
18. Prince Paul, powerful defender **protector**

Write a short definition for five spelling words.

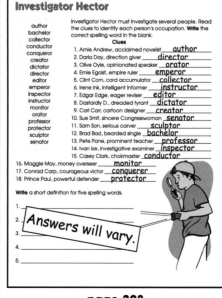

1. _____
2. Answers will vary.
3. _____
4. _____
5. _____

page 328

Double Line Graphs

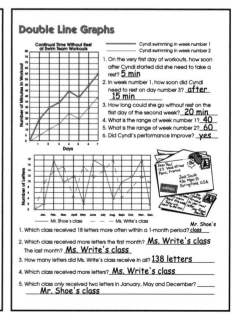

Cyndi swimming in week number 1
Cyndi swimming in week number 2

1. On the very first day of workouts, how soon after Cyndi started did she need to take a rest? **5 min**
2. In week number 1, how soon did Cyndi need to rest on day number 3? **after 15 min**
3. How long could she go without rest on the first day of the second week? **20 min**
4. What is the range of week number 1? **40**
5. What is the range of week number 2? **60**
6. Did Cyndi's performance improve? **yes**

1. Which class received 18 letters more often within a 1-month period? **class**
2. Which class received more letters the first month? **Ms. Write's class** The last month? **Ms. Write's class**
3. How many letters did Ms. Write's class receive in all? **138 letters**
4. Which class received more letters? **Ms. Write's class**
5. Which class only received two letters in January, May and December? **Mr. Shoe's class**

page 329

Learn at Home, Grade 6

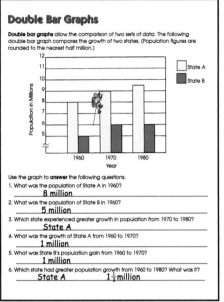

Double Bar Graphs

Double bar graphs allow the comparison of two sets of data. The following double bar graph compares the growth of two states. (Population figures are rounded to the nearest half million.)

Use the graph to **answer** the following questions.

1. What was the population of State A in 1960?
   8 million
2. What was the population of State B in 1960?
   5 million
3. Which state experienced greater growth in population from 1970 to 1980?
   State A
4. What was the growth of State A from 1960 to 1970?
   1 million
5. What was State B's population gain from 1960 to 1970?
   1 million
6. Which state had greater population growth from 1960 to 1980? What was it?
   State A   1½ million

page 330

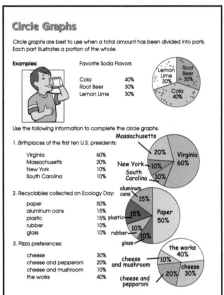

Circle Graphs

Circle graphs are best to use when a total amount has been divided into parts. Each part illustrates a portion of the whole.

Examples:

Favorite Soda Flavors

Cola	40%
Root Beer	30%
Lemon Lime	30%

Use the following information to complete the circle graphs.

1. Birthplaces of the first ten U.S. presidents:

Virginia	60%
Massachusetts	20%
New York	10%
South Carolina	10%

2. Recyclables collected on Ecology Day:

paper	50%
aluminum cans	15%
plastic	15%
rubber	10%
glass	10%

3. Pizza preferences:

cheese	30%
cheese and pepperoni	20%
cheese and mushroom	10%
the works	40%

page 331

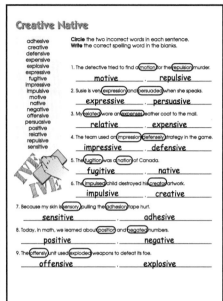

Creative Native

adhesive
creative
defensive
expensive
explosive
expressive
fugitive
impressive
impulsive
motive
native
negative
offensive
persuasive
positive
relative
repulsive
sensitive

Circle the two incorrect words in each sentence. **Write** the correct spelling word in the blanks.

1. The detective tried to find a motive for the repulsion murder.
   motive , **repulsive**
2. Susie is very expression and persuaded when she speaks.
   expressive , **persuasive**
3. My related wore an expenses leather coat to the mall.
   relative , **expensive**
4. The team used an impression defensely strategy in the game.
   impressive , **defensive**
5. The fugition was a nation of Canada.
   fugitive , **native**
6. The impulsed child destroyed his creato artwork.
   impulsive , **creative**
7. Because my skin is sensory, pulling the adhesion tape hurt.
   sensitive , **adhesive**
8. Today, in math, we learned about position and negated numbers.
   positive , **negative**
9. The offensly unit used exploded weapons to defeat its foe.
   offensive , **explosive**

page 336

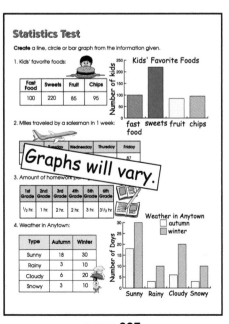

Statistics Test

Create a line, circle or bar graph from the information given.

1. Kids' favorite foods:

Fast Food	Sweets	Fruit	Chips
100	220	85	95

2. Miles traveled by a salesman in 1 week:

Graphs will vary.

3. Amount of homework per grade:

1st Grade	2nd Grade	3rd Grade	4th Grade	5th Grade	6th Grade
½ hr.	1 hr.	2 hr.	2 hr.	3 hr.	3½ hr.

4. Weather in Anytown:

Type	Autumn	Winter
Sunny	18	30
Rainy	3	10
Cloudy	6	20
Snowy	3	10

page 337

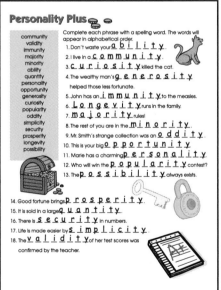

Personality Plus

community
validity
immunity
majority
minority
ability
quantity
personality
opportunity
generosity
curiosity
popularity
oddity
simplicity
prosperity
security
longevity
possibility

Complete each phrase with a spelling word. The words will appear in alphabetical order.

1. Don't waste your **a b i l i t y**.
2. I live in a **c o m m u n i t y**.
3. **c u r i o s i t y** killed the cat.
4. The wealthy man's **g e n e r o s i t y** helped those less fortunate.
5. John has an **i m m u n i t y** to the measles.
6. **L o n g e v i t y** runs in the family.
7. **m a j o r i t y** rules!
8. The rest of you are in the **m i n o r i t y**.
9. Mr. Smith's strange collection was an **o d d i t y**.
10. This is your big **o p p o r t u n i t y**.
11. Marie has a charming **p e r s o n a l i t y**.
12. Who will win the **p o p u l a r i t y** contest?
13. The **p o s s i b i l i t y** always exists.
14. Good fortune brings **p r o s p e r i t y**.
15. It is sold in a large **q u a n t i t y**.
16. There is **s e c u r i t y** in numbers.
17. Life is made easier by **s i m p l i c i t y**.
18. The **v a l i d i t y** of her test scores was confirmed by the teacher.

page 342

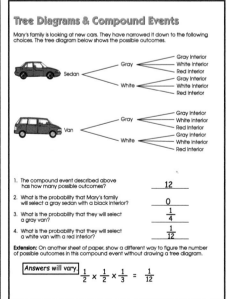

Tree Diagrams & Compound Events

Mary's family is looking at new cars. They have narrowed it down to the following choices. The tree diagram below shows the possible outcomes.

1. The compound event described above has how many possible outcomes?   **12**
2. What is the probability that Mary's family will select a gray sedan with a black interior?   **0**
3. What is the probability that they will select a gray van?   **¼**
4. What is the probability that they will select a white van with a red interior?   **1/12**

Extension: On another sheet of paper, show a different way to figure the number of possible outcomes in this compound event without drawing a tree diagram.

Answers will vary. $\frac{1}{2} \times \frac{1}{2} \times \frac{1}{3} = \frac{1}{12}$

page 343

Integers

Solve the problems. **Write** your answers here.

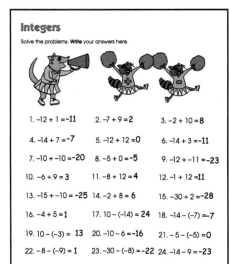

1. −12 + 1 = **−11**   2. −7 + 9 = **2**   3. −2 + 10 = **8**

4. −14 + 7 = **−7**   5. −12 + 12 = **0**   6. −14 + 3 = **−11**

7. −10 + −10 = **−20**   8. −5 + 0 = **−5**   9. −12 + −11 = **−23**

10. −6 + 9 = **3**   11. −8 + 12 = **4**   12. −1 + 12 = **11**

13. −15 + −10 = **−25**   14. −2 + 8 = **6**   15. −30 + 2 = **−28**

16. −4 + 5 = **1**   17. 10 − (−14) = **24**   18. −14 − (−7) = **−7**

19. 10 − (−3) = **13**   20. −10 − 6 = **−16**   21. −5 − (−5) = **0**

22. −8 − (−9) = **1**   23. −30 − (−8) = **−22**   24. −14 − 9 = **−23**

25. −16 − (−4) = **−12**   26. 20 − 30 = **−10**   27. −10 − 4 = **−14**

page 348

Overview Test

1. **Write** 7,245,208.07 in words __Seven million, two hundred forty-five__ __thousand, two hundred eight and seven hundredths__

2. Round 3,657.189 . . .
to the nearest hundredth. __3,657.19__
to the nearest whole number. __3,657__

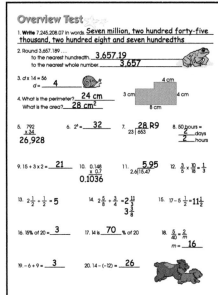

3. $d \times 14 = 56$
$d =$ __4__

4. What is the perimeter? __24 cm__
What is the area? __28 cm²__

5. 792
× 34
26,928

6. $2^5 =$ __32__

7. 28 R9
23)653

8. 50 hours =
__2__ days
__2__ hours

9. 15 ÷ 3 × 2 = __21__

10. 0.148
× 0.7
0.1036

11. **5.95**
2.6)15.47

12. $\frac{3}{5} \times \frac{10}{18} = \frac{1}{3}$

13. $2\frac{1}{2} \div \frac{1}{2} =$ **5**

14. $2\frac{5}{8} + \frac{3}{4} = 2\frac{11}{3}$ $3\frac{3}{8}$

15. $17 - 5\frac{1}{2} = 11\frac{1}{2}$

16. 15% of 20 = __3__

17. 14 is __70__ % of 20

18. $\frac{5}{40} = \frac{2}{m}$
$m =$ __16__

19. −6 + 9 = __3__

20. 14 − (−12) = __26__

page 349

Mapping Mania

Refer to a map of Canada and the United States to complete the following.

1. A group of islands close to each other is called an archipelago. Name the archipelago that extends southwest from Alaska. __Aleutian Islands__

2. What state is made up of an archipelago? __Hawaii__

3. Why are Texas, Louisiana, Mississippi, Alabama and Florida known as the Gulf states? __They border the Gulf of Mexico.__

4. The Great Lakes hold $\frac{1}{5}$ of all surface freshwater in the world. Name the American states and Canadian province that border these lakes. __Minnesota,__ __Wisconsin, Michigan, Illinois, Indiana, Ohio, Pennsylvania, New York, Ontario__

5. What Canadian province retains its French heritage and language? __Quebec__

6. Name the Canadian Maritime Provinces. __New Brunswick, Nova Scotia,__ __Prince Edward Island, Newfoundland__

7. Name the oceans that border Canada. __Pacific, Atlantic, Arctic__

8. Name the American state that borders two oceans. __Alaska__
Name the oceans. __Pacific and Arctic__

9. Name the state made up of two peninsulas. __Michigan__

10. Name the three major mountain chains found in North America. __Rocky Mountains, Appalachians, Coastal/Cascades__

11. Locate a map with time zones. Find the number of time zones within the contiguous United States. Name them. __4 Pacific, Mountain,__ __Central, Eastern__

12. Name the states that have the Mississippi River as a border. __Minnesota, Wisconsin,__ __Iowa, Illinois, Missouri, Kentucky, Tennessee, Arkansas, Mississippi,__ __Louisiana__

Challenge!
There is one place in North America where you could get into a boat at one state capital, sail to the nearby capital of a Canadian province and continue along the coast to another state capital. Name the three capitals. __Olympia, WA; Victoria__ __British Columbia; Juneau, Alaska__

page 350

Mapping Mania

Refer to a map of Central America and South America to complete the following.

1. Name the large peninsula in Mexico that separates the Gulf of Mexico from the Caribbean. __Yucatán__

2. Name the four nations that still have possessions in the Caribbean region. __Netherlands, U.S., United Kingdom, France__

3. Which Central American country is not officially Spanish speaking? (It was formerly British Honduras.) __Belizé__

4. In 1949, this Central American country abolished its army. Today, it is one of the most stable countries in Latin America. Its president won a Nobel Peace Prize in 1987 for working to end fighting in Central America. It lies west of Panama and south of Nicaragua. Identify the country. __Costa Rica__

5. Name the countries that border the Gulf of Mexico. __United States,__ __Cuba, Mexico__

6. Which South American countries lie on the equator? __Ecuador,__ __Colombia, Brazil__

7. Does any South American country lie completely outside the tropics? If so, which one? __Uruguay__

8. Name the cape at the southern tip of South America. __Cape Horn__

9. Name three countries in South America where Spanish is not the official language. __Guyana, Suriname, French Guiana__

10. In 1935, one of the great scientists in history, Charles Darwin, spent a month in the Galápagos Islands, part of Ecuador. His visit was the inspiration for the theory of natural selection that revolutionized science. Give the absolute and relative location of the Galápagos. __0.30° S, 90.30°W; approximately__ __850 miles due west of Quito, Ecuador__

11. Name the only country in South America without a coastline. __Paraguay__

page 351

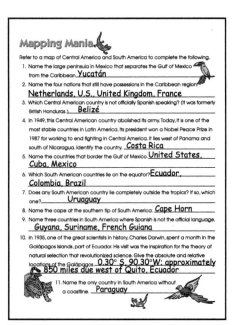

Learn at Home, Grade 6

Write Government Officials

The government needs to hear from kids just like you! Our nation's leaders and the leaders of other countries need to hear our concerns. Most government officials welcome letters and want to know your thoughts.

Write letters that clearly state what you are concerned about and why you are concerned. Using the information that you have learned will help influence the people who make decisions about the laws and funding that govern the safety of our planet.

NO MATTER HOW YOUNG YOU ARE YOU CAN MAKE A DIFFERENCE.

Here are some addresses of where to write to our government officials.

Representative _____
US House of Representatives
Washington DC 20515

Senator _____
US Senate
Washington DC 20510

(You will need to know the names of your state's Senators and Representatives.)

President _____
The White House
1600 Pennsylvania Ave.
Washington DC 20500
(Begin your letter, "Dear Mr. President.")

If you wish to write to the leaders of other foreign countries, request the proper address from:

(Country's Name) Embassy
The United Nations,
United Nations Plaza
New York, NY 10017

Organizations to Contact

The Acid Rain Foundation
1630 Blackhawk Hills
St. Paul, MN 55122

Acid Rain Information
Clearinghouse Library
Center for Environmental Information, Inc.
33 S. Washington St.
Rochester, NY 14608

Adopt-A-Stream Foundation
P.O. Box 5558
Everett, WA 98201

Air Pollution Control
Bureau of National Affairs Inc.
1231 25th St. NW
Washington DC 20037

Alliance To Save Energy
1925 K St. NW
Suite 206
Washington DC 20036

American Association of Zoological Parks and Aquariums
Oglebay Park
Wheeling, WV 26003

American Wind Energy Association
1730 N Lynn St.
Suite 610
Arlington, VA 22209

Canadian Coalition On Acid Rain
112 St. Clair Ave. West
Suite 504
Toronto, Ontario, Canada
M4V 2Y3

Center for Marine Conservation
1725 DeSales St. NW
Suite 500
Washington DC 20036

Friends of the Earth
530 Seventh St. SE
Washington DC 20003

Global Releaf, c/o the American Forestry Association
P.O. Box 2000
Washington DC 20013

Greenpeace
1436 U Street NW
Washington DC 20009

Household Hazardous Waste Project
901 S. National Ave.
Box 108
Springfield, MO 65804

National Association of Recycling Industries
330 Madison Ave.
New York, NY 10017

National Clean Air Coalition
530 7th St. SE
Washington DC 20003

National Wildlife Federation
1412 16th St. NW
Washington DC 20036

Public Affairs Office
US Environmental Protection Agency
Washington DC 20036

Renew America
1400 16th St. NW
Suite 710
Washington DC 20036

Save the Manatee Club
500 N. Maitland Ave.
Suite 200
Maitland, FL 32751

U.S. Environmental Protection Agency
401 M St. SW
Washington DC 20460

United Nations Environment Programme
North American Office
Room DC2-0803, United Nations
New York, NY 10017

Learn at Home, Grade 6